Managing Trade-offs in Adaptable Software Architectures

Managing Trade-offs in Adaptable Software Architectures

Edited by

Ivan Mistrik

Nour Ali

Rick Kazman

John Grundy

Bradley Schmerl

AMSTERDAM • BOSTON • HEIDELBERG • LONDON
NEW YORK • OXFORD • PARIS • SAN DIEGO
SAN FRANCISCO • SINGAPORE • SYDNEY • TOKYO

Morgan Kaufmann is an imprint of Elsevier

Morgan Kaufmann is an imprint of Elsevier
50 Hampshire Street, 5th Floor, Cambridge, MA 02139, United States

Library of Congress Cataloging-in-Publication Data
A catalog record for this book is available from the Library of Congress

British Library Cataloguing-in-Publication Data
A catalogue record for this book is available from the British Library

ISBN: 978-0-12-802855-1

For information on all Morgan Kaufmann publications
visit our website at https://www.elsevier.com/

Working together
to grow libraries in
developing countries

www.elsevier.com • www.bookaid.org

Publisher: Todd Green
Acquisition Editor: Todd Green
Editorial Project Manager: Lindsay Lawrence
Production Project Manager: Priya Kumaraguruparan
Cover Designer: Maria Inês Cruz

Typeset by SPi Global, India

Contents

Contributors

N. Ali
University of Brighton, Brighton, United Kingdom

M. Abdelrazek
Deakin University, Melbourne, VIC, Australia

S. Andrade
Federal Institute of Education, Science, and Technology of Bahia; Federal University of Bahia, Salvador, Bahia, Brazil

F. Arcelli Fontana
University of Milano-Bicocca, Milan, Italy

P. Avgeriou
University of Groningen, Groningen, Netherlands

R. Bahsoon
University of Birmingham, Birmingham, United Kingdom

N. Bencomo
Aston University, Birmingham, United Kingdom

A. Bennaceur
The Open University, Milton Keynes, United Kingdom

P. Boxer
Boxer Research Limited, London, United Kingdom

J. Cámara
Carnegie Mellon University, Pittsburgh, PA, United States

K. Canavera
George Mason University, Fairfax, VA, United States

R. Capilla
Rey Juan Carlos University, Madrid, Spain

C. Carrillo
Polytechnic University of Madrid, Madrid, Spain

R. de Lemos
University of Kent, United Kingdom; CISUC, University of Coimbra, Portugal

N. Esfahani
Google Inc, Mountain View, CA, United States

D. Garlan
Carnegie Mellon University, Pittsburgh, PA, United States

J. Grundy
Deakin University, Melbourne, VIC, Australia

A. Ibrahim
Deakin University, Melbourne, VIC, Australia

R. Kazman
Carnegie Mellon University, Pittsburgh, PA; University of Hawaii, Honolulu, HI, United States

R. Macêdo
Federal University of Bahia, Salvador, Bahia, Brazil

S. Mahdavi-Hezavehi
University of Groningen, Groningen, Netherlands; Linnaeus University, Växjö, Sweden

S. Malek
University of California, Irvine, Irvine, CA, United States

I. Mistrik
Independent Software Researcher, Heidelberg, Germany

G.A. Moreno
Carnegie Mellon University, Pittsburgh, PA, United States

H.A. Müller
University of Victoria, Victoria, BC, Canada

B. Nuseibeh
The Open University, Milton Keynes, United Kingdom; Lero—The Irish Software Research Centre, Limerick, Ireland

O. Ozcan
Bilkent University, Ankara, Turkey

P. Potena
Fondazione Bruno Kessler, Trento, Italy

C. Raibulet
University of Milano-Bicocca, Milan, Italy

M. Salama
University of Birmingham, Birmingham, United Kingdom

B. Schmerl
Carnegie Mellon University, Pittsburgh, PA, United States

H. Sozer
Ozyegin University, Istanbul, Turkey

G. Tamura
Universidad Icesi, Cali, Colombia

B. Tekinerdogan
Wageningen University, Wageningen, The Netherlands

N.M. Villegas
Universidad Icesi, Cali, Colombia

D. Weyns
Linnaeus University, Växjö, Sweden

About the Editors

Ivan Mistrík is a researcher in software-intensive systems engineering. He is a computer scientist who is interested in system and software engineering and in system and software architecture, in particular: life cycle system/software engineering, requirements engineering, relating software requirements and architectures, knowledge management in software development, rationale-based software development, aligning enterprise/system/software architectures, value-based software engineering, agile software architectures, and collaborative system/software engineering. He has more than 40 years' experience in the field of computer systems engineering as an information systems developer, R&D leader, SE/SA research analyst, educator in computer sciences, and ICT management consultant. In the past 40 years, he has been primarily working at various R&D institutions in United States and Germany and has done consulting on a variety of large international projects sponsored by the ESA, EU, NASA, NATO, and UN. He has also taught university-level computer sciences courses in software engineering, software architecture, distributed information systems, and human-computer interaction. He is the author or co-author of more than 90 articles and papers in international journals, conferences, books, and workshops. He has written a number of editorials for special issues and edited books. He has also written over 120 technical reports and presented over 70 scientific/technical talks. He has served in many program committees and panels of reputable international conferences and organized a number of scientific workshops. He was the lead-editor of nine books between 2006 and 2015: *Rationale Management in Software Engineering*, *Rationale-Based Software Engineering*, *Collaborative Software Engineering*, *Relating Software Requirements and Architecture*, *Aligning Enterprise/System/Software Architectures*, *Agile Software Architecture*, *Economics-Driven Software Architecture*, *Relating System Quality and Software Architecture*, and *Software Quality Assurance*.

Nour Ali has been a Principal Lecturer at the University of Brighton since Dec. 2012. She holds a Ph.D. in Software Engineering from the Polytechnic University of Valencia-Spain for her work in Ambients in Aspect-Oriented Software Architecture. She is a Fellow of the UK Higher Education Academy (HEA). Her research area encompasses service-oriented architecture, software architecture, self-adaptation, and mobile systems. In 2014, the University of Brighton granted her a Rising Stars award in Service Oriented Architecture Recovery and Consistency. She is currently the Principal Investigator for the Royal Society Newton grant, "An Autonomic Architectural Approach for Health Care Systems," and is the Knowledge Supervisor for the Knowledge Transfer Partnership project for migrating legacy software systems using architecture centric approach. She has also been the Principal Investigator for an Enterprise Ireland Commercialisation Project in Architecture Recovery and Consistency and co-investigator in several funded projects. Dr. Ali serves on the Programme Committee for several conferences (e.g., ICWS, ICMS, and HPCC) and journals (e.g., JSS, or JIST). She has co-chaired and co-organized several workshops such as the IEEE International Workshop on Engineering Mobile Service Oriented Systems (EMSOS) and the IEEE Workshop on Future of Software Engineering for/in the Cloud. She was the co-editor of the JSS Special Issue on the Future of Software Engineering for/in the Cloud published in 2013 and has co-edited three books including *Agile and Lean Service-Oriented Development: Foundations, Theory, and Practice*, published in 2012.

She is the Application Track chair for International Conference on Web Services (ICWS 2016). Her personal website is: http://www.cem.brighton.ac.uk/staff/na179.

John Grundy is Professor of Software Engineering and Pro-Vice Chancellor ICT Innovation and Translation at Deakin University, Australia. Previously he was Dean of the School of Software and Electrical Engineering and also Director of the Swinburne University Centre for Computing and Engineering Software Systems (SUCCESS). Before coming to Swinburne, he was Head of Department for Electrical and Computer Engineering at the University of Auckland, New Zealand. His teaching is mostly in the area of team projects, software requirements and design, software processes, distributed systems, and programming. His research areas include software tools and techniques, software architecture, model-driven software engineering, visual languages, software security engineering, service-based and component-based systems and user interfaces. He has authored over 300 publications and supervised over 50 Ph.D. and Masters by research students. He provides consulting work for a range of companies which have included, among many others, Data61, DST Group, Mailguard, Thales Australia, CA Labs, XSol Ltd, Orion Health Ltd, Peace Software Ltd, and Whitecloud Systems Ltd.

Rick Kazman is a Professor at the University of Hawaii and a Principal Researcher at the Software Engineering Institute of Carnegie Mellon University. His primary research interests are software architecture, design and analysis tools, software visualization, and software engineering economics. Kazman has created several highly influential methods and tools for architecture analysis, including the *SAAM* (software architecture analysis method), the *ATAM* (architecture tradeoff analysis method), the *CBAM* (cost-benefit analysis method), and the *Dali* and *Titan* tools. He is the author of over 200 publications, and co-author of several books, including *Software Architecture in Practice*, *Designing Software Architectures: A Practical Approach*, *Evaluating Software Architectures: Methods and Case Studies*, and *Ultra-Large-Scale Systems: The Software Challenge of the Future*. His publications have been cited over 16,000 times, making him one of the most cited authors in all of software engineering.

Bradley Schmerl is a Principal Systems Scientist in the Institute for Software Research at Carnegie Mellon University, USA. He has been involved in research in self-adaptive systems for over 20 years, starting with his Ph.D. at Flinders University in South Australia, which investigated using configuration management techniques to manage dynamically changing systems. He was a Lecturer at Flinders University and an Assistant Professor at Clemson University in South Carolina before joining Carnegie Mellon in 2000. He is involved in research using software architecture models as a basis for reasoning about self-adapting systems, including using utility theory to select appropriate strategies that balance multiple quality and business priorities. He has co-authored over a dozen journal and conference papers on self-adaptation, co-organized the Second Workshop on Self-Organizing Architectures in 2011, co-edited the Special Issue on "State of the Art in Self-Adaptive Systems" of the *Journal of Software and Systems* in 2012, and was program chair for the 2015 International Symposium on Software Engineering for Adaptive and Self-Managing Systems.

Foreword by David Garlan

The idea of a system that adapts itself while it is running is as old as the notion of computation. But for many years the complexity of creating such systems hardly justified their value. Systems typically ran in predictable, stable environments, and their requirements and fault models were fairly well prescribed.

But over the past couple of decades, many things have driven system designers to reconsider the proposition of self-adapting software systems. Today systems must function in complex environments built out of infrastructure, components, services, and other systems that are not under direct control of the original system's developers. Requirements may change. Environments change, particularly in the presence of mobility. System configurations must be optimized to satisfy multiple (often conflicting) quality goals dictated by business context. And, at the same time, the need to deploy systems with 24/7 availability has moved out of the niche system category (telephone system, energy grid, etc.) into mainstream software.

About a decade and a half ago, people began to realize that to account for this new reality, it was important to understand how to make systems more resilient, more malleable, and more extensible, without compromising quality, cost of development, and cost of deployment—and, significantly, without taking systems offline. Old solutions of simply throwing more system administrators at the problem were becoming increasingly cost-prohibitive. And engineering fault tolerance and system reconfiguration directly into the system was leading to unsustainable complexity.

What emerged was a blossoming of a new focus on the software engineering of self-adaptive systems that could rise to the challenges of modern contexts. Almost simultaneously there emerged new venues for discussing such issues: the ACM Workshops on Self-Healing Systems (WOSS), the International Conference on Autonomic Computing (ICAC), the international workshop on self-adaptive software (IWSAS), and others. And, within the domain of commercial systems, we began to see myriad new (albeit special-purpose) mechanisms for adaptation: automated server monitoring and repair in Internet-based systems, adaptive performance through cloud computing platforms, and micro-services to support rapid, and frequent, deployment of functional enhancements.

Additionally, a major advance in our thinking about such systems emerged through the recognition that one way to address the challenges of self-adaptation was to take a control systems perspective on the problem. Specifically, a system could be made self-adaptive by adding sensors to monitor its runtime state, actuators to change it at runtime, and a separate reasoning mechanism to decide when it is appropriate to adapt the system, and how best to do so. This was famously referred to (in some circles) as the MAPE-K loop, or monitor-analyze-plan-execute using a shared base of knowledge.

This perspective (among others) helped researchers and developers consider the architectures of self-adaptive systems as first-class areas of study. And while the overall MAPE-K control architecture tends to encompass most such efforts, numerous new challenges emerge in order to get the details right.

Monitoring: What does it mean to have sufficient situational awareness, and what can one do when such information is unavailable or highly uncertain? How can one sift through large volumes of low-level system observations to derive higher-level views of system behavior and state?

Analysis: How can a system determine when adaptation is necessary? How can it identify the part of the system that needs to be adapted? How do you prioritize the possible problems that need to be addressed when several are detected? To what extent should the system focus on faults, and to what extent on homeostatic improvement? What are appropriate measures of system quality that take into account multiple dimensions of concern (e.g., cost, performance, security, availability)? How do you recognize "softer" problems, where the system is out of balance with respect to competing quality attributes (e.g., sacrificing deployment cost to improve performance)?

Planning: How can one determine an appropriate adaptation strategy that considers the inherent trade-offs between different quality dimensions that might be affected? How can one balance the need for rapid response to critical problems, while still support longer-range system improvement? How can one provide assurance that adaptation will make a system better, and not worse? How can one provide guarantees about coverage of potential problems? How can one build planning mechanisms that are proactive in anticipating problems and correcting them before they do damage? How do you reason about uncertainty, given the fact that we may not know precisely the state of the system, environment, or even the outcomes of repair actions?

Execution: How can you build systems so their actuation interface provides more flexibility to the adaptive process? How can you support concurrent adaptations of the same system?

Knowledge: What kinds of information are most useful to the adaptation process? How can you strike a balance between abstract views of the system and detailed enough information to make informed decisions about adaptation? Can cooperating adaptive systems share knowledge to improve the adaptation behavior of the ensemble?

In addition to these kinds of challenges, new forces in technology are raising interesting questions about positioning adaptive systems in today's ecosystems. For example, increasingly computing systems must work in the context of physical devices and technologically rich environments. Such systems, sometimes referred to as the Internet of Things or cyber-physical systems, raise the question of how to combine what we have learned about software adaptation with more traditional disciplines of physical control. As another example, systems today must take into account the capabilities of the humans that interact with them. Humans may be clients of the adaptive system, but also might be viewed as components in the overall adaptation process. Indeed, in principle humans can serve in any of the MAPE-K roles—for example, providing contextual information to the system, assisting with adaptation, or performing physical actions to achieve some desired result.

It is clear that much remains to be done, and what we do know today will need to evolve with the shifting landscape of technology and its use in our world. The chapters in this book span the entire field: from engineering of adaptive systems, to reasoning about them, to exploring their use in emerging frontiers. Despite this diversity, however, across all of these chapters is a broad concern with the question of balancing trade-offs. The moment you go down the path of adaptation, you are faced with questions about how best to reconcile conflicting goals and requirements: of timely response with optimal repair, of multiple system qualities that must be balanced to provide overall utility, of automated versus human-assisted adaptation, of localized versus distributed control, of human-assisted versus stand-alone adaptation. Balancing trade-offs thus provides a common theme underlying these chapters, and, in fact, any serious treatment of self-adaptation. As such, this book provides both a broad perspective and deep exploration of many of these issues, serving as an excellent starting point for someone who wants to know more about the field, as well for researchers and practitioners who want a more in-depth examination of recent research and its potential.

David Garlan

Foreword by Nenad Medvidovic
Behold the Golden Age of Software Architecture

In the mid-to-late 1990s, I had the fortune of witnessing a great deal of activity and innovation that, today, is sometimes referred to as the "golden age" of software architecture research. As a community, we were trying to understand the phenomena underlying software systems' architectures, develop abstractions to capture those phenomena, construct models to embody the abstractions properly and effectively, analyze the models for interesting and important properties, and, finally, figure out how to implement systems that would inherit all of the positive and none of the negative characteristics we encountered along the way. This resulted in a seeming whirlwind of notations, techniques, tools, patterns, styles, and reference architectures. It was an incredibly exciting and fun time if you were a software architecture researcher. The rest, as they say, has been history.

An issue that emerged somewhat more slowly and deliberately by comparison to the above was architectural adaptation. One question was always there: Once you build the system, you will inevitably change it, so what does that do to the architecture? That question, however, turned out to have a more compelling counterpart: What do you have to do to and with the architecture to make it support the change in the system? As a result of multiple years of investigating this question, several colleagues and I came up with what we have since named (hopefully for obvious reasons) the "figure 8" model, shown below.

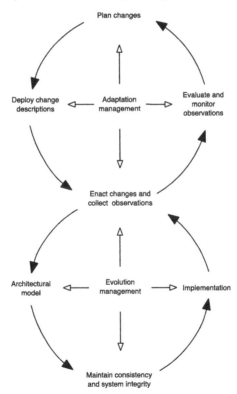

The model recognized the dichotomy and tight interconnection between the system and its architecture. The upper portion of the diagram—adaptation management—was intended to capture the lifecycle of adaptive software systems. The original vision was that the lifecycle may have humans in the loop or it may be autonomous. The lower portion of the diagram—evolution management—was intended to capture the software mechanisms employed to change the system.

The objective here is not to explain the entire model; the interested reader can find more details in the original papers that introduced the model [1,2], as well as subsequent publications that have reflected and expounded upon it [3,4]. The important takeaway is that the approach was architecture-based: changes were *always* formulated in, and reasoned over, an explicit architectural model that resided on the implementation platform along with the implemented system itself. Furthermore, changes to the architectural model were directly reflected in modifications to the system's implementation. The key to the "figure 8" was ensuring that the architectural model and the implementation remained consistent with one another throughout the system's life span.

The "figure 8" model was followed by and it inspired several other architecture-based software adaptation models that shared its basic traits: the models looked at the adaptation problem at a very high level and tried to prescribe activities and provide mechanisms for addressing the problem in a general way. However, the details remained largely unaddressed. The models captured *what* and *when* an engineer, or an automated agent, would have to do, and *why*. However, the existing models left unspecified many details of *how* these activities would be accomplished. They also tended not to specify precisely what would happen to the system's properties as its architecture is adapted and how trade-offs among those properties should be handled. In that sense, although these architecture-based adaptation models are usually comprehensive in scope, targeting broad classes of software systems and adaptation scenarios, they aimed to solve what is fundamentally the simpler portion of the problem, leaving the harder portion unaddressed.

The actual details of *how* to adapt a system by modifying its architecture in order to accomplish a given objective turn out to require more focused, targeted solutions because those solutions depend on many, varying factors. The good news is that such solutions can typically be "plugged into" the general-purpose adaptation models—a perfect symbiosis. This book aims to provide just that: a broad cross-section of state-of-the-art solutions to the problem of *how* quality trade-offs are managed in adaptable software architectures. The reader will find a great variety of methods, techniques, and tools that can be adopted wholesale, adapted for different scenarios, or indeed, plugged into one or more of the existing adaptation models. The reader may also walk away feeling that there is still much work left to be done on this problem. If so, that will not be an inaccurate impression. Software adaptation is a remarkably complex phenomenon and it must be and will be studied for some time. The upside is that this is a very exciting area to work in, proving wrong those who think that the "golden age" of software architecture has passed. So, dive in, read, learn, and get inspired!

Nenad Medvidovic
University of Southern California
Los Angeles, CA, USA

REFERENCES

[1] P. Oreizy, N. Medvidovic, R.N. Taylor, Architecture-based runtime software evolution, in: Proceedings of the 20th International Conference on Software Engineering (ICSE'98), Kyoto, Japan, April 1998.

[2] P. Oreizy, M.M. Gorlick, R.N. Taylor, D. Heimbigner, G. Johnson, N. Medvidovic, A. Quilici, D.S. Rosenblum, A.L. Wolf, An architecture-based approach to self-adaptive software, IEEE Intell. Syst. Appl. 14 (3) (1999) 54–62.

[3] P. Oreizy, N. Medvidovic, R.N. Taylor, Runtime software adaptation: framework, approaches, and styles, in: Proceedings of the 30th International Conference on Software Engineering (ICSE 2008), Leipzig, Germany, 2008.

[4] R.N. Taylor, N. Medvidovic, E.M. Dashofy, Software Architecture: Foundations, Theory, and Practice, John Wiley & Sons, Hoboken, NJ, 2009. ISBN-10: 0470167742, ISBN-13: 978-0470167748.

Foreword by Paris Avgeriou

The software architecture community realized from the very beginning (more than 2 decades ago) that functionality was not the main challenge; we could get that right, sooner or later, in an incremental and iterative manner. The real focus for researchers and the main pain point in industrial architecture practice was and still remains how to tame quality attributes. Form (architecture) does follow function, but form has some trouble following quality.

The problem of achieving requirements for quality attributes qualifies as a "wicked problem," and it is a multifaceted one. First, one cannot achieve each attribute in isolation as they are often interdependent and even contradictory. Consider, for example, the conflict between performance with almost any other quality attribute; when you try to optimize for performance, you may hurt the modifiability or security of your system. Second, a quality attribute cannot be dealt within a single component but requires system-wide measures. It would have been wonderful to have, e.g., a "reliability component" that can be simply integrated in a system, but it does not work that way; quality needs to be ensured across the system. Third, in contrast to functionality that can be very tangible and expressed simply yet effectively in use cases or user stories, quality attributes are rather elusive and often expressed in a vague way. This has been the source of frustration in innumerable discussions between development teams and other stakeholders, that started from a simple question like "What exactly does it mean for the system to be usable?" Finally, quality attributes are almost always implicitly derived from business goals. The link to business goals constitutes the rationale behind quality attributes; just like the rationale behind design decisions, it can hamper system evolution if it remains implicit.

However, all is not lost. The architecture community has been diligently working on methods and tools to tackle the aforementioned problems and help architects systematically manage quality attributes and their trade-offs. Software patterns for architecture and design describe in detail the quality attributes in terms of the pattern forces and further elaborate how the solution incurs both benefits and liabilities regarding those quality attributes; tactics contribute in the same direction by focusing on individual qualities. Furthermore, architecture design methods consider quality attributes as inputs and match them with candidate patterns and tactics in order to make rational decisions. Subsequently, architecture evaluation methods examine multiple quality attributes and perform explicit trade-offs by looking at related design decisions. Moreover, there are proven techniques to express quality attribute requirements in a SMART way for example by means of low-level scenarios with a tangible input and a measurable output. Additionally, there are several architecture views that frame quality attributes and modeling techniques for formal specification and verification of qualities. Finally, there are methods that elicit the relationships between quality attributes and business goals, as well as methods that study the explicit trade-off between the utility gained from achieving quality attribute requirements and the corresponding cost.

But then again, just as we thought we had tamed quality attributes, the advent and proliferation of self-adaptive systems changes the rules of the game. Self-adaptive systems are moving towards more and more flexibility where the design space is not fixed at design time but both problems and solutions can shift during runtime in an unplanned manner. Especially the new generation of self-adaptive systems that is currently emerging will increasingly face this core challenge: *uncertainty*. Our entire arsenal in the struggle towards managing quality attributes is going to be rendered obsolete as uncertainty looms in a number of ways. We may not know whether the requirements for the system quality attributes will change in the future or how they will change. We may be uncertain whether the components and services being used will remain the same and will continue operating within the same functional and quality boundaries. We cannot predict changes in the environment and other interacting systems, or changes in the mission and goals of the overall system. We cannot ensure that new configurations of the system will continue delivering the prescribed quality of service. There may be doubts whether established and confirmed design decisions are still valid under future conditions.

Current architecture design methods can only optimize the design with respect to explicit requirements and trade-offs for quality attributes; introducing variability in both problem and solution space can become extremely complicated. Similarly, architecture evaluation methods can gauge whether design decisions are sound for specific quality attributes, given that both decisions and qualities are described in a nonambiguous manner. Software patterns and tactics describe both the problem and solution space under a specific context and a "closed world assumption"; they do not take into account unforeseen changes. And what is the point of expressing quality attributes in a SMART way if the stimulus changes or if the way we measure responses takes a different form? In other words, none of the current available methods and tooling can be used as is, in the self-adaptive domain. This is why this book is very timely in shedding some light on the intricate problem and potential solutions of managing trade-offs of quality attributes in self-adaptive architectures.

I think this field will become increasingly important over the next years and the following directions are particularly promising for further research:

Intertwinement of problem and solution space. While the interrelation between requirements and architecture has long been recognized, it has remained to a large extent a "holy grail" in practice. The different metamodels and schools of thought used for expressing problem and solution spaces limit this interrelation while traces between them can be mostly constructed manually, which is prohibitively expensive. However in self-adaptive architectures, we need to come up with better traceability so that changes in the problem space can be translated more flexibly and accurately to changes in the solution space and vice versa.

Data science to the rescue. We do not have a crystal ball to predict the future, but looking at the past can often provide sound indications on where we are headed. Data science can contribute enormously to this field with tools and techniques on how systems and environments evolve over time, especially in an open source context, thereby reducing the uncertainty in the design space. Furthermore, using theory and tools from machine learning, the knowledge base of a self-adaptive architecture can be continuously updated to reflect the current situation from both the problem and the solution side.

Variability management redefined. Handling uncertainty in self-adaptation can be viewed as a variability management problem, where the sources of uncertainty are variation points, while the different potential cases of problems and solutions are the variants. Variability management theory and tools from software product lines or massively customizable software can be reused and built on, to model deviations in quality attributes in self-adaptive systems as well the impact of alternative design decisions. Emphasis needs to be given on the dependencies between the variants which can be immensely complicated.

The chapters in this book provide some initial steps towards solving these and related problems. I hope you enjoy reading this volume as much as I did, and I would strongly encourage you to work persistently on these hard problems, as this field holds both a challenging and rewarding future.

Paris Avgeriou
University of Groningen, the Netherlands

Foreword by Rogério de Lemos

Although the reasoning of software systems at the architectural level provides an effective way to handle complexity, the emerging area of self-adaptive software systems is challenging traditional approaches on how to develop, operate, and evolve software systems. However, at the same time that current practices are being challenged, opportunities emerge regarding new application areas for software system that are flexible when handling change (which may affect the system itself, its environment, or its requirements). Associated with changes, inevitably, there are uncertainties that need to be identified, analyzed, and handled, and this is the purposes of trade-off analysis in systems design. In the context of self-adaptive software systems trade-off analysis is not an exclusive development-time activity, trade-off analysis takes place also at runtime while the system is adapting itself.

Architectural-based development-time trade-off analysis is still a very much human activity, and their techniques and practices cannot be easily automated. Even if they could be automated, one would not be able to achieve the same level of thoroughness because of the lack of human insight, experience and diversity. However, there are certain benefits for moving some of the trade-off analysis from development-time to runtime, and one of these is related to the state space of uncertainties. At runtime, the state space should be smaller than that at development-time since at development-time there is little operational information of the actual system yet in the process of being designed. The amount of operational information available during runtime should be exploited in order to support trade-off analysis for adapting the software system. The development-time and runtime trade-off analyses should be complementary in order to optimize the service, and its qualities, to be delivered by the system. In order words, there are decisions currently being made at development-time related to operational uncertainties that can be deferred to runtime.

This rearrangement of trade-off analysis for handling uncertainties between development-time to runtime raises a clear challenge: how to identify what kind of analyses should be performed at development-time from those that should be performed at runtime. This identification, on its own, should establish the limits of adaptation, and this in itself already involves some kind of trade-off between adaptation and evolution. It is unquestionable that adaptation has its limits, and the decision when to stop adapting and to start a new evolution cycle is something that should be related to runtime limitations. An interesting feature to be considered in any self-adaptive software system should be the system capability of decommissioning itself when is not able to adapt anymore. Whether to deploy another redundant system, or completely stop its activities is a key decision to be made.

This book provides a timely springboard for starting a more insightful discussion on how to perform trade-off analysis in architecture-based self-adaptive software systems. New processes for trade-off analysis should be established, which should identify activities and decisions to be associated with development-time and runtime. These processes should identify what should be tailored on existing and well established practices, and identify challenges associated with the dynamic trade-off analysis to be performed during runtime. As part of development-time trade-off analysis, decisions should be made regarding the ability of the architecture in supporting runtime adaptation, and the easiness in instrumenting the software in terms of probes and effectors, for example. Regarding runtime trade-off analysis, since this has to be fully automated, some kind of decision maker should be adopted, and the literature is reach regarding synthesis techniques. The challenge is on the analysis side in which solution boundaries need to be explored in terms of their effectiveness, quality attributes and risks, for example. In this context, the promising solutions rely on games to be played between the controller and the sources of change that might affect the system. A more far reaching challenge, for the sake of the evolving software, is how to consider and incorporate into the trade-off analysis performed at development-time, the trade-off decisions, and their associated rationale, made during runtime.

Another major challenge regarding runtime trade-offs are the decision-making criteria. If a system, its requirements and environment are expected to change, also the criteria regulating decision making should be dynamic. Usually these criteria are considered static, which might lead to less than optimal decisions, in a truly dynamic environment. If that is the case, trade-off analysis tools and techniques should be capable of updating during runtime the values of the criteria. Moreover, one should not expect that a single technique, for example, utility functions, should be sufficient for a wide range of applications and contexts. The area of decision making is an area in which diversity of techniques and tools should have a positive impact since changes in the parameters of the decision-making criteria, or the techniques and tools being used, might have a great impact upon decisions. In summary, the runtime trade-off analysis should be itself resilient against changes that might affect the self-adaptive software system in which it is embedded.

Rogério de Lemos
March 2016

Preface

J. Grundy, I. Mistrik, B. Schmerl, R. Kazman, N. Ali

INTRODUCTION

Self-adaptive systems are those that, unlike traditional software systems, are engineered to be adaptable at runtime and, in fact, adapt themselves in various ways to their changing environment, users, user requirements, and related systems. Adaptation can take many forms: adaption to new data sources and remote services; adaption to changing network, hardware or related software systems; adaption in the presence of uncertainty and/or unreliability of other systems; adaption to new users and user needs; adaption of security, privacy, and trust models and implementations; adaption to improve one or more quality of service attributes; and adaption to handle catastrophic environmental events.

Engineering software systems that adapt is hard. A fundamental premise for such systems is a software architecture that encapsulates, and is designed for in some way, adaptation. Some architectures support a wide variety of adaptation, while others are more limited. In either circumstance, there will be inherent trade-offs that need to be made by the architects to achieve the necessary kinds of adaption and the supporting software and systems infrastructure required to achieve it.

Analyzing and managing these trade-offs is also very hard. A great deal of research and practice interest has been focused on this problem due to its increasing need in a wide variety of contexts. These include cloud-based systems, mobile applications, security- and safety-critical systems, and the emerging Internet of Things. Our goal in this book is to collect chapters on architecting for adaptability and, more specifically, how to manage trade-offs between functional requirements and multiple quality requirements in adaptable software architectures. The intention of this book is to collect state-of-the-art knowledge on:

- what it means to architect a system for adaptability;
- software architecture for self-adaptive systems;
- what trade-offs are involved and how can one balance these;
- general models of self-adaptive systems;
- architectural patterns for self-adaptive systems;
- how to intertwine business goals and software quality requirements with adaptable software architectures;
- how quality attributes are exhibited by the architecture of the system;
- how to connect the quality of a software architecture to system architecture or other system considerations;
- what are the major challenges of engineering adaptive software architectures;
- what techniques are required to achieve quality management in architecting for adaptability;
- the best ways to apply adaptation techniques effectively in systems such as cloud, mobile, cyber-physical, and ultra-large-scale/internet-scale systems;

- the approaches that can be employed to assess the value of total quality management in a software development process, with an emphasis on adaptable software architecture; and
- case studies of successful (or unsuccessful but useful lessons learned) application of trade-offs in designing, developing, and deploying adaptive systems.

The book is arranged into four parts. Part I reviews key concepts and models for self-adaptive software architectures. This includes key approaches to architecting systems for adaptation; tackling uncertainty when architecting self-adaptive systems; viewpoint modeling for dynamically modifiable software systems; and adaptive security for software systems. Part II focuses on analysis and trade-offs in self-adaptive software systems. This includes the use of automation in terms of inference techniques to support architecting of adaptable systems; managing trade-offs when dealing with the human element of adaptive systems; elicitation and evaluation of discovered trade-offs when architecting such systems; analysis for self-adaptive software architectures; and adaptive architectures for scalable software-as-a-service based systems. Part III examines the management of trade-offs for self-adaptive software architectures. A systematic mapping study reviews the large body of work in this area to date and formulates key contributions and research gaps. Also in this part is a requirements-driven approach to mediation solutions. Finally, Part IV addresses the issue of quality assurance for self-adaptive software architectures. Quality evaluation mechanisms are reviewed, compared, and contrasted.

PART I: CONCEPTS AND MODELS FOR SELF-ADAPTIVE SOFTWARE ARCHITECTURES

Chapter 1 is by the editors and provides a review of the concepts of self-adaptive software architectures, their history, key features, some of the key challenges in managing trade-offs, and what we see as some of the major outstanding areas for research and practice in this domain. We first review some of the key prior work in architecting self-adaptive systems that has been published to date. We then discuss the body of work that has looked at the issue of managing trade-offs when designing such self-adaptive software systems. Trade-off management at run time in particular is then discussed including many outstanding challenges that exist in this domain. We then outline a set of research challenges that should lead us as a community to a better vision for managing trade-offs in self-adaptive systems.

Chapter 2, by Villegas, Tamura, and Muller, provides an overview of architecting software systems for runtime self-adaptation: concepts, models, instrumentation and challenges. In this chapter the authors introduce practitioners, researchers, and students to foundational concepts and reference models associated with the architecture of self-adaptive software. It also presents challenges related to the design of software architectures that enable self-adaptation of software systems at execution time. They first introduce a running example to illustrate the studied concepts. They then explore the meanings of adaptation and self-adaptation as well as the differences between these two concepts. They explain fundamental concepts for architecting self-adaptive software systems and then present a set of reference models and architectures relevant to the engineering of self-adaptive software. Finally they discuss major challenges regarding the architecting of complex software systems for self-adaptation.

Chapter 3, by Hezavehi, Avgeriou, and Weyns, provides a classification of current architecture-based approaches. In this chapter the authors review the state-of-the-art of architecture-based approaches tackling uncertainty in self-adaptive systems with multiple quality requirements, propose a classification framework for this domain, and classify the current approaches according to their new framework. To do this they conducted a systematic literature review by performing an automatic search on 27 selected venues and books in the domain of self-adaptive systems. From detailed analysis of this review they propose a novel classification framework for uncertainty and its sources in the domain of architecture-based self-adaptive systems with multiple quality requirements. They map their identified primary studies into their new framework and present the classified results. Results from this review will help researchers to understand the current state of research regarding uncertainty in architecture-based self-adaptive systems with multiple concerns, and identity areas for improvement in the future.

Chapter 4, adaptability viewpoint for modeling dynamically configurable software architectures, is authored by Tekinerdogan and Sozer. In this chapter the authors introduce an "adaptability viewpoint" that can be used for modeling dynamically configurable software architectures. They then illustrate the use of the viewpoint for a demand-driven supply chain management system. To represent runtime adaptability concerns more explicitly, the authors argue that an explicit dedicated architectural view is required to model the decomposition of the architecture based on the runtime adaptability concern. To this end they introduce a new runtime adaptability viewpoint that can be used for modeling dynamically configurable software architectures. This viewpoint has been defined via domain analysis of dynamic configurability and software architecture viewpoint modeling. The viewpoint is based on a meta-model that defines the underlying semantics. The authors first provide a background about architecture viewpoints and then introduce their supply chain system case study as a motivating example where runtime adaptability becomes a critical concern. They describe key related concepts and a meta-model for their runtime adaptability viewpoint and then introduces a concrete notation and a method for applying this viewpoint. The case study is then described by application of the viewpoint.

Chapter 5 is authored by Almorsy, Grundy, and Ibrahim, and describes a new framework for supporting adaptive security for software systems. In this chapter the authors discuss the needs for adaptive software security, and key efforts that have been made to date in this area. They then introduce a novel runtime adaptive security engineering approach that enables adapting software security capabilities at runtime based on new security objectives, risks/threats, and requirements, as well as newly reported vulnerabilities. The authors then categorize the source of adaptation in terms of manual adaptation (managed by end users), and automated adaption (automatically triggered by the supporting platform). They describe the application of their approach to a large case study and discuss its strengths, limitations, and areas for further enhancement.

PART II: ANALYZING AND EVALUATING TRADE-OFFS IN SELF-ADAPTIVE SOFTWARE ARCHITECTURES

Chapter 6, by Malek, Canavera, and Esfahani, describes the use of automated inference techniques to assist with construction of adaptable software architectures. The authors state that state-of-the-art in engineering self-adaptive software systems involves manual construction of numerous models, which are then used at runtime for making and effecting adaptation decisions. They show that the construction of such models is unwieldy and impractical for use by practitioners and describe an alternative approach for engineering adaptive software that aims to alleviate the challenges of manually developing such models using inference techniques to automatically derive the models necessary for building an adaptive architecture. A machine-learning approach is used to automatically derive the models predicting the impact of architectural change on the system's quality objectives. These types of models are used to make adaptation decisions to fix problems that may arise at runtime. A data-mining approach is then used to derive automatically the models expressing the probabilistic dependencies between the architectural elements of the system. These types of models are used to ensure changes in the running software do not create inconsistency, and jeopardize its functionality. The chapter discusses some remaining research challenges and areas of future research in employing automated inference techniques in the construction of adaptive architectures.

Chapter 7 focuses on evaluating trade-offs of human involvement in self-adaptive systems, and is authored by Cámara, Moreno, Garlan, Moreno, and Schmerl. In this chapter the authors we identify various roles that can perform in cooperating with self-adaptive systems. They focus on humans as effectors—doing tasks which are difficult or infeasible to automate—and describe how they modified their own self-adaptive framework to involve human operators in this way. This involved choosing suitable human models and integrating them into the existing utility trade-off decision models of their tool. They used probabilistic modeling and quantitative verification to analyze the trade-offs of involving humans in adaptation. They then complement their study with experiments to show how different business preferences and modalities of human involvement may result in different outcomes.

Chapter 8, principled eliciting and evaluation of trade-offs when designing self-adaptive systems architectures, is by Andrade and Macêdo. The authors present a systematic approach for design and analysis of self-adaptive systems architectures. This approach enables the representation of refined knowledge as structured design spaces and relies on the use of multiobjective optimization mechanisms to elicit and evaluate the involved quality attributes trade-offs. The authors present the key requirements for an automated approach for software architecture design and analysis and detail the underlying mechanisms and technologies adopted. They describe in detail how they have used their infrastructure to automate the design of self-adaptive systems. The authors validate their approach for effectiveness by using particular optimization performance indicators, as well as in functional prototypes of self-adaptive web servers and elastic platforms for distributed MapReduce jobs.

Chapter 9, by Kazman and Boxer, focuses on an approach for analyzing the architectures of software-intensive ecosystem. This chapter describes the core-periphery structures of the systems participating in software ecosystems, and approaches the analysis of their behavior from the perspective of the market behaviors that they are expected to support. The authors propose a key driver of the "wickedness" of these systems' behaviors is the accelerating pace at which an ecosystem is expected to respond to new kinds of demand. This makes it necessary to extend the concept of "architecture" to include the resultant processes of dynamic alignment. It then becomes necessary to analyze architecture in a way that includes the context of use of systems. The authors propose the use of a multisided matrix to represent the variety of forms of dynamic alignment demanded by self-adaptive systems, and describes an extension to the architecture trade-off analysis method as a means of discovering the risks inherent in architectural decisions made to support a software-intensive ecosystem.

Chapter 10, architectural perspective for design and analysis of scalable software as a service architecture, is authored by Tekinerdogan and Ozcan. In this chapter the authors discuss one of the major challenges in designing and maintaining SaaS computing systems, the design for and analysis of scalability. To address this they propose the scalability perspective for supporting the design and analysis of scalable SaaS architectures. They argue that in order to address quality concerns in software architecture design, an important approach is to define architectural perspectives that include a collection of activities, tactics, and guidelines that require consideration across a number of the architectural views. Their proposed architectural perspective can assist software architects in designing, analyzing, and communicating decisions made regarding scalability as well as any trade-offs with other concerns. They illustrate the scalability perspective on an industrial case study and discuss the lessons learned from this application of the technique.

PART III: MANAGING TRADE-OFFS IN SELF-ADAPTIVE SOFTWARE ARCHITECTURES

Chapter 11 is by Salama, Bencomo, and Bahsoon, and provides a systematic mapping study of managing trade-offs in self-adaptive architectures. The authors conducted this systematic mapping study to identify and analyze research related to analyzing and managing trade-offs for self-adaptive software architectures. They argue that self-adaptation has been driven by the need to achieve and maintain quality attributes in the face of continuously changing and emerging requirements, as well as the uncertain demand at runtime. Designing architectures that exhibit a good trade-off between multiple attributes is challenging, especially in the case of self-adaptive software systems, due to the complexity, heterogeneity and ultra-large scale of the modern software systems. Their study aims at collecting research work that explicitly addresses trade-off management for self-adaptive software architectures, to obtain a comprehensive overview on the current state of research on this specialized area. They selected 20 primary studies and analyzed these to classify software paradigms, quality attributes considered, and the properties that drive trade-off management. The results show constant interest in finding solutions for trade-offs management at design-time and runtime. The authors findings call for a foundational framework in analyzing and managing trade-offs for self-adaptive software architectures that can explicitly consider specific multiple quality attributes, the runtime dynamics, the uncertainty of the environment and the complex challenges of modern, ultra-large scale systems in particular software paradigms.

Chapter 12 is by Bennaceur and Nuseibeh and discusses the many facets of mediation. The authors discuss the concept of "mediation," which aims to enable dynamic composition of multiple components by making them interact successfully in order to satisfy given requirements. They argue that through dynamic composition, software systems can adapt their structure and behavior in dynamic and heterogeneous environments such as ubiquitous computing environments. Their chapter provides a review of existing mediation approaches and their key characteristics and limitations. The authors claim that only a multifaceted approach that brings together and enhances the solutions of mediation from different perspectives is viable in the long term. They then discuss how requirements can help identify synergies and trade-offs between these approaches and drive the selection of the appropriate mediation solution.

PART IV: QUALITY ASSURANCE IN SELF-ADAPTIVE SOFTWARE ARCHITECTURES

Chapter 13 is authored by Raibulet, Arcelli, Capilla, and Carrillo, and provides an overview of quality evaluation mechanisms for self-adaptive systems. In this chapter the authors aim to identify general guidelines for the evaluation of self-adaptive systems independent of their type, application domain, or implementation details. Evaluation is an important concern for building and monitoring the quality of software. The complex nature of self-adaptive systems demands continuous monitoring of their behavior and execution of runtime changes, which challenge the quality of their adaptations in dynamic environments. The characteristics of self-adaptive systems demand a continuous evaluation of their performances and improvement of the adaptation process. The authors propose a new taxonomy for the evaluation of the quality of self-adaptive systems based on five dimensions: scope, time, mechanisms, perspective, and type. They have identified the main available evaluation approaches and analyzed them using their proposed taxonomy. They discuss several trade-offs concerning each dimension in the taxonomy, trade-offs which need to be addressed during system evaluation.

Finally, Chapter 14 by Rogério de Lemosa and Pasqualina Potenac provides a discussion of identifying and handling uncertainties in the feedback control loop, a common feature of many adaptive systems. In this chapter they discuss how uncertainty is associated to different sources (e.g., the environment) and appears in different forms (e.g., as noise in variables or imperfections in techniques being used). They present the MAPE-K control loop, where uncertainty is normally handled by a decision maker at the plan stage. However, depending on the complexity of the stages of the MAPE-K control loop, uncertainties need also to be handled at other stages. The authors claim that uncertainties should be considered as a nonfunctional property that should be collectively handled at the different stages of the feedback control loop. One advantage of this approach is that it leads to a more accurate estimation of the system quality attributes since uncertainties are handled in the context where they arise, beneficial for trade-off analysis. Their approach relies on the identification of internal and external sources of uncertainty for a given stage, and promotes error propagation analysis as a method for analyzing the propagation of uncertainties.

We hope that you enjoy this book as much as we have in editing it. We thank the anonymous reviewers for all of their time in reviewing all of the chapters in this book. All chapters were reviewed by at least four reviewers, and many went through two or even three rounds of revision, many quite substantial revision. We thank the Elsevier Editorial team for their professional and very helpful approach that makes many of the chores associated with academic publishing much more bearable. And finally we sincerely thank the authors for their research efforts, willingness to respond to extensive feedback from the reviewers and editorial team, and without whose excellent contributions this would not have been possible.

MANAGING TRADE-OFFS IN ADAPTABLE SOFTWARE ARCHITECTURES

B. Schmerl*, R. Kazman*,†, N. Ali‡, J. Grundy§, I. Mistrik¶

Carnegie Mellon University, Pittsburgh, PA, United States* University of Hawaii, Honolulu, HI, United States†
University of Brighton, Brighton, United Kingdom‡ Deakin University, Melbourne, VIC, Australia§
Independent Software Researcher, Heidelberg, Germany¶

1.1 INTRODUCTION

As the field of software architecture enters into its third decade of formal study, it is moving from its traditional and foundational focus on the nature of an architecture in terms of a system's structure and behavior, to the more general notion of software architecture as the set of design decisions made to ensure software requirements are met. Consistent with this view is the trend towards focusing software architecture documentation on meeting stakeholder needs and communicating how the software solution addresses their concerns. Usually, a software system is not isolated, but part of a larger system. When making design decisions, not only is the quality of the software architecture itself important, but the quality of the overall system also needs to be considered.

As such, software systems increasingly interact with each other and are more often part of critical civil and business infrastructure. This means that software is increasingly required to operate for long periods of time, in highly dynamic environments, where user demands may change, and where systems' interaction and business goals may evolve. Software architectures, in addition to the design decisions that led to them, also must react and evolve to ensure old and new requirements are met, and that the systems they represent operate reliably.

Design decisions are fundamentally about trade-offs. When deciding between architectural alternatives, architects need to consider how each alternative affects the functional and quality requirements of the software being designed. Often, functional requirements can be architected in a number of ways; the choice of architecture is made by trading off different software qualities. The architecture trade-off analysis method (ATAM) [1,2] by the Software Engineering Institute defines a method for conducting architectural trade-offs for classical quality attributes such as performance, availability, and modifiability. However, this method works best for systems with fixed business goals, behaviors, and bounded environments. Furthermore, the trade-offs are done manually with multiple stakeholders.

For over 15 years, there has been increasing research in the field of adaptable software architectures—where systems are able to change their topology and behavior to adapt to changing circumstances (e.g., changing environments and requirements). For example, in 1997, Robert

Laddaga [3] defined self-adaptive software as software that "evaluates its own behavior and changes behavior when the evaluation indicates that it is not accomplishing what the software is intended to do, or when better functionality or performance is possible." Oreizy et al. [4] proposed an architecture-based approach for the construction of self-adaptive systems that relies on software agents, explicit representation of software components, the environment, messaging, and event services. To be able to act autonomously, the software needs to evaluate potential adaptations, taking into consideration trade-offs in new circumstances to make adaptations that are best for meeting the system's requirements.

There are at least two critical aspects of managing trade-offs for self-adaptive systems. First, how do we design systems to be adaptable in the presence of other quality attributes? Through methods like ATAM we have a reasonable understanding of how to manage design trade-offs for performance, availability, maintainability etc., but we have little idea about how to integrate the notion of adaptability in this process. Second, how do we manage these trade-offs at runtime so that when the self-adaptive system needs to decide on an adaptation, it can make appropriate trade-offs dynamically and autonomously?

Despite extensive research on self-adaptive systems, there are still many challenges that need to be addressed. This book contains a set of chapters on the state of the art of managing trade-offs in self-adaptive software systems. In this chapter, we summarize some of the prior work on this topic and lay out a set of challenges that need to be addressed to realize a principled approach to trade-off management in self-adaptive systems.

This chapter is organized as follows. Section 1.2 discusses prior work in architecting self-adaptive systems. Section 1.3 discusses work in managing trade-offs when designing self-adaptive software systems. Trade-off management at runtime is discussed in Section 1.4. Finally, Section 1.5 outlines a set of research challenges that should lead to a better vision for managing trade-offs in self-adaptive systems.

1.2 BACKGROUND

In recent years there has been a fundamental shift in software development, away from stovepipe applications that are intended to run on a small cluster of computers, to large distributed software applications that service many clients through public facing interfaces. These highly distributed systems often run on cloud systems and implement big data analytics, meaning that software architects must consider scale and autonomy as primary concerns in developing software. Furthermore, the use of agile development methods and the emergence of DevOps (bringing together development and operation) means that software must be designed with zero downtime, that is, it must run continuously. Moreover, as the software requirements and business needs evolve, and as new, unanticipated threats and security vulnerabilities emerge, the software itself must adapt to meet these challenges. Therefore, it is no longer feasible for many systems to architect them assuming a static set of requirements or a fixed and known environment—systems need to restructure or reconfigure to meet this new and uncertain world.

Historically, the changes required to meet the challenges above have required human intervention in the form of re-engineering the systems through updates, or reconfiguring the system. However, such human intervention cannot scale because adaptations to meet new demands or threats must happen extremely quickly, or the inherent complexity and distribution of modern systems means that the systems are too large and complex to understand. Therefore, there is a need for software to become self-adaptive, meaning that software must be able to autonomously change structure and/or behavior to respond to changing conditions, and must do so reliably and without unnecessarily degrading quality of service (QoS) [5,6].

We can think of the design of self-adaptive systems from two perspectives. On one hand, individual self-adaptive systems contain knowledge of the system's goals and constraints, and adapt themselves to maintain, as far as possible, the goals under changing conditions. On the other hand, because software systems increasingly exist in large interconnected ecosystems, collective self-adaptive systems consist of multiple autonomous elements that are coordinating to achieve a common set of goals. Both kinds of adaptation have received extensive investigation.

The areas of intelligent agents [7], reflective computing [8], and control theory [9] have provided inspiration for approaches to constructing individual adaptive systems. Furthermore, several architectures and mechanisms to enable adaptation have been proposed, including the widely adopted IBM autonomic computing approach [10]. The latter proposes an architectural pattern for self-adaptation called the MAPE-K loop, which enumerates the activities that should be considered and coordinated when designing autonomic systems: monitoring the system and the environment, analyzing the situation to determine if the system needs to change, planning what to do, and then executing an adaptation on the system; all of these activities involve accessing some knowledge base of the system or part of the system being managed, and in many cases its environment and context. This approach considers self-adaptive systems as adding a closed control loop around the systems they manage. In the control loop, a specific control component (e.g., the "autonomic manager" in the autonomic computing approach, or the "meta-component" in reflective approaches) is responsible for each of these activities.

Collective adaptation requires coordinating adaptation among multiple self-adaptive systems. Centralized approaches to this do not scale, but there is a variety of patterns for coordinating multiple controllers and control loops that have been investigated [11,12]. A control approach to designing self-adaptive system is only one possible approach. Although this approach is overwhelmingly favored in existing self-adaptive systems research, other approaches using negotiation and market-oriented mechanisms have also been studied [7]. These approaches involve autonomic components cooperating to adaptively converge on specific suitable configurations, possibly respecting specific global goals [13]. In the past few years, a number of proposals have also suggested that adaptation in distributed systems can be achieved with decentralized self-organization [14]. However, this raises the issue of properly controlling and predicting the possible emergence of unexpected behaviors.

Research to date has primarily focused on approaches to engineering self-adaptive systems, trying to distil generalized examples of architectures to implement self-adaptation. While these approaches have resulted in engineering a number of successful self-adaptive systems, there has been little research on how to decide which style of self-adaptation is suitable in what cases, how these different styles support or inhibit other system qualities, and how to conduct trade-offs to decide the best architectural approach in specific cases. Furthermore, there is a lack of architectural tactics that can be applied generally, in the same sense as architectural tactics for achieving other qualities (e.g., reliability, performance) [15]. Some work [16,17] describes patterns for different domains (e.g., service-oriented architecture and self-protection). Again, there is no discussion of how to choose these patterns in the presence of multiple quality concerns.

1.3 TRADE-OFFS IN ADAPTIVE SYSTEMS DESIGN

Trade-offs occur in all designs of nontrivial systems, whether these systems are computational or not. Trade-offs are inherent in the design process and resulting artifacts, arising from the properties of components and their interactions. Trade-offs are, therefore, among the most important design decisions that an architect has to make.

A trade-off is an architectural decision that affects two or more system properties, making at least one property better and at least one property worse. Every system, and every system's design, is constrained: by computational resources, by development time, by development team effort, and by investment dollars. And so the concerns and priorities of different groups of stakeholders cannot always be fully met when designing the system. In such cases, the architect needs to make a decision, to value and support one property of the system over another.

For example, the architect might decide to rush a system to market, knowing full well that it will not easily scale. Or the architect might choose to implement ultra-high availability, using backup servers, storage, and networks, knowing that this will unnecessarily increase the cost, or reduce the profitability, of the system. Or the architect might choose to design and implement a very strong encryption scheme on communications over the internet, knowing that this will negatively impact system throughput and latency. These are all risky decisions and any of them might backfire on the architect and doom the project. Trade-offs must, therefore, be carefully considered. And virtually every *technical* trade-off—for performance, or security, or availability—must be balanced against the ubiquitous trade-offs of cost and schedule [18] that all organizations must face.

Having to make a trade-off in your architecture design does not necessarily mean that you will be unable to satisfy the goals of your stakeholders, but it does mean that some stakeholders will inevitably be more satisfied than others. Your manager, for example, wants to keep costs and schedule as low as possible, while your end users want as much performance and usability and security as possible, preferably with no downtime ever. System administrators want systems that are easy to install, upgrade, and backup. And so forth.

A good design is one that satisfies the architectural drivers—the primary functionality, quality attribute goals, architectural concerns, and constraints—of the stakeholders that the system is meant to serve [5]. A good design does not, in most cases, need to optimize for any one of those drivers, at the expense of the others. As Simon explained [19], designs only need to *satisfice* for most properties and for most users: that is, the system designs typically only need to be "good enough," rather than optimal.

In all software systems, trade-offs come in two possible flavors:

1. "static" or nonruntime decisions, made during the design, implementation, and evolutionary maintenance of a system, which are relatively difficult and expensive to change, requiring extensive development effort, and
2. "dynamic" or runtime decisions, that we can automatically make, monitor, and adapt to as the system is executing. This is the realm of self-adaptive systems.

Trade-offs of type 1 are no different than trade-offs in nonself-adaptive systems. We make these decisions and we live with them, or we pay the price in terms of refactoring and re-engineering costs or technical debt [17,20]. Trade-offs of type 2 are those properties that we can manage and reason about at runtime, such as performance, scalability, availability, security, and so forth. Such type 2 changes—adaptations—may be necessitated because of changes in the environment (e.g., the failure of a network channel), changes in resources (e.g., new servers coming online or being removed), or changes in user demand.

1.4 RUNTIME TRADE-OFFS IN SELF-ADAPTIVE SYSTEMS

Even when *adaptability* is designed into a system, there may be a number of adaptations that can apply when the software encounters a situation in which it needs to adapt. For example, adapting to address low response time in a modern IT system might involve choosing between scaling up, scaling out, or focusing service on important clients; or, reducing battery consumption in an autonomous robotics system might involve switching to less-accurate sensing hardware and localization algorithms, or changing the mission profile of the robot to do fewer tasks. Furthermore, the choice of the best adaptation depends on several factors, including the context in which the system resides, the future environment that the system is likely to encounter, and the business context and goals that the system is trying to achieve or maintain.

It may be theoretically possible to enumerate *all* the possible states that a system can be in and predetermine the appropriate trade-off for each state, in which case the runtime decision is a simple look-up that maps the current state to the best configuration. However, this approach is complicated by various factors of uncertainty that make the state space extremely large.

First, there is considerable uncertainty involved in understanding the current context in which the system finds itself. To overcome this, the system must sense itself and its environment, but this cannot be done with absolute certainty. For example, self-adaptive systems usually abstract the state of the system into runtime models (e.g., architectural models [21]), and this abstraction necessarily loses some detail. Second, the environment itself needs to be monitored and abstracted, and because the environment is typically out of the control of the system, there will be limitations in what knowledge the system can ascertain about it. For example, if the number of requests increases, how can we discern if this is due to an increase in the popularity of the application, or whether the system is undergoing a denial of service attack? How do we know if this change in environment is a durable shift that must be addressed with more permanent adaptations, or if it is temporary? How can we be sure that the adaptation we choose will have the desired effect, or impact, on the system to address the concerns? Because of these (and other) sources of uncertainty [22], these decisions need to be made and evaluated at runtime.

To make the appropriate choice, a self-adaptive system must, at runtime, trade-off multiple concerns in this environment of uncertainty.

As many of these trade-offs involve understanding and managing the quality of the system in addition to the functionality of the system, the use of software architecture models at runtime has been proposed and used to provide self-adaptive capabilities [4,23–25].

The use of architectural models as the central knowledge for runtime adaptation is embodied in a framework called Rainbow [26]. The Rainbow framework uses software architectures and a reusable infrastructure to support self-adaptation of software systems. Fig. 1.1 shows the adaptation control loop of Rainbow. Probes are used to extract information from the target system and its environment that update an architecture model via gauges, which abstract and aggregate this system-level information to detect architecture-relevant events and properties. Gauges and probes together comprise the *monitoring* aspect of the MAPE-K loop. The *analysis* aspect of MAPE-K is implemented in Rainbow as architecture evaluators, which check for properties in the model, including satisfaction of constraints and quality attributes in the model, and triggers adaptation if any violation is found. The adaptation manager, on receiving the adaptation trigger, chooses the "best" strategy to execute, thus covering *planning* in MAPE, and passes it on to the strategy executor, which executes the strategy on the target system via effectors.

The adaptation manager may initially discover that several strategies are applicable, and so must perform a trade-off to choose between them. The trade-off is captured by predicting the impact each strategy will have on each quality attribute, and then prioritizing some qualities over others to score the strategy. The best strategy is chosen on the basis of stakeholder utility

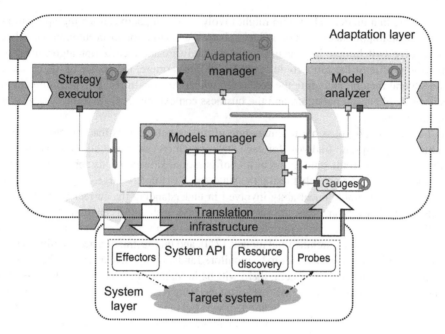

FIG. 1.1

The Rainbow framework.

preferences and the current state of the system, as reflected in the architecture model. The underlying decision making model is based on decision theory and utility [27]; varying the utility preferences allows the adaptation engineer to affect which strategy is selected. Each strategy, which is written using the Stitch adaptation language [28], is a multi-step pattern of adaptations in which each step evaluates a set of condition-action pairs and executes an action, namely a *tactic*, on the target system with variable execution time. A tactic defines an action, packaged as a sequence of commands (operators). It specifies conditions of applicability, expected effect and cost-benefit attributes to relate its impact on the quality dimensions. Operators are basic commands provided by the target system that implement a particular change.

As a framework, Rainbow can be customized to support self-adaptation for a wide variety of system types. Customization points are indicated by the cut-outs on the side of the architecture layer in Fig. 1.1. Different architectures (and architectural styles), strategies, utilities, operators, and constraints on the system may all be defined to make Rainbow reusable in a variety of situations.

In addition to providing an engineering basis for creating self-adapting systems, Rainbow also provides a basis for their analysis. By separating concerns, and formalizing the basis for adaptive actions, it is possible to reason about fault detection, diagnosis, and repair. For example, many of the standard metrics associated with classical control systems can, in principle, be carried over: settling time, convergence, overshoot, etc. In addition, the focus on utility as a basis for repair selection provides a formal platform for principled understanding of the effects of repair strategies, and for reasoning about trade-offs at runtime.

In summary, Rainbow uses architectural models of a software system as the basis for reasoning about whether the system is operating within an acceptable envelope. If this is not the case, Rainbow chooses appropriate adaptation strategies to return the system to an acceptable operating range. The key concepts of this approach are thus:

(a) the use of abstract architecture models representing the runtime structures of a system, that make reasoning about system-wide properties tractable;
(b) detection mechanisms that identify the existence and source of problems at an architectural level;
(c) a strategy definition language called Stitch that allows architects to define adaptations that can be applied to a system at runtime; and
(d) a means to choose appropriate strategies to fix problems, taking into consideration multiple quality concerns to achieve an optimal balance among all desired properties.

In order to conduct trade-offs at runtime, Rainbow uses utility preferences and impact predictions to choose the strategy that will have the best result according to the business goals of the system. This approach is detailed in Refs. [28–30], and is summarized here. First, applicable strategies are chosen based on whether they apply in the given context. For example, if the system is not under attack, then there is no need to examine strategies that deal with attacks; or, if server resources have been depleted, then there is no point in choosing strategies that add servers. Next, each applicable strategy is examined to determine its predicted impact on the current state of the system. Each tactic in a strategy is assigned an impact on each of the qualities of interest. For example, a tactic to add a server will have a positive impact on response time but a negative impact on cost. Each strategy forms a tree of tactics guarded by conditions and probabilities that the branch will be taken. This tree is traversed and an overall impact on each quality is calculated as a combination of the tactics. These impacts are then assigned a value utility based on utility functions defined for the business context, and then combined using preference weights to determine an overall score for the strategy. The strategy with the highest score is then executed by Rainbow.

Naturally, doing this trade-off at runtime is dependent on (a) accurate models of the state of the system, (b) accurate models of impact, and (c) accurate quantification of utilities and preferences. Recent work on Rainbow has begun to address (a) and (b). Accurate models of the system have been addressed partially in Ref. [31], where theoretical limits on knowledge about the health states of parts of the system that are unobservable have been determined. In Ref. [32], context sensitive and probabilistic models of tactic impact, and how to modify the impact calculation using probabilistic model checking have been defined.

Despite these advances in using trade-offs to make adaptation choices at runtime, there remain some limitations. First, a decision is made considering only the cost and benefits, but not the risk. A more nuanced approach to decision making might choose a less risky but less impactful strategy over a strategy that has a high impact but might fail. Second, utility and preferences need to be quantified, which is often hard for stakeholders to do accurately. Improving this approach using a ranking scheme might be easier to specify and still provide good results in choosing the most appropriate adaptation at runtime. Linking this runtime decision making to design time rationale for architecture tactics (as is discussed in Section 1.3), is also likely to be a worthwhile advance.

1.5 CHALLENGES AND THE ROAD AHEAD

In this chapter we have reviewed the state of the art in managing trade-offs in self-adaptive systems. While using trade-offs in designing software architectures has received a lot of investigation, incorporating adaptability as a quality attribute, and how it affects other quality attributes has received less attention. Also, while mechanisms and formalisms for trading off quality attributes at runtime to decide the best adaptation has emerged in the past decade, the ability to manage these trade-offs at runtime and adapt the trade-offs has yet to gain traction.

The challenges ahead for taking an architectural perspective on adaptation, and using this as a basis for managing this trade-off among quality attributes, can be divided into the following questions.

1.5.1 HOW TO ARCHITECT FOR ADAPTABILITY?

While a lot of work has been done on architecting systems for reliability, performance, etc., and the styles, analysis, and patterns are well understood, how to architect an *adaptable* system is still largely done in an a hoc manner. There has been considerable work on elaborating the design of autonomy following the MAPE loop, but this represents only one way in which adaptability could be designed. Software architects need principled approaches for designing for adaptability to address the concern of modern software systems. This involves addressing the following concerns:

What are good software architectures or architecture styles for self-adaptive systems? Architectural approaches to self-adaptation have been dominated by elaborations or variations of the MAPE loop, which at its essence represents a control loop approach. However, this approach is not necessarily the only approach, and may not be the best approach in some contexts. We need a good catalog of styles from other communities. For example, Ref. [33] discusses a pattern-based style from the agent community as an alternative. Other approaches to self-organization that are biologically inspired might also be applied [34]. The challenges in all these cases are what are the strengths and weaknesses of each style, in what cases and domains do they apply, and how do they enhance or inhibit other qualities such as performance and security?

What architectural patterns enhance adaptability? Architectural styles for adaptability are perhaps most useful when adaptability is a primary concern. Architectural patterns (or tactics) are building blocks that can be used to design part of a system to enhance a quality attribute. There are a number of approaches that can be considered as patterns for implementing self-adaptation. For example hot swapping of component, micro-rebooting, and component isolation all have requirements and rules that must be satisfied by the components and connectors that make up the tactics. Notions such as component isolation, quiescence, and tranquility might also be considered parts of patterns. These need to be cataloged and examined considering the same questions as for architectural styles. Some patterns for reliability and fault tolerance (like failing safe) also need to be examined in the context of adaptability.

How to quantify adaptability? One requirement for doing good design is being able to analyze the design to ensure that it has the properties the designer requires. For example, in the area of performance, queuing theory has been useful in establishing properties such as throughput, response time, and whether there is sufficient load; designs for real time systems can be analyzed with rate monotonic analysis to reason about task deadlines being met. In these cases, the quality attributes can be measured quantifiably, and compared with alternative designs. We need equivalent metrics for adaptability. There has been little work on this. In Ref. [35] the authors develop adaptability metrics for business processes that examines a number of alternative implementations of a particular service, and how often the service is used in the business process. Much work needs to be done to develop more comprehensive and general metrics. It may be possible to extend methods for quantifying the resilience and reliability of systems to deal with adaptability.

1.5.2 ADAPTABILITY IN MODERN SYSTEMS

A key driver of self-adaptive systems described in Section 1.1 is that it is often a consequence of the need for continuous operation. This is particularly the case in the domains of cloud computing, service-based systems, cyber-physical systems, and ultra-large-scale systems. The main question for all of these domains is how do we consider adaptability as a first class concern, and trade it off with other concerns that must be met by the systems in these domains. There has been some discussion of self-adaptation in each of these domains, and each domain has its own approach.

1.5.2.1 Cloud computing

Cloud computing is characterized by the use of remote computing to provide computing resources. Often, the cloud is used to provide scale of computation, where services are duplicated over multiple remote servers to provide enough resources for the software to provide service. Third party providers "rent" resources to clients so that clients do not need to provide or manage these resources in house. Because providing these resources has a cost, clients typically do not want to pay for more resources than are being used. This leads many cloud providers to provide autonomous management services that scale resource usage based on the use of the applications. This is termed *elasticity*, where infrastructure resources grow and shrink with application demands. Clients have some control over the elasticity used for their applications, to balance cost and performance.

Elasticity is a form of self-adaptation, and is usually characterized by two different tactics: *scaling up* and *scaling out*. Scaling up is used to expand the resources (storage, CPU cores, etc.) of the machines that are already being used by an application. Scaling out adds more machines into the pool of machines that can be used by an application. While these are the most common forms of self-adaptation used in cloud computing, other forms of adaptation can be applied in other contexts that use cloud computing. For example, in big data applications, database partitioning can be changed to account for scaling associated with different types of queries.

Cloud computing providers, in giving their application customers control over some of the parameters of elasticity, allow them some ability to trade-off the different concerns of cost and performance to in turn meet their own clients' needs. They can define rules that indicate what forms of scaling should happen when monitored conditions happen. However, this control is limited. As discussed in Ref. [36], cloud providers need to be careful about what they can monitor to maintain the intellectual property and privacy of the applications they are hosting. So, monitoring is typically limited so that it does not provide visibility into application-level information. This in turn limits the kinds of rules that can be written. For example, an application developer might want to write rules that are based on the types of jobs in various queues in their application (because different types of jobs might take different amounts of processing). However, they might only be able to monitor and adapt to the *number* of jobs because the type of job is an application-level concern.

More generally, cloud computing is divided into several levels—Infrastructure, Platform, and Software. Each level has its own adaptation rules and trade-offs that can be conducted. For example, at the infrastructure level a developer might be concerned with adaptations that involve the number of machines and their capacity, at the platform level a developer might be concerned with adaptations that change partitioning in databases or thread counts in web servers, and at the software level they might be concerned with more application-specific adaptations. However, each of these levels provides adaptation facilities isolated to those levels. Adaptations, and therefore trade-offs, need to be carefully coordinated between the layers at deployment, but thereon run without the knowledge of what might be happening in other levels. Thus, a key challenge is how to coordinate these layers and allow trade-offs and information to cross these levels.

1.5.2.2 Service-based adaptation to QoS

Service-based adaptations (SBAs) are built by composing small and loosely coupled entities called services that interact in a distributed environment. Service provider organizations usually administer services hosted on their servers or on the cloud, and can build their own services by composing services provided by other service providers. A service-oriented architecture style has been successful as it promises to allow systems to dynamically adapt at runtime and integrate distributed components [19]. Adaptation of service-based applications is achievable as services can be discovered, selected, and composed at runtime. Several approaches are based on selecting services for achieving one specific quality. It is more complex to select services to achieve multiple qualities simultaneously as it can create an NP-Hard problem [37]. To solve this, several approaches have proposed using artificial intelligence optimization techniques: multi-agent systems for bidding candidate services to find a good service composition focusing on cost [38], genetic algorithm based approaches [39,40] which work fine with a scalable number of services and find nearly optimal solutions, or ant colony based approaches [41]. Approaches have used models as knowledge to self-adapt the SBA. Mostly, QoS SBA adaptation is based on workflow models such as Business Process Models (or business specification languages such as Business Process Execution Language) [42] or use design time variability models along with business processes to define service compositions [18].

The above are not based on architecture at runtime solutions to adaptation. Approaches that are architecture based are MUSIC [43] and SASSY [44]. MUSIC uses component based models and variability models at design time and at runtime generate service-based models. In SASSY, structural and behavioral architecture models are used to represent the SBA. QoS architectural patterns are stored in a library and to adapt, adaptation patterns that define how to incorporate an architectural pattern into a configuration to achieve QoS are followed. For example, a fault tolerance architectural pattern that considers availability and execution time. When multiple QoS objectives need to be fulfilled a nearly optimal solution is provided.

1.5.2.3 Cyber-physical systems

Cyber-physical systems are those systems where software concerns and physical concerns have equal prominence. In traditional control systems, physical issues dominate, and so those are given priority over software issues. However, as the control of different physical processes needs to be integrated and combined with more complex software, the controls (or adaptations) that need to be exerted on the system become more complex to manage. For example, in a smart building we might have control systems for climate control (HVAC - Heating, Ventilation, and Air Conditioning), lighting, emergency and security, and energy consumption.

Traditionally, these would be separate control systems, but more recently there is a need for these to be closely integrated. This need might come about, for example, if a building needs to achieve some green or sustainable properties. In such a system, controlling the climate might affect all the other control systems. Thus, a key challenge is how to integrate these separate controls into ones that can achieve more global properties—how do we bridge the different providers, expertise, regulations, etc. that are characteristic in each domain to understand and manage the trade-offs among them to guarantee the global properties?

Because cyber-physical systems have an impact on physical objects in an environment, safety becomes a real concern. In such situations, it becomes even more important for runtime trade-offs to guarantee that certain safety constraints will never be violated, regardless of the trade-offs on other dimensions. For example, in a factory handling dangerous materials, we would never want to trade power to a device transporting the material over concerns for energy standards. While these kinds of constraints arise in other domains, they become critical in this domain. One avenue for exploring this might be to incorporate concerns from the fault tolerance community regarding failure modes and effects analysis [45] and adaptations like failing safely and redundancy.

Another concern in cyber-physical systems is their need to self-adapt to the constraint resources in the devices or their environment. For example, the battery or power of the devices change, therefore the systems have to evaluate trade-offs to keep functioning in these conditions. Self-adaptive software architecture approaches are emerging to aid in allowing systems to choose suitable architectural configurations that satisfy the resources at runtime [27,46]. A critical challenge that needs exploration is how do we provide self-adaptation architectural approaches without negatively affecting the resources of these cyber-physical systems?

REFERENCES

[1] P. Clements, R. Kazman, M. Klein, Evaluating Software Architectures: Methods and Case Studies, Addison-Wesley, Boston, MA, 2001.
[2] R. Kazman, M.H. Klein, P.C. Clements, ATAM: a method for architecture evaluation, Technical report CMU/SEI-2000-TR-004, 2000.
[3] R. Laddaga, Active software, in: Proceedings of the First International Workshop on Self-Adaptive Software (IWSAS 2000), Springer-Verlag, New York, Inc., Secaucus, NJ, USA, 2000, pp. 11–26
[4] P. Oreizy, M.M. Gorlick, R.N. Taylor, D. Heimbigner, G. Johnson, N. Medvidovic, A. Quilici, D. S. Rosenblum, A.L. Wolf, An architecture-based approach to self-adaptive software, IEEE Intell. Syst. 14 (3) (1999) 54–62.
[5] H. Cervantes, R. Kazman, Designing Software Architectures: A Practical Approach, Addison-Wesley, Boston, MA, 2016.
[6] M. Salehie, L. Tahvildari, Self-adaptive software: landscape and research challenges, ACM Trans. Auton. Adapt. Sys. 4 (2) (2009).
[7] N.R. Jennings, An agent-based approach for building complex software systems, Commun. ACM 44 (4) (2001) 35–41.
[8] T. Wantanabe, A. Yonezawa, Reflection in an object-oriented concurrent language, in: Proceedings of the ACM Conference on Object-Oriented Programming Systems, Languages, and Applications, 1988, pp. 306–315.
[9] T. Abdelzaher, Y. Diao, J.L. Hellerstein, C. Lu, X. Zhu, Introduction to control theory and its application to computing systems, in: Performance Modeling and Engineering, Springer, New York, 2008, pp. 185–215.
[10] J.O. Kephart, D.M. Chess, The vision of autonomic computing, Computer 36 (1) (2003) 41–50.
[11] M. Puviani, G. Cabri, F. Zambonelli, A taxonomy of architecture patterns for self-adaptive systems, in: Proceedings of the International C* Conference on Computer Science & Software Engineering (C3S2E13), Porto, Portugal, July, 2013, pp. 77–85.

[12] D. Weyns, B. Schmerl, V. Grassi, S. Malek, R. Mirandola, C. Prehofer, J. Wuttke, J. Andersson, H. Giese, K. Goeschka, On patterns for decentralized control in self-adaptive systems, in: Software Engineering for Self-Adaptive Systems II, Lecture Notes in Computer Science, vol. 7475, Springer, Berlin, Heidelberg, 2012, pp. 76–107.

[13] G. Andrighetto, G. Governatori, P. Noriega, L.W.N. Van der Torre, Normative multi-agent systems, Dagstuhl Follow-Ups, vol. 4, Schloss Dagstuhl-Leibniz-Zentrum fuer Informatik, Wadern, 2013.

[14] F. Zambonelli, M. Viroli, A survey on nature-inspired metaphors for pervasive service ecosystems, Int. J. Pervasive Comput. Commun. 7 (13) (2011) 186–204.

[15] L. Bass, P. Clements, R. Kazman, Software Architecture in Practice, third ed., Addison-Wesley Professional, Boston, MA, 2012.

[16] H. Gomaa, K. Hashimoto, M. Kim, S. Malek, D.A. Menascé, Software adaptation patterns for service-oriented architectures, in: Proceedings of the 25th ACM Symposium on Applied Computing, Dependable and Adaptive Distributed Systems, Sierre, Switzerland, March 22–26, 2010.

[17] L. Xiao, Y. Cai, R. Kazman, R. Mo, Q. Feng, Identifying and quantifying architectural debts, in: Proceedings of the International Conference on Software Engineering (ICSE) 2016, (Austin, TX), May, 2016.

[18] J. Asundi, R. Kazman, M. Klein, Using economic considerations to choose among architecture design alternatives, Technical report CMU/SEI-2001-TR-035, Software Engineering Institute, Carnegie Mellon University, 2001.

[19] H. Simon, The Sciences of the Artificial, second ed., MIT Press, Cambridge, MA, 1981.

[20] R. Kazman, Y. Cai, R. Mo, Q. Feng, L. Xiao, S. Haziyev, V. Fedak, A. Shapochka, A case study in locating the architectural roots of technical debt, in: Proceedings of the International Conference on Software Engineering (ICSE) 2015, Florence, Italy, May, 2015.

[21] M. Shaw, D. Garlan, Software Architecture: Perspectives on an Emerging Discipline, Prentice Hall, Upper Saddle River, NJ, 1996.

[22] N. Esfahani, E. Kouroshfar, S. Malek, Taming uncertainty in self-adaptive software, in: Proceedings of the 19th ACM SIGSOFT Symposium and the 13th European Conference on Foundations of SEngineering (ESEC/FSE '11), ACM, New York, NY, USA, 2011, pp. 234–244.

[23] D. Garlan, B. Schmerl, J. Chang, Using gauges for architecture-based monitoring and adaptation, in: Proceedings of the Working Conference on Complex and Dynamic Systems Architecture, Brisbane, Australia, 12–14 December, 2001.

[24] D. Garlan, S.-W. Cheng, B. Schmerl, Increasing system dependability through architecture-based self-repair, in: R. de Lemos, C. Gacek, A. Romanovsky (Eds.), Architecting Dependable Systems, Springer-Verlag, Berlin, Heidelberg, 2003.

[25] P. Oreizy, N. Medvidovic, R.N. Taylor, Architecture-based runtime software evolution, in: Proceedings of the 20th International Conference on Software Engineering (ICSE '98), IEEE Computer Society, Washington, DC, USA, 1998, pp. 177–186.

[26] D. Garlan, S.-W. Cheng, A.-C. Huang, B. Schmerl, P. Steenkiste, Rainbow: architecture-based self adaptation with reusable infrastructure, Computer 37 (10) (2004) 46–54.

[27] N. Ali, C. Solis, Self-adaptation to mobile resources in service oriented architecture, in: Proceedings of the 2015 IEEE International Conference on Mobile Services (MS), New York, NY, 2015, pp. 407–414.

[28] S.-W. Cheng, D. Garlan, Stitch: a language for architecture-based self-adaptation, in: D. Weyns, J. Andersson, S. Malek, B. Schmerl (Eds.), State of the Art in Self-Adaptive Systems, J. Syst. Softw. 85 (12) (2012) (Special Issue).

[29] S.-W. Cheng, Rainbow: cost-effective software architecture-based self-adaptation, Ph.D. Thesis, Institute for Software Research technical report CMU-ISR-08-113, Carnegie Mellon University, Pittsburgh, PA, May 2008.

[30] B. Schmerl, J. Cámara, J. Gennari, D. Garlan, P. Casanova, G.A. Moreno, T.J. Glazier, J.M. Barnes, Architecture-based self-protection: composing and reasoning about denial-of-service mitigations, in: HotSoS 2014: 2014 Symposium and Bootcamp on the Science of Security, Raleigh, NC, USA, 8–9 April, 2014.

[31] P. Casanova, D. Garlan, B. Schmerl, R. Abreu, Diagnosing unobserved components in self-adaptive systems, in: Proceedings of the 9th International Symposium on Software Engineering for Adaptive and Self-Managing Systems, Hyderabad, India, 2–3 June, 2014.

[32] J. Cámara, A. Lopes, D. Garlan, B. Schmerl, Adaptation impact and environment models for architecture-based self-adaptive systems, in: Science of Computer Programming, 2016. http://dx.doi.org/10.1016/j.scico.2015.12.006.

[33] J.L. Fernandez-Marquez, G. Di Marzo Serugendo, P.L. Snyder, G. Valetto, F. Zambonelli, A pattern-based architectural style for self-organizing software systems, in: N. Suri, G. Cabri (Eds.), Adaptive, Dynamic, and Resilient Systems, CRC Press, Boca Raton, FL, 2014.

[34] Y. Brun, Building biologically-inspired self-adapting systems, in: B.H. Cheng et al., (Eds.), Proceedings of the Schloss Dagstuhl Seminar 08031: Software Engineering for Self-Adaptive Systems, 2008.

[35] R. Mirandola, D. Perez-Palacin, P. Scandurra, M. Brignoli, A. Zonca, Business process adaptability metrics for QoS-based service compositions, in: Service Oriented and Cloud Computing: 4th International European Conference (ESOCC 2015), LNCS, vol. 9306, Springer, New York, September 2015.

[36] A. Gandhi, P. Dube, A. Karve, A. Kochut, L. Zhang, Adaptive, model-driven autoscaling for cloud applications, in: Proceedings of the 11th International Conference on Autonomic Computing, June 18–20, 2014.

[37] D. Ardagna, B. Pernic, Global and local QoS constraints guarantee in web service selection, in: Proceedings of the IEEE International Conference on Web Services (ICWS '05), IEEE Computer Society, Washington, DC, 2005, pp. 805–806.

[38] V. Nallur, R. Bahsoon, A decentralized self-adaptation mechanism for service-based applications in the cloud, IEEE Trans. Softw. Eng. 39 (5) (2013) 591–612.

[39] G. Canfora, M. Di Penta, R. Esposito, M. Luisa Villani, An approach for QoS-aware service composition based on genetic algorithms, in: Proceedings of the Conference on Genetic and Evolutionary Computation, 2005, pp. 1069–1075.

[40] H. Liu, F. Zhong, B. Ouyang, J. Wu, An approach for QoS-aware web service composition based on improved genetic algorithm, in: Proceedings of the 2010 International Conference on Web Information Systems and Mining (WISM), vol. 1, 23–24 October, 2010, pp. 123–128.

[41] W. Zhang, C.K. Chang, T. Feng, H.-y. Jiang, QoS-based dynamic web service composition with ant colony optimization, in: Proceedings of the IEEE 34th Annual Computer Software and Applications Conference, July, 2010, pp. 493–502.

[42] V. Dellini, E. Casalicchio, V. Grassi, S. Iannucci, P. Lo Presti, R. Mirandola, MOSES: a framework for QoS driven runtime adaptation of service-oriented systems, IEEE Trans. Softw. Eng. 38 (5) (2012) 1138–1159.

[43] S. Hallsteinsen, K. Geihs, N. Paspallis, F. Eliassen, G. Horn, J. Lorenzo, A. Mamelli, G.A. Papadopoulos, A development framework and methodology for self-adapting applications in ubiquitous computing environments, J. Syst. Softw. 0164-121285 (12) (2012) 2840–2859.

[44] D. Menasce, H. Gomaa, S. Malek, J.P. Sousa, SASSY: a framework for self-architecting service-oriented systems, IEEE Softw. 28 (6) (2011) 78–85.

[45] J.B. Bowles, R.D. Bonnel, Failure mode, effects, and criticality analysis, in: Annual Reliability and Maintainability Symposium, Tutorial Notes, 1993, pp. 1–36.

[46] G.G. Pascual, M. Pinto, F. Fuentes, Self-adaptation of mobile systems driven by the common variability language, Futur. Gener. Comput. Syst. 47 (2015) 127–144.

CONCEPTS AND MODELS FOR SELF-ADAPTIVE SOFTWARE ARCHITECTURES

ARCHITECTING SOFTWARE SYSTEMS FOR RUNTIME SELF-ADAPTATION: CONCEPTS, MODELS, AND CHALLENGES

2

N.M. Villegas*, G. Tamura*, H.A. Müller[†]

Universidad Icesi, Cali, Colombia[*] University of Victoria, Victoria, BC, Canada[†]

2.1 INTRODUCTION

Self-adaptive software systems modify their own structure or behavior at runtime to regulate the satisfaction of functional and nonfunctional requirements that change over time, for instance when affected by changes in the system's context of execution (e.g., when facing a sudden and unusually large increment of user requests that causes the agreed upon throughput to be violated) [1–5]. For modifying the software structure or behavior, either at a coarse- or fine-grained level, and both at design time and runtime, most of the approaches rely on the structure or behavior determined by the software architecture. As a result, software architecture is among the most critical enablers for both adaptation and self-adaptation as a means to regulate requirements satisfaction, in particular of nonfunctional ones, under changing contexts of execution.

In traditional software engineering, as summarized succinctly by the Software Engineering Institute (SEI) in 2006, architecture design usually starts from a set of architecturally significant requirements [6]. Designed as the footprint for the solution, the architecture is expected to guarantee requirements satisfaction, without special consideration of changes in context that can violate assumptions regarding the immutability of requirements. In contrast, from the self-adaptive software engineering point of view, even though architects depart also from functional and nonfunctional requirements, they focus precisely on context changes that could violate the satisfaction of these requirements at execution time, including the expected quality attributes. For systems facing this kind of context changes, the designed architecture must enable the software to be *self-aware*, that is, it must include components that enable the system to dynamically reconfigure its own structure or behavior at runtime. This implies, among others, to monitor its own behavior with respect to its current goals (e.g., nonfunctional requirements), and modify its own structure based on an internal, but explicit, representation of itself.

This chapter discusses the meaning of software design-time adaptation, and runtime self-adaptation, and their implications for the task of architecting this kind of software systems. Of course, architecting software systems that are self-adaptive at runtime implies the understanding of the way the satisfaction of nonfunctional requirements can be affected by internal and external context variables that may not be fully characterized at design time. Once the meaning of architecting a particular system for runtime self-adaptation is understood, architectural drivers can be identified and thus the architecture of the self-adaptive system can be designed more realistically to successfully cope with changes on requirements and context conditions happening at runtime. To achieve this, software engineers produce architectural artifacts in the form of concrete models derived from reference models. Moreover, these models must be operable at runtime to be used in the implementation of self-adaptation mechanisms that reconfigure the system's architecture or behavior, thus providing the means for self-awareness, and realizing self-adaptation [7].

The goal of this chapter is to introduce practitioners, researchers, and students to foundational concepts and reference models associated with the architecting of self-adaptive software, as well as to present challenges related to this task. Besides contributing novel discussions about (self)adaptation, we compile and summarize research work that has been conducted by researchers in the field, including our own.

This chapter is organized as follows. Section 2.2 introduces the running example used in this chapter to illustrate the studied concepts. Section 2.3 explores the meanings of adaptation and self-adaptation as well as the differences between these two concepts, and their implications for architecting adaptive and self-adaptive software systems. Section 2.4 explains fundamental concepts that must be understood for architecting self-adaptive software systems. Section 2.5 presents reference models and architectures relevant to the engineering of self-adaptive software. Section 2.6 discusses major challenges on architecting software systems for self-adaptation. Finally, Section 2.7 summarizes and concludes the chapter.

2.2 MOTIVATION: A WEB-MASHUP APPLICATION

To illustrate the concepts and challenges on (self)adaptation analyzed in this chapter, we use a web-mashup application as a running example. This application is built by combining existing services of the Twitter social network platform,[1] and generic weather services accessible programmatically through REST and WSDL interfaces. It is worth noting that—without loss of generality or complexity—it is possible to apply and analyze (self)adaptation concepts even in relatively simple applications based on the orchestration of functionalities offered through software components and services, such as this web mashup. In other words, the fundamental (self)adaptation problems are just as challenging when the software complexity is reduced.

Basically, the web mashup application implements a `weather-for-a-twitter-user` functionality, by composing the location service of a Twitter user (i.e., the city/country as stored in the user's profile) with a weather service. We can choose from different available weather information providers, such as WebServiceX,[2] Google,[3] Yahoo,[4] VisualWebservice,[5] and the US National Weather Service.[6]

---

[1] https://dev.twitter.com/docs/api.
[2] http://www.webservicex.net/ws/WSDetails.aspx?CATID=12&WSID=56.
[3] http://code.google.com/p/java-weather-api.
[4] http://weather.yahooapis.com/forecastrss.
[5] http://www.visualwebservice.com/wsdl/wsf.cdyne.com/Weather.asmx%3FWSDL.
[6] http://www.weather.gov/forecasts/xml/DWMLgen/wsdl/ndfdXML.wsdl.

The web mashup is partially based on two examples available on the Internet, which provide components for two basic functionalities:[7]

- Twitter: For a given user, retrieves and decodes the public profile information. This includes the user's registered city and country.
- Weather: Retrieves the weather conditions on a given location as a pair city-country, using the WSDL weather information service from WebServiceX.

The core components of these two examples are reused and their required services composed as illustrated in Fig. 2.1. In this figure, we follow the Service-Component Architecture (SCA) specification, which is a computing model for realizing distributed Service Oriented Architecture (SOA) applications [8, 9].

The fundamental concept of SCA is the notion of *component*, a gray-box software artifact with well-defined *provided interfaces* (or services), *required interfaces* (service references), and exposed *properties*. Components can contain other components hierarchically (thus called *composites*) and can be implemented using different programming constructs and languages. To exchange information among them, components communicate either by wiring directly their respective interfaces, or by binding their interfaces through communication protocols such as SOAP, RMI, JMS, or REST.

For a given user (the `userId` exposed property in the figure), the Twitter-Weather mashup component (`TWMashup`) requests the user profile from Twitter using the `twitter` service. Once obtained, this profile uses the XML Twitter profile decoder component (`Decoder`) to obtain the registered location as a city-country pair. Finally, it uses this location to obtain the corresponding weather information through the *weather* service.

Using this web-mashup application, the following sections introduce different requirements scenarios that help analyze (self)adaptation concepts and reference models.

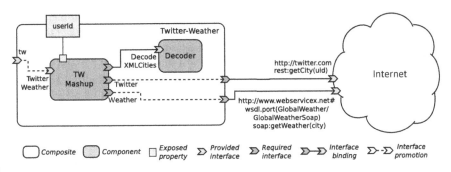

FIG. 2.1

The Twitter-Weather web-mashup application architecture.

[7]http://websvn.ow2.org/listing.php?repname=frascati&path=%2Ftags%2Ffrascati%2F\frascati-1.4%2Fexamples%2Ftwitter and http://websvn.ow2.org/listing.php?repname=\frascati&path=%2Ftags%2Ffrascati%2Ffrascati-1.4%2Fexamples%2Fweather.

2.3 ADAPTATION VS. SELF-ADAPTATION

This section presents an analysis of the difference between the concepts *adaptation* and *self-adaptation*. This analysis is important to understand differences in engineering self-adaptive and adaptive software.

2.3.1 BASIC DEFINITIONS

Even though several software engineering publications and research communities treat the terms *adaptation* and *self-adaptation* as synonyms, we believe that understanding the difference between these two concepts is key to effectively architect software systems that have to adapt to context changes *at runtime*. In general, this chapter is based on the idea that adaptation takes place at (re)design time and is performed by a software engineer in charge of maintenance tasks (i.e., software maintenance from a traditional software engineering perspective [10]). In contrast, self-adaptation happens at runtime and aims to minimize human intervention by making the software to perform the adaptation by itself [3, 11, 12].

According to Merriam-Webster,[8] adaptation, in a general sense, can be defined as (i) "the process of changing to fit some purpose or situation," or (ii) "the process of adjusting to environmental conditions." From a software engineering perspective, adaptation has been defined as the process of changing the system to accommodate changes in its environment [13]. It is important to note that these definitions do not imply that the adaptation must be dynamic nor, in the case of software, must take place at runtime. Indeed, Heineman defines the term adaptation as the manual modification of components by software engineers [14].

Self-adaptation, in turn, has been defined by several software engineering research communities as "the process through which a software system adjusts its own behavior in response to the perception of the environment and the system itself" [3, 15]. This self-adaptive behavior is realized by a software subsystem that is usually known as the controller or adaptation mechanism [12, 16], which implies that it must happen at runtime while maximizing automation and minimizing human intervention.

Analogously, in the same way that we treat the terms *adaptation* and *self-adaptation* as different concepts, we also establish a clear difference between the terms *adaptive software* and *self-adaptive software*, even though the second one can be considered as a subcategory of the first one. As Laddaga [11], we argue that any piece of software code that is relatively easy to modify can be qualified as *adaptive*, recalling that adaptation is the process of adapting it, performed by a human. That is, the implied modification requires fundamental human intervention (e.g., at the source code level) and, as a result, recompiling and interrupting the system execution. In contrast, *self-adaptive* software performs self-adaptation by evaluating its own behavior and environment and adjusting itself, at runtime, when this evaluation indicates that the system is no longer fulfilling its functional or nonfunctional requirements, without interrupting its execution. Such adjustments can happen due to changes in requirements or in the environment, including users and system context changes. An adaptive software can be converted into a self-adaptive one if enabled with self-awareness capabilities. These capabilities are instrumented for instance through an adaptation mechanism that monitors its

---

[8]http://www.merriam-webster.com.

environment—including its own execution health and requirements, analyzes the satisfaction of requirements in light of environmental situations, plans a strategy to adapt itself depending on the results of the analysis, and implements this strategy to reconfigure itself as required. All these tasks must take place at runtime and be supported by a knowledge base comprising information gathered at design time and runtime. In other words, self-adaptive software is enabled to perform self-adaptation because of its self-aware capabilities, thus eliminating (or reducing at minimum) the need for human intervention and execution interruption.

Having established these conceptual differences, next we illustrate the implications of architecting software systems for adaptation (adaptive software) versus architecting software systems for self-adaptation (self-adaptive software), using the subject system described in Section 2.2.

2.3.2 ARCHITECTING SOFTWARE FOR ADAPTATION AND SELF-ADAPTATION

Adaptation—and also self-adaptation—processes are triggered usually when some of the nonfunctional requirements are not fulfilled by a developed software system, for instance under unexpected circumstances of execution. This incorrect behavior can be detected and corrected by a human by means of observing and evaluating the software requirements satisfaction, and adjusting the source code to make the software satisfy its functional and nonfunctional requirements under the unexpected conditions. Of course, this procedure implies the recompilation and redeployment of the application. Dramatic consequences can result if the unexpected circumstances affect nonfunctional requirements and demand a more drastic redesign of the system. We characterize this procedure as an adaptation process, given that it is performed mainly by humans; it would be a self-adaptation process if the detection and correction would be performed by the software itself, and with minimum human intervention.

We examine the differences between adaptation and self-adaptation in more detail by analyzing concrete examples of both processes, based on the motivational running example introduced in the previous section.

2.3.2.1 Architecting for adaptation

Assume that the Twitter-Weather mashup of our case study stops reporting the weather for the cities the Twitter users are located in. The developer detects that the weather service used in the mashup, WebserviceX, has been unavailable for the last day because of an infrastructure maintenance. To correct this problem, she performs an adaptation process as follows. The developer finds the Yahoo weather service available on the Internet, and proceeds to adapt her mashup application code. Basically, she has to determine how to obtain results from the weather service, for both the current one (i.e., WebserviceX) and the new one (i.e., Yahoo). Then, she has to modify (i.e., adapt) the code to compute the required parameters for the new service, and process its results appropriately.

However, if the Yahoo weather service becomes also unavailable, the developer must readapt the code again, this time to invoke the Google weather service. In order to avoid changing the weather service invocation used in the code and recompiling it every time the service used in the code is unavailable, the developer could even decide to guard the service invocation on each of the three alternative weather services with a condition, checking service availability and using the one of the three that is available, in an if-then-else chain.

2.3.2.2 Architecting for self-adaptation

In the case of architecting for self-adaptation, the problem of the possible weather service unavailability is expected to be addressed exactly as the possibility of facing an otherwise completely unexpected circumstance in which the system's requirements satisfaction would be compromised. Architecting the solution for self-adaptation means that it is the software itself, not the human (i.e., developer, system administrator, or system operator), that must detect whenever this circumstance happens, and in response, decide to perform an adaptation on itself to maintain requirements satisfaction, at runtime and without interrupting its execution. Therefore, in contrast to the adaptation case, architecting the solution for self-adaptation implies fundamentally to enable the software system to be self-aware and self-managed, as proposed in the vision of Autonomic Computing [17]. Self-awareness implies, beyond equipping the software system with the components that realize the system's functional requirements (i.e., target system components), to integrate it with components comprising the self-adaptation mechanism, as depicted in the lower part of Fig. 2.2, namely:

1. Monitor: Detects events from the system's context that may compromise the system requirements satisfaction. For instance, detecting that the weather service of WebserviceX is unavailable.
2. Analyzer: Receives events detected by the monitor and analyze whether it is necessary to perform an adaptation on the system itself (thus called self-adaptation). For instance, determining that WebserviceX has been unavailable for an unacceptable amount of time, thus requiring some corrective action.
3. Planner: Synthesizes the adaptation plan. For instance, to change the WebserviceX weather service invocation by one to the Yahoo weather service.
4. Executor: Realizes the adaptation plan in the actual software system, without interrupting its execution.

Moreover, in our example, for the self-adaptation plan synthesizer to be more maintainable and less coupled to the particular adaptation logic of each weather service that could be used in the mashup, the next key architectural decision is to use the *Adapter* design-pattern [18]. Indeed, as part of the architecting process

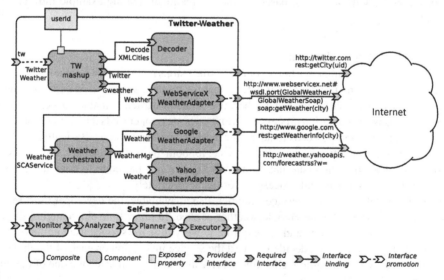

FIG. 2.2

The Twitter-Weather architecture designed for self-adaptation.

for self-adaptation of our mashup application, we anticipate that existing weather information services, available on the Internet, have different method signatures and thus different service interfaces to ask for and deliver the weather information. Thus, we apply the *Adapter* design-pattern by introducing a generic weather service interface, which is implemented by each of the concrete adapters (cf. the weather services in Fig. 2.2). These concrete adapters allow the weather service invoker to be able to use any of the existing weather services independently of their particular service interfaces and implementations (i.e., Adaptees). Additionally, the weather orchestrator component (cf. WeatherOrchestrator in Fig. 2.2) is responsible for providing the generic weather service (through the interface WeatherSCAService), from the different weather service providers. The WebServiceXWeatherAdapter component (and corresponding weather adapters for Google and Yahoo) is responsible for translating the generic weather invocation, and respective response, to each of the particular weather providers interface specifications.

Once developed and deployed, the self-adaptation mechanism of our mashup allows the system to self-adapt at runtime, whenever the monitor detects significant periods of the weather service unavailability. Human intervention would be necessary only to deploy components implementing new weather service adapters. Nevertheless, the deployment of these components can be realized transparently for the users (i.e., without interrupting the system services execution) using extended SCA frameworks such as the one proposed by Tamura et al. [5, 19].

2.3.2.3 Implications of self-adaptation

In the previous sections we described how to solve the problem of service unavailability using two similar strategies (i.e., adaptation and self-adaptation) that produce very different solutions. The plain adaptation solution involved the use of several conditional statements, which could be coded as in Listing 2.1.

LISTING 2.1

The adaptation solution

```
 1 public Weather obtainWeather() {
 2    Weather w;
 3    ...
 4    if (webservicexWeather.methodForWebServiceXisAvailable()) {
 5       p = prepareParametersForWebServiceXWeather(...);
 6       w = translateResult(webservicexWeather.methodToObtainWeather(p)
          );
 7    }
 8    else if (yahooWeather.methodForYahooisAvailable()) {
 9       p = prepareParametersForYahooWeather(...);
10       w = translateResult(yahooWeather.methodToObtainWeather(p));
11    }
12    else if (googleWeather.isAvailable()) {
13       p = prepareParametersForGoogleWeather(...);
14       w = translateResult(googleWeather.methodToObtainWeather(p));
15    }
16    ...
17    return w;
18 }
```

In this solution, the application logic is adapted by the developer by modifying the application source code and recompiling and redeploying it, for each time a new weather service is added. Thus, it is possible to argue that the service availability conditions (cf. lines 4, 8, and 12) replace the functionality of the self-adaptation's monitor and analyzer components, and the service invocations themselves (cf. lines 6, 10, and 14) make the planner and executor components unnecessary. Naturally, as illustrated in the code, these service invocations require the previous instructions for mapping and translating the actual parameters to the ones required by each of the weather service providers, as well as the following instructions for translating their responses to the expected weather information. In fact, in Listing 2.1 we have presented the code for mapping and translating parameters and return values. A similar, but more standardized way of invoking the different weather services results from the application of the *Adapter* design pattern, which we proposed as part of the architectural decisions in the self-adaptation strategy. However, there are fundamental differences between these two strategies:

- Adaptation time and responsibility: in the adaptation strategy, the actual adaptation of the application code is performed at (re)design time and is realized by a human, requiring recompilation, redeployment, and restarting of the application; in the self-adaptation strategy, the adaptation is performed at runtime, and realized by the software itself without recompilation, redeployment, or restarting. In the first case, the adaptation decision and responsibility is assumed and performed by the developer, given that the software itself is not aware of its own structure (i.e., components, services, bindings), nor of its behavior (e.g., fulfillment status of its nonfunctional requirements), and thus, it has no possibilities to act upon or modify itself (i.e., self-adapt). In the second case, the adaptation decision is a function completely of the software itself.
- Separation of concerns as enabler for dynamic reconfiguration: from Fig. 2.2 and Listing 2.1, it is evident that in the self-adaptation strategy the code for performing the adaptation is clearly separated from the code that implements the application logic, whereas in the plain adaptation one there is no adaptation code. Monitoring components are executed in independent threads, reporting changing-context events to the analyzer, while the application logic is executed in a different thread of control flow. Planner and executor logic, located in different components, allow the complete substitution of the application logic components, if needed. Thus, separation of concerns, both between application and adaptation logic, and among the adaptation logic components, is a critical enabler for the dynamic reconfiguration and self-adaptation of the application components. Furthermore, intertwining all of the adaptation logic with the application logic would render the system more challenging to maintain.
- Maintainability and policy-driven behavior: as a result of the separation of concerns, the self-adaptation strategy not only promotes maintainability and decoupled components, but also the policy-driven specification of behavior. For instance, the decision of changing the weather service provider should involve the notion that web services may have an associated cost of use and also differentiated preferences by users. Thus, changing the weather service should not depend solely on a simple check of service unavailability, but on a set of comprehensive conditions that could include monitoring the unavailability for a certain amount of (maximum acceptable) time, or the observation of repeating a series of short unavailability periods in a given time frame.
- Feedback control: in terms of the process, the plain adaptation strategy can be seen as a closed loop controlled and performed by a human. That is, the human monitors, analyzes, and determines whether the software application code requires to be adapted. If an adaptation is required to accomplish a given goal, the human performs the adaptation by modifying, recompiling and

redeploying the application code. Then, she starts the loop again, evaluating whether the source code adaptation accomplished the desired goal. However, the resulting software in general has no feedback control implemented in it, by definition, only conditional statements or similar control-flow structures. In contrast, the self-adaptation mechanism of self-adaptive software systems is by itself a closed loop, in which human intervention is eliminated or reduced to the minimum. This mechanism permanently monitors the software application behavior, analyzes whether an adaptation is needed, and plans and executes it in the software application components, if required. Thus, instead of chained conditional statements guarding method invocations, the self-adaptation strategy replaces the actual method invocations and its defining components by the required ones, as needed, through component redeployment and service rebinding operations at the architecture level.

Performing adaptation processes by hand to adaptive software is a challenging task. However, our goal in this chapter is to focus on architecting self-adaptive software. From the previous sections and discussions, it should be clear that the main difference between adaptive and self-adaptive software is that the latter is aware of its own status about the accomplishment of its goals, and is able to modify itself at runtime, without human intervention. In the following sections, we analyze and discuss the most important aspects that architects of self-adaptive systems ought to consider.

2.4 FOUNDATIONAL CONCEPTS FOR ARCHITECTING SELF-ADAPTIVE SOFTWARE

This section presents foundational concepts on architecting software systems for self-adaptation.

2.4.1 FUNDAMENTAL DIMENSIONS OF SELF-ADAPTIVE SOFTWARE

We characterize self-adaptive software through a set of dimensions or elements that play an important role in the architectural design of this kind of software systems. These dimensions are defined as follows [7]:

1. Self-adaptation goal: The main reason for the system to be self-adaptive. These goals can be defined through one or more of the self-* properties defined in Autonomic Computing (e.g., self-configuring, self-healing, self-optimizing, self-protecting, self-managing) [17], the regulation of quality of service (QoS) properties (e.g., nonfunctional requirements), or the preservation of functional requirements. In the context of our example (cf. Section 2.2), a self-adaptation goal is the self-healing property, since the system is able to detect the failure associated with the service that becomes unavailable and to recover from this situation.

2. Structure of self-adaptive software: Self-adaptive systems have two well-defined subsystems (although sometimes indistinguishable, depending on the level of separation of concerns applied): (i) the self-adaptation mechanism (also known as self-adaptation controller or autonomic manager) and (ii) the managed system (also known as target system). The architecture of these two subsystems not only must be explicitly designed and maintained, but also must coexist in a proper manner, albeit not necessarily on the same processor. In our example, the target system corresponds to the mashup application (cf. the Twitter-Weather composite depicted in Fig. 2.2), which is

clearly separated from the self-adaptation controller (cf. the `Self-Adaptation Mechanism` composite in the same figure).

3. Reference inputs: The set of values with corresponding types that are used to specify the self-adaptation goal to be achieved and maintained in the managed system by the self-adaptation mechanism. As presented in [7], reference inputs are specified as (a) one or more reference values (e.g., a physically or logically measurable property); (b) some form of contract (e.g., QoS, service level agreements (SLA), or service level objectives (SLO)); (c) goal-policy-actions; (d) constraints defining computational states (according to the particular proposed definition of state); or even (e) functional requirements (e.g., logical expressions as invariants or assertions, regular expressions).

4. Measured outputs: The set of values with corresponding types that are measured in the managed system. These measurements must be specified, monitored and compared against the reference inputs to evaluate whether the self-adaptation goal has been achieved. Often, measured outputs are specified through (a) continuous domains for single variables or signals; (b) logical expressions or conditions for contract states; and (c) conditions expressing states of system malfunction. Most common options for monitoring measured outputs are (a) measurements on physical properties from physical devices (e.g., CPU temperature); (b) measurements on logical properties of computational elements (e.g., request processing time in software or CPU load in hardware); and (c) measurements on external context conditions (e.g., user location or weather conditions). For the self-adaptive system of our case study, measure outputs are in the form of conditions expressing states of system malfunction (e.g., service unavailability).

5. Computed control actions: Correspond to the means used by the self-adaptation mechanism to affect or modify the managed system to achieve the self-adaptation goal. In general, computed control actions can be (a) continuous signals that affect behavioral properties of the managed system; (b) discrete operations affecting the computing infrastructure executing the managed system (e.g., host system's buffer allocation and resizing operations; modification of process scheduling in the CPU); (c) discrete operations that affect the processes of the managed system directly (e.g., processes-level service invocation, process execution operations-halt/resume, sleep/respawn/priority modification of processes); and (d) discrete operations affecting the managed system's software architecture (e.g., managed system's architecture reconfiguration operations such as deploying/undeploying components, binding/unbinding services). The nature of these controller outputs is related to the extent of the intrusiveness of the self-adaptation mechanism with respect to the managed system. In our example, the self-adaptation mechanism relies on discrete operations that affect the software architecture. Particularly, it uses service unbinding and binding operations to connect to a new weather service after the current one becomes unavailable.

6. Observable adaptation properties: Correspond to characteristics that can be observed on the self-adaptation mechanism to evaluate its quality. Properties of the self-adaptation controller are (a) stability, (b) accuracy, (c) settling-time, (d) small-overshoot, (e) robustness, (f) termination, (g) consistency (in the overall system structure and behavior), (h) scalability, and (i) security. For the managed system, the identified properties result from the self-adaptation process: (a) behavioral/functional invariants and (b) QoS conditions, such as performance (i.e., latency, throughput, capacity); dependability (i.e., availability, reliability, maintainability, safety, confidentiality, integrity); security (i.e., confidentiality, integrity, availability); and safety (i.e., interaction complexity and coupling strength).

2.4.2 SELF-ADAPTATION GOALS

Adaptation goals are the main reasons for a system to be self-adaptive [7]. These goals are generally defined in terms of the self-* properties, as defined in the Autonomic Computing vision [17], as well as in terms of nonfunctional and functional requirements. This section presents definitions for the self-* properties and most commonly addressed nonfunctional requirements, from the perspective of self-adaptive software architecture design.

The purpose of self-adaptation can be characterized as the need for the continuous satisfaction of functional requirements, and the regulation of nonfunctional requirements under changing conditions on requirements and execution contexts [7]. The continuous satisfaction of requirements at runtime may be affected by two main factors [20]: (i) changes in goals (i.e., requirements evolve according to changes in business goals, for example, a renegotiation of SLAs, and changes in user preferences, for example, when the situation of the user changes); and (ii) changes in the environment, which include changes in the system itself (e.g., unavailability caused by a service failure) and changes in the external environment (e.g., peaks of transactions caused by seasonal events such as the Black Friday).

2.4.2.1 Self-properties as self-adaptation goals

Autonomic Computing, as envisioned by IBM [17], refers to the capability of computing systems to manage themselves according to goals and policies defined by system administrators. The essential purpose of Autonomic Computing is self-management, which is realized through self-adaptation, exposing one or more of the following four properties that are commonly known as the self-* or self-management properties: self-configuration, self-optimization, self-healing, and self-protection. In the context of architecting software systems for self-adaptation, these properties can be defined as follows:

1. Self-configuration: This property refers to the automatic configuration of the system architecture at runtime. Self-configuration is generic in the sense that it can be used to realize any other self-* property, or even any self-adaptation goal achievable through the automatic reconfiguration of the system architecture (of both the structure of the managed system and of the self-adaptation mechanism). Systems with self-configuration capabilities reconfigure themselves automatically, based on high level policies, and reconfiguration symptoms and strategies.
2. Self-optimization: The capability of the system to continuously improve the satisfaction of nonfunctional properties (i.e., quality attributes such as performance, or resource usage such as power consumption, or SLA profit) through the self-configuration of the system architecture according to changes in business goals and environmental situations.
3. Self-healing: The capability of the system to detect, diagnose and repair malfunctions by itself, at runtime. In particular, failures originating in the software architecture can be fixed through self-reconfiguration.
4. Self-protection: The capability of the system to protect itself against malicious attacks or intrusions, adopting secure configurations through self-adaptation.

As we already mentioned, concerning the self-* properties, the self-adaptation goal for our web mashup example is self-healing.

2.4.2.2 Nonfunctional requirements as self-adaptation goals

This subsection presents nonfunctional requirements that are commonly defined as self-adaptation goals in self-adaptive software. For each nonfunctional requirement, we give its definition and a set of related quality attributes. The following selected definitions are borrowed from the framework for evaluating quality-driven self-adaptive software that we proposed previously [7].

1. Performance: Refers to system responsiveness, that is, the time required for the system to respond to processing events, or inversely, the event processing rate in a time interval. Identified factors that affect performance are latency (the time the system takes to respond to a specific event); throughput (the number of events that can be completed in a given time interval; and capacity (a measure of the amount of work the system can perform).
2. Dependability: Defines the level of reliance that can be placed on the services the software system delivers. Adaptation goals associated with dependability are availability (readiness for usage); reliability (continuity of service); maintainability (capacity to self-repair and evolve); safety (from a dependability point of view, nonoccurrence of catastrophic consequences from an external environment perspective); confidentiality (immune to unauthorized disclosure of information); integrity (nonimproper alterations of the system structure, data and behavior).
3. Security: Concerns of security are defined in terms of confidentiality (protection from disclosure); integrity (protection from unauthorized modification); and availability (protection from destruction).
4. Safety: The level of reliance that can justifiably be placed on the software system as not generator of accidents. Safety is concerned with the occurrence of accidents, defined in terms of external consequences. The following two properties of critical systems can be used as indicators of system safety: interaction complexity and coupling strength. In particular, interaction complexity is the extent to which the behavior of one component can affect the behavior of other components.

Referred to our example, availability, as a nonfunctional requirement, is the most important self-adaptation goal. In this case, the self-adaptation mechanism must guarantee is the readiness for usage of the mashup application, even when some services may be unavailable at any moment of the system execution.

2.4.3 SELF-ADAPTATION FUNDAMENTAL PROPERTIES

Properties inherent to self-adaptive software are qualities (or characteristics) that can be observed on self-adaptation mechanisms. These properties, one of the main contributions of our research on self-adaptive software, are key for evaluating the quality of self-adaptation mechanisms [7]. Therefore, these properties should be considered when making design decisions on architecting self-adaptive software.

1. Stability: Represents the degree in which the self-adaptation process makes the observed target system behavior to converge toward the self-adaptation goal, and to stabilize around it. An unstable self-adaptation process will repeat self-adaptation tasks without reaching stability.
2. Accuracy: Represents how close the observed target system behavior approximates the self-adaptation goal, in its stable state.

3. Settling time: Represents how fast the self-adaptation process makes the observed target system behavior reach the self-adaptation goal.

4. Resource overshoot: Refers to how well the self-adaptation process performs under given conditions in terms of the amount of resources used in excess to achieve a required settling-time, before reaching a stable state.

5. Robustness: Applies to both the target system and the self-adaptation mechanism. From the perspective of the target system, robustness implies that the target system must remain stable and guarantee accuracy, short settling time, and small resource overshoot, even if its current state differs from the expected state in some measurable way. From the perspective of the self-adaptation mechanism, robustness refers to the capability of the self-adaptation mechanism to operate within desired limits even under unforeseen conditions.

6. Termination: Guarantees that the execution of the self-adaptation mechanism will finish, even if the target system does not reach the self-adaptation goal.

7. Consistency (also known as integrity): Aims at ensuring the structural and behavioral integrity of the target system after performing a self-adaptation process. For instance, when a self-adaptation plan is based on dynamic reconfiguration of software architecture, consistency must guarantee sound interface bindings between component services (e.g., component and service-based structural/behavioral compliance) and ensure that when a component is replaced dynamically by another one, the execution will continue without affecting the function of the system.

8. Atomicity: Guarantees that the self-adaptation process is executed atomically.

9. Durability: Guarantees that the final result of the self-adaptation process endures over time (i.e., especially after restarting the target system).

10. Security: Ensures that not only the target system, but also the data and components shared with the self-adaptation mechanism, are protected from disclosure (confidentiality), modification (integrity), and destruction (availability).

2.4.4 SENSORS AND EFFECTORS

In Autonomic Computing, sensors and effectors constitute what has been defined as the manageability interface. Through this interface, one or more autonomic managers manage or control the managed resources or components. A manageability interface is composed of one or more manageability endpoints (also known as touchpoints), whose functions are to expose the state and management operations of the managed resource or component. An autonomic manager is a software component that implements an intelligent control loop. This loop, which is referred to as Monitoring-Analysis-Planning-Execution and shared Knowledge (MAPE-K) loop (cf. Section 2.5) comprises four phases—monitoring, analysis, planning, and execution—that operate over a knowledge base.

Similarly, when architecting software systems for self-adaptation, components intended to be dynamically adapted at runtime must implement a self-adaptation interface composed of sensors and effectors. The functionality of sensors is twofold. First, they allow the gathering of context information from the environment, and second, they expose the state of the self-adaptive component to other components or systems. Effectors expose the methods that implement the self-adaptation operations on the component. Architectures of self-adaptive software must implement standard and interoperable self-adaptation interfaces using specifications such as WSDL, REST, and RMI. In our example, sensors allow the self-adaptive system to monitor the availability of the multiple weather services, whereas effectors are part of the execution phase of the MAPE-K loop and correspond to a method that invokes a dynamic binding reconfiguration.

2.4.5 UNCERTAINTY AND DYNAMIC CONTEXT

The dynamic capabilities of self-adaptive software are highly affected by the entities in the execution environment, including system requirements and the system itself. The observable characteristics of these entities are known as context information. According to Whittle et al. [21], the uncertainty inherent in self-adaptation is generated by two main sources. The first one, *environmental uncertainty*, is the uncertainty due to changing environmental conditions. The second one, *behavioral uncertainty*, originates from changes in software requirements or in the system behavior. Therefore, context monitoring in self-adaptive software concerns not only entities external to the system, but also entities within the boundaries of the system and system requirements.

So far, most monitoring mechanisms for supporting context-aware and self-adaptive systems have been based on the classical definition of context [7]. This definition characterizes context as *"any information that describes the situation of entities that can affect the system's behavior"* [22]. It is important to point out that this definition, given by Dey in 1999, did not consider changes in the states of these entities while the system that is intended to be context-aware is in execution. On the contrary, in the case of self-adaptive software, which by definition is significantly affected by uncertainty, context is not simply the state of a predefined environment with fixed entities, but part of an interacting process with a continuously changing and uncertain environment. Therefore, architecting software systems for runtime self-adaptation must involve an operational definition in which context, and their requirements monitoring, are modeled as first-class entities, in such a way that its changing states can be acquired from the environment, manipulated along its life cycle explicitly by taking into account its dynamic nature, and provisioned based on changes on requirements [23].

Dynamic context differs from *static context* in aspects related to its modeling and management. Concerning context modeling, static context specifies, at design-time, relevant context entities, and the interactions among them, which remain immutable at runtime. The birthday and gender of a user are instances of static context. Therefore monitoring mechanisms based on static context keep track of entities specified at design-time. Once the system is in execution, the addition of new entities is not supported by the static context specification. On the contrary, dynamic context requires modeling techniques that support changes in the specification of context entities and corresponding monitoring requirements at runtime. For example, location, product, and service preferences are instances of highly dynamic context.

Concerning context management, monitoring strategies that keep track of static context are determined at design-time and remain fixed at runtime, whereas monitoring strategies that manage dynamic context are required to change over time, at runtime. Dynamic context management is key to leverage the dynamic capabilities of self-adaptive systems and manage the uncertainty that can affect their behavior. Furthermore, the architecture of context management infrastructures must also be reconfigured at runtime to support changes in context monitoring requirements generated by high levels of uncertainty. Coping with uncertainty is perhaps the most complex aspect of architecting software systems for runtime adaptation. In our example, a manifestation of uncertainty is the modification of the current self-adaptation goal of availability, by another goal of performance. In particular, to satisfy the new goal, new sensors would have to be deployed to monitor, for example, the latency of the weather service configured to be consumed.

2.5 REFERENCE MODELS FOR ARCHITECTING SELF-ADAPTIVE SOFTWARE

In this section we analyze, from the software architecture perspective, representative reference models that have been proposed for engineering self adaptive software systems. A reference model is a standard decomposition of a known kind of problems into distinguishable parts or components, each having well defined functionalities and control/data flow [24]. We start with the feedback-loop reference model of control theory, which has been instantiated in several ways for different self-adaptive software systems. More abstractly, it has served directly or indirectly as a foundation for defining the structure of the reference models analyzed in this section.

2.5.1 THE FEEDBACK LOOP MODEL OF CONTROL THEORY

In control theory, the feedback loop is a generic model designed with the goal of automatically controlling the dynamic behavior of a system (thus called *target system*). As such, it has been used to automate a large number of processes in diverse fields of engineering [25]. More recently, it also has been adopted as a model for self-adaptation in computing and software engineering [26, 27].

As depicted in Fig. 2.3, the feedback loop model clearly distinguishes and separates the *controller* from the target system. To control the dynamic behavior of the target system, the model regularly compares the *measured outputs* (A) of the target system behavior to the control objectives given as *reference inputs* (B), yielding the *control error* (C), and then adjusting the *controlling inputs* (D) accordingly for the target system to behave as defined by the reference input. The target system's measured output can also be affected by external *disturbances* (E), or even by the *noise* (F) caused by the system self-adaptation. *Transducers* (G) translate the signals coming from sensors, as required by the comparison element (H).

To compute the controlling inputs, the representative mechanism in control theory is the *system transfer function,* a mathematical model built upon the physical properties and characteristics of the target system. For instance, depending on these characteristics, in classic control the transfer function can be built with proportional, derivative and integral (PID) terms. The parameters in a PID controller have special significance given that there exist precise and sophisticated methods for tuning their values in a specific controller.

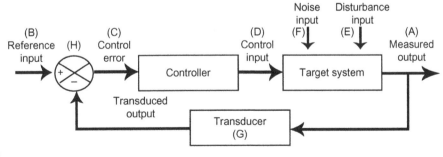

FIG. 2.3

Block diagram of a general feedback control system.

Source: Modified from J.L. Hellerstein, Y. Diao, S. Parekh, D.M. Tilbury, Feedback Control of Computing Systems, Wiley, Chichester, 2004.

2.5.2 **THE MAPE-K MODEL**

Even though the application of control theory and its feedback-loop model to industrial processes is well understood, it requires to be adapted for its application to the control of software systems. First, the system's transfer function, which represents the target system's behavior model, is defined in terms of continuous mathematics. Second, this theory relies on measurements taken from, and actions performed into, physical, self-contained and self-performing artifacts, that is, on variables in the continuous-time domain (e.g., sensors, gauges and valves/actuators for temperature, pressure and other variables). In contrast, models for software systems are usually built using discrete formalisms, given that they are composed of intangible artifacts with discrete-time behavior and not always well characterized properties. Moreover, to fully exploit the possibilities of software self-adaptation from the software architecture perspective, the output of the self-adaptation mechanism must be based on some kind of discrete operations rather than on controlling signals to be transduced by electro-mechanical devices. For instance, it would be more appropriate for this output to be a plan of ordered instructions to be instrumented by the software actuators on the target software components.

Inspired by the human autonomous nervous system, IBM researchers adapted the feedback-loop model to define the *autonomic element* as a building block for developing self-managing and self-adaptive software systems. They synthesized this adaptation in the form of the so-called MAPE-K loop model, as depicted in Fig. 2.4. The purpose of this model is to develop autonomous controlling mechanisms to regulate the satisfaction of dynamic requirements, specifically in software systems [17, 26, 28].

In Fig. 2.5 we illustrate our interpretation of the MAPE-K loop, mapped from the general feedback-loop block diagram. To autonomously regulate the satisfaction of the system requirements (cf. *reference control input*s in the figure), which vary with context changes, a `Monitor` gathers information from the internal and the external contexts. This information, in the form of *control symptoms*, is analyzed by

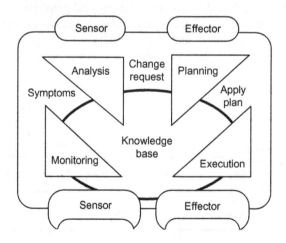

FIG. 2.4

The MAPE-K loop.

Source: Based on J.O. Kephart, D.M. Chess, The vision of autonomic computing, Computer 36 (1) (2003) 41–50.

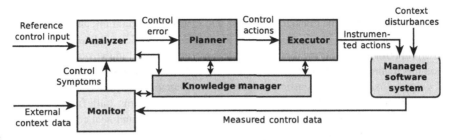

FIG. 2.5

The MAPE-K loop as adapted from the feedback loop.

Source: From G. Tamura, QoS-CARE: a reliable system for preserving QoS contracts through dynamic reconfiguration, PhD Thesis, University of Lille 1—Science and Technology and University of Los Andes, May 2012.

the `Analyzer`, which compares them to the *reference control input*, yielding a *control error*. Based on this difference, the `Planner` element computes *control actions* to be instrumented by the `Executor` in the managed software system. A `KnowledgeManager` manages relevant information, such as adaptation policies, thresholds, and rules, shared with the other MAPE-K loop elements. The measured control data can also be affected by *context disturbances* caused, for instance, by the system adaptation itself [20, 26].

The concrete responsibilities for each of the MAPE-K loop elements are as follows:

1. Monitor: Monitoring elements are responsible for sensing changes in both, the managed application's internal variables corresponding to QoS properties (e.g., measured QoS data), and also the external context (i.e., measured from outside the managed application). Based on these changes, monitors must notify relevant context events to the analyzer. Relevant context events are those derivable from system requirements (e.g., from QoS contracts).

2. Analyzer: The analyzer, based on the high-level requirements to fulfill, and the context events notified by monitors, determines whether a system adaptation must be triggered. This would occur, for instance, when the notified events signal changes that (may) violate the reference control inputs. Context analyzers can be based on either, multi-event or single-event pattern matchers, as discussed in [29]. Multi-event matchers produce complex events based on single events that accumulate over time. These single events are produced by single-event matchers, which identify partial matches in the flow of the monitored events.

3. Planner: Once notified with a reconfiguration event from the context analyzer, the planner selects a strategy to fulfill the new requirements, using the accumulated knowledge in the shared Knowledge Manager. By applying the selected strategy, the planner computes the necessary control actions to be instrumented in the managed software system. An important difference between the feedback and the MAPE-K loops is that, in the former, the control actions are continuous signals for physical actuators (e.g., resistors and motors), whereas in the latter, they are sequences of discrete operations (thus called reconfiguration plans). These discrete operations are then interpreted by the executor.

4. Executor: Upon reception of a reconfiguration plan, the executor interprets each of the operations specified in the plan and effects them in the managed software system. This implies to translate or adequate the reconfiguration actions to the ones implemented by the particular runtime component platform that executes the managed software system.

5. (Reconfiguration) Knowledge Manager: The reconfiguration knowledge manager makes explicit the relevant knowledge about the managed software application configuration, and how to perform its reconfiguration at runtime. In a feedback loop, the controller encodes fundamental knowledge about the properties of the physical plant or target system to control in the system transfer function. Based on this mathematical model of the target system, and its response to context disturbances, control properties such as short settling-time, stability, accuracy, and small resource-overshoot can be guaranteed on a controller [25, 26]. In contrast to physical systems, built from materials with well known standard properties such as conductance, capacitance, and heat conduction, software systems are developed with software components with no standardized properties. Thus, in the case of the MAPE-K loop (i.e., in the software systems domain), the knowledge manager, provided by the adaptation designer, must supply the lack of information about the properties of the managed software application, in order to make adequate decisions for its adaptation.

Referring to our case study, using the MAPE-K model to design the architecture produces the solution already explained in Section 2.3.2.2, and illustrated in Fig. 2.2. The monitor regularly checks the availability of the currently selected weather service provider (e.g., WebserviceX). When it accumulates evidence of service unavailability, notifies the analyzer with the respective information. If this evidence justifies changing the provider, the analyzer notifies the planner about this need. The planner, depending on the reported information and the availability of the other two providers (e.g., Yahoo and Google weather), generates a reconfiguration (i.e., adaptation) plan to solve the unavailability problem. This plan basically must link the interface of the required "weatherMgr" service of the "WeatherOrchestrator" component, unlink it from the provided "weather" service of the "WebserviceXWeatherAdapter," and linking it to the provided "weather" service of the selected provider (i.e., "GoogleWeatherAdapter" or "YahooWeatherAdapter").

2.5.3 KRAMER AND MAGEE'S SELF-MANAGEMENT REFERENCE MODEL

Inspired by the reference architecture defined by the artificial intelligence and robotics community [30], Kramer and Magee proposed a three-layer reference model for self-managed systems. Each of the layers has defined responsibilities at different abstraction levels. These responsibilities correspond to: goal management, change management, and component control, being executed in independent threads of control [31, 32], as depicted in Fig. 2.6.

The *component control layer* is responsible for implementing the functionalities of a feedback loop to control the operational-level actions the system has to accomplish, such as a particular task or function. These functionalities would include, for instance, self-tuning algorithms, and the capability of identifying situations for which the current configuration of components is not designed to deal with. In this latter case, this layer reports this situation to higher layers.

The *change management layer* has the responsibility of handling decentralized configuration management, identifying inconsistencies in the system (i.e., component configuration) state, and reestablishing a satisfactory stable state. It also reacts to events reported by the component-control layer, for instance by executing plans that set new control behaviors in that layer in response to new objectives. These new objectives could have been introduced by the layer above. The change management layer can introduce new components to the layer below, as well as modify component interconnections and parameters of operation. However, all of the actions in this layer are prespecified in adaptation plans. If it detects a situation for which a plan does not exist, it must ask the higher layer for such a plan. A

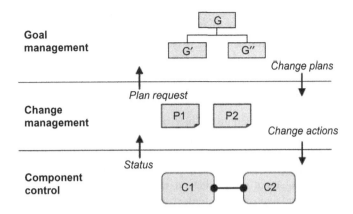

FIG. 2.6

The three-layer reference architecture for self-management.

Source: From J. Kramer, J. Magee, Self-managed systems: an architectural challenge, in: Proceedings of the 2007 Workshop on the Future of Software Engineering (FOSE 2007), IEEE Computer Society, 2007, pp. 259–268.

similar situation occurs when a new goal is required for the system, which implies the higher layer to introduce new plans into this layer.

Finally, the *goal management layer* is responsible for the global planning to achieve high-level goals. This layer produces plans required by lower layers by considering the current component configuration state, and the specification of the (possibly new) high-level goal. Changes in the environment, such as context conditions not considered in the current reconfiguration plans would involve reconsideration of planning in this layer.

This reference model can be applied in our case study as follows. The component control layer can be implemented exactly as described in the MAPE-K model section (cf. final part of Section 2.5.2). That is, this layer is comprised of a MAPE-K loop that solves the system unavailability by reconfiguring (i.e., adapting) the weather service. This is achieved by unlinking this service from the unavailable one (e.g., the one from WebserviceX), and then relinking it to one that is available, among the ones registered in the reconfiguration subsystem (e.g., the ones from Google and Yahoo). However, if both of these are also unavailable, the component control layer notifies the change management layer about this situation. In response, this layer could introduce two new software components and two new reconfiguration rules into the component control layer. The new components provide the functionalities for consuming the weather services from VisualWebservice,[9] and the US National Weather Service,[10] for instance. The new reconfiguration rules would allow the component control layer to make use of the new registered weather services. Finally, the user could specify a new goal for the system, for instance requiring not only high availability but also lowest response time, among the registered weather services. To satisfy this new goal, the management layer should generate new software components and reconfiguration rules for the layers below. Some of the new software components would monitor the new context variables of interest, namely those measuring the response time of the registered weather services. Other software components would implement the new logic for choosing the weather service that satisfies the new

---

[9]http://www.visualwebservice.com/wsdl/wsf.cdyne.com/Weather.asmx%3FWSDL.

[10]http://www.weather.gov/forecasts/xml/DWMLgen/wsdl/ndfdXML.wsdl.

established conditions. The new reconfiguration rules would allow the layers below to make use of the new software components. However, the model does not specify how it would use these new components when their functionality affects or replaces directly the behavior of the model's own feedback loop elements, in this case, the monitor and analyzer of the component control layer.

2.5.4 THE DYNAMICO REFERENCE MODEL

Dynamic Adaptive, Monitoring and Control Objectives model (DYNAMICO) is a reference model inspired by classic control theory that explicitly addresses: (i) the achievement of self-adaptation goals and their usage as the reference control objectives; (ii) the separation of control concerns by decoupling the different feedback loops required to satisfy the reference objectives as context changes; and (iii) the specification of context management as an independent control function to preserve the contextual relevance with respect to internal and external context changes.

The model is composed of three types of feedback loops, as depicted in the high level view that presents Fig. 2.7. Each of these feedback loops manages each of the three levels of dynamics that characterize highly *context-dependent* self-adaptation: (i) the control objectives feedback loop (CO-FL) (cf. CO-FL in the figure), (ii) the target system adaptation feedback loop (A-FL) (cf. A-FL in the figure),[11] and (iii) the dynamic monitoring feedback loop (M-FL) (cf. M-FL in the figure). As a reference model, DYNAMICO provides guidelines for designing the software architecture of self-adaptive software that is highly sensitive to changes in context situations and self-adaptation goals. Thus, the model is tailored

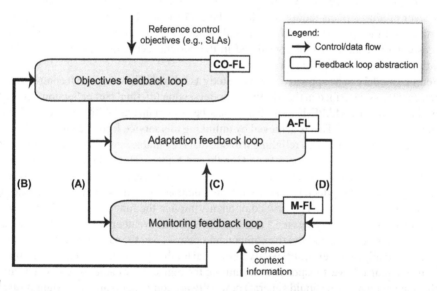

FIG. 2.7

The three levels of dynamics in a context-driven self-adaptive software systems..

Source: From N.M. Villegas, G. Tamura, H.A. Müller, L. Duchien, R. Casallas, DYNAMICO: A Reference Model for Governing Control Objectives and Context Relevance in Self-Adaptive Software Systems, vol. 7475 of LNCS, Springer, Berlin, 2013, pp. 265–293.

---

[11]Based on the analysis of the differences between the concepts of self-adaptation and adaptation (cf. Section 2.3), this feedback loop is associated with self-adaptation and not with adaptation.

for architecting self-adaptive systems prone to be adapted not only in their structure, but also in their monitoring infrastructure, as a result of adaptations in their control objectives. In this sense, this reference model emphasizes the need for checking if these three levels of dynamics have to be addressed in the architectural design. Moreover, it defines the elements and functionalities, as well as the control and data interactions to be implemented, not only among the three types of feedback loops, but also among the internal elements of each feedback loop. The reference model characterizes the interactions among the three types of feedback loops in such a way that the model can be applied partially, that is, omitting any of its feedback loops, targeting self-adaptive systems where supporting changes in any of the three levels of dynamics is a crucial requirement.

The separation of concerns among the three levels of dynamics made explicit by DYNAMICO is particularly crucial for cases in which the self-adaptation goals are modified significantly. For instance, referring to our case study, changing the objective of high-availability to high-performance requires the self-adaptation of not only the managed system, but also the monitoring infrastructure, to preserve the relevance of the self-adaptation mechanism with respect to the modified control objectives. However, the automatic reconfiguration of the monitoring infrastructure is impractical having the context manager (i.e., including the monitoring infrastructure) tightly coupled to the self-adaptation mechanism. Similarly, the explicit control of changes in self-adaptation goals (i.e., control objectives) requires separate instrumentation. Fig. 2.8 depicts a detailed view of the feedback loops for the three levels of dynamics presented in Fig. 2.7. These feedback loops are explained in the following sections.

2.5.4.1 The control objectives feedback loop (CO-FL)

The CO-FL (cf. CO-FL in Fig. 2.8) addresses the first level of dynamics specified by DYNAMICO. It governs changes in control objectives (e.g., SLAs) with the collaboration of the A-FL and the M-FL. We define requirements and self-adaptation properties as system variables to be controlled. We refer to these variables as *control objectives* and *self-adaptation goals* interchangeably. Moreover, control objectives are subject to change by user-level (re)negotiations at runtime and therefore must be addressed in a consistent and synchronized way by the self-adaptation mechanism (i.e., A-FL) and the context manager (i.e., M-FL). For example, as with the Kramer and Magee scenario defined for our case study (cf. final part of Section 2.5.3), the user could introduce the response time in the CO-FL, thus requiring not only high availability but also lowest response time, among the registered weather services. Therefore, the context monitors must keep track of a new context variable, the response time of the registered weather services. Both availability and response time must be managed explicitly as the control objectives for the adaptive system. Thus, both reference inputs, the A-FL reference control input and the M-FL reference context input, are derived automatically from control objectives and fed into the corresponding feedback loops, as illustrated by interaction (A) in Fig. 2.8.

2.5.4.2 The adaptation feedback loop (A-FL)

The A-FL, the second level of dynamics, regulates the target system requirements satisfaction and the preservation of self-adaptation properties. Recalling our self-adaptation scenario (cf. Section 2.2), the system availability represent a nonfunctional requirement. Due to changing objectives, the satisfaction of this requirement and the one introduced in the CO-FL (cf. Section 2.5.4.1) depend on the adaptive capabilities of the mashup application. For example, under the initial goal, the system reconfigures itself to change the weather service provider. After the control objective modification, the response time of the registered weather service providers becomes a new context variable to be monitored. Thus, according to the available services and their current response times, the A-FL will trigger the adaptation

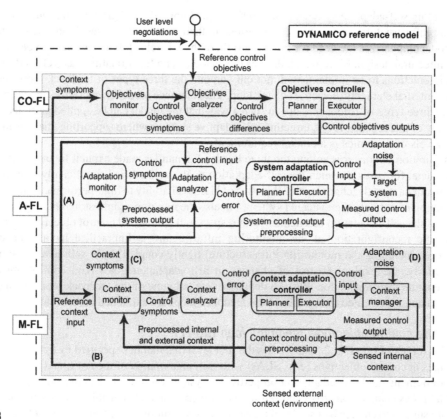

FIG. 2.8

The DYNAMICO reference model with a detailed view of the controllers for the three abstract levels of dynamics presented in Fig. 2.7.

Source: From N.M. Villegas, G. Tamura, H.A. Müller, L. Duchien, R. Casallas, DYNAMICO: A Reference Model for Governing Control Objectives and Context Relevance in Self-Adaptive Software Systems, vol. 7475 of LNCS, Springer, Berlin, 2013, pp. 265–293.

of the system by relinking the weather service to the one being available and with better response time. For this, the A-FL gathers measurements from the target system and registered weather services through context monitors provided by the M-FL (cf. Label (C) in Fig. 2.8).

2.5.4.3 The context monitoring feedback loop (M-FL)

The M-FL in Fig. 2.8 represents a dynamic context manager, the third level of dynamics specified by DYNAMICO. The reference context inputs correspond to the context monitoring requirements and are derived from the CO-FL reference control objectives. In our case study the reference control objectives are defined as nonfunctional requirements. Thus, the context monitoring requirements are derived from the metrics and conditions defined for these requirements and, as a result, monitors for measuring the response time of the registered weather services would be deployed in the managed system. The context analyzer decides about the adaptation of the monitoring strategy. The context adaptation controller is responsible for defining and triggering the execution of the adaptation plan to adjust the context manager (i.e., the target system of the M-FL).

In summary, referring to our case study and compared to the Kramer and Magee's reference model, DYNAMICO's CO-FL and A-FL supply the functionalities of the three layers of their model. Nonetheless, the M-FL in DYNAMICO solves effectively the problem of incorporating the functionalities of the new monitoring components in the model's feedback loop. That is, the feedback loops of Kramer and Magee's reference model are designed to adapt the managed system structure and behavior, but not its own adaptation logic.

2.5.5 THE AUTONOMIC COMPUTING REFERENCE ARCHITECTURE (ACRA)

The ACRA, depicted in Fig. 2.9, provides a reference architecture to organize and orchestrate self-adaptive (i.e., autonomic) systems using autonomic elements, where an autonomic element is basically an implementation of the MAPE-K model. ACRA was proposed as the foundation for realizing the Autonomic Computing vision [28]. In this vision, ACRA-based autonomic systems are defined as a multiple-layer hierarchy of MAPE-K elements, which correspond to orchestrating managers and resource managers, controlling managed resources.

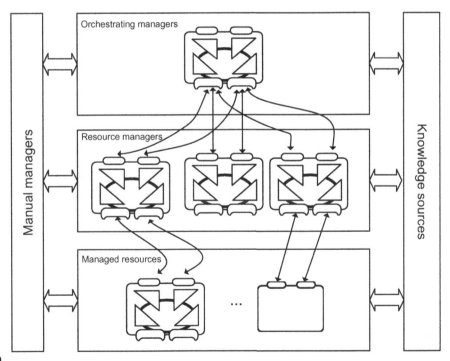

FIG. 2.9

The autonomic computing reference architecture (ACRA).

Source: Based on IBM Corporation, An architectural blueprint for autonomic computing, tech. rep., IBM Corporation, 2006.

ACRA differs from the previously analyzed models in two important ways. First, those models are based either on a single MAPE-K loop element or on a three-layer structure of MAPE-K loop elements, whereas ACRA is based on a multiple-layer hierarchy in which each layer adds autonomic control over the layers below it. Second, each layer on each of the three-layered models has specific responsibilities of control, whereas ACRA defines mainly generic responsibilities of orchestration and resource management for its multiple layers.

Referring to our case study, the ACRA model is applied very differently compared to the DYNAMICO and Kramer and Magee models. Starting with the lowest layer, ACRA would define the weather services as managed resources. For each of the registered weather services in the reconfiguration mechanism, it would dedicate a MAPE-K loop, to control it as a managed resource, even though they are external services. In the layer above, ACRA would specify the "resource managers" to control the weather services. Then, the orchestrating managers would be responsible for coordinating not only the multiple feedback loops execution and interactions, but also the information exchange among them. The purposes of each of the layers in ACRA, as applied to our case study, could be similar to those of Kramer and Magee's reference model.

Yet another scheme for controlling self-adaptation of software systems has been proposed by distributing and then combining the MAPE-K loop elements in different machines. Examples of these decentralized architectural variants are the proposals by Vromant et al. [33] and Weyns et al. [34]. Furthermore, even though the MAPE-K and feedback loops have been recognized as fundamental design elements for self-adaptation, their visibility is usually hidden in the related approaches. In many cases, the self-adaptation mechanisms are intertwined with the managed applications, rendering them as hard to reuse and manipulate, and more importantly, as unanalyzable and uncomparable in their inherent properties [7, 27, 32, 35]. To alleviate this problem, Müller et al. advocate to make feedback loops explicit and highly visible as first class entities in self-adaptive architectures [27]. Thus, when studying the architecture of an existing self-adaptive system, the feedback architectures discussed in this section are easily recognized and characterized by experienced software engineers.

2.6 MAJOR ARCHITECTURAL CHALLENGES IN SELF-ADAPTATION

Architectural challenges concern the design of both the target system as well as the self-adaptation mechanisms.

1. Concerning visibility of control: Making control loops explicit requires, beyond the consolidation of architecture knowledge in the form of different MAPE configurations as patterns, practical interface definitions (signatures and APIs), message formats, and protocols. Making control explicit and exposing self-adaptive properties are important aspects to assure self-adaptation mechanisms [12, 27].

2. Concerning separation of concerns: Recalling the DYNAMICO reference model presented in Section 2.5.4, the separation of concerns between the monitoring process, the self-adaptation controller, and the management of control objectives (self-adaptation goals) is still an open challenge. This challenge is crucial for governing the consistency between self-adaptation mechanisms and control objectives, while preserving the relevance of context monitoring of the self-adaptation mechanism [20].

3. Concerning distribution and decentralization: In complex self-adaptive software (i.e., systems composed of several feedback loops with multiple interactions among them), distribution and decentralization are considered important architectural drivers. Distribution is used to deal with issues such as latency, concurrency, and partial failures. Decentralization is important to guarantee robust execution in situations where partial failures can occur. According to [12, 36], a number of interesting challenges exist regarding self-adaptive control schemes, including: (i) Pattern applicability: In what circumstances and for what systems are the different patterns of control applicable? Which quality attribute requirements hinder or encourage which patterns? What styles and domains of software are more easily managed with which patterns? (ii) Pattern completeness: What is the complete set of patterns that could be applied to self-adaptation? (iii) QoS analysis: For decentralized approaches, what techniques can we use to guarantee system-wide quality goals? What are the coordination schemes that can enable guaranteeing these qualities?

4. Concerning the process of architecting the system: (i) Reference architectures for self-adaptive systems that address issues such as structural arrangements of control loops (e.g., sequential, parallel, hierarchical, decentralized), interactions among control loops, data flow around the control loops, tolerances, trade-offs, sampling rates, stability and convergence conditions, hysteresis specifications, context uncertainty [3], and the preservation of self-adaptation properties on both the target system and the self-adaptation mechanism [7]; (ii) patterns that characterize control-loop schemes and elements, along with associated obligations; and (iii) development of reference models and architectures, as well as further validation of existing ones in industrial settings.

2.7 SUMMARY

This chapter began with an analysis of the difference between the terms adaptation and self-adaptation, and then presented foundational concepts and reference models that facilitate the architectural design of self-adaptive software. Furthermore, the chapter presented a list of research challenges. This chapter is useful for students, researchers and practitioners to acquire a general understanding on the engineering of self-adaptive software systems, in particular of its architectural design.

REFERENCES

[1] R. Laddaga, Guest editor's introduction: creating robust software through self-adaptation, IEEE Intell. Syst. 14 (3) (1999) 26–29.

[2] R. Laddaga, Active software, in: Proceedings of the First International Workshop on Self-Adaptive Software, IWSAS 2000, Springer-Verlag, New York, NY, 2000, pp. 11–26.

[3] B.H. Cheng, R. Lemos, H. Giese, P. Inverardi, J. Magee, J. Andersson, B. Becker, N. Bencomo, Y. Brun, B. Cukic, G. Marzo Serugendo, S. Dustdar, A. Finkelstein, C. Gacek, K. Geihs, V. Grassi, G. Karsai, H.M. Kienle, J. Kramer, M. Litoiu, S. Malek, R. Mirandola, H.A. Müller, S. Park, M. Shaw, M. Tichy, M. Tivoli, D. Weyns, J. Whittle, Software engineering for self-adaptive systems: a research roadmap, Springer-Verlag, Berlin, 2009, pp. 1–26.

[4] M. Salehie, L. Tahvildari, Self-adaptive software: landscape and research challenges, ACM Trans. Auton. Adapt. Syst. 4 (14) (2009) 1–14:42.

[5] G. Tamura, R. Casallas, A. Cleve, L. Duchien, QoS contract preservation through dynamic reconfiguration: a formal semantics approach, Sci. Comput. Program. 94 (3) (2014) 307–332.

[6] L. Bass, J. Bergey, P. Clements, P. Merson, I. Ozkaya, R. Sangwan, Comparison of requirements specification methods from a software architecture perspective, tech. rep, 2006.

[7] N.M. Villegas, H.A. Müller, G. Tamura, L. Duchien, R. Casallas, A framework for evaluating quality-driven self-adaptive software systems, in: Proceedings of the Sixth International Symposium on Software Engineering for Adaptive and Self-Managing Systems (SEAMS 2011), ACM, New York, NY, 2011, pp. 80–89.

[8] M. Beisiegel, H. Blohm, D. Booz, M. Edwards, O. Hurley, et al., Service component architecture, assembly model specification, tech. rep, Open Service Oriented Architecture Collaboration, 2007.

[9] M.P. Papazoglou, P. Traverso, S. Dustdar, F. Leymann, Service-oriented computing: state of the art and research challenges, Computer 40 (2007) 38–45.

[10] P. Bourque, R.E. Fairley (Eds.), Guide to the software engineering body of knowledge—SWEBOK v3.0, 2014th ed, IEEE CS, ashington, DC, 2014.

[11] R. Laddaga, Active software, Self-Adaptive Software, Springer, Berlin, 2001, pp. 11–26.

[12] R. de Lemos, H. Giese, H.A. Müller, M. Shaw, J. Andersson, M. Litoiu, B. Schmerl, G. Tamura, N. M. Villegas, T. Vogel, D. Weyns, L. Baresi, B. Becker, N. Bencomo, Y. Brun, B. Cikic, R. Desmarais, S. Dustdar, G. Engels, K. Geihs, K.M. Göschka, A. Gorla, V. Grassi, P. Inverardi, G. Karsai, J. Kramer, A. Lopes, J. Magee, S. Malek, S. Mankovskii, R. Mirandola, J. Mylopoulos, O. Nierstrasz, M. Pezzè, C. Prehofer, W. Schäfer, R. Schlichting, D.B. Smith, J.P. Sousa, L. Tahvildari, K. Wong, J. Wuttke, Software engineering for self-adaptive systems: a second research roadmap, 7475, Springer, Berlin, 2013, pp. 1–32.

[13] N. Subramanian, L. Chung, Software architecture adaptability: an NFR approach, in: Proceedings of the Fourth International Workshop on Principles of Software Evolution, IWPSE '01, ACM, New York, NY, 2001, pp. 52–61.

[14] G.T. Heineman, Adaptation and software architecture, in: Proceedings of the Third International Workshop on Software Architecture, ISAW '98, ACM, New York, NY, 1998, pp. 61–64.

[15] P. Oreizy, M.M. Gorlick, R.N. Taylor, D. Heimbigner, G. Johnson, N. Medvidovic, A. Quilici, D.S. Rosenblum, A.L. Wolf, An architecture-based approach to self-adaptive software, IEEE Intell. Syst. 14 (3) (1999) 54–62.

[16] Y. Brun, G.D.M. Serugendo, C. Gacek, H.M. Giese, H. Kienle, M. Litoiu, H.A. Müller, M. Pezzè, M. Shaw, Engineering self-adaptive systems through feedback loops, 5525 of Lecture Notes in Computer Science, Springer-Verlag, Berlin, 2009, pp. 48–70.

[17] J.O. Kephart, D.M. Chess, The vision of autonomic computing, Computer 36 (1) (2003) 41–50.

[18] E. Gamma, R. Helm, R. Johnson, J. Vlissides, Design patterns: elements of reusable object-oriented software, Addison-Wesley Longman Publishing, Boston, MA, 1995.

[19] G. Tamura, QoS-CARE: a reliable system for preserving QoS contracts through dynamic reconfiguration, PhD Thesis, University of Lille 1—Science and Technology and University of Los Andes, May 2012.

[20] N.M. Villegas, G. Tamura, H.A. Müller, L. Duchien, R. Casallas, DYNAMICO: a reference model for governing control objectives and context relevance in self-adaptive software systems, 7475 of LNCS, Springer, Berlin, 2013, pp. 265–293.

[21] J. Whittle, P. Sawyer, N. Bencomo, B.H.C. Cheng, J.-M. Bruel, RELAX: a language to address uncertainty in self-adaptive systems requirement, Requir. Eng. 15 (2) (2010) 177–196.

[22] G.D. Abowd, A.K. Dey, P.J. Brown, N. Davies, M. Smith, P. Steggles, Towards a better understanding of context and context-awareness, in: Proceedings of the First International Symposium on Handheld and Ubiquitous Computing (HUC 1999), 1707 of LNCS, Springer, Berlin, 1999, pp. 304–307.

[23] N.M. Villegas, H.A. Müller, Managing dynamic context to optimize smart interactions and services, Springer-Verlag, Berlin, Heidelberg, 2010, pp. 289–318.

[24] L. Bass, P. Clements, R. Kazman, Software architecture in practice, Addison-Wesley, Reading, MA, 2003.

[25] K. Ogata, Modern control engineering, third edition, Prentice Hall, Upper Saddle River, NJ, 1996.

[26] J.L. Hellerstein, Y. Diao, S. Parekh, D.M. Tilbury, Feedback control of computing systems, John Wiley & Sons, Chichester, 2004.

[27] H. Müller, M. Pezzè, M. Shaw, Visibility of control in adaptive systems, in: Proceedings of the Second International Workshop on Ultra-Large-Scale Software-Intensive Systems (ULSSIS 2008), 2008, pp. 23–26.

[28] I.B.M. Corporation, An architectural blueprint for autonomic computing, IBM Corporation, 2006.

[29] D.C. Luckham, The power of events: an introduction to complex event processing in distributed enterprise systems, Addison-Wesley Longman Publishing, Boston, MA, 2001.

[30] E. Gat, On three-layer architectures, MIT/AAAI, Palo Alto, CA, 1998, pp. 1–26.

[31] J. Kramer, J. Magee, Dynamic structure in software architectures, SEN 21 (6) (1996) 3–14.

[32] J. Kramer, J. Magee, Self-managed systems: an architectural challenge, in: Proceedings of the 2007 Workshop on the Future of Software Engineering (FOSE 2007), IEEE Computer Society, 2007, pp. 259–268.

[33] P. Vromant, D. Weyns, S. Malek, J. Andersson, On interacting control loops in self-adaptive systems, in: Proceedings of the Sixth International Symposium on Software Engineering for Adaptive and Self-Managing Systems (SEAMS 2011), ACM, New York, NY, 2011, pp. 202–207.

[34] D. Weyns, S. Malek, J. Andersson, On decentralized self-adaptation: lessons from the trenches and challenges for the future, in: Proceedings of the 2010 ICSE Workshop on Software Engineering for Adaptive and Self-Managing Systems (SEAMS 2010), ACM, New York, NY, 2010, pp. 84–93.

[35] H.A. Müller, H.M. Kienle, U. Stege, Autonomic computing: now you see it, now you don't–design and evolution of autonomic software systems, 5413 Lecture Notes in Computer Science, Springer, Berlin, 2009, pp. 32–54.

[36] D. Weyns, B. Schmerl, V. Grassi, S. Malek, R. Mirandola, C. Prehofer, J. Wuttke, J. Andersson, H. Giese, K.M. Göschka, On patterns for decentralized control in self-adaptive systems, Software Engineering for Self-Adaptive Systems—II, Springer, Berlin, 2013, pp. 76–107.

A CLASSIFICATION FRAMEWORK OF UNCERTAINTY IN ARCHITECTURE-BASED SELF-ADAPTIVE SYSTEMS WITH MULTIPLE QUALITY REQUIREMENTS

S. Mahdavi-Hezavehi[*,†]**, P. Avgeriou**[*]**, D. Weyns**[†]

University of Groningen, Groningen, Netherlands[*] Linnaeus University, Växjö, Sweden[†]

3.1 INTRODUCTION

Software systems are subject to continuous changes due to new requirements and the dynamics of the system context. Engineering such complex systems is often difficult as the available knowledge at design time is not adequate to anticipate all the runtime conditions. Missing or inaccurate knowledge may be due to different types of uncertainty such as vagueness regarding the availability of resources, operating conditions that the system will encounter at runtime, or the emergence of new requirements while the system is operating. We define uncertainty in a software system as the circumstances in which the system's behavior deviates from expectations due to dynamicity and unpredictability of a variety of factors existing in software systems.

One way to deal with this uncertainty is to design systems that adapt themselves during runtime, when the knowledge is accessible. Self-adaptive systems are capable of autonomously modifying their runtime behavior to deal with dynamic system context, and changing or new system requirements in order to provide dependable, and recoverable systems [1]. In this research, we focus on architecture-based approaches ([2,3,34]), which are widely used to support self-adaptation. Architecture-based self-adaptive systems achieve this capability by means of using reflective software architecture models. In order to manage a system, an architecture-based self-adaptive system is equipped with adaptation software that uses models of the system, its environment, and goals when monitoring the running system, to detect problems, identify solutions, and apply adaptation actions to modify the system.

However, incorporating self-adaptation into a system may lead to further uncertainty in its own right: defective adaptation actions or unforeseen consequences of adaptation on the system can result

Managing Trade-offs in Adaptable Software Architectures. http://dx.doi.org/10.1016/B978-0-12-802855-1.00003-4

in unexpected system behavior. This is further aggravated in the case of self-adaptive systems that need simultaneously to fulfill multiple quality requirements without interrupting the system's normal functions, and deal with a growing number of both adaptation scenarios and requirements trade-offs [4]. This implies that the system should be able to prioritize the adaptation actions, choose the optimal adaptation scenarios, adapt the system, and presumably handle the positive or negative chain of effects caused by the adaptation of certain requirements. However, when the number of system quality requirements increases, so does the number of adaptation alternatives. Therefore, the decision making, as well as the handling of requirements trade-offs becomes more complex. If the problem is not handled properly, over time uncertainty provokes inconsistency in certain subsystems, and the accumulated inconsistencies may result in unforeseen circumstances, and possibly in unexpected system behavior.

Over the past years, numerous approaches have been proposed to quantify and mitigate existing uncertainty in self-adaptive systems. However, the concept of uncertainty and its different types and categories are hardly ever studied in the domain of architecture-based self-adaptive systems with *multiple quality requirements*. As a result, identification, investigation, and consequently selection of suitable approaches for tackling uncertainty in this domain may be problematic. To alleviate this problem, in this paper we present a framework to classify existing uncertainty concepts for architecture-based solutions in self-adaptive systems with multiple quality requirements. To create the framework, we systematically review all the papers that propose approaches to deal with uncertainty and its sources. Subsequently, we study these approaches according to the proposed classification framework in order to facilitate their potential comparison and selection. This classification framework may further be used to propose new solutions tackling the uncertainty problem more efficiently in the future.

This paper is organized as follows: in Section 3.1 we present background and related work. In Section 3.2 we introduce our research questions, discuss both the search strategy, and data extraction method. In Section 3.3 we present the results of the study, and extensively answer the research questions. In Section 3.4 we discuss the results of the study including main findings, limitations of the study, and threats to validity. Finally, Section 3.5 concludes the paper.

3.1.1 BACKGROUND

In this section, we present a brief description for self-adaptive systems, architecture-based self-adaptation, architecture-based self-adaptive systems with multiple quality requirements, and uncertainty in architecture-based self-adaptive systems.

3.1.1.1 Self-adaptive systems

Self-adaptive systems are capable of modifying their runtime behavior in order to achieve system objectives. Unpredictable circumstances such as changes in the system's environment, system faults, new requirements, and changes in the priority of requirements are some of the reasons for triggering adaptation actions in a self-adaptive system. To deal with these uncertainties, a self-adaptive system continuously monitors itself, gathers data, and analyzes them to decide if adaption is required. The challenging aspect of designing and implementing a self-adaptive system is that not only must the system apply changes at runtime, but also fulfill the system requirements up to a satisfying level. Engineering such systems is often difficult as the available knowledge at design time is not adequate to anticipate all the runtime conditions. Therefore, designers often prefer to deal with this uncertainty at runtime, when more knowledge is available.

3.1.1.2 Architecture-based self-adaptation

Architecture-based self-adaptation [3] is one well recognized approach that deals with uncertainties by supporting modifiable runtime system behavior. The essential functions of architecture-based self-adaptation are defined in the MAPE-K (i.e., monitor, analyze, plan, execute, and knowledge component) reference model [5]. By complying with the concept of separation of concerns (i.e., separation of domain specific concerns from adaptation concerns), the MAPE-K model supports reusability and manages the complexity of constructing self-adaptive systems. This makes the MAPE-K model a suitable reference for designing feedback loops and developing self-adaptive systems [6]. One well-known architecture-based self-adaptive framework is Rainbow [2]. Rainbow uses an abstract architectural model to monitor software system runtime specifications, evaluates the model for constraint violations, and if required, performs global or module-level adaptations. Calinescu et al. [7] present a quality of service management framework for self-adaptive services-based systems, which augments the system architecture with the MAPE-K loop functionalities. In their framework, the high-level quality of service requirements are translated into probabilistic temporal logic formulae which are used to identify and enforce the optimal system configuration while taking into account the quality dependencies. Moreover, utility theory can be used [4,8] to dynamically compute trade-offs (i.e., priority of quality attributes over one another) between conflicting interests, in order to select the best adaptation strategy that balances multiple quality requirements in the self-adaptive system.

3.1.1.3 Architecture-based self-adaptive systems with multiple quality requirements

Similar to any other software system, architecture-based self-adaptive systems should fulfill a variety of quality attributes in order to support a desired runtime system behavior and user experience. To design and develop such self-adapting systems, it is important to analyze the tradeoffs between multiple quality attributes at runtime, and ensure a certain quality level after adaptation actions. This means that not only requirements with higher priorities, which define the system's goal, should be met; but also quality attributes of the system should be fulfilled at an acceptable level. After all, a systems' overall quality is a desired combination of several runtime and design time requirements. However, when the number of adaptation dimensions increases, representing the choices for adaptation, and updating and maintaining trade-offs becomes problematic [4]. Therefore, the majority of current architecture-based self-adaptive systems approaches do not address trade-offs analysis explicitly, and specifically the negative impacts of the applied adaptation method on multiple quality attributes, which deteriorates systems' overall quality in complex software systems. A recent survey [9] summarizes the state of the art in architecture-based adaptation in general, and handling multiple requirements in particular.

3.1.1.4 Uncertainty in architecture-based self-adaptive systems

Uncertainty in an architecture-based self-adaptive system, or self-adaptive systems in general, can be studied from a number of different perspectives. The first and foremost genre of uncertainty is the dynamicity and unpredictability of a variety of factors existing in software systems. In fact, this type of uncertainty justifies the need for design and development of self-adaptive systems. An architecture-based self-adaptive system should be able to investigate a solution space, choose the optimal adaptation action, and adapt the system while fulfilling quality requirement of the system in a specified satisfying level. However, in a system with multiple objectives and quality goals the decision making process for selecting the optimal adaptation action is quite complex; which leads us to the second genre of uncertainty in architecture-based self-adaptive systems: consequences of self-adaptation in a software system. Incorporating a self-adaptation capability into a software system may produce even more complexity and undesirable effects in the system. Not only the self-adaptive system should deal with a growing solution space for adaptation, but it also needs to handle possible negative effects of adaptation on the system. Adversely affecting quality requirements of the system, noise in sensing and imperfect application of adaptation actions are examples of uncertainties which are aftermaths of self-adaptation in a system. Lastly, the concept of uncertainty itself and its characteristics are vaguely described and interchangeably used to refer to a variety of notions in domain of architecture-based self-adaptive systems with multiple quality requirements; this poses more ambiguity to the topic of uncertainty in this domain.

3.1.2 **RELATED WORK**

During the past decade, several studies have been conducted to address uncertainty issue in different phases of software systems life cycle. Rotmans et al. [10] attempt to harmonize the uncertainty terminology by proposing a conceptual framework (i.e., uncertainty matrix which considers uncertainty from three different dimensions: location, level of uncertainty, and nature of uncertainty), which helps to identify and characterize uncertainty in model-based decision support activities. Although the uncertainty matrix presented in that paper can be used as a guideline in the domain of self-adaptive systems as well; we found it difficult to use their detailed taxonomies and definitions of uncertainty dimensions, as it is mainly applicable to the field of model-based decision support. Following the same theme of uncertainty dimensions (i.e., location, level, and nature of uncertainty) [11] present a taxonomy for uncertainty in the modeling of self-adaptive systems. In their work, they also provide an extensive list of examples for sources of uncertainty, which is extracted from the literature. Nonetheless, the authors do not manage to provide descriptions for the sources of uncertainty. In Ref. [12], the authors present terminology and a topology of uncertainty and explore the role of uncertainty at different stages of a water management modeling process. However, their terminology is substantially inspired by the work of Rotmans et al. [10], and their field of research is remarkably different from our domain of interest; which makes it difficult to apply their work in the domain of self-adaptive systems. In Ref. [13], the author argues that in today's software systems uncertainty should be considered as a first-class concern throughout the whole system life cycle, and discusses a number of sources of uncertainty affecting software systems. What we think is missing in this work is the mapping of these sources of uncertainty into the previously discussed dimensions and taxonomies of uncertainty in the literature. Esfahani and Malek [14] mostly focus on sources of uncertainty, and present an extensive list of sources with examples. Moreover, they investigate uncertainty characteristics (reducibility versus irreducibility, variability versus lack of knowledge, and spectrum of uncertainty), and sources of uncertainty characteristics in their work; however the connection between these characteristics and dimensions of uncertainty is unclear. Lastly, Ramirez et al. [15] provide a definition and taxonomy for uncertainty in dynamically adaptive systems. The presented taxonomy describes common sources of uncertainty and their effect on requirements, design and runtime phases of dynamically adaptive systems. The main focus of this paper is sources of uncertainty as well.

Investigating the current state of research regarding uncertainty in software systems, and identifying gaps and inconsistencies in the literature, motivated us to conduct an exhaustive review of the topic in domain of architecture-based self-adaptive systems with multiple quality requirements. We argue that it is crucial to systematically study and grasp current approaches, investigate different dimensions of uncertainty to precisely comprehend the problem statement (i.e., uncertainty definition, dimensions, sources, etc.), and to identify issues which need to be resolved in order to propose approaches that can be tailored and reused in a variety of systems. The classification framework we present aims to provide a consistent and comprehensive overview of uncertainty and its specifications in domain of architecture-based self-adaptive systems with multiple quality requirements.

3.2 STUDY DESIGN

In this study, we aim at identifying, exploring, and classifying the state of the art on architecture-based methods handling uncertainty in self-adaptive systems with multiple quality requirements. Therefore, we perform a systematic literature review [16] to collect and investigate existing architecture-based methods, and to answer a set of predefined research questions. The first step of conducting a systematic literature review is to create a protocol,[1] in which all the steps and details of the study are specified. In this section, we report parts of the protocol and its execution: we present our research questions, a generic overview of the process and the search strategy which we use to search through selected databases, inclusion and exclusion criteria for filtering the collected papers, data extraction procedure, and the data synthesis method we used to answer the research questions and propose the classification framework.

3.2.1 RESEARCH QUESTIONS

We pose the following research questions to investigate the current architecture-based approaches tackling uncertainty in self-adaptive systems with multiple quality requirements.

(1) What are the current architecture-based approaches tackling uncertainty in self-adaptive systems with multiple requirements?
(2) What are the different uncertainty dimensions which are explored by these approaches?
    (a) What are the options for these uncertainty dimensions?
(3) What sources of uncertainties are addressed by these approaches?
(4) How are the current approaches classified according to the proposed uncertainty classification framework?

By answering research question 1, we get an overview of current architecture-based approaches tackling uncertainty. "Architecture-based" implies that the approach presented in the study should provide architectural solutions (e.g., architectural models) to handle and reason about the dynamic behavior of the system. To be more specific, the software system that is subject of adaption (i.e., the managed system) should be equipped with adaptation software that uses architectural models of the system, its environment, and goals when monitoring the running system and adapt the managed system at runtime when needed. In particular, it should be possible to map the components of the adaptation software to MAPE-k functionalities. With multiple requirements, we refer both to approaches that handle more than one adaptation concern (e.g., adapt for reliability and security) and approaches that consider a single adaptation concern (e.g., reliability) but also the effects on one or more other concerns (e.g., performance overhead). The answer to this research question will be a list of current studies, related venues and books in which they have been published, year of publication, and authors' names.

---

[1]The protocol is available at: http://www.cs.rug.nl/search/uploads/Resources/book_chapter_protocol.pdf.

Research question 2 aims to identify and investigate possible dimensions for uncertainty. Dimensions refer to different aspects of uncertainty in self-adaptive systems with multiple quality requirements. For instance, we are interested in figuring out whether or not locations (e.g., environment, the managed system, components of the adaptation software) in which the uncertainty manifests itself are a commonly discussed subject, or if phases of systems life cycle in which the existence of uncertainty is acknowledged, etc. are discussed in the selected papers or not. The answer to this research question will help us to derive the most significant and common aspects of uncertainty in this domain.

Research question 2.a aims to understand the dimensions of uncertainty resulting from answering the previous research question, on a more concrete level. By answering this research question, we come up with a list of common categories and options for each of the aforementioned dimensions. For instance, we intend to come up with a list of possible locations in which the uncertainty appears in a self-adaptive system, or identify in which particular phases of systems life cycle the existence of uncertainty is acknowledged or the problem is tackled.

The source of uncertainty is one of the most important dimensions of uncertainty, Therefore, we investigate it in more depth in research question 3. By answering this research question, we aim to identify and list common sources of uncertainty, from which the uncertainty originates. Sources of uncertainty refer to a variety of circumstances, which affect and deviate system behavior from expected behavior in the future. For example, changes in the environment or system requirements are considered as sources of uncertainty. The list of sources of uncertainty will be a separate part of the final classification framework. Answers to research questions 2 and 3 help to compose the classification framework, which is the main contribution of this study.

Finally, we pose research question 4 to indicate how the proposed uncertainty classification framework can be used to study and classify current approaches tackling uncertainty in the domain of self-adaptive systems with multiple quality requirements. Essentially, we investigate the usefulness of the proposed classification framework by analyzing selected primary studies and mapping them to the framework.

To sum up, by answering the aforementioned research questions, we aim to present an overview of existing architecture-based approaches tackling uncertainty in self-adaptive systems with multiple requirements. In addition, we strive to identify common dimensions, characteristics of those dimensions, and sources, which are treated in the literature, and propose a comprehensible classification framework for uncertainty in self-adaptive systems with multiple quality requirements. Finally, we use the proposed framework as the basis for further analysis of extracted data from the selected papers to present a statistical overview of the current research in this domain.

3.2.2 SEARCH STRATEGY

In this section, we present the main steps we performed in order to identify, filter, and include all the relevant papers in our study. An extended and more detailed description of our search strategy can be found in the protocol.

3.2.2.1 Search scope and automatic search

The scope of the search is defined in two dimensions: publication period and venues. In terms of publication period, we limited the search to papers published over the period Jan. 1, 2000 to Jul. 20, 2014. We chose this start date because the development of successful self-adaptive software hardly goes back to a decade ago; after the advent of autonomic computing [17]. Note that even though some major venues on self-adaptive systems started to emerge after 2005 (e.g., International Symposium on Software Engineering for Adaptive and Self-Managing Systems), we chose to start the search in the year 2000 to avoid missing any studies published in other venues.

Since the number of published papers in this domain is over several thousand, manual search was not a feasible approach to search databases [18]. Therefore, we used the automatic search method to search through selected venues. By automatic search we mean search performed by executing search strings on search engines of electronic data sources (i.e., IEEE Xplorer, ACM digital library, SpringerLink, and ScienceDirect). An advantage of automatic search is that it supports easy replication of the study.

One of the main challenges of performing an automatic search to find relevant studies in the domain of self-adaptive systems was a lack of standard, well-defined terminology in this domain. Due to this problem, and to avoid missing any relevant paper in the automatic search, we decided to use a more generic search string and include a wider number of papers in the initial results. We used the research questions and a stepwise strategy to obtain the search terms; the strategy is as follows:

(1) Derive main terms from the research questions and the topics being researched.
(2) If applicable, identify and include alternative spellings and synonyms for the terms.
(3) When database allows, use "advance" or "expert" search option to insert the complete search string.
  (a) Otherwise, use Boolean "or" to incorporate alternative spellings and synonyms, and use Boolean "and" to link the major terms.
(4) Pilot different meaningful combinations of search terms.
(5) Check the pilot results with the "quasi-gold" standard which is a set of manually derived primary studies from a given set of studies (see below for further explanation).
(6) Organized discussions between researchers to adjust the search terms, if necessary.

As a result, the following terms were used to formulate the search string:

Self, Dynamic, Autonomic, Manage, Management, Configure, Configuration, Configuring, Adapt, Adaptive, Adaptation, Monitor, Monitoring, Heal, Healing, Architecture, Architectural.

The search string consists of three parts based on the combination of key terms: Self AND Adaptation AND Architecture. The alternate terms listed above are used to create the main search string. This is done by connecting these keywords through logical OR as follow:

> (self **OR** dynamic **OR** autonomic) **AND** (manage **OR** management **OR** configure **OR** configuration **OR** configuring **OR** adapt **OR** adaptive **OR** adaptation **OR** monitor **OR** monitoring **OR** analyze **OR** analysis **OR** plan **OR** planning **OR** heal **OR** healing **OR** optimize **OR** optimizing **OR** optimization **OR** protect **OR** protecting) **AND** (architecture **OR** architectural)

Although manual search is not feasible for databases where the number of published papers can be enormous, we still incorporated a manual search (i.e., "quasi-gold" standard [19]) into the search process to make sure that the search string works properly. To establish the "quasi-gold" standard, we manually searched three different venues. To perform the manual search, we looked into papers' titles, keywords, abstracts, introductions, and conclusions. The manually selected papers were cross-checked with the results of automatic search to ensure that all the relevant papers are found during the automatic search. This means that papers found for "quasi-gold" standard should be a subset of automatic results. This step (i.e., creating "quasi-gold" standard) ensures validity of the created search string.

In total, we have selected and included 51 papers derived from 27 different venues and books. To be more specific, the venues include 13 different conferences, 4 workshops, 7 journals, and 3 books.

3.2.2.2 Overview of search process

We adopted a four-phased search process to search the selected venues and books, filter results, and collect relevant papers. The different steps of the process are shown in Fig. 3.1.

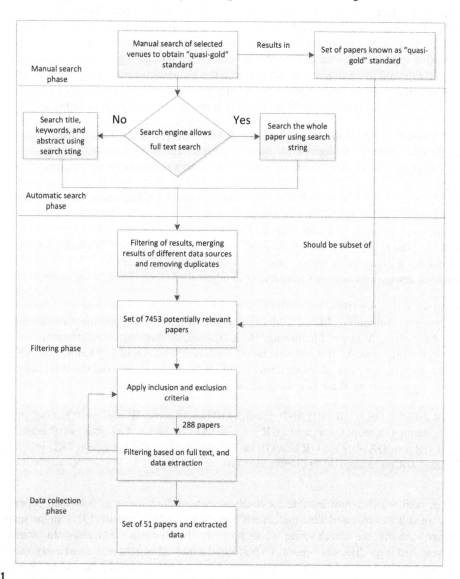

FIG. 3.1

Search process.

In the first phase (i.e., manual search), we manually searched three selected venues (see Table 3.18) to create the "quasi-gold" standard. The final set of papers from this phase should be cross checked with the automatic results in the filtering phase. In the next phase (i.e., automatic search), we performed the automatic search of selected venues (see Table 3.19). Depending on the search engines' capabilities, different search strategies were picked. If the search engine allowed, we used the search string to search the full paper; otherwise, titles, abstracts and keywords were searched. In the filtering phase, we filtered the results based on titles, abstracts, keywords, introductions, and conclusions, and also removed the duplicate papers.

We ended up having 7453 potentially relevant papers, which then were compared with the "quasi-gold" standard. Since the "quasi-gold" standard papers were a subset of potentially relevant papers, we proceeded to the next step and started filtering the papers based on inclusion and exclusion criteria. At this point, we started reading the whole papers as it was not possible to filter some of the papers only based on abstract, introduction, and conclusion. Therefore, for certain papers we also started extracting and collecting data simultaneously. Finally, we included 51 papers as our primary studies, and finished the data extraction for all of the papers.

3.2.2.3 *Refining the search results*
We used the following inclusion and exclusion criteria to filter our extracted set of papers.

3.2.2.3.1 Inclusion criteria
To be selected, a paper needed to cover all the following inclusion criteria:

(1) The study should be in the domain of self-adaptive systems.
(2) The method presented to manage systems adaptability should be architecture-based. This implies that the study should provide architectural solutions (e.g., architectural models) to handle and reason about the dynamic behavior of the system. In other words, it should be possible to map components of the systems adaptation logic to MAPE-k functionalities.
(3) The study should tackle multiple quality requirements, either as a goal of adaptation or as a consequence of applying a self-adaptation method.

3.2.2.3.2 Exclusion criteria
A paper was excluded if it fulfilled one of the following exclusion criteria:

(1) Study is editorial, position paper, abstract, keynote, opinion, tutorial summary, panel discussion, or technical report. A paper that is not a peer-reviewed scientific paper may not be of acceptable quality or may not provide reasonable amount of information.
(2) The study in not written in English.

3.2.3 DATA EXTRACTION
We used our selected primary studies to collect data and answer the research questions. Our data extraction approach was semistructured. We created initial uncertainty dimensions and source classification schemas (see Tables 3.1 and 3.2) based on the literature, namely the work by Perez-palacin et al. [11], Refsgaard et al. [12], Rotmans et al. [10], David Garlan [13], Esfahani and Male [14], and

Table 3.1 Uncertainty Dimensions Initial Classification Schema

Uncertainty Dimension	Dimension Descriptions
Location [10]	"It is an identification of where uncertainty manifests itself within the whole model complex."
Nature [10]	"Specifies whether the uncertainty is due to the imperfection of our knowledge, or is due to the inherent variability of the phenomena being described."
Level/spectrum ([10,14])	"Indicates where the uncertainty manifests itself along the spectrum between deterministic knowledge and total ignorance."
Sources [14]	"Factors challenge the confidence with which the adaptation decisions are made." Refers to a variety of uncertainties originating from system models, adaptation actions, systems goals, and executing environment

Table 3.2 Sources of Uncertainty Initial Classification Schema

Uncertainty Source	Descriptions
Model	Refers to a variety of uncertainties originating from system models
Goals	Refers to a variety of uncertainties originating from system's goal-related complications
Environment	Refers to a variety of uncertainties originating from environmental circumstances

Ramirez et al. [15]. Our intent was to extend and complete both the dimension and source classifications schemas based on data we extract from the primary studies.

We also recorded comments to capture additional observations about certain papers or data fields; the comments were used to solve any disagreements among researchers, if necessary.

3.2.4 DATA ITEMS

Table 3.3 lists the data fields we used to extract useful data from the primary studies in order to answer our research questions (RQ). Descriptions of the data fields are provided in Tables 3.1 and 3.2.

Table 3.3 Data Form Used for Data Extractions

Item ID	Data Field	Purpose
F1	Author(s) name	RQ1
F2	Title	RQ1
F3	Publication year	RQ1
F4	Venue	RQ1
F5	Location	RQ2
F6	Nature	RQ2
F7	Level/spectrum	RQ2
F8	Emerging time	RQ2
F9	Sources	RQ3

3.2.5 QUALITY ASSESSMENT OF SELECTED PAPERS

We use a quality assessment (QA) method to assess the quality of all the selected papers that were included in this review. We adopted the quality assessment mechanism (i.e., definitions and quality assessment questions) used by Dybå and Dingsøyr [20] as follows:

(1) *Quality of reporting*: Papers' rationale, aim, and context should be clarified.
  (a) *QA1*: Do the authors clarify the aims and objectives of the paper, and is there a clear rationale for why the study is undertaken?
  (b) *QA2*: Is there an adequate description of the context in which the research was carried out?
(2) *Rigor*: A thorough and appropriate approach is applied to key research methods in the paper.
  (a) *QA3*: Is there an adequate justification and clear description for the research design?
(3) *Credibility*: The papers' findings are well presented and meaningful.
  (a) *QA4*: Has sufficient data been presented to support the finding, are the findings are stated clearly?
  (b) *QA5*: Do the researcher examine their own potential bias and influence during the formulation of research questions and evaluation of results?
  (c) *QA6*: Do the authors discuss the credibility and limitations of their findings?

The quality assessment mechanism of Dybå and Dingsøyr covers also relevance (i.e., explores the value of the paper for the related community) of papers. However, in this systematic review we have only included papers published in high quality venues that are relevant to our domain of interest, thus further investigation of usefulness of the papers for the community is unnecessary.

To assess the quality of the papers, each paper is evaluated against the abovementioned quality assessment questions. Answers to each of the questions can be either "yes," "to some extend" or "no," and then numerical values are assigned to the answers (1 = "yes," 0 = "no," and 0.5 = "to some extent"). The final quality score for each primary paper is calculated by summing up the scores for all the questions. The results of quality assessment are used in the synthesis phase to support the validity of included papers in this review. The scores assigned to the selected papers are presented in Section 3.3.1.

3.3 RESULTS

In this section, we present a basic analysis of our results through various tables and charts, and then answer the research questions.

3.3.1 QUALITY OF SELECTED PAPERS

Our list of venues (Table 3.19) for automatic search includes the list of venues searched by Weyns et al. [9]. In that systematic literature review, the authors included a list of high quality primary studies in the domain of self-adaptive systems, software architectures, and software engineering. Furthermore, to broaden the search scope and extend the list of venues, we used Microsoft Academic Search[2] to find more relevant venues in the domains of self-adaptive systems and software architecture, and included them in the study. However, to verify the quality of selected papers furthermore, we assessed all the papers based

---

[2]http://academic.research.microsoft.com/.

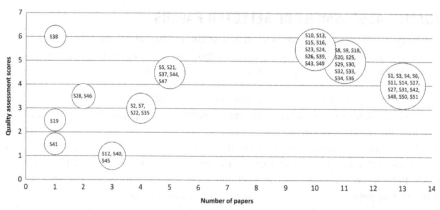

FIG. 3.2

Quality assessment of selected papers.

on the method described in Section 3.2.5. In Fig. 3.2, we indicate all the selected papers and their associated quality assessment scores. Bubbles located between scores 4 and 4.5 contain papers with an average quality, those located between scores 5 to 6 contain papers with a higher quality, and the rest of the papers were of a lower quality of reporting. The results suggest that the selected papers for this study are of relatively high quality: 18 papers are located score 4 or 4.5, and 22 papers score from 5 to 6.

3.3.2 RQ1: WHAT ARE THE CURRENT ARCHITECTURE-BASED APPROACHES TACKLING UNCERTAINTY IN SELF-ADAPTIVE SYSTEMS WITH MULTIPLE REQUIREMENTS?

In this study, we included 51 papers in total (see Table 3.17 for complete list of papers). Fig. 3.3 shows the number of included papers per venue with publication numbers equal or higher than two. Software Engineering for Adaptive and Self-Managing Systems conference (SEAMS) and Software Engineering

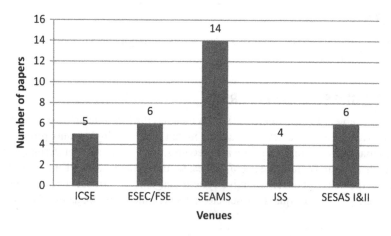

FIG. 3.3

Number of published papers per venue.

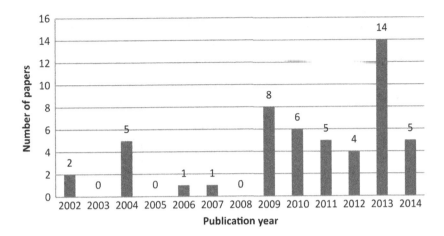

FIG. 3.4

Number of published papers per year.

for Self-Adaptive Systems (SESAS) volumes I and II have the most number of selected papers with 14 publications and 6 papers respectively.

From Fig. 3.4, we can see that most of the studies started to appear around 2009; suggesting that architecture-based approaches tackling uncertainty in self-adaptive systems with multiple quality requirements were not widely studied before the year 2008. Since architecture-based approaches have been used in the domain of self-adaptive system even before 2009, we speculate that uncertainty in self-adaptive systems with multiple quality requirements has been understudied before the year 2009.

3.3.3 RQ2: WHAT ARE THE DIFFERENT UNCERTAINTY DIMENSIONS WHICH ARE EXPLORED BY THESE APPROACHES?

We used the initial classification schema of uncertainty dimensions (see Table 3.1) to extract data from the selected papers, and then gradually extended that initial classification schema to create our framework. Table 3.4 presents a list of significant dimensions we found in the literature, descriptions of the dimensions, and possible options for each of the dimensions.

As indicated in Table 3.4, we found five different noteworthy dimensions of uncertainty (i.e., location, nature, level, emerging time, and sources). This implies that current architecture-based approaches in the domain of self-adaptive systems with multiple quality requirements examine uncertainty from five distinct perspectives. The fact that these dimensions were extracted from the literature suggests that any effective solution tackling uncertainty should at least address these dimensions in order to thoroughly explore underlying uncertainty in self-adaptive systems, and afterwards, propose solutions to tackle uncertainty.

Notice that the primary dimensions descriptions listed in Table 3.1 were refined into those presented in Table 3.4. Although undertaking the systematic review did not change the core of the definitions presented in the primary classification schema, it did help to refine the definitions in order to be further applicable in the domain of architecture-based self-adaptive systems and to fit into the final classification framework.

Table 3.4 Classification Framework for Dimensions of Uncertainty and Its Options

Uncertainty Dimension	Description	Options	Descriptions
Location	Refers to the locale, where uncertainty manifests itself within the whole system	Environment	Refers to execution context and humans interacting with, or affecting the system
		Model	Refers to a variety of conceptual models representing the system
		Adaptation functions	Refers to functionalities performed as part of MAPE-K model
		Goals	Refers to specification, modeling and alteration of system goals
		Managed system	Refers to the application specific system, which is being monitored and adapted
		Resources	Refers to a variety of essential factors and components which are required by the self-adaptive system in order to operate normally
Nature	Specifies whether the uncertainty is due to the imperfection of available knowledge, or is due to the inherent variability of the phenomena being described	Epistemic	The uncertainty is due to the imperfection of our knowledge, which may be reduced by more research and empirical efforts
		Variability	The uncertainty is due to inherent variability in the system complex including randomness of nature, human behavior, and technological surprises
Level/ spectrum	Indicates the position of uncertainty along the spectrum between deterministic knowledge and total ignorance	Statistical uncertainty	Statistical uncertainty refers to deterministic knowledge in the uncertainty spectrum and is any uncertainty that can be described adequately in statistical terms.
		Scenario uncertainty	A scenario is a plausible description of how the system and or its driving forces may develop in the future. Scenarios do not forecast what will happen in the future; rather they indicate what might happen.
Emerging time	Refers to time when the existence of uncertainty is acknowledged or uncertainty is appeared during the life cycle of the system.	Runtime	Refers to the uncertainties appearing after systems deployment, which also includes system evolution over time.
		Design time	Refers to the uncertainties manifesting themselves during any software development phases carried out before system deployment.
Sources	Refers to a variety of circumstances affecting the adaptation decision, which eventually deviate system's performance from expected behavior		See Table 3.5

3.3.3.1 RQ2.a: What Are the Options for These Uncertainty Dimensions?

In Table 3.4, we also provide detailed descriptions for each of the options listed for uncertainty dimensions. Furthermore, we expanded the options list by adding new options (i.e., managed system, and sources) to the primary schema. By providing a full list of options and their descriptions, this table can be used as a guideline for researchers to avoid any ambiguity while addressing dimensions options in their work.

We note that the dimension "level of uncertainty" may also include recognized ignorance (i.e., acknowledging uncertainty, but not proposing any remedy), and total ignorance (i.e., completely ignoring the existence of uncertainty) as options. However, these two options do not apply for any of the primary studies: all the studies acknowledge the existence of uncertainty and propose solutions to handle it.

3.3.4 **RQ3: WHAT SOURCES OF UNCERTAINTIES ARE ADDRESSED BY THESE APPROACHES?**

Finally, to answer this research question, we used the initial classification schema for sources of uncertainty (see Table 3.2) for data extraction and created an extended list of sources of uncertainty. In Table 3.5 we present the extended list, along with the descriptions for the options and examples from literature. The sources of uncertainty refer to a variety of circumstances from which the uncertainty originates. Furthermore, we added one more column, "classes of uncertainty", which is only used for grouping purposes: sources of uncertainties with similar origins are grouped in the same class of uncertainty. This helps making a long list of sources of uncertainty easier to analyze in the next section.

In this table, specific examples from the literature are provided to help with the comprehensibility of sources.

3.3.5 **RQ4: HOW ARE THE CURRENT APPROACHES CLASSIFIED ACCORDING TO THE PROPOSED UNCERTAINTY CLASSIFICATION FRAMEWORK?**

From 51 selected papers, 12 papers discuss one class of uncertainty. Environment is the most-addressed class of uncertainty, and adaptation functions is the least (see Table 3.6).

The rest of the papers (39 out of 51) discuss multiple classes of uncertainty. A variety of combinations of classes of uncertainty are discussed in the literature; "Environment, Goal, and Adaptation functions" is the most addressed set of classes of uncertainty, for details see Table 3.7.

From Tables 3.6 and 3.7, we can conclude that the majority of existing studies (39 papers) explore different classes of uncertainty, and do not focus on proposing solutions to tackle certain class of uncertainty and its sources. We can also observe that "Environment" and "Goal" seems to be the most important classes of uncertainty, and the majority of researchers are interested in tackling uncertainties emanating from environmental circumstances and self-adaptive system's goal related complications.

Regarding the nature of uncertainty (see Table 3.8), 35 papers (68.6%) discuss uncertainty due to variability, and only two papers tackle uncertainty due to lack of knowledge (i.e., epistemic). Although 14 papers address both variability and lack of knowledge as the nature of uncertainty in self-adaptive systems; variability seems to be the main source from which uncertainty originates, as 35 primary studies' main focus is only variability.

Table 3.5 Sources of Uncertainty

Class of Source of Uncertainty	Options (for Sources of uncertainty)	Description	Example
Model uncertainty	Abstraction	Uncertainty caused by omitting certain details and information from models for the sake of simplicity	Simplifying assumptions [14]
	Incompleteness	Uncertainty caused by parts (of models, mechanisms, etc.) that are knowingly missing because of a lack of (current) knowledge	Model structural uncertainty [11]
	Model drift	Uncertainty caused by a discrepancy between the state of models and the represented phenomena	Violation of requirements in models [21]
	Different sources of information	Uncertainty caused by differences between the representations of information provided by different sources of information. Uncertainty may be due to different representations of the same information, or result of having different sources of information, or both	Granularity of models [22]
	Complex models	Uncertainty caused by complexity of runtime models representing managed sub systems	Complex architectural models [23]
Adaptation functions uncertainty	Variability space of adaptation	Uncertainty caused by the size of the variability space that the adaption functions need to handle. This type of uncertainty arises from striving to capture the whole complex relationship of the system with its changing environment in a few architectural configurations which is inherently difficult and generates the risk of overlooking important environmental states [4]	Being unable to foresee all possible environment states as well as all the system configurations in the future [24]
	Sensing	Uncertainty caused by sensors which are inherently imperfect	Noise in sensing [14]
	Effecting	Uncertainty caused by effectors of which the effects may not be completely deterministic	Futures parameter value [14]
	Automatic learning	Uncertainty caused by machine learning techniques of which the effects may not be completely predictable.	Modeling techniques [22]
	Decentralization	Uncertainty due to decision making by different entities of which the	Decentralized control in a traffic jams monitoring system [25]

Continued

Table 3.5 Sources of Uncertainty—cont'd

Class of Source of Uncertainty	Options (for Sources of uncertainty)	Description	Example
		effects may not be completely predictable	
	Changes in adaptation mechanisms	Uncertainty due to required dynamicity of adaptation infrastructure to maintain its relevance with respect to the changing adaptation goals [26]	Additional monitoring infrastructure [26]
	Fault localization and identification	Uncertainty caused by inaccurate localization and identification of faults in the managed system	Identifying and ranking faulty component [27]
Goals uncertainty	Goal dependencies	Dependencies between goals, in particular quality goals, may not be captured in a deterministic manner, which causes uncertainty	Conflict resolution between competing quality attributes [28]
	Future goal changes	Uncertainty due to potential changes of goals that could not be completely anticipated	Rapid evolution [13]
	Future new goals	Uncertainty due to the potential introduction of new goals that could not be completely anticipated	Rapid evolution [13]
	Goal specification	Uncertainty due to lack of deterministic specifications of quality goals	Quality goals priorities changes [29]
	Outdated goals	Uncertainty caused by overlooking outdated goals	Addressing goals which are irrelevant to the system [30]
Environment uncertainty	Execution context	Uncertainty caused by the inherent unpredictability of execution contexts	Mobility [13]
	Human in the loop	Uncertainty caused by the inherent unpredictability of human behavior	Objectives [14]
	Multiple ownership	Uncertainty caused by lack of proper information sharing, conflicting goals, and decision making policies by multiple entities that own parts of the system	Uncertain execution time and failure rate of a component operated by a third-party organization [31]
Resources uncertainty	New resources	Uncertainty caused by availability of new resources in the system	Availability of new services in the system [32]
	Changing resources	Uncertainty caused by dynamicity of resources in the system	Resources mobility [33]
Managed system uncertainty	System complexity and changes	Uncertainty caused by complexity and dynamicity of nature of the managed system	Complex systems and complex architectural models [23]

Table 3.6 List of Papers Discussing Single Class of Uncertainty

Class of Uncertainty	Number of Papers	Study Numbers
Environment	4	S20, S34, S37, S38
Goal	3	S4, S29, S41
Model	3	S11, S16, S23
Adaptation functions	2	S5, S14

Table 3.7 List of Papers Discussing Combinations of Classes of Uncertainty

Classes of Uncertainty	Number of Papers	Study Numbers
Environment, goal, adaptation functions	9	S8, S9, S25, S31, S32, S43, S44, S45, S49
Environment, goal	8	S7, S15, S18, S33, S46, S47, S51
Environment, adaptation functions	3	S17, S42, S50
Environment, model, adaptation functions	3	S13, S12, S19
Environment, model	2	S3, S24
Environment, goal, adaptation function, model	2	S26, S10
Environment, goal, managed system	2	S27, S36
Environment, goal, model	2	S30, S40
Adaptation function, model, goal	1	S48
Goal, adaptation function	1	S39
Environment, resources	1	S2
Environment, resources, adaptation functions	1	S21
Environment, goal, resources	1	S1
Environment, adaptation functions, goal, managed system	1	S35
Environment, adaptation functions, goal, resources	1	S22
Environment, model, managed system	1	S6
Goal, adaptation function, resources	1	S28

Table 3.8 List of Papers and Nature of Uncertainty

Nature	Number of Papers	Study Numbers
Variability	35	S1, S2, S4, S5, S6, S7, S8, S9, S10, S14, S15, S16, S17, S18, S19, S20, S21, S22, S25, S28, S29, S31, S34, S36, S37, S38, S39, S40, S41, S43, S45, S47, S48, S49, S51
Variability, epistemic	14	S3, S11, S12, S13, S24, S26, S27, S30, S32, S33, S35, S42, S46, S50
Epistemic	2	S23, S44

Table 3.9 List of Papers and Level of Uncertainty

Level	Number of Papers	Study Numbers
Scenario	28	S1, S3, S4, S6, S8, S10, S11, S15, S16, S17, S18, S19, S20, S22, S23, S24, S25, S29, S31, S32, S35, S36, S37, S40, S44, S48, S50, S51
Scenario, statistical	12	S5, S7, S21, S27, S30, S33, S34, S38, S39, S46, S47, S49
Statistical	7	S9, S12, S13, S14, S26, S42, S43
Not specified	4	S2, S28, S41, S45

Regarding the level of uncertainty (see Table 3.9), most of the primary studies (i.e., 28 papers) explore uncertainty at the scenario level, 7 papers use only statistical methods to investigate uncertainty, and 12 papers use a combination of both scenarios and statistical methods. Investigating uncertainty at the scenario level is easier to understand, it helps to anticipate potential system behavior in presence of uncertainty, and estimates how the quality requirements may be affected; on the downside it lacks rigorous analysis of system state. Statistical methods, however, can use runtime knowledge to accurately calculate system status in presence of uncertainty, and also enable finding the best adaptation option with the least side effects on quality requirements. Therefore, we envision that using a combination of both scenario and statistical levels will be the most advantageous option for handling multiple quality requirements.

Regarding emerging time, Table 3.10 indicates that most of the existing approaches (i.e., 36 papers) postpone the treatment of uncertainty to the runtime phase. This is not surprising as researchers are mostly interested to study requirements trade-offs at runtime. In 13 papers, uncertainty is treated in both design and runtime. One common way of dealing with uncertainty in these approaches is to acknowledge the existing uncertainty and anticipate probable solutions at design time, but tackle the uncertainty in the runtime phase when more knowledge is available. Finally, we found two papers in which uncertainty is explored and tackled only at design time.

Regarding the sources of uncertainty, we note that in some cases there might be an overlap between two or more of the listed sources (e.g., human in the loop, and multiple ownership) definitions; in these cases, we have assigned the primary studies to the most relevant sources. In some cases it is not clear

Table 3.10 List of Papers and the Uncertainty Treatment Time

Emerging Time	Number of Papers	Study Numbers
Runtime	36	S1, S2, S4, S5, S8, S10, S14, S16, S17, S19, S20, S21, S23, S25, S26, S27, S28, S29, S30, S31, S32, S33, S34, S35, S37, S38, S39, S41, S42, S43, S45, S46, S47, S48, S49, S51
Runtime, design time	13	S6, S7, S9, S11, S12, S13, S15, S18, S22, S24, S36, S44, S50
Design time	2	S3, S40

from the paper which source is the most relevant one; in these cases we list the source as hybrid and indicate which multiple sources are applicable. Furthermore listing papers under certain types of sources does not necessarily indicate that the paper provides a solution to tackle uncertainty originating from those particular sources. It means that the paper discusses uncertainty due to those sources; however, it may or may not propose solutions to resolve uncertainty emerging from one or multiple of those sources.

The most common types of sources of uncertainty in the literature are environmental sources (addressed in 38 papers). From Table 3.11, we see that execution context and human in the loop are respectively the most and the least common sources of uncertainty from the environment uncertainty class. This is not a surprise since the most commonly addressed nature of uncertainty is variability, and variability normally occurs in the execution context of the self-adaptive systems.

Although S6, S18, and S44 address uncertainty originating from environmental sources as well, we could not decide to which source they should be assigned. Therefore, we recoded sources discussed in S6 and S18 as hybrid sources, as they both can be considered uncertainty originating from system and/or environment. Regarding S44, the environmental fact causing the uncertainty is considered as "complexity," despite the rest of the papers which explore the uncertainty due to the dynamicity of the environment.

Table 3.12 lists sources from the goal uncertainty class. Addressed by twelve papers, future goal changes seem to be the most studied goal-related uncertainty in the literature. This suggests that researchers are mainly concerned with the ability of the self-adaptive system to handle its current goals and the potential changes in the future; adding new goals to the system (i.e., future new goals) does not seem to be as important. In Table 3.12 we also list different sets of sources that we found in the literature; however, the numbers of papers addressing these sets of sources are rather low.

Both S39 and S40 address the sources achieving stakeholder's objectives and meeting quality of service which can be considered a form of goal uncertainty class. However, we did not assign them to any of our listed sources as it was unclear which sources would be the most relevant. What we noticed from the analysis of goal uncertainty sources is that, although all the included primary studies somehow deal with multiple quality requirements, the trade-off analysis gained little attention in the literature. From 51 selected primary studies, only 8 paper address goal dependencies. In addition, the potential negative impact of self-adaptation on systems quality requirements is not explicitly explored as sources of uncertainty.

Table 3.11 List of Papers Addressing Environment Uncertainty Sources

Types of Environment Uncertainty Source	Number of Papers	Study Numbers
Execution context	30	S1, S3, S7, S8, S9, S11, S13, S17, S19, S20, S24, S25, S26, S27, S30, S31, S32, S33, S34, S35, S36, S37, S38, S40, S42, S43, S45, S46, S47, S51
Execution context, human in the loop	4	S2, S10, S22, S50
Human in the loop	1	S21

Table 3.12 List of Papers Addressing Goal Uncertainty Sources

Types of Goals Uncertainty Source	Number of Papers	Study Numbers
Future goal changes	12	S7, S10, S18, S22, S26, S27, S28, S30, S31, S32, S33, S36
Goal dependency	8	S15, S41, S43, S44, S46, S47, S49, S51
Future new goals	3	S1, S4, S8
Future goal changes, future new goals	2	S38, S45
Goal dependency, future new goals	1	S9
Goal dependency, future goal changes	1	S25
Goal specification, goal dependency	1	S13
Future goal changes, outdated goals	1	S29

Table 3.13 indicates sources of uncertainty from adaptation functions class. The most commonly discussed (i.e., addressed by 10 papers) source is variability of solution space. This shows that the current focus of research is mainly on providing assurances for applying the best adaptation actions in a system. Self-adaptive systems should be capable of exploring the solution space, and selecting the best solution to adapt the systems with minimum negative side effect on other systems functionalities and quality aspects. Interestingly, the next most common source is fault localization and identification in a system. This suggests that although the most significant source of uncertainty is the selection of most

Table 3.13 List of Papers Addressing Adaptation Function Uncertainty Sources

Types of Adaptation Functions Uncertainty Source	Number of Papers	Study Numbers
Variability of solution space	10	S9, S13, S15, S25, S26, S39, S42, S43, S44, S48
Fault localization and identification	5	S10, S17, S21, S22, S28
Decentralization	4	S1, S19, S32, S45
Variability of solution space, fault localization and identification	3	S5, S8, S14
Changes in adaptation mechanisms	2	S31, S35
Variability of solution space, decentralization	1	S11
Sensing	1	S12
Decentralization, multiple ownership	1	S49
Adaptation action's effects	1	S50

suitable approach for adaptations, in many cases the problem itself, which triggers the need for adaptation, is not identified properly and therefore causes more uncertainty in the system. Sensing and adaptation actions affects are the least common sources from this class of uncertainty. Note that although investigation of adaptation action effects is a major part of resolving the uncertainty due to variability of solution space, and also is a key factor in exploring adaptation effects on quality requirements and handling trade-offs, it has only been explicitly addressed in one paper. These results again confirm the lack of sufficient research on quality requirements trade-off analysis.

Table 3.14 presents sources from the model uncertainty class. Our results indicate that uncertainty due to differences in sources of information is the most commonly addressed source in this class. However, we could not find any source which is explored in a significantly higher number of papers; all of the sources from model uncertainty class are discussed in almost equal (low) number of papers.

Table 3.15 presents sources of uncertainty from the resources class. Four papers address changing resources as the origin of uncertainty in self-adaptive system, and one paper deals with newly arrived resources as an uncertainty sources.

Finally, four papers (i.e., S6, S27, S35, and S36) state that sources of uncertainty may be due to systems' circumstances. Complexity in the system is considered as the source of uncertainty in S6, and S27, while systems changes are considered as the sources of uncertainty in S35, and S36.

3.4 DISCUSSION

In this section, we first present a discussion about sources of uncertainty, and then list the main findings derived from our results and provide implications for researchers.

Table 3.14 List of Papers Addressing Model Uncertainty Sources

Types of Model Uncertainty Source	Number of Papers	Study Numbers
Different sources of information	3	S3, S16, S19
Model drift	2	S7, S20
Incompleteness	3	S11, S12, S48
Abstraction	2	S23, S26
Incompleteness, abstraction	2	S24, S30
Erroneous models	1	S40
Complex models	1	S6

Table 3.15 List of Papers Addressing Resource Uncertainty Sources

Types of Resource Uncertainty Source	Number of Papers	Study Numbers
Changing resources	4	S2, S21, S22, S28,
New resources	1	S1

3.4.1 ANALYSIS OF DERIVED SOURCES OF UNCERTAINTY BASED ON UNCERTAINTY DIMENSIONS

One of the major goals of this study was to deliver a comprehensive and well-organized list of commonly addressed sources of uncertainty in self-adaptive systems with multiple quality requirements. Therefore, we believe it is also essential to analyze the derived sources of uncertainty and investigate how each one of these sources is handled. In the following, we explore the sources of uncertainty (see Table 3.5) based on emerging time, level, and nature dimensions. Note that although we performed the same analysis for all classes of sources listed in Table 3.5, we have omitted results of minor significance.

3.4.1.1 Environment uncertainty

From 35 papers (see Table 3.11) that addressed sources of uncertainty originating from environment, 10 papers (i.e., S1, S8, S10, S17, S19, S20, S25, S31, S37, and S51) deal with uncertainty at scenario level, due to variability in the context, at runtime. This indicates that variability in the execution context and human behavior are the most common sources of uncertainty, and are mainly handled at runtime. It also shows that researchers mostly use scenarios to understand systems behavior at runtime and resolve the uncertainty. This is an interesting finding as it suggests that statistical methods may be used at runtime to benefit from available knowledge, and study the solutions space to improve the decision making process in self-adaptive systems.

3.4.1.2 Goals uncertainty

From 29 papers (see Table 3.12), in which sources of uncertainty originate from goals, eight papers (i.e., S1, S4, S8, S10, S25, S29, S31, and S51) deal with uncertainty due to variability of goals. In these papers, researchers use scenarios to explore how variability may affect the system goals, and deal with the goal uncertainty at runtime. Furthermore, we found that four papers (i.e., S18, S15, S22, and S36) deal with this type of uncertainty both at design and runtime. This indicates that only in a small number of papers (i.e., four papers) researchers manage to touch the issue of goals uncertainty at design time, and in most cases it is postponed to runtime. Despite the fact that more knowledge about system's status is accessible at runtime, statistical solutions are not commonly used to propose rather accurate solutions for handling goals uncertainty at self-adaptive systems with multiple quality requirements. However, a remarkable number of papers (i.e., S7, S27, S30, S33, S38, S46, S47, and S49) use a combination of statistical methods and scenarios to deal with goals uncertainty.

3.4.1.3 Adaptation functions uncertainty

Following the same pattern we found in previous sections, from 28 papers (see Table 3.12) in which adaptation functions uncertainty sources are addressed, 11 papers (i.e., S1, S8, S10, S17, S19, S25, S31, S32, S35, S48, S49) deal with this class of uncertainty due to variability issues, at scenario level, and at runtime. Interestingly, we found four papers (i.e., S14, S26, S42, and S43) in which statistical methods are used at runtime to deal with adaptation functions uncertainty sources with both variability and epistemic natures. This indicates that although statistical methods are rarely used at runtime, they are favored methods when dealing with adaptation functions uncertainty; specifically, uncertainty due to variability of solution space and fault localization at runtime. Uncertainty due to variability of the solution space is in fact one of the main challenges which needs to be handled when dealing with multiple requirements in self-adaptive systems. The system should be able to manage (i.e., identify, investigate) an increasing number of possible scenarios for adaptation, and predict their effects on quality attributes and select the best adaptation actions. Therefore, it is very crucial to design a self-adaptive system in a way that it collects the most relevant data at a given time and use the right tools to predict the system's behavior in order to handle the quality attributes trade-offs.

3.4.1.4 Model uncertainty

From 14 papers, in which model uncertainty is addressed, six papers (i.e., S3, S11, S12, S24, S26, and S30) deal with model uncertainty sources due to both variability and lack of knowledge (i.e., epistemic). This is interesting because we have only found 14 papers investigating uncertainty due to combination of both variability and lack of knowledge, and in nearly half of them source of uncertainty is related to models. This shows that lack of knowledge greatly affects credibility of models, and generates uncertainty in self-adaptive systems with multiple quality requirements. From these six papers, three of them (i.e., S11, S12, and S24) deal with uncertainty at both design and runtime, two papers at runtime (i.e., S26, S30), and one paper (i.e., S3) at design time.

It might be interesting for researchers to find methods to use runtime knowledge to constantly adjust and update models. Updated and accurate models are better representatives of the actual self-adaptive systems and ultimately improve the decision making process and trade-off analysis.

3.4.2 MAIN FINDINGS AND IMPLICATIONS FOR RESEARCHERS

The following paragraphs elaborate on the main findings, while the end of each paragraph provides implications for researchers in terms of future directions.

3.4.2.1 Model uncertainty is investigated in both design and runtime

We found that among those approaches which deal with both design time and runtime phases of the system's life cycle, model uncertainty is the most commonly addressed class of uncertainty (see Tables 3.10 and 3.14). From 51 studies, 13 papers (i.e., S6, S7, S9, S11, S12, S13, S15, S18, S22, S24, S36, S44, S50) consider uncertainty in both design and runtime phases, and 5 of these 13 studies (i.e., S6, S7, S11, S13, S24) investigate different types of model uncertainty. This indicates that, although many researchers are focusing on models at runtime to tackle the uncertainty issue, dealing with this particular type of uncertainty (i.e., model uncertainty) is not completely postponed to runtime. In other words, researchers strive to use the available knowledge at design time and probably anticipate system behavior in the future in order to be able to start dealing with model uncertainty as soon as possible (i.e., design time). Although our results cannot prove the efficiency of this way of combining both design and runtime solutions in dealing with model uncertainty, it confirms its popularity.

3.4.2.2 Uncertainty is often explored at scenario level regardless of emerging time

Our results show that most of the current studies (i.e., 17 papers) deal with uncertainty at scenario level (see Table 3.16) at runtime. Researchers frequently try to understand the current state, foresee future behavior of the system, and demonstrate system state during and after application of uncertainty remedy only through scenarios. Surprisingly, approaches expanding through both design time and runtime phases also lack statistical methods. This means that despite the availability of knowledge at runtime, most of these approaches do not consider using statistical methods to reassess their assumptions

Table 3.16 Emerging Time Versus Level of Uncertainty

Emerging Time	Level		
	Scenario	Statistical	Both
Runtime	17 papers	4 papers	11 papers
Both	9 papers	3 papers	1 paper
Design time	2 papers	None	None

regarding systems' runtime state in face of uncertainty. Most of the current approaches simply study uncertainty at scenario level (i.e., showcase the behavior of system in the future) through examples, and do not provide rigorous techniques (e.g., probabilistic methods) to support these scenarios. It may be interesting for researchers to further explore incorporating runtime information into statistical methods to mathematically strengthen their anticipations of system behavior.

3.4.2.3 Uncertainty starting to get acknowledged in both design and runtime

Our results indicate that over a decade ago, researchers were focused on solving uncertainty related issues mainly at runtime. This means that both identification of uncertainty and tackling the uncertainty were postponed to the runtime phase. However, around the year 2009 (see Fig. 3.5) researchers started to acknowledge the uncertainty in design time as well. In order to deal with uncertainty in a more structured manner, we propose that researchers investigate whether certain sources of uncertainty can be handled specifically in design or runtime.

3.4.2.4 Current approaches mainly focus on tackling uncertainty due to variability through approaches in both design and runtime

Variability may emerge in system requirements, execution environment, or may be a result of dynamicity of self-adaptive systems solutions space. Our results indicate that the main focus of current research is on the variability issues rather than problems originating from lack of knowledge in

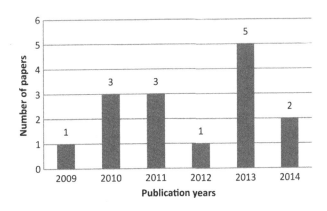

FIG. 3.5

Number of papers acknowledging uncertainty in design time per year.

self-adaptive systems (see Tables 3.8 and 3.10). Therefore, more investigation is required to distinguish the differences in characteristics of variability in different circumstances, and possibly propose tailored solutions capable of dealing better with uncertainty due to variability.

3.4.2.5 *Most commonly addressed source of uncertainty is dynamicity of environment*
Not surprisingly, changes in the environment are considered as the main reason behind uncertainty in self-adaptive systems (see Table 3.11). This is because at the design time, engineers can not anticipate the potential changes in the environment in the future as it is out of their control, and most of the decision making process should be postponed to runtime when more information is available.

3.4.2.6 *Future goal changes is the second most important uncertainty source*
From the selected primary studies, we can see that researchers consider changes of system goals as one of the main sources of uncertainty in self-adaptive systems. However, studies rarely explore details of these changes and how changes in one or two goals affects other goals of the system (i.e., requirements trade-offs) explicitly. Therefore, the first step toward handling the requirements trade-offs may be the thorough monitoring of the requirements; this means that adequate data on how the systems' requirements, intentionally or unintentionally, are affected by the adaptation actions (or human's intervene) should constantly be collected, and then the data should properly be analyzed in order to make the best decision and fulfill the requirements at a desired level.

3.4.3 LIMITATIONS OF THE REVIEW AND THREATS TO VALIDITY
In this section, we discuss the limitations and risks that may have potentially affected the validity of the systematic literature review and represent solutions we used to mitigate these threads.

3.4.3.1 *Bias*
The pilot search indicates that, it is not always easy to extract relevant information from the primary studies. Therefore, there may be some bias and inaccuracy in the extracted data and creation of the classification framework. This is especially prominent for establishing the sources of uncertainty classification due to existing overlap of certain sources definitions. To mitigate this, we included a list of examples from the literature to clarify the sources and help the reader to better comprehend them. Moreover, we had discussions among researchers and asked experts to judge the accuracy of data when the researchers could not reach a consensus on certain extracted data occasionally.

3.4.3.2 *Domain of study*
One of the main risks of performing a systematic literature review in the domain of self-adaptive systems is lack of a common terminology. This problem emanates from the fact that research in this field is to a large extend still in an exploratory phase. The lack of consensus on the key terms in the field implies that in the searching phase, we may not cover all the relevant studies on architecture-based self-adaptation [9]. To mitigate the risk, we used a generic search string containing all the mostly used terms, and we avoided a much narrowed search string to prevent missing papers in the automatic search. In addition, we established "quasi-gold" standard to investigate the trustworthiness of the created search string. Furthermore, we had a look at the references of the selected primary studies to figure out if we have missed any well-known paper due to the fact that they are out of the search scope. If applicable (i.e., if they match the search scope), we included them in our final set of selected primary studies.

3.5 CONCLUSION AND FUTURE WORK

We conducted a systematic literature review to survey the current state of research regarding uncertainty in architecture-based self-adaptive systems with multiple quality requirements. Our results present a classification framework for concept of uncertainty and its different types and categories, and sources of uncertainty in this domain. Furthermore, we investigate the usefulness of the proposed classification framework by analyzing the selected primary studies, and mapping them to the framework. Our work may be interesting for researchers in field of self-adaptive systems as it offers an overview of the existing research and open areas for future work.

Analysis of the selected primary studies suggests that although researchers consider changes of system goals as one of the main sources of uncertainty in architecture-based self-adaptive systems with multiple quality requirements, studies rarely explore details of these changes explicitly and often overlook how changes in one or two of the goals may affect other goals of the system (i.e., requirements trade-offs).

Our results also indicate that uncertainty in architecture-based self-adaptive systems with multiple quality requirements is often explored at scenario level regardless of emerging time of the uncertainty. This means that despite the availability of sufficient knowledge at runtime, most existing approaches do not consider using statistical methods to reassess their assumptions regarding systems' runtime state in face of uncertainty, or incorporate runtime information into statistical methods to mathematically strengthen their anticipations of system behavior in the future. This implies that statistical methods can further be used to more efficiently handle quality requirements and their trade-offs in architecture-based self-adaptive systems tackling uncertainty.

For our future work, we plan to particularly focus on uncertainty and its potential influences on quality attributes. To be more specific, we plan to identify types of requirements for which uncertainty in architecture-based self-adaptive systems is more relevant, and investigate the relationship between uncertainty and quality requirements tradeoffs.

Another direction for future work is to focus on proposing methods that are designed to handle a specific class of uncertainty (i.e., uncertainty originating from certain sources) and its sources rather than covering a variety of classes and their sources to a limited degree. Different sources of uncertainty assigned to one class are more likely to overlap, and therefore, focusing on a specific class of uncertainty may result in proposing more structured and efficient methods dealing with multiple sources of uncertainty and their potential interplay.

APPENDIX

Table 3.17 Primary Studies Included in the Review				
Study #	Title	Authors	Year	Venues
1	Architecture-driven self-adaptation and self-management in robotics systems	G. Edwards, J. Garcia, H. Tajalli, D. Popescu, N. Medvidovic, G. Sukhatme, and B. Petrus	2009	ICSE
2	Self-adaptation for everyday systems	S. Hallsteinsen, E. Stav, and J. Floch	2004	SIGSOFT

Continued

Table 3.17 Primary Studies Included in the Review—cont'd

Study #	Title	Authors	Year	Venues
3	Adapt cases: extending use cases for adaptive systems	M. Luckey, B. Nagel, C. Gerth, and G. Engels	2011	SEAMS
4	A case study in software adaptation	G. Valetto and G. Kaiser	2002	WOSS
5	Diagnosing architectural run-time failures	P. Casanova, D. Garlan, B. Schmerl, and R. Abreu	2013	SEAMS
6	Adaptation and abstract runtime models	T. Vogel and H. Giese	2010	SEAMS
7	Dealing with nonfunctional requirements for adaptive systems via dynamic software product-lines	C. Ghezzi and A. Sharifloo	2013	LNCS
8	A case study in goal-driven architectural adaptation	W. Heaven, D. Sykes, J. Magee, and J. Kramer	2009	LNCS
9	Designing search based adaptive systems: a quantitative approach	P. Zoghi, M. Shtern, and M. Litoiu	2014	SEAMS
10	Rainbow: architecture-based self-adaptation with reusable infrastructure	D. Garlan, S.-W. Cheng, A.-C. Huang, B. Schmerl, and P. Steenkiste	2004	JC
11	Models at runtime to support the iterative and continuous design of autonomic reasoners	F. Chauvel, N. Ferry, and B. Morin	2013	JC
12	Context-aware reconfiguration of autonomic managers in real-time control applications	R. Anthony, M. Pelc, W. Byrski	2010	ICAC
13	Taming uncertainty in self-adaptive software	N. Esfahani, E. Kouroshfar, and S. Malek	2011	SIGSOFT
14	Architecture-based run-time fault diagnosis	P. Casanova, B. Schmerl, D. Garlan, and R. Abreu	2011	LNCS
15	Requirements and architectural approaches to adaptive software systems: a comparative study	K. Angelopoulos, V.E. Souza, and J. Silva Pimentel	2013	SEAMS
16	An architecture for coordinating multiple self-management systems	D. Garlan, B. Schmerl, and P. Steenkiste	2004	WICSA
17	Robust, secure, self-adaptive and resilient messaging middleware for business critical systems	H. Abie, R.M. Savola, and I. Dattani	2009	CW
18	A development framework and methodology for self-adapting applications in ubiquitous computing environments	S. Hallsteinsena, K. Geihsb, N. Paspallisc, F. Eliassend, G. Horna, J. Lorenzoe, A. Mamellif, and G.A. Papadopoulosc	2012	JSS
19	Architecting self-aware software systems	F. Faniyi, P. Lewis R. Bahsoon, and X. Yao	2014	WICSA
20	High-quality specification of self-adaptive software systems	M. Luckey and G. Engels	2013	SEAMS
21	Implementing adaptive performance management in server applications	Y. Liu and I. Gorton	2007	SEAMS
22	A framework for distributed management of dynamic self-adaptation in heterogeneous environments	M. Zouari, M. Segarra, and F. André	2010	ICCIT

Continued

Table 3.17 Primary Studies Included in the Review—cont'd

Study #	Title	Authors	Year	Venues
23	A language for feedback loops in self-adaptive systems: executable runtime megamodels	T. Vogel and H. Giese	2012	SEAMS
24	Learning revised models for planning in adaptive systems	D. Sykes, D. Corapi, J. Magee, J. Kramer, A. Russo, and K. Inoue	2013	ICSE
25	gocc: a configuration compiler for self-adaptive systems using goal-oriented requirements	H. Nakagawa	2011	SEAMS
26	A learning-based approach for engineering feature-oriented self-adaptive software systems	A. Elkhodary	2010	SIGSOFT
27	Towards run-time adaptation of test cases for self-adaptive systems in the face of uncertainty	E. Fredericks, B. DeVries, and B. Cheng	2014	SEAMS
28	Model-based adaptation for self-healing systems	D. Garlan and B. Schmerl	2002	WOSS
29	Improving context-awareness in self-adaptation using the DYNAMICO reference model	G. Tamura, N. Villegas, H. Müller, L. Duchien, and L. Seinturier	2013	SEAMS
30	FUSION: a framework for engineering self-tuning self-adaptive software systems	A. Elkhodary, N. Esfahani, and S. Malek	2010	SIGSOFT
31	DYNAMICO: a reference model for governing control objectives and context relevance in self-adaptive software systems	N. Villegas, G. Tamura, H. Müller, L. Duchien, and R. Casallas	2013	LNCS
32	On decentralized self-adaptation: lessons from the trenches and challenges for the future	D. Weyns, S. Malek, and J. Andersson	2010	ICSE
33	Improving architecture-based Self-adaptation through Resource Prediction	S. Cheng, V. Poladian, D. Garlan, B. Schmerl	2009	LNCS
34	Evolving an adaptive industrial software system to use architecture-based self-adaptation	J. Camara, P. Correia, R. de Lemos, D. Garlan, P. Gomes, B. Schmerl, R. Ventura, and J. Cámara	2013	SEAMS
35	Towards practical runtime verification and validation of self-adaptive software systems	G. Tamura, N. Villegas, H. Müller, J. Sousa, B. Becker, G. Karsai, S. Mankovskii, M. Pezzè, W. Schäfer, L. Tahvildari, and K. Wong	2013	LNCS
36	Model-driven engineering of self-adaptive software with EUREMA	T. Vogel and H. Giese	2014	TAAS
37	Achieving dynamic adaptation via management and interpretation of runtime models	M. Amoui, M. Derakhshanmanesh, J. Ebert, and L. Tahvildari	2012	JSS
38	Towards self-adaptation for dependable service-oriented systems	V. Cardellini, E. Casalicchio, V. Grassi, F. Lo Presti, and R. Mirandola	2009	LNCS

Continued

Table 3.17 Primary Studies Included in the Review—cont'd

Study #	Title	Authors	Year	Venues
39	Architecture-based self-adaptation in the presence of multiple objectives	S. Cheng, D. Garlan, and B. Schmerl	2006	SEAMS
40	QUAASY: QUality Assurance of Adaptive SYstems	M. Luckey, C. Gerth, C. Soltenborn, and G. Engels	2011	ICAC
41	Using CVL to support self-adaptation of fault-tolerant service compositions	A. Nascimento, C. Rubira, and F. Castor	2013	SASO
42	Online model-based adaptation for optimizing performance and dependability	K. Joshi, M. Hiltunen, R. Schlichting, W. Sanders, and A. Agbaria A	2004	SIGSOFT
43	On the relationships between QoS and software adaptability at the architectural level	D. Perez-Palacin, R. Mirandola, and J. Merseguer	2014	JSS
44	Quality attribute tradeoff through adaptive architectures at runtime	J. Yang, G. Huang, W. Zhu, X. Cui, and H. Mei	2009	JSS
45	Towards automated deployment of distributed adaptation systems	M. Zouari and I. Rodriguez	2013	LNCS
46	A self-optimizing run-time architecture for configurable dependability of services	M. Tichy and H. Giese	2004	LNCS
47	Model-driven assessment of QoS-aware self-adaptation	V. Grassi, R. Mirandola, and E. Randazzo	2009	LNCS
48	Evaluation of resilience in self-adaptive systems using probabilistic model-checking	J. Camara and R. De Lemos	2012	SEAMS
49	Managing nonfunctional uncertainty via model-driven adaptivity	C. Ghezzi, L. Pinto, P. Spoletini, and G. Tamburrelli	2013	ICSE
50	Coupling software architecture and human architecture for collaboration-aware system adaptation	C. Dorn and R. Taylor	2013	ICSE
51	Qos-driven runtime adaptation of service oriented architectures	V. Cardellini, E. Casalicchio, V. Grassi, F. Lo Presti, and R. Mirandola	2009	SIGSOFT

Table 3.18 List of Manually Searched Venues to Create the "Quasi-Gold" Standard

Venues
International Conference on Software Engineering
Software Engineering for Adaptive and Self-managing
Systems Transactions on Autonomous and Adaptive Systems

Table 3.19 List of Automatically Searched Venues and Books

Conference proceedings and symposiums	International Conference on Software Engineering (ICSE)
	IEEE Conference on Computer and Information Technology (IEEECIT)
	IEEE Conference on Self-Adaptive and Self-Organizing Systems (SASO)
	European Conference on Software Architecture (ECSA)
	International Conference on Autonomic Computing (ICAC)
	International Conference on Software Maintenance (CSM)
	International Conference on Adaptive and Self-adaptive Systems and Applications (ADAPTIVE)
	Working IEEE/IFIP Conference on Software Architecture (WICSA)
	International Conference of Automated Software Engineering (ASE)
	International Symposium on Architecting Critical Systems (ISARCS)
	International Symposium on Software Testing and Analysis (ISSTA)
	International Symposium on Foundations of Software Engineering (FSE)
	International Symposium on Software Engineering for Adaptive & Self-Managing Systems (SEAMS)
Workshops	Workshop on Self-Healing Systems (WOSS)
	Workshop on Architecting Dependable Systems (WADS)
	Workshop on Design and Evolution of Autonomic Application Software (DEAS)
	Models at runtime (MRT)
Journals/transactions	ACM Transactions on Autonomous and Adaptive Systems (TAAS)
	IEEE Transactions on Computers (TC)
	Journal of Systems and Software (JSS)
	Transactions on Software Engineering and Methodology (TOSEM)
	Transactions on Software Engineering (TSE)
	Information & Software Technology (INFSOF)
	Software and Systems Modeling (SoSyM)
Book chapters/lecture notes/ special issues	Software Engineering for Self-Adaptive Systems (SefSAS)
	Software Engineering for Self-Adaptive Systems II (SefSAS)
	ACM Special Interest Group on Software Engineering (SIGSOFT)
	Assurance for Self-Adaptive Systems (ASAS)

REFERENCES

[1] R. de Lemos, H. Giese, H.A. Müller, M. Shaw, J. Andersson, M. Litoiu, J. Wuttke, Software engineering for self-adaptive systems: a second research roadmap, in: R. de Lemos, H. Giese, H.A. Müller, M. Shaw (Eds.), Software Engineering for Self-Adaptive Systems II, Springer, Berlin, Heidelberg, 2013, pp. 1–32. Retrieved from, http://link.springer.com/chapter/10.1007/978-3-642-35813-5_1.

[2] D. Garlan, B. Schmerl, P. Steenkiste, Rainbow: architecture-based self-adaptation with reusable infrastructure, in: IEEE Proceedings of International Conference on Autonomic Computing, 2004, pp. 276–277, http://dx.doi.org/10.1109/ICAC.2004.1301377.

[3] P. Oreizy, N. Medvidovic, R.N. Taylor, Architecture-based runtime software evolution. in: Proceedings of the 20th International Conference on Software Engineering, 1998, pp. 177–186, http://dx.doi.org/10.1109/ICSE.1998.671114.

[4] S.-W. Cheng, D. Garlan, B. Schmerl, Architecture-based self-adaptation in the presence of multiple objectives. in: ACM Proceedings of the 2006 International Workshop on Self-Adaptation and Self-Managing Systems, 2006, pp. 2–8, http://dx.doi.org/10.1145/1137677.1137679.

[5] Autonomic Computing, W. Paper, T. Edition, An architectural blueprint for autonomic computing. *IBM White Paper*. June 2005.

[6] D. Weyns, S. Malek, J. Andersson, FORMS: unifying reference model for formal specification of distributed self-adaptive systems. ACM Trans. Auton. Adapt. Syst. 7 (1) (2012) 1–61, http://dx.doi.org/10.1145/2168260.2168268.

[7] R. Calinescu, L. Grunske, M. Kwiatkowska, R. Mirandola, G. Tamburrelli, Dynamic QoS management and optimization in service-based systems, IEEE Trans. Softw. Eng. 37 (3) (2011) 387–409.

[8] W.E. Walsh, G. Tesauro, J.O. Kephart, R. Das, Utility functions in autonomic systems, in: IEEE Proceedings of International Conference on Autonomic Computing, 2004, pp. 70–77, http://dx.doi.org/10.1109/ICAC.2004.1301349.

[9] D. Weyns, T. Ahmad, Claims and evidence for architecture-based self-adaptation: a systematic literature review, Software Architecture, (2013). Retrieved from, http://link.springer.com/chapter/10.1007/978-3-642-39031-9_22.

[10] W.E. Walker, P. Harremoës, J. Rotmans, J.P. van der Sluijs, M.B. van Asselt, P. Janssen, M.P. Krayer von Krauss, Defining uncertainty: a conceptual basis for uncertainty management in model-based decision support, Integrated assessment 4 (1) (2003) 5–17.

[11] D. Perez-Palacin, R. Mirandola, Uncertainties in the modeling of self-adaptive systems: a taxonomy and an example of availability evaluation, In Proceedings of the 5th ACM/SPEC international conference on Performance engineering (2014) 3–14. ACM.

[12] J.C. Refsgaard, J.P. van der Sluijs, A.L. Højberg, P.A. Vanrolleghem, Uncertainty in the environmental modelling process—a framework and guidance. Environ. Model. Softw. 22 (11) (2007) 1543–1556, http://dx.doi.org/10.1016/j.envsoft.2007.02.004.

[13] D. Garlan, Software engineering in an uncertain world. in: Proceedings of the FSE/SDP Workshop on Future of Software Engineering Research—FoSER'10, 2010, p. 125, http://dx.doi.org/10.1145/1882362.1882389.

[14] N. Esfahani, S. Malek, Uncertainty in self-adaptive software systems, in: R. de Lemos, H. Giese, H.A. Müller, M. Shaw (Eds.), Software Engineering for Self-Adaptive Systems II, Springer, Berlin, Heidelberg, 2013, pp. 214–238. Retrieved from, http://link.springer.com/chapter/10.1007/978-3-642-35813-5_9.

[15] A.J. Ramirez, A.C. Jensen, B.H.C. Cheng, A taxonomy of uncertainty for dynamically adaptive systems. in: ICSE Workshop on Software Engineering for Adaptive and Self-Managing Systems (SEAMS), 2012, http://dx.doi.org/10.1109/SEAMS.2012.6224396.

[16] B. Kitchenham, S. Charters, Guidelines for performing systematic literature reviews in software engineering, (2007). Retrieved from, http://www.citeulike.org/group/14013/article/7874938.

[17] J.O. Kephart, D.M. Chess, The vision of autonomic computing, J. Chem. Theory Comput. 36 (1) (2003) 41–50, http://dx.doi.org/10.1109/MC.2003.1160055.

[18] M.S. Ali, M. Ali Babar, L. Chen, K.-J. Stol, A systematic review of comparative evidence of aspect-oriented programming, Inf. Softw. Technol. 52 (9) (2010) 871–887. Retrieved from, http://www.sciencedirect.com/science/article/pii/S0950584910000819.

[19] H. Zhang, M. Ali Babar, On Searching Relevant Studies in Software Engineering, British Informatics Society, Keele, 2010. Retrieved from, http://ulir.ul.ie/handle/10344/730.

[20] T. Dybå, T. Dingsøyr, Empirical studies of agile software development: a systematic review. Inf. Softw. Technol. 50 (9–10) (2008) 833–859, http://dx.doi.org/10.1016/j.infsof.2008.01.006.

[21] C. Ghezzi, A.M. Sharifloo, Dealing with non-functional requirements for adaptive systems via dynamic software product lines, in: R. de Lemos, H. Giese, H.A. Müller, M. Shaw (Eds.), Software Engineering for Self-Adaptive Systems II, Springer, Berlin, Heidelberg, 2013, pp. 191–213. Retrieved from, http://link.springer.com/chapter/10.1007/978-3-642-35813-5_8.

[22] L. Cheung, L. Golubchik, N. Medvidovic, G. Sukhatme, Identifying and addressing uncertainty in architecture-level software reliability modeling, in: Parallel and Distributed Processing Symposium, 2007. IPDPS 2007. IEEE International (2007) 1–6. IEEE.

[23] T. Vogel, H. Giese, Adaptation and abstract runtime models, in: Proceedings of the 2010 ICSE Workshop on Software Engineering for Adaptive and Self-Managing Systems—SEAMS '10, ACM Press, New York, NY, 2010, pp. 39–48, http://dx.doi.org/10.1145/1808984.1808989.

[24] F. Chauvel, N. Ferry, B. Morin, N. Bencomo, R.B. France, S. Götz, B. Rumpe (Eds.), Models@Runtime to Support the Iterative and Continuous Design of Autonomic Reasonersvol. 1079, 2013, pp. 26–38. Retrieved from, http://ceur-ws.org/Vol-1079/mrt13_submission_20.pdf.

[25] D. Weyns, S. Malek, J. Andersson, On decentralized self-adaptation: lessons from the trenches and challenges for the future, in: Proceedings—International Conference on Software Engineering, Department of Computer Science, Katholieke Universiteit Leuven, Leuven, 2010, pp. 84–93. Retrieved from, http://www.scopus.com/inward/record.url?eid=2-s2.0- 77954577834&partnerID=40&md5=1f389e0a603761b96aa46db6bf06e287.

[26] N.M. Villegas, G. Tamura, H.A. Müller, L. Duchien, R. Casallas, DYNAMICO: a reference model for governing control objectives and context relevance in self-adaptive software systems, in: R. de Lemos, H. Giese, H.A. Müller, M. Shaw (Eds.), Software Engineering for Self-Adaptive Systems II, Springer, Berlin, Heidelberg, 2013, pp. 265–293. Retrieved from, http://link.springer.com/chapter/10.1007/978-3-642-35813-5_11.

[27] P. Casanova, D. Garlan, B. Schmerl, R. Abreu, Diagnosing Architectural Run-Time Failures, (2013). pp. 103–112. Retrieved from, http://dl.acm.org/citation.cfm?id=2487336.2487354.

[28] P. Zoghi, M. Shtern, M. Litoiu, Designing search based adaptive systems: a quantitative approach. in: Proceedings of the 9th International Symposium on Software Engineering for Adaptive and Self-Managing Systems, ACM, 2014, pp. 7–16, http://dx.doi.org/10.1145/2593929.2593935.

[29] N. Esfahani, E. Kouroshfar, S. Malek, Taming uncertainty in self-adaptive software, in: Proceedings of the 19th ACM SIGSOFT Symposium and the 13th European Conference on Foundations of Software Engineering, ACM, 2011, pp. 234–244, http://dx.doi.org/10.1145/2025113.2025147.

[30] G. Tamura, N.M. Villegas, H.A. Muller, L. Duchien, L. Seinturier, Improving context-awareness in self-adaptation using the DYNAMICO reference model. in: ICSE Workshop on Software Engineering for Adaptive and Self-Managing Systems (SEAMS), 2013. http://dx.doi.org/10.1109/SEAMS.2013.6595502.

[31] C. Ghezzi, L.S. Pinto, P. Spoletini, G. Tamburrelli, Managing non-functional uncertainty via model-driven adaptivity. in: 35th International Conference on Software Engineering (ICSE), 2013. http://dx.doi.org/10.1109/ICSE.2013.6606549.

[32] G. Edwards, J. Garcia, H. Tajalli, D. Popescu, N. Medvidovic, G. Sukhatme, B. Petrus, Architecture-driven self- adaptation and self-management in robotics systems. in: ICSE Workshop on Software Engineering for Adaptive and Self-Managing Systems, SEAMS '09, 2009. http://dx.doi.org/10.1109/SEAMS.2009.5069083.

[33] S. Hallsteinsen, E. Stav, J. Floch, Self-adaptation for everyday systems. in: Proceedings of the 1st ACM SIGSOFT Workshop on Self-Managed Systems, ACM, 2004, pp. 69–74, http://dx.doi.org/10.1145/1075405.1075419.

[34] J. Kramer, J. Magee, Self-managed systems: an architectural challenge. In Future of Software Engineering, (2007). FOSE'07, pp. 259–268. IEEE.

AN ARCHITECTURE VIEWPOINT FOR MODELING DYNAMICALLY CONFIGURABLE SOFTWARE SYSTEMS

4

B. Tekinerdogan*, H. Sozer[†]

Wageningen University, Wageningen, The Netherlands* Ozyegin University, Istanbul, Turkey[†]

4.1 INTRODUCTION

Dynamic system configurability defines the ability to modify and extend a system while it is running. This is an important requirement for an increasing number of software-intensive systems in which it is not possible or economically feasible to stop the complete system and modify it to meet new requirements. Dynamic configurability is not only important during operation of the system but can also be useful during development time. In fact, many systems are now being developed in an incremental manner in which dynamic configurability is also useful during the incremental integration of the components in the system.

Dynamic software architectures support reconfigurations of their structures during execution and as such aid system evolution. A current practice to model software architectures is usually based on architecture views to separate the concerns and as such support the modeling, understanding, communication, and analysis of the software architecture for different stakeholders. An architecture view is a representation of a set of system elements and relations associated with them to support a particular concern [14]. Architectural views conform to viewpoints that represent the conventions for constructing and using a view. Given the complexity of applications where necessary new viewpoints have been defined to address new concerns. In this paper we focus on dynamic configurability in software architecture. Considering the existing viewpoint approaches we can observe that the modeling of dynamic configurability is not explicitly considered. This seems to be the case for quality concerns in general. The ISO/IEC 42010 [2] standard intentionally does not define particular viewpoints to address the different concerns. In the Views and Beyond (V&B) approach, quality concerns appear to be implicit in the different views and specific viewpoints have to be introduced to represent quality concerns [3–6]. Software architecture analysis approaches have been introduced [7] to analyze the software architecture and provide guidelines for adapting it with respect to the quality concern. However, the difficulty here is that these approaches usually apply a separate quality model, such as Markov models, queuing networks or process algebra, to analyze the quality properties. Although these models represent precise calculations they do not depict the decomposition of the architecture and an additional translation from the evaluation of the quality model needs to be performed [8].

To represent runtime adaptability concerns more explicitly, preferably an explicit dedicated architectural view is required to model the decomposition of the architecture based on the runtime adaptability concern. In this context, we introduce the *runtime adaptability viewpoint* that can be used for modeling dynamically configurable software architectures. The viewpoint has been defined after a domain analysis to both dynamic configurability and software architecture viewpoint modeling. The viewpoint is based on a metamodel that defines the underlying semantics. Further we provide the necessary notation for supporting software architects in modeling dynamic configurability concerns of software architectures. We illustrate the viewpoint for a demand-driven supply chain management (DDSCM) system in which the dynamic configurability plays an important aspect.

The remainder of this paper is organized as follows. Section 4.2 provides background information regarding architecture viewpoints. Section 4.3 introduces the case study as a motivating example where runtime adaptability becomes a relevant concern. Section 4.4 presents the related concepts and a metamodel for runtime adaptability viewpoint. Section 4.5 introduces a concrete notation and a method for applying this viewpoint. Section 4.6 describes the application of the viewpoint for the case study. Section 4.7 presents the related work and finally Section 4.8 provides the conclusions.

4.2 ARCHITECTURE VIEWPOINTS

Software architecture is an abstract representation that serves various purposes including the understanding of the system, communication among the stakeholders, guideline for supporting the life cycle activities, support for organizational concerns such as work allocation, budget planning and development structure of the software development project [9].

In practice, software architecture is modeled and documented using *architecture views*, which are basically representations of a system for particular concerns. In the literature, initially a fixed set of viewpoints have been proposed to document the architecture [10–13]. Because of the different concerns that need to be addressed for different systems, the current trend recognizes that the set of views should not be fixed but multiple viewpoints might be introduced instead. The ISO/IEC 42010 standard [2] indicates in an abstract sense that an architecture description consists of a set of views, each of which conforms to a viewpoint realizing the various concerns of the stakeholders. The V&B approach as proposed by Clements et al. is another multiview approach [14] that proposes the notion of architectural style similar to the notion of architectural viewpoint. For addressing the general concerns, we shall use the viewpoints in the V&B approach [14]. In this approach, typically the notions of view category and style are used to define viewpoints. Hereby, three different view categories are identified:

- *Module view* category that is used for documenting a system's principal units of implementation
- *Component and connector (C&C)* category that is used for documenting the system's units of execution
- *Deployment view* category that is used to document the relationships between a system's software and its development and execution environments

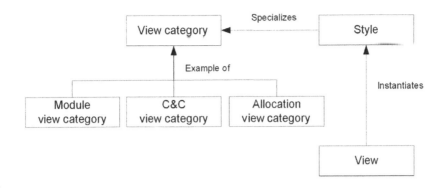

FIG. 4.1

Relations among view category, style, and view in the V&B approach.

Although the V&B approach has defined a predefined set of architectural styles it is also possible to define new styles for particular concerns. Views are instantiations of styles. The relations between view category, style and view is depicted in Fig. 4.1.

To define new viewpoints, the guidelines and templates of the recommended standard for architecture description can be adopted [2].

4.3 CASE STUDY: DDSCM SYSTEMS

A supply chain is defined as a system consisting of organizations, people, activities, information, and resources involved in moving a product or service from supplier to customer. Supply chain activities transform natural resources, raw materials, and components into a finished product that is delivered to the end customer [15]. Due to the increased global competition many companies are forced to improve their efficiency of the supply chain using systematic supply chain management (SCM) approaches. A conceptual model for SCM is shown in Fig. 4.2.

The underlying idea for SCM is based on the observation that practically every product that reaches an end user represents the cumulative effort of multiple organizations defining the supply chain. SCM, as such, is the active management of supply chain activities to maximize customer value and achieve a sustainable competitive advantage [15]. SCM activities typically include the management of the flow of materials, information, and finances in a process from supplier to manufacturer to wholesaler to retailer to consumer. Further, SCM involves coordinating and integrating these flows both within and among companies. To provide an effective SCM it is important to develop the appropriate software architecture for it [16–19].

In SCM, we can identify different entities that require input, process this input, and deliver this to the next entity. The overall supply chain network consists of organizations moving a product or service from supplier to customer. Currently, an increasing number of organizations focus on so-called DDSCMs [17]. The main motivation for DDSCM is to manage and optimize the material and information flow that propagates up the supply chain from the source of demand to the suppliers. Usually customer demand is rarely stable and likewise businesses must forecast demand to properly position inventory and other resources.

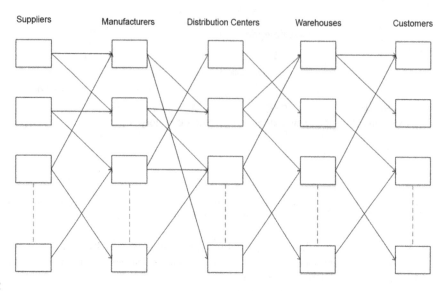

FIG. 4.2

A conceptual model of supply chain management.

To meet the requirements for DDSCMs, the corresponding software system and likewise the architecture must be dynamically adaptable. We can identify the following important components in a SCM system:

- *Enterprise resource planning (ERP) systems*—providing services for purchase management, production management, and sales management, in particular for manufacturers and trading companies
- *Warehouse management systems (WMS)*—providing services for logistics, in particular for wholesalers
- *Transport management systems (TMS)*—providing services for transport booking, planning, and monitoring

The deployment architecture for a general SCM system is presented in Fig. 4.3. The architecture follows the guidelines of the so-called supply-chain operations reference model which is a process reference model for SCM [15]. The architecture consists of five different node types: *supplier, manufacturer, distributor, warehouse,* and *retailer.* Note that each node has three similar components including *report engine, message conversion engine,* and *data communication engine.* Further each node has also its' specific type of components. Finally, a manufacturer node is connected to an ERP system, a distributor to a TMS, and a warehouse to a WMS. To model DDSCMs, the components and nodes need to be dynamically configurable. This means that for example, a supplier node can be replaced by another supplied node, or a copy of the report engine can be transferred to the other nodes etc. In the following section, we introduce a metamodel for runtime adaptability viewpoint to capture such dynamic configuration capabilities.

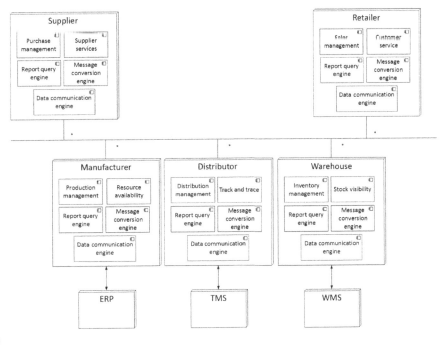

FIG. 4.3

General deployment view for supply chain management system.

4.4 METAMODEL FOR RUNTIME ADAPTABILITY VIEWPOINT

In Fig. 4.4 we show the conceptual model for architectural view modeling. In fact, the conceptual model is based on the ISO/IEC recommended standard for architectural description [2] but it enhances the standard to explicitly depict quality concerns and defines their relation to architectural views. The left part of the figure shows basically the definition of the architectural drivers. A system has one or more stakeholders who have interest in the system with respect to one or more concerns. Concerns can be functional or quality related. The right part of the figure focuses on the architectural views for the different concerns. Each system has an architecture, which is described by an architectural description. The architectural description consists of a set of views that correspond to their viewpoints. Viewpoints aim to address the stakeholder's concerns. Functional concerns will define the dominant decomposition along architectural units that are mainly functional in nature. On the other hand, quality concerns will define the dominant decomposition of the architecture along architectural units that explicitly represent quality concerns. Runtime adaptability is a specific quality concern that is addressed by runtime adaptability view. Run-adaptability is not directly considered in the other viewpoints.

To define the foundation for the runtime adaptability viewpoint we have performed a domain analysis regarding architectural frameworks introduced for dynamic configurability. These frameworks employ different adaptation mechanisms. We have reviewed these mechanisms and we focus on

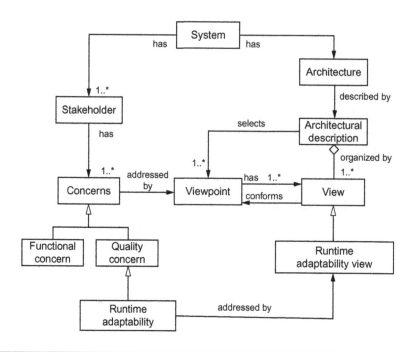

FIG. 4.4

Conceptual model for architectural views and the relation of runtime adaptability.

Based on IEEE Standard: ISO/IEC 42010:2007 Recommended practice for architectural description of software-intensive systems (ISO/IEC 42010), July 2007.

the adaptation capabilities that they can provide. For providing adaptability, one also needs to decide on the type of adaptation mechanism. However, we decided not to integrate this in the viewpoint because we aim to provide a generic viewpoint in which we address only *what* can be adapted. We did not wish to fix the mechanisms. The viewpoint is agnostic to the adaptation mechanisms and as such could be used together with existing adaptation frameworks. However, our approach allows the extension of the viewpoint to include also the mechanisms for adaptation.

Existing frameworks assume either a component-based architecture [20–25] or service-oriented architecture (SOA) [26]. So, reconfigured architectural elements are components, connectors, or services. We have observed that the majority of the existing approaches mainly focus on the C&C view to depict the runtime structure and reason about dynamic adaptation [20–23,25,27]. Hence, the proposed viewpoint mainly relies on the C&C viewpoint as defined by the V&B approach [14]. The following figure depicts a metamodel of the viewpoint as described in this approach (Fig. 4.5).

In the C&C viewpoint, there are two basic types of elements: *component* types that represent principal processing units and data stores, and *connector* types that represent interaction mechanisms. Each of these elements has two properties: a *name* that suggests its functionality, and a *type* that determines the general functionality and constraints for the element. Every component has one or more *ports*. These ports have *names* that suggest the corresponding interface of the component. On the other hand, every connector has two or more *roles*. These roles have *names* that suggest the interacting parties. There is an *attachment* relation defined between a port and one or more roles.

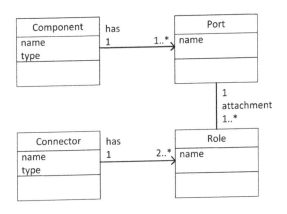

FIG. 4.5

A metamodel of the C&C viewpoint as described by V&B approach [14].

As stated in the V&B approach many C&C styles allow C&Cs to be created or destroyed as the system is running. For example, in client-server based systems new server instances might be created as the number of client requests increases. In a peer-to-peer system, new components may dynamically join or leave the peer-to-peer network. In principle, any C&C style supports the dynamic creation and destruction of elements.

In addition to the C&C views, allocation views [14] are also highly relevant for runtime adaptability. These views document a mapping between software elements and nonsoftware elements in the context of the system [14]. In particular, deployment views constitute a type of allocation view, which describes a mapping between software elements and hardware elements in the computing platform. These views conform to the deployment style and they are relevant for dynamic reconfiguration because the allocation of software elements can be dynamic. Three types of dynamic relations are defined for deployment views in the V&B approach [14]: (1) *migrates-to*: a software element can move from one processor to another processor, (2) *copy-migrates-to*: a software element can be copied to another processor and different copies can execute on different processors at the same time, (3) *execution-migrates-to*: a software element can be copied to another processor, where only one of the copies can be executed at a time. The corresponding metamodel is depicted in Fig. 4.6. Migration relations are mainly triggered by changing application profiles and operational context for supporting quality concerns such as performance, availability, reliability, and security [14]. For example, performance improvements can be achieved by deploying some components together when the frequency of intercommunication is increased. Some components can be migrated for isolating them from the other components to improve reliability [4] or security. Resource utilization and hardware faults can also trigger a migration.

To support the viewpoint for runtime adaptability and dynamic configurability we have integrated the metamodels of Figs. 4.5 and 4.6 as shown in Fig. 4.7.

Dynamic configurability is facilitated in three ways (1) adaptation of elements by change of mode, state, parameters [20,28,29], (2) replacement of elements [22,23,26] leading to a structural change [28,29], (3) migration of elements to different nodes. In general, formal specifications for dynamic software architectures utilize the second one; they define reconfigurations as a series of C&C

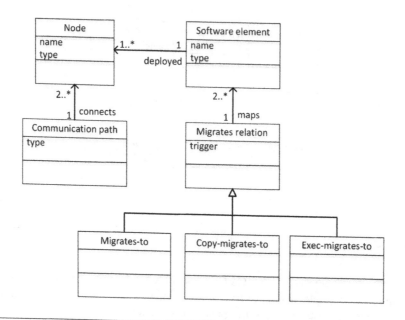

FIG. 4.6

A metamodel of the deployment style as described by V&B approach.

addition/removal operations [30]. To differentiate between elements that can be subject to configurability, we have introduced adaptable components and adaptable connectors. Such a distinction is also being made in existing frameworks [22]. In some of the existing approaches, communication is assumed to be asynchronous and architectural elements are assumed to be stateless and independent [26]. However, in some other approaches, architectural elements can be interdependent and they can be stateful [22,23]. This makes a difference because adaptable components that are stateful provide means for loading and storing state information [22,25]. In principle, connectors can also involve rich semantics [14] just like components. For this reason, we also distinguished between stateful and stateless connectors in our viewpoint as depicted in the metamodel.

4.5 RUNTIME ADAPTABILITY VIEWPOINT

Once we have identified the important concepts regarding runtime adaptability and defined the metamodel we can define the corresponding viewpoint. Defining a new architectural viewpoint implies writing a *viewpoint guide*. This is similar to the notion of *style guide* as defined in Ref. [14]. The *viewpoint guide* includes the vocabulary of the architectural element and relation types, and describes the rules for how that vocabulary can be used. The adaptability viewpoint guide that we have defined is shown in Table 4.1. Hereby, we focus on capturing the adaptability capabilities of the managed system [31], rather than the adaptation mechanism involved [32]. The viewpoint guide for dynamic configurability is largely the same as for the viewpoints that address functional concerns. The important difference here is that the architectural elements now are used to explicitly represent dynamic

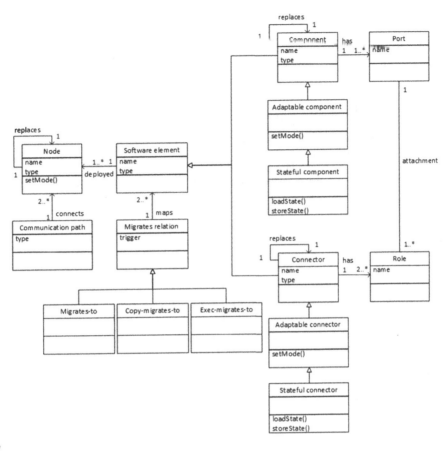

FIG. 4.7

A metamodel of the viewpoint for dynamic configurability.

configurability properties in the software architecture. These properties are aligned with the introduced metamodel.

Note that the viewpoint provides two complementary ways in terms of notation. The first option is to use visual representations of different element types. These representations are created by minor alterations (like a stereotype definition) of the commonly used representations [14].

The second option is to represent relations by mapping the involved elements with each other in a table, which provides another overview of these relations. There are three such tables to represent (1) relations among C&Cs, (2) relations between C&Cs and nodes, and (3) relations among nodes.

The first table includes the set of C&Cs both in the rows and the columns. The cells on the diagonal are used for marking possible adaptations of the corresponding C&C with symbol A. If a C&C can be replaced by another C&C, the corresponding cell is marked with the symbol R. If there is also a state transfer during replacement, the symbol RS is used instead. A C&C can be replaced with a replica in a different state. In this case, again the RS symbol is marked in the corresponding cell on the diagonal.

Table 4.1 Runtime Adaptability Viewpoint

Viewpoint Element	Description
Name	Runtime adaptability viewpoint: C&C viewpoint U deployment style
Element types	• Adaptable component (AC): represents a component that can be adapted • Stateful component (SC): represents an AC that keeps state information to be considered when replaced by another component • Adaptable connector (ACN): represents a connector that can be adapted • Stateful connector (SCN): represents an ACN that keeps state information to be considered when replaced by another connector • Adaptable node (AN): represents a processing element that can be tuned at runtime • The other types as they are defined for the C&C viewpoint and deployment style
Relation types	• *Replaces* relation as defined by the metamodel • *Migrates* relations as defined by the metamodel • The other types as they are defined for the C&C viewpoint and deployment style
Properties of elements	Mode: the active mode among the possible set of modes that can be activated by runtime adaptation
Properties of relations	Mode: the active mode among the possible set of modes that can be activated by runtime adaptation
Topology constraints	Same as the C&C viewpoint and deployment style
Notation	

Continued

Table 4.1 Runtime Adaptability Viewpoint—cont'd

Viewpoint Element	Description		
	Mapping Table	Type	Cell Marking
	C&C to C&C	Adapted	A
		Replaces	R
		Replaces /w State	RS
	C&C to Node	Deployed-to	D
		Migrates-to	M
		Copy-migrates-to	CM
		Exec-migrates-to	EM
	Node to Node	Adapted	A
		Replaces	R
Relation to other views/ viewpoints	Same as the C&C viewpoint and deployment style		

The second table includes the set of C&Cs in the rows and the set of nodes in the columns. Symbols in the cells define where each C&C is initially deployed, and where it can be potentially migrated. There is symbol for each migration type as defined by the metamodel.

The third table includes the set of nodes both in the rows and the columns. The cells on the diagonal are used for marking possible adaptations of the corresponding node with symbol A. If a node can be replaced by another node, then the corresponding cell is marked with the symbol R.

In the following subsection, we introduce a method for applying this viewpoint. Then, in the following section, we shall provide an example application of the viewpoint in the context of the SCM case study.

4.5.1 METHOD FOR APPLYING THE ADAPTABILITY VIEWPOINT

So far, we have defined the runtime adaptability viewpoint that can be used to define runtime adaptability views for particular applications. In this section we provide the method for applying the viewpoint as shown in Fig. 4.8. The method starts with defining the C&C view as well as the deployment view. Based on these provided two views, the nodes, the components, and the connectors will be analyzed and their characteristics will be identified with respect to the requirements for runtime adaptability. The characterization will be based on the possible properties as defined in the metamodel and viewpoint. As such, components will be, for example, characterized as regular component, adaptable component, or stateful component. After the characterization of the separate elements the relations will be considered including the node-to-node, C&C-to-node, and C&C-to-C&C relations. These will be again defined based on the relations defined in the viewpoint. Subsequently, the runtime adaptability view will be defined that meets the characterization of the architectural elements and the identified adaptability relations. The presented view is evaluated and if needed necessary iterations will be carried out.

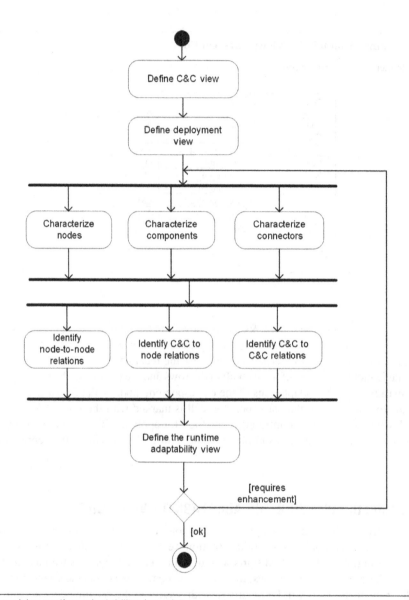

FIG. 4.8

Method for applying runtime adaptability viewpoint.

4.6 CASE STUDY—ADAPTABILITY VIEW OF THE SCM SOFTWARE ARCHITECTURE

We have applied the runtime adaptability viewpoint for documenting possible runtime adaptations that can take place in the SCM software architecture. Fig. 4.9 depicts some of these adaptations.

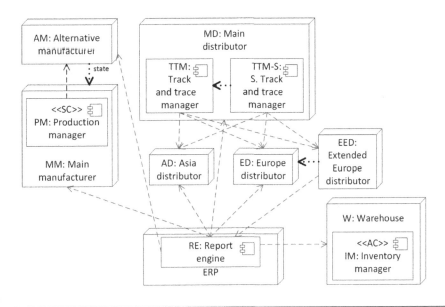

FIG. 4.9

Adaptability view for part of the SCM software architecture.

Hereby, eight nodes are shown. Two of them (MM and AM) are dedicated for manufacturing process. Four of them (MD, AD, ED, EED) are dealing with distribution. One node (W) is used for storage, and another one (ERP) is keeping the overall management system and related components. Different types of runtime adaptability relations can be seen here. For instance, we can see that TTM-S component can replace TTM component. Tracking and tracing functionalities can change depending on the goods that are distributed in a SCM system. TTM provides only the basic functionalities. TTM-S is used for sensitive products like food and medicine that has to be tracked with respect to many attributes such as shelf life, temperature, etc.

It can be observed in the figure that the view quickly gets cluttered with many relations depicted to represent different types of runtime adaptations. As a complementary notation, table-based views can be used to capture runtime adaptability options for the overall SCM software architecture. This approach leads to more readable and scalable documentation for systems that involve a high number of adaptation relations.

In the following, we document runtime adaptability for the same system with three tables that conform to the viewpoint notation listed in Table 4.1. Tables 4.2–4.4 list runtime adaptability relations between C&Cs and nodes, among C&Cs, and among nodes, respectively.

Table 4.2 shows runtime adaptability relations among C&Cs. Here, we can see that IM is an adaptable component. TTM-S can replace TTM. We can also see that PM can be replaced with a replica of itself in a different state.

Table 4.3 defines runtime adaptability relations between C&Cs and nodes. Hereby, C&Cs are listed in the rows and nodes are listed in the columns. The cells marked with D show the initial deployment of C&Cs: PM on MM, TTM and TTM-S on MD, IM on W, and RE on ERP. We see that PM can migrate to

Table 4.2 Runtime Adaptability Relations Among C&Cs

C&C	C&C				
	PM	TTM	TTM-S	RE	IM
PM	RS				
TTM					
TTM-S		R			
RE					
IM					A

Table 4.3 Runtime Adaptability Relations Between C&Cs and Nodes

C&C	Node							
	MM	AM	MD	AD	ED	EED	W	ERP
PM	D	M						
TTM			D	CM	CM	CM		
TTM-S			D	CM	CM	CM		
RE	CM	CM	CM	CM	CM	CM	CM	D
IM							D	

Table 4.4 Runtime Adaptability Relations Among Nodes

Node	Node							
	MM	AM	MD	AD	ED	EED	W	ERP
MM								
AM	RS							
MD								
AD								
ED								
EED					R			
W								
ERP								

AM. On the other hand, a copy of RE can migrate to all the nodes except ERP. We also see that copies of TTM and TTM-S can migrate to the nodes AD, ED, and EED.

Table 4.4 shows runtime adaptability relations among nodes. There are two such relations. First, EED can replace ED. Second, AM can replace MM. State information must also be transferred for this replacement.

We have adopted tables since the visual representation is less scalable. For large cases, the table representations will also have limitations. For this, we might need additional tool support.

4.7 RELATED WORK

In this paper we have defined a viewpoint for modeling dynamically configurable software architectures. The viewpoint has been defined based on a domain analysis of the existing runtime adaptability mechanisms. The introduced abstractions can be extended if needed and more refined viewpoints can be defined. However, it should be noted that an architectural view represents the gross level abstraction of the system and likewise should preferably not include implementation details. In the following, provide a review of related studies in two different categories: (i) modeling of quality concerns in software architecture including adaptability, and (ii) architectural modeling techniques and frameworks introduced for supporting runtime adaptability.

4.7.1 QUALITY CONCERNS IN SOFTWARE ARCHITECTURE MODELING

Separating quality concerns at the architecture design modeling phases has been also addressed earlier with the notion of so-called *attribute-based architectural style* (ABAS). ABAS refers to prepackaged units of architectural design and analysis. The purpose of ABAS is to enhance precise reasoning about architectural design which is achieved by explicitly associating a *reasoning framework* with an architectural style. The reasoning framework shows how to reason about the design decisions comprised by the style. The reasoning frameworks are based on quality attribute-specific models, which exist in the various quality attribute communities. ABASs are quality attribute *specific* and consider only one quality attribute at a time. Our work could be compared to the idea presented in ABAS, that is, define the architectural model for particular quality concerns. The difference is that we focus on the notion of architectural viewpoint. We do not provide a reasoning framework but this could be a complementary and useful elaboration on our work as well as the other viewpoint approaches in general.

Aspect-oriented software development (AOSD) [1,33] promotes the separation of crosscutting concerns principle [34–36] to increase modularity. Hereby, crosscutting concerns are separately represented as first-class abstractions (aspects) and woven into the *base code*. In our approach we have applied the separation of concerns principle to separate the views for quality concerns. Similar to crosscutting concerns in AOSD, quality concerns seem to crosscut the elements in the functional views. By separating these quality concerns and providing explicit abstractions in the viewpoints, we have supported an enhanced description of the architecture.

Architectural perspectives [37] are a collection of activities, tactics, and guidelines to modify a set of existing views to document and analyze quality properties. Architectural perspectives as such are basically guidelines that work on multiple views together. An analysis of the architectural perspectives and our approach shows that the crosscutting nature of quality concerns can be both observed *within* an architectural view and *across* architectural views. Both approaches focus on providing a solution to the crosscutting problem. We have chosen for providing separate architectural viewpoints for quality concerns. It might be interesting to look at integrating the guidelines provided by the *architectural perspectives* and the definition/usage of the viewpoints developed by our approach. In that sense the approaches can also be considered as complimentary to each other.

Architectural tactics [38] aim at identifying architectural decisions related to a quality attribute requirement and composing these into an architecture design. Defining explicit viewpoints for quality concerns can help to model and reason about the application of architectural tactics.

Several software architecture analysis approaches have been introduced for addressing quality properties. They usually perform either static analysis of formal architectural models or they apply a set of scenario-based architecture analysis methods [7]. The goal of these approaches is to assess whether or not a given architecture design satisfies desired concerns including quality requirements. The main aim of the viewpoint definitions in our approach, on the other hand, is to communicate and support the architectural design with respect to quality concerns. As such our work can directly support the architectural analysis to select feasible design alternatives.

4.7.2 ARCHITECTURAL APPROACHES FOR RUNTIME ADAPTABILITY

Oreizy et al. [25] discuss the use of existing architectural styles to represent dynamically adaptable software architectures. In particular, they describe how runtime changes can be facilitated by the Weaves and C2 architectural styles. However, they do not propose a dedicated view for dynamic adaptation. Many existing frameworks like PLASMA [21] and Rainbow [20] mainly focus on the C&C view to depict the runtime structure and reason about dynamic adaptation. Contract-based adaptive software architecture [22] is a framework that facilitates dynamic adaptation by dynamic recomposition of components. They define the adaptable class/component concept for replaceable components. They also introduce a handle class/component that is inspired from the bridge pattern. This provides a layer of transparency between the application code and the dynamic replacement process. It is assumed that adaptable components provide a means for loading and storing state. They propose the specification of adaptation policy of the application in a so-called application contract. However, they do not also propose a model or view for the representation of the overall architecture.

Self-architecting software systems [26] is a framework for dynamic service-oriented systems. It is based on functionally equivalent services, which can be replaced based on their desired properties, for example, QoS levels. It employs basic elements of SOAs. The list of services is registered to a service directory. These services are discovered and selected based on so-called service activity schemas that express system requirements. They employ an extension of xADL and finite state models to represent the software architecture. A software adaptation pattern is specified as a list of steps to be performed for adaptation. However, they do not propose a view for explicitly representing the dynamic adaptation. There is a coordinator component for each client. Communication is asynchronous. Services are stateless and independent.

Rainbow [20] is a framework that supports architecture-based adaptation. It introduces a language for specifying adaptation techniques as first-class adaptation concepts. The basic idea is that the adaptation strategies depend on the architectural style of the target system. It augments the notion of style with operators that define style-specific reconfiguration options.

The K-component model [23] was introduced to support dynamic adaptation. Dynamic reconfiguration of software architecture is modeled as graph transformations. These adaptation models are specified as adaptation contracts, separate from the implementation. Types of supported dynamic reconfigurations are limited to C&C replacement.

According to a survey on formal specification of dynamic software architectures [30], three approaches stand out: graph-based; process algebra; and logic-based description languages. These approaches provide a formal basis for the description of types of changes, rules for selection of changes and their application. Four phases are identified for dynamic architectural changes: change initiation, selection of architectural transformation; implementation of transformation; assessment of architecture after transformation. Basic changes are listed as C&C addition and removal. Those basic changes can be composed by sequencing, choice, and iteration.

Dynamic software product lines (DSPL) [39] extend conventional product line approaches to support runtime variability. Therefore, they are considered as a systematic approach for developing adaptive systems [39]. However, existing DSPL approaches mainly focus on extensions of feature models and orthogonal variability diagrams [40] for modeling and documentation. Extensions of the architectural models have not been considered for creating a dedicated view for runtime adaptability.

4.8 CONCLUSION

Dynamic software architectures support reconfigurations of their structures during execution and as such aid system evolution useful during the incremental integration of the components in the system. In this paper we have addressed the problem of dynamic configurability from the modeling perspective. In this context we have proposed an architecture viewpoint for runtime adaptability. The viewpoint has been defined based on a well-defined metamodel that includes the concepts related to component-based runtime structure, architecture deployment, and runtime adaptability. Unlike existing general purpose architecture viewpoints, the proposed viewpoint can support the architect in modeling the concerns for runtime adaptability and as such support the communication among stakeholders and the analysis of the architecture. We have illustrated the viewpoint for a DDSCM. In our future work, we shall investigate the trade-off of runtime adaptability with time performance and scalability, and also study the integration of the various different viewpoints with the runtime adaptability viewpoint that we have proposed.

REFERENCES

[1] R. Chitchyan, A. Rashid, P. Sawyer, J. Bakker, M.P. Alarcon, A. Garcia, B. Tekinerdogan, S. Clarke, A. Jackson, Survey of aspect-oriented analysis and design, in: R. Chitchyan, A. Rashid (Eds.), AOSD-Europe Project Deliverable No. AOSD-Europe-ULANC-9, 2005.

[2] ISO/IEC 42010:2007 Recommended practice for architectural description of software-intensive systems (ISO/IEC 42010), July 2007.

[3] H. Sözer, B. Tekinerdogan, Introducing recovery style for modeling and analyzing system recovery, in: Proceedings of the 7th Working IEEE/IFIP Conference on Software Architecture, 2008, pp. 167–176.

[4] H. Sözer, B. Tekinerdogan, M. Akşit, FLORA: a framework for decomposing software architecture to introduce local recovery, J. Softw. Pract. Exp. 39 (10) (2009) 869–889.

[5] B. Tekinerdogan, H. Sözer, Defining architectural viewpoints for quality concerns, in: Proceedings of the 5th European Conference on Software Architecture, 2011, pp. 26–34.

[6] B. Tekinerdogan, H. Sözer, Variability viewpoint for introducing variability in software architecture viewpoints, in: Proceedings of the 2nd International Workshop on Variability in Software Architecture, 2012, pp. 163–166.

[7] L. Dobrica, E. Niemela, A survey on software architecture analysis methods, IEEE Trans. Softw. Eng. 28 (7) (2002) 638–654.

[8] H. Boudali, H. Sözer, M. Stoelinga, Architectural availability analysis of software decomposition for local recovery, in: Proceedings of the 3rd International Conference on Secure Software Integration and Reliability Improvement, 2009, pp. 14–22.

[9] B. Tekinerdogan, Software architecture, in: T. Gonzalez, J.L. Díaz-Herrera (Eds.), Computer Science Handbook, second ed., Computer Science and Software Engineering, vol. I, Taylor and Francis, London, 2014.

[10] C. Hofmeister, R. Nord, D. Soni, Applied Software Architecture, Addison-Wesley, New York, NJ, 2009.

[11] P. Kruchten, The 4 + 1 view model of architecture, IEEE Softw. 12 (6) (1995) 42–50.

[12] P. Kruchten, The Rational Unified Process: An Introduction, second ed., Addison-Wesley, Boston, MA, 2000.

[13] A.J. Lattanze, Architecting Software Intensive Systems: A Practitioner's Guide, CRC Press, Taylor & Francis Group, Boca Raton, FL, 2009.

[14] P. Clements, F. Bachmann, L. Bass, D. Garlan, J. Ivers, R. Little, P. Merson, R. Nord, J. Stafford, Documenting Software Architectures: Views and Beyond, second ed., Addison-Wesley, Boston, 2010.

[15] R.G. Poluha, Application of the SCOR Model in Supply Chain Management, Cambria Press, Amherst, NY, 2007.

[16] B. Chaibdraa, J. Müller, Multiagent Based Supply Chain Management, Springer, New York, NY, 2006.

[17] K. Kumar, Technology for supporting supply chain management: introduction, Commun. ACM 44 (6) (2001) 58–61.

[18] J. Li, L. Yuan, J. Guo, Business integrated architecture for dynamic supply chain management with web service, in: Proceedings of the International Conference on New Trends in Information and Service Science, 2009, pp. 356–361.

[19] V. Misra, M.I. Khan, U.K. Singh, Supply chain management systems: architecture, design, vision, J. Strateg. Innov. Sustain. 6 (4) (2010) 102–108.

[20] D. Garlan, S.-W. Cheng, A.-C. Huang, B. Schmerl, P. Steenkiste, Rainbow: architecture-based self-adaptation with reusable infrastructure, IEEE Comput. 37 (10) (2004) 46–54.

[21] H. Tajalli, J. Garcia, G. Edwards, N. Medvidovic, PLASMA: a plan-based layered architecture for software model-driven adaptation, in: Proceedings of the IEEE/ACM International Conference on Automated Software Engineering, 2010, pp. 467–476.

[22] A. Mukhija, M. Glinz, Runtime adaptation of applications through dynamic recomposition of components, in: Proceedings of the 18th International Conference on Architecture of Computing Systems Conference on Systems Aspects in Organic and Pervasive Computing, 2005, pp. 124–138.

[23] J. Dowling, V. Cahill, The K-component architecture meta-model for self-adaptive software, in: Proceedings of the Third International Conference on Metalevel Architectures and Separation of Crosscutting Concerns, 2001, pp. 81–88.

[24] J. Kramer, J. Magee, Self-managed systems: an architectural challenge, in: Proceedings of the Future of Software Engineering, 2007, pp. 259–268.

[25] P. Oreizy, M.M. Gorlick, R.N. Taylor, D. Heimbigner, G. Johnson, N. Medvidovic, A. Quilici, D.S. Rosenblum, A.L. Wolf, An architecture-based approach to self-adaptive software, IEEE Intell. Syst. 14 (3) (1999) 54–62.

[26] D. Menascé, H. Gomaa, S. Malek, J. Sousa, SASSY: a framework for self-architecting service-oriented systems, IEEE Softw. 28 (6) (2011) 78–85.

[27] D. Garlan, J.M. Barnes, B.R. Schmerl, O. Celiku, Evolution styles: foundations and tool support for software architecture evolution, in: Proceedings of the 7th Working IEEE/IFIP Conference on Software Architecture (WICSA'09), 2009, pp. 131–140.

[28] P.K. McKinley, S.M. Sadjadi, E.P. Kasten, B.H.C. Cheng, Composing adaptive software, IEEE Comput. 37 (7) (2004) 56–64.

[29] N.M. Villegas, H.A. Müller, G. Tamura, L. Duchien, R. Casallas, A framework for evaluating quality-driven self-adaptive software systems, in: Proceedings of the 6th International Symposium on Software Engineering for Adaptive and Self-Managing Systems, 2011, pp. 80–89.

[30] J.S. Bradbury, J.R. Cordy, J. Dingel, M. Wermelinger, A survey of self-management in dynamic software architecture specifications, in: Proceedings of the 1st ACM SIGSOFT Workshop on Self-Managed Systems, 2004, pp. 28–33.

[31] J.O. Kephart, D.M. Chess, The vision of autonomic computing, IEEE Comput. 36 (1) (2003) 41–50.

[32] S. Kell, A survey of practical software adaptation techniques, J. Univers. Comput. Sci. 14 (13) (2008) 2110–2157.

[33] T. Elrad, R. Fillman, A. Bader, Aspect-oriented programming, Commun. ACM 44 (10) (2001) 29–32.

[34] E.W. Dijkstra, On the role of scientific thought, in: E.W. Dijkstra (Ed.), Selected Writings on Computing: A Personal Perspective, Springer-Verlag, New York, NY, 1982, pp. 60–66.

[35] J. Bakker, B. Tekinerdogan, M. Aksit, Characterization of early aspects approaches, in: Workshop on Early Aspects: Aspect-Oriented Requirements Engineering and Architecture Design, Held in Conjunction With AOSD Conference, 2005.

[36] M. Aksit, B. Tekinerdogan, L. Bergmans, The six concerns for separation of concerns, in: Proceedings of Workshop on Advanced Separation of Concerns, European Conference on Object-Oriented Programming, Budapest, Hungary, 2003.

[37] N. Rozanski, E. Woods, Software Systems Architecture—Working With Stakeholders Using Viewpoints and Perspectives, Addison-Wesley, Boston, 2005.

[38] F. Bachmann, L. Bass, M. Klein, Architectural tactics: a step toward methodical architectural design, Technical report CMU/SEI-2003-TR-004, Carnegie Mellon University, Pittsburgh, PA, 2003.

[39] M. Hinchey, S. Park, K. Schmid, Building dynamic software product lines, IEEE Comput. 45 (10) (2012) 22–26.

[40] R. Capilla, J. Bosch, P. Trinidad, A. Ruiz-Cortes, M. Hinchey, An overview of dynamic software product line architectures and techniques: observations from research and industry, J. Syst. Softw. 91 (2014) 3–23.

[41] M. Klein, R. Kazman, L. Bass, S.J. Carriere, M. Barbacci, H. Lipson, Attribute-based architectural styles, in: Proceedings of the First Working IFIP Conference on Software Architecture, San Antonio, TX, February, 1999.

updated quickly to adjust to these as well as any emergent security threats. A delay in patching newly discovered vulnerabilities means a loss of money.

An analysis of this scenario identifies many challenges including: security requirements differ from one customer to another; each customer's security requirements may change over time based on current operational environment security and business objectives; Galactic system security must be integrated with customers' deployed security controls in order to achieve coherent security operational environment; and new security vulnerabilities may be discovered in the Galactic system at any time. Using traditional security engineering techniques would require SwinSoft to conduct a lot of system maintenance iterations to deliver system patches that block vulnerabilities and adapt the system to every new customer needs.

A better security engineering approach that addresses these challenges should: enable each customer to specify and enforce their security requirements based on their current security needs; security should be applied to any arbitrary system component/entity; no predefined/hardcoded secure points or capabilities, usually built at design time; security specification should be supported at different levels of abstraction based on software customers' experience, scale, and engineers' capabilities. Integration of security controls with system entities should be supported at different levels of abstraction, from the system as one unit to a specific system method. The security engineering approach should ease the integration with third-party security controls. System and security specifications should be reconfigurable at runtime.

5.3 SECURITY ENGINEERING STATE-OF-THE-ART

Existing security engineering efforts focus on capturing and enforcing security requirements at design time, security retrofitting (maintenance), and adaptive security engineering. On the other hand, most industrial efforts focus on delivering security platforms to help software developers in implementing their security requirements using readymade standard security algorithms and mechanisms. Some of the key limitations we found in these efforts include: (i) these efforts focus mainly on design-time security engineering—that is, how to capture and enforce security requirements during software development phase; (ii) limited support to dynamic and adaptive security and require design-time preparation. Fabian et al. [1] introduce a detailed survey of the existing security engineering efforts but did not highlight limitations of these approaches. We discuss key efforts in these areas.

5.3.1 DESIGN-TIME SECURITY ENGINEERING

Software security engineering aims to develop secure systems that remain dependable in the face of attacks [3]. Security engineering activities include: identifying security objectives that systems should satisfy; identifying security risks that threaten system operation; elicitation of security requirements that should be enforced on the system to achieve the expected security level; developing security architectures and designs that deliver the security requirements and integrates with the operational environment; and developing, deploying, and enforcing the developed or purchased security controls. Below, we summarize the key efforts in the security engineering area.

5.3.1.1 Early-stage security engineering

The early-stage security engineering approaches focus mainly on security requirements engineering including security requirements elicitation, capturing, modeling, analyzing, and validation at design time from the specified security objectives or security risks. Below we discuss some of the key existing security requirements engineering efforts.

Knowledge acquisition in automated specification (KAoS) [4] is a goal-oriented requirements engineering approach. KAoS uses formal methods for models analysis [5]. KAoS was extended to capture security requirements [6] in terms of obstacles to stakeholders' goals. Obstacles are defined in terms of conditions that when satisfied will prevent certain goals from being achieved. This is helpful in understanding the system goals in details but it results in coupling security goals with system goals.

Secure i* [7,8] introduces a methodology based on the i* (agent-oriented requirements modeling) framework to address security and privacy requirements. The secure i* focuses on identifying security requirements through analyzing relationships between users, attackers, and agents of both parties. This analysis process has seven steps organized in three phases of security analysis as follows: (i) attacker analysis focuses on identifying potential system abusers and malicious intents; (ii) dependency vulnerability analysis helps in detecting vulnerabilities according to the organizational relationships among stakeholders; (iii) countermeasure analysis focus on addressing and mitigating the vulnerabilities and threats identified in previous steps.

Secure TROPOS [9–11] is an extension of the TROPOS requirements engineering approach that is based on the goal-oriented requirements engineering paradigm. TROPOS was initially developed for agent-oriented security engineering. TROPOS introduces a set of models to capture the system actors (actors' model) and their corresponding goals (goal model: hard goals represent the actor functional requirements and soft-goals represent the actor nonfunctional requirements). These goals are iteratively decomposed into subgoals until these subgoals are refined into tasks, plans, and resources. Secure TROPOS is used to capture security requirements during the software requirements analysis. Secure TROPOS was appended with new notations. These included: (i) *security constraints:* restriction related to certain security issue like: privacy, integrity…etc.; (ii) *security dependency:* this adds constraints for the dependencies that may exist between actors to achieve their own goals and defines what each one expects from the other about the security of supplied or required goals; and (iii) *security entities:* are extensions of the TROPOS notations of entities like goals, tasks, and resources as follows: secure goal: means that the actor has some soft-goal related to security (no details on how to achieve) this goal will be achieved through a secure task; secure task: is a task that represents a particular way of satisfying a secure goal; secure resource: is an informational entity that's related to the security of the system; and secure capability: means the capability of an actor to achieve a secure goal.

Misuse cases [12,13] capture use cases that the system should allow side by side with the use cases that the system should not allow which may harm the system or the stakeholders operations or security. The misuse cases focus on the interactions between the system and malicious users. This helps in developing the system expecting security threats and drives the development of security use cases.

5.3.1.2 Later-stage security engineering

Efforts in this area focus on how to map security requirements (identified in the previous stage) on system design entities at design time and how to help in generating secure and security code specified. Below we summarize the key efforts in this area organized according to the approach used or the underlying software system architecture and technology used.

UMLsec [14–16] is one of the first model-driven security engineering efforts. UMLsec extends UML specification with a UML profile that provides stereotypes to be used in annotating system design elements with security intentions and requirements. UMLsec provides a comprehensive UML profile but it was developed mainly for use during the design phase. Moreover, UMLsec contains stereotypes for predefined security requirements (such as secrecy, secure dependency, critical, fair-exchange, no upflow, no downflow, guarded entity) to help in security analysis and security generation. UMLsec is supported with a formalized security analysis mechanism that takes the system models with the specified security annotations and performs model checking. UMLsec [17] has recently got a simplified extension to help in secure code generation.

SecureUML [18] provides UML-based language for modeling role based access control (RBAC) policies and authorization constraints of the model-driven engineering (MDE) approaches. This approach is still tightly coupled with system design models. SecureUML defines a set of vocabulary that represents RBAC concepts such as roles, role permissions, and user-assigned roles.

Satoh et al. [19] provides end-to-end security through the adoption of model-driven security using the UML2.0 service profile. Security analysts add security intents (representing security patterns) as stereotypes for the UML service model. Then, this is used to guide the generation of the security policies. It also works on securing service composition using pattern-based by introducing rules to define the relationships among services using patterns. Shiroma et al. [20] introduce a security engineering approach merging model-driven security engineering with patterns-based security. The proposed approach works on system class diagrams as input along with the required security patterns. It uses model transformation techniques (mainly ATL—atlas transformation language) to update the system class diagrams with the suitable security patterns applied. This process can be repeated many times during the modeling phase. One point to be noticed is that the developers need to be aware of the order of security patterns to be applied (i.e., authentication then authorization, then...).

Delessy et al. [21] introduce a theoretical framework to align security patterns with modeling of Service-Oriented Architecture SOA systems. The approach is based on a security patterns map divided into two groups: (i) abstraction patterns that deliver security for SOA without any implementation dependencies and (ii) realization patterns that deliver security solutions for web services' implementation. It appends metamodels for the security patterns on the abstract and concrete levels of models. Thus, architects become able to develop their SOA models (platform independent) including security patterns attribute. Then generate the concrete models (platform dependent web services) including the realization security patterns. Similar work introduced by Schnjakin et al. [22] to use security patterns in capturing security requirements and then enforce these requirements using predefined security patterns.

Hafner et al. [23] introduce the concept of security-as-a-service (SeAAS) where a set of key security controls are grouped and delivered as a service to be used by different web-based applications and services. It is based on outsourcing security tasks to be done by the SeAAS component. Security services are registered with SeAAS and then it becomes available for consumers and customers to access whenever needed. A key problem of the SeAAS is that it introduces a single point of failure and a bottleneck in the network. Moreover, it did not provide any interface where third-party security controls can implement to support integration with the SeAAS component. The SECTET project [24] focuses on the business-to-business collaborations (such as workflows) where security needs to be incorporated between both parties. The solution was to model security requirements (mainly RBAC policies) at high level and merged with the business requirements using SECTET-PL [25]. These modeled security requirements are then used to automate the generation of implementation and configuration of the realization security services using WS-security as the target applications are assumed to be SOA-oriented.

We have also determined different industrial security platforms that have been developed to help software engineers realizing security requirements through a set of provided security functions and mechanisms that the software engineers can select from. Microsoft has introduced more advanced extensible security model—Windows Identity Foundation [26] to enable service providers delivering applications with extensible security. It requires service providers to use and implement certain interfaces in system implementation. The Java Spring framework has a security framework—Acegi [27]. It implements a set of security controls for identity management, authentication, and authorization. However, these platforms require developers' involvement in writing integration code between their applications and such security platforms. The resultant software systems are tightly coupled with these platforms' capabilities and mechanisms. Moreover, using different third-party security controls requires updating system source code to add necessary integration code.

5.3.2 SECURITY RETROFITTING

Although a lot of security engineering approaches and techniques do exist as we discussed in the last section, the efforts introduced in the area of security reengineering and retrofitting are relatively limited. This comes, based on our understanding, from the assumption that security should not be considered as an afterthought and should be considered from the early system development phases. Thus, research and industry efforts focus mainly on how to help software and security engineers in capturing and documenting security in system design artifacts and how to enforce using MDE approaches. Security maintenance is implicitly supported throughout updating design-time system or security models. In the real world, system delivery plans are dominated by developing business features that should be delivered. This leads to systems that miss customers expected or required security capabilities. These existing legacy systems lack models (either system or security or both) that could be used to conduct the reengineering process. The maintenance or reengineering of such systems is hardly supported by existing security (re)engineering approaches.

Research efforts in the security retrofitting area focus on how to update software systems in order to extend their security capabilities or mitigate security issues. Abdulkarim et al. [28] discussed the limitations and drawbacks of applying the security retrofitting techniques including cost and time problems, technicality problems, issues related to the software architecture and design security flaws. Hafiz and Johnson [29,30] propose a security on demand approach, which is based on a developed catalog of security-oriented program transformations to extend or retrofit system security with new security patterns that have been proved to be effective and efficient in mitigating specific system-security vulnerabilities. These program transformations include adding policy enforcement point, single access point, authentication enforcer, perimeter filter, decorated filter and more. A key problem with this approach is that it depends on predefined transformations that are hard to extend especially by software engineers.

Ganapathy et al. [31,32] propose an approach to retrofit legacy systems with authorization security policies. They used concept analysis techniques (locating system entities using certain signatures) to find fingerprints of security-sensitive operations performed by system under analysis. Fingerprints are defined in terms of data structures (such as window, client, input, Event, Font) that we would like to secure their access and the set of APIs that represent the security-sensitive operations. The results represent a set of candidate join-points where we can operate the well-known "reference monitor" authorization mechanism.

Ganapathy et al. [33] present a practical tool to inject security features that defend against low-level software attacks into system binaries. The authors focus on cases where the system source code is not available to system customers. The proposed approach focuses on handling buffer overflow related attacks for both memory heap and stack.

Welch and Stroud [34] introduce a security reengineering approach based on java reflection concept. Their security reengineering approach is based on introducing three metaobjects that are responsible for authentication, authorization, and communication confidentiality. These metaobjects are weaved with the system objects using java reflection. However, this approach focuses only on adding predefined types of security attributes and do not address modifying systems to block reported security vulnerabilities.

5.3.3 ADAPTIVE APPLICATION SECURITY

Several research efforts target to enable systems to adapt their security capabilities at runtime. Elkhodary and Whittle [35] survey adaptive security systems. Extensible security infrastructure [36] is a framework that enables systems to support adaptive authorization enforcement through updating in memory authorization policy objects with new low-level C code policies. It requires developing wrappers for every system resource that catch calls to such resource and check authorization policies. Strata Security API [37] where systems are hosted on a strata virtual machine which enables interception of system execution at instruction level based on user security policies. The framework does not support securing distributed systems and it focuses on low-level policies specified in C code.

The SERENITY project [38–40] enables provisioning of appropriate security and dependability mechanisms for ambient intelligence systems at runtime. The SERENITY framework supports: definition of security requirements in order to enable a requirements-driven selection of appropriate security mechanisms within integration schemes at runtime; provide mechanisms for monitoring security at runtime and dynamically react to threats, breaches of security, or context changes; and integrating security solutions, monitoring, and reaction mechanisms in a common framework. SERENITY attributes are specified on system components at design time. At runtime, the framework links serenity-aware systems to the appropriate security and dependability patterns. *SERENITY does not support dynamic or runtime adaptation for new unanticipated security requirements neither adding security to system entities that was not secured before and become critical points.*

Morin et al. [41] propose a security-driven and model-based dynamic adaptation approach to adapt applications' enforced access control policies in accordance to changes in application context—that is, applying context-aware access control policies. Engineers define security policies that take into consideration context information. Whenever the system context changes, the proposed approach updates the system architecture to enforce the suitable security policies. *The key limitation of this work is that it focuses mainly on access control policies and requires design-time preparation of the software.*

Mouelhi and others [41] introduce a model-driven security engineering approach to specify and enforce system access control policies at design time based on aspect-oriented programming (AOP)-static weaving. These adaptive approaches require design-time preparation (to manually write integration code or to use specific platform or architecture). *They also support only limited security objectives, such as access control. Unanticipated security requirements are not supported. No valida-tion that the target system (after adaptation) correctly enforces security as specified.*

Yuan et al. [42] introduce a more comprehensive survey of efforts in the area of self-protecting software systems. They have also outlined the key research gaps in the existing techniques. This in-cludes: (i) lack of comprehensive self-protecting systems either from the monitoring, planning, exe-cution perspective, or from the software stack perspective—that is, host, network, and software; (ii) lack of an integrated solution that supports both design-time and runtime security, (iii) support of more security adaptation patterns. Our approach focus is the first problem, which is to extend a given soft-ware system with necessary security monitors (using user-defined metrics and properties), security analysis (using formalized vulnerability signatures), planning (using models for manual adaptation and rules for automated adaptation), and execution (using AOP). Furthermore, we generate a set of integration test cases to verify that the specified adaptations (realized by security controls' integration with the software system) are functioning as expected. The big picture of our approach is available in Ref. [43]. In this chapter we focus mainly on how adaptation can be specified (manually/automatically) and how such adaptations can be realized.

5.4 RUNTIME SECURITY ADAPTATION

We identified two potential types of security adaptation: *manual adaptation*: usually triggered manu-ally by security engineers/administrators based on change in security goals, security threats, and risks; and *automated adaptation*: triggered automatically based on specified adaptation rules fired when a certain metric exceeds a user-defined threshold, a property is violated, or a new vulnerability was reported.

Our approach, outlined in Fig. 5.2, is based on externalizing the software security capabilities from the software so that we can easily change such security capabilities without the need to change the software itself. At the same time being able to integrate (inject) such new capabilities within the soft-ware at any arbitrary system entity. This is abstracted to end users by a set of domain-specific visual

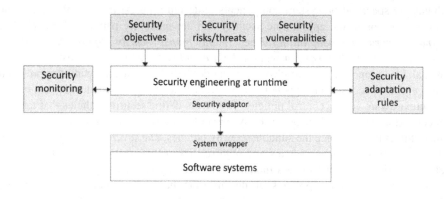

FIG. 5.2

Block diagram of our adaptive security approach.

languages (DSVLs) at different levels of abstraction to help them describe their security needs, software details, and mapping security to system entities at the right level of abstraction for different stakeholders. This helps in speeding up the software change time to ad hoc security needs. The security vulnerability analysis is based on formalized signatures that describe bad code smells we need to look for in a given system. The same idea is used in the security monitoring component. All these inputs (requirements for adaptation) are realized/executed using the same execution component (MDSE@R, security engineering at runtime).

5.4.1 SUPPORTING MANUAL ADAPTATION USING MDSE@R

The MDSE@R approach [44,45] targets externalizing all security engineering activities so we can define and change system security at any time, while being able to integrate these new security capabilities on the system at runtime. MDSE@R is based on two key concepts: (i) MDE, using DSVL models at different levels of abstraction to describe system and security details; and (ii) AOP, which enables dynamic runtime weaving of interceptors and system code based on configuration files that specify the required security point-cuts in the system. Fig. 5.3 shows an overview of how to apply MDSE@R in engineering security for a given system at runtime, as discussed here.

Build system-description model (SDM): A detailed SDM (Fig. 5.3(1), see Fig. 5.9 for an example) made up of a set of models delivered by the system provider. This describes various details of the target software application. Our SDMs include: system features (using use case diagrams), system architecture (using component diagrams), system classes' model (using class diagrams), system behavior model (using sequence diagrams), system deployment (using deployment diagrams), and system context (using component diagrams). We have selected these models as they cover all system perspectives that may be required in order to specify system security. The use of many of these submodels is optional. It depends on how many of the system details the system provider exposes to their customers and how many details customers' security engineers will need in enforcing the required security on the target system. Security engineers may be interested in specifying security on system entities (using

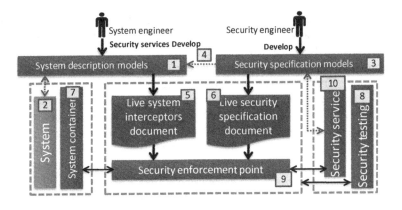

FIG. 5.3

Security engineering at runtime.

system components and/or classes models), on system status (using system behavior model), on system hosts (using system deployment model), or external system interactions (using system context model). Moreover, system customers can specify security on coarse-grained level (using system component model), or on fine-grained level (using system class models). The SDMs can be synchronized with the running system instance using models@runtime synchronization techniques [25,26], or manually by the system provider. Some of such system-description information can be reverse-engineered, if not available, from the target system (Fig. 5.3(2)).

Build security specification model (SSM): A set of models developed and managed by security engineers (Fig. 5.3(3)) to specify the security needs that must be satisfied in the target system. They include a set of submodels that capture the details required during the security engineering process including: security goals and objectives, security risks and threats, security requirements, security architecture for the operational environment, and security controls to be enforced. These models deliver different levels of abstractions and enable separation of concerns between customer stakeholders including business owners, security analysts, security architects and implementers. The key mandatory model in the SSMs set is a security controls model. This is required in generating interceptors and security aspect code.

System-security models weaving: A many-to-many mapping between the SDMs and SSMs is developed by the customer security engineers (Fig. 5.3(4)). One or more security concepts (security objective, security requirement, and/or security control) is mapped to one or more system model entities (system-level, feature-level, component-level, class-level, and/or method-level entities). Mapping a security concept on a higher level system entity implies a delegation to the underlying levels. Whenever a security specification is mapped to a system feature, this implies that the same security specification is mapped on the feature related components, classes, and methods.

The few steps discussed so far helps in addressing the planning phase in security adaption. New security requirements (objectives, risks, etc.) can easily be reflected on the SSM described earlier. The next steps related to enforcing (executing) the specified security, and are automated by MDSE@R without any involvement from the security or system engineers. Whenever a mapping is defined or updated between a SSM and a SDM, the underlying MDSE@R framework propagates such changes as follows:

Update Live System Interceptors' Document (Fig. 5.3(5))—this maintains a list of point-cuts where security controls should be weaved/integrated with the target software application entry points. This document is updated based on the modeled security specifications and the corresponding system entities where security should be applied. *Update a Live Security Specification Document* (Fig. 5.3 (6))—this maintains a list of security controls to be applied at every point-cut defined in the system interceptors' document. *Update the system container* (Fig. 5.3(7))—this is responsible for injecting interceptors defined in the system interceptors' document into the target system at runtime using dynamic weaving AOP. Any call to a method, with a matching in the interceptors' document, will be intercepted and delegated to a central security enforcement point. *Test current system security* (Fig. 5.3(8))—this validates that the target system is currently enforcing the specified security levels. The security-testing component makes sure that the intended security is correctly integrated with the target application at runtime. MDSE@R generates and fires a set of security integration test cases. This is done before MDSE@R gives confirmation to security engineers that required security is now enforced. *Security enforcement point* (Fig. 5.3(9))—this acts as a bridge between the target system (system container) and the security controls that deliver the required security. The security enforcement point uses the live security specification document to determine, and initiate, security control to be enforced on a given, intercepted, request. *Security services* (Fig. 5.3(10)) are the application security controls (deployed in the system operational environment) that are integrated with the security enforcement point. This enables the security enforcement point to communicate with these services via APIs implemented by each service.

Thus, MDSE@R covers manually adaptation scenarios. A given set of security objectives and requirements are reflected on the SSM, and MDSE@R will make sure to automatically inject (or may be leave out) these security requirements as needed. For legacy systems, this might seem infeasible, but we have used static aspect oriented to modify system binaries and add calls to our security enforcement point.

5.4.2 AUTOMATED ADAPTATION USING VULNERABILITY ANALYSIS AND MITIGATION

Another key trigger for security adaption is the discovery of a new vulnerability in the software. In our approach [46–48], we assume that this requires automated adaptation of the enforced security to (virtually) patch the reported security until the software vendor develops a real patch. In this section we discuss how we can do the vulnerability analysis, and then using a set of rules to come up with necessary adaptation actions to block such vulnerability. Fig. 5.4 summarizes the interactions between the vulnerability analysis component, security mitigation component, and the software. Our vulnerability analysis approach depends on a formalized vulnerability definition schema that covers many concepts of software security weaknesses (flaws) such as vulnerability signature—what are the key things in the software when found, it means that the system suffers from such vulnerability, and mitigation actions—what adaptation we need to apply to patch the vulnerability.

Formalizing vulnerability signatures helps automating the vulnerability analysis process. Ideally, a formal vulnerability signature should be specified on an abstract level far from the source code and programming language details, enabling locating of possible vulnerability instances in different programs written in different programming languages. We use Object Constraint Language (OCL) as a well-known, extensible, and formal language to specify semantic rather than syntactical signatures of security weaknesses. To support specifying and validating OCL-based vulnerabilities' signatures, we have developed a system-description metamodel, shown in Fig. 5.5. This model is inspired from

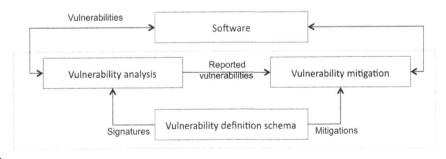

FIG. 5.4

Automated vulnerability analysis and mitigation.

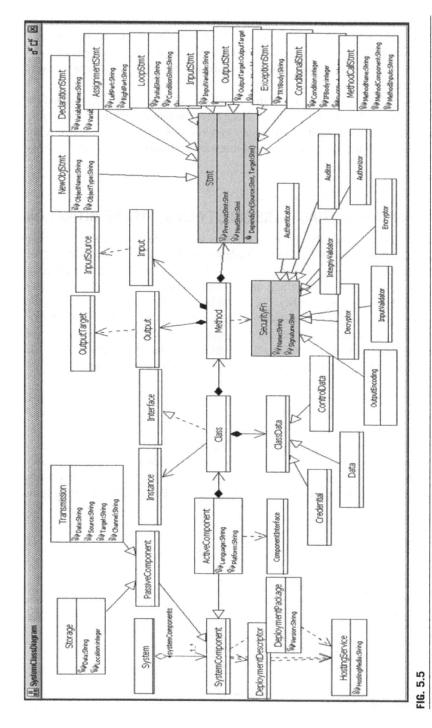

FIG. 5.5

Software description metamodel.

our analysis of the nature of the existing security vulnerabilities. It captures the main entities in any object-oriented program and relationships between them including components, classes, instances, inputs, input sources, output, output targets, methods, method bodies, statements, for example, if-else statements, loops, new objects, etc. Each entity has a set of attributes such as method name, accessibility, variable name, variable type, method call name. This model helps conducting semantic analysis of the specified vulnerability signatures. Table 5.1 shows examples of vulnerability signatures specified in OCL and using our SDM.

SQL Injection - SQLI: Any method statement "*S*" of type "*MethodInvocation*" where the callee function is "*ExecuteQuery*" and one of the *parameters* passed to it, is assigned to "*identifier*" coming from one of the input sources. Taint analysis "*IsTainted*" can be defined as an OCL function that adds every variable assigned to a user input parameter to a suspected list.
Cross-Site Scripting - XSS signature: Any method statement "*S*" of type assignment statement where left part is of type "*output target*" for example, text, label, grid, etc. and right part uses input from the input sources or tainted identifier as just discussed.
Authentication bypass: Any public method that has statement "*S*" of type "*MethodInvocation*" where the callee method is marked as Authentication function while this method call can be skipped using user input as part of the bypassing condition.
Improper authorization: Any public method that has statement "*S*" that uses input data X without being sanitized, authorized.

5.4.2.1 OCL-based vulnerability analyzer

Given that vulnerability signatures become now formally specified using OCL, the static vulnerability analysis component simply traverses the given program looking for code snippets with matches to the given vulnerabilities' signatures.

Table 5.1 Example Vulnerability Signatures

Vulnerability	Vulnerability Signature
SQLI	Context Method Inv SQLICheck: self.Statements->exists(S | S.StatementType = 'MethodInvocation' and S.MethodName = 'ExecuteSQL' and S.Parameters.exists(P | self.IsTainted(P.ParameterName) = true)
XSS	Context Method Inv SQLICheck: self.Exists(S | S.StatementType = 'Assignment' and S.RightPart.Contains(InputSource) and S.LeftPart.Contains(OutputTarget))
Authentication bypass	Context Method Inv SQLICheck: self.IsPublic == true and self->Exists(S | S.StatementType = 'MethodInvocation' and S.IsAuthenitcationFn == true and S.Parent == IFElseStmt and S.Parent.Condition.Contains(InputSource))
Improper authorization	Context Method Inv SQLICheck: self.IsPublic == true and self.Contains(S| S.Exists(X| X.StatementType = 'InputSource' and X.IsSanitized = false or X.IsAuthorized == False)

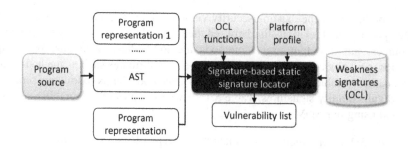

FIG. 5.6

OCL-based vulnerability analysis.

The architecture of our formal and scalable static vulnerability analysis component, as shown in Fig. 5.6, is based on our formalized vulnerability signature concept.

Program source code: We should have source code or binaries (dlls, exes—de-compilation is used to reverse engineer source code) of the application to be analyzed.

Abstract program representation: Source code is transformed into an abstract syntax tree (AST) representation. This abstracts language-specific source code details away from specific language constructs. Extracting source code AST requires using different language parsers (currently support C++, VB.Net, and C#). Then, we perform more abstract transforming from AST to SDM that conforms to the model.

OCL functions: Represent a library of predefined functions that can be used in specifying vulnerability signatures and in identifying matches to these signatures. This includes control flow, data flow, string patterns, program taint analysis, etc.

Signature locator: This is the main component in our vulnerability analysis tool. It receives the abstract service/application model and outputs the list of discovered vulnerabilities in the given system along with their locations in code. At analysis time, it loads the platform (C#, VB, PHP) profile based on the details of the program under analysis. Then, it loads the existing weaknesses defined in the weaknesses' signatures database, based on the target program platform/language. The signature locator transforms these signatures into C# methods that check different program entities based on the specified vulnerability signature. We use Application Vulnerability Description Language to represent the identified vulnerabilities in XML format to support interoperability with existing vulnerability databases such as National Vulnerabilities Database.

5.4.2.2 Vulnerability mitigation

Discovered application/service security vulnerabilities can be mitigated in different approaches including: modifying application source code to block the identified problems (patches); however, this solution will be hard to approach in public accessible software systems—for example, cloud systems—as it may take long time to deliver patched version. A quick solution is to use Web application firewall (WAF) to filter requests/responses that exploit such vulnerabilities; however, WAF has many limitations including it does not help in output validation, cryptography storage, and mitigating improper authorization.

Our approach supports integrating different security controls including identity management, authentication controls, authorization controls, input validation, output encoding, WAF, cryptography controls, etc. In our approach, each vulnerability mitigation action specifies a security control type/ family to be used in mitigating the related vulnerability, its required configurations, and application/service entity where the security control will be integrated with (hosting service—webserver or operating system, components, classes, and methods). Thus, a reported SQLI vulnerability in a method (M) that belongs to component (C) can be mitigated by adding input sanitization control (Z) on component (C) that removes SQL keyword from every single request to the method (M). In Table 5.2, we show examples of mitigation actions for some of the known security vulnerabilities. These actions should be specified in XML and included as a part of the formalized vulnerability definition.

5.4.2.3 Vulnerability mitigation component

The analysis component outputs a list of the discovered vulnerabilities in the software system (Fig. 5.7 (1)). Each entry in this list has a service/application vulnerable entity (method, class, or component) along with the list of discovered vulnerabilities in this entity. Given this list of vulnerabilities, the security vulnerability mitigation manager queries the vulnerability definition schema database (Fig. 5.7 (2)) to retrieve the appropriate actions to be taken in order to mitigate each of such reported vulnerabilities. Examples of the retrieved actions are shown in Table 5.2. Using these two lists (vulnerable software entities and mitigation actions), the vulnerability mitigation manager (Fig. 5.7(3)) decides the patching level (component level, class level, or method level) using, for example, HttpModules, object

Table 5.2 Example Vulnerability Mitigation Rules/Actions

Vulnerability	Security Control	Entity Level
SQLI	Input sanitization	Method level
XSS	Input encoding	Component level
Authentication bypass	WAF	Component level
Improper authorization	Authorization	Method level

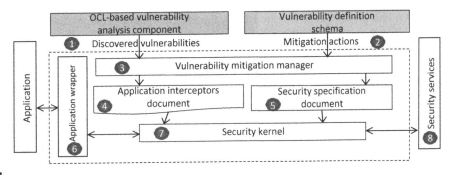

FIG. 5.7

Vulnerability mitigation component.

interceptor using dependency injection, or method-level interception using dynamic weaving AOP respectively. The rest of the steps to enforce the right security control at the right place are as described in the MDSE@R section.

5.5 USAGE EXAMPLE

To demonstrate the capabilities of our new MDSE@R security engineering approach we revisit our example discussed in Section 5.2, the ERP system "Galactic" developed by SwinSoft and procured by Swinburne and SwinMarket. The two customers using the Galactic ERP system have their own distinct security requirements to be enforced on each of their Galactic ERP application instances. We illustrate this security engineering scenario using screen dumps from our prototype tool.

5.5.1 TASK 1—MODEL GALACTIC SYSTEM DESCRIPTION—ONE-TIME TASK

This task is done during or after the system is developed. SwinSoft decides the level of application details to provide to its customers in the Galactic system model. Fig. 5.8 shows that SwinSoft provides its customers with description of system features including customer, employee, and order management features (Fig. 5.8B), system architecture including presentation, business logic layer, and data access layer (Fig. 5.8C), system classes including CustomerBLL, OrderBLL, EmployeeBLL (Fig. 5.8D), and system deployment including web tier, application tier, and data tier (Fig. 5.8E). SwinSoft uses the provided UML profile (Fig. 5.8A) to specify the dependences and relations between system features and components, and components and their classes. Fig. 5.8A shows the UML profile we built to extend UML with security properties (what security controls/requirements/objectives) are mapped to a given system entity; and to store the traceability information between different system artifacts—for example, system features to realization components, components to classes, etc.

5.5.2 TASK 2—MODEL SWINBURNE SECURITY NEEDS

This step is conducted by Swinburne and SwinMarket security engineers during their repetitive security management process. In our scenario, Swinburne security engineers document Swinburne security objectives that must be satisfied by Galactic system. This is done using a high-level security-objectives model (Fig. 5.9A). This model can be revisited at any time to incorporate changing Swinburne security objectives. Security engineers refine these security objectives in terms of security requirements that must be enforced on the Galactic system, developing a security requirements model. This model keeps track of the detailed security requirements and their link back to the high-level security objectives (Fig. 5.9B). This example shows user authentication requirements to be enforced on the Galactic application and its hosting server.

Swinburne security engineers next develop a detailed security architecture including other existing IT systems. This security architecture (Fig. 5.9C) identifies the different security zones (Big Boxes) that cover Swinburne network and the allocation of IT systems, including Galactic, as either one unit or in terms of system components according to the Galactic deployment model. The security architecture also shows the security services, security mechanisms and standards that should be deployed. Swinburne security engineers finally specify the security controls (i.e., the real implementations) for the security

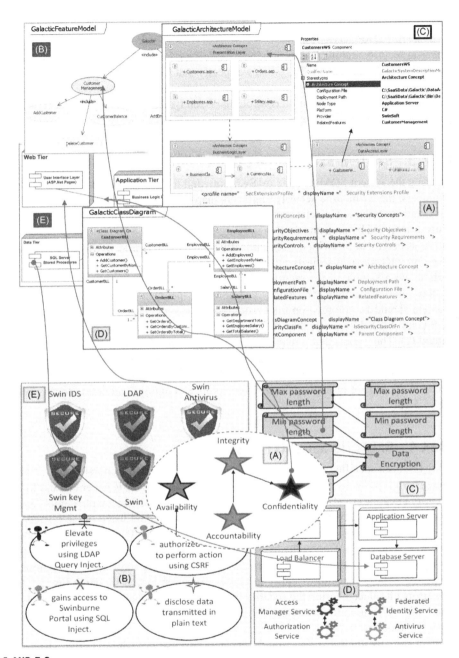

FIG. 5.8 AND 5.9

Examples of Galactic software definition model (*upper panel*) and examples of Swinburne security specification model (*lower panel*).

services modeled in the security architecture model (Fig. 5.9D). This includes SwinIPS Host Intrusion Prevention System, LDAP access control, and SwinAntivirus. These are used to realize the security requirements and security architecture as previously specified. Each SSM maintains traceability information to parent models' entities. In Fig. 5.9D, we specify that LDAP "realizes" the *AuthenticateUser* requirement. Whenever MDSE@R finds a system entity with a mapped security requirement *AuthenticateUser* it adds LDAP as its realization control, that is, an LDAP authentication check is run before the entity is used, for example, before a method or web service is called or module loaded.

5.5.3 TASK 3—SYSTEM-SECURITY WEAVING

After developing the system SDMs—done by SwinSoft, and the security SSMs—done by Swinburne security engineers, the Swinburne security engineers map security attributes (in terms of objectives, requirements, and controls) to Galactic system specification details (in terms of features, components, classes). This is achieved by drag and drop of security attributes to system features in our toolset. Any system feature, structure, or behavior can dynamically and at runtime reflect different levels of security based on the currently mapped security attributes on it.

Fig. 5.9E shows a sample of the security objectives, requirements, and controls mapped to CustomerBLL class. In this example the security engineer has specified that the *AuthenticateUser* security requirement should be enforced on the CustomerBLL class (1). Such a requirement is achieved using LDAP control (3). Moreover, they have specified Forms-based authentication on the GetCustomers method (2). This means that a request to a method in the CustomerBLL class will be authenticated by the caller's Windows identity, but a request to the GetCustomers method will be authenticated with a Forms-based identity. MDSE@R uses security attributes mapped to system entities to generate the full set of methods' call interceptors and entities' required security controls, as shown in Fig. 5.13.

5.5.4 TASK 4—GALACTIC SECURITY TESTING

Once security has been specified and interceptors and configurations are generated, MDSE@R makes sure that the system is correctly enforcing security as specified. MDSE@R generates and fires a set of required security integration test cases. Our test case generator uses the system interceptors and security specification documents to generate a set of test cases for each method listed in the interception document. The generated test case contains a set of security assertions (one for each security property specified on a given system entry). During the firing phase, the security enforcement point is instrumented with logging transactions to reflect the calling method, called security control, and the returned values. Security engineers should check the security test cases execution log, as shown in Fig. 5.10, to make sure that no errors introduced during the security integration with Galactic entities. Fig. 5.11 shows a sample run of Galactic after weaving Forms-based authentication control when calling GetCustomers method.

SwinMarket security engineers go through the same process as Swinburne did when specifying their security requirements. However, SwinMarket specifies their requirements, context, security controls, and IT applications. This results in quite different generated security enforcement controls.

Both Swinburne and SwinMarket security engineers can modify the security specifications while their Galactic applications are in use. MDSE@R framework updates interceptors in the target systems and enforces changes to the security specification for each system as required. For example, the

Test Case Name	Message
Authentication testing	Authentication control "forms-based authentication" is plugged-in
Authorization testing	Authorization control is not plugged-in

FIG. 5.10

Sample test cases firing log.

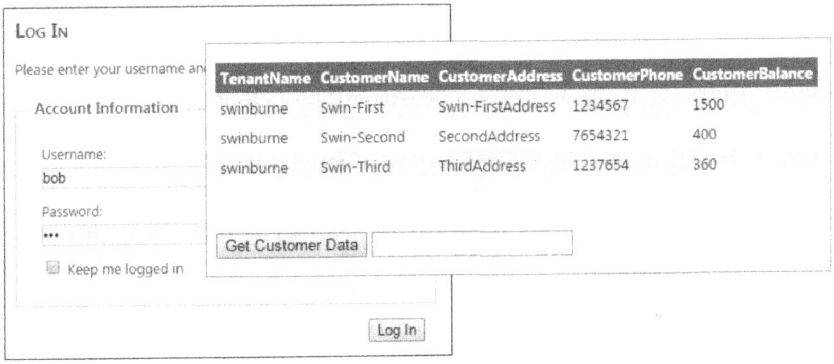

FIG. 5.11

Testing Galactic with injected form-based authentication.

Swinburne Galactic security model can be updated with a Shibboleth single sign-on security authentication component. The updated interceptors and security specification are applied to the running Galactic deployment, which then enforces this authentication protocol instead of the Forms approach as above.

5.5.5 TASK 5—GALACTIC CONTINUOUS VULNERABILITY ANALYSIS AND MITIGATION

We have applied the vulnerability analysis tool on Galactic ERP system (and many other applications), and using the mitigation actions, summarized in Table 5.2. Table 5.3 shows the number of reported vulnerability instances grouped by vulnerability type. We applied the vulnerability analysis

Table 5.3 Number of Reported Vulnerabilities											
SQLI			XSS			Authentication Bypass			Improper Authorization		
TP	FP	FN	TP	FP	FN	TP	FP	FN	TP	FP	FN
2	0	0	3	1	1	4	0	0	2	1	0
TP, true positives; FP, false positives; FN, false negative.											

incrementally—that is, SQLI analysis, then XSS, and so on. For each of these reported vulnerabilities, we have checked that the proper security control(s) was integrated successfully as specified in the actions table, Table 5.2, and that the reported vulnerability is no longer exploitable.

5.6 DISCUSSION

Our approach is based on promoting security engineering from design time to runtime by externalizing security engineering activities including capturing objectives, requirements controls, and realization from the target system implementation. This permits both security to be enforced and critical points to secure to evolve at runtime (supporting adaptive security at runtime). Using a common security interface helps integrating different security controls without a need to develop new system-security control connectors. Moreover, a key benefit reaped from MDSE@R approach is to the support model-based security management. Enterprise-wide security requirements, architecture and controls are maintained and enforced through a centralized SSM instead of low-level scattered configurations and code that lack consistency and are difficult to modify. Thus any update to the enterprise security model will be reflected on all IT systems that use our security engineering platform. This is another key issue in environments where multiple applications must enforce the same security requirements. Having one place to manage security reduces the probability of errors, delays, and inconsistencies. Moreover, automating the propagation of security changes to underlying systems simplifies the enterprise security management process.

One may argue that MDSE@R may lead to a more vulnerable system as we did not consider security engineering during design time. Our argument is that at design time we need to think more about building secure systems. However, given that we continue to discover a lot of vulnerabilities in systems even those with design-time security consideration, we have supported our approach with both continuous vulnerability analysis and mitigation. The vulnerability analysis component is based on formal vulnerability definition schema that includes vulnerability signature and mitigation actions. Using abstract representation instead of source code helps to generalize/abstract our analysis from programming language and platform details. It also helps to make the approach more scalable for larger applications.

AOP is always suspected as a source of potential security attacks [49] given that a malicious user might be able to plug vulnerable aspect code that can alter the innovation parameter, redirect the request or discard it completely. Moreover, using AOP to integrate security aspects as a cross cutting concern is also questionable given that these security aspects could lead to inconsistent update of system properties. However, the authors did not stop using AOP to develop their permission model, they have suggested a set of recommendations when using AOP such as dealing woven code, define appropriate language extension, and analyze weaver components for potential flaws. To avoid such issues, we disable the write permission on the interceptor document and security handlers. Thus only our platform will have write access to these documents.

Security adaptation of existing software systems: The security engineering of existing services (extending system-security capabilities) has three possible scenarios: (i) systems that already have their SDMs, we can use MDSE@R directly to specify and enforce security at runtime; (ii) systems without SDMs, we reverse engineer parts of system models (specifically the class diagram) using MDSE@R. Then we can use MDSE@R to engineer required system security. Finally, systems with built-in security, in this case we can use MDSE@R to add new security capabilities only. MDSE cannot help modifying or disabling existing security. We have built another tool (re-aspects) to leave out existing built-in security methods and partial code using modified AOP techniques.

Security and performance trade-off: The selection of the level of details to apply security on depends on the criticality of the system. In some situations like web applications, we may intercept calls to the presentation layer only (webserver) while considering the other layers secured by default (not publicly accessible). In other cases, such as integration with a certain web service or using third-party component, we may need to have security enforced at the method level (for certain methods only). Security and performance trade-off is another dilemma to consider. The more security validations and checks the more resources required. MDSE@R enables adding security only whenever needed. Thus, when we believe that the system operational environment we can reduce the security controls required which improves system performance and vice versa. So the trade-off between performance and security is now at the hand of system/security admins.

Hybrid vulnerability analysis: From our experience in developing signatures of the OWASP Top 10 vulnerabilities (most frequently reported vulnerabilities) we determined that:

1. the accuracy of our vulnerability analysis depends heavily on the accuracy of the specified vulnerability signatures;
2. it is better to use dynamic analysis tools with certain vulnerabilities, such as cross site reference forgery, because these vulnerabilities can be handled by the web server. This means static analysis may result in high FP, if used;
3. some vulnerabilities can be easily identified and located by static analysis such as SQLI and XSS vulnerabilities; and
4. some vulnerabilities such as DOM-based SQL and XSS vulnerabilities need a collaborating static and dynamic analysis to locate them.

We believe that combining static and dynamic analysis is needed to increase the precision and recall rates. Static analysis approaches usually result in high false positives as they work on source code level—that is, the vulnerability may be addressed on the component or the application level. Employing dynamic vulnerability analysis can solve this problem. However, dynamic vulnerability analysis approaches cannot help locating specific code snippets where vulnerabilities exist. Moreover, they do not help testing code coverage by generating all possible test cases.

Virtual patching trade-off: From our experiments in the mitigation actions and security controls integrations, we found that although the use of WAFs is a straightforward solution, it is not always feasible to use WAF to block all discovered vulnerabilities. The selection of the entity level to apply security controls on (application, component, method, etc.) impacts the application performance—that is, instead of securing only vulnerable methods, we intercept and secure (add more calls) the whole component requests. A key point that worth mentioning is that the administration of security controls should be managed by the service/cloud provider admins. We focus on integrating controls within vulnerable entities. Our vulnerability mitigation component works online without a need for manual integration with the applications/services under its management. The overhead added by the mitigation action can be easily saved if the service developers worked out a new service patch. In this case, the vulnerability analysis component will not report such vulnerability. Thus, the mitigation component will not inject security controls.

Pros & cons: The key benefits of our adaptation approach are: (i) we support both manual security adaptation and rule-based adaptation. Most of the existing efforts either focus on engineering systems to support adaptiveness with either intensive development required, or limiting the approach to specific security properties—for example, access control; (ii) our approach also takes into consideration different sources of adaptation including: new security requirements, current system status (using security monitors), and/or reported security vulnerabilities. Most of the existing efforts consider only one source: either new security requirements or monitored system status but not reported vulnerabilities; and (iii) we adopt security externalization and MDE techniques, which make it easier to change system-security capabilities whenever needed and at system, component, and method levels based on user experience and needs. The security model itself can be shared between different systems. Thus, an enterprise security model can be easily managed.

5.7 CHAPTER SUMMARY

In this chapter we discussed our adaptive security engineering approach, which enable adapting software security capabilities at runtime based on the new security objectives, risks/threats, requirements as well as the newly reported vulnerabilities. We categorize the source of adaptation in terms of manual adaptation (managed by end users), and automated adaption (automatically triggered by the platform). The platform makes use of the formal vulnerability definition schema, the formal signature-based security analysis, externalization of security engineering using AOP, and MDE techniques.

APPENDIX
PLATFORM IMPLEMENTATION

The architecture of our approach is aggregate of two key components: the security engineering at runtime (MDSE@R) and the security vulnerability analysis. Both of them are end-user oriented—that is, both depend on end-user specifications in terms of security objectives, requirements, controls, properties, vulnerabilities, and mitigation action. Both components are discussed below in more details.

MDSE@R: MODEL-DRIVEN SECURITY ENGINEERING AT RUNTIME

The architecture of the MDSE@R platform is shown in Fig. 5.12. It consists of a system-description modeling tool (1), a security specification modeling tool (2), a repository for the system and security models (3), a library of registered security controls and extensible security patterns that can be used by security engineers in enforcing their security needs (4), a system container that manages system execution and intercepts requests and function calls for system entry points at runtime (5), and a security test case generator (6) that is used to test the integration of configured application with required security controls.

The system-description modeler (1) was developed as an extension of Microsoft VS 2010 modeler with an UML profile to enable system engineers modeling their systems' details with different perspectives including system features, components, deployment, and classes. The UML profile defines

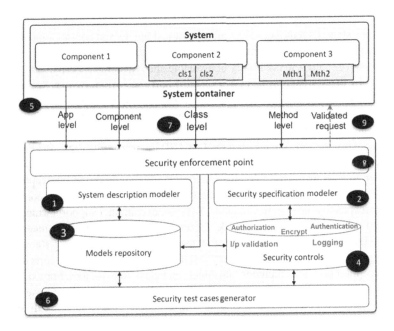

FIG. 5.12

MDSE@R architecture.

stereotypes and attributes to maintain the track back and foreword relations between entities from different models. Moreover, a set of security attributes to maintain the security concepts (objectives, requirements, and controls) mapped to system entities. The minimum level of details expected from the system provider is the system deployment model. MDSE@R uses this model to reverse engineer system classes using .Net Reflections.

The *security specification modeler tool* (2) is a VS 2010 plug-in. It enables application customers, represented by their security engineers, to specify the security attributes and capabilities that must be enforced on the system and/or its operational environment. The security modeler delivers a set of security DSVLs. The security-objectives DSVL captures customer's security objectives and the relationships between them. Each objective has a criticality level and the defense strategy to be followed: preventive, detective, or recovery. The Security requirements DSVL captures customer's security requirements and relationships between requirements including composition and referencing relations. The Security Architecture DSVL captures security architectures and designs of the customer operational environment in terms of security zones and security level for each zone; security objectives, requirements, and controls to be enforced in each layer; components and systems to be hosted in each layer; security services, mechanisms, and standards to be deployed in each layer or referenced from other layers. The security controls DSVL captures details of security controls that are registered and deployed in the customer environment and relationships between these and the security requirements they cover. The system models, security models, interception documents, and security specification documents are maintained under one repository (3). We use Visual Studio T4 Templates and code generation language to generate these documents from the software and SSMs and mapping between both sets of models. T4 templates are a mixture of text blocks and control logic that can generate a text file. The control logic is written as program code in C#.

The *security controls database* is a library of available and registered security patterns and controls. It can be extended by the system providers or by a third-party security provider. Security controls implement certain APIs as defined by the security enforcement point in order to be able to integrate with target security control systems. Having a single enforcement point with a predefined interface for each security control category enables security providers to integrate with systems without having to redevelop adopters for every system. We adopted the OWASP Enterprise Security API library as a part of MDSE@R security controls database.

To support runtime security enforcement, MDSE@R uses a combined interceptor and AOP approach. Whenever a client or application component makes request to any system component method, this request is intercepted by the system container. The system container supports wrapping of both new developments and existing systems. For new development, SwinSoft system engineers should use the Unity application block delivered by Microsoft PnP team to intercept calls to registered classes. This is a .NET-based implementation of the dependency injection design pattern. It supports dynamic runtime injection of interception points on methods, attributes, and class constructors. For existing systems we adopted Yiihaw AOP for C#, where we can modify application binaries (dll and exe files) to add security aspects at any arbitrary method (in our implementation we add a call to our security enforcement point).

The *security test case generator* (6) uses the NUnit testing framework to partially automate security controls and system integration testing. We developed a test case generator library that generates a set of security test cases for authentication, authorization, input validation, and cryptography for every enforcement point defined in the interceptors' document. MDSE@R uses NUnit library to fire the generated test cases and notifies security engineers via test case execution result logs. At runtime, whenever a request for a system resource is received (7), the system container checks for the requested method in the live interceptors' document. If a matching found, the system delegates this request with the given parameters to the default interception handler—security enforcement point (8).

The security enforcement point (9) is a class library that we developed to act as the default interception handler and the mediator between the system and the security controls. Whenever a request for a target application operation is received, it checks the system-security specification document to enforce the particular system-security controls required. It then invokes such security controls through APIs published in the security control database (4). The security enforcement point validates a request via the appropriate security control(s) configured and specified, for example, imposes authentication, authorization, encryption, or decryption of message contents. The validated request is then propagated to the method for execution (10).

Both system and security modeling tools are based on VS 2010 Modeling SDK that enables developing DSVLs integrated with VS IDE. To develop each DSVL, we developed a metamodel for the DSL domain and specified the corresponding shapes that visualize each domain model concept. Then we specified the mapping between the domain concepts' attributes and the shape compartments. Finally we developed code generation templates that generate the system live interceptors' document and the security specification document from the system and security models. Our modeling tools use a repository to maintain models developed either by the system engineers or by the security engineers. It also maintains the system live interceptors' document and security specification document. Examples of

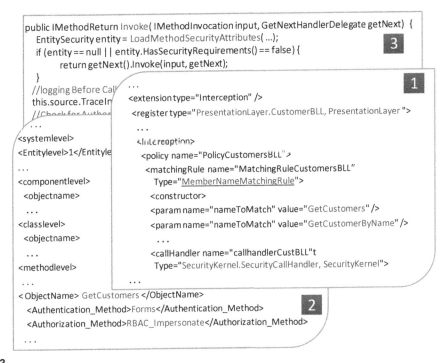

```
public IMethodReturn Invoke( IMethodInvocation input, GetNextHandlerDelegate getNext) {
    EntitySecurity entity = LoadMethodSecurityAttributes( ...);
    if (entity == null || entity.HasSecurityRequirements() == false) {
        return getNext().Invoke(input, getNext);                                    [3]
    }
    //logging Before Call
    this.source.TraceIn...
    //Check for Authori...
    ...
<systemlevel>
<Entitylevel>1</Entityle...
...
<componentlevel>
 <objectname>
   ...
<classlevel>
 <objectname>
   ...
<methodlevel>
   ...
< ObjectName> GetCustomers </ObjectName>
    <Authentication_Method>Forms</Authentication_Method>
    <Authorization_Method>RBAC_Impersonate</Authorization_Method>
    ...
```

```
...                                                               [1]
<extension type="Interception" />
 <register type="PresentationLayer.CustomerBLL, PresentationLayer ">
   ...
 <interception>
  <policy name="PolicyCustomersBLL">
   <matchingRule name="MatchingRuleCustomersBLL"
     Type="MemberNameMatchingRule">
    <constructor>
     <param name="nameToMatch" value="GetCustomers" />
     <param name="nameToMatch" value="GetCustomerByName" />
      ...
    <callHandler name="callhandlerCustBLL"t
     Type="SecurityKernel.SecurityCallHandler, SecurityKernel">
```

[2]

FIG. 5.13

Examples of MDSE@R weaved system interceptors and security specification files.

these documents are shown in Fig. 5.13. Examples of MDSE@R weaved system interceptors and security specification files. This example shows a sample of the Galactic interceptors' document generated from the specified security-system mapping. It informs the system container to intercept GetCustomers and GetCustomerByName methods (1); a sample of Swinburne security specification file defining the security controls to be enforced on every intercepted point (2); and a sample of the security enforcement point API that injects the necessary security control calls before and after application code is run (3).

VULNERABILITY ANALYSIS AND MITIGATION

We developed a GUI, as shown in Fig. 5.14, to assist security experts in capturing vulnerability signatures' in OCL. This provides vulnerability signature editing, validity checking, and testing these signatures' specifications on simple target applications. We use an existing OCL parser to parse and validate signatures against our system-description metamodel. Once validated, the vulnerability signature is stored in our weakness signatures database. To parse the given program source code and generate a system abstract model, we use **NReFactory** .NET parser Library, which parses source code and generates its corresponding AST (it supports VB.Net and C#. We are currently working on parsers for PHP and Java). Applications without source code—that is, only binaries are available—are decompiled using **ILSPY**. This is currently supported for C# and VB.NET. We developed a class library to

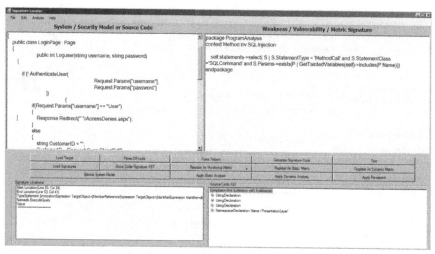

FIG. 5.14

Snapshot of the vulnerability analysis tool.

transform the generated AST into a more abstract (summarized) representation that conforms to our SDM. Our signature locator has an OCL translator that translates a given OCL signature into a corresponding C# class with a signature matching method that checks the passed in system entity looking for matches to specified signatures. The OCL functions library maintains a set of functions that extend the system-description metamodel entities capabilities and can be used during the vulnerability analysis phase. This includes control-flow analysis, data-flow analysis, and tainted-data analysis. These functions can be extended with further analysis functions based on future vulnerability analysis needs. The OCL to C# transformer performs a transformation for these functions as well as new OCL signatures once defined. Program slicing and taint analysis techniques (core techniques in program and security analysis area) can be easily captured in OCL. Platforms' profiles are specified in XML documents that contain information about specific platforms' details. It is used to set the context of the signature locator according to the software.

REFERENCES

[1] B. Fabian, S. Gürses, M. Heisel, T. Santen, H. Schmidt, A comparison of security requirements engineering methods, Requir. Eng. 15 (2010) 7–40.

[2] R. Barnett, WAF virtual patching challenge: securing WebGoat with ModSecurity, (2009).

[3] R. Anderson, Security Engineering: A Guide to Building Dependable Distributed Systems, John Wiley and Sons, New York, NY, 2001.

[4] A. Dardenne, A.v. Lamsweerde, S. Fickas, Goal-directed requirements acquisition, in: Selected Papers of the Sixth International Workshop on Software Specification and Design, 1993.

[5] H.S.F. Al-Subaie, T.S.E. Maibaum, Evaluating the effectiveness of a goal-oriented requirements engineering method, in: Proceedings of the Fourth International Workshop on Comparative Evaluation in Requirements Engineering (CERE'06—RE'06 Workshop), 2006.

[6] A. Lamsweerde, S. Brohez, et al., System goals to intruder anti-goals: attack generation and resolution for security requirements engineering, in: Proceedings of the RE'03 Workshop on Requirements for High Assurance Systems, Monterey, 2003, pp. 49–56.

[7] L. Liu, E. Yu, J. Mylopoulos, Secure ¡*: engineering secure software systems through social analysis, Int. J. Softw. Inform. 3 (2009) 89–120.

[8] L. Liu, E. Yu, J. Mylopoulos, Security and privacy requirements analysis within a social setting, in: Proceedings of the 11th IEEE International Requirements Engineering Conference, 2003.

[9] H. Mouratidis, P. Giorgini, Secure Tropos: a security-oriented extension of the Tropos methodology, Int. J. Softw. Eng. Knowl. Eng. 17 (2007) 285–309.

[10] H. Mouratidis, J. Jurjens, From goal-driven security requirements engineering to secure design, Int. J. Intell. Syst. 25 (2010) 813–840.

[11] R. Matulevičius, N. Mayer, H. Mouratidis, E. Dubois, P. Heymans, N. Genon, Adapting secure tropos for security risk management in the early phases of information systems development, in: Proceedings of the 20th International Conference on Advanced Information Systems Engineering, 2008, pp. 541–555.

[12] G. Sindre, A. Opdahl, Eliciting security requirements with misuse cases, Requir. Eng. 10 (2005) 34–44.

[13] D.G. Firesmith, Security use cases, J. Object Technol. 2 (3) (2003) 53–64.

[14] J. Jürjens, Towards development of secure systems using UMLsec, in: Fundamental Approaches to Software Engineering, vol. 2029, Springer, Berlin, Heidelberg, 2001, pp. 187–200.

[15] J. Jurjens, J. Schreck, Y. Yu, Automated analysis of permission-based security using UMLsec, in: Proceedings of the 11th International Conference on Fundamental Approaches to Software Engineering, 2008, pp. 292–295.

[16] J. Jürjens, UMLsec: extending UML for secure systems development, in: Proceedings of the 5th International Conference on the Unified Modeling Language, 2002.

[17] L. Montrieux, J. Jurjens, C.B. Haley, Y. Yu, P.-Y. Schobbens, H. Toussaint, Tool support for code generation from a UMLsec property, in: Proceedings of the IEEE/ACM International Conference on Automated Software Engineering, Antwerp, Belgium, 2010.

[18] T. Lodderstedt, D. Basin, J. Doser, SecureUML: a UML-based modeling language for model-driven security, in: Proceedings of the 5th International Conference on the Unified Modeling Language, Dresden, Germany, 2002, pp. 426–441.

[19] F. Satoh, Y. Nakamura, N.K. Mukhi, M. Tatsubori, K. Ono, Methodology and tools for end-to-end SOA security configurations, in: IEEE Congress on Services—Part I, 2008, pp. 307–314.

[20] Y. Shiroma, H. Washizaki, Y. Fukazawa, A. Kubo, Model-driven security patterns application based on dependences among patterns, in: Proceedings of the International Conference on Availability, Reliability, and Security, Krakow, 2010, pp. 555–559.

[21] N.A. Delessy, E.B. Fernandez, A pattern-driven security process for SOA applications, in: Proceedings of the Third International Conference on Availability, Reliability and Security, 2008, pp. 416–421.

[22] M. Schnjakin, M. Menzel, C. Meinel, A pattern-driven security advisor for service-oriented architectures, in: Proceedings of the 2009 ACM Workshop on Secure Web Services, Chicago, Illinois, USA, 2009.

[23] M. Hafner, M. Memon, R. Breu, SeAAS—a reference architecture for security services in SOA, J. Univers. Comput. Sci. 15 (2009) 2916–2936.

[24] M. Alam, Model driven security engineering for the realization of dynamic security requirements in collaborative systems, in: T. Kühne (Ed.), Models in Software Engineering, vol. 4364, Springer, Berlin, 2007, pp. 278–287.

[25] M. Alam, R. Breu, M. Hafner, Modeling permissions in a (U/X)ML world, in: Proceedings of the First International Conference on Availability, Reliability and Security, 2006, 8 pp.

[26] V. Bertocci, Programming Windows Identity Foundation, Microsoft Press, Redmond, WA, 2010.

[27] L. Peng, Y. Zhao-Lin, Analysis and extension of authentication and authorization of Acegi security framework on spring, Comput. Eng. Des. (6) (2007) 1313–1316.

[28] L.A. Abdulkarim, Z. Lukszo, Information security implementation difficulties in critical infrastructures: smart metering case, in: Proceedings of the International Conference on Networking, Sensing and Control, 2010, pp. 715–720.

[29] M. Hafiz, R.E. Johnson, Improving perimeter security with security-oriented program transformations, in: ICSE Workshop on Software Engineering for Secure Systems, 2009, pp. 61–67.

[30] M. Hafiz, R.E. Johnson, Security-oriented program transformations, in: Proceedings of the 5th Annual Workshop on Cyber Security and Information Intelligence Research: Cyber Security and Information Intelligence Challenges and Strategies, Oak Ridge, Tennessee, 2009.

[31] V. Ganapathy, D. King, T. Jaeger, S. Jha, Mining security-sensitive operations in legacy code using concept analysis, in: Proceedings of the 29th International Conference on Software Engineering, 2007.

[32] P. O'Sullivan, K. Anand, A. Kothan, M. Smithson, R. Barua, A.D. Keromytis, Retrofitting security in COTS software with binary rewriting, in: Proceedings of the 26th IFIP International Information Security Conference (SEC), Lucerne, Switzerland, 2011.

[33] V. Ganapathy, T. Jaeger, S. Jha, Retrofitting legacy code for authorization policy enforcement, in: Proceedings of the 2006 IEEE Symposium on Security and Privacy, 2006, pp. 15–229.

[34] I.S. Welch, R.J. Stroud, Re-engineering security as a crosscutting concern, Comput. J. 46 (2003) 578–589.

[35] A. Elkhodary, J. Whittle, A survey of approaches to adaptive application security, in: Proceedings of the 2007 International Workshop on Software Engineering for Adaptive and Self-Managing Systems (SEAMS '07), 2007, pp. 1–16.

[36] B. Hashii, S. Malabarba, R. Pandey, et al., Supporting reconfigurable security policies for mobile programs, in: Proceedings of the 9th International World Wide Web Conference on Computer Networks, Amsterdam, The Netherlands, 2000, pp. 77–93.

[37] K. Scott, N. Kumar, S. Velusamy, et al., Retargetable and reconfigurable software dynamic translation, in: Proceedings of the International Symposium on Code Generation and Optimization, San Francisco, California, 2003.

[38] F. Sanchez-Cid, A. Mana, SERENITY pattern-based software development life-cycle, in: 19th International Workshop on Database and Expert Systems Application, 2008, pp. 305–309.

[39] F. Sanchez-Cid, A. Mana, Patterns for automated management of security and dependability solutions, in: Proceedings of the 18th International Conference on Database and Expert Systems Applications, 2007.

[40] A. Benameur, S. Fenet, A. Saidane, S.K. Sinha, A pattern-based general security framework: an eBusiness case study, in: Proceedings of the 11th IEEE International Conference on High Performance Computing and Communications, 2009, pp. 339–346.

[41] B. Morin, T. Mouelhi, F. Fleurey, Security-driven model-based dynamic adaptation, in: Proceedings of the IEEE/ACM International Conference on Automated Software Engineering, Antwerp, Belgium, 2010.

[42] E. Yuan, N. Esfahani, S. Malek, A systematic survey of self-protecting software systems, ACM Trans. Auton. Adapt. Syst. 8 (2014) 17.

[43] M. Almorsy, A. Ibrahim, J. Grundy, Adaptive security management in SaaS applications, in: S. Nepal, M. Pathan (Eds.), Security, Privacy and Trust in Cloud Systems, Springer, Berlin, 2014, pp. 73–102.

[44] M. Almorsy, J. Grundy, A.S. Ibrahim, MDSE@R: model-driven security engineering at runtime, in: Proceedings of the 4th International Symposium on Cyberspace Safety and Security, Melbourne, Australia, 2012.

[45] M. Almorsy, J. Grundy, SecDSVL: a domain-specific visual language to support enterprise security modelling, in: 2014 Australian Conference on Software Engineering, Sydney, 2014.

[46] M. Almorsy, J. Grundy, A.S. Ibrahim, Supporting automated vulnerability analysis using formalized vulnerability signatures, in: Proceedings of the 27th IEEE/ACM International Conference on Automated Software Engineering, Essen, Germany, 2012.

[47] M. Almorsy, J. Grundy, A.S. Ibrahim, Automated software architecture security risk analysis using formalized signatures, in: Proceedings of the 36th International Conference of Software Engineering, San Francisco, 2013, pp. 300–309.

[48] M. Almorsy, J. Grundy, A. Ibrahim, VAM-aaS: online cloud services security vulnerability analysis and mitigation-as-a-service, in: X.S. Wang, I. Cruz, A. Delis, G. Huang (Eds.), Web Information Systems Engineering—WISE 2012, Springer, Berlin, 2012, pp. 411–425.

[49] B.D. Win, F. Piessens, W. Joosen, How secure is AOP and what can we do about it? in: Proceedings of the 2006 International Workshop on Software Engineering for Secure Systems, Shanghai, China, 2006.

ANALYZING AND EVALUATING TRADE-OFFS IN SELF-ADAPTIVE SOFTWARE ARCHITECTURES

AUTOMATED INFERENCE TECHNIQUES TO ASSIST WITH THE CONSTRUCTION OF SELF-ADAPTIVE SOFTWARE

S. Malek*, K. Canavera[†], N. Esfahani[‡]

University of California, Irvine, Irvine, CA, United States[*] George Mason University, Fairfax, VA, United States[†]
Google Inc, Mountain View, CA, United States[‡]

6.1 INTRODUCTION

As software engineers have developed new techniques to address the complexity associated with the construction of modern-day software systems, an equally pressing need has risen for mechanisms that automate and simplify the management of those systems after they are deployed, that is, during runtime. It is estimated that one-half of a company's total IT budget is spent on managing and troubleshooting its IT infrastructure [1,2]. According to Ganek [3], vice president of IBM Corporation's Software Group, "the spiraling cost of managing the increasingly complex computing systems is becoming a significant inhibitor that threatens to undermine the future growth and societal benefits of information technology."

To mitigate the difficulty of managing ever increasingly complex software, approaches that enable substantially higher levels of automation have become appealing. A vision of *autonomic computing* [4] promoting the development of *self-adaptive software* has started to emerge. A self-adaptive software is capable of automatically modifying its behavior at runtime to achieve certain functional or quality of service objectives [5,6]. This vision, however, has remained largely elusive. The overarching problem is that enabling a software system to manage automatically itself at runtime tends to exacerbate the complexity of constructing the software in the first place [5,7]. This has been the key obstacle that has hindered adoption of self-adaptation capabilities in real world products. This chapter aims to explore and, at least partially, answer the following question: What automated techniques and tools could be developed to assist the developers with construction of dependable self-adaptive software?

More specifically, there are three issues with the existing approaches that heavily contribute to the problem outlined above and form the focus of this project: (1) *Manually intensive*: Existing techniques

Managing Trade-offs in Adaptable Software Architectures. http://dx.doi.org/10.1016/B978-0-12-802855-1.00006-X

place a heavy burden on the engineer to manually construct numerous models (e.g., queuing network models, Markov models), which are used at runtime to assess the impact of adaptation choices on the system's quality objectives (e.g., response time, availability). This is a daunting task, especially when one considers the complexity of today's software systems, and the fact that most practitioners are not adept at those modeling languages. (2) *Fragile*: The manually constructed models make the management logic fragile to any change in the running software that was not account for in their construction. This challenges the engineer with yet another daunting task of thinking about all possible runtime conditions prior to system deployment. (3) *Inefficient*: the manually constructed models are often static and coarse-grained, and thus do not provide the level of detail that is necessary for efficient decision-making and fast adaptation of the system.

In our research over the past few years [8–12], we have tackled the complexity of engineering self-adaptive software by pursuing an alternative approach. The premise guiding our research is that any technique aimed at alleviating the complexity of runtime management at the expense of exacerbating the complexity of developing the software in the first place is not a plausible solution. The resulting solution heavily draws on inference techniques, such as machine learning [13] and data mining [14], to derive *automatically* the models necessary for building a self-adaptive software system. In particular, our work so far has followed two complementary thrusts: (1) A machine learning approach for goal management: we have used machine learning techniques to automatically derive the models predicting the impact of adaptation actions (i.e., enabling a particular capability at runtime, such as caching or authentication) on the system's quality objectives (e.g., response time, availability) [9,11]. These types of models are used to make management decisions to fix problems that may arise at runtime and achieve the system's objectives, that is, goals. (2) A data mining approach for change management: we have used data mining techniques to derive automatically the models expressing the probabilistic dependencies between the components in the system [8,10,12]. These types of models are used to ensure changes in the running software do not create inconsistency, and jeopardize the system's functionality.

In this chapter, we provide an overview of several challenges with the state-of-the-art, outline an inference-based approach for engineering adaptive software that aims to address these challenges, specific elements of which have appeared in several disjoint publications [8–12], and elaborate on the areas of future research. The contributions of an inference-based approach are threefold. (1) Automatic derivation of the models for runtime management of applications significantly reduces the manual engineering effort. (2) The ability to automatically adjust and fine-tune the runtime models to emerging patterns of behavior makes self-adaptive software developed in this manner resilient to unexpected changes that may occur at runtime. (3) The highly detailed and dynamic models learned using the proposed approach improve the efficiency of both making decisions and effecting changes.

The remainder of this chapter is organized as follows. Section 6.2 describes a running example that is used for illustration of challenges as well as explanation of the approach. Section 6.3 demonstrates the challenges of engineering self-adaptive software, particularly with respect to the manual construction of models for goal management and change management. Section 6.4 provides an overview of the overarching approach devised in our research. Sections 6.5 and 6.6 describe our automated inference techniques for goal management and change management, respectively. Finally, Sections 6.7 provides an overview of the related work, and Section 6.8 wraps up the chapter with the concluding remarks.

6.2 MOTIVATING APPLICATION

Two major paradigm shifts are increasingly defining the future of computing. Self-management capabilities are sought after in both of these paradigms. First is the migration of software to mobile, pervasive, and cyber-physical settings. Since these environments are known to be highly dynamic and unpredictable, it is difficult to determine the best configuration for the software prior to its deployment, forcing some of those decisions to be made at runtime. Second, software is increasingly provisioned from parts that are developed, maintained, and operated by independent parties, that is, *service-orientation*. Here, no single stakeholder oversees and controls all parts, which may change over time. Yet, by assembling the whole, one commits to achieve a certain goal, formalized in a contract that defines a service-level agreement. The software in these paradigms is expected to operate under changing situations and conditions, and the only way that can be achieved is to employ dependable self-management capabilities.

For the purpose of motivating and describing the research, we use a service-oriented software, called travel reservation system (TRS), but note that the principles and techniques developed as part of this project will be applicable in other domains as well. TRS is a web-based portal for preparing and making travel reservations. TRS relies on several internal and external services. Fig. 6.1 shows only a small subset of its architecture for illustration purposes. The actual software developed by an external organization is significantly larger than what is depicted here. TRS needs to be self-adaptive to deal with unexpected situations, such as failure of services in meeting their advertised service-level agreements. To that end, TRS may choose from numerous runtime solutions at its disposal, such as swap service providers that do not meet their service-level agreements, enable caching to improve performance during a traffic spike, change authentication protocol to thwart a security attack. The adaptation logic of TRS also needs to balance trade-offs, for example, improving security may degrade response time. The approach described in this chapter tackles the complexity of enabling a system such as TRS to become self-adaptive.

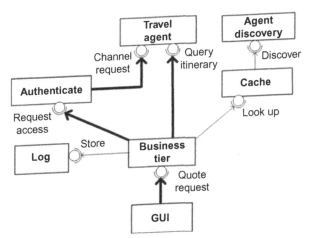

FIG. 6.1

Subset of travel reservation system's software architecture. The bold path indicates the *get price quote* scenario.

6.3 SHORTCOMINGS WITH THE STATE-OF-THE-ART

Two seminal frameworks have highly influenced the way self-adaptive software systems are conceptualized. First is *MAPE-K* from IBM [4], which advocates an architecture consisting of four types of components that operate on the managed system and provide *monitoring, analysis, planning,* and *execution (MAPE)* capabilities. MAPE components share various models using what is known as *knowledgebase,* resulting in MAPE-K. Second framework is the so-called three-*layer architecture* [6], where the three layers provide separation of concern as follows: (1) *goal management* at the top is responsible for ensuring the managed application satisfies its quality objectives, such as response time and availability, by developing new configurations. (2) *Change management* below that is responsible for executing the steps necessary to "safely" transition the software system to a new configuration. (3) *Component control* at the bottom provides the low-level facilities, such as (un)binding software modules in the runtime environment.

Our approach targets the challenges of realizing models that comprise the MAPE-K's *knowledgebase.* Moreover, in our research so far, we have focused on *goal management* and *change management* layers, mainly because those currently pose the greatest challenge. There are numerous existing platforms (middleware solutions) [15–19] for realizing component control capabilities that could benefit from the concepts described here. The remainder of this section provides an overview of the state-of-the-art in goal management and change management, in particular their shortcomings, which motivate this research.

6.3.1 GOAL MANAGEMENT

Most existing approaches (e.g., [20,21]) to goal management leverage manually constructed analytical models. These models are used together with the monitored data to predict the impact of adaptation choices on system's quality objectives, that is, goals. For instance, queuing network models [22] and hidden Markov models [23] have been used extensively for assessing the system's performance and reliability properties, respectively. When there are several quality attributes of interest, a utility function representing the desirable trade-offs is also used [24,25]. The output from goal management is a new configuration for the software, often in the form of a new software architecture [26].

There are three issues with the existing approaches:

Manually intensive—they place a heavy burden on the engineers to construct manually analytical models, especially when one considers the complexity of today's software systems. These models often need to be customized to the unique characteristics of each application, and provide little opportunity for reuse. Further exacerbating the situation is the fact that practitioners are not adept at those modeling languages (e.g., queuing networks, Markov chains).
Fragile—any analytical model inevitably relies on some simplifying assumptions by the virtue of being an abstract representation of a system or its environment. For instance, in the construction of a queuing network model, an engineer may make some assumptions as to the main sources of delay in the system. If any of those assumptions are not borne out or become invalidated due to some unexpected events or conditions, the analysis, and hence the adaptation decisions become inaccurate.

Inefficient—most formulations of goal management problem that aim to optimize the system's quality objectives by finding the best configuration are NP-complete (e.g., [20,21]). That is, at the state-of-the-art, it is not possible to prune the search space without trading off optimality. Referring to TRS example of Fig. 6.1, let us assume that *Cache*, *Authenticate*, and *Log* are all optional components that could be installed at runtime. Given a response time problem and a queuing network model of the system, there is no mechanism to find the best configuration by discriminating among the $2^{Optional\ components} = 2^3 = 8$ architectures, other than evaluating all. The state-of-the-art is brute force exploration of the configuration space, and takes a long time to solve in any sizable system with many adaptation choices.

6.3.2 CHANGE MANAGEMENT

In the change management literature [27], *transaction* is defined as an exchange of information between two components by which the state of a component is affected. A *dependent transaction* is a transaction whose completion depends on the completion of consequent transactions. It is commonly accepted that to ensure a component remains in a consistent state during/after adaptation, it should not be changed in the middle of a (dependent) transaction. Fig. 6.2 shows the transactions comprising the *get price quote* scenario of TRS. Here, *T4* is an independent transaction, while *T1* is a dependent transaction. Consider a situation in which *Business Tier* component is replaced after sending request *e2*, but before receiving response *e2'*. Since the newly installed component does not have the same state as the

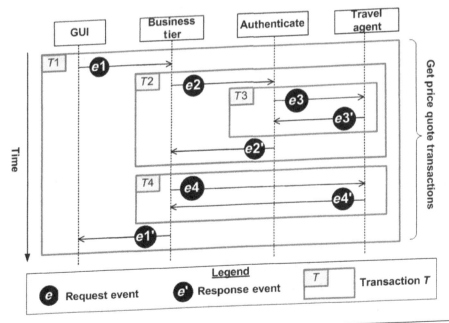

FIG. 6.2

Dependent transactions comprising TRS's *get price quote* scenario.

old one, it may not be able to handle $e2'$ and initiate $T4$, resulting in an inconsistency, and potentially the system's failure.

Even if the component is stateless, inconsistency problems may arise. Consider a stateless compression component that compresses and decompresses data using two interfaces that are reverse of one another. Replacing this component with one that uses a different type of compression algorithm in the middle of a transaction could break the system's functionality, since the decompression cannot be performed on data that was compressed using the old component. By the same reasoning, state transfer in the case of stateful components is not sufficient to address inconsistency due to adaptation. Moreover, it breaks the *black-box* treatment of components—the premise underlying this line of research is to avoid placing restrictions or making changes to the internal logic of components [27,28].

The state-of-the-art for safe adaptation of system is *quiescence* [27]. A component is in quiescence and can be adapted if (1) it is *inactivated*, meaning it is not participating in any transaction, and (2) all of the components that may initiate transactions requiring services of that component are *passivated*. A component is *passive* if it continues to receive and process transactions, but does not initiate any new transactions. At runtime, the decision about which part of the system should be passivated to replace a component is made using a *component dependency model*, such as that showed in Fig. 6.1. For instance, to change the *Authenticate* component, the *Business Tier* and *GUI* components need to be passivated, since those are the components that may initiate a transaction on the *Authenticate* component.

Interestingly, a similar set of issues as that facing goal management can be observed here as well:

Manually intensive—quiescence requires the engineer to develop manually not only models of the component dependencies, but also the logic necessary for controlling the internal behavior of components, that is, for passivating them. This problem is exacerbated in emerging systems where the dependencies become known at runtime, such as service-oriented software, as well as systems where the component's implementation is not available, such as systems composed of commercial-off-the-shelf components.

Fragile—component dependency models, such as Fig. 6.1, are tightly coupled with the application logic. As the system evolves, the internal logic of components may change, leading to inaccurate dependency models, which if used for making changes may break the system's consistency.

Inefficient—quiescence is known to be very disruptive [28]. This is particularly true for changing a component that is depended upon by many others, as they all have to be passivated. In the worst case, updating a component that all other component may indirectly initiate a transaction on is equivalent to stopping the entire system. Thus, quiescence has the potential of significantly slowing down the system.

6.4 OVERVIEW OF INFERENCE-BASED TECHNIQUES

Our research aims to address the shortcomings outlined in the previous section by fundamentally changing the way self-adaptive software is designed and developed. Our objective is to do away with manually intensive processes by providing the techniques and tools that can empower a software system to *learn* automatically how to manage itself. A byproduct of this automation is that fragility and inefficiency issues can also be dealt with. We have followed a two-pronged research agenda as follows:

1. *Learning-based approach for goal management*: We have developed a novel method of automatically deriving the models necessary for reasoning about adaptation choices using machine learning techniques. The result of learning is a set of relationships between the *adaptation alternatives* in the system and the *quality attributes* of interest (e.g., response time, availability). The novelty with respect to existing approaches is that the models used for making adaptation decisions are generated automatically, minimizing the required manual effort. The same process used to derive the initial models can be used to adjust them to emerging events and conditions at runtime. Moreover, using the learned models, it is possible to prune the search space significantly without compromising the quality of decisions.

2. *Mining-based approach for change management*: We have developed an approach for mining the execution history of a software system to derive a set of rules expressing the probabilistic relationships between occurrences of transactions in the system. Given a set of transactions currently running in the system, these rules can be used to predict the probability with which a component can be changed at a point in time without jeopardizing the system's functionality, while minimizing the interruptions. Finally, by continuously monitoring the transactions and the accuracy of predictions, the approach provides the means to adjust the rules as new patterns of interaction emerge.

The following two sections describe the two facets of this research agenda in more detail. Interested reader may find additional details in our prior publications on these topics [8–12].

6.5 LEARNING-BASED APPROACH FOR GOAL MANAGEMENT

The objective of learning in goal management is to derive a model that can quantify the impact of the *adaptation alternatives* on the *quality attributes* of interest (e.g., response time, availability). The adaptation alternatives correspond to variation points in the software that could be exercised at runtime. Each variation point is what we call a *feature*, a concept that we have borrowed from software product line engineering [29–31], except here we propose to use features as units of adaptation. We refer to the quality attributes monitored from the running system as *metrics*. Here, we assume one of the existing technologies (e.g., [32–34]) is used to measure and collect the required metrics from the running software system.

Fig. 6.3A shows a feature model representing the variability in a subset of TRS. Here, there are four features in the system and one common *core*. The features in the example use two kinds of relationships: *dependency* and *mutual exclusion*. Feature modeling supports several other types of relationships (see [35]) that are also supported in our approach, but elided for brevity. The use of feature as an abstraction makes the approach independent of a particular adaptation methodology. For example, features may correspond to configuration parameters that are stored in configuration files (Fig. 6.3B), aspects that are dynamically weaved to the running system (Fig. 6.3C), or modification of the system's software architecture at well-defined variation points (Fig. 6.3D).

As depicted in Fig. 6.4, and further described in the following section, the approach consists of two cycles.

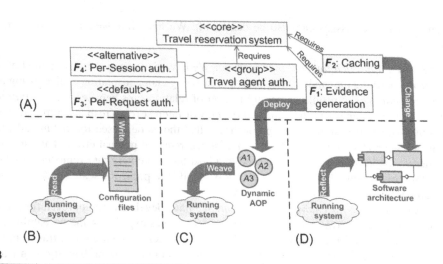

FIG. 6.3

(A) Feature model of TRS. Features may map to (B) parameters in a configuration file, (C) aspects that are (un) weaved with the running system, and (D) parts of the architecture providing the corresponding capabilities.

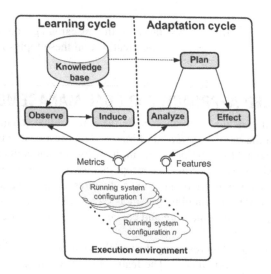

FIG. 6.4

Overview of the learning-based approach for making adaptation decisions.

6.5.1 LEARNING CYCLE

The learning cycle starts prior to system's deployment, and continues as needed throughout its operation. Prior to deployment, a benchmark or simulation environment is used to execute the software system in different feature combinations, and collect metrics (e.g., response time) from the running system. The metrics collected from benchmarks are used to induce a preliminary model that can predict the system's behavior under different configurations. The relationships identified through learning could be represented as functions that quantify the impact of features on metrics. In other words, features are *independent* variables, while metrics are *dependent*.

Modern machine learning techniques, such as *support vector machine* (SVM) [36], are capable of identifying the interactions among the independent variables, that is, features. A *feature interaction* occurs when the effect of two or more features being enabled is different from the sum of their individual effects.

The following steps comprising the learning cycle are executed for each benchmarked configuration (see Fig. 6.4). Based on the metrics collected from the running system, *observe* normalizes the data in preparation for learning, and *induce* learns the properties associated with a particular system variation and stores that in the *knowledgebase*, such that informed adaptation decisions can be made at runtime.

Based on the collected observations, the *induce* activity constructs a function that estimates the impact of making a feature selection on the metrics. Induce executes two steps to obtain these functions. The first step is a *significance test* that determines the features with the most significant impact on each metric. This allows for substantial reduction in the number of independent variables that learning needs to consider for each metric. After the significance test, the learning algorithm is employed, which given the normalized observations, derives the functions relating the impact of features on metrics. In an experiment in which we applied SVMs regression [36] to data obtained from TRS, we were able to derive the following function estimating the impact of features on the system's response time, indicated as G_1:

$$G_1 = 1.553F_1 - 0.673F_2 + 0.709F_3 + 0.163F_1F_3 - 0.843$$

Here each feature is assigned a coefficient that is effective only when the feature is enabled (i.e., it is set to "1"). The function estimates the impact of features on the system's response time. The learned functions are stored in the knowledge base for use in the adaptation cycle.

A similar process could be applied at runtime to fine-tune the models to conditions and events that may change the system's behavior. We keep track of the *prediction errors* by collecting the gap between predicted and actual impact of adaptations on the metrics. Once the prediction error reaches a certain threshold, it is taken as an indicator that new patterns of behavior are emerging, and the models are adjusted by initiating a new round of learning (*induce* activity *in* Fig. 6.4) using the collected data.

6.5.2 ADAPTATION CYCLE

As depicted in Fig. 6.4, the *adaptation cycle* uses the automatically inferred models to satisfy the quality objectives by executing the following three activities:

- Based on the metrics collected from the running system, *Analyze* calculates the achieved quality attributes to determine if a quality objective is violated.
- In case of a violation, *Plan* is invoked to search for a new configuration that restores the system's quality objectives. The search problem could be formulated in different ways. One possibility is to find a feature selection that satisfies all quality objectives, while a more sophisticated approach is to optimize (minimize/maximize) the quality objectives. When optimizing, utility functions representing the user preferences with respect to trade-offs among the quality objectives may be used [24,37].

- Given a new configuration, *Effect* determines the adaptation steps to place the system in that configuration. An adaptation step is to enable, disable, or swap a feature. The steps have to abide by the feature constraints (i.e., dependency, mutual exclusion). As discussed in Section 6.6, each adaptation step at this layer itself is realized as a set of changes in the running software by the change management layer.

An important contribution of our approach is that the adaptation cycle can use the learned models to prune the search space significantly, without compromising quality (accuracy) of decisions. Learned models provide two opportunities to generate dynamically an optimization problem tailored to the situations that may arise at runtime:

1. Given a violated quality objective, the learned model is used to eliminate all of the features with no significant impact on that objective. We call the set of features that may affect a given objective as *significant features*. They represent our decision variables.
2. Significant features may affect other quality objectives, the set of which we call the *conflicting objectives*. To detect the conflicts, again the learned models are used, except this time backtracked. For each significant feature, the other objectives that the feature affects are found.

Therefore, the learned models allow us to focus the decision on a subset of the system's features and objectives. This is in contrast to the state-of-the-art, where manually constructed models do not provide a convenient mechanism for discriminating among the features and objectives. By representing each feature as a binary decision variable, this problem could be formulated as a *linear-programming problem* [38], which when solved using a constraint solver provisions the *optimal* solution. Interested reader can find the detailed formulation of this problem as a linear-programming problem in our prior publication [9,11].

6.5.3 EXPERIMENTAL RESULTS

We have shown the feasibility of some of the key facets of the approach in a controlled execution of TRS [9,11]. These experiments were performed on an instance of TRS consisting of 78 features and 8 quality objectives to understand better the characteristics of the learning cycle. We used *SVM* [36] to induce a model predicting the impact of adaptations on the system's response time. We also developed a queuing network model, which assumes that workload and service demand parameters follow an exponential distribution. We chose queuing network, since it is a commonly used approach in the literature [39] for assessing a system's response time. Fig. 6.5 shows the results under two different scenarios:

Similar context—here the system is evaluated in a setting that is comparable to that used during the training. As shown in Fig. 6.5A, both approaches achieve good level of accuracy under expected execution conditions, which serves as preliminary evidence that through machine learning it is possible to learn complex interaction between the system's features and its quality attributes.

Unexpected situation with emerging pattern—here the system faces an unexpected change, which results in a new behavioral pattern (i.e., change in the impact of features on metrics). In this scenario, we simulated occurrence of an unexpected behavior by manually injecting a database index failure, in which the index of a database table used by the *Business Tier* component fails,

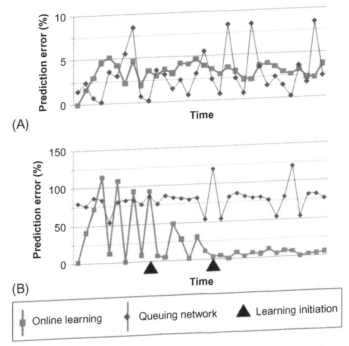

FIG. 6.5

Accuracy of learning: (A) similar context, (B) emerging pattern caused by a database index failure.

and forces a full table scan. Fig. 6.5B shows that as a result of the index failure, a new pattern of behavior emerges, and both online learning and queuing network approaches perform poorly at the beginning. However, online learning gradually adjusts the models to the new behavior in two rounds of learning. As a result, the error rate drops from an average of 54% to less than 5%, at which point the system reaches an acceptable threshold and no additional learning is performed. In contrast, the prediction error of queuing network model remains on average at 80%, since the model presumes the existence of a table index, that is, service demand of the queue representing the database in the model has become inaccurate.

We also conducted experiments involving the adaptation cycle. The results have been very promising. We compared the decisions made using the learned models against state-of-the-art, that is, manually constructed queuing network models. In both cases, we used commercially available linear-programming solvers [38]. Fig. 6.6 shows that the proposed approach achieves significant speed-ups over the state-of-the-art in the nine experiments. This is attributed to the fact that learned models allow the adaptation cycle to prune the search space significantly, by eliminating insignificant features and irrelevant objectives (recall Section 6.5.2). At the same time, although the pruning allowed for only a small subset of each system to be optimized, the quality of solutions developed using the proposed approach were on average within 3% of those resulting from optimizing the entire system.

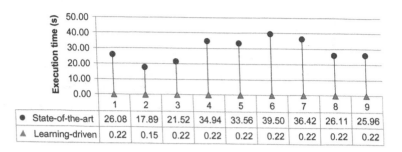

	1	2	3	4	5	6	7	8	9
● State-of-the-art	26.08	17.89	21.52	34.94	33.56	39.50	36.42	26.11	25.96
▲ Learning-driven	0.22	0.15	0.22	0.22	0.22	0.22	0.22	0.22	0.22

FIG. 6.6

Execution time in making decisions.

6.5.4 NOTEWORTHY RESEARCH CHALLENGES AND RISKS

While our experiments indicate that a learning-based approach is indeed feasible, there are several topics of special importance that need further investigation.

6.5.4.1 Extraneous and confounding variables

Two important risks to knowledge inferred through machine learning are *extraneous* and *confounding variables* [40]. *Extraneous variables* are factors other than features that may also bear an effect on the behavior of the system. An example of an extraneous variable alluded to earlier is the system's workload, which may impact some of the system's quality attributes, such as response time. A *confounding variable* is a special type of an extraneous variable that correlates positively or negatively with both dependent and independent variables. Unlike extraneous variables that introduce an error in the model, a confounding variable could result in identifying incorrect relationships. There are several possible approaches to deal with such problems. One technique is to include factors other than features (e.g., workload) that may influence the behavior of the software in the learning process as additional independent variables. Additionally, there are several known techniques [41] for testing the causality of the learned models that deserve further research.

6.5.4.2 Overhead of monitoring and learning

Another issue is the computational complexity of learning. Note that the use of feature-oriented adaptation model pioneered in our prior work [9,42] already offers two opportunities for tackling this issue: (1) Learning operates on *feature selection space*, which is significantly smaller than the traditional architectural configuration space. The features encode the engineer's domain knowledge of the adaptation choices that are practical in a given application, and thus significantly reduce the number of independent variables. (2) By using the feature relationships (e.g., mutual exclusions, dependencies), one could further reduce the feature selection space to a subset that is valid with respect to those constraints. Yet, learning in systems with very large number of features and many contextual parameters could become prohibitively expensive. One possible solution is to develop a *significance test* that would occur at the outset of learning. The test determines whether a feature in isolation has an impact on each metric. This allows for substantial reduction in the number of independent variables, and performance gains, but potentially at the expense of slight degradation in the accuracy of learned models.

Another related issue is determining how much data needs to be collected for machine learning to produce accurate models of the system's behavior. For that purpose, the *learning accuracy threshold* provided by most modern machine learning algorithms provides a good starting point.

6.5.4.3 Adaptation in the presence of uncertainty

The quality of adaptation decisions depends on the accuracy of an inferred model. When there are unanticipated changes, our approach is forced to make some decisions using the inaccurate models. An important issue is whether the decisions made during this period of time could exacerbate the violated objectives. Here, again, the feature-oriented adaptation paradigm provides us with an opportunity to address this issue. Our experience shows that while an inferred model may fail to predict accurately the *magnitude* of impact on metrics, it gets the *general direction* of impact (i.e., positive vs. negative) correctly. For instance, the fact that *cache* feature improves the system's response time, regardless of any other factor, is a property that is learned. Hence, even in the presence of inaccurate models, the approach will make decisions that are good, but not necessarily optimal, until the knowledgebase is refined.

Another potential avenue of future research is to investigate opportunistic self-training as a way of detecting emerging behaviors before adaptation decisions are made—for instance, a self-training process that takes place using a shadow clone of the running system during periods of low utilization.

6.5.4.4 Structure of learned model

In some cases, using functions to model the impact of features on metrics is not feasible. For instance, in the case of discrete metrics, classification-based techniques [40] are more suitable, as they can efficiently represent such relationships in the form of decision trees [43]. To that end, suitability of various machine learning techniques to different types of quality objectives should be explored. A few notable examples include SVMs [36], neural networks [44], decision trees [43], CART [45], MARSplines [46], etc. A follow on issue that would need to be investigated is how to make decisions using models derived from different learning techniques.

6.6 MINING-BASED APPROACH FOR CHANGE MANAGEMENT

Once goal management finds a new feature selection, change management is invoked to put it into effect. As depicted in Fig. 6.3, there are many ways of conceptualizing features, but regardless, at the change management layer, changes in features manifest themselves in terms of changes to the software components comprising the running software. For clarity, in this section, we assume the solution selected by the goal management layer has already mapped to a set of software components that need to be changed.

According to quiescence, to ensure safe adaptation, a component should not be adapted in the middle of a dependent transaction. It achieves this by first passivating (halting) all components that may initiate a transaction on the component that is being adapted. However, as you may recall from Section 6.3.2, the existing approach has three issues: (1) manually intensive, requiring the engineer to model the component dependencies, (2) fragile, since when the software evolves, the models become inaccurate representation of dependencies, and (3) inefficient, due to the severe disruptions caused by passivation.

We have developed an alternative approach that alleviates these shortcomings [8,10]. We assume the events intended for the component that is being adapted can be buffered during the change, and delivered afterward. The key insight is that the quiescence constraint that a component can only be adapted when it is not participating in a dependent transaction is overly constraining, since there are also certain times within the execution of a transaction that a component can be safely adapted. More specifically, a component can be safely adapted unless it has already participated in a dependent transaction that will require services of that component again to complete. For instance, *Authenticate* component in Fig. 6.2 can be safely adapted either prior to $e2$ or after $e2'$ without the need to wait for the top-level transaction (TLT) $T1$ to complete. As another example, *Business Tier* component can be safely adapted either prior to $e1$ or after $e1'$, but not in between, since it participates twice in the transaction $T1$.

The research challenge then is developing a detailed model of the system's transactions, such as Fig. 6.2, that would allow us to make such refined decisions about *when* components can be safely changed. At first blush, it may seem that simply tagging events comprising the dependent transactions (i.e., establishing sessions) would solve this problem, but that breaks the black-box treatment of components. We have developed an approach that learns the details of dependent transactions by mining the execution history of a software system. The result of mining is a set of rules expressing the probabilistic relationships between occurrences of transactions, and consequently involvement of corresponding components in servicing those transactions. Given a set of transactions currently running in the system, these rules can be used to predict the probability with which a component can be safely changed at any point in time. Finally, by continuously monitoring the transactions and the accuracy of predictions, the approach provides the means to adjust the rules as new patterns of interaction emerge.

6.6.1 MINING FOR RUNTIME DEPENDENCIES

Fig. 6.7 shows the steps comprising our approach. Mining operates on an *event log* of the system, which contains the events and the time at which they occur in the system. Similar to prior research [27,28], we assume events, which mark the beginning and end of transactions, can be observed in a running software system. For instance, looking at Fig. 6.2, it is reasonable to assume the *GUI* component can determine the beginning and end of dependent transaction $T1$ in terms of request $e1$ and response $e1'$. What is missing is the ability to infer automatically the causal relationship among the transactions that happen in between, and whether those transactions are initiated in response to $T1$, given that there may be multiple concurrently running dependent transactions at any point in time.

As shown in Fig. 6.7, the first step is to *construct baskets*. A *basket* is a set of events that occur close together in time. A new basket is formed for each transaction if its beginning, end, or both do not fall within the beginning and end of another transaction. In reference to Fig. 6.2, a new basket would be created for $T1$, as its beginning and end (determined by $e1$ and $e1'$) do not fall within any other transactions. As such, a basket is created for each "top-level" transaction, but not the transactions that those TLTs initiate. All transactions beginning and ending within the time frame of a basket are added to that basket. In the example of Fig. 6.2, all three transactions $T2$, $T3$, and $T4$ are added to $T1$ basket, represented as $b_{T1}=\{T1,T2,T3,T4\}$.

Using this process, an entire segment of a software system's event log can be transformed into a set of baskets representing the occurrence of transactions together in time. Several data mining approaches, such as *apriori* [47], *Eclat* [48], and *FP-growth* [49], can then be used to process baskets

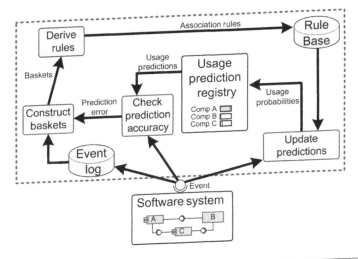

FIG. 6.7

Overview of mining-based approach for change management.

constructed in this way to derive a set of *transaction association rules (TARs)*. TARs are probabilistic rules for predicting the occurrence of transactions. A TAR is a rule of the form $A \rightarrow B{:}p$. It states that the occurrence of transaction set A implies the occurrence of transaction set B with probability p. As shown in Fig. 6.7, TARs derived in this way are stored in the *rule base* for use during system's adaptation at runtime.

Given a sufficiently large usage history, the approach compensates for concurrently running transactions. Consider the scenario in which a user is performing the TLT $T1$ as shown in Fig. 6.2, when a second user initiates another TLT $T5$ overlapping partially in time with $T1$ and itself initiating a transaction $T6$ that falls wholly within the beginning and end times of both $T1$ and $T5$. The proposed approach will include $T6$ in both b_{T1} and b_{T5} baskets. However, since transactions $T6$ and $T5$ are truly independent, the false placement of $T6$ in b_{T1} is a random event that is not likely to occur in a significantly large number of baskets, and thus safely ignored by modern data mining algorithms.

6.6.2 USING THE MINED DEPENDENCIES

As shown in Fig. 6.7, a *usage prediction registry* for every component in the system is maintained. This registry stores the probability that the component will imminently be used as a result of transactions running in the system. When an event (indicating the beginning or end of a transaction) occurs, the *update predictions* activity consults the rule base for any TARs that are *satisfied*. A TAR is satisfied if all of the transactions on its left-hand side have been initiated and currently running. If so, it is expected that the transactions predicted by the rule (i.e., right-hand side) will occur with a probability p. Those predictions are used to update the registries for components that handle those transactions.

However, since a value may already be present in the registry, the probability p cannot simply be placed in there. Instead, three cases must be considered and appropriate update mechanisms would need to be developed: (1) *Independent*: The new TAR is independent of the TARs that are already affecting the registry, that is, no transactions on the left-hand sides of the TARs are shared. (2) *Dependent*: The new TAR is dependent on the TARs that are already affecting the registry, that is, the left-hand side of the new TAR is a superset of the left-hand side of the previous TARs. (3) *Overlapping*: The left-hand side of the new TAR shares some transactions with the left-hand side of the previous TARs.

Each registry keeps track of the TARs that combine to create the overall usage probability of a component at any point in time. When an event signifies the termination of a transaction, the usage prediction registry also has to be updated. Thereby, the probability values in usage prediction registries change as events that begin and end transactions are observed.

The usage probability of a component together with the recent history of its participation in running transactions are taken to determine the time for enacting the changes. In one extreme, a component that has already participated in a running transaction, and irrespective of its usage probability in future, is not changed until the transaction ends. This approach provides safety guarantee, even if the mined rules are inaccurate. Alternatively, to achieve faster adaptation, but at the expense of slightly higher risk, the component may be adapted if its usage probability reaches either zero or less than an acceptable threshold. As mentioned earlier, since a new transaction requiring the services of the component may start while it is being changed, the events intended for the component would have to be buffered, and delivered after it is replaced. Therefore, even if a component has not participated in any running transaction, and thus there is no risk of inconsistency, the usage probability may still be taken into consideration to minimize the interruptions. Compared to quiescence, the proposed approach reduces interruptions, as it does not require passivation of any part of the system, and allows for changes to occur in the middle of transactions.

Over time, changes that occur in the software system may render the TARs in the rule base incomplete or inaccurate. For instance, components may be updated with new or modified functionality that alter their interaction patterns. As shown in Fig. 6.7, the *check prediction accuracy* activity denotes the process of monitoring the accuracy of usage predictions at runtime. When the predictions become inaccurate, it initiates a new round of data mining-based on the recently collected event log.

6.6.3 EXPERIMENTAL RESULTS

We have developed a prototype of the approach using an implementation of *Apriori* provided in WEKA [50]. We performed extensive experimentation on runtime adaptation of an emergency response software system, the details of which can be found in our publications [8,10,12]. To evaluate the approach, we used several versions of the emergency response system with different concurrency levels. We used a baseline version of the system with a single user. We then repeated the evaluations on higher concurrency systems to evaluate the susceptibility of the approach to concurrency errors. The 80 and 137 experiments were simulated by using hyperactive dummy users, as the system never naturally reached that level of concurrency error. We intentionally use very low confidence and support thresholds. We chose confidence value of 0.05 and support threshold of 0.045.

Table 6.1 shows what percentage of all recorded transactions where actually erroneous duplicates caused by concurrency, as well as the average number of these erroneously recorded transactions per TLT. As expected, with increased concurrency, the number of erroneously recorded transactions grows. Each experiment had roughly eight true transactions per TLT. The effectiveness of our rule pruning heuristics can also be observed from Table 6.1.

Table 6.1 Experimental Systems Used in Evaluation, and Effects of TAR Pruning Heuristics

# of Users	# of TLT Observed	Concurrency Errors		# of TAR	
		Rate (%)	Per Itemset	Initial	Remain
1	500	0.00	0.00	38,582	1683
10	1628	1.69	0.13	34,050	2190
28	2787	4.51	0.35	38,248	2331
40	3330	10.94	0.92	38,460	1758
80	11,920	36.32	4.19	35,168	3126
137	3543	60.77	11.26	31,442	3143

The quality of differentiating active and inactive components can be viewed with a *receiver operating characteristic (ROC) curve*, often used to evaluate a binary classifier, as shown in Fig. 6.8. In this experiment, we change the usage probability threshold, which indicates the likelihood of the component being used before the currently active transactions end. In essence, the threshold indicates the level of inaccuracy the user may be willing to tolerate with respect to the adaptation of the system's components. The ROC curve, thus, depicts the change in the ratio of true positive (TP) to false positive (FP) as different thresholds are chosen.

It can be seen how the TP and FP rates respond by moving the threshold. The ROC curve shows that the approach does an incredible job of achieving TPs despite changes in the threshold. The comparison of the different experiments also shows the effect of concurrency on the approach. With many users in the system, there are many more observations that allow the approach to predict usage of a component,

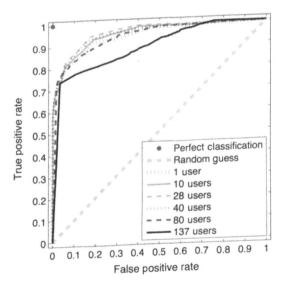

FIG. 6.8

ROC curve for determining safe adaptation of components under different levels of concurrency.

when the component is actually used. Therefore, as concurrency increases, the approach keeps the high quality in differentiating active and inactive components. However, when we approach 137 users, the concurrency error rate is roughly 60% and active components are constantly used until the transactions they participate in subside, making it more difficult to identify situations in which the components can be adapted. In such extreme scenarios, a passive approach, such as the one advocated in our research, needs to fall back on an active approach, such as quiescence, that forces some of the components to halt execution.

6.6.4 NOTEWORTHY RESEARCH CHALLENGES AND RISKS

In spite of the promising results that have shown the feasibility of a mining-based approach for the construction of change management capabilities, as outlined in our prior publications [8,10,12], several challenging issues remain. We provide an overview of these topics to frame a future research agenda for the community.

6.6.4.1 Long-living transactions and high workload

As described in Section 6.6.1, given sufficiently large number of baskets, mining can account for the anomalies caused by concurrency. However, there are two extreme cases that challenge the mining approach: (1) When there are long-living TLTs that are always running in the system, resulting in many wrong baskets. (2) When the system has an exceptionally high workload, resulting in many TLTs overlapping in time, and thus increasing the possibility of placing events in wrong baskets. One plausible approach to mitigate these challenges is to use known measurement techniques [51] for evaluating the *entropy* and *variance* of data (i.e., baskets), which would allow us to detect baskets that are problematic to be treated differently.

6.6.4.2 Overhead of mining and updating predictions

Another issue of importance is the overhead of mining, in particular at runtime. Since due to changes in the system, it is likely that only a subset of TARs become inaccurate, it would be important to develop a partial mining approach, where the event log is pruned to include only the information that is relevant for updating the affected TARs. Another source of overhead is the computational complexity of updating the usage prediction registries for components. One possible approach to reduce this overhead is to adopt a just-in-time policy, where only when it is decided to update a component, the usage predictions are calculated. Future research also needs to devise and employ efficient data structures, such as specialized *hash tables* and *map-reduce functions*, for achieving fast update of registries.

6.6.4.3 Transaction coverage and other forms of mining

The accuracy of mined rules depends on the availability of a sufficiently large usage history of the software, exercising the interactions among the system's component. Such data could either be collected through benchmark of the system or its previous deployments. However, determining how much data is needed to allow for generation of accurate rules is challenging. The notion of *component interaction coverage metric* [52] provides a good starting point in addressing this issue. Another interesting avenue of research is emerging forms of mining, such as the use of *data stream mining* [53], which allows the mining to be performed incrementally and based on the real-time stream of monitoring data.

6.7 RELATED WORK

Over the past decade, many frameworks and technologies intended to support the construction of self-adaptive systems have been developed (see recent surveys [5–7,54–56]). In Section 6.3, we described the shortcomings with the most relevant research. Here we outline other related work.

Numerous approaches [4,6,15,16,19] have advocated the use of software architectures in the construction of self-adaptive software. IBM's autonomic computing architecture [4] advocates hierarchies of feedback-control loop (i.e., MAPE-K discussed in Section 6.3). Oreizy et al. present the architecture-based approach to runtime adaptation and evolution management in their seminal work [19]. Garlan et al. describe the Rainbow framework [15], a style-based approach for developing reusable self-adaptive systems. Georgiadis et al. [16] propose a decentralized adaptation approach, where each self-organizing component manages its own adaptation with respect to the overall system goal. These works form the foundation of our research, manifested by the key role of architecture in the proposed approach.

Several models of adaptation other than architecture-based have also been proposed, such as parametric [57,58], component-based [17], aspect-oriented [59,60], and feature-oriented [61–63]. The work outlined in this chapter have also used feature-orientation as a method of modeling the dynamic variability in software, but unlike these approaches we propose to use learning to identify the impact of features on quality objectives.

Automated inference techniques have been applied extensively in the construction of adaptive software (e.g., [64–70]), but not in the context of self-adaptive software. The distinction between adaptive and self-adaptive software lies in the feedback-control loop. An adaptive software has an *external* feedback-control loop, that is, between the software and the domain (environment) in which it is deployed. For instance, a robotic software system is often adaptive; based on the data collected from the environment, it reasons and reacts accordingly. On the other hand, a self-adaptive software has an *internal* feedback-control loop, that is, between the management subsystem (meta-level logic) and the managed subsystem (application logic).

Providing assurances in effecting runtime changes is a topic that has been studied extensively in the past (e.g., [17,28,71–73]). Most relevant is *tranquility* [28], which also aims to reduce the interruptions caused by quiescence. However, unlike the proposed research, tranquility is specific to a proprietary middleware, called *Draco*, and makes an unrealistic assumption that not only components can provide a list of transactions they have already participated in the past, but also transactions they will participate in future. This is an issue that we have overcome through data mining techniques.

6.8 CONCLUSION

Self-adaptive software systems rely on several types of models to reason about the adaptation of the software at runtime. The majority of existing literature and approaches targeted at the engineering of adaptive software systems require manual development of models for use at runtime. Manual development of models, however, is a time-consuming, laborious task. In addition, keeping manually constructed models in sync with the changing software system at runtime, and in a timely fashion, is a challenge. Finally, since it is difficult to build manually models that capture the fine-grained behavior of the managed software system, reasoning about adaptation decisions using such models introduces further uncertainty in the autonomic management of software.

In this chapter, we first illustrated the shortcomings of manually constructed models, in light of the prior research, and with respect to two exemplary self-adaptation concerns occurring at the goal management and change management layers. We further provided an overview of a body of recent research that has attempted to address these challenges through automated means of inferring the models. Namely, we provided an overview of two complementary thrusts of research: (1) A machine learning approach to automatically derive the models predicting the impact of architectural change (i.e., enabling a particular capability at runtime, such as caching or authentication) on the system's quality objectives (e.g., response time, availability). These types of models are used to make adaptation decisions to fix problems that may arise at runtime. (2) A data mining approach to derive automatically the models expressing the probabilistic dependencies between the architectural elements (components) of the system. Finally, we described a set of research challenges that we have come across in our own experiences of employing automated inference techniques for the construction of self-adaptive software, which we hope to frame future research directions for the community of researchers.

ACKNOWLEDGMENTS

We would like to acknowledge the contributions of Ahmed Elkhodary in the development of our learning-based approach for goal management. This work was supported in part by awards CCF-1252644 from the National Science Foundation, D11AP00282 from the Defense Advanced Research Projects Agency, W911NF-09-1-0273 from the Army Research Office, HSHQDC-14-C-B0040 from the Department of Homeland Security, and FA95501610030 from the Air Force Office of Scientific Research.

REFERENCES

[1] D.A. Patterson, A. Brown, P. Broadwell, G. Candea, M. Chen, J. Cutler, P. Enriquez, A. Fox, E. Kiciman, M. Merzbacher, D. Oppenheimer, N. Sastry, W. Tetzlaff, J. Traupman, N. Treuhaft, Recovery-oriented computing (ROC): motivation, definition, techniques, and case studies, U.C. Berkeley computer science technical report, UCB//CSD-02-1175, University of California, Berkeley, CA, 2002.

[2] Yankee Group Report. How much is an hour of downtime worth to you? Must-Know Business Continuity Strategies, Yankee Group, Boston, MA, 2002, pp. 178–187.

[3] A.G. Ganek, T.A. Corbi, The dawning of the autonomic computing era, IBM Syst. J. 42 (1) (2003) 5–18.

[4] J.O. Kephart, D.M. Chess, The vision of autonomic computing, IEEE Comput. 36 (2003) 41–50.

[5] B. Cheng, R. De Lemos, H. Giese, P. Inverardi, J. Magee, J. Andersson, B. Becker, N. Bencomo, Y. Brun, B. Cukic, G. Di Marzo Serugendo, S. Dustdar, A. Finkelstein, C. Gacek, K. Geihs, V. Grassi, G. Karsai, H.M. Kienle, J. Kramer, M. Litoiu, S. Malek, R. Mirandola, H.A. Müller, S. Park, M. Shaw, M. Tichy, M. Tivoli, D. Weyns, J. Whittle, Software engineering for self-adaptive systems: a research roadmap, in: Software Engineering for Self-Adaptive Systems, LNCS Hot TopicsSpringer, Berlin, 2009, pp. 1–26.

[6] J. Kramer, J. Magee, Self-managed systems: an architectural challenge, in: International Conference on Software Engineering, Vancouver, Canada, May, 2007.

[7] R. De Lemos, H. Giese, H.A. MüLler, M. Shaw, J. Andersson, L. Baresi, B. Becker, N. Bencomo, Y. Brun, B. Cukic, R. Desmarais, S. Dustdar, G. Engels, K. Geihs, K.M. Goeschka, A. Gorla, V. Grassi, P. Inverardi, G. Karsai, J. Kramer, M. Litoiu, A. Lopes, J. Magee, S. Malek, S. Mankovskii,

R. Mirandola, J. Mylopoulos, O. Nierstrasz, M. Pezzè, C. Prehofer, W. Schäfer, R. Schlichting, B. Schmerl, D.B. Smith, J.P. Sousa, G. Tamura, L. Tahvildari, N.M. Villegas, T. Vogel, D. Weyns, K. Wong, J. Wuttke, Software engineering for self-adaptive systems: a second research roadmap, in: Dagstuhl Seminar Proceedings, Number 10431, 1862-4405Schloss Dagstuhl - Leibniz-Zentrum fuer Informatik, Wadern, 2011.

[8] K.R. Canavera, N. Esfahani, S. Malek, Mining the execution history of a software system to infer the best time for its adaptation, in: 20th ACM SIGSOFT International Symposium on the Foundations of Software Engineering (FSE 2012), Cary, North Carolina, November, 2012.

[9] A. Elkhodary, N. Esfahani, S. Malek, FUSION: a framework for engineering self-tuning self-adaptive software systems, in: 18th ACM SIGSOFT International Symposium on the Foundations of Software Engineering (FSE 2010), Santa Fe, NM, November, 2010.

[10] N. Esfahani, E. Yuan, K.R. Canavera, S. Malek, Inferring software component interaction dependencies for adaptation support, ACM Trans. Auton. Adapt. Syst. 10 (4) (2016).

[11] N. Esfahani, A. Elkhodary, S. Malek, A learning-based framework for engineering feature-oriented self-adaptive software systems, IEEE Trans. Softw. Eng. 39 (11) (2013) 1467–1493.

[12] E. Yuan, N. Esfahani, S. Malek, Automated mining of software component interactions for self-adaptation, in: 9th International Symposium on Software Engineering for Adaptive and Self-Managing Systems (SEAMS 2014), Hyderabad, India, June, 2014.

[13] E. Alpaydın, in: Introduction to Machine Learning, Adaptive Computation and Machine Learning, MIT Press, Cambridge, MA, 2004.

[14] P. Tan, M. Steinbach, V. Kumar, Introduction to Data Mining, Addison-Wesley, Boston, MA, 2006.

[15] G. Garlan, et al., Rainbow: architecture-based self-adaptation with reusable infrastructure, IEEE Comput. 37 (2004) 46–54.

[16] I. Georgiadis, J. Magee, J. Kramer, Self-organising software architectures for distributed systems, in: Workshop on Self-healing Systems, Charleston, SC, November, 2002.

[17] H. Gomaa, M. Hussein, Software reconfiguration patterns for dynamic evolution of software architectures, in: Working IEEE/IFIP Conference on Software Architecture, 2004.

[18] S. Malek, M. Mikic-Rakic, N. Medvidovic, A style-aware architectural middleware for resource-constrained distributed systems, IEEE Trans. Softw. Eng. 31 (5) (2005) 256–272.

[19] P. Oreizy, N. Medvidovic, R.N. Taylor, Architecture-based runtime software evolution, in: International Conference on Software Engineering, Kyoto, Japan, April, 1998.

[20] M. Bennani, D. Menasce, Resource allocation for autonomic data centers using analytic performance models, in: IEEE International Conference on Autonomic Computing, Seattle, WA, June, 2005.

[21] V. Cardellini, E. Casalicchio, V. Grassi, F. Lo Presti, R. Mirandola, Qos-driven runtime adaptation of service oriented architectures, in: 7th Joint Meeting of the European Software Engineering Conference and the ACM SIGSOFT Symposium on the Foundations of Software Engineering (ESEC/FSE '09), Amsterdam, The Netherlands, August, 2009.

[22] G. Gross, C.M. Harris, Fundamentals of Queuing Theory, second ed., John Wiley & Sons, New York, NY, 1985.

[23] L.R. Rabiner, A tutorial on hidden Markov models, Proc. IEEE 77 (1989) 257–286.

[24] R. Das, I. Whalley, J.O. Kephart, Utility-based collaboration among autonomous agents for resource allocation in data centers, in: 5th International Joint Conference on Autonomous Agents and Multiagent Systems, Hakodate, Japan, 2006.

[25] W.E. Walsh, G. Tesauro, J.O. Kephart, R. Das, Utility functions in autonomic systems, in: International Conference on Autonomic Computing (ICAC 2004), New York, NY, USA, May, 2004.

[26] R.N. Taylor, N. Medvidovic, E. Dashofy, Software Architecture Foundations, Theory, and Practice, John Wiley & Sons, Hoboken, NJ, 2008.

[27] J. Kramer, J. Magee, The evolving philosophers problem: dynamic change management, IEEE Trans. Softw. Eng. 16 (1990) 1293–1306.

[28] Y. Vandewoude, P. Ebraert, Y. Berbers, T. D'Hondt, Tranquility: a low disruptive alternative to quiescence for ensuring safe dynamic updates, IEEE Trans. Softw. Eng. 33 (2007) 856–868.

[29] D. Batory, Feature models, grammars, and propositional formulas, in: 9th International Conference on Software Product Lines, Rennes, France, September, 2005.

[30] P. Clements, L. Northrop, in: Software Product Lines: Practices and Patterns, SEI Series in Software Engineering Addison-Wesley, Boston, MA, 2001.

[31] S. Trujillo, D. Batory, O. Diaz, Feature oriented model driven development: a case study for portlets, in: 29th International Conference on Software Engineering, Minneapolis, MN, 2007.

[32] B. Lowekamp, N. Miller, D. Sutherland, T. Gross, P. Steenkiste, J.A. Subhlok, Resource query interface for network-aware applications, Clust. Comput. 2 (1999) 139–151. Baltzer.

[33] A. Mos, J. Murphy, COMPAS: adaptive performance monitoring of component-based systems, in: Workshop on Remote Analysis and Measurement of Software System (RAMSS), Edinburgh, Scotland, May, 2004.

[34] B. Tierney, B. Crowley, D. Gunter, M. Holding, J. Lee, M. Thompson, A monitoring sensor management system for grid environments, in: IEEE International Symposium on High Performance Distributed Computing, Pittsburgh, PA, August, 2000.

[35] K. Kang, S. Cohen, et al., Feature-oriented domain analysis (FODA) feasibility study, Technical report CMU/SEI-90-TR-21, Software Engineering Institute, Pittsburgh, PA, 1990.

[36] A.J. Smola, B. Schölkopf, A tutorial on support vector regression, Stat. Comput. 14 (2004) 199–222.

[37] J.O. Kephart, R. Das, Achieving self-management via utility function, IEEE Internet Comput. 11 (1) (2007) 40–48.

[38] L.A. Wolsey, Integer Programming, John Wiley & Sons, New York, 1998.

[39] C. Ghezzi, G. Tamburrelli, Predicting performance properties for open systems with KAMI, in: International Conference on Quality of Software Architecture, June, 2009.

[40] M. Kantardzic, Data Mining: Concepts, Models, Methods, and Algorithms, John Wiley & Sons, Hoboken, NJ, 2003.

[41] J. Pearl, Causality: Models, Reasoning and Inference, Cambridge University Press, Cambridge, 2000.

[42] A. Elkhodary, S. Malek, N. Esfahani, On the role of features in analyzing the architecture of self-adaptive software systems, in: 4th International Workshop on Models at Runtime, Denver, Colorado, October, 2009.

[43] Y. Yuan, M.J. Shaw, Induction of fuzzy decision trees, Fuzzy Sets Syst. 69 (2) (1995) 125–139.

[44] D. Kriesel, A Brief Introduction to Neural Networks, University of Bonn/Epsilon, Bonn, 2005.

[45] J. Gehrke, Classification and regression trees (C&RT), Encyclopedia of Data Warehousing and Mining, 2008, 192–195.

[46] J.H. Friedman, Multivariate adaptive regression splines, Ann. Stat. 19 (1) (1991) 1–67.

[47] R. Agrawal, R. Srikant, Fast algorithms for mining association rules in large databases, in: 20th International Conference on Very Large Data Bases (VLDB), Santiago, Chile, September, 1994, pp. 487–499.

[48] M.J. Zaki, Scalable algorithms for association mining, IEEE Trans. Knowl. Data Eng. 12 (3) (2000) 372–390.

[49] J. Han, J. Pei, Y. Yin, R. Mao, Mining frequent patterns without candidate generation, Data Min. Knowl. Disc. 8 (1) (2004) 53–87.

[50] WEKA 3: Data mining software in Java. http://www.cs.waikato.ac.nz/ml/weka.

[51] S. Farzi, A.B. Dastjerdi, Data quality measurement using data mining, Int. J. Comput. Theor. Eng. 2 (1) 2010 115–118.

[52] A.W. Williams, R.L. Probert, A measure for component interaction test coverage, in: ACS/IEEE International Conference on Computer Systems and Applications (AICCSA 2001), Beirut, Lebanon, June, 2001.

[53] M. Gaber, A. Zaslavsky, S. Krishnaswamy, Mining data streams: a review, ACM SIGMOD Rec. 0163-5808, 34 (1) (2005) 18–26.

[54] J. Andersson, R. De Lemos, S. Malek, D. Weyns, Modeling dimensions of self-adaptive software systems, Lecture Notes on Computer Science Hot Topics, in: B.H.C. Cheng, R. De Lemos, H. Giese, P. Inverardi, J. Magee (Eds.), Software Engineering for Self-Adaptive Systems, Springer, New York, 2009.

[55] J. Andersson, R. de Lemos, S. Malek, D. Weyns, Modeling dimensions of self-adaptive software systems, in: B.H.C. Cheng, R. de Lemos, H. Giese, P. Inverardi, J. Magee (Eds.), Software Engineering for Self-Adaptive Systems, Lecture Notes on Computer Science Hot Topics, Springer, Berlin, 2009.

[56] J. Andersson, R. De Lemos, S. Malek, D. Weyns, Reflecting on self-adaptive software systems, in: ICSE 2009 Workshop on Software Engineering for Adaptive and Self-Managing Systems, Vancouver, Canada, May, 2009.

[57] M. Salehie, L. Tahvildari, Self-adaptive software: landscape and research challenges, ACM Trans. Auton. Adapt. Syst 4 (2) (2009) 1–42.

[58] D. Menasce, M. Bennani, H. Ruan, On the use of online analytic performance models in self-managing and self-organizing computer systems, in: Self-Star Properties in Complex Information Systems, 3460 Springer, New York, 2005.

[59] T. Ryutov, L. Zhou, C. Neuman, T. Leithead, K. Seamons, Adaptive trust negotiation and access control, in: ACM Symposium on Access Control Models and Technologies, 2005, pp. 139–146.

[60] B. Morin, O. Barais, G. Nain, J.-M. Jzquel, Taming dynamically adaptive systems with models and aspects, in: 31st International Conference on Software Engineering, Vancouver, Canada, May, 2009.

[61] B. Morin, F. Fleurey, N. Bencomo, J.-M. Jzquel, A. Solberg, V. Dehlen, G. Blair, An aspect-oriented and model-driven approach for managing dynamic variability, in: ACM/IEEE 11th International Conference on Model Driven Engineering Languages and Systems, Toulouse, France, October, 2008.

[62] S. Hallsteinsen, M. Hinchey, S. Park, K. Schmid, Dynamic software product lines, IEEE Comput. 41 (4) (2008) 93–95.

[63] J. Lee, K. Kang, A feature-oriented approach to developing dynamically reconfigurable products in product-line engineering, in: Software Product Lines Conference, August, 2006.

[64] P. Trinidad, A. Ruiz-Cortes, J.P. Na, Mapping feature models onto component models to build dynamic software product lines, in: International Workshop on Dynamic Software Product Line, 2007.

[65] J.C. Georgas, R.N. Taylor, Towards a knowledge-based approach to architectural adaptation management, in: Workshop on Self-Healing Systems, Newport Beach, CA, October, 2004.

[66] D. Kim, S. Park, Reinforcement learning-based dynamic adaptation planning method for architecture-based self-managed software, in: International Workshop on Software Engineering for Adaptive and Self-Managing Systems, Vancouver, Canada, May, 2009.

[67] K. Rieck, P. Laskov, Language models for detection of unknown attacks in network traffic, J. Comput. Virol. 2 (4) (2007) 243–256.

[68] M. Sabhnani, G. Serpen, Application of machine learning algorithms to KDD intrusion detection dataset within misuse detection context, in: International Conference on Machine Learning: Models, Technologies and Applications, 2003, pp. 209–215.

[69] D. Sykes, et al., From goals to components: a combined approach to self-management, in: International Workshop on Software Engineering for Adaptive and Self-Managing Systems, Leipzig, Germany, May, 2008.

[70] G. Tesauro, N.K. Jong, R. Das, M.N. Bennani, A hybrid reinforcement learning approach to autonomic resource allocation, in: International Conference on Autonomic Computing, Washington, DC, June, 2006.

[71] G. Tesauro, Reinforcement learning in autonomic computing: a manifesto and case studies, IEEE Internet Comput. 11 (1) (2007) 22–30.

[72] H. Gomaa, K. Hashimoto, M. Kim, S. Malek, D.A. Menasce, Software adaptation patterns for service-oriented architectures, in: 25th ACM Symposium on Applied Computing (SAC 2010), Dependable and Adaptive Distributed Systems track, Sierre, Switzerland, March, 2010.

[73] A.J. Ramirez, D.B. Knoester, B.H.C. Cheng, P.K. McKinley, Applying genetic algorithms to decision making in autonomic computing systems, in: International Conference on Autonomic Computing, 2009, pp. 97–106.

[74] J. Zhang, B.H.C. Cheng, Model-based development of dynamically adaptive software, in: International Conference on Software Engineering (ICSE), Shanghai, China, May, 2006.

[75] N. Esfahani, S. Malek, J.P. Sousa, H. Gomaa, D.A. Menasce, A modeling language for activity-oriented composition of service-oriented software systems, in: ACM/IEEE 12th International Conference on Model Driven Engineering Languages and Systems (MODELS 09), Denver, Colorado, October, 2009.

EVALUATING TRADE-OFFS OF HUMAN INVOLVEMENT IN SELF-ADAPTIVE SYSTEMS

7

J. Cámara*, D. Garlan*, G.A. Moreno*, B. Schmerl*

Carnegie Mellon University, Pittsburgh, PA, United States*

7.1 INTRODUCTION

Modern society increasingly relies upon software-intensive systems to support a wide range of tasks in multiple application domains, such as energy, transportation, and communications. Despite the critical nature of many of these systems, it is increasingly difficult to obtain guarantees about their ability to provide service that can justifiably be trusted in the presence of changes in their environment (e.g., resource availability), or within the system itself (e.g., faults). The growing complexity of these systems and the high degree of uncertainty in the environment in which they operate are two of the main factors that contribute to their lack of predictability.

Early attempts to address this situation involved human oversight, which is expensive and has often been considered unreliable due to the fact that humans are liable to err and have difficulty in reacting in a timely manner when situations that demand changes to the system at run time arise. In contrast, approaches developed over the last decade in the area of self-adaptive systems [1–3] advocate for the full automation of mechanisms to adapt the structure and behavior of a system at runtime to overcome some of the limitations associated with human oversight. Self-adaptive approaches often rely on closed-loop control, eliminating the human factor from the solution.

Although fully automated adaptation has proven successful in a variety of application domains, this class of approach may be suboptimal in some situations (e.g., when information required for decision-making is difficult to capture and/or analyze), or may simply be insufficient to effect changes in the system (e.g., when adaptations involve physical changes that cannot be automated).

Among self-adaptive approaches, one of the most successful paradigms to date is MAPE-K, which includes activities to monitor and analyze a software system and its environment, and if the situation demands it, plan and execute adaptations. MAPE-K systems rely on a knowledge base that can include models of a system's environment, goals, and architecture [3, 4]. The different activities in the MAPE-K loop can benefit from human involvement in a variety of ways:

Managing Trade-offs in Adaptable Software Architectures. http://dx.doi.org/10.1016/B978-0-12-802855-1.00007-1

- Monitoring can receive information from humans (acting as sophisticated sensors) that would otherwise be difficult to automatically monitor (e.g., operators can indicate whether there is an ongoing anomaly based on context information that is not captured by the models included in the knowledge base).
- Analysis and planning can incorporate into the decision-making process input (e.g., recommendations, validation) from application domain experts who have additional insight about the best way of adapting the system.
- Execution can employ humans as system-level effectors to execute adaptations when changes to the system cannot be fully automated, or as a fallback mechanism.

Despite the benefits that involving humans in adaptation can bring, it is worth noticing that their behavior is influenced by factors external to the system that affect their effectiveness at carrying out different tasks, such as fatigue, or training level. These factors need to be carefully considered if we want to enable systems to discriminate situations in which human involvement is preferable over fully automated adaptations.

Analyzing the trade-offs of involving humans in adaptation demands new approaches to support systematic reasoning about the way in which the behavior of human participants affects the outcome of adaptations. In this chapter, we describe a formal framework to analyze trade-offs in self-adaptation at two levels: (i) reasoning about business concerns in the context of other (potentially conflicting) business properties; and (ii) reasoning about the effectiveness of automated *vs.* human-driven adaptations with respect to a set of business concerns and preferences.

The core of the framework consists of an extended version of a language to express adaptation models with elements that capture some of the main factors affecting human behavior. Moreover, we show how adaptation models expressed in this language can be encoded as stochastic multiplayer games (SMGs), a formalism amenable to automated verification that can be employed to analyze human-system-environment interactions.

We explore the topics discussed in this chapter using an extension of the Stitch language [5] employed by the Rainbow framework for self-adaptation [4] with elements inspired from opportunity-willingness-capability (OWC) models employed in *cyber-human systems* (CHS) [6] that capture major factors that influence human-system interactions. We illustrate our approach in the domain of security, employing as a motivating scenario the mitigation of denial of service (DoS) attacks in Znn.com, a simple news site system that has been extensively used to assess different research advances in self-adaptive systems.

In the remainder of this chapter, Section 7.2 describes the example that we employ to illustrate our approach, and Section 7.3 discusses related work. Section 7.4 provides an overview of trade-off analysis in self-adaptation as embodied in Stitch. Next, Section 7.5 describes our human model and its integration in adaptation models described using Stitch. Section 7.6 describes probabilistic modeling and analysis of adaptation models including humans in the loop. Finally, Section 7.7 concludes the chapter, indicating research avenues to explore in future work.

7.2 MOTIVATING SCENARIO

Before detailing the formal framework to reason about trade-offs of human involvement in adaptation, we introduce an example that will be used to illustrate the approach.

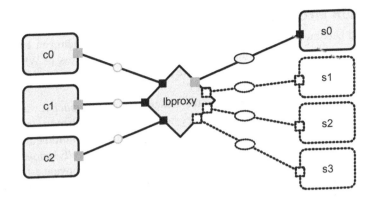

FIG. 7.1

Znn.com system architecture.

Znn.com [7] is a case study portraying a representative scenario for the application of self-adaptation in software systems embodying the typical infrastructure for a news website. It has a three-tier architecture consisting of a set of servers that provide contents from back-end databases to clients via front-end presentation logic (Fig. 7.1). The system uses a load balancer to balance requests across a pool of replicated servers, the size of which can be adjusted according to service demand. A set of clients makes stateless requests, and the servers deliver the requested contents.

From time to time, Znn.com can experience spikes in requests that it cannot serve adequately, even at maximum pool size. These spikes can result either from legitimate client traffic caused by a popular event (*slashdot effect*), or by DoS attacks in which malicious clients try to overwhelm system capacity in order to render system services unavailable.

7.2.1 SYSTEM OBJECTIVES

Regarding Znn.com's objectives, users of the system are concerned with experiencing service without any disruptions, whereas the organization is interested in minimizing the cost of operating the infrastructure (including not incurring additional operating costs derived from DoS attacks). For users, service disruption can be mapped to specific run time conditions such as (i) experienced response time for legitimate clients, and (ii) user annoyance, often related to disruptive side effects of defensive tactics. For the organization, we map cost to the specific resources being operated in the infrastructure at runtime (e.g., number of active servers). Moreover, in addition to keeping costs below budget, the organization is also interested in minimizing the fraction of that cost that corresponds to resources consumed by malicious clients. Hence, we identify minimizing the presence of malicious clients as an additional objective.

In short, we identify four quality objectives for Znn.com: legitimate client response time (R), user annoyance (A), cost (C), and client maliciousness (M).

7.2.2 ADAPTATION MECHANISMS

When response time becomes too high due to spikes in requests, the system can employ two general approaches for dealing with the situation: absorb excess traffic or suppress it. While the former approach is better suited to situations in which legitimate user traffic has increased due to a popular event, the latter is indicated for dealing with DoS attacks.

Znn.com can absorb excess traffic employing the tactics: (i) *adding capacity*, which commissions a new replicated web server to share the load; and (ii) *reducing service*, which reduces the level of service to *text only* (Znn.com has two fidelity levels: *high*, which includes full multimedia content; and *text only*, which does not provide any multimedia content). These tactics are *fully automated*, and are good at improving the performance of the system without increasing the annoyance to legitimate users. However, employing these tactics comes at a price, since they do not deal with reducing the cost derived from resources consumed by potentially malicious clients, and they can even result in an increment of the cost of operating the system (in the case of adding capacity).

Alternatively, Znn.com can eliminate excess traffic by enacting the tactics: (i) *blackholing*, which adds the IP addresses of clients that are deemed to be attacking the system to a blacklist that blocks their requests; and (ii) *throttling*, which limits the rate of requests accepted from potentially malicious clients. Eliminating excess traffic from potentially malicious clients is an approach that to be effective requires accurately identifying the attackers. Znn.com relies upon the judgment of a human operator to enact these tactics. In general, well-trained operators will be effective at eliminating traffic from malicious clients, but poorly trained operators can increase user annoyance if they cause service disruption to legitimate clients due to mistakes in malicious client identification.

7.3 RELATED WORK

Deciding whether humans should be involved in the execution of adaptation is no easy task, since their behavior and the outcome of their actions can be affected by transient factors such as changing levels of attention and load, fixed attributes (e.g., level of expertise in carrying out a particular task), or even their physical context (e.g., access to different locations, timing issues). These factors constitute an additional source of uncertainty affecting the self-adaptive system (classified by Esfahani and Malek as *uncertainty due to human in the loop* [8]) that needs to be managed if we want to answer the following questions:

Q1: How can the outcome of adaptation be predicted if human actors are involved in its execution?
Q2: How can it be determined whether human actors should be involved in adaptation?

While answering **Q1** calls for employing models of human characteristics sufficient for representing the probabilistic nature of human behavior and its interaction with the system, **Q2** also demands exploring mechanisms suitable to compare candidate solutions that might include human-system collaborations, as well as fully automated adaptations.

Some existing approaches in self-adaptation that automatically generate adaptation plans at run time are able to propose candidate solutions by analyzing trade-offs among different qualities [9], consider uncertainty when tuning the operation of the system (e.g., by dynamically adjusting parameters [10, 11]), or fall back to a graceful degradation of the system by relaxing constraints in system requirements [12]. However, despite their consideration of uncertainty as a first-order element, most of these approaches do not systematically consider the trade-offs of alternative solutions in the context of multiple quality concerns. Hence, these approaches are not natural candidates for analyzing the trade-offs of involving humans in adaptation in a context-sensitive manner.

Other approaches in self-adaptation that rely on selection of adaptation strategies defined by a designer at development time [4, 13] are also able to rank candidate solutions by analyzing trade-offs among different quality concerns. Moreover, these approaches are sometimes able to deal with some aspects of uncertainty and timing [4]. These proposals are limited to ranking and selecting fully automated adaptations, since the knowledge models they employ are unable to capture the multiple facets of uncertainty derived from human behavior that affect the outcome of adaptations.

While the aforementioned approaches focus on fully automated adaptations, Dorn and Taylor [14] introduce a framework that enables a system adaptation manager to reason about the effects of software-level changes on human interactions and vice versa by mapping a model of what they describe as *human architecture* (described in a language called hADL) to a model of the system's architecture updated at runtime. This approach focuses on the collaboration topology and is able to compare collaboration-(un)aware adaptations in order to select the best course of action, although it does not explicitly consider uncertainty derived from human behavior as a major factor affecting the outcome of adaptations.

Outside of the scope of self-adaptive systems, some approaches in the business process modeling domain include some aspects of human involvement, providing constructs for describing human activities in business processes and their dependencies [15, 16]. These languages primarily target service-oriented architectures and have limited support for other common architectural styles.

Eskins and Sanders [6] introduce a definition of a Cyber-Human Systems (CHS) and the Opportunity-Willingness-Capability (OWC) ontology for classifying CHS elements with respect to system tasks. This approach provides a structured and quantitative means of analyzing cyber security problems whose outcomes are influenced by human-system interactions, reflecting the probabilistic nature of human behavior.

If we contrast questions **Q1** and **Q2** with the characteristics of the related approaches described in this section, we can list a set of requirements that a suitable approach to our problem should satisfy:

R1: The approach must include a value system that enables candidate solution trade-off analysis, allowing context-sensitive adaptation.

R2: The approach must be able to consider uncertainty as a primary factor that affects the effectiveness of tasks or adaptations.

R3: The approach must consider timing delays that capture the notion of task or adaptation latency.

R4: The approach must be able to represent and enable the analysis of human participant behavior.

R5: The approach must provide support for a variety of architectural styles.

Although the approaches described in this section partially satisfy these requirements (see Table 7.1), in this chapter we describe an approach that combines the strengths of the Rainbow framework for self-adaptation [4] and the OWC ontology described in [6]. On the one hand, Rainbow includes a value system based on utility to rank candidate adaptations, explicit time delays to observe the effects of adaptation actions executed on the target system, and it is able to account for uncertainty in the selection of adaptive actions. On the other hand, OWC models provide the concepts required to capture human factors that can influence adaptation, some of which are of a probabilistic nature.

In previous work [17], we presented an analysis technique based on model checking of SMGs to quantify the potential benefits of employing different types of algorithms for self-adaptation.

Table 7.1 Requirements Satisfied by Related Approaches

Area	Approach	R1	R2	R3	R4	R5
Self-adaptive systems	Sykes et al. [9]	✓				✓
	Calinescu et al. [10]		✓	✓		
	Epifani et al. [11]		✓	✓		
	Cheng et al. [4]	✓	✓	✓		✓
	Oreizy et al. [13]	✓				✓
	Dorn and Taylor [14]	✓				✓
Business process modeling	BPMN [16]			✓	✓	
	WSBPEL4People [15]			✓	✓	
Cyber-human systems	Eskins and Sanders [6]		✓		✓	

Specifically, we showed how the technique enables the comparison of alternatives that consider tactic latency information for proactive adaptation with those that are not latency-aware. The work in [18] places this analysis technique in the context of human-in-the-loop adaptation, extending SMG models with elements that encode an extended version of Stitch adaptation models with OWC constructs. That work focuses on a simple scenario, does not explore trade-off analysis with respect to multiple quality concerns, and involved two versions (automated and human) of the same adaptation tactic. In this chapter, we extend our study to consider trade-off analysis at two different levels: (i) discriminating cases in which the involvement of human actors in execution leads to an improvement in system qualities, providing the basis to combine human-based and automated adaptations; and (ii) deciding about human involvement in a context-sensitive manner, selecting different adaptations for different preferences over business concerns. Moreover, we explore human involvement in self-adaptation in the domain of self-protecting systems, illustrating our approach in a richer adaptation scenario (a comprehensive description is provided in [19]), both in terms of tactics and dimensions of concern.

7.4 ANALYZING TRADE-OFFS IN SELF-ADAPTATION

In this section, we show how elevating the reasoning to an architectural level can provide a principled basis for analyzing the trade-offs among potentially conflicting business objectives. To illustrate this point, we first introduce the main concepts behind the Stitch language for self-adaptation, which will be used as the vehicle to explore the questions discussed in the remainder of this chapter.

7.4.1 ADAPTATION MODEL

Although many proposals rely on closed-loop control exploit architectural models for adaptation [4, 13, 20], in this chapter we use some of the high-level concepts in Stitch [5] as a reference framework to illustrate our approach. Stitch is the language employed by the Rainbow framework [4] to describe automated repairs based on an architectural description of the underlying target system. Rainbow has among its distinct features an explicit architecture model of the target system, a collection of adaptation tactics, and utility preferences to guide adaptation.

We assume a model of adaptation that represents adaptation knowledge employing the following high-level concepts[1]: (i) tactics, or primitive actions that correspond to a single step of adaptation; (ii) strategies, which encapsulate an adaptation process, where each step is the conditional execution of a tactic; and (iii) utility profile, which drives the selection of strategies at runtime based on a set of utility functions and preferences.

7.4.1.1 Tactic

A tactic is a primitive action that corresponds to a single step of adaptation. Tactics require three parts to be specified: (1) the *condition*, which specifies when a tactic is applicable; (2) the *action*, which defines the script for making changes to the system; and (3) the *effect*, which specifies the expected effect that the tactic will have.

Listing 7.1 shows an example tactic for activating a set of servers in Znn.com. Line 3 specifies the applicability condition, which says that the tactic may be executed if (i) there is a client experiencing a response above the maximum acceptable threshold (predicate cHiRespTime defined in line 1), and (ii) there are enough servers available to activate. Lines 4–7 specify the action, which is to select a set of servers among those currently inactive (line 5), and enable them (line 6). Line 8 states that the intended effect of the tactic is achieved only if all clients experience a response time below the maximum acceptable threshold.

Tactics have an associated cost/benefit impact on the different dimensions of concern in the system. Table 7.2 shows the impact on different properties of the tactics employed in Znn.com, as well as an indication of how the tactic affects the utility for every particular dimension of concern (the number of upward or downward arrows is directly proportional to the magnitude of utility increments and decrements, respectively).[2] While all tactics reduce the response time experienced by legitimate clients,

---

> **LISTING 7.1**
>
> Tactic for activating a server in Znn.com
>
> ```
> 1  define boolean cHiRespTime = exists c:T.ClientT in M.components |
>         c.experRespTime>M.MAX_RESPTIME;
> 2  tactic enlistServers (int n) {
> 3      condition { cHiRespTime && set.Size(s : T.ServerT in M.components | !s.isArchEnabled)>=n;}
> 4      action {
> 5          set servers = Set.randomSubset(Model.findServices(T.ServerT), n);
> 6          for (T.ServerT freeSvr : servers) { M.enableServer (freeSvr, true); }
> 7      }
> 8      effect { !cHiRespTime; }
> 9  }
> ```

---

[1]We use a simplified version of Stitch [5] to illustrate the main ideas in this chapter.
[2]To obtain the impact on the different quality dimensions of tactics in practice, the approach relies on expert knowledge or field data about similar existing systems, although nothing prevents the use of machine learning techniques to obtain that information. In this chapter we consider fixed cost/benefit impacts for illustration purposes, although Stitch also supports the specification of sophisticated impact models that are context-sensitive, and can capture probabilistic aspects in the outcome of tactic executions [21].

Table 7.2 Tactic Cost/Benefit on Qualities and Impact on Utility Dimensions

Tactic	Response Time (R)		Malicious Clients (M)		Cost (C)		User Annoyance (A)	
	ΔAvg. Resp. Time (ms)	ΔU_R	ΔMal. Clients (%)	ΔU_M	ΔCost (usd/h)	ΔU_C	ΔU. Annoyance (%)	ΔU_A
enlistServers	−1000	↑↑↑	0	=	+1.0	↓↓↓	0	=
lowerFidelity	−500	↑↑	0	=	−0.1	↑	0	=
blackholeAttacker	−1000	↑↑↑	−100	↑↑↑	0	=	+50	↓↓
throttleSuspicious	−500	↑↑	0	=	0	=	+25	↓

some of them (e.g., enlistServers and blackholeAttacker) cause a more drastic reduction, resulting in higher utility gains in that particular dimension. Regarding the presence of malicious clients, tactic blackholeAttacker is the most effective, whereas other tactics (e.g., enlistServers) do not have any impact. With respect to cost, tactic enlistServers increases the operating cost and reduces utility in this dimension, since it employs additional resources to absorb incoming traffic. Finally, tactics blackholeAttacker and throttleSuspicious impact negatively on user annoyance, since there is a risk that incorrect detection of malicious clients will lead to annoying a fraction of legitimate clients by blackholing or throttling them.

7.4.1.2 Strategy

A strategy encapsulates an adaptation process, where each step is the conditional execution of a tactic. Strategies are characterized in Stitch as a tree of condition-action-delay decision nodes, where delays correspond to a time window for observing tactic effects. System feedback (through the dynamically updated architectural model of the system) is used to determine the next tactic at every step during strategy execution.

Listing 7.2 shows the Stitch code for a simple adaptation strategy in Znn.com that deals with degraded performance by activating additional servers and reducing the fidelity of the contents served[3]: line 1 specifies the applicability condition that needs to be satisfied for the strategy to be eligible for execution (in this case, predicate cHiRespTime indicates that there are clients experiencing a response time above the acceptable threshold). In the body of the strategy, node t0 (line 2) executes tactic enlistServers if the guard cHiRespTime evaluates to true. To account for the delay in observing the outcome of tactic execution in the system (settling time), t0 specifies a time window of 30 s, after which, if the tactic's intended effect (as defined in the tactic script—Listing 7.1, line 8) is observed, successful tactic completion (keyword success, line 3) leads to the end of strategy execution in normal conditions through node t1 (keyword done). Otherwise, if the intended tactic effect is not observed after the delay window expires

---

[3]Although strategies can be complex decision trees involving multiple executions of multiple tactics with different orderings, we provide here a simple example for illustration purposes.

LISTING 7.2

Strategy for absorbing excess traffic.

```
1  strategy Outgun [cHiRespTime] {
2      t0: (cHiRespTime) −> enlistServers(1) @[30000 /*ms*/] {
3          t1: (success) −> done;
4          t2: (fail) −> lowerFidelity() @[2000 /*ms*/] {
5              t2a: (success) −> done;
6              t2b: (fail) −> TNULL;
7          }
8      }
9  }
```

(keyword fail, line 4), the strategy attempts to reduce response time by executing the tactic lowerFidelity and waiting 2 s to observe its effect, exiting through node t2a if the tactic succeeds. If the intended effect of lowerFidelity is not observed, the strategy exits with an error status via node t2b (line 6).

7.4.1.3 Utility profile

In Stitch, the selection of strategies at run time is driven by utility functions and preferences, which are sensitive to the context of use and able to consider trade-offs among multiple potentially conflicting objectives. The different qualities of concern are characterized as utility functions that map architectural properties capturing quality attributes to utility values.

Utility functions are defined by an explicit set of value pairs (with intermediate points linearly interpolated). Table 7.3 summarizes the utility functions for Znn.com. Function U_R maps low response times (up to 100 ms) to maximum utility, whereas values above 2000 ms are highly penalized (utility below 0.25), and response times above 4000 ms provide no utility. In this case, utility and mapped property values across all quality dimensions are inversely proportional, although this is not necessarily true in general.

Utility preferences capture business preferences over the quality dimensions, assigning a weight to each of them. We consider two scenarios in Znn.com, whose priority concerns are summarized in Table 7.4.

Table 7.3 Utility Functions for Znn.com

U_R	U_M	U_C	U_A
0:1.00	0:1.00	0:1.00	0:1.00
100:1.00	5:1.00	1:0.90	100:0.00
200:0.99	20:0.80	2:0.30	
500:0.90	50:0.40	3:0.10	
1000:0.75	70:0.00		
1500:0.50			
2000:0.25			
4000:0.00			

Table 7.4 Utility Preferences for Znn.com Scenarios

Scenario	Priority	w_{U_R}	w_{U_M}	w_{U_C}	w_{U_A}
1	Minimizing number of malicious clients	0.15	0.6	0.1	0.15
2	Optimizing good client experience	0.3	0.3	0.1	0.3

7.4.2 ADAPTATION STRATEGY SELECTION

A situation that demands adaptation can generally be addressed in different ways by executing alternative adaptation strategies, many of which may be applicable under the same run time conditions (e.g., excess traffic under high workload can be either absorbed or eliminated). Since different strategies impact run time quality attributes in various ways, there is a need to choose a strategy that will result in the best outcome with respect to achieving the system's desired quality objectives.

To enable decision-making for selecting strategies we use the utility functions and preferences introduced in the previous section. By evaluating all applicable strategies against the different quality objectives, we obtain an aggregate expected utility value for each strategy by using the specified utility preferences. The strategy selected for execution by the adaptation manager is the one that maximizes expected utility.

The aggregated impact on utility of a strategy is obtained by: (i) computing the aggregate impact of the strategy on the system's state, (ii) merging aggregated strategy impact with current system state to obtain the expected state after strategy execution, (iii) mapping expected state to utilities, and (iv) combining all utilities using utility preferences.

As an example of how the utility of a strategy is calculated, let us assume that the adaptation cycle is triggered in system state [1500, 90, 2, 0], indicating response time, percentage of malicious clients, operating cost, and user annoyance level, respectively. We focus on the evaluation of strategy Outgun.

To obtain the aggregate impact on system state of a strategy, we need to estimate the likelihood of selecting different tactics at run time due to the uncertainty in their selection and outcome within the strategy tree. To this end, Rainbow uses a stochastic model of a strategy, assigning a probability of selection to every branch in the tree.[4] Fig. 7.2 shows how the aggregate impact on state is computed from the leaves to the root of the strategy tree: the aggregate impact of each node is computed by adding the aggregate impact of its children, reduced by the probability of their respective branches, with the cost-benefit attribute vector of the tactic in the node (if any). In the example, the impact contributed by nodes t0 and t2 correspond to the cost-benefit vectors of the associated tactics, whereas leaf nodes make no changes to the system and therefore have no impact.

Once the aggregate impact of the strategy is computed, it is merged with the current system state to obtain the expected system state after strategy execution:

$$[1500, 90, 2, 0] + [-1250, 0, +0.95, 0] = [250, 90, 2.95, 0]$$

Next, we map the expected conditions to the utility space:

$$[U_R(250), U_M(90), U_C(2.95), U_A(0)] = [0.975, 0, 0.11, 1.0]$$

---

[4]By default, probabilities are divided equally among the branches, although they can be progressively adjusted in accordance with information collected from system executions.

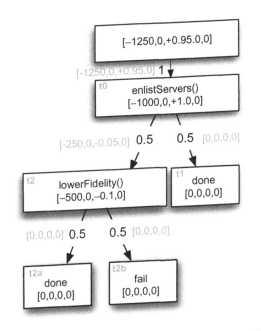

FIG. 7.2

Calculation for aggregate impact of strategy Outgun. Grayed out tuples adjacent to tree branches indicate aggregate impact corresponding to the child subtree (including adjustments due to branch probabilities).

And finally, all utilities are combined into a single utility value by making use of the utility preferences. Hence, if we assume that we are in Scenario 2, the aggregate utility for strategy Outgun would be:

$$0.975 * 0.3 + 0 * 0.3 + 0.11 * 0.1 + 1.0 * 0.3 = 0.6035$$

Utility scores are computed similarly for all strategies. In this case, strategies Eliminate and Outgun score 0.81 and 0.6, respectively, thus Eliminate would be selected.

7.5 ANALYZING TRADE-OFFS OF INVOLVING HUMANS IN ADAPTATION

In the previous section, we described a language to express adaptation models that can be analyzed to evaluate trade-offs among different concerns in self-adaptation. In this section, we first present a candidate model for quantifying how human involvement in adaptation can affect business objectives. This model is inspired by the OWC ontology described in [6]. Next, we describe how the concepts behind Stitch and the proposed OWC model can be combined to capture descriptions of adaptations that involve collaborations among the system and its human participants. This extension enables the evaluation of trade-offs of involving humans in adaptation with respect to a given set of concerns and preferences expressed in a utility profile.

7.5.1 HUMAN MODEL

Attributes of human actors that might affect interactions with the system are captured in a model inspired by an OWC ontology described in the context of CHSs [6]. The OWC ontology provides a structured way of defining and grouping human model elements for different (adaptation) tasks that can be refined to incorporate other models, enabling fine-grained reasoning about certain aspects of humans interacting with the system. OWC models extend the description of the underlying system's architecture, and can incorporate multiple human actor types (e.g., human actor roles specialized in different tasks), each of which can have multiple instances (e.g., operators with different levels of training in a particular task). Attributes of human actor types fall into three categories:

7.5.1.1 Opportunity

Opportunity captures the applicability conditions of the adaptation tactics that can be executed by human actors on the target system as constraints imposed on the human actor (e.g., by the physical context—is there an operator physically located on site?).

Example 7.1. We consider a tactic to have a human operator manually select malicious clients to blackhole (blackholeAttacker) in a DoS attack scenario. Opportunity elements are $OE^{blackholeAttacker} = \{L,B\}$, where L represents the operator's location, and B tells us whether the operator is busy doing something else:

- $L.state \in \{operator\ on\ location\ (ONL),\ operator\ off\ location\ (OFFL)\}$.
- $B.state \in \{operator\ busy\ (OB),\ operator\ not\ busy\ (ONB)\}$.

Using $OE^{blackholeAttacker}$, an opportunity function for the tactic $f_O{}^{blackholeAttacker} = (L.state == ONL) \wedge (B.state == ONB)$ can be used to constrain its applicability only to situations in which there is an operator on location who is not busy (e.g., in a meeting).

7.5.1.2 Willingness

Willingness captures transient factors that might affect the disposition of the operator to carry out a particular task (e.g., load, stamina, stress). Continuing with our example, willingness elements in the case of the blackholeAttacker tactic can be defined as $WE^{blackholeAttacker} = \{S\}$, where $S.state \in [0,10]$ represents the operator's stress level. A willingness function mapping willingness elements to a probability of tactic completion can be defined as $f_W{}^{blackholeAttacker} = pr_W(S.state)$, with $pr_W : S \rightarrow [0,1]$.

7.5.1.3 Capability

Capability captures the likelihood that the human participant will successfully carry out a particular task, which is determined by relatively stable attributes of the human actor, such as training level. In our example, we define capability elements as $CE^{blackholeAttacker} = \{T\}$, where T represents the operator's level of training (e.g., $T.state \in [0,1]$). We define a capability function that maps training level to a probability of successful tactic performance as $f_C{}^{blackholeAttacker} = pr_C(T.state)$, with $pr_C : T \rightarrow [0,1]$. This models the fact that better trained operators are more effective at eliminating malicious users and less likely to blackhole legitimate clients, resulting in better reductions in the percentage of malicious clients with little or no increase in user annoyance.

7.5.2 INTEGRATING HUMAN AND ADAPTATION MODELS

Incorporation of OWC elements for adaptation execution in Stitch affects the specification of different elements in adaptation tactics and strategies.

7.5.2.1 Tactics

In tactics involving humans, constraints that affect the applicability of a tactic can be derived either from the human model (opportunity elements), or properties of the architecture itself (e.g., are there any available servers to activate?). In general, applicability conditions of these tactics will be a combination of both. In Listing 7.3, the condition block of tactic blackholeAttacker (line 4) combines opportunity elements from the human model (operator on location and not busy—predicate ONLNB, defined in line 1), with a predicate defined over the properties of the architecture (legitimate clients are experiencing a high response time—cHiRespTime).

The action block of these tactics can execute automated operations, as in the case of tactic enlistServers (Listing 7.1), and also notify human actors to perform a task. The action block of tactic blackholeAttacker (Listing 7.3, lines 5 and 6) first selects an available operator (line 5), and next it notifies the selected operator that she has to blackhole potentially malicious clients via a text message (line 6).

7.5.2.2 Strategies

Tactics, both fully automated ones and those involving humans, can be combined to achieve better outcomes in adaptation strategies. Listing 7.4 shows strategy Eliminate for eliminating excess traffic from potentially malicious clients first by notifying an operator (via tactic blackholeAttacker, line 5)

LISTING 7.3

Tactic for blackholing malicious clients via human operator.

```
1  define boolean ONLNB=exists o:operatorT in M.participants | o.onLocation && !o.busy;
2  ...
3  tactic blackholeAttacker(){
4    condition {ONLNB && cHiRespTime;}
5    action {ao=Set.RandomSubSet({select o:operatorT in M.participants | o.onLocation && !o.busy},1);
6           notify(ao,"Blackhole_potentially_malicious_clients");}
7    effect {!cHiRespTime;}
8  }
```

LISTING 7.4

Strategy to eliminate excess traffic inZnn.com

```
1  define boolean unhandledMalicious=exists c:T.ClientT in M.components | c.maliciousness>M.MAL_THR && !c.isBlackHoled;
2  define boolean unhandledSuspicious=exists c:T.ClientT in M.components | c.maliciousness > M.SUS_THR and !c.isThrottled;
3  ...
4  strategy Eliminate [unhandledMalicious || unhandledSuspicious] {
5    t0: (unHandledMalicious) −> blackholeAttacker () @[300000] {
6      t0a: (success) −> done;
7      t0b: (unHandledSuspicious) −> throttleSuspicious () @[300000] {
8        t1a: (success) −> done;
9        t1b: (default) −> fail; }
10   }
11 }
```

to manually block traffic from malicious clients. If the assigned time window of 5 min expires and the intended effect of the tactic (!cHiRespTime, Listing 7.3) is not observed, the strategy notifies an operator to execute the throttleSuspicious tactic as a fallback, throttling suspicious clients (line 7).

7.6 REASONING ABOUT HUMAN-IN-THE-LOOP ADAPTATION

When defining a collection of adaptation strategies and their associated utility profile, we need to guarantee not only that the system will carry out reasonable choices under all possible circumstances, but also that the effect of those choices combined with the behavior of human participants will have a reasonable impact on business concerns. To provide such guarantees, we use a formal model based on an abstraction of the extended Stitch profile for human-in-the-loop adaptation presented in Section 7.5.1 that enables us to reason about: (i) the choices made by the adaptation manager for adaptation strategy selection, and (ii) the impact of the execution of selected adaptation strategies on the target system.

Our modeling approach for human-in-the-loop adaptation consists of describing an SMG in which we consider that one of the players is the adaptive system (including both automated adaptation mechanisms and human actors) and the other is the environment within which the system operates. The goal of the system player is to maximize accrued utility during the system's execution (encoded formally as a reward structure), while we consider the environment to be an antagonistic player that tries to minimize that same reward. SMG analysis enables the quantification of the maximum utility reward that the system player is able to guarantee in the most adverse conditions of the environment ((i.e., a worst-case scenario).

In the remainder of this section, we first introduce some background on model checking SMGs, the formal technique that we use to formally reason about human involvement in adaptation. Next, we provide a description of our Znn.com model implemented in the probabilistic model-checker PRISM-games [22], as well as the analysis and results that we obtained for human-in-the-loop adaptation analysis.

7.6.1 MODEL CHECKING STOCHASTIC MULTIPLAYER GAMES

Automatic verification techniques for probabilistic systems such as probabilistic model checking provide a means to model and analyze systems that exhibit stochastic behavior, effectively enabling reasoning quantitatively about probability and reward-based properties (e.g., about the system's use of resources, or time).

Competitive behavior may also appear in (stochastic) systems when some component cannot be controlled, and could behave according to different or even conflicting goals with respect to other components in the system. In such situations a natural fit is modeling a system as a game between different players, adopting a game-theoretic perspective. Automatic verification techniques have been successfully used in this context, for instance for the analysis of security [23] or communication protocols [24].

Our approach to analyzing human involvement in adaptation builds upon a recent technique for modeling and analyzing SMGs [25]. In this approach, systems are modeled as turn-based SMGs, meaning that in each state of the model, only one player can choose between several actions, the outcome of which can be probabilistic. Players can either cooperate to achieve the same goal, or compete to achieve their own goals.

The approach includes a logic called rPATL for expressing quantitative properties of SMGs, which extends the probabilistic logic PATL [26]. PATL is itself an extension of ATL [27], a logic extensively used in multiplayer games and multiagent systems to reason about the ability of a set of players to collectively achieve a particular goal. Properties written in rPATL can state that a coalition of players has a strategy[5] which can ensure that either the probability of an event's occurrence, or an expected reward measure, meets some threshold.

rPATL is a branching-time temporal logic that incorporates the coalition operator $\langle\langle C \rangle\rangle$ of ATL, and the reward operator R^r_{Max} from [28] to reason about goals related to rewards. An extended version of the rPATL reward operator $\langle\langle C \rangle\rangle R^r_{max=?}[F^\star \phi]$[6] enables the quantification of the maximum accrued rewards. An example of a property employing the reward maximization operator is $\langle\langle phone \rangle\rangle R^{time}_{max=?}[F$ empty_battery], meaning "the value of the maximum operation time that a cell phone can guarantee before its battery is fully discharged, independently of the behavior of its environment."

Reasoning about strategies is a fundamental aspect of model checking SMGs, which enables checking for the existence of a strategy that is able to optimize an objective expressed as a property including an extended version of the rPATL reward operator. The checking of such properties also supports strategy synthesis, enabling us to obtain the corresponding optimal strategy. An SMG strategy resolves the choices in each state, selecting actions for a player based on the current state and a set of memory elements.[7]

7.6.2 FORMAL MODEL

Our game is played in turns by two players that are respectively in control of the behavior of the environment (env) and the Znn.com system, including human actors (sys), who are assumed to share goals with the system. The SMG model consists of the following parts.

7.6.2.1 Player definition

Listing 7.5 illustrates player definition in the SMG. Player env is in control of all the (asynchronous) actions that the environment can take (defined in the environment module), while system player sys controls all the actions that belong to the human actor and the target system, whose behavior is specified in the processes ha_system, as well as Outgun and Eliminate (adaptation strategies for absorbing and eliminating excess traffic, respectively). Moreover, the system player controls the synchronization of actions between adaptation strategies and the target system, thus modeling the triggering of adaptation tactics. Global variable turn (line 4) is used to explicitly encode alternating turns between the system and environment players.

---

[5]The term *strategy* employed in the context of SMGs refers to a *game strategy* (referred to also as *policy* or *adversary*) as defined in [25], and should not be confused with Stitch adaptation strategies.
[6]The variants of $F^\star \phi$ used for reward measurement in which the parameter $\star \in \{0, \infty, c\}$ indicate that, when ϕ is not reached, the reward is zero, infinite or equal to the cumulated reward along the whole path, respectively.
[7]See [25] for more details on SMG strategy synthesis.

LISTING 7.5

Player definition for the Znn.com SMG.

```
1   player sys ha_system, Eliminate, Outgun, [blackholeAttacker], [throttleSuspicious], [enlistServers],
        [lowerFidelity] endplayer
2   player env environment endplayer
3   const ENVT=0; const SYST=1;
4   global turn:[ENVT..SYST] init ENVT;
```

LISTING 7.6

Environment module.

```
1   const MAX_TIME; // Exercution time frame [0,MAX_TIME]
2   module environment
3     t:[0..MAX_TIME] init 0;
4     [] (turn=ENVT) & (t<MAX_TIME) -> (t'=t+1) & (turn'=SYST);
5   endmodule
```

7.6.2.2 Environment

The environment process (Listing 7.6) controls the evolution of variables in the execution context that are out of the system's control. For the sake of simplicity, we assume in our model a simple behavior of the environment that only keeps track of time, although additional behavior controlling other elements (e.g., network delay) can be encoded (please refer to [17] for further details illustrating the modeling of adversarial environment behavior in turn-based SMGs).

7.6.2.3 Human model

Listing 7.7 shows the encoding of the OWC elements corresponding to an operator in the Znn.com system. Opportunity elements (line 2) indicate whether the operator is on location and/or busy. These predicates are used to guard the execution of tactics blackholeAttacker and throttleSuspicious in the model (Listing 7.8, line 19). The willingness function of the operator (line 6) is inversely proportional to her stress level, declared in line 5. The capability function (line 9) corresponds to the training level of the operator in this case.

LISTING 7.7

Human actor model encoding for a Znn.com operator.

```
1    // Opportunity elements
2    global op_onLocation:bool init true, op_busy: bool init false;
3    // Willingness elements and function
4    const MAX_STRESS_LEVEL, INIT_STRESS_LEVEL;
5    global op_stressLevel: [0..MAX_STRESS_LEVEL] init INIT_STRESS_LEVEL;
6    formula op_f_w=(MAX_STRESS_LEVEL−op_stressLevel) / MAX_STRESS_LEVEL;
7    // Capability elements and function
8    const double op_trainingLevel;
9    formula op_f_c= op_trainingLevel;
10   // Combined WC probability for tactic BlackholeAttacker
11   formula ba_wc_prob = op_f_c * op_f_w;
```

LISTING 7.8

Target system extended with human actors module.

```
1   // EnlistServer Tactic cost/benefit attribute vector functions
2   formula es_f_rt = rt−1000 >=0 ? (rt−1000<=MAX_RT? rt−1000 : MAX_RT) : 0;
3   formula es_f_as=as<MAX_SERVERS ? as+1:as;
4   // BlackholeAttacker Tactic cost/benefit attribute vector functions
5   formula ba_f_rt = rt−1000 >=0 ? (rt−1000<=MAX_RT? rt−1000 : MAX_RT) : 0;
6   formula ba_f_mc = ba_wc_prob*mc > 0 ? (ba_wc_prob*mc < 100? floor(ba_wc_prob*mc) : 100) : 0;
7   formula ba_f_ua = ua+(1−ba_wc_prob)*50 >=0 ? (ua+(1−ba_wc_prob)*50<=100?
        floor(ua+(1−ba_wc_prob)*50) : 100) : 0;
8   ...
9   formula cost=as * cost_per_server;
10  ...
11  module ha_system
12  rt : [0..MAX_RT] init init_rt; // Response time
13  as : [0..MAX_SERVERS] init init_as; // Active servers
14  mc : [0..100] init init_mc; // Malicious clients
15  ua : [0..100] init init_ua; // level of annoyance
16  cnt_es :[0..MAX_TIME] init 0;
17  cnt_ba :[0..MAX_TIME] init 0;
18  // Tactic triggers
19  [blackholeAttacker] (turn=SYST) & (op_onLocation) & (!op_busy) & (mc>0) & (cnt_ba=0) −>
        (cnt_ba'=1) & (op_busy'=true);
20  [enlistServers] (turn=SYST) & (as<MAX_SERVERS) & (cnt_es=0) −> (cnt_es'=1) & (turn'=ENVT);
21  // Tactic latency counter update
22  [] (turn=SYST) & (cnt_ba>0) & (cnt_ba<ba_latency) −> (cnt_ba'=cnt_ba+1) & (turn'=ENVT);
23  [] (turn=SYST) & (cnt_es>0) & (cnt_es<es_latency) −> (cnt_es'=cnt_es+1) & (turn'=ENVT);
24  // Tactic completion (after latency period expires)
25  [] (turn=SYST) & (cnt_ba=ba_latency) −> (cnt_ba'=0) & (rt'=ba_f_p) & (mc'=ba_f_mc) &
        (ua'=ba_f_ua) & (op_busy'=false) & (turn'=ENVT);
26  [] (turn=SYST) & (cnt_es=es_latency) −> (rt'=es_f_rt) & (cnt_es'=cnt_es+1) & (as'=es_f_as) &
        (cnt_es'=0) & (turn'=ENVT);
27  // Do nothing
28  [] (turn=SYST) & (cnt_es=0) & ... & (cnt_ba=0) −> (turn'=ENVT);
29  endmodule
```

7.6.2.4 System
The combined behavior of the target system and human actors is described in module ha_system (Listing 7.8). The module incorporates a collection of variables encoding the different system qualities of concern, as well as the aspects relevant to the applicability conditions of tactics (e.g., values of predicates used in the condition block of a tactic). Lines 12–17 illustrate how the different variables are initialized:

- rt, as, mc, and ua encode the response time, number of active servers, percentage of malicious clients, and level of user annoyance in the system, respectively.
- cnt_es and cnt_ba are counters used to keep track of the latency of tactics enlistServers and blackholeAttacker, respectively.[8]

The model also includes commands that specify the effect of executing the different tactics as updates on its variables. In particular, there are three commands per tactic in the module. We focus on tactic blackholeAttacker to illustrate how tactic execution is modeled:

---

[8]We do not describe the code corresponding to tactics lowerFidelity and throttleSuspicious in Listing 7.8 for the sake of clarity.

- *Tactic trigger* (line 19): Triggers tactic execution when: (i) an operator is on location and not busy, (ii) the estimated percentage of malicious clients is above zero, and (iii) the latency counter for the tactic is zero, meaning that the tactic is not being executed. As a consequence, the operator is flagged as busy and the latency counter is activated (cnt_ba'=1).
- *Tactic latency counter update* (line 22): If the tactic counter is active, but still has not reached the tactic's latency value, the counter is incremented in one unit.
- *Tactic completion* (line 25): When the tactic's latency counter expires, the command updates variables rt, mc, and ua according to the encoding of the impact of the tactics on the different quality dimensions (lines 5–7), which are affected by the probability ba_wc_prob (determined by the willingness and capability elements defined in Listing 7.7). The latency counter is reset, and the busy status of the operator is set to false.

The encoding used for the enlistServers tactic (lines 20, 23, and 26) follows the same structure, but without any OWC elements encoded in the guards or updates of the commands.

Every command in the module includes a predicate in the guard to ensure that the command is triggered only during the system player's turn (turn=SYST), and an additional predicate in the post state that yields the turn to the environment player (turn'=ENVT). Moreover, an additional command (line 28) lets the process progress without any variable updates when none of the latency periods for the tactics are active. Note that in our model, we assume sequential execution of tactics (in accordance with Stitch semantics).

7.6.2.5 Adaptation logic

Modules Eliminate and Outgun model the adaptation logic placed in the controller, according to the description of their respective Stitch strategies described in Listings 7.4 and 7.2. Each of the commands corresponds to a tactic that can be executed in the target system via synchronization on shared action names with trigger commands in the ha_system module (Listing 7.8, lines 19–20).

Module Eliminate (Listing 7.9) models the strategy to eliminate excess traffic with the help of a human operator. The command on line 3 encodes the triggering of tactic blackholeAttacker,[9] which sets the value of the timestamp variable ba_trigger_t that indicates at which time point the tactic was triggered. This variable is used on the guard of the command encoding the execution of

---

LISTING 7.9

Eliminate and Outgun adaptation strategy modules.

```
1   module Eliminate
2   ba_trigger_t:[0..MAX_TIME] init 0;
3   [blackholeAttacker] (turn=SYST) -> (ba_trigger_t'=t);
4   [throttleSuspicious] (turn=SYST) & (t=ba_trigger_t+ba_settling) & (ba_fail) -> true;
5   endmodule
6
7   module Outgun
8   es_trigger_t:[0..MAX_TIME] init 0;
9   [enlistServers] (turn=SYST) -> (es_trigger_t'=t);
10  [lowerFidelity] (turn=SYST) & (t=es_trigger_t+es_settling) & (es_fail) -> true;
11  endmodule
```

---

[9]We abstract away predicates unhandledMalicious and unhandledSuspicious (Listing 7.4, lines 4, 5), which we assume to be true in the scenarios encoded in our model.

throttleSuspicious (line 4) to determine whether the settling time for observation of the previous tactic's effect has already expired. If this is the case, and the blackholing of malicious clients by the human operator is not successful (ba_fail), the command executes, triggering the throttleSuspicious tactic, consistently with the Stitch code in Listing 7.4, line 4.

Module Outgun (Listing 7.9, line 7) follows a similar PRISM encoding that models the automatic strategy to absorb excess traffic in Znn.com.

7.6.2.6 Utility profile
Utility functions and preferences are encoded using formulas and reward structures that enable the quantification of the utility of a given game state. Formulas compute utility on the different dimensions of concern, and reward structures weigh them against each other by using the utility preferences of a given scenario.

Listing 7.10 illustrates in lines 1–5 the encoding of utility functions using a formula for linear interpolation based on the points defined for utility function U_M in the second column of Table 7.3. Lines 7–10 show how a reward structure can be defined to compute a single utility value for any state by using the utility preferences defined for a particular scenario.

7.6.3 ANALYSIS
SMG models of human-in-the-loop adaptation can be exploited to determine: (i) the expected outcome of human involvement in adaptation, and (ii) the conditions under which such involvement improves over fully automated adaptation. To analyze these two aspects of human involvement, we use rPATL specifications that include reward-specific operators aimed at checking quantitative properties over SMG models. Specifically, our technique enables us to statically analyze a particular region of the state space, which first has to be discretized to check rPATL properties. Obtaining the results of the analysis for each state in the discrete set requires an independent run of the model checker in which model parameters are instantiated with variable values corresponding to that state.

7.6.3.1 Strategy utility
The expected utility value of an adaptation strategy (potentially including nonautomated tactics) is quantified by checking the reachability reward property:

$$u_{mau} \triangleq \langle\langle sys \rangle\rangle R^{rGU}_{max=?}[F^c \ t=\text{MAX\_TIME}].$$

LISTING 7.10

Utility reward structure for Znn.com DoS scenarios.

```
1   formula uM = (mc>=0 & mc <=5? 1:0)
2     +(mc>5 & mc <=20? 1+(0.80−1)*((mc−5)/(20−5)):0)
3     +(mc>20 & mc <=50? 0.80+(0.40−0.80)*((mc−20)/(50−20)):0)
4     +(mc>50 & mc <=70? 0.40+(0.00−0.40)*((mc−50)/(70−50)):0)
5     +(mc>70 ? 0:0);
6   ...
7   rewards "rGU"
8     scenario=1 : 0.15*uR +0.6*uM +0.1*uC +0.15*uA;
9   ...
10  endrewards
```

The property obtains the maximum accrued utility value (i.e., corresponding to reward rGU—Listing 7.10) that the system player can achieve until the end of execution (t=MAX_TIME).

Fig. 7.3A depicts strategy utility analysis results for the different adaptation strategies in a DoS scenario in which the priority is to eliminate malicious clients (Scenario 1 in Table 7.4). In the figure, a discretized region of the state space is projected over the dimensions that correspond to the training level of a human actor, and the percentage of malicious clients (with values in the range [0,1] and [0,100], respectively). Each point in the mesh represents the maximum accrued utility that the system can achieve on the model instanced for a time frame of 15 min. The initial state of the scenario corresponds to 0 stress level of the operator, a response time is 2000 ms, 0% of user annoyance, and 2 active servers. Tactic cost/benefit values and the utility profile employed are those described in Section 7.4, whereas the latency value employed for tactics blackholeAttacker and throttleSuspicious is 5 min (this latency models the time that the human operator takes to decide which clients have to be blackholed or throttled). Time delays to observe the effect of tactic executions in the different strategies are those indicated in the Stitch code shown in Listings 7.4 and 7.2, respectively.

In the top left of Fig. 7.3, the plot shows that the utility obtained by the strategy Outgun in this scenario is not affected by the level of training of the human operator because the tactics employed

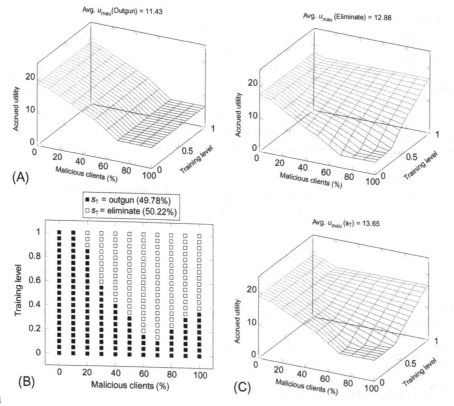

FIG. 7.3

Results for Scenario 1 (minimizing number of malicious clients): (A) outgun (top left) and eliminate (top right) strategy utility, (B) strategy selection (bottom left), and (C) combined utility (bottom right).

by the strategy are fully automated. Moreover, the utility that can be obtained decreases progressively with increasing levels of malicious clients. This is consistent with the fact that strategy Outgun employs only tactics that try to improve user experience without dealing with malicious users (e.g., adding new servers), and in Scenario 1, the main contribution to utility results from low levels of malicious clients.

The top right of Fig. 7.3 depicts the utility obtained by strategy Eliminate. In contrast with strategy Outgun, the plot shows how increasing levels of training yield better results. When the percentage of malicious clients is low, the impact of training on utility is negligible because there are few or no malicious clients to deal with. However, the outcome of the execution of tactics blackholeAttacker and throttleSuspicious in situations with increasing levels of malicious clients can vary significantly depending on the level of training of the human operator, who has to judge which clients will be affected by the tactics. Poorly trained operators may erroneously apply countermeasures to legitimate clients, being less efficient at reducing the percentage of malicious clients while increasing the level of annoyance in legitimate clients when blackholing or throttling.

Fig. 7.4 shows the results for Scenario 2, in which the top priority is optimizing the experience of legitimate clients, independently of the level of malicious clients making use of system resources.

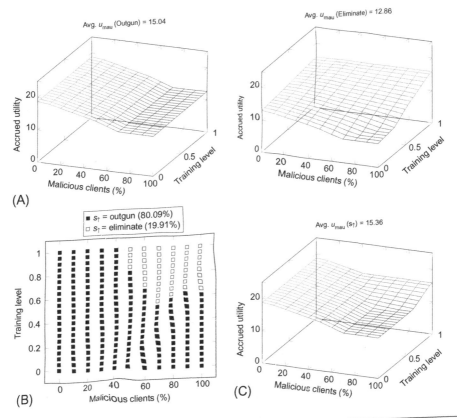

FIG. 7.4

Results for Scenario 2 (optimizing experience of legitimate clients): (A) outgun (top left) and eliminate (top right) strategy utility, (B) strategy selection (bottom left), and (C) combined utility (bottom right).

The top left plot of the figure shows how strategy Outgun still experiences a reduction in the utility with increasing levels of malicious users (similarly to Scenario 1). However, in this scenario the reduction in utility is less pronounced than in Scenario 1 because in this case the main contribution to utility results from optimizing legitimate client experience, and efficiency at reducing the percentage of malicious clients is not as relevant.

7.6.3.2 Strategy selection

Given a repertoire of adaptation strategies S, we can analyze their expected outcome in a given situation by computing their expected accrued utility according to the procedure described above. Based on this information, the different strategies can be ranked to select the one that maximizes the expected outcome in terms of utility. Hence the selected strategy $s_\uparrow$ can be determined according to:

$$s_\uparrow \triangleq \arg \max_{s \in S} u_{mau}(s)$$

where $u_{mau}(s)$ is the value of property u_{mau} (maximum accrued utility, cf. Section 7.6.3.1) evaluated in a model instantiated with the adaptation logic of strategy s.

Fig. 7.3B shows the results of the analysis of strategy selection in Scenario 1. The states in which human involvement via strategy Eliminate is chosen (50.22% of states) are represented in white, whereas states in which the automated strategy Outgun is selected (49.78%) are colored in black. The figure shows how progressively higher levels of malicious clients make human involvement preferable even when the level of training of the operator is limited (0.3–0.4) because, even under these conditions, Eliminate is still better at improving utility than Outgun. This is explained by the fact that the top priority in Scenario 1 is minimizing the number of malicious clients, and Outgun does not employ any tactics for dealing with them. However, it is worth noting that when the training level is very low, the improvement on user experience provided by Outgun can outweigh the moderate improvement in utility provided by inefficient executions of Eliminate (even if the percentage of malicious clients is high). This situation can be observed in the area in which training levels are below 0.4 and the percentage of malicious clients are in the range 80–100%.

Fig. 7.3C shows the combined accrued utility mesh that results from the selection process (i.e., every point in the mesh is computed as $u_{mau}(s_\uparrow)$). The average improvement is 16.3% over the Outgun strategy, and 5.6% over Eliminate. Note that the minimum accrued utility never goes below the achievable utility level of the automatic approach, over which improvements are made in the areas in which the strategy involving human actors is selected.

Fig. 7.4B shows the results of the analysis of strategy selection in Scenario 2. In this case, the plot shows how Outgun is selected in more than 80% of the states. This represents a remarkable increment in the selection of the automated strategy with respect to Scenario 1, which is explained by the different priorities that exist in Scenario 2 (improving legitimate client experience, independently of the percentage of malicious clients). Indeed, it can be observed that the selection of Eliminate in this scenario is justified only in the area in which both the percentage of malicious clients and the training level of the operator are high.

Fig. 7.4C shows the combined accrued utility mesh in Scenario 2. In this case, the improvement in utility obtained by the combined approach with respect to the individual strategies is not too far from those in Scenario 1, but transposed (the improvement over Outgun is 2%, and 16.2% for Eliminate).

This is motivated by the better alignment of the priorities in Scenario 2 and the target of strategy Outgun (improving client experience), whereas the priorities of Scenario 1 are better aligned with the target of Eliminate (dealing with malicious clients).

7.7 CONCLUSION

In this chapter, we have described an approach that employs formal reasoning to analyze trade-offs in self-adaptation at two different levels: (i) reasoning about business concerns in the context of other (potentially conflicting) business properties; and (ii) reasoning about the effectiveness of automated versus human-driven adaptations with respect to the different business concerns.

We have focused on human involvement in the execution stage of MAPE-K systems, in which human actors adopt the role of system-level effectors. We have shown how to incorporate concepts from CHS that model the probabilistic aspects of human behavior into a language tailored to describe runtime adaptation (Stitch) that supports systems described in a variety of architectural styles, as well as the specification of timing delays and probabilistic outcomes in adaptation tasks. We have also shown how such specifications can be encoded into SMG models amenable to analysis via model checking. We illustrated our approach in the context of Znn.com, a benchmark system in the self-adaptive systems community that embodies the typical infrastructure of a dynamically scalable web infrastructure. Our results showed that our approach can: (i) discriminate cases in which the involvement of human actors in execution leads to an improvement of system utility, providing the basis to combine human-based and automated adaptations; and (ii) decide about human involvement in a context-sensitive manner, selecting different adaptations for different preferences over business concerns.

Concerning future work, our current models assume that actors and system are working in cooperation to achieve goals. In fact, the interaction may be more subtle than that; Eskins and Sanders point out that humans may have their own motivations that run counter to policy [6]. To capture this possibility, we plan on extending the encoding of SMGs to model human actors as separate players. In particular, we intend to assess the impact on the application of our technique across different domains of various degrees of separation between the goals of human actors and those of the system. To this end, we shall explore different scenarios that include models of operators with different incentives, such as economic compensation models (e.g., per-task payments vs. fixed income), or operators with different goals who have to make use of shared platforms and resources. Moreover, we shall extend our approach to formally model and analyze human involvement in other stages of MAPE-K, studying how to best represent human-controlled tactic selection, and human-assisted knowledge acquisition.

In this chapter, we have described our approach on a simple OWC model that maps attributes of human operators to simple values for illustrative purposes. However, pragmatic solutions across different application domains might entail different instances of human models based on more nuanced representations of human operators [29, 30]. An additional future direction of research involves considering alternative models of human operators employed in different application domains, and exploring their use in the context of self-adaptive systems involving humans.

ACKNOWLEDGMENTS

This work was supported in part by awards N000141310401 and N000141310171 from the Office of Naval Research, CNS–0834701 from the National Science Foundation, the National Security Agency, and in collaboration with the Software Engineering Institute, a federally funded research and development center operated by Carnegie Mellon University. The views and conclusions contained herein are those of the authors and should not be interpreted as representing the official policies, either expressed or implied, of the Office of Naval Research, the Software Engineering Institute, or the U.S. Government.

REFERENCES

[1] B.H.C. Cheng, R. de Lemos, H. Giese, P. Inverardi, J. Magee, J. Andersson, B. Becker, N.Bencomo, Y. Brun, B. Cukic, G.D.M. Serugendo, S. Dustdar, A. Finkelstein, C. Gacek, K. Geihs, V. Grassi, G. Karsai, H.M. Kienle, J. Kramer, M. Litoiu, S. Malek, R. Mirandola, H.A. Müller, S. Park, M. Shaw, M. Tichy, M. Tivoli, D. Weyns, J. Whittle, Software engineering for self-adaptive systems: a research roadmap, in: B.H.C. Cheng, R. de Lemos, H. Giese, P. Inverardi, J. Magee (Eds.), Software Engineering for Self-Adaptive Systems [Outcome of a Dagstuhl Seminar], Volume 5525 of Lecture Notes in Computer Science, Springer, Berlin, 2009, pp. 1–26.

[2] M.C. Huebscher, J.A. McCann, A survey of autonomic computing—degrees, models, and applications, ACM Comput. Surv. 40 (3) (2008) 1–28.

[3] J.O. Kephart, D.M. Chess, The vision of autonomic computing, IEEE Comput. 36 (1) (2003) 41–50.

[4] D. Garlan, S.-W. Cheng, A. Huang, B. Schmerl, P. Steenkiste, Rainbow: architecture-based self-adaptation with reusable infrastructure, IEEE Comput. 37 (10) (2004) 46–54.

[5] S.-W. Cheng, D. Garlan, Stitch: a language for architecture-based self-adaptation, J. Syst. Softw. 85 (12) (2012) 2860–2875.

[6] D. Eskins, W.H. Sanders, The multiple-asymmetric-utility system model: a framework for modeling cyber-human systems, in: Eighth International Conference on Quantitative Evaluation of Systems, QEST 2011, Aachen, Germany, September 5–8, 2011, IEEE Computer Society, 2011, pp. 233–242.

[7] S. Cheng, Evaluating the effectiveness of the rainbow self-adaptive system, in: ICSE Workshop on Software Engineering for Adaptive and Self-Managing Systems, 2009, pp. 132–141.

[8] N. Esfahani, S. Malek, Uncertainty in self-adaptive software systems, in: R. de Lemos, H. Giese, H. Muller, M. Shaw (Eds.), Software Engineering for Self-Adaptive Systems II, Volume 7475 of Lecture Notes in Computer Science, Springer, New York, 2013, pp. 214–238.

[9] D. Sykes, W. Heaven, J. Magee, J. Kramer, Exploiting non-functional preferences in architectural adaptation for self-managed systems, in: S.Y. Shin, S. Ossowski, M. Schumacher, M.J. Palakal, C. Hung (Eds.), Proceedings of the 2010 ACM Symposium on Applied Computing (SAC), Sierre, Switzerland, March 22–26, 2010, ACM, 2010, pp. 431–438.

[10] R. Calinescu, M.Z. Kwiatkowska, Using quantitative analysis to implement autonomic IT systems, in: J. M. Atlee, P. Inverardi (Eds.), Proceedings of the 31st International Conference on Software Engineering, ICSE 2009, May 16–24, 2009, Vancouver, Canada, IEEE, 2009, pp. 100–110.

[11] I. Epifani, C. Ghezzi, R. Mirandola, G. Tamburrelli, Model evolution by run-time parameter adaptation, in: J. M. Atlee, P. Inverardi (Eds.), Proceedings of the 31st International Conference on Software Engineering, ICSE 2009, May 16–24, 2009, Vancouver, Canada, IEEE, 2009, pp. 111–121.

[12] J. Whittle, P. Sawyer, N. Bencomo, B.H.C. Cheng, J. Bruel, RELAX: a language to address uncertainty in self-adaptive systems requirement, Requir. Eng. 15 (2) (2010) 177–196.

[13] P. Oreizy, M. Gorlick, R. Taylor, D. Heimhigner, G. Johnson, N. Medvidovic, A. Quilici, D. Rosenblum, A. Wolf, An architecture-based approach to self-adaptive software, IEEE Intell. Syst. Appl. 14 (3) (1999) 54–62.

[14] C. Dorn, R.N. Taylor, Coupling software architecture and human architecture for collaboration-aware system adaptation, in: D. Notkin, B.H.C. Cheng, K. Pohl (Eds.), Proceedings of the 35th International Conference on Software Engineering, ICSE '13, San Francisco, CA, USA, May 18–26, 2013, IEEE/ACM, 2013, pp. 53–62.

[15] L. Clement, D. Konig, V. Mehta, R. Mueller, R. Rangaswamy, M. Rowley, I. Trickovic, WS-BPEL extension for people BPEL4People, 2010. http://docs.oasis-open.org/bpel4people/bpel4people-1.1.html.

[16] P. Wohed, W.M.P. van der Aalst, M. Dumas, A.H.M. ter Hofstede, N. Russell, On the suitability of BPMN for business process modelling, in: S. Dustdar, J.L. Fiadeiro, A.P. Sheth (Eds.), Proceedings of the Fourth International Conference on Business Process Management, BPM 2006, Vienna, Austria, September 5–7, 2006 Volume 4102 of Lecture Notes in Computer Science, Springer, Berlin, 2006, pp. 161–176.

[17] J. Cámara, G.A. Moreno, D. Garlan, Stochastic game analysis and latency awareness for proactive self-adaptation, in: G. Engels, N. Bencomo (Eds.), Proceedings of the Ninth International Symposium on Software Engineering for Adaptive and Self-Managing Systems, SEAMS 2014, Hyderabad, India, June 2–3, 2014, ACM, 2014, pp. 155–164.

[18] J. Cámara, G.A. Moreno, D. Garlan, Reasoning about human participation in self-adaptive systems, in: P. Inverardi, B.R. Schmerl (Eds.), Proceedings of the 10th IEEE/ACM International Symposium on Software Engineering for Adaptive and Self-Managing Systems, SEAMS 2015, Florence, Italy, May 18–19, 2015, IEEE, 2015, pp. 146–156.

[19] B.R. Schmerl, J. Cámara, J. Gennari, D. Garlan, P. Casanova, G.A. Moreno, T.J. Glazier, J.M. Barnes, Architecture-based self-protection: composing and reasoning about denial-of-service mitigations, in: L.A. Williams, D. M. Nicol, M.P. Singh (Eds.), Proceedings of the 2014 Symposium and Bootcamp on the Science of Security, Hot-SoS 2014, Raleigh, NC, USA, April 08–09, 2014, ACM, 2014, p. 2.

[20] J. Kramer, J. Magee, Self-Managed Systems: An Architectural Challenge, in: L.C. Briand, A.L. Wolf (Eds.), International Conference on Software Engineering, ISCE 2007, Workshop on the Future of Software Engineering, FOSE 2007, May 23–25, 2007, 2007, pp. 259–268.

[21] J. Cámara, A. Lopes, D. Garlan, B. Schmerl, Impact models for architecture-based self-adaptative systems, in: Proceedings of the 11th International Symposium on Formal Aspects of Component Software, FACS 2014, Bertinoro, Italy, September 10–12, 2014, Volume 8997 of Lecture Notes in Computer Science, Springer, Berlin, 2014, pp. 89–107.

[22] T. Chen, V. Forejt, M.Z. Kwiatkowska, D. Parker, A. Simaitis, PRISM-games: a model checker for stochastic multi-player games, in: N. Piterman, S.A. Smolka (Eds.), Proceedings of the 19th International Conference on Tools and Algorithms for the Construction and Analysis of Systems, TACAS 2013, Held as Part of the European Joint Conferences on Theory and Practice of Software, ETAPS 2013, Rome, Italy, March 16–24, 2013, Volume 7795 of Lecture Notes in Computer Science, Springer, Berlin, 2013, pp. 185–191.

[23] S. Kremer, J. Raskin, A game-based verification of non-repudiation and fair exchange protocols, in: K. G. Larsen, M. Nielsen (Eds.), Proceedings of the 12th International Conference on Concurrency Theory, CONCUR 2001, Aalborg, Denmark, August 20–25, 2001, Volume 2154 of Lecture Notes in Computer Science, Springer, Berlin, 2001, pp. 551–565.

[24] W.V.D. Hoek, M. Wooldridge, Model checking cooperation, knowledge, and time—a case study, Res. Econ. (2003) 200–203.

[25] T. Chen, V. Forejt, M.Z. Kwiatkowska, D. Parker, A. Simaitis, Automatic verification of competitive stochastic systems, Formal Methods Syst. Des. 43 (1) (2013) 61–92.

[26] T. Chen, J. Lu, Probabilistic alternating-time temporal logic and model checking algorithm, in: J. Lei (Ed.), Proceedings of the Fourth International Conference on Fuzzy Systems and Knowledge Discovery, FSKD 2007, August 24–27, 2007, Haikou, Hainan, China, vol. 2, IEEE Computer Society, 2007, pp. 35–39.

[27] R. Alur, T.A. Henzinger, O. Kupferman, Alternating-time temporal logic, J. ACM 49 (5) (2002) 672–713.

[28] V. Forejt, M.Z. Kwiatkowska, G. Norman, D. Parker, Automated Verification Techniques for Probabilistic Systems, in: M. Bernardo, V. Issarny (Eds.), Formal Methods for Eternal Networked Software Systems—11th International School on Formal Methods for the Design of Computer, Communication and Software Systems, SFM 2011, Bertinoro, Italy, June 13–18, 2011, Advanced Lectures, Volume 6659 of Lecture Notes in Computer Science, Springer, Berlin, 2011, pp. 53–113.

[29] J. Rasmussen, Mental models and the control of action in complex environments, in: D. Ackermann, M.J. Tauber (Eds.), Mental Models and Human-Computer Interaction 1 [Selected Papers of the Sixth Inter-disciplinary Workshop in Informatics and Psychology, Schärding, Austria, June 1987], North-Holland, 1990, pp. 41–69.

[30] J. Rasmussen, The role of hierarchical knowledge representation in decisionmaking and system management, IEEE Trans. Syst. Man Cybernet. 15 (2) (1985) 234–243.

PRINCIPLED ELICITING AND EVALUATION OF TRADE-OFFS WHEN DESIGNING SELF-ADAPTIVE SYSTEMS ARCHITECTURES

S. Andrade*,†, R. Macêdo†

Federal Institute of Education, Science, and Technology of Bahia, Salvador, Bahia, Brazil*
Federal University of Bahia, Salvador, Bahia, Brazil†

8.1 INTRODUCTION

Over the past few years, advances in areas such as virtualization, big data storage, and high performance computer networks have changed the way we develop modern software-intensive distributed systems [1–3]. Requirements for scalability, fault tolerance, and adaptability—to mention just a few—become substantially more critical in scenarios such as cloud computing environments [4], cyber-physical systems [5], QoS-aware web services [6], and applications for mobile devices [7]. In such scenarios, operational environments and workloads highly uncertain and dynamic introduce a number of shortcomings in those architectures that commit to nonadaptive solutions, taken in the early stages of software design. As a consequence, the delivered service easily degrades when conditions deviate from those assumed in design-time.

Moving one or more activities of the software development process—previously undertaken offline by designers and developers—to runtime allows for endowing software systems with self-management or self-adaptation capabilities [8–10]. Such activities—now undertaken online solely by the system itself or assisted by the operator—require the adoption of some infrastructure for system and environment monitoring, reasoning about the needs for adaptation, generation of effective adaptation plans, and enacting of adaptation changes in the running system.

Over the past years, several mechanisms for enabling self-adaptation have been proposed by different research communities, including the use of graph grammars [11], machine learning [12], control theory [13, 14], intelligent agents [15], event-condition-action rules [16, 17], and models at runtime [18]. As a consequence, being informed about all alternative candidate architectures, making judicious decisions about trade-offs, and performing early rigorous analysis of quality attributes are still quite challenging tasks, even for skilled architects.

This chapter presents an approach for principled eliciting and evaluation of trade-offs when designing software architectures. Such an approach provides the underpinnings for the systematic

Managing Trade-offs in Adaptable Software Architectures. http://dx.doi.org/10.1016/B978-0-12-802855-1.00008-3

representation of refined design knowledge in terms of well-structured design spaces [19], as well as for the use of multiobjective optimization techniques [20] as a rigorous mechanism to reveal and analyze design trade-offs. For that purpose, we developed a new modeling language—named DuSE [21]—which provides the constructs for describing well-structured design spaces for a given domain application. Such design space entails the domain's prominent architectural concerns, possible solutions for each concern, and associated architecture evaluation metrics.

A design space—when instantiated for a given problem from the application domain—yields an application-specific design space: a potentially huge search space containing all possible candidate architectures for such a problem. For those application domains where effective architectures are the result of subtle and ingenious combinations of architectural tactics, finding out such solutions by manual exploration of design spaces is quite unlikely. Therefore, the adoption of multiobjective optimization may leverage the eliciting of those candidate architectures which exhibit optimal trade-offs in the fulfillment of conflicting quality attributes.

The aforementioned infrastructure was conceived, designed, and implemented to be domain-independent and, therefore, amenable to be reused to capture refined design knowledge across different application domains. Such an infrastructure was instantiated in order to create SA:DuSE [22]—a specific design space aimed at capturing the most prominent architectural concerns when designing self-adaptive systems based on control-theoretical feedback loops [14]. SA:DuSE enables the automated design of architectures that adopt different solutions for five design dimensions: control cardinality, control law, control tuning, control adaptation, and interloop interaction. Each candidate architecture—representing a particular combination of solutions for the cited dimensions—is evaluated regarding four domain-specific quality attributes: average settling time, average overshoot, control robustness, and control overhead.

Our approach has been validated regarding three different aspects, all of them evaluated in two representative self-adaptive scenarios: an adaptive web server and an elastic platform for distributed MapReduce jobs. First, we investigated to which extent SA:DuSE effectively captures the expected trade-offs when designing feedback control loops for such scenarios. To achieve this, we evaluated the optimality and diversity of results from a single optimization run by using the *hypervolume* performance indicator. We also undertook statistical tests to find out the minimum number of iterations required to produce sufficiently optimal solutions. Second, we investigated with which accuracy the values of average settling time and average overshoot—predicted by SA:DuSE—are actually observed in real prototypes of three candidate architectures in each scenario. Such candidates were implemented on top of Apache httpd web server (for the adaptive web server scenario) and Apache Hadoop (for the elastic platform for distributed MapReduce jobs scenario). Finally, we undertook a quasi-experiment that investigated whether our approach improves the design self-adaptive systems architectures in terms of architectural complexity and control effectiveness, when compared to a traditional architecture design process.

The remainder of this chapter is organized as follows. Section 8.2 presents the most prominent requirements for an automated approach for software architecture design and analysis. Section 8.3 presents our approach, detailing the rationale which guided its inception, the underlying mechanisms and technologies adopted, and how we have used such an infrastructure to automate the design of self-adaptive systems architectures. Section 8.5 discuss the evaluation activities we have undertaken in order to assess the proposed approach. Finally, Section 8.6 presents the conclusions and draws the venues for future investigation.

8.2 REQUIREMENTS FOR AUTOMATED ARCHITECTURE DESIGN AND ANALYSIS

Although software architectures undergo continuous evolution in diverse stages of a software development process, their primary inception occurs in early stages of design, as by-product of a software architecture design process [23]. Fig. 8.1 depicts the usual stages defined in a software architecture design process. In the requirement analysis stage, major functional and nonfunctional requirements are elicited and then verified for any architecturally significant impact. Such requirements are passed as input for the decision making stage, where the well-orchestrated use of distilled design knowledge enables the judicious choice of those architectural tactics that yields a candidate architecture that effectively fulfill the desired quality attributes. The candidate architecture is then analyzed—regarding distinct quality attributes—and a new design cycle is undertaken if results show that further improvements may be achieved.

The aforementioned architecture design process may be instantiated in different ways. It may implement very agile cycles or a more bureaucratic approach; the analysis stage may include only manual inspections/reviews or be assisted by evaluation tools; and qualitative and/or quantitative aspects may be taken into account during analysis activities. Our approach aims at automating such a process by providing the underlying infrastructure for: (i) the systematic capture of refined design knowledge—supporting, therefore, the use of well-structure design spaces in the decision making stage; and (ii) a more rigorous approach for trade-off eliciting and analysis—by adopting multiobjective optimization mechanisms in the architecture analysis stage.

Under such perspective, we identified a set of six requirements that should be addressed by an automated process for architecture design and analysis, described as follows.

R1: Design knowledge should be systematically represented in a well-structured design space. Such a requirement enables the automatic design of architectures implementing any combination of architectural tactics defined for a given application domain. That helps ensuring that all candidate

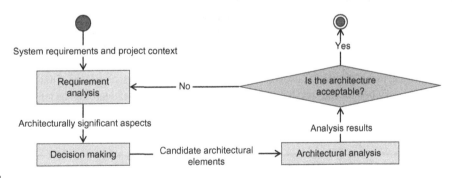

FIG. 8.1

Usual stages defined in a software architecture design process. Architecturally significant requirements—yielded in the Requirements Analysis stage—are passed as inputs to the decision making stage. Refined architectural knowledge is then applied in order to produce a given candidate architecture (decision making stage's output). Such a candidate is analyzed regarding the fulfillment of different quality attributes in the Architectural Analysis stage. The process repeats until an acceptable candidate architecture is obtained.

architectures—including those subtle and ingenious—will be taken into account during the decision making stage.

R2: Impacts of architectural tactics on quality attributes should be quantitatively measurable by accurate evaluation models. While the use of qualitative analysis enables a more thorough investigation about amorphous aspects like design rationale, fully automated design processes must rely on a set of evaluation models which quantitatively inform how good is a candidate architecture in the achievement of the desired quality attributes.

R3: Alternative architectures regarding a particular trade-off should be amenable to rigorous eliciting and evaluation. In general, architectural decisions are strategically taken in order to induce desired properties in the final solution. When such properties are conflicting, different candidate architectures provide different balances in the fulfillment of such quality attributes. Having such trade-offs explicitly identified and rigorously evaluated is mandatory if we are to prospect principled processes for software design and analysis.

R4: The adopted architectural modeling notation should be rigorous enough to support the automated process. The decision making stage must produce models described in a notation/language that fulfill the minimum requirements of ambiguity and accuracy in order to support the automatic analysis activities adopted in the process.

R5: Mechanisms for feeding analysis results back to the upcoming cycle should be adopted. As in nonautomated architecture design processes, candidate architectures are expected to be evolved until the minimum requirements for the quality attributes at hand are sufficiently fulfilled.

R6: The automated architecture design and analysis approach should be domain-independent. We expect such an approach be amenable to be adopted in a range of application domains. While some particular domains may require some uncommon model manipulations, we believe a set of common architectural changes (e.g., addition/removal of a component/connector and change of an element's property) is likely to support the automatic design of architectures for a broad class of application domains.

As for the self-adaptive systems domain in particular, it is worth mentioning that automated approaches for architecture design and analysis may play two different roles. First, as an off-line mechanism to come up with effective architectures—as in any other application domain to which a systematic design space is available. Second, as an online infrastructure responsible for continuously finding out an effective new architecture (adaptation) given the new conditions observed in the environment and in the system itself. The work we present in this chapter focuses on the first role aforementioned. A number of new requirements should be introduced when focusing on the second role, such as constraints regarding the temporal predictability of adaptations and the detection of those system states in which adaptation can be safely enacted.

8.3 THE DuSE APPROACH FOR AUTOMATED ARCHITECTURE DESIGN AND ANALYSIS

DuSE is an automated software architecture design process—proposed by us and initially described in [21, 22]—which provides the underpinnings for the systematic representation of refined architecture design knowledge for a given application domain. Furthermore, is enables the use of rigorous multi-objective optimization mechanisms to elicit and evaluate the involved trade-offs when designing architectures for a particular system of such a domain.

8.3.1 **THE RATIONALE**

During the DuSE inception, a number of underlying new and existing technologies and mechanisms have been selected and integrated in order to effectively fulfill the aforementioned requirements for automated architecture design and analysis approaches. Such decisions are described below, along with the reasons for their adoption and the requirements addressed by each decision.

D1: Use of models as underlying technology for systematizing the representation of design knowledge. Since we wanted our approach to be automatic, the forging of new architectures was supported by a machine-consumable representation of the possible architectural tactics (design space)—described in a model that captures the prominent design dimensions and solutions for a given domain application at hand. To support this, we designed a new modeling language—also named DuSE—which provides all the constructs required to define a design space for a given application domain. Such a decision addresses requirements R1 and R4, as it supports the well-structured representation of design spaces in a modeling notation (meta object facility—MOF and unified modeling language—UML) which is rigorous enough to achieve the approach's goals.

D2: Use of meta-models as enabling mechanism for domain-independence. The generic architecture optimization engine we devised performs all its operations based on constructs from the meta-model level of the language used when creating the design space model. That allows for reusing the whole architecture optimization infrastructure across a range of application domains, varying only the particular design space guiding the process. The DuSE language is described in MOF [24] and all generated candidate architectures are described in UML [25]. We decided to base our approach in MOF and UML languages because of their wide use in industry and high expressiveness when modeling software architectures. Such decision addresses requirement R6.

D3: Use of a posteriori preference articulation to reveal architectural trade-offs. Multiobjective optimization problems in which two or more objectives are potentially conflicting may be addressed by a priori or a posteriori approaches. In a priori approaches, a preference vector is defined in advance to indicate the weights that will govern the fulfillment of the multiple objectives. The problem is then reduced to a single objective one where different weights yield solutions exhibiting varying trade-offs when meeting the objectives. However, finding out an optimal solution depends highly on the adopted weight vector, often set up subjectively, based on previous experience and, therefore, amenable to bias. In our work, we rely on a posteriori preference articulation, where the output of an optimization run is a set of equally optimal architectures (named Pareto-front [20]), differing only at which objective is favored. Such decision addresses requirement R3 and sets the stage for addressing requirement R2.

D4: Use of highly scalable optimization mechanisms, even at the cost of nonguaranteed optimality. It's commonly agreed that, for some intricate application domains, the set of all architectural tactics available for use in the design stage is potentially huge. Manually evaluating all possible combinations of tactics in order to come up with an effective architecture for a problem at hand is obviously unlikely. On the other hand, we believe the most outstanding architectures may result from subtle and nonnaive combinations, which abide in regions of such huge design space hardly found by manual exploration. Our approach adopts multiobjective evolutionary optimization mechanisms in order to cope with huge design spaces without incurring in exponentially large search times. Even though that implies in nonguaranteed optimality, we believe that finding out near-optimal architectures in a reasonable time already constitutes valuable results. Such decision addresses requirement R5.

8.3.2 THE APPROACH

DuSE aims at supporting the automated design of software architectures by systematically representing refined design knowledge for a given application domain and adopting multiobjective optimization mechanisms to enable the principled eliciting and evaluation of design trade-offs. Although such an approach has been initially conceived to support the design of self-adaptive systems, the decisions mentioned in Section 8.3.1 make it amenable to use in any application domain for which a design space has been created. The domain-independent operation of our approach is described as follows.

In order to make DuSE domain-independent, we designed a generic meta-modeling infrastructure which provides the means for specifying a new design space for an application domain of interest. Such a design space entails the architectural changes that represent all possible tactics implementing alternative solutions for a set of design concerns considered prominent in the application domain. Furthermore, a design space specifies a set of quality attributes and its corresponding evaluation metrics. Each candidate architecture—a valid combination of tactics for each design concern—may then be evaluated regarding the different quality attributes present in the design space.

Since such design spaces may easily span a huge number of candidate architectures, we use multiobjective optimization mechanisms to automatically reveal those candidates that represent (near-) optimal trade-offs between the involved quality attributes. The whole optimization mechanism we propose operates at the meta-modeling level of the design space representation and it is, therefore, amenable to be used across a range of application domains.

Fig. 8.2 describes the design workflow we propose. Qualified architects use distilled design knowledge to specify: (i) a domain-specific UML profile; (ii) the most prevalent design dimensions and their corresponding alternative solutions in such a domain; and (iii) the quality metrics which evaluate candidate architectures regarding desired attributes. These tasks are performed once per application domain, at the *design space inception* stage (Fig. 8.2A).

Henceforth—in the *design space usage* stage (Fig. 8.2B)—the domain-specific design space (DuSE instance) and UML profile can be used by (novice) architects either to manually explore redesign alternatives for a given initial system or to hand over such task to the multiobjective optimization engine provided by DuSE.

A concrete design space and its quality attributes are specified by using a modeling language—also named DuSE—we have designed for such a purpose. A supporting UML profile is also defined for the application domain at hand, enabling the annotations that drive the automated design process. A *design space* (e.g., for the application domain of distributed and concurrent systems) is defined as a set of *ndesign dimensions* representing specific design concerns in such a domain (e.g., concurrency strategy, caching algorithm, and event dispatching model).

Definition 8.1. A *design space* is a tuple $ds = \langle DD, QM, P \rangle$, where DD is a nonempty totally ordered set of design dimensions, QM is a nonempty totally ordered set of quality metrics, and P is the accompanying UML profile for such an design space.

Each design dimension holds a set of *variation points*, which represent alternative solutions for such a concern (e.g., leader-followers or half-sync/half-async; for the concurrency strategy dimension).

Definition 8.2. A *design dimension* is a tuple $dd = \langle VP, targetElementsExp \rangle$, where VP is a nonempty totally ordered set of variation points and *targetElementsExp* is an object constraint language (OCL) expression which returns—when evaluated on an initial UML architectural model M—the elements of M that demand a decision about the architectural concern represented by dd. Such elements are named *target elements* of dd with respect to M and denoted by *targetElements(dd,M)*.

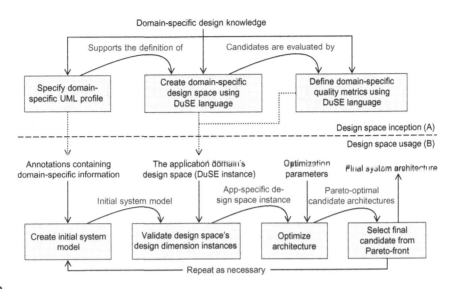

FIG. 8.2

DuSE-based architecture design process. In the *design space inception* stage (A) domain-specific design knowledge is systematically captured, by an experienced architect, in a new DuSE design space. Afterwards, in the *design space usage* stage (B), architects may submit initial models to be modified according the knowledge captured in a given DuSE design space.

The *targetElementsExp* expression uses annotations from the associated UML profile to detect, in the initial model, the architectural *loci* that demand decisions about such a concern. For instance, in the distributed and concurrent systems domain, an initial model may require the choice of a particular concurrency strategy for two different service components. Therefore, two instances of the concurrency strategy design dimension are created to capture the decisions for those architectural *loci*.

Definition 8.3. A *design dimension instance* is a tuple $ddi = \langle M,dd,te \rangle$, where M is an initial UML architectural model, dd is a design dimension, and te is a target element of dd with respect to M.

A variation point describes the architectural elements that must be added to, removed from, or changed in the initial model in order to implement such a particular solution.

Definition 8.4. A *variation point* is a tuple $vp = \langle C,postConditionExp \rangle$, where C is a totally ordered set of architectural changes and *postConditionExp* is an OCL expression evaluated after all changes in C are applied in the initial model. Such an expression must return true for valid architectures or false otherwise.

Definition 8.5. An *architectural change c* is a single indivisible operation that, when applied to a model M, results in a model $M' \neq M$. An architectural change c may represent an element addition, element removal or element's property change.

The set of all design dimension instances generated by ds, when evaluated in M, provides the underlying search space in which our approach perform the optimization activities.

Definition 8.6. An *application specific design space* is a tuple $asds = \langle M, ds, DDI \rangle$, where M is an initial UML architectural model, ds is a design space, and DDI is a partially ordered set of design dimension instances, defined as:

$$DDI = \bigcup^{dd \in ds.DD} \left(\bigcup^{te \in dd.targetElements(M)} ddi = \langle M, dd, te \rangle \right) \tag{8.1}$$

The ultimate decision space may then be specified in terms of an application specific design space.

Definition 8.7. The *architectural decision space* $\mathcal{D}_{asds}$ for a given application specific design space $asds$ is the Cartesian product of all variation point indexes of design dimensions associated to each design dimension instance in $asds.DDI$:

$$\begin{aligned} \mathcal{D}_{asds} = &\{1, 2, \ldots, |asds.DDI_1.dd.VP|\} \\ &\times \{1, 2, \ldots, |asds.DDI_2.dd.VP|\} \\ &\times \cdots \\ &\times \{1, 2, \ldots, |asds.DDI_{|DDI|}.dd.VP|\} \end{aligned} \tag{8.2}$$

A vector $\mathbf{x} \in \mathcal{D}_{asds}$ is named *candidate vector*. The architectural model resulting from the valid application of all changes of variation points whose indexes are described in $\mathbf{x}$ is named *candidate architecture*. The subset of $\mathcal{D}_{asds}$ formed only by those candidate vectors resulting in valid architectures is named architectural feasible space ($\mathcal{F}_{asds}$).

Therefore, a candidate architecture (a location in such an n-dimensional space) is formed by the initial model modified with the merge of all architectural changes provided by all involved variation points.

Finally, a quality metric may be defined for a given design space.

Definition 8.8. A *quality metric* is a tuple $qm = \langle \Phi, g \rangle$. Φ is a function $\Phi : \mathcal{F}_{asds} \rightarrow \mathcal{V}$, where $\mathcal{F}_{asds}$ is an architectural feasible space and $\mathcal{V}$ is a set supporting measurements at least in interval scale [26]. g must take the value 1 or -1 indicating, respectively, whether the metric should be maximized or minimized. The *architectural objective space* $\mathcal{O}_{asds}$ is defined as the Cartesian product $\mathcal{V}_1 \times \mathcal{V}_2 \times \cdots \times \mathcal{V}_n$, where $\mathcal{V}_i$ is the image of the function Φ_i (evaluation of the ith metric of $asds.ds.QM$).

As a consequence of such an infrastructure, huge design spaces may easily be spawned even for small input models, motivating the adoption of meta-heuristics and multiobjective optimization approaches. The number of different candidate vectors in $\mathcal{D}_{asds}$ (including those resulting in invalid architectures) is given by:

$$\prod_{dd \in ds.DD} |dd.VP|^{|dd.targetElements(M)|} \tag{8.3}$$

Once a concrete design space is defined, architects can submit initial models to manual design space exploration or rely on the multiobjective optimization engine we provide (*design space usage* stage). The domain-independent optimization engine we provide handles all required steps to forge candidate architectures for a given set of design space locations, evaluate their quality regarding the attributes defined for the design space, and find out a set of Pareto-optimal architectures.

Let $\Phi_{asds.ds.QM}(M_c)$ be the function that evaluate all quality metrics in $asds.ds.QM$ with respect to a candidate architecture M_c:

$$\begin{aligned} &\Phi_{QM} : \mathcal{F}_{asds} \rightarrow \mathcal{O} \\ &\Phi_{QM}(M_r) \mapsto (-g_1 \cdot \Phi_1(M_r), -g_2 \cdot \Phi_2(M_r), \ldots, -g_n \cdot \Phi_n(M_r)) \end{aligned} \tag{8.4}$$

Let $T : x' \rightarrow M_c$ be the function that produces the candidate architecture M_c associated to a candidate vector $x' \in \mathcal{F}_{asds}$. The optimization problem may then be stated as:

$$\overset{\prec}{\min_{x' \in \mathcal{F}_{asds}}} \Phi_{QM}(T(x')) \qquad (8.5)$$

where $\overset{\prec}{\min}$ denote minimization for Pareto optimality [20].

8.3.3 TOOL SUPPORT

Our approach is fully supported by DuSE-MT[1] —a cross platform open source tool we develop to integrate the functionalities of creating design spaces and submitting models for automatic design and analysis. The tool was implemented in C++ and makes use of Qt[2] toolkit's computational reflection capabilities to provide a meta-model-agnostic core which accepts new modeling languages as plug-ins. The DuSE language was, therefore, implemented as one of such plug-ins and its meta-model is depicted in Fig. 8.3.

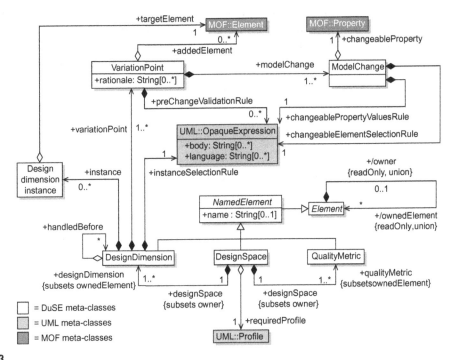

FIG. 8.3

DuSE meta-model for domain-independent design space specification. The DuSE meta-classes implement the constructs required to systematically capture a domain's refined design knowledge (design dimensions, variation points, model changes, and so on) and evaluation metrics.

---

[1]Website: http://duse.sf.net. Development repository: http://wiki.ifba.edu.br/duse-mt.
[2]http://www.qt.io.

By having the DuSE meta-model implemented as a DuSE-MT plug-in, users are able to create new design spaces for a particular application domain by merely creating a new model and selecting the DuSE language as meta-model (rather than, e.g., UML or MOF). All expressions for identifying a design dimension's target elements and specifying pre- and postconditions are defined in JavaScript, since that Qt already provides scripting capabilities with minimal coding demands.

Fig. 8.4 presents some functionalities of the DuSE-MT tool. The *Model Inspector* (panel 1) enable users to visualize the initial model submitted to optimization or the resulting candidate architecture for a given design space location. Such a location may be either manually selected in the *Design Space* tab (panel 4) or selected from the output of an optimization run (panel 5). Whenever a model's element is selected in the Model Inspector, its properties may be visualized and modified in the *Property Editor* (panel 2). Scripts written in JavaScript may be created and executed in the *Interpreter Console* (panel 3). The values of the design space's quality metrics for the model shown in the Model Inspector may be visualized in the panel 6. Finally, panel 7 presents the DuSE-MT's welcome dashboard.

DuSE-MT's architecture was conceived to ease the tool evolution in distinct ways. First—as already mentioned—the tool is meta-model-agnostic and, therefore, supports the seamlessly integration of new user defined languages, implemented as plug-ins. Second, even though we currently adopt the NSGA-II algorithm [27] as optimization back-end, alternative evolutionary mechanisms may be easily integrated also as DuSE-MT plug-ins. Third, our approach poses no constraints on the kind

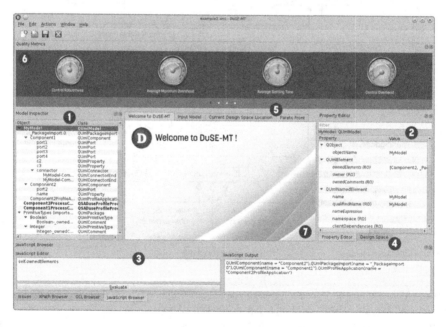

FIG. 8.4

The DuSE-MT tool and the GUI elements supporting our automated architecture design and analysis approach: (1) the initial model or the candidate architecture for a particular design space location; (2) properties of a selected model element; (3) scripting console; (4) panel for manual design space exploration; (5) architectures resulting from an optimization run; (6) quality attribute values for a given candidate architecture; and (7) welcome dashboard.

of models used to evaluate the design space's quality attributes. Such metrics may range from simple expressions written in JavaScript to interfacing with external tools like simulators or statistical toolkits.

8.4 AUTOMATING THE DESIGN AND ANALYSIS OF SELF-ADAPTIVE SYSTEMS ARCHITECTURES

A number of efforts from the software engineering for self-adaptive systems community [28] have addressed the issue of providing principled engineering approaches, leveraging the systematic capture of design knowledge and enabling the early reasoning of self-adaptation quality attributes. In this section we describe how the generic design space and architecture optimization infrastructure presented in Section 8.3 was instantiated to support the automatic design of architectures for self-adaptive systems which employ control theory as the governing law of their feedback loops.

Fig. 8.5 presents the common elements of a feedback control system. The *target system* is a software system with a *system output*—$y(t)$—which represents the quality attribute (e.g., average service response time or CPU utilization) intended to be controlled. Such attribute is directly influenced by a *system input* signal—$v(t)$, which manipulates, for instance, buffer sizes or the number of threads in a pool. The goal is to retain the system output as close as possible to a *reference input*, which represents the desired service level specified by the administrator. Uncertainties in the operating environment (e.g., changing workloads or hardware failures) introduce a *disturbance input* signal—$d(t)$—which makes it harder to derive accurate models for system input-output relationships. *Noise input* signals—$n(t)$—produced by sensors with high stochastic sensitivity may further complicate the control goals. Dealing with unmodeled and unforeseen disturbances and noises has motivated the idea where the *measured output*—$m(t) = y(t) + n(t)$—is fed back to the controller. By calculating how much the measured output deviates from the reference input (*control error*—$e(t)$), the feedback controller makes

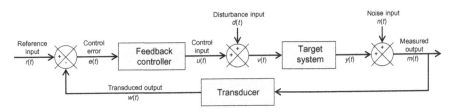

FIG. 8.5

Basic elements of a feedback control loop. The goal is to retain the target system's output $y(t)$ as close as possible to a reference value $r(t)$ by enacting changes in a target system's input $v(t)$. Feedback control uses the measured output $m(t)$ to calculate a control error $e(t)$, which serves as input for a particular control law adopted by the feedback controller.

use some specific control law to decide about the *control input* signal—$u(t)$—to be applied in the target system. A transducer is commonly used in cases demanding unit conversion and/or delay handling.

The use of control theory as the enabling mechanism for endowing software systems with self-adaptation capabilities has been the focus of many current research efforts [29–34]. Such researches have been contributing to increasing our confidence on the benefits of control theory—and its accompanying rigorous foundations for design and analysis of feedback loops—when designing self-adaptive systems. On the other hand, the required preliminary understanding of basic system dynamics modeling, analysis in the frequency domain, and the vast array of available control approaches [14] make it harder for novice architects to fully consider design alternatives, make judicious decisions, and be aware of the impact of decisions on software's quality attributes. The result is an application domain quite rich and promising, but also undisciplined and ad-hoc regarding the use of refined design and analysis knowledge.

Our work tries to mitigate such a problem by promoting a systematic capture of design knowledge related to the use of control theory when designing self-adaptive systems. For that purpose, the aforementioned design space and architecture optimization infrastructure was instantiated to create SA: DuSE—a particular design space devoted to the self-adaptive systems domain.

Table 8.1 presents the five design dimensions and their corresponding variation points captured in the SA:DuSE design space. Dimension DD1 entails the control cardinality adopted in the candidate architecture. In single-input single-output (SISO) approaches, each control input in the target system has its own controller, which is responsible for retaining a single measured output as close as possible the its corresponding reference value. On the other hand, multiple-input multiple-output (MIMO) approaches, adopt a single controller for all control inputs and all measured outputs present in the target system. SISO approaches are usually easier to be designed, at the cost of reduced control performance in systems with a strong relationship between multiple inputs and outputs.

Dimension DD2 captures the control law adopted by each controller in the candidate architecture. Seven different control laws were represented in this dimensions: five variations of SISO laws (proportional, integral, proportional-integral, proportional-derivative, and proportional-integral-derivative) and two variations of MIMO laws (static state feedback control and dynamic state feedback control). Architectures representing invalid combinations of variation points for dimensions DD1 and DD2 are automatically detected and discharged during optimization runs.

Dimension DD3 captures the tuning method which should be used to adjust the parameters of each controller added by DD1's variation points. The tuning methods represented in this dimension are: four variations of the Chien-Hrones-Reswich method, the Ziegler-Nichols method, the Cohen-Coon method, and the linear-quadratic regulator method.

Dimension DD4 entails the adaptability mechanism adopted for each controller in the candidate architecture. Adaptive control is usually required in highly dynamic and uncertain environments, where the parameter values found off-line by tuning methods no longer imply in an acceptable control performance, given the new operational conditions. Five mechanisms are captured in this dimensions: fixed gain (no adaptation), gain scheduling, model identification adaptive control, model reference adaptive control, and reconfiguring control. Further details about such mechanisms may be found at [35].

Finally, dimension DD5 captures six interloops arrangements for systems where multiple feedback control loops are in place. These arrangements are derived from the work of Weyns at al. [36] and define different trade-offs between interloop communication overhead and the fulfillment of global adaptation goals. The arrangements captured in this dimensions are: independent loops (no cooperation), information sharing, coordinated control, regional planning, master/slave, and hierarchical control.

Table 8.2 presents the quality attributes and evaluation metrics defined in the SA:DuSE design space. Metrics M1 (average settling time) and M2 (average overshoot) are originated from the control theory and, therefore, have predictive purposes. On the other hand, metrics M3 (control effectiveness)

Table 8.1 Overview of Architectural Tactics Captured in the SA:DuSE Design Space

Design Dimension	Variation Point
DD1: Control cardinality	VP11: Single-input single-output
	VP12: Multiple-input multiple-output
DD2: Control law	VP21: Proportional
	VP22: Integral
	VP23: Proportional-integral
	VP24: Proportional-derivative
	VP25: Proportional-integral-derivative
	VP26: Static state feedback
	VP27: Dynamic state feedback
DD3: Tuning method	VP31: Chien-Hrones-Reswick with 0% overshoot and disturbance rejection goal
	VP32: Chien-Hrones-Reswick with 0% overshoot and reference tracking goal
	VP33: Chien-Hrones-Reswick with 20% overshoot and disturbance rejection goal
	VP34: Chien-Hrones-Reswick with 20% overshoot and reference tracking goal
	VP35: Ziegler-Nichols
	VP36: Cohen-Coon
	VP37: Linear-quadratic regulator
DD4: Control adaptability	VP41: Fixed gain (no adaptation)
	VP42: Gain schedule
	VP43: Model identification adaptive control
	VP44: Model reference adaptive
	VP45: Reconfigurable control
DD5: Multiple loops interaction	VP51: Independent loops
	VP52: Information sharing
	VP53: Coordinated control
	VP54: Regional planning
	VP55: Master/slave
	VP56: Hierarchical control

and M4 (control overhead) were defined by us as dimensionless quantities and serve only for comparative purposes.

The average settling time (M1) is the time elapsed from a control actuation to the time when the system stabilizes its measured output (steady-state value). This metrics is intended to be minimized since high settling times usually imply in violations in service level agreements and multiple loop interference. The average overshoot (M2) is the normalized maximum amount by which the system output exceeds its steady-state value. This metric is also intended to be minimized, since high overshoots usually imply in waste of resources.

The control effectiveness (M3) is the extent to which the controller keeps presenting acceptable control performance even when operational conditions deviate from those considered when tuning the controller. This evaluation metric is the average value of the weighted mean (controlled by β^E

Table 8.2 Overview of Quality Attributes and Metrics Captured in the SA:DuSE Design Space

Quality Attribute	Evaluation Metric
M1: Average settling time	$$\dfrac{\sum_i \left(\dfrac{-4}{\log r_i}\right)}{n}$$
M2: Average overshoot	$$\dfrac{\sum_i M_{P_i}}{n}; \text{ where } M_{p_i} \approx \begin{cases} 0 & \text{real dominant pole } p_{1_i} \geq 0 \\ |p_{1_i}| & \text{real dominant pole } p_{1_i} < 0 \\ r_i^{\pi/|\theta|} & \text{real dominant poles } p_{1_i}, p_{2_i} = re_i^{\pm j_i \theta} \end{cases}$$
M3: Control effectiveness	$$\dfrac{\sum_i E_i(c)}{n}; \text{ where } E_i(c) = \beta^E \cdot E_{r_i}(c) + (1 - \beta^E) \cdot E_{m_i}(c)$$
M4: Control overhead	$$\dfrac{\sum_i O_i(c)}{n}; \text{ where } O_i(c) = \beta^O \cdot O_{r_i}(c) + (1 - \beta^O) \cdot O_{m_i}(c)$$

parameter) of the effectiveness given by the ith loop robustness (E_{r_i}) and the effectiveness given by the ith interloop arrangement (E_{m_i}). E_{r_i} generates a value between 0 and 1, according to the variation point selected for design dimension DD4 (0 for fixed gain, increasing to 1 in Reconfigurable Control). Similarly, E_{m_i} produces a value between 0 and 1, according to the interloop arrangement selected for design dimension DD5. Independent loops (no cooperation) are expected to decrease the global control effectiveness (0), increasing to a maximum effectiveness (1) when selecting Hierarchical Control. The control overhead (M4) adopts a similar approach to estimate computational and communication overhead.

8.4.1 RUNNING EXAMPLES

This section presents two self-adaptation scenarios widely investigated nowadays and that have been used to evaluate our approach. The first one, depicted in Fig. 8.6, represents a self-adaptive web server. The self-adaptive systems architect is in charge of designing an effective feedback control loop which controls the server's memory and CPU utilization by regulating two impacting parameters: IMaxRW (the number of working threads serving client requests) and IKATimeout (the number of seconds to wait for a new request until the server closes the current connection). These two parameters affect both memory and CPU utilization (measurable, respectively, from the IMemUtilization and ICPUUtilization interfaces) and the architect would have to consider alternative solutions (degrees of freedom) for a number of design dimensions in order two fulfill the expected quality attributes (e.g., small average settling time and average overshoot).

Fig. 8.6A and 8.6B present two examples of candidate architectures generated by SA:DuSE. The former adopts MIMO control (VP12), with dynamic state feedback as control law (VP27) and LQR as tuning method (VP37). The later, on the other hand, adopts two SISO controllers (VP11), both with Proportional-Integral as control law (VP23) and using, respectively, Ziegler-Nichols (VP35) and Cohen-Coon (VP36) as tuning methods. For both candidate architectures, no control adaptation has been adopted (VP41) and no interloop arrangements have been applied (VP51) since one single loop

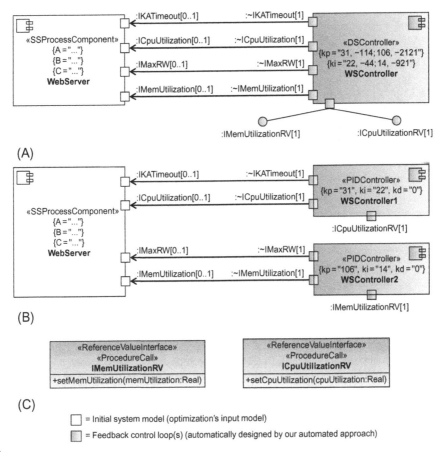

FIG. 8.6

(A) Candidate architecture representing an initial web server model endowed with a single MIMO controller.
(B) Candidate architecture representing an initial web server model endowed with two SISO controllers. (C)
Interfaces for adjusting the reference values for memory and CPU utilization.

is in place. These two candidate architecture exhibit specific values for the four metrics defined in SA:
DuSE. Other variation points' combinations yield different candidate architectures, with different balances in the fulfillment of the quality attributes.

The second self-adaptation scenario, depicted in Fig. 8.7, is an elastic cluster for the distributed execution of MapReduce jobs. The entire cluster, depicted as the `ElasticCluster` component, entails a set of `NodeManager` components representing each storing/processing node in the cluster. Such scenario poses a number of self-adaptation challenges since multiple loops may operate at different levels. For instance, each cluster's node may adopt a local feedback loop which controls the node throughput (measurable from the `INodeThrput` interface) by regulating the maximum number of map tasks which simultaneously operate on that node (parameter `IMaxMappers`). In addition, a cluster-wide feedback control loop may control the total job throughput by regulating the number of nodes operating in

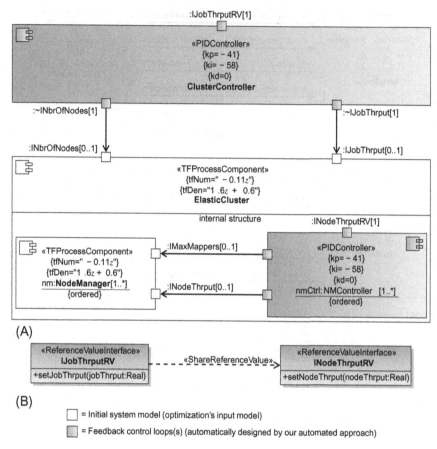

FIG. 8.7

(A) Candidate architecture representing an initial elastic cluster model for MapReduce applications endowed with two nested SISO controllers. (B) Interfaces for adjusting the reference values for job throughput and node throughput.

the cluster. In spite of finding out effective combinations of variation points, architects must in this case be also concerned about issues regarding multiple loops interactions. Part of such concerns are automatically handled when optimizing models with the SA:DuSE design space, marking candidate architectures with pernicious combinations as invalid.

8.5 EVALUATION

We have evaluated our approach for automated architecture design and analysis regarding different aspects. First, the performance of optimization runs and the SA:DuSE effectiveness in capturing the most prominent trade-offs when designing self-adaptive systems based on control theory were evaluated by using performance indicators from the multiobjective optimization field (experiment 1). Second, the predictive capabilities of SA:DuSE's quality metrics were evaluated by comparing the metric values presented by the optimization's output with observations of real prototypes implementing candidate architectures (experiment 2). Third, the impact of our approach in the effectiveness and complexity of resulting architectures—when compared to a traditional architecture design process—were investigated in a quasi-experiment (experiment 3). This chapter focuses on the description of the experiment 1. A comprehensive report on experiment 3 may be found at [37].

The experiment 1 aimed at evaluating the following research questions:

RQ1.1: Do the design dimensions defined in the SA:DuSE design space actually capture the multiobjective aspect of the design of self-adaptive systems architectures?

RQ1.2: Do the solutions yielded by the multiobjective architecture optimization mechanism we proposed actually represent effective architectures and provide alternatives in the fulfillment of involved quality attributes?

To answer RQ1.1, we undertook 31 optimization runs for each of the two example applications described in Section 8.4.1. Replication was needed because of the inherent nondeterministic nature of evolutionary optimization algorithms. We then calculated the Pareto-front (set of equally optimal architectures) of the merge of all 31 optimization run's outputs. We call this the *reference Pareto-front* P^* and assume it is a nice representative of the global Pareto-front (usually unknown because its actual discovery requires a complete design space exploration).

Fig. 8.8 depicts the scatter plot matrix for the population of architectures resulting from the optimization runs using the elastic cluster architecture (presented in Section 8.4.1) as initial model. The matrix's main diagonal presents—for each quality metric—the histograms of solutions in the Pareto-front and of dominated solutions. The remaining cells present the projection of the final population with respect to the quality metrics indicated at the cell's row and column. For instance, the scatter plot at the first column and second row depicts solutions using average settling time values in the abscissa and average overshoot values in the ordinate. Solutions in the Pareto-front are presented as diamonds, while the dominated ones are depicted as circles. A partial Pareto-front—regarding only the two quality metrics involved in a given cell—is shown as diamonds connected by a line. As indicated in the figure's legend, the solution color represents the interloop arrangement adopted by such an architecture. Finally, the solution size denotes the architecture's control robustness (the bigger, the more robust).

The outcome of our approach provides useful insights and supports the self-adaptive systems architect in several aspects. First, we observe that architectures exhibiting short average settling times are quite rare in the final population, making it harder for novice architects to find out such effective solutions by manually scouring the design space or by performing random searches. Second, the outcome reveals pronounced trade-offs between two pairs of quality attributes: (i) average settling time and average overshoot (first column, second row); and (ii) control robustness and control overhead (third column, fourth row). The Pareto-fronts for such combinations are smooth, providing alternative solutions regarding the fulfillment of such quality attributes. No significant trade-off has been found in other quality metric pairs. Third, the rigorous identification of Pareto-optimal solutions prevents novice architects from adopting those combinations of control law, tuning technique, and control adaptation mechanism that lead to inferior architectures. Finally, the metric values presented by solutions in the

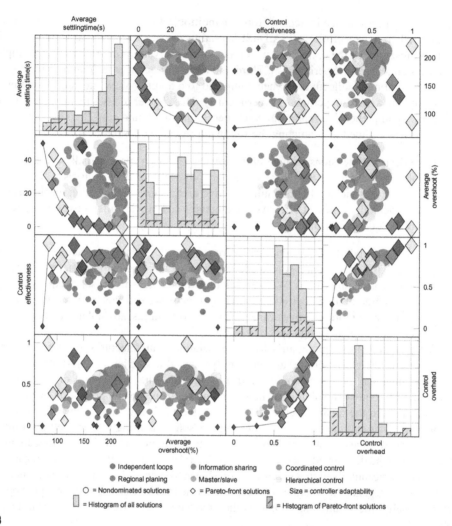

FIG. 8.8

Scatter plot matrix for the reference Pareto-front P^* for the elastic cluster initial architectural model.

Pareto-front allow for the early analysis of the dynamics exhibited by real prototypes implementing such architectures.

During the 31 optimization runs, 334,800 candidate architectures have been evaluated (probably including repeated ones) and the reference Pareto-front P^* presented 18 optimal candidates. Fig. 8.9 shows, for a single optimization run, the values of the hypervolume [20] metric for each optimization iteration i. The hypervolume calculates the extent of the search space covered by an optimization run. By comparing the hypervolume of a single optimization run with the one calculated for the reference Pareto-front, we can estimate how close of such optimal architectures are the solutions yielded by a single optimization run. This tell us how much we can rely on the output of a single

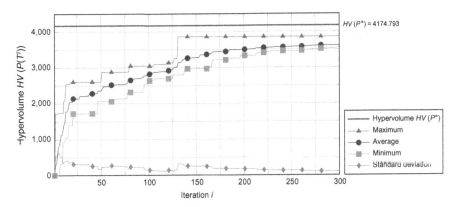

FIG. 8.9

Convergence of hypervolume metric during optimization iterations of the elastic cluster model for distributed execution of MapReduce jobs.

optimization run regarding the effectiveness of the resulting candidates in the fulfillment of involved quality attributes. Fig. 8.9 presents the minimum, average, maximum, and standard deviation values for the hypervolume of the resulting population at each iteration i—$HV(P(T^i))$, compared to the hypervolume value obtained from the reference Pareto-front—$HV(P*)$.

We conclude that the hypervolume of a single optimization run converges, in average, to $\overline{HV}(P(T^{300})) = 3612.8311$, nearly 85.53% of the reference Pareto-front's hypervolume. We also noticed that the hypervolume becomes sufficiently close (95%) to its final value at iteration 169. Keep running the optimization beyond such number of iterations produces no significantly enhanced candidate architectures. In order to better evaluate the convergence of the hypervolume metric for a single optimization run we investigated—at every iteration i—the null hypothesis that the average hypervolume is less or equal than 95% of its final value—$H_0 : \overline{HV}(P(T^i)) \leq 0.95 \cdot \overline{HV}(P(T^{300}))$. The goal was to find out, with a given significance level α, the first iteration where H_0 is rejected (its hypervolume exceeds 95% of its final value).

Table 8.3 presents the results of the statistical tests undertaken. For each iteration i, we used the Anderson-Darling test to verify whether the hypervolume values for the 10 replications are uniformly distributed (p-value ≥ 0.5). The Levene test investigates where the hypervolume values are homoscedastic (also p-value ≥ 0.5). If both conditions are satisfied, the H_0 may be evaluated by a parametric test (use adopted the t-test). Otherwise, a nonparametric test should be applied (we adopted the *Wilcoxon Signed Rank* test). We conclude that, with a significance level $\alpha = 0.05$, we claim the hypervolume reaches 95% of its final value at the 213th iteration. With a significance level $\alpha = 0.01$, the convergence happens at the 215th iteration.

8.6 CONCLUSIONS AND FUTURE WORK

Software architectures play a paramount role in the fulfillment of nonfunctional requirements and their design is usually driven by the use of refined experience, domain-specific knowledge, and

Table 8.3 Hypothesis Test's Results of the Hypervolume Convergence in the Elastic Cluster Model for Distributed Execution of MapReduce Jobs

Iteration i	$\overline{HV}(P(Ti))$	Anderson-Darling p-Value	Levene p-Value	Used Test	p-Value
...					
212	3512.200411	0.113852	0.274383	t-Test	0.101512
213	3533.574236	0.152420	0.260664	t-Test	0.046263
214	3533.574236	0.152420	0.260664	t-Test	0.046263
215	3539.272402	0.047992	0.320262	Wilcoxon SR	0.009520
216	3539.272402	0.047992	0.320262	Wilcoxon SR	0.009520
...					

well-informed decision making. In this chapter, we presented a novel approach for systematically representing distilled architecture design knowledge through the use of a meta-modeling infrastructure for the definition of domain-specific design spaces. Multiobjective optimization approaches were then adopted to leverage the discovery of (local-)optimal architectures. We described how such an infrastructure has been used to support the automated design and analysis of feedback control loops for self-adaptive systems.

On the other hand, we assume that an initial input model for the system being redesigned is available and minimally annotated. How hard this task is depends on the skills of the architect designing the domain-specific design space and UML profile. Future work include the use of alternative optimization methods, the definition of design space navigation traces to document design rationale, and the integration of our process with the prospection of design theories. Additionally, moving such architecture optimization engine to runtime may constitute a useful infrastructure to support Dynamic Adaptive Search-Based Software Engineering.

REFERENCES

[1] M.A. Heroux, Software challenges for extreme scale computing: going from petascale to exascale systems, Int. J. High Perform. Comput. Appl. 23 (4) (2009) 437–439. http://dx.doi.org/10.1177/1094342009347711.
[2] L.M. Northrop, Does scale really matter? Ultra-large-scale systems seven years after the study (keynote), in: Proceedings of the 35th International Conference on Software Engineering, ICSE '13, May 18–26, 2013, San Francisco, CA, USA, 2013, p. 857. http://dl.acm.org/citation.cfm?id=2486902.
[3] V. Sarkar, W. Harrod, A.E. Snavely, Software challenges in extreme scale systems, J. Phys. Conf. Ser. 180 (1) (2009) 012045. http://stacks.iop.org/1742-6596/180/i=1/a=012045.
[4] L.M. Vaquero, L. Rodero-Merino, R. Buyya, Dynamically scaling applications in the cloud, SIGCOMM Comput. Commun. Rev. 41 (1) (2011) 45–52. http://doi.acm.org/10.1145/1925861.1925869.
[5] M. Conti, S.K. Das, C. Bisdikian, M. Kumar, L.M. Ni, A. Passarella, G. Roussos, G. Tröster, G. Tsudik, F. Zambonelli, Looking ahead in pervasive computing: challenges and opportunities in the era of cyber-physical convergence, Pervasive Mobile Comput. 8 (1) (2012) 2–21. http://dx.doi.org/10.1016/j.pmcj.2011.10.001.
[6] E.D. Nitto, C. Ghezzi, A. Metzger, M.P. Papazoglou, K. Pohl, A journey to highly dynamic, self-adaptive service-based applications, Autom. Softw. Eng. 15 (3–4) (2008) 313–341. http://dx.doi.org/10.1007/s10515-008-0032-x.

[7] T. Kunz, An architecture for adaptive mobile applications based on mobile code, in: Proceedings of the 17th IASTED International Conference on Applied Informatics, February 15–18, 1999, Innsbruck, Austria, 1999, pp. 308–311.

[8] M.C. Huebscher, J.A. McCann, A survey of autonomic computing—degrees, models, and applications, ACM Comput. Surv. 40 (3) (2008) 7:1–7:28. http://doi.acm.org/10.1145/1380584.1380585.

[9] J.O. Kephart, D.M. Chess, The vision of autonomic computing, IEEE Comput. 36 (1) (2003) 41–50. http://doi.ieeecomputersociety.org/10.1109/MC.2003.1160055.

[10] M. Salehie, L. Tahvildari, Self-adaptive software: landscape and research challenges. ACM Trans. Auton. Adapt. Syst. (TAAS) 4 (2) (2009) 14:1–14:42. http://dx.doi.org/10.1145/1516533.1516538.

[11] D.L. Mtayer, Describing software architecture styles using graph grammars, IEEE Trans. Softw. Eng. 24 (7) (1998) 521–533. http://dblp.uni-trier.de/db/journals/tse/tse24.html#Metayer98.

[12] N. Esfahani, A.M. Elkhodary, S. Malek, A learning-based framework for engineering feature-oriented self-adaptive software systems, IEEE Trans. Softw. Eng. 39 (11) (2013) 1467–1493. http://doi.ieeecomputersociety.org/10.1109/TSE.2013.37.

[13] M.M. Kokar, K. Baclawski, Y.A. Eracar, Control theory-based foundations of self-controlling software, IEEE Intell. Syst. Appl. 14 (3) (1999) 37–45.

[14] D.M. Tilbury, S. Parekh, Y. Diao, J.L. Hellerstein, Feedback Control of Computing Systems, Wiley IEEE Press, Hoboken, NJ, USA, 2004. http://opac.inria.fr/record=b1119042 ISBN 0-471-26637-X.

[15] H.V.D. Parunak, S.A. Brueckner, Software engineering for self-organizing systems, in: D. Weyns, J.P. Müller (Eds.), Proceedings of the 12th International Workshop on Agent-Oriented Software Engineering (AOSE 2011), AAMAS 2011, Taipei, Taiwan, 2011.

[16] S. Cheng, D. Garlan, B. Schmerl, Architecture-based self-adaptation in the presence of multiple objectives, in: Proceedings of the 2006 International Workshop on Self-Adaptation and Self-Managing Systems, ACM Press, New York, NY, USA, 2006, pp. 2–8.

[17] D. Gil de la Iglesia, A formal approach for designing distributed self-adaptive systems, Ph.D. thesis, Linnaeus University, 2014.

[18] T. Vogel, H. Giese, A language for feedback loops in self-adaptive systems: Executable runtime megamodels, in: Proceedings of the 7th International Symposium on Software Engineering for Adaptive and Self-Managing Systems, SEAMS 2012, June 4–5, 2012, Zurich, Switzerland, IEEE, Washington, DC, USA, 2012, pp. 129–138. http://dx.doi.org/10.1109/SEAMS.2012.6224399.

[19] M. Shaw, The role of design spaces, IEEE Softw. 29 (1) (2012) 46–50. http://dx.doi.org/10.1109/MS.2011.121.

[20] K. Deb, D. Kalyanmoy, Multi-Objective Optimization Using Evolutionary Algorithms, John Wiley & Sons, Inc., New York, NY, USA, 2001. ISBN 047187339X.

[21] S.S. Andrade, R.J. de Araújo Macêdo, Architectural design spaces for feedback control concerns in self-adaptive systems (S), in: Proceedings of the 25th International Conference on Software Engineering and Knowledge Engineering, June 27–29, 2013, Boston, MA, USA, 2013, pp. 741–746.

[22] S.S. Andrade, R.J. de Araújo Macêdo, A search-based approach for architectural design of feedback control concerns in self-adaptive systems. in: Proceedings of the Seventh IEEE International Conference on Self-Adaptive and Self-Organizing Systems, SASO 2013, September 9–13, 2013, Philadelphia, PA, USA, 2013, pp. 61–70. http://dx.doi.org/10.1109/SASO.2013.42.

[23] C. Hofmeister, P. Kruchten, R. Nord, H. Obbink, A. Ran, P. America, Generalizing a model of software architecture design from five industrial approaches, in: Proceedings of the Fifth Working IEEE/IFIP Conference on Software Architecture, WICSA 2005, pp. 77–88. http://dx.doi.org/10.1109/WICSA.2005.36.

[24] OMG, OMG Meta Object Facility (MOF) Core Specification, Version 2.4.1. Object Management Group, 2011. http://www.omg.org/spec/MOF/2.4.1.

[25] OMG, OMG Unified Modeling Language (OMG UML), Superstructure, Version 2.4.1. Object Management Group, 2011. http://www.omg.org/spec/UML/2.4.1.

[26] S.S. Stevens, On the theory of scales of measurement, Science 103 (2684) (1946) 677–680. http://dx.doi.org/10.2307/1671815.

[27] K. Deb, A. Pratap, S. Agarwal, T. Meyarivan, A fast and elitist multiobjective genetic algorithm: NSGA-II. IEEE Trans. Evol. Comput. 6 (2) (2002) 182–197. http://dx.doi.org/10.1109/4235.996017.

[28] R. de Lemos, H. Giese, H.A. Müller, M. Shaw, J. Andersson, M. Litoiu, B.R. Schmerl, G. Tamura, N.M. Villegas, T. Vogel, D. Weyns, L. Baresi, B. Becker, N. Bencomo, Y. Brun, B. Cukic, R. Desmarais, S. Dustdar, G. Engels, K. Geihs, K.M. Göschka, A. Gorla, V. Grassi, P. Inverardi, G. Karsai, J. Kramer, A. Lopes, J. Magee, S. Malek, S. Mankovski, R. Mirandola, J. Mylopoulos, O. Nierstrasz, M. Pezzè, C. Prehofer, W. Schäfer, R.D. Schlichting, D.B. Smith, J.P. Sousa, L. Tahvildari, K. Wong, J. Wuttke, Software engineering for self-adaptive systems: a second research roadmap, in: International Seminar on Software Engineering for Self-Adaptive Systems II, October 24–29, 2010, Dagstuhl Castle, Germany, Revised Selected and Invited Papers, 2010, pp. 1–32. http://dx.doi.org/10.1007/978-3-642-35813-5_1.

[29] R. Hebig, H. Giese, B. Becker, Making control loops explicit when architecting self-adaptive systems, in: Proceedings of the Second International Workshop on Self-Organizing Architectures, SOAR '10, ACM, Washington, DC, USA, 2010, pp. 21–28. ISBN 978-1-4503-0087-2.

[30] H.C. Lim, S. Babu, J.S. Chase, S.S. Parekh, Automated control in cloud computing: challenges and opportunities, in: Proceedings of the First Workshop on Automated Control for Datacenters and Clouds, ACDC '09, ACM, New York, NY, USA, 2009, pp. 13–18. http://doi.acm.org/10.1145/1555271.1555275.

[31] H.C. Lim, S. Babu, J.S. Chase, Automated control for elastic storage, in: Proceedings of the Seventh International Conference on Autonomic Computing, ICAC '10, ACM, New York, NY, USA, 2010, pp. 1–10. http://doi.acm.org/10.1145/1809049.1809051.

[32] H. Müller, M. Pezzè, M. Shaw, Visibility of control in adaptive systems, in: Proceedings of the Second International Workshop on Ultra-Large-Scale Software-Intensive Systems, ULSSIS '08, ACM, New York, NY, USA, 2008, pp. 23–26. http://doi.acm.org/10.1145/1370700.1370707.

[33] T. Patikirikorala, A.W. Colman, J. Han, L. Wang, A systematic survey on the design of self-adaptive software systems using control engineering approaches, in: Proceedings of the Seventh International Symposium on Software Engineering for Adaptive and Self-Managing Systems, SEAMS 2012, June 4–5, 2012, Zurich, Switzerland, 2012, pp. 33–42. http://dx.doi.org/10.1109/SEAMS.2012.6224389.

[34] D. Weyns, M.U. Iftikhar, J. Söderlund, Do external feedback loops improve the design of self-adaptive systems? A controlled experiment, in: M. Litoiu, J. Mylopoulos (Eds.), Proceedings of the Eighth International Symposium on Software Engineering for Adaptive and Self-Managing Systems, SEAMS 2013, May 20–21, 2013, San Francisco, CA, USA, IEEE/ACM, Washington, DC, USA, 2013, pp. 3–12. http://dl.acm.org/citation.cfm?id=2487341.

[35] I. Landau, R. Lozano, M. M'Saad, A. Karimi, Adaptive Control: Algorithms, Analysis and Applications, Communications and Control Engineering, Springer, New York, NY, USA, 2011. http://books.google.com.br/books?id=fb1GVyJHeBgC.

[36] D. Weyns, B.R. Schmerl, V. Grassi, S. Malek, R. Mirandola, C. Prehofer, J. Wuttke, J. Andersson, H. Giese, K.M. Göschka, On patterns for decentralized control in self-adaptive systems, in: R. de Lemos, H. Giese, H.A. Müller, M. Shaw (Eds.), International Seminar on Software Engineering for Self-Adaptive Systems II, October 24–29, 2010, Dagstuhl Castle, Germany, Revised Selected and Invited Papers, Volume 7475 of Lecture Notes in Computer Science, Springer, New York, NY, USA, 2010, pp. 76–107. http://dx.doi.org/10.1007/978-3-642-35813-5_4.

[37] S.S. Andrade, R.J. de A Macdo, Assessing the benefits of search-based approaches when designing self-adaptive systems: a controlled experiment. J. Softw. Eng. Res. Dev. 3 (1) (2015) 1–27. http://dx.doi.org/10.1186/s40411-015-0016-z.

ANALYZING THE ARCHITECTURES OF SOFTWARE-INTENSIVE ECOSYSTEMS

P. Boxer*, R. Kazman[†,‡]

Boxer Research Limited, London, United Kingdom* *Carnegie Mellon University, Pittsburgh, PA, United States*[†]
University of Hawaii, Honolulu, HI, United States[‡]

9.1 INTRODUCTION

An ecosystem is a community of managerially and operationally independent organizations interacting with each other and with their environment. Software-intensive ecosystems—ecosystems in which the behaviors of the participating organizations are themselves dependent on software because of the intensive use they make of it—are an increasingly important social, financial, and political force in the world. We find examples of software-intensive ecosystems in industries concerned with such things as transport, healthcare, defense, government, and communications.

These software-intensive ecosystems are different from traditional "closed-world" software systems that can be analyzed independently of the contexts in which they are embedded. Such ecosystems exhibit ultra-large-scale characteristics: they are constantly evolving, they have no centralized control, they have many heterogeneous elements, their requirements are inherently conflicting and unknowable, failures are normal, and the boundary between people and systems is blurred [1]. In software ecosystems, unlike systems-of-systems, the participating organizations may be in competition with each other. And the emergent properties of such ecosystems could not have been predicted by the designers of the software systems on which they depend. For example, performance problems due to unanticipated demands on the ecosystem, or unanticipated interactions between parts of the ecosystem, are a common form of emergent property that challenge designers.

A number of key drivers underlie this change, challenging the former "closed-world" perspective on software engineering which underlies system and system-of-system design. Among these are the tempo at which the ecosystems are themselves expected to evolve, the ubiquity and criticality of the software on which they depend, and the entanglement not only between software systems and the way they are used by people, but also between interoperating software systems that are themselves managerially and operationally independent of each other [2].

To understand the behaviors of such ecosystems, the analysis of their architectures must not separate the software systems from the organizational contexts-of-use that depend on them. New ways are needed for analyzing the patterns in how the parts of the ecosystem interact, and to what ends. This is

Managing Trade-offs in Adaptable Software Architectures. http://dx.doi.org/10.1016/B978-0-12-802855-1.00009-5

the case even where the interactions between the organizations within the ecosystem primarily concern the use of software itself, such as is to be found in the Microsoft and iPhone ecosystems [3].

9.1.1 THE CHALLENGE OF "WICKEDNESS"

Understanding the behavior of ecosystems presents a form of "wicked" problem [4]. Wicked problems have a number of characteristics. Every wicked problem is essentially unique while also being a symptom of other problems. It has no definitive formulation; there is neither clarity over when it will no longer be a problem nor an immediate or ultimate test of a solution. There are no well-described set of potential solutions and numerous ways of explaining its causes. While every implemented solution has consequences, therefore, solutions are not true-or-false, but good-or-bad. The final twist, however, is that the planner (designer) has no right to be wrong. As Rittel and Webber said: "As we seek to improve the effectiveness of actions in pursuit of valued outcomes, as system boundaries get stretched, and as we become more sophisticated about the complex workings of open societal systems, it becomes ever more difficult to make the planning idea operational" [4]. With wicked problems, we simply cannot draw a "closed-world" box around the ecosystem and analyze it, even though that is what is expected of us. This presents us with a challenge not just at the level of the ecosystem, but also at the level of the software systems on which it depends.

In particular, consider the characteristic: "Every implemented solution has consequences." The nature of this characteristic appears to undermine our ability to do any meaningful analysis of an ecosystem. Where does one stop analyzing consequences? On the other hand, simply not analyzing ultra-large scale software-intensive ecosystems is an unpalatable option. Society is increasingly dependent on them, for example, the social networking communities enabled by the internet, the patterns of energy production, distribution and use enabled by the Smart Grid, the interconnected networks of healthcare providers, users, and organizations, or the forms of military response enabled by networked capabilities.

Let us briefly consider just one of these examples. The US Army, in considering the impact of such wicked problems concluded that a different approach to problem solving was needed by a commander (as the planner/designer) that was *inductive* in nature, concerned with producing a well-framed problem hypothesis (what the Army calls a "mission objective") and an associated design for engaging with it— a conceptual approach for the problem. Thus as much attention had to be paid to the way the problem was framed—the way the boxes were defined—as to the subsequent analysis of what was placed within and between those boxes. The conclusion reached was as follows:

> The issue is whether a commander should begin by analyzing the mission objective, or whether complexity compels the commander to first understand the operational problem, and then — based upon that understanding — design a broad approach to problem solving. The answer to this question depends upon the problem and the mission objective. If the problem is structured so that professionals can agree on how to solve it, and the mission objective received from higher headquarters is properly framed and complete, then it makes sense to begin with the analysis of the mission objective (breaking it down into specified, implied, and essential tasks). However, if the problem is unstructured (professionals cannot agree on how to solve the problem), or the mission objective received from higher headquarters is not properly framed (it is inappropriate for this problem), or higher headquarters provided no clear guidance (permissive orders), then it is crucial to begin by starting to identify and understand the operational problem systemically.

Another way of stating the challenge, therefore, is to improve our systemic understanding of the organizational contexts-of-use into which software systems are being deployed, before analyzing any proposed architectures or architectural changes for such systems.

9.1.2 ANALYZING COMPLEMENTARITY WITHIN ECOSYSTEMS

The early work on sociotechnical systems defined enterprises as composite systems combining technological and social systems [5]. Analysis of the technological system involved "establishing a systematic picture of the tasks and task interrelations required by a technological system," revolving around the establishment and control of the boundaries of this technological system and the way it interacted with its environment. But analysis of the social system involved establishing the nature of the social relations between the people engaged in the tasks defined by the technological system. The boundaries around these social systems related to the way in which meaning was shared within these boundaries [6]. The technological and social systems were therefore *complementary*: the behavior of each type of system was entangled in the behavior of the other, and the behavior of neither system could be defined independently of the other [7]. The composite system that was the enterprise therefore involved managing the alignment between these two complementary systems to meet a shared goal. This sociotechnical system was defined as being open, so that this alignment process had to be dynamic in order to be able to change and adapt to changes in its environment [8].

With software-intensive ecosystems we are dealing with multiple enterprises that are managerially and operationally independent of each other, but that are still necessarily sociotechnical [9]; their software-intensive nature tells us something about the technological systems that they use. As a result, any analysis of software-intensive ecosystems has to be able to account for the behaviors of the complementary technological and social systems, and also has to be able to account for their alignment.

In this we examine the architectural characteristics of adaptability that follow from this characterization of the problem of understanding ecosystems. We do this as a means of motivating how traditional architectural analysis can be extended to take account of complementarity. Such an analysis can give us insight into the properties of an ecosystem and can help us reason about the alignment of the technological systems within the ecosystem with the goals of the stakeholders within its many social systems (an example of the complexity of which can be seen with the Smart Grid [10,11]). For any organization that is planning on creating a substantial piece of an ecosystem, it is prudent to examine the architecture for this piece, to ensure that it will meet the organization's goals and will be appropriately adaptive to change from within and without.

9.2 THE METROPOLIS MODEL AND CORE-PERIPHERY STRUCTURES

The entanglement of the technological and social systems within an ecosystem demands an approach that can understand the impact of software not only on the technological systems, but also on the corresponding social systems with their associated alignment processes. This understanding is necessary to considering consequences for software development. The Metropolis Model [12] provides a starting point for understanding how software systems are constructed, maintained, and operated.

At the heart of this model is the distinction between the core and the periphery, which has been often noted as a key architectural construct in complex software systems [13]. The core-periphery architectural pattern provides the maximum opportunity for developers (and the producers and consumers sometimes called *prosumers*—of content) at the periphery to embed the behavior of a system into their own contexts-of-use, enabling the activities of the eventual customers and end-users within the larger ecosystem. Examples of cores include the Linux kernel, the Android platform, Facebook's application platform, the Apache core, iPhone's iOS platform, Hadoop Common, and so forth. Each of these "cores" provides an abstraction upon which the actual end-user-facing functionality is built. The core itself provides little or no end-user value, but rather provides the architectural foundation upon which others build value. The core is typically relatively small, compared with the size of the periphery. It controls access to the platform's resources and hence provides the means to achieve the system's most important quality attributes (performance, modifiability, availability, security, etc.).

For example, the core (iOS) platform of the iPhone enables application developers and users to develop uses independently that can in turn taken up within a wide variety of contexts-of-use. Making GPS location data accessible to users and application developers on the iPhone platform has spawned a wide variety of location-based services. A simple diagram showing the relationships defined by the Metropolis Model is given in Fig. 9.1.

We can apply the core-periphery distinction to the way modularity and its associated interdependencies are defined for a software system. For modules in the core, tight coupling between them creates mutual dependencies. In the periphery, coupling is much looser creating a measure of independence in the way modules can be used. The strength of the core-periphery pattern is therefore the relatively few constraints it imposes at the periphery on how modules may be used and combined, and how it allows their use to be modified. A core-periphery structure is less over-determining of its use at the periphery than it is at the core. This under-determination at the periphery frees stakeholders to use systems in ways that have not been anticipated in their original design. This enables novel compositions of systems (such as the mashups that appear regularly in web-based and open-source applications), but it also leads to emergent system properties.

The core-periphery distinction applied to the software describes patterns of *necessary* dependency. It can also be applied to the social systems within an ecosystem, describing the ways in which stakeholders align their behaviors to each other. For example, according to the mirroring hypothesis [14], differences in the ways software modules are coupled will also tend to be mirrored by the organizations

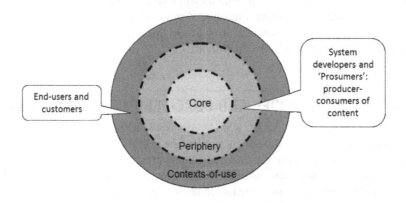

FIG. 9.1

Metropolis model roles and relationships.

that develop them, even if these "organizations" are open-source communities or other ad hoc collections of interested individuals. And even in open-source communities there is a subset of all developers, called *committers*, who have primary responsibility for the core functionality, integrity, and evolution of the overall system [3]. The core-periphery distinction applied to a social system thus describes patterns of *chosen* dependency reflecting choices made by stakeholders, in contrast to the necessary dependencies in software systems.

Together, the chosen and necessary dependencies described by the core-periphery distinction reflect the complementary forms of dependency associated with the technological and social systems within an ecosystem. The challenge in analyzing the adaptability of the architecture of an ecosystem therefore involves describing how necessary and chosen dependencies interact, bringing their complementarity within a unifying framework.

9.3 THE CHALLENGE TO ARCHITECTURE ANALYSIS

Architecture analysis has been used for over two decades as a risk analysis and risk mitigation technique. The central tenet of architecture analysis is that one can profitably analyze the proposed architecture for a software system before it has been built, or before major changes to it are made [15]. In doing so, potential risks to the system may be discovered and mitigated at a low cost (relative to the cost of these risks going undiscovered until the system is developed and fielded). This has been shown over many years, by many researchers (e.g., [16–18]). In this chapter we focus on extending the architecture tradeoff analysis method (ATAM) [19], as it is the most widely adopted method and it has already been shown to be effective in analyzing larger contexts, such as systems-of-systems [20].

The ATAM and its various progeny [21–23] have adopted the use of software system scenarios to elaborate and reify the quality attributes demanded of the system. This technique has shown itself to be well suited to understanding and analyzing the architectural characteristics of the single systems (and of directed and acknowledged systems-of-systems[1]) needed to deliver those attributes. It has been employed countless times over the past decade, in hundreds of large companies and government organizations.

A quality-attribute scenario is a description of a stimulus-response pair: some portion of the system is stimulated and the system responds in a specified, measurable way. The impact of scenarios, like use-cases, can be traced through a software system. These scenarios, in addition to describing the *direct* interaction of some end-user with the software system, also describe a quality attribute of the system (e.g., a latency goal) within the context-of-use defined by the scenario. The achievement of these quality-attribute-related responses brings benefit to the stakeholders in the behavior of the system. For example, a correct response might be of great value to an end-user stakeholder if it arrives predictably within 100 ms, of moderate value if it arrives predictably within 1 s, and of little value if it arrives unpredictably or if it predictably arrives within 10 s.

---

[1]Both directed and acknowledged systems-of-systems have a single design authority over the development of their composition from their (managerially and operationally independent) constituent systems. When deployed into an operational space, these systems-of-systems operate concurrently alongside other systems-of-systems using overlapping sets of constituent systems, collectively forming a collaborative system-of-systems [17]. These collaborative systems-of-systems create distinctly different demands on systems of governance [24].

We can use scenarios to trace through the core-periphery interactions when trying to identify, measure, and understand the benefits radiating out to end-users at the periphery on the basis of their direct uses of the system. Scenarios such as these are necessary to analyze a shared infrastructure, such as a core. Such scenarios might illuminate contention for resources; consider, for example, understanding the load on an operating system kernel when multiple processes are operating and competing for shared resources. On a larger scale, cloud computing platforms such as Amazon's EC2 support large numbers of simultaneous users, each of which could request thousands of server instances [http://aws.amazon.com/ec2/]. And social computing platforms such as Facebook have over 250 million active users each day [http://www.facebook.com/press/info.php?statistics], each of whom will consume core resources, potentially interacting through applications that are built on top of Facebook's core application platform.

This is depicted in Fig. 9.2, where three different scenarios are shown at the periphery. Each scenario sits within a particular context-of-use, and connects some end-user input—a stimulus—to an output (perceived by a potentially different end-user). Consider, for example, the connecting lines for each scenario: $\alpha_1\beta_1$, $\alpha_2\beta_2$, and $\alpha_3\beta_3$. These might represent different contexts-of-use in which end-users are making voice-over-IP (VoIP) connections, for example conferencing, or saying hello to a colleague on the other side of the world, or giving a seminar. The end-users within each scenario might be employing different software, but in the end they must use, and share, some resources at the core—name servers, protocol translators, routers, satellite links, IP stacks, fiber-optic cables, etc. Furthermore, the stakeholder perspective on each of these scenarios could be that the VoIP call would only be of value if latency and jitter were both kept within specified ranges.

In a software-intensive ecosystem, the under-determining effects of core software systems on their periphery free end-users to act independently of each other, but also enable new kinds of interactions between end-users. The scenarios associated with these interactions are not necessarily directly related to their use of any given system, and may involve multiple core systems that can be operationally and managerially independent of each other. For example, Facebook's location features allow users and service providers to interact with each other in ways that are only made possible by their use of a smartphone.

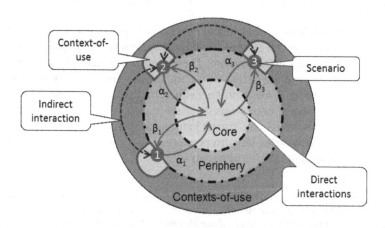

FIG. 9.2

Scenarios over a core-periphery structure.

This creates a much larger and more complex environment defined by interactions that are *indirect* (from the perspective of the core software systems). For example, the actors within scenarios 1, 2, and 3 in Fig. 9.2 may belong to different research institutions, but are all involved in a single research collaboration for which a number of core systems become a key enabling element. It is the dominance of these indirect interactions over direct interactions that are the distinguishing characteristic of an ecosystem and that increase the demands on the adaptability of an ecosystem's architecture.

9.3.1 MULTISIDED INTERACTIONS

This more complex environment is represented in Fig. 9.3 as a matrix of *multisided interactions* in which the sets of columns correspond to sets of direct interactions associated with direct use of particular core technological systems (e.g., particular uses of VoIP or screen-sharing) that are operationally and managerially independent of each other. The rows correspond to the indirect interactions associated with particular forms of social collaboration across multiple core systems (e.g., a research collaboration or a marketing project). Thus the matrix represents interactions between the technological and social systems within the larger ecosystem.

A new challenge arises therefore for architecture analysis: what is the impact of these *indirect* interactions on the architecture of the operationally and managerially independent core systems (VoIP, Screen-sharing, etc.)? From the perspective of the core systems, each row is a collaborative system-of-systems in which *indirect effects* dominate its behaviors.

For example, in Fig. 9.3, consider the indirect effects that might arise where the end-users in the research collaboration are combining the use of VoIP, screen-sharing, and file-sharing systems. Multiple X's in a column represent the architectural challenges facing the technological system. For example, many users of the VoIP systems will be competing for resources, such as computation and bandwidth, affecting latency. Or the developers of those applications may have chosen a common protocol affecting the development time of individual systems. Or charging schemes may affect an

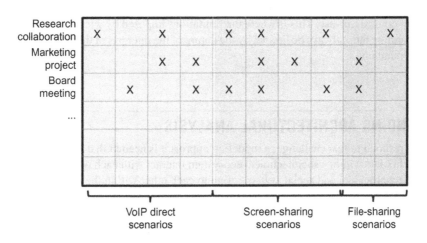

FIG. 9.3

Multisided interactions.

end-user's choice of combined systems to employ (e.g., as a result of differential charging schemes for relatively time-sensitive internet-traffic such as VoIP packets, and relatively non-time-sensitive traffic, such as file sharing).

Such considerations are of real concern to core providers because these indirect interactions can collectively have a huge effect on the performance and behavior of the core. As an example, Google Maps imposes resource restrictions on the services that it provides to other organizations, in an effort to moderate worst-case resource usage [http://www.zdnet.com/blog/google/google-maps-api-team-says-stop-it/429].

But decisions made affecting the capabilities of core systems will also impact on the way they can participate in the indirect interactions chosen by stakeholders. The variety and scale of these indirect interactions arising between stakeholders within the social system will determine the emergent qualities of the ecosystem. But multiple X's in a row represent social collaborations that also present architectural challenges: how will the systems interoperate, and how will the collaboration manage that interoperation within its larger context?

To summarize, the presence and impact of these indirect interactions is an *essential* characteristic of software-intensive ecosystems, arising from the entanglement of the technological and social systems. To understand these ecosystems, and to analyze them, we therefore need to be able to characterize a pragmatically representative set of the interactions between many independent actors across independent systems [25]. But if we just analyze the direct impact of the $\alpha\beta$ paths of each direct interaction (vertical in the matrix) with the core-periphery architecture of any given system—what we do in traditional architectural analysis—we shall not understand the collective impact of the indirect interactions (horizontal in the matrix) between many such direct interactions across many systems caused by the social collaborations taking place within the larger sociotechnical ecosystem. We shall thus not be in a position to analyze the potential emergent effects and behaviors arising from the way the core systems are used within this larger context. We must therefore be able to analyze the multisidedness of demands arising from these indirect interactions. This analysis will always be a sample of such demands, and hence effort must be taken when creating the multisided matrix to ensure that the indirect interactions collected are pragmatically representative of the population of users and usages across their variety of contexts-of-use. This is where the limitations imposed by wickedness emerge. Any systemic understanding must always be limited by the nature of the interests of the stakeholders driving the need for understanding.

9.4 EXTENDING ARCHITECTURAL ANALYSIS

To be able to respond to this challenge, a modeling approach is needed that can represent the way the multiple stakeholders within a sociotechnical ecosystem interact with each other. The multisided ways in which the technological and social systems align to each other within the ecosystem need to be described and analyzed. To give three examples from our own experience:

- The suppliers of orthotic services within the UK National Healthcare System wanted to change the ways in which orthotics clinics were managed and regulated in order to improve the quality of care that they provided and reduce the underuse of their services by the larger ecosystem [26].

- A supplier of unmanned aerial vehicles (UAVs) needed to understand the way the use of these UAVs was changing within the context of the missions arising within operational theater. Their understanding of this dynamic then determined what kinds of architectural change needed to be made to the UAV systems themselves [27].
- A government department supplying on-line search capabilities in support of an eGovernment initiative needed to understand how citizens' questions were changing. The department's understanding of how this dynamic impacted on the way departments needed to collaborate then determined what kind of architectural change was needed to the search capabilities [28].

In each case, it was necessary to analyze the way indirect interactions between enterprises (clinics, mission commanders, collaborating departments) and their customers (patients' conditions, adversaries' threats, citizens' questions) created multisided demands on the supporting technological systems. This involved distinguishing the stakeholders in the technological systems supplying products and services, and the stakeholders in the social systems identified with the horizontal collaborations creating indirect demands on those products and services. And it involved being able to model the impact of new and anticipated forms of collaboration on demands as well as on the way the supporting technological systems were used [29]. Again, this modeling could never represent all possible demands, but our intention was to represent a pragmatically valid sample of the known and anticipated forms of demand, to drive the analyses.

But these software-intensive ecosystems are "wicked": any models of multisidedness are also hypotheses about what forms of multisidedness should be supported by any given technological systems within it on the basis of the view they take of the larger ecosystem. And this view depends on a prior analysis both of way the current technological systems can be aligned to the social systems of demand, and also of the way these demands are themselves changing. For example, Facebook makes its application platform available to developers who then create applications that add value to Facebook users. But these applications often weave together much more than just Facebook resources—they might incorporate Google maps, demographic data from the census.gov, Twitter feeds, personal information from other web-sites, and so forth. The forms of alignment are constantly changing and evolving. We can never completely master such evolutionary pressures (as Rittel and Weber warned in their original discussion of wickedness, nearly 40 years ago), but the analysis that we can do endeavors to capture the dimensions and degrees of wickedness as accurately as possible.

9.4.1 ELICITING MODELS OF MULTISIDEDNESS

An analysis of a software-intensive ecosystem starts from an analysis of the way forms of value are created within the ecosystem. That is, we must understand value as it pertains to the social systems *creating demand* rather than solely to the technological systems supplying products and services [30]. Consider, for example, the case of the orthotics clinics. The value was in the way treatments impacted on the patient's condition through the life of the condition within the context of the patient's life. For the UAVs, the value was in the way the UAVs could be combined with other assets to produce operational effects on threats with much greater timeliness and proportionality. And for the government departments responding to citizens' questions, the value was in the ability to respond to greater numbers and varieties of questions without commensurate increases in staffing levels.

These forms of value arise within specific contexts, giving rise to indirect demands on the supporting technological systems. The scope of an analysis of an ecosystem is therefore bounded by the analysis of the relationships between these indirect demands, the direct demands they give rise to, and the activities of the technological systems through which the demands are ultimately satisfied. This scoping starts with defining the relevant customer situations giving rise to indirect demands. The varieties of collaboration that respond to these indirect demands are then analyzed in terms of the multisidedness of demands they generate on the supporting technological systems [25]. In the case of the orthotics clinics, this meant understanding the referral pathways through which demands for treatment were defined. For the UAVs, it involved understanding how the tempo and nature of threats were changing within the context of unconventional warfare. And for the government it meant understanding how the nature of the questions varied over time with respect to the changing concerns of citizens.

The corresponding analysis of the supporting technological systems and the processes by which their use is aligned to the multisidedness of demands involves modeling tasks, resources, organizational processes, and governance. Different methods of conceptual or structural modeling are constrained by the different categories of things and relationships between things that they make it possible to represent [31]. These determine the forms of knowledge that can be represented in particular domains [32,33]. Many such frameworks exist, for example, Zachman [34], DoDAF [35], or Federal Enterprise Architecture [36]. The characteristic of all of these frameworks, however, is that they model physical and digital structures and behaviors, and the accountability hierarchies under which these operate. Thus they assume a single unifying architecture for a single organization (whether virtual or not).

Our method of analysis used for eliciting models of multisidedness admits multiple organizations, adding representations for network relationships across these organizations, and for the organization of customers' contexts-of-use [37]. This enables the relationships between multiple organizations to be modeled, aligned to different definitions of demand, for example, reflecting different ways of organizing multiepisode treatments [26], using UAVs in concert with other assets [38], or collaborating across government [28].

This extended representation [39] allows us to analyze the different forms of alignment with respect to different forms of demand through analyzing patterns of simple relations across the underlying models. These patterns enable us to represent the way underlying technological systems are aligned to the ultimately social contexts-of-use through a set of layers, producing a stratified analysis [26,40]. The structural characteristics of this stratification then reveals different kinds of risk associated with the way their constituent parts within and between layers interoperate [41].

The multisided matrix therefore represents one layer within this stratification, being the intersection between these two analyses: of the way the technological systems respond to direct demands, and of the way the social systems of collaboration generate indirect demands.

9.4.2 MULTISIDED ATAM

The nine steps of the ATAM, as it currently exists, are as follows:

Phase 1:
1. Present the ATAM.
2. Present business drivers.
3. Present architecture.

4. Identify architectural approaches.
5. Generate quality-attribute utility tree.
6. Analyze architectural approaches.

Phase 2:

7. Brainstorm and prioritize scenarios.
8. Analyze architectural approaches.
9, Present results.

To analyze a software-intensive ecosystem a number of steps must be modified in order to take into account the complementary nature of its technological and social systems The steps of the ATAM remain the same, but how we carry out those steps changes.

The presentation of business drivers in the ATAM (step 2) has previously assumed a single technological system directly supplying products or services. In an ecosystem, there is another set of "business drivers" that are more difficult to elicit and prioritize as they emerge from the social collaborations of end-users. These business drivers are associated not just with the customer's business, but also with the other stakeholders with which the customer collaborates in responding to the customer's customers. Identifying them means elaborating the architecturally significant characteristics of the collaborations in which the customer participates. These are represented by indirect interactions reflecting the different forms of collaboration supported by the technological systems, following the process described in Ref. [26].

The presentation of the architecture (step 3) will always be a snapshot, since the ecosystem is continually changing, but like the analysis of business drivers, it will be based on the prior elicitation process. Thus the analysis of collaborations from which the multisided matrix is derived will need to document the way in which architectural constraints are placed on them, and the way the technological and social systems are dynamically aligned. Both the underlying technological systems and the social systems defining these collaborations are outputs of the elicited models of multisidedness described earlier. The multisided matrix therefore represents the particular ways in which these systems complement each other, representing the layer in the stratification where these two systems meet. From the perspective of a multisided ATAM therefore, the social layers of the overall stratification represent the indirect interactions giving rise to the direct demands on the technological systems.

The most important change in a multisided ATAM is therefore this elicitation of the indirect interactions, followed by their prioritization. In the ATAM there are two techniques for eliciting and prioritizing scenarios: the quality-attribute utility tree (step 5) and scenario brainstorming and prioritization (step 7). In the multisided ATAM, step 7 must be modified to elicit two sets of scenarios, describing direct and indirect interactions, distinguishing the interests of the stakeholders in the technological systems and in the social systems of collaboration respectively. The rows of the multisided matrix therefore define indirect scenarios presenting a set of stimuli and responses in the same way as the columns, but for different kinds of scenario. For the orthotics clinics, these indirect scenarios were the different kinds of referral situation emerging from the referral pathways through which demands for treatment were defined. For the UAVs, the indirect scenarios were different types of threat situation needing to be countered, and for eGovernment it meant understanding the different types of collaboration needed to respond to different types of questions from citizens.

Returning to the small-scale example in Fig. 9.3, each column for VoIP stream, screen-sharing, and file-sharing session must have direct scenarios with associated stimuli and responses defining their direct scope across the rows. But since the rows themselves represent indirect scenarios (the point of which is to satisfy a social demand arising in the larger ecosystem, for which its technological systems had potentially never been designed), we must consider both dependencies and alignment processes between the direct scenarios along a row, each of which presents an interoperability requirement and a potential contention for shared resources between operationally and managerially independent systems. Consider, for example, the Research Collaboration in the first row in Fig. 9.4.

Perhaps an end-user in this interaction wishes to capture the content of a screen-sharing session and share that with other end-users. Such a scenario imposes an interoperability requirement between the screen-sharing and file-sharing systems. This might be accomplished via a separate system function (i.e., this interoperability requirement might have been anticipated by the architects and implemented) or it might be accomplished via a user interaction (e.g., the user saves a file from the screen-sharing session, and then copies this file to a separate device from which it is file-shared with another user). If the former, then the system may be said to have an *indirect scope* defined by the systems it can enable to interoperate, shown in Fig. 9.4 as a separate set of columns.

Whether the response to this intersystem portion of the indirect scenario is automated or manual, it has a number of important effects on the quality-attribute responses of the collaboration as a whole that must be taken into consideration:

- its latency must be considered when analyzing the performance of the ecosystem as a whole;
- if the interoperation is accomplished by a system function, that function might be a single point of failure, thus compromising availability;
- if the interoperation is accomplished by a user, that use might be a security risk for the system (by writing the information on a sheet of paper, or by transferring it using unsecured channels); and
- if the interoperation is anticipated to change frequently, this might be a modifiability risk for the system.

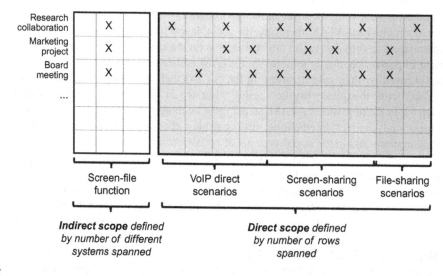

FIG. 9.4

Functions with direct and indirect scope.

Furthermore, the set of rows (the indirect scenarios) in the multisided matrix define the *environment* under which each individual row is evaluated. Referring once again to Fig. 9.4, the Research Collaboration will be sharing and competing for resources with the Marketing Project, the Board Meeting, and perhaps other indirect interactions which collectively may be modeled as stochastic processes.

The consideration of such a complex set of indirect scenarios then proceeds as any other scenarios would be analyzed in the traditional version of the ATAM: by mapping each scenario to a documented set of architectural approaches, and probing for risks associated with the mapping. In the above case we might probe for interoperability, availability, security, and performance risks. However, there is one important difference with the traditional ATAM scenario analysis: the rows of the multisided matrix describe the environment within which each direct scenario is analyzed. This analysis process will be exemplified in the next section.

9.5 AN EXAMPLE ANALYSIS

In this section we provide an example showing how the multisided ATAM was approached, using a prototype system.

This system is a prototype integrated grid supercomputing infrastructure for distributed high performance computing, in which the emphasis is on the variety of collaborations that can be supported. While the specific details of the system have been fabricated, the technical challenges identified are representative of those faced by the real system as it builds on the existing capabilities of the TeraGrid, particularly with reference to the role of Science gateways in supporting collaboration across science communities supported from gateways [https://www.teragrid.org/web/science-gateways/home].

To analyze this system, a multisided matrix was elicited through structured interviews with strategic stakeholders, in order to establish a pragmatically representative set of indirect interactions. A portion of the multisided matrix is shown in Fig. 9.5. The indirect scenarios will be described in Section 5.9.1.

Each row of the multisided matrix describes an indirect scenario with a set of end-to-end stimuli and responses addressing different quality-attribute concerns. But recall that each row requires the orchestration of independent systems. An X in a cell of the matrix describes a single use of a single system (which includes its stimulus-response behavior). The entire row is a collection of these systems, appropriately interoperating, via human or system mediation. Finally, each column in the matrix describes a set of potential simultaneous demands on the systems—a set of simultaneously occurring stimuli with associated response goals. We shall use this information in probing for risks in the ecosystem architecture.

Consider the example view of the grid-based high performance computing architecture presented in Fig. 9.6, in which the services to end-users all have an indirect scope spanning multiple data providers (DPs), for example the research institutions within the Southern Earthquake Centre; and resource providers (RPs) or example facilities provided by TeraGrid, each of which is operationally and managerially independent. An example of the type of scenario being considered is physics-based earthquake wave propagation simulations [42], with their associated challenges of managing large-scale scientific workflows [43] with their associated semantics [44]. Data transformation is concerned with aligning time-series physics calculations across different mesh sizes, and data visualization involves animated renderings of terrain deformations [45].

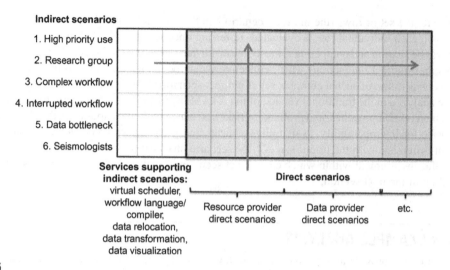

FIG. 9.5

The elicited multisided matrix.

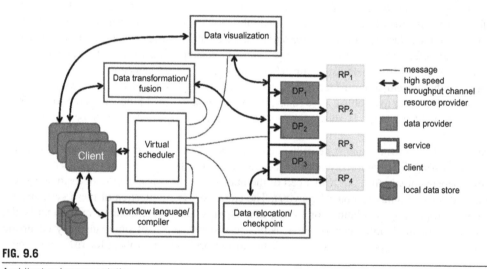

FIG. 9.6

Architectural representation.

9.5.1 EXAMPLE INDIRECT SCENARIOS

Consider the following scenarios which were a subset of those collected from the Utility tree and scenario brainstorming exercises:

1. A new job request from a high priority user occurs that spans multiple RPs. Within 15 min, an administrator reviews current usage and availability of resources suitable to accommodate this request, and enters the job into the job queue with high priority. The job is dispatched within 3 min and completes execution within its deadline (6 h).

2. An international research group schedules a regularly run job that employs six RPs and two DPs, all from different organizations. The schedule contains legacy-based estimates of the resources required from each of the providers, and the bandwidth required to move the data so that it is available "just in time" at each RP. The job executes as scheduled and terminates within 4 h.

3. Three collaborating scientists submit a workflow entailing three related jobs at different remote sites, each of which needs different processing capabilities (speed, memory, cache size, etc.). The system automatically matches two of the three jobs to resources that satisfy their execution requirements. The third job requests resources beyond what is available. The system matches this request to the best available RP and notifies the user of the anticipated response time, given this allocation, within 30 min. The user can then choose to accept the allocation or cancel the workflow.

4. While a long-running collaborative scientific simulation employing four RPs at remote sites is executing one RP is shut down because it has lost its air conditioning. Jobs executing on this RP are suspended, relocated to an alternate RP, and restarted. Users of the workflow are notified within 10 min and the workflow is reconstituted within 20 min. Users can then choose to accept this new workflow or resubmit the job (or a portion of it, resuming from a checkpoint).

5. A team of scientists collaborating on an analysis requiring intensive simulation submit a 10-h (scheduled) job for execution that runs 100 interdependent jobs at three different RP sites. This job involves a large amount of data staging from six other RP and DP sites, and transfers of computed data between these sites. The job was scheduled to use 50% of the resources at site 1 throughout its execution cycle, but, due to slow arrival of data, a site monitor determines that site 1 is consistently only using 50% of its resources over the first hour of the job, and alerts the users. The users in turn contact a system administrator who suspends the job, determines that the source of the bottleneck is a single DP, re-allocates two additional DPs to share the load, and restarts the job from the latest checkpoint. Execution completes with less than a 2 h delay.

6. A team of seismologists concerned about an impending earthquake in a highly populated area needs to use multiple sets of sensor data to anticipate forthcoming events. These scientists need to run concurrent simulations of 1000 predictive models at different levels of fidelity within 6 h, to generate recommendations for civil defense authorities.

9.5.2 PERFORMING THE ANALYSIS

To see how this elicited information is employed let us first consider the evaluation of indirect scenario 6 in Section 5.9.1. The architect traced out the steps involved in satisfying this scenario using the architectural representation depicted in Fig. 9.6:

- a user first interacts with the Workflow language and compiler component to define the programs to be run and their (data) dependencies; the Workflow language/compiler provides an executable script that ensure that programs are executed in the correct order and that data is transferred, stored, and transformed appropriately;
- this script is transferred to the virtual scheduler, which begins allocating resources in an attempt to meet the specified 6 h deadline;
- the virtual scheduler allocates jobs to a set of organizationally independent RPs and DPs;
- the data relocation/checkpoint service is used to transfer data among the independent RPs and to perform periodic checkpoints (to provide snapshots of stable intermediate results in case of processing failures or interruptions);

- the data transformation/fusion service is used to translate data formats and to fuse data sets so that different programs, RPs, and DPs can exchange data and interoperate; and
- when the jobs have all completed the results are sent to the data visualization service and then returned to the requesting user.

The purpose of the multisided ATAM is to discover risks in the architectural decisions that have been made and in decisions that have not been made as they apply to the row collaborations. In the course of evaluating scenario 6, a number of risks were noted:

1. The virtual scheduler employs "best effort" scheduling; it allocates jobs fairly, according to the pool of jobs to execute, the pool of available resources, and the priorities of the jobs. However, the policies for job prioritization are unclear, particularly since the system is not "owned" by a single organization.
2. The virtual scheduler is a single service and hence represents a single point of failure for the system.
3. The performance characteristics of Workflow language/compiler are unknown for very large jobs; it is possible that the calculation of the workflow itself could consume significant time, putting the deadline for the job at risk.
4. Combining data relocation and fusion into a single service component adds unnecessary complexity and if the component fails both services are disabled.
5. The data relocation/checkpoint service is a single point of failure and potential performance bottleneck; if this service is split and/or distributed into multiple service components then it will become a potential complexity risk for the system as a whole.
6. The data transformation/fusion service is a single point of failure and a potential performance bottleneck.
7. There is no system-wide standard protocol for reporting service failures and outages.

These risks could be discerned purely through an examination of the indirect scenario as it was mapped onto the architectural representation. Additional risks could be found when considering the "environment" of scenario 6, which is to say the other scenarios (1–5) that may be competing with scenario 6 for resources. Based on a consideration of this environment, additional risks were discovered. The risks identified below emerged during the process of elicitation as a consequence of bringing the separate parts of the analysis together. The emergence of such insights is intrinsic to an ATAM-like process. More detailed analysis of risks arising from the absence of interoperabilities across the wider ecosystem is beyond the scope of this but an example of their analysis within a different ecosystem is detailed in Ref. [46].

8. The worst-case performance characteristics of the system are not well understood. Scenarios 1, 2, and 5 all have deadlines. Scenarios 3 and 4 will impose additional loads on the system. Without a system-wide policy and processes for resource reservation, negotiation, arbitration, or bidding, it is unclear at best how the worst-case behaviors of the system will be controlled within the context of concurrent research collaborations.
9. Scenarios 3 and 4 both involve user responses. While waiting for these responses resources (that could otherwise have been used) may be allocated but not used. This represents a performance and availability risk for the system.
10. The anticipated distribution of job requests that the system will face is not well understood. This needs to be studied and statistically characterized in order to understand how the variability in

indirect demands on the system will impact on its performance. The impact of such variability will be on the economics of supporting emergent forms of collaboration, risks to existing collaborations arising from new forms of interoperability, and of course performance issues arising from changing loads on the different parts of the system.

What else can we learn from this collection of scenarios? The risks identified above relate to the systems supporting horizontal collaborations. These systems are themselves sociotechnical, so that a number of risks arose during the analysis due to a consideration of the *human* elements in these collaborations. For example, scenarios 1 and 5 require the actions of a system administrator. This person is, then, a potential performance bottleneck if these scenarios, and others like them, occur concurrently. In scenario 3, the actions of the collaborating scientists could lock valuable resources while the system waits for the users to make a decision, preventing other users in the ecosystem from employing them. In the analysis of scenario 4 it was noted that some RPs require data in different formats. This presents an interoperability risk (since a human would need to introduce a format translation as a repair mechanism), and a performance risk (since the computation will need to be suspended until the human has acted and the data transformation has completed). The analysis therefore presents us with the challenge of levels of detail: how much refinement is needed to satisfy the interests of the stakeholders in the analysis process itself? This brings us back to the importance of prioritization. The methods described here have to serve those priorities, but cannot determine them.

9.5.3 DISCUSSION

Clearly the analysis that we have just described builds upon the existing ATAM techniques. But the analysis goes beyond what would be done in an ATAM in several important ways, beginning with the multisided matrix. The elicitation of the multisided matrix causes the analysts to consider not just direct scenarios (which the traditional ATAM considered), but also indirect scenarios. A consideration of indirect scenarios requires analysis of the system as a sociotechnical ecosystem, including humans as both principals and agents, and including many resources that are not under direct control of any single authority. These humans both determine and become part of the execution of the system and may themselves represent performance, availability, security, interoperability, or other kinds of risks.

The resulting steps for the multisided ATAM are as follows, with the modified steps shown in italics:

Phase 1:
1. Present the ATAM.
2. *Present ecosystem business drivers.*
3. *Present ecosystem architecture.*
4. Identify architectural approaches.
5. Generate quality-attribute utility tree.
6. Analyze architectural approaches.
Phase 2:
7. *Brainstorm and prioritize direct and indirect scenarios.*
8. Analyze architectural approaches.
9. Present results.

Each of these changes is a departure from the traditional ATAM, which was focused on analyzing the architectures of systems under the control of a single organization (or a known, finite number of organizations) with reasonably well understood requirements. The analysis of ecosystem architecture forces us to relax those assumptions and, in doing so, creates new obligations for analysis [47].

9.6 CONCLUSIONS/FUTURE RESEARCH

In this we have examined the architectural characteristics of software-intensive ecosystems, to suggest how traditional architectural analysis can be extended to address the complementary nature of their technological and social systems, reflected in the multisidedness of demands on the use of technological systems. We have argued that, in fact, such analysis must be extended. It must be extended to account for how dynamic processes of alignment, in response to rapidly changing demands, can be made sufficiently adaptive to the wicked (ill-structured) nature of ecosystems.

We have proposed the use of a multisided matrix to represent the variety of forms of dynamic alignment and, given this information, have proposed an extension to the ATAM that allows us to analyze software ecosystems. Such an analysis can give us insight into the properties of an ecosystem and can help us reason about the dynamic alignment of the ecosystem with the goals of its many stakeholders. In the early years of ATAM, the challenge was to define effective architectures for the use of software systems. Now this challenge extends to analyzing the effectiveness of embedding these software systems within sociotechnical ecosystems.

In addition to the application of ATAM to multisidedness, several other forms of analysis can be based on the data elicited to generate the multisided matrix. These evaluate the impact of adaptable architectures—architectures which are structurally agile—on the performance of the larger ecosystem [48]:

1. A structural analysis of potential hazards arising from both technological and social system architectures, using a dependency structure matrix to identify core-periphery characteristics in both technological and social systems [13].
2. A stratification analysis of the processes aligning the technological and social systems to new and/or different forms of demand. This identifies the hazards to aligning systems to different forms of demand (e.g., in evaluating the risks facing military operational capabilities in a changing threat environment [49]).
3. An economic analysis of the consequences of changes in demand on the use of the architecture (e.g., in assessing the value of investment in eGovernment search capabilities to support greater responsiveness to citizens [24], and in assessing the value of investing in UAV capabilities to support greater agility in military force structures [46]). This quantifies the impact on the overall cost of ecosystem performance of increasing the adaptability of its supporting systems [11,50,51].

REFERENCES

[1] L. Northrop, et al., Ultra-Large-Scale Systems: The Software Challenge of the Future, Software Engineering Institute, Carnegie Mellon University, Pittsburgh, 2006.
[2] L. Coyle, et al., Guest editor's introduction: evolving critical systems, Computer 43 (5) (2010) 28–33.

[3] S. Jansen, A. Finkelstein, S. Brinkkemper, A sense of community: a research agenda for software ecosystems, in: 31st International Conference on Software Engineering (New Ideas and Emerging Results Track), IEEE CS Press, Vancouver, Canada, 2009.

[4] H. Rittel, M. Webber, Dilemmas in the general theory of planning, Policy Sci. 4 (1973) 155–169.

[5] F.E. Emery, E.L. Trist, Socio-technical systems, in: C.W. Churchman, M. Verhulst (Eds.), Management Science, Models and Techniques, Pergamon, London, 1960, pp. 83–97.

[6] E.J. Miller, A.K. Rice, Systems of Organization: The Control of Task and Sentient Boundaries, Tavistock, London, 1967.

[7] H. Atmanspacher, H. Romer, H. Walach, Weak quantum theory: complementarity and entanglement in physics and beyond, Found. Phys. 32 (3) (2002) 379–406.

[8] L.v. Bertalanffy, The theory of open systems in physics and biology, Science 111 (1950) 23–29

[9] G. Walker, et al., A Review of Sociotechnical Systems Theory: A Classic Concept for New Command and Control Paradigms, Human Factors Integration Defence Technology Centre, 2007.

[10] National Energy Technology Laboratory, Advanced Metering Infrastructure, NETL, 2008.

[11] R. Kazman, L. Bass, G. Moreno, Architecture evaluation without an architecture: experience with the smart grid, in: Proceedings of 33rd International Conference on Software Engineering (ICSE 33), Honolulu, Hawaii, 2011.

[12] R. Kazman, H.-M. Chen, The metropolis model: a new logic for the development of crowdsourced systems, Commun. ACM 52 (7) (2009) 76–84.

[13] J. MacCormack, C. Baldwin, J. Rusnak, The architecture of complex systems: do core-periphery structures dominate? MIT Sloan School of Management, 2010, Working paper 4770-10.

[14] L. Colfer, C.Y. Baldwin, The mirroring hypothesis: theory, evidence and exceptions, Harvard Business School working paper, 2009.

[15] D. Falessi, et al., Decision-making techniques for software architecture design: a comparative survey, ACM Comput. Surv. (2010).

[16] P. Bengtsson, J. Bosch, Architecture level prediction of software maintenance, in: 3rd European Conference on Software Maintenance and Reengineering (CSMR 99), Amsterdam, Netherlands, 1999.

[17] N. Lassing, D. Rijsenbrij, H. van Vliet, How well can we predict changes at architecture design time? J. Syst. Softw. 65 (2003) 141–153.

[18] P. Tarvainen, Adaptability evaluation of software architectures: a case study, in: 31st Annual International Computer Software and Applications Conference, Beijing, 2007.

[19] P. Clements, R. Kazman, M. Klein, Evaluating Software Architectures: Methods and Case Studies, Addison-Wesley, USA, 2001.

[20] R. Kazman, M. Gagliardi, W. Wood, Scaling up software architecture analysis, J. Syst. Softw. 85 (2013) 1511–1519.

[21] H.-M. Chen, R. Kazman, A. Garg, BITAM: an engineering-principled method for managing misalignments between business and IT architectures, J. Sci. Comput. Program. 57 (1) (2005) 5–26.

[22] M. Barbacci, et al., Quality attribute workshops, Software Engineering Institute technical report, CMU/SEI, 2003.

[23] M. Moore, et al., Quantifying the value of architectural design decisions: lessons from the field, in: Proceedings of the 25th International Conference on Software Engineering (ICSE 25), Portland, OR, 2003.

[24] P. Boxer, P. Kirwan, H. Sassenburg, The impact of governance approaches on SoS environments, in: IEEE International Systems Conference, IEEE, San Diego, CA, 2010.

[25] P. Boxer, et al., Systems-of-systems engineering and the pragmatics of demand, in: Second International Systems Conference, IEEE, Montreal, QC, 2008.

[26] B. Cohen, P. Boxer, Why critical systems need help to evolve, Computer 43 (5) (2010).

[27] P.J. Boxer, Evaluating platform architectures within ecosystems: modeling the relation to indirect value, School of Engineering and Information Sciences, Middlesex University, London, 2012.

[28] P. Boxer, H. Sassenburg, The Swiss eGov Case: "Metadata 2010," CMU/SEI-2010-SR-003 Unlimited distribution, Pittsburgh, 2010.

[29] C.Y. Baldwin, Where do transactions come from? Modularity, transactions, and the boundaries of firms, Ind. Corp. Chang. 17 (1) (2008) 155–195.

[30] C.K. Prahalad, V. Ramaswamy, The Future of Competition: Co-Creating Unique Value With Customers, Harvard Business School Press, Boston, 2004.

[31] J.F. Sowa, Knowledge Representation: Logical, Philosophical, and Computational Foundations, Brooks/Cole, Pacific Grove, CA, 2000.

[32] A. Amin, P. Cohendet, Architectures of Knowledge: Firms, Capabilities and Communities, Oxford University Press, Oxford, 2004.

[33] R. Hopkins, K. Jenkins, Eating the IT Elephant: Moving From Greenfield Development to Brownfield, IBM, Indianapolis, IN, 2008.

[34] J.A. Zachman, A framework for information systems architecture, IBM Syst. J. 26 (3) (1987) 276–292.

[35] U.S. Department of Defense, DoD Architecture Framework Version 2.0, 2009.

[36] The Office of Management and Budget, Federal Enterprise Architecture Consolidated Reference Model V2.3, 2007.

[37] P. Boxer, S. Garcia, Limits to the use of the Zachman framework in developing and evolving architectures for complex systems of systems, SATURN, SEI, Pittsburgh, 2009.

[38] P. Boxer, Valuing Multi-Sided Systems, CMU/SEI-2009-SR-012 Unlimited distribution (in draft), Pittsburgh, 2009.

[39] P.J. Boxer, S. Garcia, Enterprise architecture for complex system-of-systems contexts, in: 3rd International Systems Conference, IEEE, Vancouver, BC, 2009.

[40] P.J. Boxer, Building organizational agility into large-scale software-reliant environments, in: 3rd International Systems Conference, IEEE, Vancouver, BC, 2009.

[41] W.B. Anderson, P. Boxer, Modeling and analysis of interoperability in systems of systems environments, in: IDGA Systems of Systems Engineering Forum, 2009.

[42] E. Deelman, et al., Managing large-scale workflow execution from resource provisioning to provenance tracking: the cybershake example, in: IEEE e-Science and Grid Computing, Amsterdam, The Netherlands, 2006.

[43] E. Deelman, Y. Gil, Managing large-scale scientific workflows in distributed environments: experiences and challenges, in: IEEE e-Science and Grid Computing, Amsterdam, Netherlands, 2006.

[44] Y. Gil, et al., Wings for Pegasus: a semantic approach to creating very large scientific workflows, in: OWL: Experiences and Directions 2006, Athens, GA, 2006.

[45] A. Chourasia, et al., Insights gained through visualization for large scale earthquake simulations: discovering the unexpected, Comput. Graph. Appl. 2 (6) (2007) 28–33.

[46] W. Anderson, P. Boxer, Modeling and analysis of interoperability in systems of systems environments, CrossTalk, 2008.

[47] P.J. Boxer, Leading organisations without boundaries: "Quantum" organisation and the work of making meaning, Org. Social. Dyn. 14 (1) (2014) 130–153.

[48] P.J. Boxer, The Architecture of Agility: Modeling the Relation to Indirect Value Within Ecosystems, Lambert Academic Publishing, Saarbrücken, Germany, 2012.

[49] W. Anderson, P. Boxer, L. Brownsword, An Examination of a Structural Modeling Risk Probe Technique, 2006, CMU/SEI-2006-SR-017, Pittsburgh, 2006.

[50] J. Asundi, R. Kazman, M. Klein, Using economic considerations to choose among architecture design alternatives, Software Engineering Institute technical report, CMU/SEI, Pittsburgh, 2001.

[51] R. Nord, et al., Integrating the Architecture Tradeoff Analysis Method (ATAM) With the Cost Benefit Analysis Method (CBAM), CMU/SEI, Pittsburg, PA, 2003.

ARCHITECTURAL PERSPECTIVE FOR DESIGN AND ANALYSIS OF SCALABLE SOFTWARE AS A SERVICE ARCHITECTURES

10

B. Tekinerdogan*, O. Ozcan[†]

Wageningen University, Wageningen, The Netherlands[*] Bilkent University, Ankara, Turkey[†]

10.1 INTRODUCTION

Different from traditional enterprise applications that rely on the infrastructure and services provided and controlled within an enterprise, cloud computing is based on services that are hosted on providers over the Internet. Hereby, services are fully managed by the provider, whereas consumers can acquire the required amount of services on demand, use applications without installation and access their personal files through any computer with Internet access. Recently, a growing interest in cloud computing can be observed thanks to the significant developments in virtualization and distributed computing, as well as improved access to high-speed Internet and the need for economical optimization of resources. The services that are hosted by cloud computing approach can be broadly divided into three categories: Infrastructure-as-a-Service (IaaS), Platform-as-a-Service (PaaS), and Software-as-a-Service (SaaS) [1,2]. Research on cloud computing has focused on different issues, one of which is the need for adaptability. Within the context of cloud computing adaptability manifests itself primarily as requirements for scalability. Designing and maintaining SaaS computing systems for scalability can be considered as one of the key concerns in SaaS since it affects both the cloud consumers and cloud producers. Scalability can be defined as the ability of a system, network, or process to handle a growing amount of work in a capable manner or its ability to be enlarged to accommodate that growth [3,4]. A system whose performance improves after adding hardware, proportionally to the capacity added, is said to be a scalable system.

Scalability is an important quality concern that has a systemic, global impact on the overall system, both from the cloud consumer and the cloud producer. Hence it is important to address this concern early on at the software architecture design level. In the literature, the basic components required for cloud computing and its conceptual reference architecture are given. Based on these existing reference architectures one could derive multiple different application architectures, but the overall guidance for designing an architecture for a particular quality concern is left to the application architect.

Designing a cloud architecture that is scalable is not a trivial task and involves many different design decisions.

To address quality concerns in software architecture design, an important approach is to define so-called architectural perspectives [5] that include a collection of activities, tactics [6,7] and guidelines that require consideration across a number of the architectural views. Several architectural perspectives have been defined for selected quality concerns but scalability for cloud systems has not been explicitly addressed. In this chapter we propose the *Scalability Perspective* for supporting the design and analysis of scalable SaaS architectures. The proposed architectural perspective can assist software architects in designing, analyzing, and communicating the decisions regarding scalability as well as the trade-offs with other concerns. We illustrate the scalability perspective for a real industrial case study and discuss the lessons learned.

The remainder of the chapter is organized as follows. In Section 10.2, we describe the background on Software as a Service Architecture. Section 10.3 presents the work on software architecture perspectives [5] on which the approach in this chapter builds. Section 10.4 presents the case study that we shall use as a running example throughout the chapter. Section 10.5 discusses the proposed software architecture perspective for scalability. Section 10.6 discusses the related work and finally Section 10.7 concludes the paper.

10.2 SOFTWARE AS A SERVICE ARCHITECTURE

A study of the computing literature reveals a number of reference architectures for SaaS. Based on the literature [1,2,8–10], we have defined a reference architecture for SaaS as given in Fig. 10.1, which is a hybrid view including both the deployment view and layered view. In SaaS systems the thin clients rent

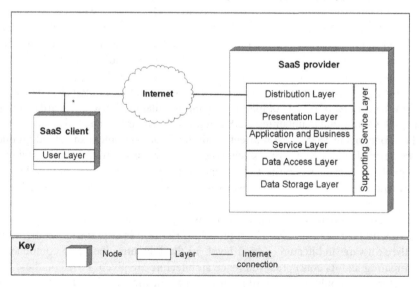

FIG. 10.1

SaaS reference architecture.

and access the software functionality from providers on the Internet. As such the cloud client includes only one layer User Layer which usually includes a web browser and/or the functionality to access the web services of the providers. This includes, for example, data integration and presentation. The SaaS providers usually include the layers of Distribution Layer, Presentation Layer, Business Service Layer, Application Service Layer, Data Access Layer, Data Storage Layer, and Supporting Service Layer.

Distribution Layer defines the functionality for load balancing and routing. *Presentation Layer* represents the interfacing to the users. The *Application and Business Service Layer* represents services such as identity management, application integration services, and communication services. *Data Access Layer* represents the functionality for accessing the database through a database management system. *Data Storage Layer* includes the databases. Finally, the *Supporting Service Layer* includes functionality that supports the horizontal layers and may include functionality such as monitoring, billing, additional security services, and fault management. Each of these layers can be further decomposed into sublayers.

Although Fig. 10.1 describes the common layers for SaaS reference architecture, it deliberately does not commit on specific *application architecture*. The application architecture can have multiple nodes in which the layers are allocated in different ways. This results in various design alternatives. Figs. 10.2 and 10.3 show two different application architectures derived from the reference architecture in Fig. 10.1. The design in Fig. 10.2 supports the need for multitenancy by adopting a single database management system with a shared database and shared schemas for the tenants. In the alternative in

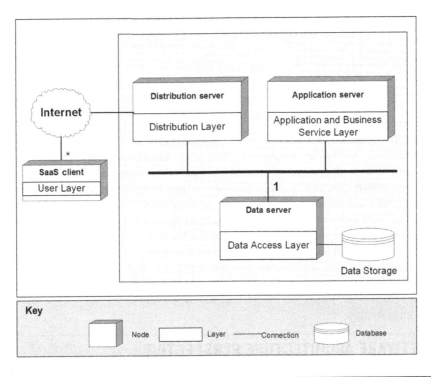

FIG. 10.2

SaaS application architecture alternative with shared data servers.

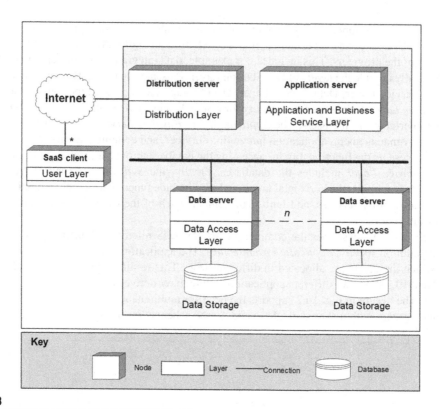

FIG. 10.3

SaaS application architecture alternative with separate single distribution and single application server.

Fig. 10.3 the data storage is not shared but a separate data server provided for each tenant is provided. Obviously these design models are not the only alternatives and a considerable number of other design alternatives may be derived from the same reference SaaS architecture. Each of these alternatives will perform different with respect to scalability. SaaS application designers must be able to explicitly compare, evaluate, and select among various alternatives based on the required scalability requirements. While designing SaaS architectures, software engineers apply their knowledge, experience, and intuition to compare the design alternatives and design the feasible scalable architecture. However, this process is primarily implicit and lacks explicit modeling support. As such, the lack of an active guidance for the design of scalable SaaS architecture can lead to a nonoptimal SaaS system which will impede the realization of the desired scalability levels.

10.3 SOFTWARE ARCHITECTURE PERSPECTIVE

For supporting the design of software architecture proper modeling and design approaches should be adopted. A common practice in software architecture design is to model and document different *architectural views* for describing the architecture according to the stakeholders' concerns [11]. An architectural view is a representation of a set of system elements and relations associated with them to support a particular concern. Having multiple views helps to separate the concerns and as such support the modeling, understanding, communication, and analysis of the software architecture for different stakeholders. Architectural views conform to viewpoints that represent the conventions for constructing and using a view. An architectural framework organizes and structures the proposed architectural viewpoints.

For supporting the architecture design Rozanski and Woods propose an architecture framework consisting of seven different viewpoints: *Functional, Information, Concurrency, Development, Deployment* and *Operational,* and *Context* viewpoints for architecture design [5]. The *Functional viewpoint* defines the functional elements of the system, their responsibilities, interfaces, and interactions. The *Information viewpoint* represents the way that the architecture stores, manipulates, manages, and distributes information. The *Concurrency viewpoint* illustrates the concurrency structure of the system and identifies the parts of the systems which should execute concurrently, and shows these are coordinated and controlled. The *Development viewpoint* describes the architecture that supports the system development. The *Deployment viewpoint* defines the environment into which system will be deployed. The *Operational viewpoint* describes how the system will be operated, managed, and supported. The *Context viewpoint* describes the relationships, dependencies, and interactions between the system and its environment such as external systems, people, and groups.

Rozanski and Woods state that quality concerns are crosscutting on these viewpoints and as such creating a viewpoint for a given quality concern seems less appropriate. As such, they define several architectural perspectives for selected quality concerns whereby each relevant perspective is applied to some or all views. In this way, the architectural views provide the description of the architecture, while the architectural perspectives can help to analyze and modify the architecture to ensure that system exhibits the desired quality properties.

Rozanski and Woods [5] define *Security, Performance and Scalability, Availability and Resilience, Evolution, Accessibility, Development Resource, Internationalization, Location, Regulation,* and *Usability* perspectives. For example, the *Security* perspective describes the ability of the system reliably control, monitor, and audit who can perform which activity on which resources, detect and recover from failures. The *Performance* and *Scalability* perspective defines the ability of the system to be executed in desired performance profile and to handle increased processing volumes. The *Availability* and *Resilience* perspective describes the ability of the system to be fully or partly operational as and when required and to effectively handle failures that could affect system availability. For a detailed analysis of these and the other perspectives we refer to [5].

Each perspective is defined using the following description:

- the perspective description in brief in *desired quality*;
- the perspective's *applicability to views* to show which views are to be affected by applying the perspective;
- the *concerns* which are addressed by the perspective;
- an explanation of *activities for applying the perspective* to the architectural design;
- the *architectural tactics* as possible solutions when the architecture doesn't exhibit the desired quality properties the perspective addresses [6,7];
- some *problems and pitfalls* to be aware of and risk-reduction techniques; and
- checklist of things to consider when applying and reviewing the perspective to help make sure correctness, completeness, and accuracy.

Similar to the provided perspectives by Rozanski and Woods we could in principle define novel architectural perspectives for various quality concerns. In this chapter we focus on scalability of cloud-based systems for which we shall propose a novel architectural perspective in the following sections.

10.4 CASE STUDY

In this section we describe a case study on cloud hotel management system (CHMS) that we shall use as a running example throughout the paper. The system provides various services to support the management of hotel departments. Important stakeholders of the system are guests, hotel managers, and travel agencies. For modeling the architecture it would be first required to define the architecture views. We shall illustrate two important example views for this case study. The development view of the system is shown in Fig. 10.4.

As shown in the figure, the system consists of nine subsystems including Reservation and Booking, Room, Points of Sale (POS), Guest, Accounting, Agency, Channel, General, and Report Management. Reservation and Booking Management module includes services for supporting the reservation and booking of hotel rooms. Room Management module includes services related to the management of hotel rooms, such as room availability, room schema, room status, room wakening list, and other activities. POS Management module includes services for managing the product selling and delivery operations made by the guests. Guest Management module keeps track of the information about guests that stays in a hotel. Accounting Management module manages all of the accounting operations that are performed in the hotel. Agency Management module manages all the information about travel agencies and the sales information. Channel Management module keeps track of selling channels and administrators. General Management module includes general services that are used by the other modules. Finally, Report Management module manages the generation of various types of reports.

In practice, most of the hotels serve only during a limited amount of time (e.g., only during summer season) and as such developing/buying, installing, and maintaining a standalone software solution for

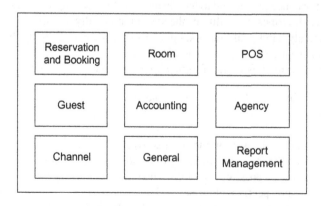

FIG. 10.4

Development view of the CHMS.

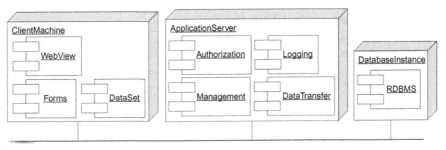

FIG. 10.5

Deployment view of the CHMS.

such a small period is less feasible and costly. Hence, it has been decided to develop a cloud-based solution instead, whereby hotels can rent the required services from the cloud provider that provides the various services for hotel management.

Another architecture view of the system is the deployment view which shows the allocation of software modules to nodes. Fig. 10.5 shows the deployment view of the case study. In the system multiple tenants can connect simultaneously to CHMS via a travel agency or a hotel. Example scenarios here could be the booking of hotel rooms, downloading invoices, searching customers, checking customer details, and generating reports.

In addition to the functional requirements the system needs to meet several quality requirements. As stated before different quality concerns can be addressed by different architectural perspectives. For example, for addressing and modeling the impact of security concerns on the architectural views one could use the predefined *Security* perspective. For addressing availability, the corresponding *Availability and Resilience* perspective, etc. In the given case it is required that the system is scalable for various loads. To identify the scalability requirements and analyze the impact on the architectural views it would be required to adopt a corresponding scalability perspective. We present this in the next section.

10.5 SOFTWARE ARCHITECTURE PERSPECTIVE FOR SCALABILITY

Scalability of a cloud application is the ability of an application that handles the service level agreement (SLA) requirements for all customers. As long as the minimum requirements of SLA are maintained for all users, that application can be considered as a scalable cloud application. In this section we focus on scalability at the software architecture design level. In fact, one of the perspectives in the Rozanski and Woods' perspective catalog [5] is performance and scalability. The focus hereby tends to be more towards performance, and scalability for the cloud environment is not explicitly discussed. We propose the scalability perspective dedicated for scalability whereby we adopt the guidelines of Rozanski and Woods [5] for defining perspectives. The overall description of the scalability perspective is shown in Table 10.1. The impact of the scalability perspective on the architecture views is shown in Table 10.2. In the following subsections we discuss the concerns (Section 10.5.1), the activities for scalability (Section 10.5.2), and the problems and pitfalls (Section 10.5.3).

Table 10.1 Brief Description of Scalability Perspective	
Desired quality	Scalability—the ability of a system, network, or process to handle a growing amount of work in a capable manner or its ability to be enlarged to accommodate that growth
Applicability	Any system where future expansion is important. Systems with complex, unclear, or ambitious scalability requirements
Concerns	User access load, communication traffic load, data storage access load, transaction, response time, throughput, hardware resource requirements, cost, predictability, availability, and reliability
Activities	Capture the scalability requirements, create scalability models, analyze scalability models, assess against the requirements, rework the architecture
Architectural tactics	Multitiered architecture, component-based architecture, service-oriented architecture, database partitioning, scale-out, scale-up, key-value stores, dynamic provisioning, caching, replication, virtualization, load balancing, parallel processing
Problems and pitfalls	Inaccurate scalability goals, use of simple requirements for complex cases, unrealistic models, choice of inappropriate or redundant scalability approach, invalid environment, platform, and user behavior assumptions

Table 10.2 Applicability of Scalability Perspective to Architectural Views	
View	**Applicability**
Functional view	Applying this perspective leads to changes in functional elements, such as adding new elements or splitting some elements into more, and to change some of the links between elements. Also it requires determining which elements need to be scalable. The models from this view can be used to create scalability models
Information view	This view identifies shared resources, static data structure, dynamic information flow, information lifecycle, and transactional requirements. Some of the obstacles to scalability may be identified in this view. It gives information about which data can be cached or replicated, and also how the data can be partitioned. It may provide input to scalability models
Concurrency view	Application of this perspective may change the concurrency design. It may divide the work on some functional elements or it may provide solutions for excessive contention on key resources. To meet requirements of the perspective will change the concurrency design. Elements in this view can also provide input to scalability models
Development view	This view will change based on the scalability approaches chosen. There may be an increase of the number of packages. Change in layers has low possibility, yet it may happen if the architectural pattern changes
Deployment view	Scalability tactics that are chosen will affect this view and requires redefining types, specification, and quantity of hardware required, network requirements, third-party software requirements and physical constraints. Scalability models are usually created by using this view
Operational view	Applying this perspective makes performance monitoring more important, it also may cause to change the migration model

10.5.1 CONCERNS

The notion of concern refers to any matter of interest when designing a software architecture [7,12]. The primary sources for concerns are elicited from stakeholders, a person, group, or entity with an interest (concern) about the realization of the software architecture [13]. While scalability is in our case the basic quality factor we can also identify several concerns that need to be considered when reasoning about scalability. We have identified the following concerns [5,14].

User access load: The number of concurrent users who access the system, number of online users, in a given time unit [14]. Usually each system can have a limited amount of concurrent connections. User access load also affects the communication traffic load of the servers and the load on data storage access. The system should accommodate the growing user load in scalable systems.

Communication traffic load: The amount of incoming and outgoing communication messages and transactions within a given time unit [14]. Important metrics that define the communication traffic load are request per second, hits per second, and transaction per second

Data storage access load: The data storage access load of the underlying system, such as the number of data store access, and data storage sizing [14].

Transactions: A unit of work, typically encapsulating a number of operations, such as reading or writing an object.

Response time: The duration of a process between start and end time, when the system finishes and reacts to the given input [5].

Throughput: The amount of workload the system can handle within a unit time period.

Hardware resource requirements: Resource requirements imposed on hardware. These will define how much workload the system can handle, how fast the system responds to requests, and how many devices can be connected and likewise these will have a high impact on the scalability of the system.

Cost: Generally, increased level of hardware resources leads to higher throughput and better response times, but also higher costs.

Predictability: The degree to which a correct prediction of a system's state can be made either qualitatively or quantitatively. Predictability of the system's performance is important for scalability, for ensuring the scalability goals when the workload increases.

Availability: The capability of providing the intended service of the system fully or partly. An available system should effectively handle failures and maintain its operation.

Reliability: Reliability is the probability of failure or availability. A potential overload of the system due to limited scalability harms reliability.

10.5.2 ACTIVITIES FOR APPLYING SCALABILITY PERSPECTIVE

The activities for applying the scalability perspective are shown in Fig. 10.6. We discuss these in the following subsections.

10.5.2.1 Capture scalability requirements

To meet the scalability goals of a system the only way is to specify each of them clearly and unambiguously. Further, these goals should be determined accurately at the earliest phase of the system development [15] and as such one should not wait after the development of the system since this would be too late. To reveal the scalability goals the following must be clearly specified [5,16]:

Specify workload requirements: Description of workload goals should include user access load, communication traffic load, and data storage access load with the deployment information.

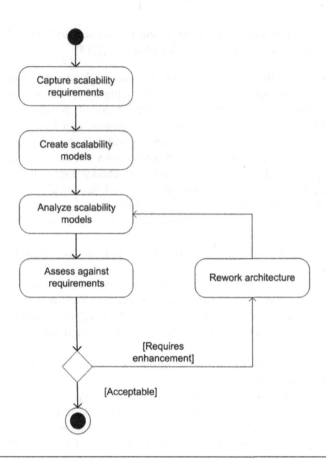

FIG. 10.6

Activity diagram for applying the scalability perspective.

Specify response time requirements: Response time goals should described with the information how much workload the system has, measurement location, and features of hardware resources during that time [5].

Specify throughput requirements: Scalability requirements should state how many requests or transactions of each kind processed and go through the system per unit time as throughput [17]. It should be determined for the steady cases when the number of incoming requests would be equal to the number of processed requests. Also, it should be determined for homogenous tasks when a system doing the same type of business operations for a given time.

Specify hardware resource requirements: Features and quantities of CPU, memory, storage, I/O, network, etc. of the system should be specified [17].

These goals and needs are determined according to certain amount of estimations, assumptions, and constraints. To be able to capture scalability requirements we follow existing requirements engineering techniques defined in the IEEE Software Engineering Book of Knowledge (SWEBOK) [18]. It defines four stages for requirements that are elicitation, analysis, specification, and validation. A more specific approach is presented in [15,16] in which the rules of GORE (goal-oriented requirements engineering) are applied to identify and analyze scalability requirements. The presented method includes the following steps: (1) specifying scaling assumptions, (2) specifying scalability goals, (3) identifying scalability obstacles, (4) assessing scalability obstacles, (5) resolving scalability obstacles.

Based on these guidelines we can derive the scalability requirements for the provided case study. An example set of the requirements for the case study are shown in Fig. 10.7.

10.5.2.2 Create scalability model

The scalability requirements define the specific scalability need of the stakeholders. To reason about the scalability requirements and support the design of the system, scalability models need to be created that explicitly depict the scalability properties. More concretely, the purpose of scalability modeling includes: (1) To make scalability requirements and estimations more understandable, visual, manageable, and easier for the stakeholders. (2) To be able to see both runtime behavior and deployment of the system with scalability features. (3) To provide a tool for scalability assessment for the stakeholders. (4) To identify resources that cannot achieve scalability.

We have chosen to adopt unified modeling language (UML) profiling mechanisms in which existing UML models are decorated with the essential scalability properties. The profile that we use is based on the OMG's general resource model (GRM) which is a framework for modeling systems with the usage of quality of service (QoS) information [19]. QoS information represents, either directly or indirectly, the physical properties of the hardware and software environments of the application represented by the model. GRM has two viewpoints, domain viewpoint and UML viewpoint. Domain

---

System shall be responsive, available, reliable, and consistent all the time.

Ninety-five percent of all visible pages for customers shall respond in 8 s or less, including infrastructure, excluding back-ends.

The load time for user interface screens shall take no longer than 2 s.

The log in information shall be verified within 5 s.

System shall response to queries within 5 s.

Fifty records of any table shall be downloaded at most 1 s. (max: 50 kb)

System shall be able to deal with 100 users at the same time.

System shall ensure that performance shall not fall below while supporting 3000 users.

System shall be fast enough to support a 1000-transaction-per-day-workload.

Under a load of 360 update transactions per minute, 95% of transactions shall return control to the user within 5 s of pressing the submit button.

Under a load of 360 update transactions per minute, 90% of service requests should return a reply to the calling program within the following times:

        Open account: 30 s; Update account details: 10 s;

        Retrieve account status: 5 s; Search operation: 5 s;

        List operation: 12 s; Filter and sort operations: 7 s;

        Display graphs, tables, calendars operation: 10 s;

        Save forms and reports operation: 6 s;

The DBMS shall support up to 100 concurrent users performing reservation transactions.

. . .

FIG. 10.7

Part of the scalability related requirements for the case study.

viewpoint describes the common structural and behavioral concepts and patterns that characterize a system. UML viewpoint defines the realization of the elements of domain model using UML. It mainly consists of a set of UML extensions, such as stereotypes, constraints, tagged values, and is supplemented by specifications of the mappings of the domain concepts to those extensions. GRM provides mostly abstract concepts that are not applied directly to elements of a UML model. It provides a basis for UML profiles so that concrete extensions can be generated. Table 10.3 shows an example set of stereotypes that we have defined in the scalability perspective.

Fig. 10.8 shows an example sequence diagram of the case study in which scalability profile is used for defining the scalability properties. The diagram shows the increase of the scalability properties together with the adopted scalability tactics. Fig. 10.9 shows an example deployment diagram with adopted stereotypes. In the figure different values related to scalability such as traffic load and access load are explicitly provided. When defining the architecture views with scalability other quality concerns besides of scalability will be taken into account. In particular the cases whereby a scalability decision has an impact on other quality concerns. The presented approach, i.e., an architectural perspective for scalability, helps to reason about the design decision for scalability and is broader than trade-off analysis approach.

10.5.2.3 Analyze scalability model

Similar to the analysis of other quality requirements, scalability analysis can be carried out at two different levels: analysis at the architecture design level, and analysis at the code level. Since architecture is critical for the success of a project, different architectural evaluation approaches have been introduced to evaluate the stakeholders' concerns. A comparison of conventional architecture analysis methods has been given by, for example, Dobrica et al. [20] and Babar et al. [21]. Kazman et al. [22] have provided a set of criteria for comparing the foundations underlying different methods, the effectiveness and usability of methods. In essence, each architecture evaluation approach takes as input the stakeholder concerns, the environment issues, and the architecture description. Based on these inputs, the evaluation results in an architecture evaluation report, which is used to adapt the architecture.

Some metrics cannot be easily evaluated at the architecture design level because of the runtime properties. As such, the evaluation of these metrics requires running code. Scalability analysis at code level analyzes the behavior of the system at various load levels, identifies scalability problems, and the

Table 10.3 Example UML Scalability Stereotypes in the Corresponding Profile

Stereotype	Description
<<SCAcontext>>	This stereotype models scalability analysis context
<<SCAstep>>	A step in a scalability analysis scenario
<<SCAhost>>	A processing resource
<<SCAresource>>	A passive resource
<<SCAopenLoad>>	An open workload
<<SCAclosedLoad>>	A closed workload
<<SCAuserAccessLoad>>	A user access workload
<<SCAcomTrafficLoad>>	A communication traffic workload
<<SCAdbAccessLoad>>	A database access workload
<<SCAtactic>>	A tactic in a scalability analysis scenario

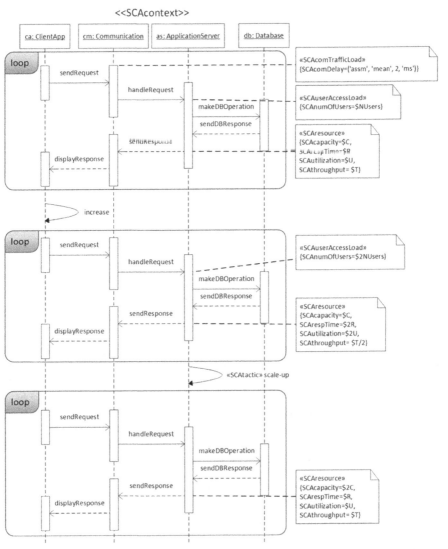

FIG. 10.8

Example sequence diagram with scalability annotations.

bottlenecks of the system. For analyzing the code in scalability perspective we can apply one or more of testing methods that involve performance testing, load testing, endurance testing, stress testing, spike testing, and scalability testing [23,24].

10.5.2.4 Assess against requirements

After analyzing the scalability models, the results will be compared against the identified requirements. The result of this is that either the models or the requirements need to be updated. Another decision could be to iterate over the analysis and testing of the models. The final decision will be to complete the

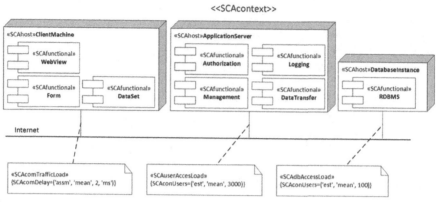

FIG. 10.9

Example annotated deployment model for CHMS.

cycle or to rework the architecture. Within this activity, no new artifacts will be generated but a process and its steps will be followed to ensure that the requirements are realized. The overall process and the decisions need to be explicitly documented.

10.5.2.5 Rework architecture

The previous step might conclude that the architecture needs to be enhanced to realize the identified scalability requirements. This will imply that several architecture views need to be adapted. Table 10.4 shows the impact of the scalability perspective on the defined architecture views of the case study.

To support the adaptation of the architecture to meet the scalability requirements we have derived several architecture tactics from the literature. Architecture tactics are defined as a characterization of architectural decisions that are used to achieve a desired quality attribute response [6]. As such a scalability architecture tactic includes architectural decisions to support scalability. Based on a literature study we have identified the following important architectural tactics for scalable SaaS:

- *Component-based architecture*
  For supporting adaptable, scalable system architecture it is worthwhile to adopt component abstractions. Component-based development will provide a reuse-based approach for defining, implementing, and composing loosely coupled independent components into systems [25,26]. In the component-based software engineering (CBSE) paradigm individual software components are independently executable and ready-to-assemble into larger systems. As such, the construction of applications is now based on using and assembling components rather than a programming process thereby targeting faster and more predictable software construction. In well-designed scalable software, the components should be separated according to their functional domain, i.e., the separation of concerns design principle should be applied and these components should have high cohesion internally and low coupling to the outside.
- *Service-oriented architecture*
  It is necessary to avoid coupling in the architecture so that a change in a part of the software system should not affect other parts [10]. Service-oriented architecture (SOA) is a software architecture design pattern that is composed of services, pieces of software providing application functionality

Table 10.4 Impact of Scalability Perspective on the Architecture Views of the Case Study

View	Applicability to the Case Study
Functional	Sessionless authorization has been applied. Field validations have been moved from database layer to client business logic layer. Data to be displayed in web view has been cached on the client device
Information	We could see that hotel, guest, and other information related with them may cause a scalability problem, since with multitenancy number of their records is high. Also, we could understand reservation data is sensitive in terms of consistency and availability, so that we have taken care of that during applying scalability tactics
Concurrency	No change has been made
Development	Layers have been reorganized. Database has been separated from the server layer and as a result, the system has client, application, and database layers
Deployment	Application layer and database has been placed on the same Amazon EC2 server machine. Database has been moved to another EC2 instance. Instead of using shared memory TCP/IP will be started to use to access database. Memory cache will be added in front of the database, the contents of the application will be reproduced, and a load balancer will be put in front of them
Operational	Performance monitoring and management has been started and metrics related to concerns have been collected and tracked periodically. It has seen that auto scaling can be needed and can be applied in the future

[27]. SOA supports low coupling, since services are unassociated units of functionality that are self-contained. SOA also provides asynchrony meaning system can perform useful work while waiting for input and output to complete, and concurrency meaning tasks can be done in parallel taking advantages of the distributed nature of hardware and software.

- *Minimize the workload on the server*
  Most of the cloud-based SaaS applications have several similar operations, such as making a request, authorization of the requests, fetching data from the database, inserting or updating or deleting data, validation of data, and making some operations, calculations, merging, etc. on data. These operations are either executed on the client or on the server. If all of these operations are executed on the server, then the server may become unresponsive, or even unavailable. Scaling-up the server solves this problem just temporarily, since as the demands grow the server always needs to be scaled-up and it is costly. Moving the workload from the server to the clients as much as possible can minimize the workload on the server [5,10].

- *Scale-up*
  To cope with dynamically increasing demands from multiple tenants, the first approach that comes to mind is scaling the system vertically (scaling-up). This means adding resources to a single node in a system, typically involving the addition of processors or memory to a single computer. In order to be scalable, the more nodes are added to the system, the higher the achievable throughput should be. When adding new hardware to the platform, the total capacity of the entire environment increases, becoming more scalable for not just a single customer, but for the entire client base. Such vertical scaling of a system also enables to use virtualization approach more effectively, as it provides more resources for the operating system (OS) and application modules to share [28].

- *Scale-out*
  The other and a popular approach that includes hardware addition is scaling horizontally (scale-out). It means adding more nodes to a system, such as adding a new server to a distributed

server cluster [29]. Vertical scalability is addressed by increasing the power of nodes whereas horizontal scalability uses more nodes for the same job. It provides a more cost effective and smooth scalability versus scale-up approach [30]. When more computing power is required, a multitenant architecture makes it easy to increase capacity. Since SaaS platform consists of many tenants and all tenants share the same application and data store, and tenants are usually distributed to servers.

- *Database partitioning*

Partitioning is the process of pruning subsets of the data from a database and moving the pruned data to other databases or other tables in the same database [9,12]. Database partitioning in SaaS means that tenant data are partitioned well in the back-end database so that processing and I/O can be done in parallel, and data can be repartitioned easily. You can partition a database by relocating whole tables, or by splitting one or more tables up into smaller tables horizontally or vertically. Horizontal partitioning means that the database is divided into two or more smaller databases using the same schema and structure, but with fewer rows in each table. Vertical partitioning means that one or more individual tables are divided into smaller tables with the same number of rows, but with each table containing a subset of the columns from the original. Partitioning is also an example of scale-out approach, since in order to improve the efficiency the number of databases or tables is increased.

- *Key-value stores*

In a multitenant environment that has high number of requests, database must be able to execute large requests with low response times and also redistribute data and load on the new hardware. To be able to satisfy these requirements of the database and scale data layer successfully key-value stores (KVS) are used [28]. KVS allow the application to store its data in a schema-less way. In KVS, data is viewed as key-value pairs and atomic access is supported only at the granularity of single keys. Since the data could be stored in a data type of a programming language, there is no need for a fixed data model. In DBMS all data within a database is treated as a whole and it is the responsibility of the DBMS to guarantee the consistency of the entire data. In the context of KVS this relationship is completely severed into key-values where each entity is considered an independent unit of data or information and hence can be freely moved from one machine to the other. Also, single key atomic access semantics naturally allows efficient horizontal data partitioning. Moreover, the design of the KVS provides dynamic provisioning in the presence of load fluctuations easily. On the other hand, traditional DBMS are more appropriate for static provisioning. Due to the above desirable properties of KVS, they have almost limitless scalability. KVS can be applied either from the beginning of the system setup or leveraging from it during using the conventional DBMS architecture.

- *Dynamic provisioning*

By adding new resources to the system or partitioning data we can guarantee scalability for a while. For sudden load fluctuations on an application or a service due to demand surges dynamic provisioning can be applied. Dynamic provisioning mechanism uses scalability approaches dynamically, i.e., a system can be scaled-up dynamically by adding more nodes or can be scaled-down by removing nodes.

- *Caching*

Caching is a common practice of storing data in a medium holding smaller amounts of data but which can deliver it faster than a secondary complete source when future requests are made [31]. The purpose of caching is to be able to serve data faster when dealing with thousands of requests per second. By serving data faster throughput of the system is increased, response time is decreased, and scalability can be satisfied. Caching can be done in any tier, but generally the application tier caches database state for quick local access. The data to be cached is determined according to percentage and time of use of data. Data that has frequent use or recent use has the priority of caching. For read-intensive applications, caching approach can provide large performance gains, great scalability as application processing time and database access is reduced. On the other hand, write-intensive applications usually do not see as a great benefit, but solutions that include modifications to caching approach exist. For SaaS systems distributed caching, the extension of caching applied to multiple servers, is used. Distributed caching is scalable because of the architecture it employs [31]. Since caching mechanism is much simpler than a DBMS, usage of distributed cache avoids the scalability problems that a database usually faces.

- *Replication*
  When running a high traffic site, one of the biggest bottlenecks becomes the database. In order to solve this problem and to achieve scalability of database, replication is applied as one of the most common techniques. In replication all or part of the data in a database is copied to another database, and then these replicas are kept synchronized with the original [14]. This increases the availability of the data, so that processes or threads that are waiting in the queue to be able to do some operation with data do not need to wait anymore. Since there are multiple copies of data, it can reach it from the next available one. Replication of data is recommended for mostly read-type operations in terms of scalability perspective. This is because for writing operations consistency of data to all of the copies need to be updated when one of them is changed, which on its turn brings another workload to the database layer. Besides of data replication we could also replicate applications. This means that components in the application layer or the whole application layer can be stored on multiple server instances. Thus, the workload on the application layer can be distributed to multiple machines and processed concurrently by each of the application instances, so a performance improvement can be satisfied and it can reply to more number of requests without performance degradation. Moreover, to support dynamically increasing demands from multitenants, the cloud service providers have to duplicate computing resources dynamically to cope with the fluctuation of requests from tenants. This is currently handled by virtualization and duplication at the application level in the existing cloud environment [32,33].

- *Virtualization*
  Virtualization refers to the act of creating a virtual (rather than actual) version of something, including (but not limited to) a virtual computer hardware platform, OS, storage device, or computer network resources. As we mentioned in the scale-up approach increasing the number of resources in the system, also increases the performance of the system which as such supports scalability. Resources can be provided to the system by not only plugging in the server machine but through virtualization. The resources of the system that is comprised of OS, memory, storage, network, etc. can be virtualized. This will allow, for example, the running of multiple systems on a single physical system or one OS on multiple physical systems. To be able to dynamically respond to increasing demands of the multitenants, virtualization is widely used in current cloud computing systems.

- *Load balancing*
  With an increased number of end users, the performance of a SaaS degrades and it will become soon necessary to distribute client requests to different servers in order to perform parallel processing and provide scalability. This process of distributing workloads across multiple

computing resources is referred as load balancing. Its purpose is to optimize resource usage, maximize throughput, minimize response time, and avoid overload of any one of the resources. In most of the existing SaaS, client requests towards web servers are distributed using a front-end load balancer [34]. To do better load balancing among partitions of a database or application servers, an effective algorithm that can migrate, distribute, and duplicate tenants among partitions through monitoring the load is highly desirable.

- *Parallel processing*

In multitenant environment the SaaS has high number of requests from users, and in order to respond to all of these requests in a very short time, an approach that improves SaaS scalability should be followed. A request is composed of many tasks, including computing operations, database access, etc. In order to be able to reduce execution time of tasks and to reduce the workload of each component, the tasks should be grouped and executed in a parallel and asynchronous manner.

- *Distributing processing in time*

Excessive usage can result in peak loads on the server which will cause low response time and scalability problems. One way to overcome this problem is reduce the system load, and postpone some of the workload to other times in your processing cycle [32]. Some of the tasks on the server occur continually at all times of day or night, and some of them are not urgent, or not need to do real-time, so these tasks can be postponed to other times. Distributing the processing time will reduce the total workload during the peak load times, and as such lead to performance and scalability improvement.

10.5.3 PROBLEMS AND PITFALLS

Given the scalability perspective we have provided an instrument to explicitly reason about scalability and guide the architecture design process. An important benefit of the perspective is of course the explicit focus on scalability. This is helpful both from the analysis and design perspective. In the end, the perspective results in architecture views in which scalability is explicitly considered which will support the communication among the stakeholders and the design decisions.

Like each architecture perspective also the scalability perspective might need to cope with problems and pitfalls. For the problems and pitfalls related to this scalability perspective we can identify the listed problems and pitfalls as defined by Rozanski and Woods [5]. These include incomplete scalability goals, unrealistic models, use of simple measures for complex cases, inappropriate partitioning, invalid environment, and platform assumptions [32], concurrency-related contention, careless allocation of resources, and disregard for network and in-process invocation differences.

10.5.3.1 Checklist

In this section, we provide a checklist to consider when applying and reviewing the perspective. The identified checklist items are based on various resources, such as [5,10,16,17]. The items [CH1]–[CH8] present the checklist for requirements and the items [CH9]–[CH19] present the checklist for architecture definition (Table 10.5).

Item	Explanation
Table 10.5 Checklist Including Questions for Applying Scalability Perspective	
[CH1]	Have you identified scalability goals with stakeholders?
[CH2]	Have you identified the platform features of the system?
[CH3]	Are scalability goals driven by business needs?
[CH4]	Does cost of your hardware requirements conform to your project budget plan?
[CH5]	Have you considered goals for user access load, communication traffic load, data access load, response time, and throughput?
[CH6]	Have you assessed your scalability goals for reasonableness?
[CH7]	Have you appropriately set expectations among your stakeholders of what is feasible in your architecture?
[CH8]	Have you defined all scalability goals within the context of a particular load on the system?
[CH9]	Have you identified possible scalability problems in your architecture?
[CH10]	Have you done sufficient analysis and testing to figure out the scalability need of the system?
[CH11]	What are the expected and maximum workloads the system can process?
[CH12]	Do you define the way how to detect the time when to apply the scalability solution?
[CH13]	Do you know to which components you will apply a scalability tactic?
[CH14]	Do you know by which tactics your architecture can be scaled when needed?
[CH15]	Have you assessed the impact of the scalability solution on functionality and other quality concerns such as performance? Is this impact acceptable?
[CH16]	Have external experts reviewed your scalability design?
[CH17]	Have you verified and validated estimations you have made for scalability goals?
[CH18]	Have you updated your scalability requirements after you validated the scalability goals estimated?
[CH19]	Have you applied the results of the scalability perspective to all of the affected views?

10.6 RELATED WORK

Scalability is not only a concern in cloud computing but has been addressed for the broader domain of distributed systems and web-based systems for a longer period. Lehrig et al. [27] provide the results of a systematic literature review in which they aim to investigate the existing definitions and metrics for scalability, elasticity, and efficiency. The identified concepts can be used by cloud consumers and providers as a common vocabulary and understanding. The concepts that we have used in this study seem to align with the concepts of the systematic literature review. The metrics of the systematic review could be used to support the analysis activities of the scalability perspective that we have provided.

Separating quality concerns at the architecture design modeling phases has been also addressed earlier with the notion of so-called *Attribute-Based Architectural Style* (ABAS) [35]. ABASs refer to prepackaged units of architectural design and analysis. The purpose of ABASs is to enhance precise reasoning about architectural design which is achieved by explicitly associating a *reasoning framework* with an architectural style. The reasoning framework shows how to reason about the design decisions comprised by the style. The reasoning frameworks are based on quality attribute-specific models, which exist in the various quality attribute communities. ABASs are quality attribute *specific* and consider only one quality attribute at a time. Our work could be compared to the idea presented in ABAS, that is, define the architectural model for particular quality concerns. Since the perspective provides also guidelines for identifying, modeling, and analyzing scalability concerns, it could be also considered as a kind of reasoning framework.

Aspect-oriented software development (AOSD) [12] promotes the separation of crosscutting concerns principle [13,39] to increase modularity. Hereby, crosscutting concerns are separately represented as first class abstractions (aspects) and woven into the *base code*. In our approach we have applied the separation of concerns principle to separate the views for quality concerns at the architecture design level [7,40]. Similar to crosscutting concerns in AOSD, quality concerns seem to crosscut the elements in the functional views. To address this problem in essence two different kinds of solutions can be provided. In our earlier work we have considered the explicit modeling of viewpoint for quality concerns [36,37]. Hereby, each quality concern such as adaptability and recoverability require a different decomposition of the architecture. To define the required decompositions for the quality concerns architectural elements and relations are defined accordingly. Earlier work on local recoverability has shown that this approach is also largely applicable. We consider this work complementary to the architectural perspectives approach. It seems that both alternative approaches seem to have merits. In our future work we shall also consider defining architecture viewpoint for scalability. The other alternative for addressing crosscutting concerns at the architecture design level is to adopt architecture perspectives promoted by Rozanski and Woods [5]. For various selected quality concerns corresponding architectural perspectives have been provided. As stated before an architectural perspective dedicated for scalability in cloud computing is currently missing.

Architectural tactics [6] aim at identifying architectural decisions related to a quality attribute requirement and composing these into an architecture design. As described in the scalability perspective architectural tactics are needed to design and rework the architecture if necessary.

Several software architecture analysis approaches have been introduced for addressing quality properties. They usually perform either static analysis of formal architectural models or they apply a set of scenario-based architecture analysis methods [20]. The goal of these approaches is to assess whether or not a given architecture design satisfies desired concerns including quality requirements. Typically these approaches tend to be general purpose and do not focus on a particular concern. The benefit of architectural perspectives and reasoning frameworks for quality concerns is the dedicated focus and analysis which will in the end provide a more precise and consistent view on the selected quality concern. As such, the architecture perspective that we have proposed for scalability can directly support the architectural modeling and analysis for scalability.

Object management group (OMG) has proposed various UML profiles, such as profile for schedulability, performance and time (SPT) [19] and profile for modeling Quality of Service and Fault Tolerance (QoS & FT) [38]. SPT profile has enabled the construction of models that can be used for making quantitative predictions regarding these characteristics. Performance profile has extended the UML metamodel with stereotypes, tagged values, and constraints, which make it possible to attach performance annotations, such as resource demands and visit ratios to a UML model. It has provided facilities for capturing performance requirements within the design context, associating performance-related QoS characteristics with selected elements of the UML model, specifying execution parameters which can be used by modeling tools to compute predicted performance characteristics, and presenting performance results computed by modeling tools or found by measurement. To support the architecture perspective we have adopted a UML profile for scalability. For reasoning about multiple quality concerns multiple profiles could be adopted but the integration of these would require further research.

10.7 **CONCLUSION**

In designing and analyzing SaaS-based systems for scalability the architect needs to be assisted with suitable modeling approaches. Architectural perspectives have shown to be of value for addressing quality concerns. In this paper we have provided a scalability perspective dedicated for SaaS systems. To design the scalability perspective we have first carried out a domain analysis to scalability and defined a scalability perspective according to the guidelines by Rozanski and Woods. The scalability perspective appeared to be really practical, especially since it forced the designers to think about the design decisions regarding the scalability. The scalability perspective was not only useful as a guidance tool for assisting the architect, but it also helped in the early analysis of the architecture. The proposed perspective has only been applied to the existing case study which is from a real industrial context. In our future work we aim to apply it for other case studies as well. Also we shall consider the trade-off analysis using the scalability perspective with the perspectives as defined for other quality concerns.

REFERENCES

[1] B. Tekinerdogan, K. Öztürk, A. Doğru, Modeling and reasoning about design alternatives of software as a service architectures, in: Proceedings of Architecting Cloud Computing Applications and Systems Workshop, 9th Working IEEE/IFIP Conference on Software Architecture, June 20–24, 2011, pp. 312–319.

[2] B. Adler, Building Scalable Applications in the Cloud: Reference Architecture & Best Practices, RightScale, Edinburgh, Scotland, 2011.

[3] A. Bondi, Characteristics of scalability and their impact on performance, in: Proceedings of the Second International Workshop on Software and Performance—WOSP'00, 2000, p. 195.

[4] C.B. Weinstock, J.B. Goodenough, On system scalability, SEI technical note, CMU/SEI-2006-TN-012, 2006.

[5] N. Rozanski, E. Woods, Software Architecture Systems Working with Stakeholders Using Viewpoints and Perspectives, first ed., Addison-Wesley, Boston, MA, 2005.

[6] F. Bachmann, L. Bass, M. Klein, Architectural tactics: a step toward methodical architectural design, Technical report CMU/SEI-2003-TR-004, Pittsburgh, PA, 2003.

[7] L. Bass, P. Clements, R. Kazman, Software Architecture in Practice, third ed., Addison-Wesley, Boston, MA, 2012.

[8] F. Chong, G. Carraro, R. Wolter, Multi-tenant data architecture, MSDN, 2006.

[9] S. Fang, Q. Tong, A comparison of multi-tenant data storage solutions for Software-as-a-Service, in: Proceedings of 6th International Conference on Computer Science & Education (ICCSE), IEEE, August 3–5, 2011, pp. 95–98.

[10] J. Gao, X. Bai, W. Tsai, Y. Huang, Scalable architectures for SaaS, in: Proceedings of IEEE 15th International Symposium on Object/Component/Service-Oriented Real-Time Distributed Computing Workshops, 2012.

[11] P. Clements, F. Bachmann, L. Bass, D. Garlan, J. Ivers, R. Little, P. Merson, R. Nord, J. Stafford, Documenting Software Architectures: Views and Beyond, second ed., Addison-Wesley, Boston, MA, 2010.

[12] R. Chitchyan, A. Rashid, P. Sawyer, J. Bakker, M.P. Alarcon, A. Garcia, B. Tekinerdogan, S. Clarke, A. Jackson, in: R. Chitchyan, A. Rashid (Eds.), Survey of Aspect-Oriented Analysis and Design, 2005. AOSD-Europe project deliverable no. AOSD-Europe-ULANC-9.

[13] M. Aksit, B. Tekinerdogan, L. Bergmans, The six concerns for separation of concerns, in: Proceedings of Workshop on Advanced Separation of Concerns, European Conference on Object-Oriented Programming, Budapest, Hungary, 2003.

[14] J. Gao, P. Pattabhiraman, X. Bai, W.T. Tsai, SaaS performance and scalability evaluation in clouds, in: Proceedings of the 6th IEEE International Symposium on Service Oriented System Engineering (SOSE), 2011, pp. 61–71.

[15] L. Duboc, E. Letier, D.S. Rosenblum, Systematic elaboration of scalability, IEEE Trans. Softw. Eng. 39 (1) (2013) 119–140.

[16] L. Duboc, E. Letier, D.S. Rosenblum, T. Wicks, A case study in eliciting scalability requirements, in: Proceedings of the 16th IEEE International Requirements Engineering Conference, September 8–12, 2008, pp. 247–252.

[17] A. Podelko, Multiple dimensions of performance requirements, in: Proceedings of the 33rd International Computer Measurement Group (CMG) Conference, December 2–7, 2007.

[18] IEEE, Guide to the Software Engineering Body of Knowledge (SWEBOK), IEEE, Piscataway, NJ, 2004.

[19] Object Management Group, UML profile for schedulability, performance and time specification, OMG document, version 1.1, formal/05-01-02, (2005).

[20] L. Dobrica, E. Niemela, A survey on software architecture analysis methods, IEEE Trans. Softw. Eng. 28 (7) (2002) 638–654.

[21] M.A. Babar, L. Zhu, R. Jeffrey, A framework for classifying and comparing software architecture evaluation methods, in: Proceedings of 5th Australian Software Engineering Conference, April, 2004, pp. 309–319.

[22] R. Kazman, G. Abowd, L. Bass, P. Clements, Scenario-based analysis of software architecture, in: Proceedings of IEEE Software, November, 1996, pp. 47–55.

[23] J.D. Meier, C. Farre, P. Bansode, S. Barber, D. Rea, Performance Testing Guidance for Web Applications, Microsoft Corporation, Seattle, US, 2007.

[24] B.M. Subraya, Integrated Approach to Web Performance Testing, IRM Press, Hershey, PA, 2006.

[25] G.T. Heineman, W.T. Councill, Component-Based Software Engineering: Putting the Pieces Together, Addison-Wesley, Boston, MA, 2001.

[26] C. Szyperski, Component Software, Addison-Wesley Professional, Boston, MA, 2002.

[27] S. Lehrig, H. Eikerling, S. Becker, Scalability, elasticity, and efficiency in cloud computing: a systematic literature review of definitions and metrics, in: Proceedings of the 11th International ACM SIGSOFT Conference on Quality of Software Architectures, 2015, pp. 83–92.

[28] D. Agrawal, A. El Abbadi, S. Das, A.J. Elmore, Database scalability, elasticity, and autonomy in the cloud, in: Proceedings of the 16th International Conference on Database Systems for Advanced Applications (DASFAA), April 22–25, Springer-Verlag, Berlin, 2011, pp. 2–15.

[29] W. Tsai, Q. Shao, Y. Huang, X. Bai, Towards a scalable and robust multi-tenancy SaaS, in: Proceedings of the Second Asia-Pacific Symposium on Internetware, ACM, New York, 2010.

[30] L. Jiang, J. Cao, P. Li, Q. Zhu, A mixed multi-tenancy data model and its migration approach for the SaaS application, in: Proceedings of IEEE Asia-Pacific Services Computing Conference (APSCC), December 6–8, 2012, pp. 295–300.

[31] I. Khan, Distributed caching on the path to scalability, MSDN Magazine (2009), July.

[32] B. Tekinerdogan, S. Bilir, C. Abatlevi, Integrating platform selection rules in the model driven architecture approach, in: Proceedings of the 2003 European Conference on Model Driven Architecture: Foundations and Applications, June 26–27, 2003, pp. 159–173.

[33] X. Sun, Q. Shao, G. Qi, Two-tier multi-tenancy scaling and load balancing, in: IEEE 7th International Conference on e-Business Engineering (ICEBE), November 10–12, 2010, pp. 484–489.

[34] D. Yuanyuan, N. Hong, W. Bingfei, L. Lei, Scaling the data in multi-tenant business support system, in: Pacific-Asia Conference on Knowledge Engineering and Software Engineering, IEEE, 2009.

[35] M. Klein, R. Kazman, L. Bass, S.J. Carriere, M. Barbacci, H. Lipson, Attribute-based architectural styles, in: Proceedings of the First Working IFIP Conference on Software Architecture, San Antonio, TX, February, 1999.

[36] H. Sözer, B. Tekinerdogan, M. Aksit, Optimizing decomposition of software architecture for local recovery, Softw. Qual. J. 21 (2) (2013) 203–240.

[37] B. Tekinerdogan, H. Sözer, Defining architectural viewpoints for quality concerns, in: Proceedings of the 5th European Conference on Software Architecture (ECSA 2011), LNCS 6903, 2011, pp. 26–34.

[38] Object Management Group, UML profile for modeling quality of service and fault tolerance characteristics and mechanisms, Request for proposal, ad/02-01-07, 2002.

[39] J. Bakker, B. Tekinerdogan, M. Aksit, Characterization of early aspects approaches, in: Workshop on Early Aspects: Aspect-Oriented Requirements Engineering and Architecture Design, Held in Conjunction with AOSD Conference, 2005.

[40] B. Tekinerdogan, ASAAM: aspectual software architecture analysis method, in: Proceedings of 4th Working IEEE/IFIP Conference on Software Architecture (WICSA), June, 2004, pp. 5–14.

MANAGING TRADE-OFFS IN SELF-ADAPTIVE SOFTWARE ARCHITECTURES

MANAGING TRADE-OFFS IN SELF-ADAPTIVE SOFTWARE ARCHITECTURES: A SYSTEMATIC MAPPING STUDY

11

M. Salama*, R. Bahsoon*, N. Bencomo[†]

University of Birmingham, Birmingham, United Kingdom[*] Aston University, Birmingham, United Kingdom[†]

11.1 INTRODUCTION

Self-adaptation has been primarily driven by the need to achieve and maintain quality attributes in the face of the continuously changing requirements and uncertain demand during run-time. Designing architectures that exhibit a good trade-off between multiple quality attributes is challenging, especially in the case of self-adaptive software systems, due to the continuously changing run-time requirements as a result of operating in dynamic, open, and uncertain contexts [1–3]. This challenge increases with the complexity of the imposed trade-offs, due to considering more quality dimensions and the conflicts that might appear between different quality attributes [1–3]. Further challenges are imposed from the need for complying to environmental, regulatory, and sustainability requirements; such as energy consumption regulations [4].

Researchers and practitioners have recognized the architecture is the appropriate level of abstraction for making such trade-offs decisions explicit [2,3]. The subject of trade-offs analysis in software architecture has received plenty of attentions over the years [2,3]. Contributions have motivated the need for systematic approaches that can inform the decision of architecting software systems [5–7]. The state-of-art and practice provide tangible evidence on the importance and wide adoption of contributions, which are grounded on systematic analysis for trade-offs [2,3]. The adoption of such analysis has demonstrated impact in various architecting domains. Examples of seminal work include Architecture Tradeoff Analysis Method (ATAM) [8], and Cost Benefit Analysis Method (CBAM) [9]. Research has encountered many efforts for analyzing and managing quality attributes trade-offs and the field has attracted a wide range of researchers and practitioners. Despite the maturity of research in this topic, we still lack a clear picture of trade-offs management approaches, which are designed for self-adaptive environments.

This paper presents a systematic mapping study examining trade-offs management, to compile relevant literature related to self-adaptive software architectures. A systematic mapping study is a methodological mean to analyze systematically a research topic, in order to provide an overview of the research area, analyze the quality and type of research conducted, and identify the gaps and research opportunities in this area [10–12]. The focus is on the studies that explicitly considered trade-offs management; i.e., modeled trade-offs, or devised management solutions; not implicit consideration for trade-offs. This study has also a specific concern about self-adaptive architectures; i.e., studies related to classical software architectures; such as [8,9] are not taken into consideration in this study. We have carefully chosen the systematic mapping study approach, as the trade-offs management topic is quite broad; cross-cutting multiple software paradigms and many self-* properties, which requires analyzing the research landscape. This mapping study mainly aims to (i) get an overview of the current state of the research on trade-offs management for self-adaptive software architectures, (ii) obtain a comprehensive understanding of the process of managing trade-offs and its related challenges with respect to self-adaptive software and different software paradigms, and (iii) identify trends and promising future research directions to support self-adaptive software architectures.

The mapping study analyzed the landscape of self-adaptive software systems, exploring the self-* properties that drive trade-offs management, and the software paradigms in which trade-offs management was considered. The study also investigated the quality attributes considered in trade-offs, reviewed the mechanisms for resolving trade-offs and analyzed them with respect to scale and operating time. More specifically, we draw our analysis based on the following dimensions: *when*, *who*, *what*, and *how*, for a comprehensive look for trade-offs management. The *when* reflects the time when trade-offs are considered and managed; i.e., design-time, or run-time. By design-time, we mean trade-offs management is considered while evaluating the architectural design alternatives and making architectural decisions. The run-time is meant to be managing trade-offs while the system is operating and the change requests are implemented. The *who* dimension is related to the actor performing the analysis at run-time and/or design-time. At design-time, architects and stakeholders are the ones involved in conducting trade-offs management. During run-time, trade-offs management might be conducted on-line while the system is operating, off-line using simulations, for example, or following an interactive mode. The *what* dimension reflects the subject of trade-offs; i.e., what is meant to be traded off. This could be different quality attributes, run-time goals or sustainability goals. The *how* dimension echoes the mechanism used to manage trade-offs; i.e., multi-objective optimization, utility theory.

The results of the study contribute to the understanding of state of the research in this area and pave the way for solutions from both academia and industry. Despite the mature and systematic treatment for trade-offs in software design and architecture fields, research in the area of self-adaptive software architectures has not sufficiently discussed trade-offs frameworks and specialized foundations, which are specifically designed for self-adaptivity and run-time requirements [13]. This calls for foundational framework for analyzing and managing trade-offs in self-adaptive software architectures, both while designing self-adaptive systems and at run-time during their operation. More specifically, we envision the need for a systematic way for managing trade-offs that can consider multiple quality attributes explicitly, the run-time dynamics and the uncertainty of the environment. Self-adaptive software architectures can hugely benefit from such focus to render cost-effectiveness and better seamless solutions. With the vision that architectures play an important role in the software sustainability and long-livety, modern complex software systems; e.g., systems of systems [14–16], ultra-large scale systems, smart cities [17–20], smart homes [21], cloud federations [22–24]; call for approaches that can cater heterogeneity of the environment, better deal with uncertainty, and scale for managing trade-offs for a sustainable and long-living software.

The manuscript is structured as follows. Section 11.2 presents a background on self-adaptive software architectures and their related trade-offs. A description of the systematic mapping study protocol is presented in Section 11.3. Section 11.4 shows the systematic mapping study process conducted. Section 11.5 presents the principal results of the analysis, the answers to the research questions, and discussions. Section 11.6 presents related surveys. New trends and research directions are discussed in Section 11.7, whereas conclusions and further work are then summarized in Section 11.8.

11.2 BACKGROUND

In this section, we give a brief background about self-adaptive software architectures and the trade-offs they encounter during operation.

Self-adaptive software systems feature the ability to adjust their behavior in response to their perception of the environment and the system itself [7,25]. The "self" prefix indicates that the system is capable to decide autonomously how to adapt or organize for accommodating changes in their contexts and environments [26]. The capability of the system to adjust its behavior in response to changes in requirements and the environment, in the form of self-adaptation, has received significant attention in the research community [27–29].

Self-adaptation has been used as a mechanism to deal with the increasing complexity of software systems and uncertainty of their environments [26]. By architecting self-adaptive systems, we tend to cover two areas: (i) architectures and models which are developed to support self-adaptive software systems and (ii) self-managed architectures which automatically configure their components in a way that is compatible with an overall architectural specification while interacting in response to the system goals. The former could include reference architectural styles and models, which are architectural in essence and tend to guide the adaptation of the system. Notable examples include the work by Oreizy et al. [30] providing a general outline of an architectural approach which includes adaptation and evolution management, the work by Garlan and Schmerl [31] describing the use of architecture models to support self-healing, and the work by Dashofy et al. [32] proposing the use of an architecture evolution manager to provide the infrastructure for run-time adaptation and self-healing. The latter, often backed up by reference architectural models, enacts architectural changes at run-time; not only implements the change internally, but also initiates, selects and assesses the change itself without the assistance of an external user [7]. As an example, the works of Kramer and Magee [33,34] have provided a context for achieving the vision of self-management at the architectural level, where the self-managed architecture components automatically configure their interaction in a way that is compatible with an overall architectural specification and achieves the goals of the system.

Software architectures that provide trade-offs management between multiple quality attributes to support decision making are essential to deal with the complexity, heterogeneity, and ultra-large scale of the modern software systems. As the complexity of systems increases, it is expected that more quality attributes need to be managed and handled for satisfaction, and therefore more conflicts will arise. Also, challenges are further imposed from the need for complying to environmental, regulatory, and sustainability requirements; such as energy consumption regulations. Research roadmaps for self-adaptive software systems [7,25] have identified several research challenges related to trade-offs to support decision making for self-adaptive systems. First, in the case of multiple conflicting goals, trade-offs should be analyzed for identifying an optimal configuration of the goals to be met. Second, trade-offs between the adaptation cost and benefit need to be taken into consideration. Third, trade-off between flexibility and assurance of meeting the critical high-level goals is required when developing self-adaptive systems due to uncertainty levels. Recently emerging self-adaptive styles; such as self-awareness; have been promoted to seamlessly manage uncertainty of the operating environment across dimensions related to goal-, time-, and interaction-awareness [35–37].

The issues discussed above call for a deeper, profounder analysis and management for trade-offs that can better cater for dynamic changes in the system and the environment, both while designing self-adaptive systems and at run-time during their operation. Designing and engineering self-adaptive systems with better trade-offs management result in having more sustainable architectures in the face of uncertainty at run-time. At run-time, better trade-offs management result in better selection of adaptation action to fulfill the continuously changing run-time requirements, which will sustain the architecture in fulfilling multiple quality attributes.

11.3 SYSTEMATIC MAPPING PROTOCOL

A systematic mapping study is "the process of identifying, categorizing, analyzing existing literatures that are relevant to a certain research topic" [10]. The aim of a systematic mapping study is to get a comprehensive overview on a particular research topic, present unbiased assessment of current literature, identify research gaps and collect evidence for future research directions [11,12,38–40]. The outcome of a mapping study is a classified portfolio of publications on the research area [41,42]; i.e., a high level map reporting the structure of existing literature related to the research field subject of interest, visualizing the status of that field with respect to pre-defined research questions, and giving a visual summary and mapping with respect to various classification categories [10].

A systematic mapping study is a form of secondary study that aims at providing an overview of the research area, and allows discovering research gaps and trends [10,42]. This form of studies, used to give an overview of a research area and designed to structure it [42], involves searching the literature in order to identify the topics covered in the literature [10]. Another form of secondary studies is the systematic literature review (SLR) that, in contrast, focuses on gathering and synthesizing evidence [42]. Although these two forms of studies have some commonalities in the process of conducting the search and studies selection, they are different in terms of goals, and thus the research process is different [38,42]. A systematic mapping study is primarily concerned with structuring a research area [38,42], while a systematic review considers only evidence and their strengths [42]. In more details, the differences are with respect to the type of research questions, analysis conducted on the literature, quality evaluation, and results [38,43]. The research questions in mapping studies are general and broad, since they aim to classify topics covered in the literature and discover research trends [38,42]. Then again, systematic reviews provide in-depth analysis to answer more specific questions [38], with the aim to aggregate evidence [42]. Given the classification conducted in systematic mapping studies, solution proposals are included in the analysis, while this category would not be included in SLRs [42]. This reflects the importance of systematic mapping studies in spotting research trends and topics currently in-progress [42].

We have chosen to conduct a systematic mapping study, as the involved topic of trade-offs management is quite broad cross-cutting multiple software paradigms and many self-* properties. We cover and classify research in the area of self-adaptive software systems following the inclusion criteria. Our focus is on analyzing and classifying research topics, as well as identifying trends and gaps in this area. The procedure of this mapping study followed the guidelines for conducting secondary studies [38], and dedicated guidelines for performing mapping studies [10]. It has been also informed by other systematic mapping studies relevant to software and architecture [40,44–46]. And, we have employed some guidelines from SLR, since some research questions cannot be answered only by mappings and required further data synthesis.

The systematic mapping study is conducted in the following steps (depicted in Fig. 11.1): (1) planning of the study, (2) search execution, (3) selection of primary studies, (4) data extraction and classification, (5) analysis and mapping.

1. Systematic mapping planning:

    In this step, we establish the plan that will be used as a basis to conduct the systematic mapping study. The following is to be defined and carried during this step:

    (a) Definition of research questions: These questions reflect the objective that the study is intended to attain.

    (b) Definition of the scope: To frame the research questions, defining the scope helps to decide the research initial boundaries and guide the course of the research.

    (c) Establishment of the search strategy: This includes the selection of search sources; e.g., indexing services, digital libraries, publication venues; that will be used to find the primary studies, as well as the search strings. Quality criteria of the journals and conferences are taken into account.

    (d) Establishment of selection criteria: The selection criteria consist of the inclusion and exclusion criteria. These are used to select the primary studies that are relevant to answer the research questions and exclude the irrelevant ones.

2. Search execution:

    In this step, the search is conducted in the search sources using the search strings, according the previously defined search strategy.

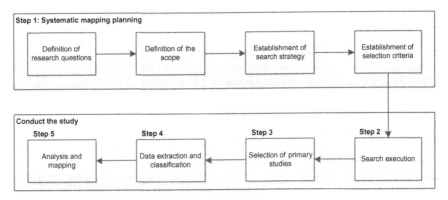

FIG. 11.1

Systematic mapping process.

3. Selection of primary studies:

   In this step, the selection criteria are applied in order to select the relevant primary studies. To conduct further examination, the titles, abstracts, introductions, and conclusions are screened for better relevance decision.

4. Data extraction and classification:

   The classification scheme is built; i.e., the clusters that will be used to form the categories of the map. The researchers read the whole paper, and look for keywords and concepts that reflect the contribution of the studies. The actual data extraction takes place, where the studies are classified using the classification scheme, with the aim of providing the set of results to address the research questions. During this process, data sheets are created to store extracted information.

5. Analysis and mapping:

   During this step, statistics are extracted from the extracted information and the visual maps are built.

11.4 SYSTEMATIC MAPPING PROCESS

Having presented the protocol for conducting a systematic mapping study, this section presents the application of the protocol to this study. The study presented in this paper focuses on the specific topic of managing trade-offs for self-adaptive architectures to support decision making and maintain quality of service. By managing trade-offs for self-adaptive software architectures, we are looking for studies that explicitly considered handling and managing trade-offs; i.e., modeled trade-offs, or devised management solutions for trade-offs. The systematic mapping was conducted according to the process presented in the aforementioned steps in Section 11.3, and completed with discussing limitations of the study.

11.4.1 STEP 1: SYSTEMATIC MAPPING PLANNING

In this step, the research questions, scope, search strategy, and selection criteria are defined and established.

11.4.1.1 Research questions

The overall research objective of the study is to give an overview of the current state of the art related to managing trade-offs for self-adaptive software architectures in research and practice. This mapping study focuses on the research questions, presented in Table 11.1 along with their motivations.

11.4.1.2 Search strategy
11.4.1.2.1 Search sources

The search process for this study is based on automated search in the following digital libraries and indexing systems: IEEE Xplore, ACM Digital Library, ScienceDirect, Web of Science, and Springer-Link (details in Table 11.2). These are considered as the largest and most complete scientific databases for conducting literature reviews [47,48] and most relevant electronic databases to computer science and software engineering [10]. The selected trustworthy search sources have direct impact on the quality of conferences and journals when retrieving the search results. As technical reports and white papers do not appear in these libraries, we consider Google Scholar for this type of publications only.

Table 11.1 Research Questions

RQ	Research Question	Motivation
RQ1	What are the studies that explicitly addressed trade-offs management for self-adaptive software architectures?	The aim of this question is to identify the existing studies that explicitly considered trade-offs management for self-adaptive software architectures and their significant contribution in this field
RQ2	What are the types of research and contribution presented in these studies?	The goal to devise this question is to find the research approaches (research types) used to conduct the studies identified, as well as the advances to the literature developed in the study (contribution types)
RQ3	What are the publication types of these studies, and their chronological distribution? Which research groups are actively contributing into this topic?	This question aims at analyzing the landscape of the published work, by examining the publication types, their chronological and geographical distributions. This allows identifying the maturity of the work, the progress over the time and the research groups heavily interested in the subject
RQ4	Which self-* properties have driven trade-offs management for self-adaptive software architectures?	Self-* properties are one of the main characteristics of self-adaptive software systems. These self-* properties drive and call for managing imposed trade-offs
RQ5	Which software paradigms have been considered in architectures trade-offs management?	Different software paradigms exhibits dissimilar trade-offs, arising from the nature of the paradigm and their environment. Understanding the nature of these software paradigms, and their environment is important to manage their associated trade-offs
RQ6	Which quality attributes are investigated in trade-offs management?	The conflict between some quality attributes that are required to be fulfilled is the main source of trade-offs. The goal here is to identify the quality attributes that were investigated and handled in trade-offs management
RQ7	Which mechanisms were used to manage trade-offs for self-adaptive software architectures? What is the time dimension of the trade-off management approaches?	This research question looks for the approaches and mechanisms that were used to manage and resolve trade-offs, and when these approaches could operate; whether during designing the system, or during run-time while the system is operating

Table 11.2 Search sources

Database	Location
IEEE Xplore	http://ieeexplore.ieee.org/
ACM Digital Library	http://dl.acm.org/
ScienceDirect	http://www.sciencedirect.com/
Web of Science	http://www.webofknowledge.com/
SpringerLink	http://link.springer.com/
Google Scholar	https://scholar.google.co.uk/

We have also identified specialized venues in the field of software architecture and self-adaptive software. The main journals are:

- ACM Transactions on Software Engineering and Methodology;
- ACM Transactions on Autonomous and Adaptive Systems;
- IEEE Transactions on Software Engineering;
- Journal of Software and Systems (Elsevier);
- Information and Software Technology (Elsevier); and
- Software and System Modelling (Springer).

For the specialized conferences, we have identified:

- International Symposium on Software Engineering for Adaptive and Self-Managing Systems (SEAMS);
- IEEE International Conference on Self-Adaptive and Self-Organizing Systems (SASO);
- Working IEEE/IFIP Conference on Software Architecture (WICSA);
- International ACM SIGSOFT Conference on the Quality of Software Architectures (QoSA); and
- European Conference on Software Architecture (ECSA).

Furthermore, in order not to miss any relevant studies, we designated the cross-referencing technique to find potentially relevant studies, by checking the references of the selected primary studies.

11.4.1.2.2 Search string

The aim of the search string is to capture all results related to trade-offs associated with architecture in the context of self-adaptive software. Trial searches were performed in each database with the intention of checking the number of returned papers and their relevance. The objective of the trial searches is to check the feasibility of the search string and adjust it accordingly.

The general search string used on all databases is:

```
(trade*) AND (architecture) AND (self-*) AND (software)
```

The first parentheses capture the different ways "trade-offs" are usually written; i.e., tradeoffs or trade-offs. The term "management" was not included, as pre-tests showed false positives because this term is frequently used in business or operational contexts. Same applies for the term "decision" as a synonym. The second one makes it explicit for architecture and the third and fourth are for self-adaptive software. Other keywords; such as design for architectures, multi-objective for trade-offs; when tried, had led to a vast wide set of irrelevant results. The simplicity and generality of the search string helps in maximizing the number of returned relevant papers, as it places as few restrictions as possible on the search string.

11.4.1.3 Selection criteria

Inclusion criteria, formalized with the aim to increase the possibilities of having relevant studies, are:

1. Papers published in conferences and journals, as full research paper, short and position paper presenting new and emerging ideas, as well as doctoral symposiums.
2. Literatures published as books, book chapters, technical reports, and white papers.
3. When similar studies were reported in several papers as work-in-progress, the most comprehensive version is considered, unless significant details were reported in the earlier version.

4. Papers presenting a technique for trade-offs management.
5. Papers evaluating architectures with multi-dimensional trade-offs.
6. Papers discussing general or particular aspects of architecture trade-offs management.

Exclusion criteria, applied on the results retrieved, are:

1. Duplicate studies.
2. Papers in the form of abstract, tutorials, posters, or presentation.
3. Abstract not available.
4. Full-text papers not accessible.
5. Papers not in English language.
6. Papers not explicitly addressing architecture trade-offs.
7. Papers focusing on trade-offs for any types of software without self-adaption.
8. Papers focusing on hardware or network architecture.

11.4.2 STEP 2: SEARCH EXECUTION

The search was executed on the databases using the search string, as specified earlier. In practice, particular settings were built for each search engine (Table 11.3 for details), since each digital library works in a specific manner. This was attempted to minimize duplications and rejections by setting the appropriate options in each search engine. In particular, a filter was applied for setting the search engine to retrieve only studies published by its own engine, and a language filter was applied, whenever available, to retrieve documents in English language only. Minimizing results by excluding irrelevant

Table 11.3 Search Strings and Settings

Database	Search String and Settings
ACM Digital Library	Searching for: (trade) AND (architecture) AND (self-) AND (software) Refinements: Publishers: ACM Content Formats: Pdf
IEEE Xplore	You searched for: ("Metadata": ((trade) AND (architecture) AND (self-) AND (software))) You Refined by: Publisher: IEEE Content Type: Conference Publications, Journals & Magazines, Books & eBooks
ScienceDirect	TITLE-ABSTR-KEY(trade* AND architecture AND self-* AND software) (All Sources(Computer Science, Engineering))
SpringerLink	"trade AND architecture AND self- AND software" within Language: English Discipline: Computer Science Sub-discipline: SWE
Web of Science	TOPIC: ((trade*) AND (architecture) AND (self-*) AND (software)) Refined by: RESEARCH AREAS: (COMPUTER SCIENCE OR ENGINEERING) Timespan: All years

disciplines was also used, whenever available. In case the search engine does not imply enough filters and large number of irrelevant results were retrieved, we used the first 200 search results ordered according to the relevance with regard to the search string. This decision was made after carefully checking up to other 150 search results after the first 200 and found complete irrelevance.

Regarding the search in the specialized venues, manual search method on target venues was not needed, after we manually ensured that the papers published in these venues were retrieved in the databases included in the automated search. A separate search was done on Google Scholar, searching only for technical reports and white papers.

The search was executed during March 2015, by the main researcher. As a result of this step, we obtained 4489 (first 200 used) from ACM Digital Library, 29 from IEEE Xplore, 5 from ScienceDirect, 5029 (first 200 used) from SpringerLink, and 28 from Web of Science. It is worth to note here that the limited number of search results—compared with some systematic mapping studies—is due to the fact that this study is focused on a very specific aspect; i.e., managing trade-offs; for self-adaptive architectures only. This reflects the fact of the narrow scope and specialization of this study; compared to systematic mapping studies with wider scope [49,50]. Table 11.4 shows the total results retrieved from each database. Bibliographic data, including abstracts, and full texts were exported and stored using EndNote [51], an efficient reference management system by Thomson Reuters, for further analysis. We have also created a sheet listing the primary sources with their meta-information.

11.4.3 STEP 3: SELECTION OF PRIMARY STUDIES

During the screening of search results, the title, abstract, introduction, and conclusion for each candidate paper were examined closely to determine the relevance of the paper. The aforementioned inclusion and exclusion criteria were applied at this stage. Since quality assessment is not a necessary task for mapping studies, as stated by Kitchenham and Charters [38], we do not use it to filter primary studies. But, we evaluated the contributions of the primary studies, as well as the scale and completeness of proposed approaches, as described later in the results (Section 11.5). Table 11.5 shows the figures of included studies from each database. This step was performed by the main researcher, and supervised by the second researcher.

After performing the selection of the primary studies retrieved by the search execution, we have applied the cross-referencing technique to find potentially relevant studies, by checking the references of the selected primary studies. These referenced papers are then taken forward to the step of primary studies selection to apply the same process.

Table 11.4 Summary of Search Results

Database	Search Results
ACM Digital Library	4489
IEEE Xplore	29
ScienceDirect	5
SpringerLink	5029
Web of Science	28

Table 11.5 Selection Summary

Database	Included Studies
ACM Digital Library	2
IEEE Xplore	6
ScienceDirect	3
SpringerLink	4
Web of Science	10

The selection of primary studies has resulted in a final list of 20 relevant papers, after removing the duplicate studies. The reference list of the primary studies is included in Appendix A. Despite the fact of the limited number of primary studies identified, we believe that our search found all primary studies that explicitly deal with trade-offs management for self-adaptive software architectures. We interpret this number of primary studies due to the narrow focus on which the study was designed; i.e., trade-offs management, that is a specific architectural aspect for self-adaptive software architectures only.

11.4.4 STEP 4: DATA EXTRACTION AND CLASSIFICATION

For each selected primary study, the whole paper was read to extract the data items listed in Table 11.6. These data items include publication year, publication type, authors' country of affiliation, research type, contribution type, software paradigm, self-* properties, traded quality attributes, as well as the mechanisms used in managing trade-offs, their scale, and time. This step was performed by the main researcher, and supervised by the second researcher reviewing the whole process, having thorough discussions and looking iteratively at the literature. The extracted data were recorded on a spreadsheet. Detailed information about the data extracted and classifications of each study is summarized in the table appearing in Appendix B.

With respect to the classification, we have chosen the following classification schemes, to analyze the research landscape:

Research type
The research type facet reflects the research approach used in the papers. To classify the types of research in the primary studies, we adopted the classification suggested by Wieringa et al. [41], as suggested by the guidelines for performing mapping studies [10] and similar to other studies [52,53]. The classification is summarized in Table 11.7.

Contribution type
This facet reflects what was developed in order to achieve advances in the focus area. Possible contributions, based on Petersen et al. [10], are summarized in Table 11.8.

Along the classification, we have allowed a paper to be associated to more than one category in a certain classification facets. This explains why the accumulated number of papers in some figures and tables appearing in Section 11.5 is more than 20.

Table 11.6 Data Extracted From Each Primary Study

Data Item	Description	Relevant RQ
Key	A key for referencing the study	None
Title	The title of the study	None
Authors	The list of authors	None
Affiliations	The affiliations of the authors	None
Publication venue	The name of the publication venue	None
Publication type	Journal paper, conference paper, technical report, book chapter	RQ3
Publication year	The publication year of the study	RQ3
Country of affiliation	The countries of the authors' affiliation	RQ3
Research type	The research approach used in the study; e.g., solution proposal, validation research, evaluation research, philosophical paper, opinion paper, experience paper	RQ2
Contribution type	The advances developed in the study; e.g., process, approach, model, tool, metric, case study, experiment, non-empirical study, literature review	RQ2
Software paradigm	The type of software that the study has considered; e.g., cloud-based, service-oriented, mobile, real-time	RQ5
Self-* property	The self-* property that the study focused on; e.g., self-managing, self-organizing, self-healing, self-configuring	RQ4
Quality attributes	The quality attributes that were investigated and handled in trade-offs management; e.g., performance, security, energy consumption, cost	RQ6
Trade-offs management mechanism	The approach used in managing and resolving trade-offs; e.g., multi-objective optimization, Pareto-optimality, utility theory	RQ7
Time dimension	The time in which the mechanism is operating; i.e., during design-time of the system, or during run-time while the system is operating	RQ7
Contribution	A brief summary about the main contribution of the study	RQ1

Table 11.7 Types of Research Facet

Category	Description
Solution proposal	Proposes new technique to solve a problem, where the technique can be either novel or significant extension of an existing technique. Applicability of the solution is supported by examples and solid arguments
Validation research	Describes investigation of a novel technique that has not been implemented yet
Evaluation research	Describes investigation of an existing technique in practice to acquire understanding of a problem. This shows how the technique is implemented in practice (solution implementation) and what the consequences are of the implementation (implementation evaluation)
Philosophical paper	Describes the nature of background and knowledge research by presenting structuring the field in form of a taxonomy or conceptual framework
Opinion paper	Describes the researcher's opinion, values, and preferences without introducing new research results
Experience paper	Describes the researcher's experience in conducting a practice

Table 11.8 Types of Contribution Facet

Category	Description
Process	Describes activities or actions and their work flow
Approach	Describes a method or approach stating the rules of how things should be done. This includes algorithms, frameworks, and infrastructures
Model	Provides a description of the real world omitting details, it has a higher degree of formality, and should have semantics and notations
Tool	Is a software tool developed to support the development of a proposed solution
Metric	Presents metrics and measurements related to trade-offs management
Case study	Presents descriptive explanation of empirical enquiries performed in an in-depth study
Experiment	Presents evaluation method or empirical evidence for an existing technique
Non-empirical study	Describes the researcher's persuasive ideas and arguments without data validation. This includes also taxonomies, research challenges, and conceptual frameworks
Literature review	Reports critical analysis of prior researched studies that summarizes, classifies, compares, and evaluates them

11.4.5 STEP 5: ANALYSIS AND MAPPING

Once the data extraction and classification task had been accomplished, the results obtained were analyzed and the systematic mapping was created. Data analysis aims to synthesize the extracted data to answer the RQs defined in Section 11.4.1.1. Descriptive statistics and frequency analysis were employed in analyzing the data. In more details, the following analyses were conducted:

- When synthesizing the data to answer RQ1, besides listing the studies that explicitly addressed trade-offs management for self-adaptive architectures and their contributions, a weighted word cloud was created to analyze the topical content of the publications.
- To answer RQ2, descriptive analyses for the distribution of the research types and the contribution types were generated.
- To analyze the characteristics of publications (RQ3), we generated the distribution of the publication types, the chronological distribution of the publications, and the geographical distribution of researchers based on their country of affiliation. Also, chronological distribution of the publications related to the publication types was considered for more thorough analysis.
- To answer RQ4, frequency analysis for the self-* properties driving trade-offs management was created. Also, the self-* properties found were mapped to the research types. This map provides the distribution of all the research types conducted with respect to the self-* properties.
- For RQ5, studies related to software paradigms are listed and the frequency analysis of these paradigms in studies was created.
- With respect to RQ6, the frequency analysis for the quality attributes investigated in trade-offs management was created. We have also considered the correlation between the quality attributes considered in trade-offs management and different software paradigms.
- To answer RQ7, the mechanisms used for trade-offs management and their related studies were tabulated, and their time dimension was analyzed using frequency analysis.

Table 11.9 Analyses Conducted	
Analysis	**Relevant RQ**
Weighted word cloud	RQ1
Distribution of the research types	RQ2
Distribution of the contribution types	RQ2
Distribution of the publication types	RQ3
Chronological distribution of the publications	RQ3
Chronological distribution of the publications related to the publication types	RQ3
Distribution of researchers based on their country of affiliation	RQ3
Frequency of self-* properties driving trade-offs management	RQ4
Systematic mapping between research types and self-* properties	RQ2, 4
Frequency of software paradigms considered for trade-offs management	RQ5
Frequency of quality attributes investigated in trade-offs management	RQ6
Correlation between quality attributes and software paradigms	RQ5, 6
Frequency of the time dimension of trade-offs management mechanisms	RQ7
Correlation between software paradigms, quality attributes, and the mechanisms for trade-offs management	RQ5, 6, 7

- In order to get a comprehensive view about the research conducted, we have created a correlation matrix, summarizing the research conducted with respect to the software paradigm, the quality attributes, and the mechanisms for trade-offs management.

The analyses conducted and their relevant RQs are summarized in Table 11.9. The results of the analysis with regard to each research questions are detailed in Section 11.5.

11.5 RESULTS AND DISCUSSIONS

This section presents the findings of the study, addressing and discussing each of the research questions listed in Table 11.1.

11.5.1 RQ1. WHAT ARE THE STUDIES THAT EXPLICITLY ADDRESSED TRADE-OFFS MANAGEMENT FOR SELF-ADAPTIVE SOFTWARE ARCHITECTURES?

This first research question aims to identify the existing studies that explicitly considered trade-offs management for self-adaptive software architectures and their significant contribution in this field. These studies are listed below, identified by the key used in Appendix A. The contributions of the primary studies are summarized below:

[**Ardagna 2008**] employed analysis-oriented models to support analyzing and reasoning about non-functional system properties; precisely performance and reliability.

[**Inoue 2008**] work resulted in optimized trade-offs between system design complexity, system performance and power impact, by proposing on-line self-test features in a multi-/many-core architecture.

[**Sousa 2008**] attempted engineering resource-adaptive software systems targeted at small mobile devices, by empowering users to control trade-offs among service-specific aspects of quality of service and coordinating resource usage among several applications.

[**Sousa 2009**] further developed their earlier research [Sousa 2008] by presenting a framework for engineering resource-adaptive systems that empowers users to control trade-offs among a set of quality aspects, and coordinates resource usage among several applications.

[**Teich 2009**] presented a paradigm of parallel computing for giving embedded systems the ability to explore and claim resources in a certain neighborhood, where the trade-off between flexibility and cost is considered.

[**Mirandola 2010**] introduced a dynamic adaptation for service-based systems that minimizes the adaptation costs and guarantees the required quality of service, based on an optimization model.

[**Sawyer 2010**] presented a research agenda for self-adaptive systems towards being able to adapt dynamically to new environmental uncertain contexts. This work called for research into how self-adaptive systems envisage run-time trade-offs of requirements that are present as the environment changes; i.e., how self-adaptive systems can have run-time flexibility to ignore temporarily some requirements in favor of others.

[**Landauer 2011**] studied trade-offs between safety and capability in the autonomic agent infrastructure of self-organizing real-time systems. This work used off-line simulations to tune the trade-off at deployment time—based on what is known or expected of the environment—as well as to monitor and change those assumptions when necessary.

[**Menasce 2011**] presented a model-driven framework targeted at dynamic settings for self-architecting service-oriented systems in which a requirements might change, taking into consideration trade-offs that reflect stakeholders' priorities.

[**Perez-Palacin 2011**] proposed an adaptation process for service-based self-adaptive systems, which guarantees a trade-off between energy consumption and quality of service offered, while maintaining suitable revenues for the service provider.

[**Peng 2012**] proposed a control-theoretic method for self-tuning software systems, combining goal models with feedback controllers, to tune dynamically the preferences of different quality requirements and make dynamic trade-off among conflicting soft goals. That was achieved through preference-based goal reasoning procedure, in order to find Pareto-optimal configurations for dynamic quality trade-off.

[**Perez-Palacin 2012**] extended their previous work [Perez-Palacin 2011] by developing an adaptation framework for service-based applications that can be used to reduce power consumption according to the observed workload. This work aimed at guaranteeing a trade-off between energy consumption and performance, using stochastic Petri nets for the modeling where their analyses give results about the trade-offs.

[**Shen 2012**] proposed a quality-driven self-adaptation approach for designing architectures of self-adaptive software systems, which incorporates design decisions as the bridge between requirements- and architecture-level adaptations. This was based on making value-based quality trade-off decisions with the aim of maximizing system-level value propositions, and using a preference-driven goal reasoner to reconfigure the run-time goal models based on the results of dynamic quality trade-off. [**Andrade 2013**] defined a model-based approach for design spaces representation and exploration which entails a search-based mechanism that points out decision trade-offs between feedback controls and performance overhead to find out a set of Pareto-optimal candidate architectures for self-adaptive software systems.

[**Sandionigi 2013**] proposed an approach for service selection in a pervasive environment, framed as a quality of service optimization problem. The approach evaluates at run-time the services optimal binding as well as the trade-off between the remote execution of software fragments and their dynamic deployment on local nodes of the computational environment.

[**Andrade 2014**] reported the results of a controlled experiment that evaluates the design of self-adaptive systems using a search-based approach, in contrast to the use of a style-based non-automated approach, for finding out subtle effective designs and providing well-informed means to reveal quality attributes trade-offs.

[**Chen 2014**] addressed trade-offs between global benefit of the cloud and local optimization of virtual machines from one side, and between global benefit of the cloud and overhead in the design for selecting an elastic strategy from another side, in order to determine dynamically and efficiently an architectural elastic strategy that produces globally-optimal benefit.

[**Perez-Palacin 2014**] proposed an approach for analyzing and evaluating trade-offs between the system adaptability and other system quality attributes, like availability or cost. The approach was based on a set of metrics that allows evaluating the system adaptability at the architecture level to guide architecture decisions on system adaptation for fulfilling system quality requirements.

[**Sutcliffe 2014**] proposed a reference architecture for context-aware adaptive system, where the heuristics and metrics of design architecture strategies are used to refine conceptual architectures in trade-off analysis to deal with non-functional requirements.

[**Andrade 2015**] reported the results of another controlled experiment, following their earlier work [**Andrade 2014**]. This experiment evaluated the design of self-adaptive systems using a search-based approach for explicitly eliciting design trade-offs, in contrast to a non-automated approach based on architectural styles catalogs, with the goal of investigating to which extent the adoption of search-based design approaches impacts on the effectiveness and complexity of resulting architectures.

In order to gain first impression on the topical content of the publications and show on which areas the studies are focused, we have created a simple weighted word cloud (see Fig. 11.2) that was generated from the abstracts of the primary studies. This was created with Tagxedo [54], which uses a stemming algorithm to filter the textual input. Observing the density of terms, the most frequently used (given other forms between brackets) are: software, system (systems), architecture (architectures, architectural), requirements (goals), quality (QoS), design, self-adaptive (adaptation, adaptive), run-time (dynamic, dynamically, on-line), and trade-offs. This reflects the generality of the type of software and systems addressed when working for trade-offs management. Same applies to the appearance of the general term of self-adaptive, compared with other self-* properties. This also reflects that trade-offs management acquired on the architecture level is interleaving with the requirements level. The distinct appearance of the word "performance" might leave the impression of its special concern among other quality attributes, though it might be used in the context of measuring the performance of the proposed work. The word "design," if added to other words such as model and framework, gives the impression of the nature of work done in the primary studies.

FIG. 11.2

Weighted word cloud.

11.5.2 RQ2. WHAT ARE THE TYPES OF RESEARCH AND CONTRIBUTION PRESENTED IN THESE STUDIES?

To answer this question, we analyzed the types of researches used in the primary studies collected, and their contributions types, as described earlier in the classification step (Section 11.4.4).

The categorization of the primary studies according to the research types appears in Fig. 11.3. The results show a significant number of solutions proposed in comparison with evaluation researches. This

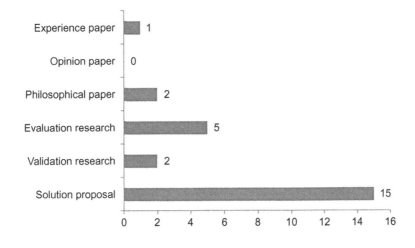

FIG. 11.3

Distribution of the research types.

indicates a relative high degree of interest in providing solutions for supporting trade-offs management. On the other hand, this research area still lacks other types of researches; such as validation research investigating new techniques to advance the research, experience papers investigating existing techniques in practice, as well as philosophical papers describing the nature of background and knowledge research and structuring the field. Further analysis about the implications of these studies appears in the plot, mapping the research types to the self-* properties (Section 11.5.4).

We have also analyzed the research studies according to their contribution type, as illustrated in Fig. 11.4. The descriptive statistics show that most of the researches proposed an approach and evaluated it by experiment, whereas other contribution types; such as tool, model, process, and metric; have lower figures.

11.5.3 RQ3. WHAT ARE THE PUBLICATION TYPES OF THESE STUDIES, AND THEIR CHRONOLOGICAL DISTRIBUTION? WHICH RESEARCH GROUPS ARE ACTIVELY CONTRIBUTING INTO THIS TOPIC?

This question aims at analyzing the landscape of the published work, by examining the publication types, their chronological and geographical distributions. This allows identifying the maturity of the work, the progress over the time and the research groups heavily interested in the subject. We analyzed the primary studies from different perspectives: (1) publication types, (2) chronological distribution of the studies, and (3) geographical distribution of the research in this area.

First, the distribution of the collected studies related to the method of publication is shown in Fig. 11.5. The results show that a significant number of publications were made through conferences

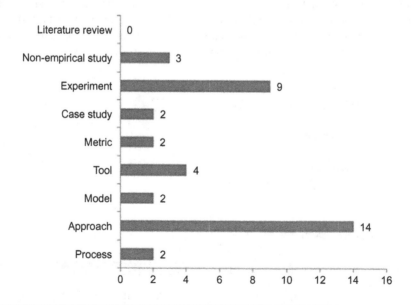

FIG. 11.4

Distribution of contribution types.

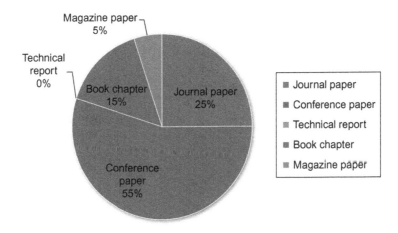

FIG. 11.5

Distribution of the publication types.

(55%), followed by a less significant number of publications (25%) in journals. A limited number of publications were found in the form of book chapters (15%) and magazines papers (5%), whereas none technical reports were published. Ideas and solutions are still being proposed in conferences, and some of them have matured and reported through journals and books. This indicates that research in this particular area is still considered maturing. Yet, no technical reports and magazine papers have reflected transition between pure research and pure practice, transferring ideas, methods, and experiences among researchers and practitioners.

Further, we analyzed the number of published studies for each year, as illustrated in Fig. 11.6. The results show that publications related to trade-offs management for self-adaptive software architecture started at 2008 with a constant and stable attention, regardless the limited number of publications. It is also worth to note that this mapping study was conducted early 2015, which interprets the decrease appearing in 2015.

For a better insight about the publications, Fig. 11.7 shows the chronological distribution of the publication types. This illustrates an overall constant figure in the number of papers published in conferences, while papers published in journals, books, and magazines maintained a lower and inconstant number. The publication of studies in conferences might indicate a shift towards more mature, complete, and technical work in the future.

Despite the narrow scope of the study topic, we analyzed the location where the collected researches were conducted. The aim is to identify the research communities that contributed to this subject, based on the number of resided researchers. Therefore, the demographic distribution of the researchers upon their affiliations was analyzed. Fig. 11.8 illustrates the distribution of this analysis. This shows that 24% of the collected papers were investigated by researchers in Italy, followed by 20% and 16% by researchers from United States and United Kingdom, respectively, whereas the rest of papers are fairly distributed amongst the other countries; Spain and Brazil (12%), and Singapore and China (8%).

By that, we have identified four main research groups (other groups of authors are not listed for their single contributions) that are working actively and providing progressive contributions, namely:

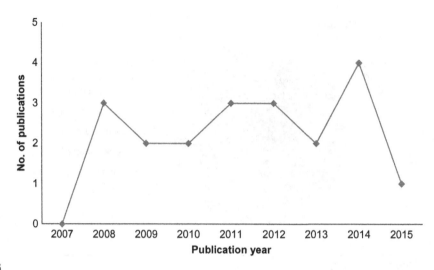

FIG. 11.6

Chronological distribution of the publications.

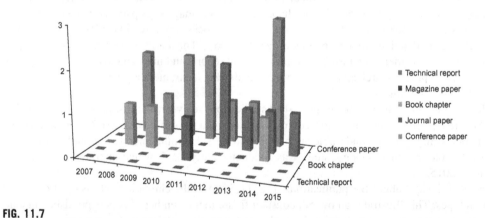

FIG. 11.7

Chronological distribution of the publication types.

- [Perez-Palacin] focused on service-based applications and proposed the use of stochastic Petri nets for modeling trade-offs between three different sets: (a) energy consumption and quality of service, (b) energy consumption and performance, (c) system adaptability and quality of service.
- [Andrade] focused on designing self-adaptive systems architectures, presenting a search-based approach to find out a set of Pareto-optimal candidate architectures and followed by a multi-objective optimization engine that relies on the Non-dominated Sorting Genetic Algorithm II.
- [Sousa] presented a framework for engineering resource-adaptive software systems targeted at small mobile devices, that empowers users to control trade-offs among some aspects of quality of service, founding their approach on the utility theory.

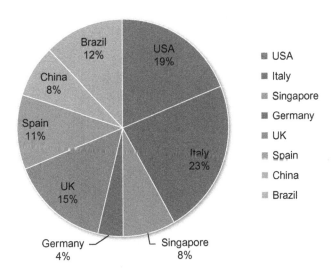

FIG. 11.8

Distribution of researchers based on their country of affiliation.

- [Shen] and [Peng] used value-based reasoning for quality-driven self-adaptation design and continued the work towards a dynamic trade-off with little human intervention.

11.5.4 RQ4. WHICH SELF-* PROPERTIES HAVE DRIVEN TRADE-OFFS MANAGEMENT FOR SELF-ADAPTIVE SOFTWARE ARCHITECTURES?

This research question provides the analysis of the self-* properties which drive trade-offs and call for their management. As self-* properties are inter-linked; e.g., self-managing might embed some self-organizing or self-optimizing capabilities; we relied in this analysis on the explicit consideration of a particular self-* property. We considered this type of simple and explicit analysis, due to the fact that each of the self-* properties exhibits its own challenges that affect trade-offs management, beside the common trade-offs among general self-adaptivity. A distinct example is the recently emerging self-awareness, which was built on top of self-adaptivity. Self-awareness aims for more efficiency in the way the self-adaptation is performed, by making the computation node aware of certain useful information; such as run-time goals, interaction with the environment and historical information [35–37].

Extracting the self-* properties from the primary studies, Fig. 11.9 presents this descriptive analysis. The results show that the majority of the research considered the general self-adaptive property. Self-managing, self-organization, and self-optimization properties received some equal attention, whereas all other properties had less attention. This indicates the generality of the trade-offs management approaches, yet specialized approaches are still required to manage trade-offs for specific self-* properties and handle their related challenges.

For profounder view of the research status, we related the self-* properties with the research types found in the literature. We have constructed a bubble plot diagram for mapping the distribution of research types with the self-* properties. Fig. 11.10 presents the bubble plot diagram illustrating this

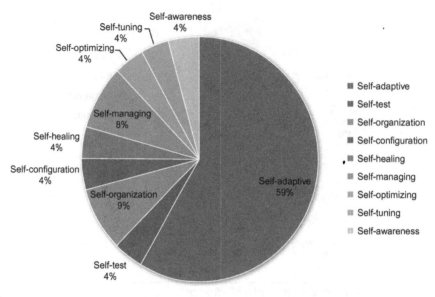

FIG. 11.9

Self-* properties driving trade-offs management.

mapping. The systematic map illustrates that the significant contribution of the research field was solution proposals for the general self-adaptive property. The self-adaptive property has also taken some attention in the validation and evaluation research types. All other self-* properties gained some attention in the solution proposal only. This view of the research field clarifies the lack of different research types, rather than solution proposals, for specific self-* properties.

11.5.5 RQ5. WHICH SOFTWARE PARADIGMS HAVE BEEN CONSIDERED IN ARCHITECTURES TRADE-OFFS MANAGEMENT?

This research question provides the analysis of software paradigms in which trade-offs management was considered. Different software paradigms and their related studies are listed in Table 11.10.

Analyzing software paradigms that were considered in trade-offs management in different researches, Fig. 11.11 shows the descriptive analysis of this distribution. The majority found were addressing general self-adaptive software and software systems. A limited special attention was given to service-based and mobile software. Single researches covered other different types of software, including cloud-based software, embedded systems, real time and pervasive applications.

One observation is that the majority of the proposed work tends to be generic and not explicitly designed for the requirements of a particular paradigm. This implies that generality can come with advantages and disadvantages. Generality can imply application and evaluation of the proposed work under different context and applications, as well as reflecting on their strengths and weaknesses in dealing with the said paradigm. This can consequently provide inputs for further improvements and extensions. On the other hand, these approaches can take simplistic assumptions, or tend to be limited when addressing the requirements of

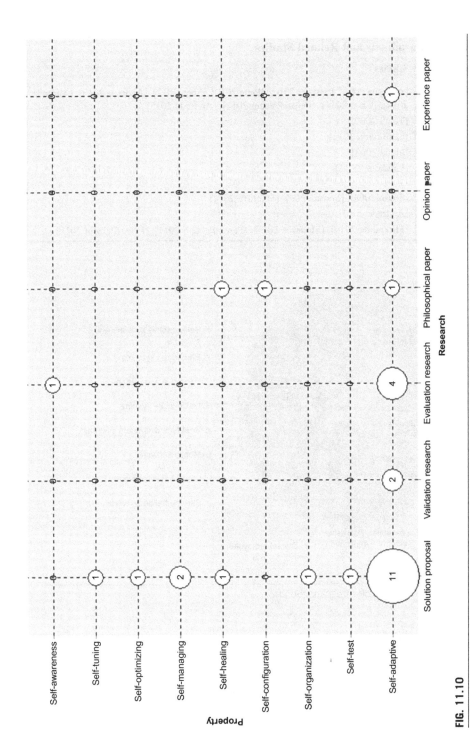

FIG. 11.10

Systematic mapping (bubble plot) for research types and self-* properties.

Table 11.10 Software Paradigms and Related Studies

Software Paradigm	Studies
Self-adaptive software and systems	[Ardagna 2008], [Sawyer 2010], [Peng 2012], [Shen 2012], [Andrade 2013], [Andrade 2014], [Chen 2014], [Perez-Palacin 2014], [Andrade 2015]
Embedded systems	[Teich 2009]
Pervasive systems	[Sandionigi 2013]
Large-scale systems	[Inoue 2008]
Real-time distributed systems	[Landauer 2011]
Mobile software	[Sousa 2008], [Sousa 2009], [Sutcliffe 2014]
Cloud-based software	[Andrade 2013]
Service-based software	[Mirandola 2010], [Menasce 2011], [Perez-Palacin 2011], [Perez-Palacin 2012]

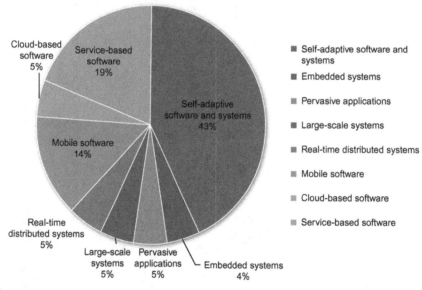

FIG. 11.11

Software paradigms considered for trade-offs management.

some paradigms, where speciality and customization is desirable for more effective adaptation. More trade-offs arising from a particular software paradigm need to be explicitly considered. For instance, considering a cloud federation, a cloud node exhibits trade-offs arising from the run-time environment and the quality goals received from other nodes in the federation. Trade-offs management that considers characteristics of particular software paradigms will result in advancing these paradigms. Yet, the validity of these observations can be subject to further empirical studies.

11.5.6 RQ6. WHICH QUALITY ATTRIBUTES ARE INVESTIGATED IN TRADE-OFFS MANAGEMENT?

As part of analyzing the details of research work done in the literature, we have listed out the quality attributes investigated in trade-offs management. Fig. 11.12 illustrates the statistics of these attributes among the primary studies. The major case of trade-offs management considered quality attributes on a general level. Special attention was given to performance and cost. Other attributes; such as safety, reliability, and adaptation cost; were considered in single research efforts.

In the case of considering specific attributes, Table 11.11 summarizes the related studies and the attributes considered. Beside quality attributes, we have also considered feedback loops in trade-offs management, for feedback loops became a crucial element of the overall architecture in engineering self-adaptive software systems [26]. Feedback loops—in all forms—can carry information about emerging or implied behavior of the system and imply new trade-off that needs to be managed. Considering multiple feedback loops, or multiple decisions from a feedback loop, or internal and external feedback loops, more trade-offs will arise and need to be managed.

Another observation is that the majority of the studies, considering specific attributes, were concerned only with two attributes for trade-offs as examples in illustrating their approaches. Examples include [Ardagna 2008] considered performance and reliability only, [Perez-Palacin 2011] and [Perez-Palacin 2012] considered performance and energy only. However, the formalism behind their trade-offs management process might not be limited to treating only two quality attributes.

Considering multiple quality attributes in trade-offs management will result in selecting better adaptation action that is able to fulfill multiple qualities. With many efforts and claims indicating the validity of this statement, we still need formal and rigorous investigations. Empirical studies provide the means for this, but no controlled experiments have been performed to provide that evidence. Afterwards, we call for more comprehensive trade-offs management approaches that consider *multiple* specific quality attributes.

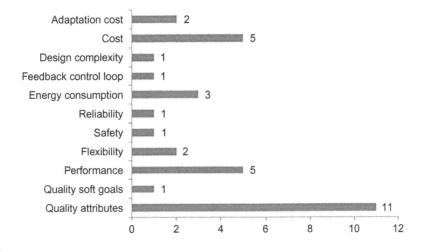

FIG. 11.12

Quality attributes investigated in trade-offs management.

Table 11.11 Studies Considering Specific Attributes

Study	Attributes
[Ardagna 2008]	Performance, reliability
[Inoue 2008]	Design complexity, performance, power impact
[Teich 2009]	Flexibility, cost
[Mirandola 2010]	Adaptation cost, quality attributes
[Landauer 2011]	Safety, resources
[Menasce 2011]	Stakeholders' priorities
[Perez-Palacin 2011]	Performance, energy
[Perez-Palacin 2012]	Energy consumption, performance
[Andrade 2013]	Feedback control loop, performance overhead
[Sandionigi 2013]	Flexibility, cost
[Chen 2014]	Global QoS, cost

As trade-offs are imposed from the recent advancements of different software paradigms, we considered the correlation between the quality attributes considered in trade-offs management and the different software paradigms. We have identified a cross-reference matrix classifying the primary studies, as depicted in Fig. 11.13.

11.5.7 RQ7. WHICH MECHANISMS WERE USED TO MANAGE TRADE-OFFS FOR SELF-ADAPTIVE SOFTWARE ARCHITECTURES? WHAT IS THE TIME DIMENSION OF THE TRADE-OFF MANAGEMENT APPROACHES?

This research question looks for the mechanisms that were used to manage trade-offs. The trade-offs mechanisms and their related studies are listed in Table 11.12.

Analyzing the extracted mechanisms, we identified that utility theory and multi-objective optimization appeared to be the most used techniques. Some efforts approached the use of stochastic Petri nets, value-based reasoning and Pareto-optimality. We have identified these mechanisms, listed as follows:

- Utility theory was used to model and quantify quality of service trade-offs [Sousa 2008, Sousa 2009, Menasce 2011] for engineering resource-adaptive software systems targeted at small mobile devices in order to coordinate resource usage among several applications.
- Stochastic Petri nets were proposed for modeling trade-offs for service-based applications [Perez-Palacin 2011, Perez-Palacin 2012, Perez-Palacin 2014].
- Multi-objective optimization was employed for optimizing trade-offs between system design complexity, system performance and power impact [Inoue 2008], for minimizing the adaptation costs while guaranteeing the quality of service [Mirandola 2010], for pointing out decision trade-offs between feedback controls and performance overhead [Andrade 2013, Andrade 2014], as well as for optimizing service selection [Sandionigi 2013].

Trade-off attributes \ Software paradigm	Service-based software	Cloud-based software	Mobile software	Real-time distributed systems	Large-scale systems	Pervasive applications	Embedded systems	Self-adaptive software & systems
Quality attributes		[Mirandola 2010], [Menasce 2011]		[Sousa 2008], [Sutcliffe 2014]			[Teich 2009]	[Sawyer 2010], [Shen 2012], [Andrade 2014], [Chen 2014], [Perez-Palacin 2014], [Andrade 2015]
Quality soft goals								[Peng 2012]
Performance		[Perez-Palacin 2012]	[Andrade 2013]	[Sousa 2009]			[Sandionigi 2013]	[Ardagna 2008], [Andrade 2013]
Flexibility					[Landauer 2011]	[Inoue 2008]		
Safety								
Reliability		[Perez-Palacin 2011]				[Inoue 2008]		
Energy consumption		[Perez-Palacin 2012]			[Landauer 2011]			[Ardagna 2008], [Andrade 2013]
Feedback control loop			[Andrade 2013]					[Ardagna 2008]
Design complexity								[Andrade 2013], [Andrade 2014]
Cost		[Perez-Palacin 2012]	[Andrade 2013]	[Sousa 2009]			[Sandionigi 2013]	[Sawyer 2010]
Adaptation cost		[Perez-Palacin 2011]						[Perez-Palacin 2014]

FIG. 11.13

Correlation of software paradigms and quality attributes.

Table 11.12 Trade-offs Management Mechanisms and Related Studies

Trade-offs Mechanism	Studies
Utility theory	[Sousa 2008], [Sousa 2009], [Menasce 2011]
Stochastic Petri	[Perez-Palacin 2011], [Perez-Palacin 2012], [Perez-Palacin 2014]
Multi-objective optimization	[Inoue 2008], [Mirandola 2010], [Andrade 2013], [Sandionigi 2013], [Andrade 2014]
Pareto-optimal solutions	[Peng 2012], [Andrade 2015]
Value-based reasoning	[Peng 2012], [Shen 2012]
Analysis-oriented method	[Ardagna 2008]
Invasive algorithms	[Teich 2009]
Requirements reflection	[Sawyer 2010]
Simulations	[Landauer 2011]
Objective functions	[Chen 2014]
Heuristics	[Sutcliffe 2014]

- Pareto-optimal solutions were also used to point out trade-offs decision using a search-based mechanism [Andrade 2015] and to find optimal configurations for dynamic quality trade-off for self-tuning [Peng 2012].
- Value-based reasoning was used to make design decisions that bridge between requirements- and architecture-level adaptations [Shen 2012] and dynamically to make trade-offs among quality requirements [Peng 2012].

Analyzing the time dimension of these mechanisms (see Fig. 11.14); i.e., when these mechanisms tend to operate; we found 50% of the mechanisms were design-time mechanisms, approximately equals to

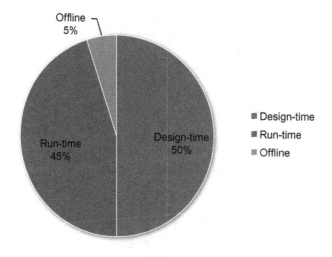

FIG. 11.14

Time dimension of trade-offs management mechanisms.

45% run-time ones and 5% off-line. The design-time and run-time mechanisms studied and analyzed above are meant to be either design decisions or run-time adaptation decisions respectively. For both types of decisions, linkage of architectures with requirements is expected to enrich and better-inform the trade-offs decisions. More precisely, design-time trade-offs management requires linkage with requirements elucidated while designing the system, and run-time trade-offs management requires run-time monitoring of requirements changes. Such linkage should, then, employ requirements reflection, as proposed in [Sawyer 2010].

To get a comprehensive view about the research landscape, we have created a correlation matrix (see Fig. 11.15), summarizing the research conducted in the primary studies with respect to the software paradigms, the quality attributes, and the mechanisms for trade-offs management.

11.5.8 LIMITATIONS OF THE STUDY

Despite the fact that this study has been conducted following mainly the systematic mapping study methodology, there are some limitations that need to be clarified:

- The limited number of search results and selected primary studies—compared with other systematic mapping studies [45]—might leave a question about the completeness and coverage of the study. However, the study was designed from the beginning to focus on a specific architectural aspect; i.e., managing trade-offs for self-adaptive software only. This reflects partly the narrow scope and specialization of this study; which is similar to the case of [55] that constructs a systematic mapping study focusing on software architecture knowledge (13 primary studies), and [56] that focused on measuring the understandability of architectural structures (25 primary studies). Obviously, the narrow scope of the systematic mapping interprets the limited number of search results and selected primary studies. Thus, we believe that we have covered much of the significant studies relevant to the topic. It is also worth to note the quality of conferences and journals of the primary studies that are used in the analysis.
- Along this study, only a set of criteria was presented to classify and analyze the research done in the topic studied. There could be other criteria to evaluate the work of these studies; such as the technical details of these studies, their efficiency and limitations. However, this requires a systematic literature review rather than a systematic mapping study [12,57].
- Some relevant papers might not have been found in the identified digital databases when executing the search, as automated searches rely on the search engine quality. However, the search sources used are considered as the largest and most complete scientific databases for conducting literature reviews [8,9] and are highly relevant electronic databases to computer science and software engineering [4]. Therefore, we are reasonably confident that significant studies have been unlikely missed.
- The search was based on meta-data (abstract, title, and keywords) only and might missed some studies that have considered trade-offs management as part of their proposed work, and have not mentioned this in their titles, abstract and keywords. Though the meta-data are specified by the authors of the papers, we reasonably rely on how well the digital databases classify and index papers.
- The search process and data extraction were performed by one researcher implying that some bias might, therefore, have been introduced in the results for many reasons; such as the background of

Trade-off attributes \ Software paradigm	Service-based software	Cloud-based software	Mobile software	Real-time distributed systems	Large-scale systems	Pervasive applications	Embedded systems	Self-adaptive software & systems
Utility theory	[Menasce 2011] Quality attributes	[Perez-Palacin 2011] Safety, adaptation cost; [Perez-Palacin 2012] Performance, energy consumption	[Sousa 2008] Quality attributes; [Sousa 2009] Flexibility, cost					[Perez-Palacin 2014] Quality attributes, adaptation cost
Stochastic petri		[Mirandola 2010] Quality attributes						[Andrade 2013] Feedback control loop, cost; [Andrade 2014] Quality attributes, cost
Multi-objective optimization		[Andrade 2013] Feedback control loop, cost			[Inoue 2008] Performance, reliability	[Sandionigi 2013] Flexibility, cost		[Peng 2012] Quality soft goals
Pareto-optimal solutions								[Andrade 2015] Quality attributes
Value-based reasoning								[Peng 2012] Quality soft goals; [Shen 2012] Quality attributes
Analysis-oriented method							[Teich 2009] Quality attributes	[Ardagna 2008] Performance, energy consumption, design complexity
Invasive algorithms								
Requirements reflection				[Landauer 2011] Performance, energy consumption				[Sawyer 2010] Quality attributes, adaptation cost
Simulations								
Objective functions								[Chen 2014] Quality attributes
Heuristics			[Sutcliffe 2014] Quality attributes					

FIG. 11.15

Correlation of software paradigms, quality attributes, and mechanisms.

the researcher and the researcher's subjectivity that affects the entire process. However, the second researcher's supervision reviewing the whole process, looking iteratively at the literature, and having thorough discussions with the third researcher lead us to believe that the effect of this error is minimal.

11.6 RELATED SURVEYS

There have been many surveys in the literature related to self-adaptive software architectures. The SLR of Weyns and Ahmad [58] was performed on the claims and evidence for architecture-based self adaptation. This study concluded that the trade-offs implied by self-adaptation have not received much attention, and evidence is mainly obtained from simple examples. Other surveys related to self-adaptive architectures include the survey of Bradbury et al. [59] that evaluated the self-managing approaches in dynamic software architecture specification, the work of Wynes et al. [60] on understanding formal methods for self-adaptive systems, and the work of Yuan et al. [61] on understanding self-protecting software systems. Some of these studies discussed the decision making process in the light of multiple quality concerns for self-adaptive systems, yet none has extensively and explicitly looked at trade-offs management.

It is worth to mention further surveys related to software architectures which reviewed topics that can indirectly contribute to trade-offs management. Examples include the systematic review conducted about software architecture evolution [62] and another one more specialized to characterize software architecture changes [63]. Sustainability evaluation of software architectures was reviewed in [64]. Another survey reviewed the reliability and availability prediction methods from the viewpoint of software architecture [65].

11.7 CHALLENGES AND RESEARCH DIRECTIONS

As modern software systems are increasingly expected to be autonomous, smarter and scalable, research in self-adaptivity faces new and unique challenges in the way software systems are architected. As discussed earlier, solutions for architecting self-adaptive software systems face numerous trades-offs across different dimensions related to quality goals, workload, time, context, and environment. Based on our study, we identify in this section challenges and research directions in managing trade-offs for self-adaptive software architectures.

- *Separation of trade-offs concerns of the managing and the managed systems.* Analyzing quality attributes considered in trade-offs management studies, existing research have not well addressed the separation of trade-offs of the managed system and the managing system of a self-adaptive software system [7,66–68]. Managed systems can have their own trade-offs; such as quality concerns and run-time goals. The managing system can be informally referred to as the "engine" for enabling self-adaptation. The trade-offs for the managing system, for example, could be related to: (i) operation efficiency, cost, and benefits of supporting multiple systems under its own management, (ii) styles for management (eg, centralized, decentralized, semi-decentralized), and (iii) the use of various trade-offs management and conflict resolution mechanisms to optimize for its operation. However, these should not be discussed in isolation of the context; that is the situation and the managed systems themselves. We call for explicit consideration and separation of trade-offs for both the managed and the managing systems to promote flexibility, scalability, and heterogeneity in the analysis.

- *Managing trade-offs of trade-offs.* Observations from primary studies that explicitly looked at trade-offs management have revealed that trade-offs are often treated without clear separation between trade-offs of the managed system and trade-offs of the managing system [7,66–68]. While it is imperative that the managing and managed systems can influence each other's trade-offs management decisions, a question that becomes relevant is how can trade-offs of trade-offs be managed. That is, trade-offs of trade-offs are dynamically encountered in the managed and the managing environment to reach a compromise. For example, it may be possible that the separation can benefit from fine-grained view of the management process, that can reveal situations where the trade-offs of both systems can be in agreement, or in conflict, and other situations leading to risks.

- *Catering for heterogeneity in systems.* Trade-offs management should cater for heterogeneity in the managed systems [69], where these systems can be of varying scale, environments, and operate under different assumptions, constraints, and optimization objectives. Consider, for the example, managing trade-offs in Systems of Systems [14–16] (e.g., smart cities [17–20], smart homes) [21] and open systems that rely on shared models and multi-tenant provision (e.g., cloud, and cloud federations) [22–24], the challenge can include scaling the trade-offs analysis and management to cater for the individual systems and the welfare of the composed system—as a whole—in the operating environment. The trade-offs management shall also look at mechanisms that can scale the identification, analysis, and mitigation of the numerous uncertainties that an operating and evolving system may exhibit.

- *The need of viewpoints for managing uncertainties when handling trade-offs.* As discussed earlier, self-adaptation has been used as a mechanism to deal with the increasing complexity of software systems and uncertainty of their environments [30]. As architectures are facing higher levels of uncertainties [7,25], future research in managing trade-offs shall better deal with uncertainty. As systems become more complex, the uncertainties can relate to various viewpoints of the system. Research shall look at identifying various viewpoints, predicting uncertainties relative to these viewpoints, performing automatic negotiation, and reconciling these viewpoints. The aim is to reach a comprehensive model that can better reflect on possible risks associated with the various viewpoints of the systems to better cope with uncertainties.

- *Dynamic run-time trade-offs management.* As run-time adaptation is heavily motivated by the autonomic management for quality of service, scalability, and improving users' satisfaction and experience [7]; while reducing operational cost and minimizing or eliminating human intervention; managing trade-offs is seen to be a *live* process with critical importance. This calls for a foundational framework in the architecture for managing run-time trade-offs, rather than acting or reacting to solve trade-offs. Such foundational work would embrace systematic modeling, analysis, management, as well as continuous refinement and control for trade-offs at run-time. Such framework is expected to act autonomously during run-time or tested off-line using simulations and the simulation results are carried out to the running architecture.

- *Building frameworks combining design-time and run-time trade-offs management.* Though we advocate the need for run-time frameworks for systematically managing trade-offs; this should not undermine the role of design-time frameworks. As an example of design-time approaches, the work of Hassan et al. [70] that allows designers to make explicit links between the possible emergence of risks and design decisions. We view these two strands as complementary; where a rich body of work on architecture trade-off analysis techniques at design-time facilitates run-time self-adaptation [31]. In more detail, design-time approaches can provide us with information related to possible trade-offs and related scenarios, while run-time frameworks are expected to increase our understanding to these trade-offs, their importance and criticality through continuous monitoring, measurement, and feedback. For instance, the work of Faniyi et al. [71] combined some properties of the ATAM and security testing using Implied Scenarios. Such combination is likely to identify new trade-offs points, and give better idea about the performance of adaptation decisions.

- *Considering individual self-* properties.* According to the analysis performed in Section 11.5.4 about the self-* properties that have driven trade-offs management for self adaptive software architectures, general self-adaptivity has received the most attention among self-* properties, whereas all other properties had less attention. An important issue in managing trade-offs is that individual self-* properties drive related trade-offs that need to be considered. This calls for building generic frameworks focusing on particular self-* properties [69,72]. The benefit of such generic frameworks is that they could be applicable to different software paradigms implementing particular self-* properties.

- *Simultaneous multiple trade-offs management.* Analyzing quality attributes considered in trade-offs management in Section 11.5.6 has revealed the consideration of quality attributes on a general level, and in case of considering specific attributes, this tends to be limited to two or three as explicit examples. For better trade-offs management, specific *multiple* quality attributes need to be considered simultaneously. A preliminary analysis of architectural primitives, performed in the light of the characteristics of self-adaptive software, arise other trade-offs. These primitives are considered as the factors influencing the selection of the suitable adaptation strategy. Examples include: (i) multiple feedback loops; as reconciling multiple feedback loops in the adaptation would lead to a better adaptation [26], (ii) environmental interaction; where a computational node with limited resources is expected to interact with other nodes for fulfilling run-time goals [36], (iii) cost/benefit of adaptation; reasoning between the cost and benefit of adaptation should be considered when making adaptation decisions, implying also the overhead of adaptation (i.e., the frequency of adaptation and the number of adaptation cycles).

- *Novel solutions to be borrowed from other disciplines.* Novel solutions could be borrowed from different disciplines; such as nature, biology, ecology, physics, economics, or cognition sciences; to reach better and more effective adaptation. We can further inform the design of the system by drawing inspiration from other disciplines for a better informed adaptation decision. An example could be engaging economics and decisions theories for handling trade-offs arising from conflicts between different quality attributes [73]. Another example could be the use of dynamic decision networks, a form of Bayesian Networks, to support decision-making in self-adaptive software [74–76]. We also draw on game theory for selecting the adaptation strategy to take a strategic decision under the run-time uncertainty while managing the run-time trade-offs [77]. In more details, adaptation strategies are evaluated for their pay-off values, and based on such evaluation, an adaptation strategy will be selected in a way to support trade-offs management between different quality requirements under uncertainty and environmental constraints. Game theory also leverages the ability handle decisions under run-time uncertainty.

- *Devised learning for managing trade-offs.* There is a great potential for Artificial Intelligence (AI) techniques to provide benefits to software engineering, and specifically in engineering self-adaptive systems [76,78]. Here, we draw on machine learning techniques to be employed to learn from historical information accumulated about the performance of adaptation action, for better future adaptation.

- *Self-aware trade-offs management.* With the recent emergence of self-awareness [35–37], we rely on combining self-awareness capabilities [36] with trade-offs management approaches to realize better informed trade-offs management for architectures operating in open, dynamic scalable environments. The different levels of self-awareness, called capabilities, (i.e., stimulus-, interaction-, time-, goal-, and meta-self-awareness) [36], are expected to enrich the decisions making process with knowledge about run-time goals, interaction goals and historical information.

11.8 CONCLUSIONS AND FUTURE WORK

The main contribution of this work is a systematic mapping study analyzing the research landscape related to managing trade-offs of self-adaptive software architectures. Hence, the aim was to draw a picture of the current state of the research in this specialized topic, to help researchers and developers identify what has been established so far, to understand which software paradigms, quality attributes, self-* properties, and techniques have seen particular emphasis, as well as what is still under research and warrant greater attention.

To this end, the study has been conducted methodologically, by employing the standard guidelines for conducting secondary studies in order to ensure the quality of the analysis. The search was conducted in five main publications databases resulting in 462 studies that have been reviewed, and 20 relevant studies have been selected as primary studies.

Our findings show some attention and growing work in trade-offs management for self-adaptive software architectures. Our observation is that there is an adoption for the general "self-adaptivity" property without a discrete specialization on self-* properties. The generality also applies to the quality attributes considered in trade-offs management. When considering certain qualities, they tend to be limited to two or three attributes, as explicit examples. It was also noted that work related to trade-offs management has covered some software paradigms. It was also observed that the published work have not moved yet towards the full maturity as publications in journals, as well as towards practice in technical report. Although the work discussed has provided much that is useful in contributing towards self-adaptive architectures, it has not yet resolved some of the general and fundamental issues in order to provide a comprehensive, systematic, and integrated approach. As a general conclusion, the current work tend to be a solution for trade-offs management that act on trade-offs; not fundamental work that changes the architectural self-adaptivity. The dynamics and uncertainty of modern software environments require us to look for novel approaches that can provide systematic design and run-time support for change and uncertainty while managing trade-offs. Design-time and run-time mechanisms should be complementary for a comprehensive trade-offs decision, both while designing the system and while the system is operating.

Future work could be devised into: (i) future directions related to the study itself, and (ii) the implications of our study in identifying gaps and motivating new research directions in the field. With respect to future directions related to the study itself, we shall complement this study with empirical and comparative evaluation for the effectiveness, efficiency, and scalability of trade-offs management mechanisms to provide quantitative assessment of representative techniques to complement our findings. It is also worth looking at other emerging domains to uncover new criteria, if possible. The investigation can provide confirmation or threats to the validity of our findings. Such analysis can help in identifying patterns for common and variable trade-off problems, to inform the design of more effective mechanisms suited for a given context, situation, and scale. It can also lead for better tuning and optimization for the trade-offs process and how conflicts could be effectively handled. In general, this will help to shed the light on the most promising directions for future research in the landscape of self-adaptive software architectures. Finally, with respect to research directions in the field subject to review, possible directions have been identified in Section 11.8.

APPENDIX A **PRIMARY STUDIES**

[1] S.S. Andrade, R.J. de Araujo Macedo, Assessing the benefits of searchbased approaches when designing self-adaptive systems: a controlled experiment, J. Softw. Eng. Res. Dev. 3 (1) (2015) 1–27, doi:10.1186/s40411-015-0016-z.

[2] S.S. Andrade, R.J. de Araujo Macedo, A search-based approach for architectural design of feedback control concerns in self-adaptive systems, in: IEEE 7th International Conference on Self-Adaptive and Self-Organizing Systems (SASO), 2013, pp. 61–70, doi:10.1109/SASO.2013.42.

[3] S.S. Andrade, R.J. de Araujo Macedo, Do search-based approaches improve the design of self-adaptive systems? A controlled experiment, in: 28th Brazilian Symposium on Software Engineering (SBES), 2014, pp. 101–110, doi:10.1109/sbes.2014.17.

[4] D. Ardagna, C. Ghezzi, R. Mirandola, Rethinking the use of models in software architecture, in: S. Becker, F. Plasil, R. Reussner (Eds.), Quality of Software Architectures Models and Architectures, Lecture Notes in Computer Science, vol. 5281, Springer, Berlin, Heidelberg, 2008 pp. 1–27, doi:10.1007/978-3-540-87879-7_1.

[5] T. Chen, R. Bahsoon, Symbiotic and sensitivity-aware architecture for globally-optimal benefit in self-adaptive cloud, in: 9th International Symposium on Software Engineering for Adaptive and Self-Managing Systems (SEAMS), ACM, 2014, pp. 85–94, doi:10.1145/2593929.2593931.

[6] H. Inoue, Y. Li, S. Mitra, VAST: virtualization-assisted concurrent autonomous self-test, in: IEEE International Test Conference (ITC), 2008, pp. 1–10, doi:10.1109/TEST.2008.4700583.

[7] C. Landauer, Abstract infrastructure for real systems: reflection and autonomy in real time, in: 14th IEEE International Symposium on Object/Component/Service-Oriented Real-Time Distributed Computing Workshops (ISORCW), 2011, pp. 102–109, doi:10.1109/ISORCW.2011.44.

[8] D. Menasce, H. Gomaa, S. Malek, J.P. Sousa, SASSY: a framework for self-architecting service-oriented systems, IEEE Softw. 28 (6) (2011) 78–85, doi:10.1109/MS.2011.22.

[9] R. Mirandola, P. Potena, Self-adaptation of service based systems based on cost/quality attributes tradeoffs, in: 12th International Symposium on Symbolic and Numeric Algorithms for Scientific Computing (SYNASC), 2010, pp. 493–501, doi:10.1109/synasc.2010.16.

[10] X. Peng, B. Chen, Y. Yu, W. Zhao, Self-tuning of software systems through dynamic quality tradeoff and value-based feedback control loop, J. Syst. Softw. 85 (12) (2012) 2707–2719, doi:10.1016/j.jss.2012.04.079.2

[11] D. Perez-Palacin, R. Mirandola, J. Merseguer, On the relationships between QoS and software adaptability at the architectural level, J. Syst. Softw. 87 (2014) 1–17, doi:10.1016/j.jss.2013.07.053.

[12] D. Perez-Palacin, R. Mirandola, J. Merseguer, QoS and energy management with Petri nets: a self-adaptive framework, J. Syst. Softw. 85 (12) (2012) 2796–2811, doi:10.1016/j.jss.2012.04.077.

[13] D. Perez-Palacin, R. Mirandola, J. Merseguer, Enhancing a QoS-based self-adaptive framework with energy management capabilities, in: Joint ACM SIGSOFT Conference – QoSA and ACM SIGSOFT Symposium – ISARCS on Quality of Software Architectures – QoSA and Architecting Critical Systems – ISARCS, ACM, 2011, pp. 165–170, doi:10.1145/2000259.2000287.

[14] C. Sandionigi, D. Ardagna, G. Cugola, C. Ghezzi, Optimizing service selection and allocation in situational computing applications, IEEE Trans. Serv. Comput. 6 (3) (2013) 414–428, doi:10.1109/tsc.2012.18.

[15] P. Sawyer, N. Bencomo, J. Whittle, E. Letier, A. Finkelstein, Requirements-aware systems: a research agenda for RE for self-adaptive systems, in: 18th IEEE International Requirements Engineering Conference (RE), 2010, pp. 95–103.

[16] L.W. Shen, X. Peng, W.Y. Zhao, Quality-driven self-adaptation: bridging the gap between requirements and runtime architecture by design decision, in: X. Bai, F. Belli, E. Bertino, C.K. Chang, A. Elci, C. Seceleanu, H. Xie, M. Zulkernine (Eds.), IEEE 36th Annual Computer Software and Applications Conference (COMPSAC), Proceedings International Computer Software & Applications Conference, 2012, pp. 185–194, doi: 10.1109/compsac.2012.29.

[17] J.P. Sousa, R.K. Balan, V. Poladian, D. Garlan, M. Satyanarayanan, User guidance of resource-adaptive systems, in: J. Cordeiro, B. Shishkov, A. Ranchordas, M. Helfert (Eds.), 3rd International Conference on Software and Data Technologies (ICSOFT), 2008, pp. 36–44.

[18] J.P. Sousa, R.K. Balan, V. Poladian, D. Garlan, M. Satyanarayanan, A software infrastructure for user-guided quality-of-service tradeoffs, in: J. Cordeiro, B. Shishkov, A.K. Ranchordas, M. Helfert (Eds.), Software and Data Technologies, Communications in Computer and Information Science, vol. 47, 2009, pp. 48–61.

[19] A. Sutcliffe, An architecture framework for self-aware adaptive systems, in: I. Mistrik, R. Bahsoon, R. Kazman, Y. Zhang (Eds.), Economics-Driven Software Architecture, Morgan Kaufmann, Boston, 2014, pp. 59–80, doi: 10.1016/B978-0-12-410464-8.00004-0.

[20] J. Teich, From dynamic reconfiguration to self-reconfiguration: invasive algorithms and architectures, in: International Conference on Field-Programmable Technology (FPT), 2009, pp. 11–12, doi:10.1109/FPT.2009.5377603.

[21] U. Abmann, S. Gotz, J.M. Jezequel, B. Morin, M. Trapp, A reference architecture and roadmap for Models@run.time systems, in: N. Bencomo, R. France, B. Cheng, U. Abmann (Eds.), Models@run.time, Lecture Notes in Computer Science, vol. 8378, Springer International Publishing, 2014, pp. 1–18.

[22] E. Alonso, M. Fairbank, Emergent and adaptive systems of systems, in: IEEE International Conference on Systems, Man, and Cybernetics (SMC), 2013, pp. 1721–1725.

[23] A. Ardini, M. Hosseini, A. Alrobai, A. Shahri, K. Phalp, R. Ali, Social computing for software engineering: a mapping study, J. Comput. Sci. Rev. 13–14 (2014) 75–93.

[24] M.R.M. Assis, L.F. Bittencourt, R. Tolosana-Calasanz, Cloud federation: characterization and conceptual model, in: IEEE/ACM 7th International Conference on Utility and Cloud Computing, IEEE Computer Society, 2014, pp. 585–590.

[25] N. Bencomo, A. Belaggoun, Supporting decision-making for self-adaptive systems: from goal models to dynamic decision networks, in: J. Doerr, A. Opdahl (Eds.), Requirements Engineering: Foundation for Software Quality, Lecture Notes in Computer Science, vol. 7830, Springer, Berlin, Heidelberg, 2013, pp. 221–236, doi:10.1007/978-3-642-37422-7_16.

[26] N. Bencomo, A. Belaggoun, V. Issarny, Dynamic decision networks for decision-making in self-adaptive systems: a case study, in: 8th International Symposium on Software Engineering for Adaptive and Self-Managing Systems (SEAMS), IEEE Press, 2013, pp. 113–122.

[27] N. Bencomo, A. Belaggoun, V. Issarny, Bayesian artificial intelligence for tackling uncertainty in self-adaptive systems: the case of dynamic decision networks, in: 2nd International Workshop on Realizing Artificial Intelligence Synergies in Software Engineering (RAISE), 2013, pp. 7–13.

[28] J. Bradbury, J. Cordy, J. Dingel, M. Wermelinger, A survey of self-management in dynamic software architecture specifications, in: 1st ACM SIGSOFT Workshop on Self-managed Systems, ACM, 2014, pp. 28–33.

[29] H.P. Breivolda, I. Crnkovicb, M. Larsson, A systematic review of software architecture evolution research, J. Inf. Softw. Technol. 54 (1) (2012) 16–40.

[30] P. Brereton, B. Kitchenham, D. Budgen, M. Turner, M. Khalil, Lessons from applying the systematic literature review process within the software engineering domain, J. Syst. Softw. 80 (4) (2007) 571–583.

[31] Y. Brun, G. DiMarzo Serugendo, C. Gacek, H. Giese, H. Kienle, M. Litoiu, H. Muller, M. Pezze, M. Shaw, Engineering self-adaptive systems through feedback loops, in: B. Cheng, R. de Lemos, H. Giese, P. Inverardi, J. Magee (Eds.), Software Engineering for Self-Adaptive Systems, Lecture Notes in Computer Science, vol. 5525, Springer, Berlin, Heidelberg, 2009, pp. 48–70, doi:10.1007/978-3-642-02161-9_3.

[32] D. Budgen, M. Turner, P. Brereton, B. Kitchenham, Using mapping studies in software engineering, in: 20th Annual Meeting of the Psychology of Programming Interest Group (PPIG 2008), Lancaster University, 2008, pp. 195–204.

[33] C. Cetina, P. Giner, J. Fons, V. Pelechano, Autonomic computing through reuse of variability models at runtime: the case of smart homes, IEEE Comput. 42 (10) (2009) 37–43.

[34] T. Chen, F. Faniyi, R. Bahsoon, P. Lewis, X. Yao, L. Minku, L. Esterle, The Handbook of Engineering Self-Aware and Self-Expressive Systems, Technical Report, University of Birmingham 2014, arXiv:1409.1793 [cs.SE].

[35] B. Cheng, K. Eder, M. Gogolla, L. Grunske, M. Litoiu, H. Muller, P. Pelliccione, A. Perini, N. Qureshi, B. Rumpe, D. Schneider, F. Trollmann, N. Villegas, Using models at runtime to address assurance for self-adaptive systems, in: N. Bencomo, R. France, B. Cheng, U. Abmann (Eds.), Models@run.time, Lecture Notes in Computer Science, vol. 8378, Springer International Publishing, 2014, pp. 101–136.

[36] B. Cheng, R. Lemos, H. Giese, P. Inverardi, J. Magee, J. Andersson, B. Becker, N. Bencomo, Y. Brun, B. Cukic, G. Marzo Serugendo, S. Dustdar, A. Finkelstein, C. Gacek, K. Geihs, V. Grassi, G. Karsai, H.M. Kienle, J. Kramer, M. Litoiu, S. Malek, R. Mirandola, H. Muller, S. Park, M. Shaw, M. Tichy, M. Tivoli, D. Weyns, J. Whittle, Software engineering for self-adaptive systems: a research roadmap, in: B. Cheng, R. Lemos, H. Giese, P. Inverardi, J.

Magee (Eds.), Software Engineering for Self-Adaptive Systems, Springer-Verlag, 2009, pp. 1–26.

[37] T. Clohessy, T. Acton, L. Morgan, Smart City as a Service (SCaaS): a future roadmap for e-government smart city cloud computing initiatives, in: IEEE/ACM 7th International Conference on Utility and Cloud Computing (UCC), 2014, pp. 836–841.

[38] E. Dashofy, A. Hoek, R. Taylor, Towards architecture-based self-healing systems, in: 1st Workshop on Self-healing Systems, ACM, 2002, pp. 21–26.

[39] T. Dyba, T. Dingsoyr, G. Hanssen, Applying systematic reviews to diverse study types: an experience report, in: 1st International Symposium on Empirical Software Engineering and Measurement (ESEM 2007), 2007, pp. 225–234.

[40] E. Engstrom, P. Runeson, Software product line testing: a systematic mapping study, J. Inf. Softw. Technol. 53 (1) (2011) 2–13.

[41] F. Faniyi, R. Bahsoon, A. Evans, R. Kazman, Evaluating security properties of architectures in unpredictable environments: a case for cloud, in: 9th Working IEEE/IFIP Conference on Software Architecture (WICSA 2011), 2014, pp. 127–136.

[42] F. Faniyi, P. Lewis, R. Bahsoon, Y. Xin, Architecting Self-Aware Software Systems, in: 11th Working IEEE/IFIP Conference on Software Architecture (WICSA'14), 2014, pp. 91–94.

[43] F. Febrero, C. Calero, M.A. Moraga, A systematic mapping study of software reliability modeling, J. Inf. Softw. Technol. 56 (8) (2014) 839–849.

[44] D. Garlan, Software architecture: a travelogue, in: International Conference on Future of Software Engineering, ACM, 2014, pp. 29–39.

[45] D. Garlan, A 10-year perspective on software engineering self-adaptive systems (keynote), in: 8th International Symposium on Software Engineering for Adaptive and Self-Managing Systems (SEAMS), IEEE Press, 2013, pp. 2–2.

[46] D. Garlan, Software architecture: a roadmap, in: Conference on the Future of Software Engineering, 2000, pp. 91–101.

[47] David. Garlan, B. Schmerl, Model-based adaptation for self-healing systems, in: 1st Workshop on Self-healing Systems, ACM, 2002, pp. 27–32.

[48] I. Georgiadis, J. Magee, J. Kramer, Self-organising software architectures for distributed systems, in: 1st Workshop on Self-healing Systems, ACM, 2002, pp. 33–38.

[49] M. Harman, The role of Artificial Intelligence in Software Engineering, in: 1st International Workshop on Realizing Artificial Intelligence Synergies in Software Engineering (RAISE), 2012, pp. 1–6.

[50] S. Hassan, N. Bencomo, R. Bahsoon, Minimizing nasty surprises with better informed decision-making in self-adaptive systems, in: 10th International Symposium on Software Engineering for Adaptive and Self-Managing Systems (SEAMS), IEEE Press, 2015, pp. 134–144.

[51] N. Huber, A. van Hoorn, A. Koziolek, F. Brosig, S. Kounev, Modeling run-time adaptation at the system architecture level in dynamic service-oriented environments, Serv. Oriented Comput. Appl. 8 (1) (2014) 73–89.

[52] M.C. Huebscher, J.A. Mccann, A survey of autonomic computing, ACM Comput. Surv. 40 (3) (2008) 1–28.

[53] IBM, An architectural blueprint for autonomic computing, Technical Report, 2003.

[54] A. Immonen, E. Niemela, Survey of reliability and availability prediction methods from the viewpoint of software architecture, J. Softw. Syst. Model. 7 (1) (2008) 49–65.

[55] R. Kazman, R. Bahsoon, I. Mistrik, Y. Zhang, Economics-driven software architecture: introduction, in: I. Mistrik, R. Bahsoon, R. Kazman, Y. Zhang (Eds.), Economics-Driven Software Architecture, Morgan Kaufmann, Boston, 2014, pp. 1–8.

[56] R. Kazman, M. Klein, P. Clements, ATAM: Method for Architecture Evaluation, Technical Report CMU/SEI-2000-TR-004, Software Engineering Institute, Carnegie Mellon University, 2000.

[57] S. Kehua, L. Jie, F. Hongbo, Smart city and the applications, in: International Conference on Electronics, Communications and Control (ICECC), 25011, pp. 1028–1031.

[58] J.O. Kephart, D.M. Chess, The vision of autonomic computing, IEEE Comput. 36 (1) (2003) 41–50.

[59] B. Kitchenham, What's up with software metrics? – a preliminary mapping study, J. Syst. Softw. 83 (1) (2010) 37–51.

[60] B.A. Kitchenham, D. Budgen, O.P. Brereton, The value of mapping studies: a participantobserver case study, in: 14th International Conference on Evaluation and Assessment in Software Engineering, British Computer Society, 2010, pp. 25–33.

[61] B. Kitchenham, P. Brereton, D. Budgen, Mapping study completeness and reliability – a case study, in: 16th International Conference on Evaluation & Assessment in Software Engineering (EASE 2012), 2012, pp. 126–135.

[62] B. Kitchenham, D. Budgen, O.P. Brereton, Using mapping studies as the basis for further research – a participant-observer case study, J. Inf. Softw. Technol. 53 (6) (2011) 638–651.

[63] B. Kitchenham, S. Charters, Guidelines for performing Systematic Literature Reviews in Software Engineering, Technical Report, Keele University, 2007.

[64] J. Klein, H. Vliet, A systematic review of system-of-systems architecture research, in: 9th international ACM Sigsoft Conference on Quality of Software Architectures, ACM, 2013, pp. 13–22.

[65] B. Knowles, L. Blair, M. Hazas, S. Walker, Exploring sustainability research in computing: where we are and where we go next, in: ACM International Joint Conference on Pervasive and Ubiquitous Computing, ACM, 2013, pp. 305–314.

[66] A. Koziolek, H. Koziolek, R. Reussner, PerOpteryx: automated application of tactics in multi-objective software architecture optimization, in: I. Crnkovic, J.A. Stafford, D. Petriu, J. Happe, P. Inverardi (Eds.), Joint ACM SIGSOFT Conference – QoSA and ACM SIGSOFT Symposium – ISARCS on Quality of Software Architectures – QoSA and Architecting Critical Systems – ISARCS (QoSA-ISARCS'11), ACM, 2011, pp. 33–42.

[67] H. Koziolek, Sustainability evaluation of software architectures: a systematic review, in: Joint ACM SIGSOFT Conference – QoSA and ACM SIGSOFT Symposium – ISARCS on Quality of Software Architectures – QoSA and Architecting Critical Systems – ISARCS (QoSA-ISARCS'11), 2011.

[68] J. Kramer, Adventures in adaptation: a software engineering playground!, in: IEEE/ACM10th International Symposium on Software Engineering for Adaptive and Self-Managing Systems (SEAMS), 2015, pp. 1–1.

[69] J. Kramer, J. Magee, Self-managed systems: an architectural challenge, in: Future of Software Engineering (FOSE'07), 2007, pp. 259–268.

[70] R. Lemos, H. Giese, H. Muller, M. Shaw, J. Andersson, M. Litoiu, B. Schmerl, G. Tamura, N. Villegas, T. Vogel, D. Weyns, L. Baresi, B. Becker, N. Bencomo, Y. Brun, B. Cukic, R. Desmarais, S. Dustdar, G. Engels, K. Geihs, K. Goschka, A. Gorla, V. Grassi, P. Inverardi, G. Karsai, J. Kramer, A. Lopes, J. Magee, S. Malek, S. Mankovskii, R. Mirandola, J. Mylopoulos, O. Nierstrasz, M. Pezze, C. Prehofer, W. Schafer, R. Schlichting, D. Smith, P.J. Sousa, L. Tahvildari, K. Wong, J. Wuttke, Software engineering for self-adaptive systems: a second research roadmap, in: R. Lemos, H. Giese, H. Muller, M. Shaw (Eds.), Software Engineering for Self-Adaptive Systems II, Lecture Notes in Computer Science, vol. 7475, Springer-Verlag, 2013, pp. 1–32.

[71] G. Lewis, E. Morris, P. Place, S. Simanta, D. Smith, L. Wrage, Engineering systems of systems, in: 2nd Annual IEEE Systems Conference, 2008, pp. 1–6.

[72] P. Lewis, A. Chandra, S. Parsons, E. Robinson, K. Glette, R. Bahsoon, J. Torresen, Yao Xin, A survey of self-awareness and its application in computing systems, in: 5th IEEE Conference on Self-Adaptive and Self-Organizing Systems Workshops (SASOW'11), 2011, pp. 102–107.

[73] Z. Li, P. Avgeriou, P. Liang, A systematic mapping study on technical debt and its management, J. Syst. Softw. 101 (2015) 193–220.

[74] Z. Li, P. Liang, P. Avgeriou, Application of knowledge-based approaches in software architecture: a systematic mapping study, J. Inf. Softw. Technol. 55 (5) (2013) 777–794.

[75] N. Medvidovic, Adapting our view of software adaptation: an architectural perspective (keynote), in: 9th International Symposium on Software Engineering for Adaptive and Self-Managing Systems (SEAMS), ACM, 2014, pp. 5–6.

[76] A. Monzon, Smart cities concept and challenges: bases for the assessment of smart city projects, in: International Conference on Smart Cities and Green ICT Systems (SMARTGREENS), 2015, pp. 1–11.

[77] E.Y. Nakagawa, D. Feitosa, K.R. Felizardo, Using systematic mapping to explore software architecture knowledge, in: ICSE Workshop on Sharing and Reusing Architectural Knowledge, ACM, 2010, pp. 29–36.

[78] R. Nord, M. Barbacci, P. Clements, R. Kazman, M. Klein, L. O'Brien, J. Tomayko, Integrating the Architecture Tradeoff Analysis Method (ATAM) with the Cost Benefit Analysis Method (CBAM), Technical Report CMU/SEI-2003-TN-038, Software Engineering Institute, Carnegie Mellon University, 2003.

[79] P. Oreizy, M.M. Gorlick, R.N. Taylor, D. Heimbigner, G. Johnson, N. Medvidovic, A. Quilici, D.S. Rosenblum, A.L. Wolf, An architecture-based approach to self-adaptive software, IEEE Intell. Syst. 14 (3) (1999) 54–62.

[80] B. Penzenstadler, A. Raturi, D. Richardson, C. Calero, H. Femmer, X. Franch, Systematic mapping study on software engineering for sustainability (SE4S), in: 18th International Conference on Evaluation and Assessment in Software Engineering, ACM, 2014, pp. 1–14.

[81] D. Petcu, Multi-cloud: expectations and current approaches, in: International Workshop on Multi-cloud Applications and Federated Clouds, ACM, 2013, pp. 1–6.

[82] K. Petersen, R. Feldt, S. Mujtaba, M. Mattsson, Systematic mapping studies in software engineering, in: 12th International Conference on Evaluation and Assessment in Software Engineering, British Computer Society, 2008, pp. 68–77.

[83] K. Petersen, S. Vakkalanka, L. Kuzniarz, Guidelines for conducting systematic mapping studies in software engineering: an update, Inf. Softw. Technol. 64 (2015) 1–18.

[84] N. Qureshi, M. Usman, N. Ikram, Evidence in software architecture, a systematic literature review, in: 17th International Conference on Evaluation and Assessment in Software Engineering (EASE'13), 2013, pp. 97–106.

[85] M. Roscia, M. Longo, G.C. Lazaroiu, Smart city by multi-agent systems, in: International Conference on Renewable Energy Research and Applications (ICRERA), 2013, pp. 371–376.

[86] M. Salama, Stability of self-adaptive software architectures, in: 30th IEEE/ACM International Conference on Automated Software Engineering (ASE 2015), Doctoral Symposium, 2015.

[87] M. Salama, R. Bahsoon, Managing run-time trade-offs for self-adaptive architectures: a game theoretical vision, in: 7th ACM/SPEC International Conference on Performance Engineering (ICPE), Vision Track, 2016.

[88] M. Salehie, L. Tahvildari, Self-adaptive software: landscape and research challenges, ACM Trans. Auton. Adapt. Syst. 4 (2) (2009) 1–42.

[89] P. Sawyer, N. Bencomo, J. Whittle, E. Letier, A. Finkelstein, Requirements-aware systems: a research agenda for RE for self-adaptive systems, in: 18th IEEE International Requirements Engineering Conference (RE 2010), 2010, pp. 95–103.

[90] S. Stevanetic, U. Zdun, Software metrics for measuring the understandability of architectural structures: a systematic mapping study, in: 19th International Conference on Evaluation and Assessment in Software Engineering, ACM, 2015, pp. 1–14.

[91] D. Tofan, M. Galster, P. Avgeriou, W. Schuitema, Past and future of software architectural decisions – a systematic mapping study, J. Inf. Softw. Technol. 56 (8) (2014) 850–872.

[92] A.N. Toosi, R.N. Calheiros, R. Buyya, Interconnected cloud computing environments: challenges, taxonomy, and survey, ACM Comput. Surv. 47 (1) (2014) 1–47.

[93] D. Weyns, T. Ahmad, Claims and evidence for architecture-based self-adaptation: a systematic literature review, in: K. Drira (Ed.), Software Architecture, Lecture Notes in Computer Science, vol. 7957, Springer, Berlin, Heidelberg, 2013, pp. 249–265.

[94] D.Weyns, M.U. Iftikhar, D.G. Iglesia, T. Ahmad, A survey of formal methods in self-adaptive systems, in: 5th International Conference on Computer Science and Software Engineering, ACM, 2012, pp. 67–79.

[95] R. Wieringa, N. Maiden, N. Mead, C. Rolland, Requirements engineering paper classification and evaluation criteria: a proposal and a discussion, J. Requir. Eng. 11 (1) (2005) 102–107.

[96] B. Williams, J. Carver, Characterizing software architecture changes: a systematic review, J. Inf. Softw. Technol. 52 (1) (2010) 31–51.

[97] E. Yuan, N. Esfahani, S. Malek, A systematic survey of self-protecting software systems, ACM Trans. Auton. Adapt. Syst. 8 (4) (2014) 1–41.

[98] EndNote, http://endnote.com/.

[99] Tagxedo, 2005, http://www.tagxedo.com/app.html.

APPENDIX B CLASSIFICATION AND DATA EXTRACTION OF PRIMARY STUDIES

Key	Publication Year	Publication Type	Country of Affiliation	Research Type	Contribution Type	Software Paradigm	Self-* Property	Trade-off Attributes	Mechanism	Time
[Ardagna 2008]	2008	Book chapter	Italy	Solution proposal	Taxonomy	Self-adaptive software	Self-adaptive	Performance, reliability	Analysis-oriented methods	Design-time
[Inoue 2008]	2008	Conference paper	United States	Solution proposal	Process, experiment	Large-scale systems	Self-test	Design complexity, system performance, power impact	Optimized hardware and software co-design	Design-time
[Sousa 2008]	2008	Conference paper	United States, Singapore	Solution proposal	Framework, experiment	Mobile software	Self-adaptive (resource-adaptive)	Quality attributes	Utility theory	Design-time
[Sousa 2009]	2009	Book chapter	United States, Singapore	Evaluation research, validation research	Framework, tool, metric	Mobile software	Self-adaptive (resource-adaptive)	Quality attributes	Utility theory	Design-time
[Teich 2009]	2009	Conference paper	Germany	Philosophical paper (vision)	Research challenges	Embedded systems	Self-organization, self-configuration	Flexibility, cost	Invasive algorithms and architectures	Run-time
[Mirandola 2010]	2010	Conference paper	Italy	Validation research	Framework	Service-based systems	Self-adaptive	Adaptation cost, quality attributes	Optimization model	Run-time
[Sawyer 2010]	2010	Conference paper	United Kingdom	Philosophical paper (vision), solution proposal	Research challenges	Self-adaptive systems	Self-adaptive	Requirements	Requirements reflection	Run-time
[Landauer 2011]	2011	Conference paper	United States	Solution proposal	Infrastructure	Real-time distributed systems	Self-organization	Safety, resources	Simulations	Off-line

Reference	Year	Publication	Country	Research	Contribution	Application domain	Self-* property	Stakeholders' priorities	Method / approach	Time
[Menasce 2011]	2011	Magazine paper	United States	Solution proposal	Framework	Service-oriented systems	Self-adaptive, self-healing, self-managing, self-optimizing	Stakeholders' priorities	Utility functions to quantify QoS trade-offs	Run-time
[Perez-Palacin 2011]	2011	Conference paper	Spain, Italy	Solution proposal	Approach	Service-based applications	Self-adaptive	Performance, energy	Stochastic Petri nets	Run-time
[Peng 2012]	2012	Journal paper	China, United Kingdom	Solution proposal	Framework, experiment	Self-adaptive software systems	Self-tuning	Quality soft goals (goals with no binary satisfaction criteria)	Value-based goal reasoning, Pareto-optimal solutions	Run-time
[Perez-Palacin 2012]	2012	Journal paper	Spain, Italy	Solution proposal, evaluation research	Framework, tool, experiment	Service-based applications	Self-adaptive	Energy consumption, performance	Stochastic Petri	Design-time
[Shen 2012]	2012	Conference paper	China	Solution proposal	Approach, experiment	Self-adaptive software systems	Self-adaptive	Quality requirements	Value-based quality trade-off decisions	Run-time
[Andrade 2013]	2013	Conference paper	Brazil	Solution proposal	Approach, tool, metric, case study	Self-adaptive systems, cloud-based services	Self-adaptive	Feedback control loop performance overhead	Multi-objective optimization approach, built upon elitist evolutionary optimization approach NSGA-II	Design-time
[Sandionigi 2013]	2013	Journal paper	Italy	Solution proposal	Approach, experiment	Pervasive applications	Self-managing	Remote execution of software fragments, dynamic deployment on local nodes of the computational environment	Optimization problem	Run-time

Continued

Key	Publication Year	Publication Type	Country of Affiliation	Research Type	Contribution Type	Software Paradigm	Self-* Property	Trade-off Attributes	Mechanism	Time
[Andrade 2014]	2014	Conference paper	Brazil	Solution proposal, evaluation research	Infrastructure, experiment	Self-adaptive systems	Self-adaptive	Quality attributes	Multi-objective optimization, on the NSGA-II algorithm to find out a set of Pareto-optimal candidate architectures	Design-time
[Chen 2014]	2014	Conference paper	United Kingdom	Solution proposal	Approach, model, experiment	Self-adaptive software	Self-adaptive	Global QoS, cost	Objective functions	Run-time
[Perez-Palacin 2014]	2014	Journal paper	Spain, Italy	Solution proposal	Approach, tool, experiment	Self-adaptive software	Self-adaptive	System adaptability, quality of service	Metrics for quantifying adaptability	Design-time
[Sutcliffe 2014]	2014	Book chapter	United Kingdom	Evaluation research	Framework, case study	Mobile software	Self-awareness	Non-functional requirements	Heuristics	Design-time
[Andrade 2015]	2015	Journal paper	Brazil	Evaluation research, experience paper	Model, experiment	Self-adaptive systems	Self-adaptive	Quality attributes	Pareto-optimal solutions	Design-time

REFERENCES

[1] A. Koziolek, H. Koziolek, R. Reussner, PerOpteryx: automated application of tactics in multi-objective software architecture optimization, in: I. Crnkovic, J.A. Stafford, D. Petriu, J. Happe, P. Inverardi (Eds.), Joint ACM SIGSOFT Conference—QoSA and ACM SIGSOFT Symposium—ISARCS on Quality of Software Architectures—QoSA and Architecting Critical Systems—ISARCS (QoSA-ISARCS), ACM, 2011, pp. 33–42.

[2] D. Garlan, Software architecture: a roadmap, in: Conference on the Future of Software Engineering, Limerick, Ireland, 2000, pp. 91–101.

[3] D. Garlan, Software architecture: a travelogue, in: International Conference on Future of Software Engineering, Hyderabad, India, ACM, 2014, pp. 29–39.

[4] B. Knowles, L. Blair, M. Hazas, S. Walker, Exploring sustainability research in computing: where we are and where we go next, in: ACM International Joint Conference on Pervasive and Ubiquitous Computing, Zurich, Switzerland, ACM, 2013, pp. 305–314.

[5] U. Abmann, S. Gotz, J.-M. Jezequel, B. Morin, M. Trapp, A reference architecture and roadmap for Models @run.time systems, in: N. Bencomo, R. France, B. Cheng, U. Abmann (Eds.), Models@run.time, Lecture Notes in Computer Science, vol. 8378, Springer International Publishing, Switzerland, 2014, pp. 1–18.

[6] B. Cheng, K. Eder, M. Gogolla, L. Grunske, M. Litoiu, H. Muller, P. Pelliccione, A. Perini, N. Qureshi, B. Rumpe, D. Schneider, F. Trollmann, N. Villegas, Using models at run-time to address assurance for self-adaptive systems, in: N. Bencomo, R. France, B. Cheng, U. Abmann (Eds.), Models@run.time, Lecture Notes in Computer Science, vol. 8378, Springer International Publishing, 2014, pp. 101–136.

[7] B. Cheng, R. Lemos, H. Giese, P. Inverardi, J. Magee, J. Andersson, B. Becker, N. Bencomo, Y. Brun, B. Cukic, G. Marzo Serugendo, S. Dustdar, A. Finkelstein, C. Gacek, K. Geihs, V. Grassi, G. Karsai, H.M. Kienle, J. Kramer, M. Litoiu, S. Malek, R. Mirandola, H. Muller, S. Park, M. Shaw, M. Tichy, M. Tivoli, D. Weyns, J. Whittle, Software engineering for self-adaptive systems: a research roadmap, in: B. Cheng, R. Lemos, H. Giese, P. Inverardi, J. Magee (Eds.), Software Engineering for Self-Adaptive Systems, Springer-Verlag, Berlin, 2009, pp. 1–26.

[8] R. Kazman, M. Klein, P. Clements, ATAM: Method for Architecture Evaluation, Software Engineering Institute, Carnegie Mellon University, Pittsburgh, Pennsylvania, 2000.

[9] R. Nord, M. Barbacci, P. Clements, R. Kazman, M. Klein, L. O'Brien, J. Tomayko, Integrating the Architecture Tradeoff Analysis Method (ATAM) with the Cost Benefit Analysis Method (CBAM), Software Engineering Institute, Carnegie Mellon University, Pittsburgh, Pennsylvania, 2003.

[10] K. Petersen, R. Feldt, S. Mujtaba, M. Mattsson, Systematic mapping studies in software engineering, in: 12th International Conference on Evaluation and Assessment in Software Engineering, University of Bari, Italy, British Computer Society, 2008, pp. 68–77.

[11] D. Budgen, M. Turner, P. Brereton, B. Kitchenham, Using mapping studies in software engineering, in: 20th Annual Meeting of the Psychology of Programming Interest Group (PPIG 2008), Open University, UK, Lancaster University, 2008, pp. 195–204.

[12] B. Kitchenham, D. Budgen, O.P. Brereton, Using mapping studies as the basis for further research—a participant-observer case study, Journal Information and Software Technology 53 (6) (2011) 638–651.

[13] P. Sawyer, N. Bencomo, J. Whittle, E. Letier, A. Finkelstein, Requirements-aware systems: a research agenda for RE for self-adaptive systems, in: 18th IEEE International Requirements Engineering Conference (RE), Sydney, Australia, 2010, pp. 95–103.

[14] G. Lewis, E. Morris, P. Place, S. Simanta, D. Smith, L. Wrage, Engineering systems of systems, in: 2nd Annual IEEE Systems Conference, Montreal, QC, Canada, 7–10 April 2008, 2008, pp. 1–6.

[15] E. Alonso, M. Fairbank, Emergent and adaptive systems of systems, in: IEEE International Conference on Systems, Man, and Cybernetics (SMC), Manchester, United Kingdom, 2013, pp. 1721–1725.

[16] J. Klein, Hv Vliet, A systematic review of system-of-systems architecture research, in: 9th international ACM Sigsoft Conference on Quality of Software Architectures, Vancouver, British Columbia, Canada, ACM, 2013, pp. 13–22.

[17] A. Monzon, Smart cities concept and challenges: bases for the assessment of smart city projects, in: International Conference on Smart Cities and Green ICT Systems (SMARTGREENS), Lisbon, Portugal, 2015, pp. 1–11.

[18] T. Clohessy, T. Acton, L. Morgan, Smart City as a Service (SCaaS): a future roadmap for e-government smart city cloud computing initiatives, in: IEEE/ACM 7th International Conference on Utility and Cloud Computing (UCC), London, UK, 2014, pp. 836–841.

[19] M. Roscia, M. Longo, G.C. Lazaroiu, Smart City by multi-agent systems, in: International Conference on Renewable Energy Research and Applications (ICRERA), Madrid, Spain, 2013, pp. 371–376.

[20] S. Kehua, L. Jie, F. Hongbo, Smart city and the applications, in: International Conference on Electronics, Communications and Control (ICECC), Ningbo, China, 2011, pp. 1028–1031.

[21] C. Cetina, P. Giner, J. Fons, V. Pelechano, Autonomic computing through reuse of variability models at run-time: the case of smart homes, IEEE Computer 42 (10) (2009) 37–43.

[22] A.N. Toosi, R.N. Calheiros, R. Buyya, Interconnected cloud computing environments: challenges, taxonomy, and survey, ACM Computing Surveys 47 (1) (2014) 1–47.

[23] M.R.M. Assis, L.F. Bittencourt, R. Tolosana-Calasanz, Cloud federation: characterisation and conceptual model, in: IEEE/ACM 7th International Conference on Utility and Cloud Computing (UCC), London, UK, IEEE Computer Society, 2014, pp. 585–590.

[24] D. Petcu, Multi-cloud: expectations and current approaches, in: International Workshop on Multi-cloud Applications and Federated Clouds, Prague, Czech Republic, ACM, 2013, pp. 1–6.

[25] Rd Lemos, H. Giese, H. Muller, M. Shaw, J. Andersson, M. Litoiu, B. Schmerl, G. Tamura, N. Villegas, T. Vogel, D. Weyns, L. Baresi, B. Becker, N. Bencomo, Y. Brun, B. Cukic, R. Desmarais, S. Dustdar, G. Engels, K. Geihs, K. Goschka, A. Gorla, V. Grassi, P. Inverardi, G. Karsai, J. Kramer, A. Lopes, J. Magee, S. Malek, S. Mankovskii, R. Mirandola, J. Mylopoulos, O. Nierstrasz, M. Pezze, C. Prehofer, W. Schafer, R. Schlichting, D. Smith, P.J. Sousa, L. Tahvildari, K. Wong, J. Wuttke, Software engineering for self-adaptive systems: a second research roadmap, in: Rd Lemos, H. Giese, H. Muller, M. Shaw (Eds.), Software Engineering for Self-Adaptive Systems II, Lecture Notes in Computer Science, vol. 7475, Springer-Verlag, Berlin, 2013, pp. 1–32.

[26] Y. Brun, G. Di Marzo Serugendo, C. Gacek, H. Giese, H. Kienle, M. Litoiu, H. Muller, M. Pezze, M. Shaw, Engineering self-adaptive systems through feedback loops, in: B. Cheng, R. de Lemos, H. Giese, P. Inverardi, J. Magee (Eds.), Software Engineering for Self-Adaptive Systems, Lecture Notes in Computer Science, vol. 5525, Springer, Berlin, Heidelberg, 2009, pp. 48–70.

[27] D. Garlan, A 10-year perspective on software engineering self-adaptive systems (keynote), in: 8th International Symposium on Software Engineering for Adaptive and Self-Managing Systems (SEAMS), San Francisco, CA, USA, IEEE Press, 2013, p. 2.

[28] N. Medvidovic, Adapting our view of software adaptation: an architectural perspective (keynote), in: 9th International Symposium on Software Engineering for Adaptive and Self-Managing Systems (SEAMS), Hyderabad, India, ACM, 2014, pp. 5–6.

[29] J. Kramer, Adventures in adaptation: a software engineering playground! in: IEEE/ACM 10th International Symposium on Software Engineering for Adaptive and Self-Managing Systems (SEAMS), Firenze, Italy, 2015, p. 1.

[30] P. Oreizy, M.M. Gorlick, R.N. Taylor, D. Heimhigner, G. Johnson, N. Medvidovic, A. Quilici, D. S. Rosenblum, A.L. Wolf, An architecture-based approach to self-adaptive software, IEEE Intelligent Systems 14 (3) (1999) 54–62,

[31] D. Garlan, B. Schmerl, Model-based adaptation for self-healing systems, in: 1st Workshop on Self-Healing Systems, Charleston, South Carolina, USA, ACM, 2002, pp. 27–32.

[32] E. Dashofy, Ad Hoek, R. Taylor, Towards architecture-based self-healing systems, in: 1st Workshop on Self-Healing Systems, Charleston, South Carolina, USA, ACM, 2002, pp. 21–26.

[33] I. Georgiadis, J. Magee, J. Kramer, Self-organising software architectures for distributed systems, in: 1st Workshop on Self-Healing Systems, Charleston, South Carolina, USA, ACM, 2002, pp. 33–38.

[34] J. Kramer, J. Magee, Self-managed systems: an architectural challenge, in: Future of Software Engineering (FOSE), Minneapolis, Minnesota, USA, 2007, pp. 259–268.

[35] P. Lewis, A. Chandra, S. Parsons, E. Robinson, K. Glette, R. Bahsoon, J. Torresen, Y. Xin, A survey of self-awareness and its application in computing systems, in: 5th IEEE Conference on Self-Adaptive and Self-Organizing Systems Workshops (SASOW), Ann Arbor, Michigan, USA, 2011, pp. 102–107.

[36] F. Faniyi, P. Lewis, R. Bahsoon, Y. Xin, Architecting self-aware software systems, in: 11th Working IEEE/IFIP Conference on Software Architecture (WICSA), Sydney, Australia, 2014, pp. 91–94.

[37] Chen T, Faniyi F, Bahsoon R, Lewis P, Yao X, Minku L, Esterle L, The handbook of engineering self-aware and self-expressive systems, University of Birmingham, 2014. doi:arXiv:1409.1793 [cs.SE].

[38] Kitchenham B, Charters S, Guidelines for performing systematic literature reviews in software engineering, Keele University, 2007.

[39] E. Engstrom, P. Runeson, Software product line testing—a systematic mapping study, Journal Information and Software Technology 53 (1) (2011) 2–13.

[40] Z. Li, P. Avgeriou, P. Liang, A systematic mapping study on technical debt and its management, Journal of Systems and Software 101 (2015) 193–220.

[41] R. Wieringa, N. Maiden, N. Mead, C. Rolland, Requirements engineering paper classification and evaluation criteria: a proposal and a discussion, J. Requir. Eng. 11 (1) (2005) 102–107.

[42] K. Petersen, S. Vakkalanka, L. Kuzniarz, Guidelines for conducting systematic mapping studies in software engineering: an update, Information and Software Technology 64 (2015) 1–18.

[43] B.A. Kitchenham, D. Budgen, O.P. Brereton, The value of mapping studies: a participant observer case study, in: 14th International Conference on Evaluation and Assessment in Software Engineering, Keele University, UK, British Computer Society, 2010, pp. 25–33.

[44] B. Kitchenham, What's up with software metrics?—A preliminary mapping study, Journal of Systems and Software 83 (1) (2010) 37–51.

[45] D. Tofan, M. Galster, P. Avgeriou, W. Schuitema, Past and future of software architectural decisions—a systematic mapping study, Journal Information and Software Technology 56 (8) (2014) 850–872.

[46] Z. Li, P. Liang, P. Avgeriou, Application of knowledge-based approaches in software architecture: a systematic mapping study, Journal Information and Software Technology 55 (5) (2013) 777–794.

[47] P. Brereton, B. Kitchenham, D. Budgen, M. Turner, M. Khalil, Lessons from applying the systematic literature review process within the software engineering domain, Journal of Systems and Software 80 (4) (2007) 571–583.

[48] T. Dyba, T. Dingsoyr, G. Hanssen, Applying systematic reviews to diverse study types: an experience report, in: 1st International Symposium on Empirical Software Engineering and Measurement (ESEM), Madrid, Spain, 2007, pp. 225–234.

[49] A. Ardini, M. Hosseini, A. Alrobai, A. Shahri, K. Phalp, R. Ali, Social computing for software engineering: a mapping study, Journal Computer Science Review 13–14 (2014) 75–93.

[50] F. Febrero, C. Calero, M.A. Moraga, A systematic mapping study of software reliability modeling, Journal Information and Software Technology 56 (8) (2014) 839–849.

[51] EndNote. X7 edn. Thomson Reuters. http://endnote.com/

[52] B. Penzenstadler, A. Raturi, D. Richardson, C. Calero, H. Femmer, X. Franch, Systematic mapping study on software engineering for sustainability (SE4S), in: 18th International Conference on Evaluation and Assessment in Software Engineering, London, England, United Kingdom, ACM, 2014, pp. 1–14.

[53] N. Qureshi, M. Usman, N. Ikram, Evidence in software architecture, a systematic literature review, in: 17th International Conference on Evaluation and Assessment in Software Engineering (EASE), Porto de Galinhas, Brazil, 2013, pp. 97–106.

[54] Tagxedo. http://www.tagxedo.com/app.html (accessed August 2005).

[55] E.Y. Nakagawa, D. Feitosa, K.R. Felizardo, Using systematic mapping to explore software architecture knowledge, in: ICSE Workshop on Sharing and Reusing Architectural Knowledge, Cape Town, South Africa, ACM, 2010, pp. 29–36.

[56] S. Stevanetic, U. Zdun, Software metrics for measuring the understandability of architectural structures: a systematic mapping study, in: 19th International Conference on Evaluation and Assessment in Software Engineering, Nanjing, China, ACM, 2015, pp. 1–14.

[57] B. Kitchenham, P. Brereton, D. Budgen, Mapping study completeness and reliability—a case study, in: 16th International Conference on Evaluation & Assessment in Software Engineering (EASE), Ciudad Real, Spain, 2012, pp. 126–135.

[58] D. Weyns, T. Ahmad, Claims and evidence for architecture-based self-adaptation: a systematic literature review, in: K. Drira (Ed.), Software Architecture, Lecture Notes in Computer Science, vol. 7957, Springer, Berlin, Heidelberg, 2013, pp. 249–265.

[59] J. Bradbury, J. Cordy, J. Dingel, M. Wermelinger, A survey of self-management in dynamic software architecture specifications, in: 1st ACM SIGSOFT Workshop on Self-Managed Systems, Newport Beach, California, USA, ACM, 2004, pp. 28–33.

[60] D. Weyns, M.U. Iftikhar, DGdl Iglesia, T. Ahmad, A survey of formal methods in self-adaptive systems, in: 5th International C* Conference on Computer Science and Software Engineering, Montreal, Quebec, Canada, ACM, 2012, pp. 67–79.

[61] E. Yuan, N. Esfahani, S. Malek, A systematic survey of self-protecting software systems, ACM Transactions on Autonomous and Adaptive Systems 8 (4) (2014) 1–41.

[62] H.P. Breivolda, I. Crnkovicb, M. Larsson, A systematic review of software architecture evolution research, J. Inform. Softw. Tech. 54 (1) (2012) 16–40.

[63] B. Williams, J. Carver, Characterizing software architecture changes: a systematic review, J. Inform. Softw. Tech. 52 (1) (2010) 31–51.

[64] H. Koziolek, Sustainability evaluation of software architectures: a systematic review, in: Joint ACM SIGSOFT Conference—QoSA and ACM SIGSOFT Symposium—ISARCS on Quality of Software Architectures—QoSA and Architecting Critical Systems—ISARCS (QoSA-ISARCS), Boulder, Colorado, USA, 2011.

[65] A. Immonen, E. Niemela, Survey of reliability and availability prediction methods from the viewpoint of software architecture, J. Softw. Syst. Model. 7 (1) (2008) 49–65.

[66] J.O. Kephart, D.M. Chess, The vision of autonomic computing, IEEE Comput. 36 (1) (2003) 41–50.

[67] IBM, An Architectural Blueprint for Autonomic Computing, White Paper, 2003.

[68] N. Huber, A. van Hoorn, A. Koziolek, F. Brosig, S. Kounev, Modeling run-time adaptation at the system architecture level in dynamic service-oriented environments, Service Oriented Computing and Applications 8 (1) (2014) 73–89.

[69] M.C. Huebscher, J.A. Mccann, A survey of autonomic computing, ACM Comput. Surveys 40 (3) (2008) 1–28.

[70] S. Hassan, N. Bencomo, R. Bahsoon, Minimizing nasty surprises with better informed decision-making in self-adaptive systems, in: 10th International Symposium on Software Engineering for Adaptive and Self-Managing Systems (SEAMS), Florence, Italy, IEEE Press, 2015, pp. 134–144.

[71] F. Faniyi, R. Bahsoon, A. Evans, R. Kazman, Evaluating security properties of architectures in unpredictable environments: a case for cloud, in: 9th Working IEEE/IFIP Conference on Software Architecture (WICSA), Boulder, Colorado, USA, 2011, pp. 127–136.

[72] M. Salehie, L. Tahvildari, Self-adaptive software: landscape and research challenges, ACM Trans. Auton. Adap. Sys. 4 (2) (2009) 1–42.

[73] R. Kazman, R. Bahsoon, I. Mistrik, Y. Zhang, Economics-driven software architecture: introduction, in: I. Mistrik, R. Bahsoon, R. Kazman, Y. Zhang (Eds.), Economics-Driven Software Architecture, Morgan Kaufmann, Boston, 2014, pp. 1–8.

[74] N. Bencomo, A. Belaggoun, Supporting decision-making for self-adaptive systems: from goal models to dynamic decision networks, in: J. Doerr, A. Opdahl (Eds.), Requirements Engineering: Foundation for Software Quality, Lecture Notes in Computer Science, vol. 7830, Springer, Berlin, Heidelberg, 2013, pp. 221–236.

[75] N. Bencomo, A. Belaggoun, V. Issarny, Dynamic decision networks for decision-making in self-adaptive systems: a case study, in: 8th International Symposium on Software Engineering for Adaptive and Self-Managing Systems (SEAMS), San Francisco, CA, USA, IEEE Press, 2013, pp. 113–122.

[76] N. Bencomo, A. Belaggoun, V. Issarny, Bayesian artificial intelligence for tackling uncertainty in self-adaptive systems: the case of dynamic decision networks, in: 2nd International Workshop on Realizing Artificial Intelligence Synergies in Software Engineering (RAISE), San Francisco, CA, USA, 2013, pp. 7–13.

[77] M. Salama, Stability of self-adaptive software architectures, in: 30th IEEE/ACM International Conference on Automated Software Engineering (ASE), Doctoral Symposium, Lincoln, NE, USA, 2015.

[78] M. Harman, The role of artificial intelligence in software engineering, in: 1st International Workshop on Realizing Artificial Intelligence Synergies in Software Engineering (RAISE), Zurich, Switzerland, 2012, pp. 1–6.

THE MANY FACETS OF MEDIATION
A REQUIREMENTS-DRIVEN APPROACH
FOR TRADING OFF MEDIATION SOLUTIONS

12

A. Bennaceur*, B. Nuseibeh*,†

The Open University, Milton Keynes, United Kingdom*
Lero—The Irish Software Research Centre, Limerick, Ireland†

12.1 INTRODUCTION

To software developers, life may sometimes seem like a scene from "Modern Times" where Charlie Chaplin is laboring away at an assembly line, frantically tightening bolts over and over again. Modern software systems are increasingly built by assembling, and reassembling, existing components—possibly distributed among many devices—so as to create innovative services. Since the components of a software system are often designed and implemented independently, software developers spend a lot of time, and effort, adding pieces of code so as to allow these components to work together and satisfy the requirements of the software system. The rapid pace of technological change combined with the increasing demands for high-quality software in reduced time and at lower cost, may overwhelm developers who have to deal with a multitude of details just to make components work together. Besides being a complex and error-prone task, enabling independently developed components to work together is both daunting and tedious. Developers should be free to spend more time creating new services and designing innovative software systems and less time tightening and retightening bolts. Therefore, we must enable independently developed software components to work together, if need be, despite the many differences in their implementations.

Middleware provides an abstraction that facilitates the communication and coordination of distributed components despite the heterogeneity of the underlying platforms, operating systems, and programming languages. However, middleware also defines specific message formats and coordination models, which makes it difficult (or even impossible) for applications using different middleware solutions to interoperate. For example, SOAP-based clients developed using Java and deployed on Mac can seamlessly access a SOAP-based Web Service developed using ASP.NET and deployed on a Windows server. However, a SOAP-based client cannot access a RESTful Web Service [1]. Furthermore, the evolving application requirements lead to a continuous update of existing middleware tools and the emergence of new approaches. For example, SOAP has long been the protocol of choice to interface Web services but RESTful Web services are somehow prevailing nowadays. As a result, application

Managing Trade-offs in Adaptable Software Architectures. http://dx.doi.org/10.1016/B978-0-12-802855-1.00012-5

299

developers have to juggle with a myriad of technologies and tools, and include *ad hoc* glue code whenever it is necessary to integrate applications implemented using different middleware.

To make heterogeneous components work together, without modifying them, intermediary software entities, called *mediators*, are used [2]. Mediators achieve interoperability by reconciling the differences in the implementations of the components involved. Hence, mediators enable compositional adaptation [3], which aims to change the behavior and the structure of a system to make it better fit its environment. Designing and implementing mediators requires dealing with many concerns: (i) coordination of the behaviors of the components so as to guarantee their correct interaction (e.g., absence of deadlocks), (ii) data translation so as to ensure meaningful information exchange between the components, and in the case of distributed components (iii) communication between the components so as to address the issues inherent in their distribution across the network (e.g., concurrency and fault tolerance).

Over the years, mediator synthesis has been the subject of a great deal of work, both theoretical and practical. First, to understand and formalize architectural connection and mismatches, then to synthesize mediators to solve these mismatches with an increasing shift toward runtime. While mediation has been a long-researched topic, the advent of mobile and ubiquitous computing technology emphasizes the need for more dynamic solutions to mediation, and compositional adaptation in general. These solutions are not only applicable at design time but also at runtime. For example, consider one representative application domain, that of emergency management, as illustrated by the European Programme for the establishment of a European capacity for Earth Observation, GMES.[1] GMES gives a special interest to the support of emergency situations (e.g., forest fire) across different European countries. Indeed, each country defines an emergency management system that encompasses multiple components that are autonomous, designed and implemented independently, and do not obey any central control or administration. Nonetheless, there are incentives for these components to be composed and collaborate in emergency situations. GMES makes a strong case of the need for solutions to enable multiple, and most likely heterogeneous, components to collaborate in order to perform the different tasks necessary for decision making. These tasks include collecting weather information, locating the agents involved, and monitoring the environment. In this context, the synthesis of mediators enables the dynamic composition of heterogeneous components whose interaction was unforeseen at design time.

In this paper we present a review of current research in mediation, presented from the perspective of its underpinning fields: *software architecture, middleware, formal methods, and Semantic Web*. Mediator synthesis is a complex challenge that can only be solved by appropriately combining different techniques and perspectives. These techniques include formal approaches for the synthesis of mediators with the support of ontology-based reasoning so as to automate the synthesis, together with middleware solutions to realize and execute these mediators. While these different techniques focus on *How* to synthesize mediators that make components interact in order to achieve a single property, requirements primarily focus is on *Why* components should be mediated and for which properties. Therefore, requirements can drive the selection of the appropriate method for synthesizing mediators. In this chapter, we present a requirements-driven approach for managing trade-offs between the different solutions to mediation in order to choose the appropriate one.

---

[1]Global Monitoring for Environment and Security—http://www.gmes.info/.

This chapter is structured as follows. Section 12.2 gives an overview of the different perspectives on mediator synthesis, which are then detailed in the following sections (12.3–12.6). Section 12.7 proposes a framework that unifies the different solutions. Section 12.8 identifies the opportunities and challenges for using requirements to drive mediation. Finally, Section 12.9 concludes the chapter.

12.2 THE DIFFERENT PERSPECTIVES ON MEDIATION

In this section we present the different approaches to mediation seen from the perspective of its underpinning fields: software architecture, middleware, formal methods, and Semantic Web. Fig. 12.1 depicts, for each perspective, the specific focus and the main technique used as well as how mediators are considered:

1. Software architecture focuses on *composition*: several software entities are put together to build a system and define its *structure* as a whole [4]. Interaction between components is abstractly described using software connectors. In other words, connectors model the exchange of information between components and the coordination of their behaviors. Hence, mediators can be conveniently represented as connectors.
2. Middleware provides an abstraction that facilitates communication and coordination between components in *distributed* systems. It naturally follows that middleware plays a crucial role in the *implementation* of connectors [5].

FIG. 12.1

The different perspectives on mediation.

3. Formal methods are mathematically based languages, techniques, and tools for specifying and verifying hardware and software systems [6]. Formal methods focus on the *behavior* of software systems, which they rigorously analyze in order to reveal potential inconsistencies, ambiguities, and incompleteness. In other words, formal methods help to verify the *absence of execution errors* in software systems. Once potential execution errors (a.k.a. mismatches) are detected, they can be solved by introducing *controllers* that force the components to coordinate their behaviors correctly.

4. The Semantic Web is an extension of the Web in which information is given well-defined *meaning*, better enabling computers and people to work in cooperation [7]. Ontologies play a key role in the Semantic Web by formally representing shared knowledge about a domain of discourse as a set of concepts, and the relationships between these concepts [8]. Ontologies have been extensively used to automate the reasoning about the information exchanged between software components, especially in ubiquitous computing environments, so as to infer the translations necessary to reconcile the differences in the syntax of this information [9].

We detail the techniques for mediation from each perspective in the following. We first adopt a software architecture perspective to present the concepts underpinning mediator synthesis. Next, we concentrate on middleware for the implementation of and deployment of mediators. Then, we describe formal solutions that analyze the behaviors of components in order to synthesize the mediator that guarantees that they can interact without errors. Finally, we present solutions based on ontologies so as to represent and reason about the meaning of the information exchanged between components at runtime and automatically synthesize mediators. Note that these perspectives are not orthogonal and some techniques can be classified in more than one perspective.

12.3 THE SOFTWARE ARCHITECTURE PERSPECTIVE: MEDIATORS AS CONNECTORS

Software architecture abstractly describes the structure of software systems in terms of components and connectors [4]. A component encapsulates some functionality to which it restricts access via an explicit interface [10]. To achieve its functionality, the component interacts with the environment and other components, that is the component's behavior. A connector regulates interactions between components [10].

One critical issue for software architecture is the design and implementation of the connectors that permit the various software components to work together properly. However, when composing two, or more, software components to form a system and those components make conflicting assumptions about their environment, *architectural mismatches* occur [11]. These assumptions relate to: (i) the interfaces and behaviors of the components involved, (ii) the behaviors and implementations of the connectors used, and (iii) the operating systems and the hardware of the devices on top of which the components are deployed.

Mediation aims to solve architectural mismatches by reconciling the conflicting assumptions that the components make about their environment. To solve the differences between the interfaces of components, the mediator must translate the actions required by each of them into actions provided by the other. Note that the mediator facilitates interaction—it is a connector—but does not provide any action itself since it does not encapsulate computation. To solve the differences between the behaviors of components, the mediator must coordinate the exchange of information between these components by controlling which action should be delivered to which component at what time. To solve the differences between the behaviors and implementations of connectors, the mediator must provide a concrete solution to coordinate the interaction patterns of these connectors acting as middleware, which not only makes the application agnostic to the operating systems, but also to the middleware used to implement other connectors.

12.3.1 CONNECTOR SYNTHESIS

It is not always possible to find an existing connector for managing interaction between heterogeneous components and it is difficult and time consuming to design and implement a new connector from scratch, especially if the components already exist and are implemented using different middleware solutions [5]. Compositional approaches for connector construction facilitate the development of mediators by reusing existing connector instances.

Spitznagel and Garlan [12] introduce a set of transformation patterns (e.g., data translation and action aggregation), which a developer can apply to basic connectors (e.g., RPC or data stream) in order to construct more complex connectors. The authors use the approach to enhance the reliability of component interactions, but state that this approach can also be used to construct mediators that solve architectural mismatches. Each transformation pattern is given a formal definition, which allows the verification of the properties of the resulting connectors. As developers are responsible for defining the transformation patterns, they must specify both the necessary translations and behavioral coordination that must be performed by the mediator, but they can easily verify that the mediator produced ensures that the interaction between components is free from deadlocks. The approach is also equipped with a tool that facilitates the implementation of mediators by reusing and composing the implementation of existing connectors, assuming existing connectors were implemented using the same middleware.

Inverardi and Tivoli [13] define an approach to compute a mediator that composes a set of pre-defined patterns in order to guarantee that the interaction of components is deadlock-free. These patterns represent simple mechanisms that the mediator executes to solve differences between the interfaces or behaviors of components and consist of: (i) renaming an action, (ii) translating one action into a sequence of actions, (iii) translating a sequence of actions into one action, (iv) re-ordering sequences of actions, (v) dropping an action, and (vi) introducing a new action. This last pattern has to be taken with reserve as it implies that the mediator is able to produce an action. The mediator either only replays the action or it can perform extra computation; the latter case being beyond interoperability achievement. However, the specification of the patterns to be used must still be done by the developers. Indeed, developers specify the necessary translations based on which the approach synthesizes the mediator that coordinates the behaviors of the components. Furthermore, the implementation of the resulting mediator is completely left up to the developer as the mediator is generated from scratch without reusing existing connector implementations.

Even though these compositional solutions facilitate the development of mediators, they are only applicable at design time. By requiring the intervention of the developer to specify the patterns necessary for the creation of mediators, they cannot cope with the increasing ubiquity and complexity of modern software systems together with the high demand for runtime support.

12.3.2 CONNECTOR SYNTHESIS IN DYNAMIC ENVIRONMENTS

Building mediators is already a difficult task when the developer provides the necessary translations. It is even more difficult when the mediators have to be synthesized and deployed dynamically as components are discovered and composed at runtime.

Chang et al. [14] define a framework that allows component developers to define connectors, called *healing connectors*, to recover from common failures of the component. The healing connectors enable the component to operate in environments that do not verify the assumptions made during the design and implementation of this component. At runtime, whenever an exception rises due to the misuse of a component, the framework deploys, on the fly, the corresponding healing connector. The framework also maintains a log of the exceptions in order to help developers create new healing connectors. Denaro et al. [15] apply the same approach to detect and repair disparities in different implementations of standard Web 2.0 APIs. The healing connectors are not defined by the developers but are included in a centralized catalogue that inventories the common errors that may occur when the API is used.

However, the proposed solutions only react to errors during the execution of a single action and do not consider the behaviors of the components. Hence, they solve architectural mismatches which are due to conflicting assumptions regarding the components' interfaces, but not due to conflicting assumptions about the components' behaviors. Furthermore, healing connectors act as translators for the case of common misuse based on the experience of developers and are not able to deal with unforeseen interactions. The implicit knowledge used by the developer to specify the translator should be modeled explicitly in order to allow computers to reason about the information exchanged by the components and infer the translations automatically.

12.3.3 ANALYSIS

Considering mediation from a software architecture perspective allows us to define the foundational concepts for the formal description, synthesis, and implementation of mediators. Mediators are connectors that enable components to work together by translating the actions of their interfaces and coordinating their behaviors. In ubiquitous computing environments, mediators must be generated on the fly to deal with the high degree of dynamism inherent in these environments. In the following, we first consider the middleware solutions that facilitate the implementation of mediators by compensating for the differences at the middleware layer. Then, we present the formal solutions to synthesizing mediators that coordinate the behaviors of functionally compatible components in order to guarantee their successful interaction. Finally, we consider semantics-based solutions to infer the translations necessary for meaningful exchange of information between components and enable the synthesis of mediators at runtime.

12.4 THE MIDDLEWARE PERSPECTIVE: MEDIATORS AS MIDDLEWARE

Middleware makes components work together by hiding the differences in hardware and operating systems, as depicted in Fig. 12.2. Middleware facilitates communication and coordination between components in distributed systems by defining [16]: (i) an Interface Description Language (IDL) for specifying the interfaces of components and the associated operations, and data types, (ii) a discovery

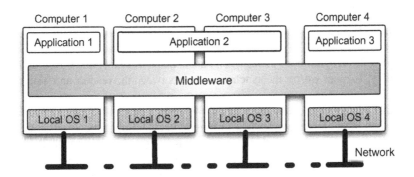

FIG. 12.2

Middleware.

Source: Based on A. Tanenbaum, M. Van Steen, Distributed Systems: Principles and Paradigms, second ed., Prentice Hall, Upper Saddle River, NJ, 2006.

protocol to address and locate the components that are available in the environment, and (iii) an interaction protocol that coordinates the behavior of different components and enables them to collaborate. While middleware solutions and implementations define diverse IDLs and message formats, their interaction protocols follow comparably few interaction patterns, a.k.a., communication paradigms/types [17] or coordination models/paradigms [16]. An interaction pattern defines the rules to coordinate the behaviors of the components. In Mehta et al. connector classification [18], these interaction patterns match with the connector types that provide communication and coordination services. The major interaction patterns are: remote procedure call (RPC), distributed shared memory (DSM), and publish/subscribe [17].

RPC represents the most common interaction pattern in distributed systems. This approach directly and elegantly supports client/server interactions with servers offering a set of operations through a service interface and clients calling these operations directly as if they were available locally. The interaction is supported by a pairwise exchange of messages from the client to the server and then from the server back to the client, with the first message containing the operation to be executed at the server and associated arguments and the second message containing any result of the operation. To interact according to RPC, the client and the server must agree on the format of the messages they exchange as well as the encoding of the data, which represent the arguments and results, enclosed in these messages. An RPC-based middleware hides the encoding together with the decoding of arguments and results as well as the passing of messages using communication modules, *stubs*, that permit the client and server to use the operations as if they were local. RPC-based middleware solutions are often associated with libraries to generate, either at compile time or runtime, the client and server stubs based on the interface definition. The strict request-reply message exchange is unnecessary when there is no result to return. RPC middleware solutions may also provide facilities for what are called asynchronous RPCs, by which a client immediately continues its execution after issuing the RPC request.

While RPC allows developers to invoke operations as if they were available locally, DSM provides developers with a familiar abstraction of reading or writing (shared) data structures as if they were in their own local address spaces. DSM is in general less appropriate for client/server interactions, where clients usually access server-held resources using an explicit interface (for reasons of modularity and protection). Still, servers can provide DSM that is shared between clients. A DSM-based middleware enables components to read and write data in the shared memory, regardless of the exact location of the data. Nevertheless, the structure of the shared data is defined at the application layer and the middleware does not provide any guarantee about when data is made available and how long it will reside in the shared memory. In other words, the synchronization between the readers and writers also needs to be managed at the application layer.

Many applications require the dissemination of information or items of interest from a large number of producers to a similarly large number of consumers. Publish/Subscribe middleware solutions provide an intermediary service, a *broker*, that efficiently ensures that information generated by producers is delivered to the consumers that want to receive it. In other words, publish/subscribe middleware solutions (sometimes also called distributed event-based middleware) allow subscribers to register their interest in an event, or a pattern of events, and ensure that they are asynchronously notified of events generated by publishers. The task of the publish/subscribe middleware is to match subscriptions against published events and ensure the correct delivery of event notifications. A given event will be delivered to potentially many subscribers, and hence publish-subscribe is fundamentally a one-to-many interaction pattern. The expressiveness of publish/subscribe middleware solutions is determined by the type of event subscriptions they support: either subscriptions are made using specific topics (also referred to as subjects) which the events belong to, or based on the content of the event.

Traditionally, middleware promotes the use of a single technology based on which all components are built, which can be based on RPC (e.g., RMI and RPC SOAP), DSM (e.g., Linda and LIME), or Publish/Subscribe (e.g., JMS and AMQP). However, given the diversity of modern software systems that need to be dealt with, ranging from small-scale sensors to large-scale Internet applications, there is no one-size-fits-all middleware capable of coping with them all [19]. As a result, new middleware solutions have been proposed to enable interaction across middleware and hence facilitate the implementation of mediators between independently developed components that feature differences at both the application and middleware layers. We first present solutions based on the definition of middleware that provides developers with an abstraction which allows them to build components that are able to interact using different middleware solutions, i.e., *universal middleware*. We then consider solutions to directly translate messages from one middleware to the other, i.e., *middleware bridges*. Finally, we consider solutions to translate between different middleware solutions using an intermediary model or infrastructure, i.e., *service buses*.

12.4.1 UNIVERSAL MIDDLEWARE

Universal middleware solutions provide the developer with an abstraction that masks the differences that may exist at the middleware layer. Solutions include polymorphic middleware such as PolyORB [20] and reflective middleware such as ReMMoC [21].

PolyORB [20] is a middleware solution that decouples the interaction pattern used to implement the application from the middleware used for the actual achievement of this interaction. First, PolyORB supports several interaction patterns, called *application personalities*, based on which applications can be developed. Second, PolyORB supports different communication protocols called *protocol personalities*, e.g., SOAP and GIOP. The relation between the application and protocol personalities is handled via an intermediary protocol into which any application personality can be translated and which can be translated into all protocol personalities. Before deploying the component, it is configured with the appropriate personalities. Hence, it is not possible to select the appropriate protocol personality dynamically according to the running environment.

Reflective middleware for mobile computing (ReMMoC) [21] is a reflective middleware solution that provides a WSDL-based interface to develop components. ReMMoC implements a set of plugins to transform the primitives of the WSDL interface into calls to other middleware technologies, in particular SOAP, CORBA, and STEAM (a publish/subscribe middleware). At runtime, a component implemented using ReMMoC can discover and interact with components implemented using different middleware solutions by dynamically loading the necessary plugin.

An approach based on universal middleware has many flaws. First, it cannot be applied to legacy components, as it requires at least one of the interacting components to be developed using the universal middleware. Second, the universal middleware must support any possible middleware and hence requires continual maintenance in order to cope with the evolution of middleware solutions or the emergence of new ones.

12.4.2 MIDDLEWARE BRIDGES

To deal with interoperability between existing components, the most straightforward solution is to develop a middleware solution that implements direct translation between the messages of two middleware solutions. The middleware bridge takes messages from one middleware in a specific format and then marshals them to the format of the other middleware.

There exist several examples of middleware bridges: OrbixCOMet[2] is a middleware bridge between DCOM and CORBA and SOAP2CORBA[3] ensures interoperability between SOAP and CORBA in both directions. However, the implementation of middleware bridges is a complex task: developers have to deal with a lot of details involving the format of the messages used by each middleware and their correlation; therefore, developers must have a thorough understanding of the middleware at hand. As a result, solutions that help developers define middleware bridges have emerged. These solutions consist in defining a framework whereby the developer provides a declarative specification of the message translation between middleware, based on which the actual transformations are computed. z2z [22] introduces a domain-specific language to describe the message format and the communication protocol of each middleware as well as the translation logic to make them work together, and then generates the corresponding bridge. The approach has several benefits. First, it increases the level of reusability as the developer can use the individual specifications of middleware to develop different bridges. Second, the developer does not have to deal with all the message fields since z2z is able to complete default and optional fields automatically. Finally, z2z verifies that all the required fields of a message have been treated before sending it. However, the bridge cannot be modified at runtime.

Starlink [23] uses the domain-specific models defined by z2z to specify bridges, but it deploys and interprets them at runtime. More specifically, Starlink uses the message specification associated with each middleware to generate a *parser*, which is able to process the messages sent using this middleware into an *abstract message*, and a *composer*, which is able to produce the appropriate middleware

---

[2]http://documentation.progress.com/output/Iona/orbix/gen3/33/html/orbixcomet33_pguide/.
[3]http://soap2corba.sourceforge.net/.

message out of an abstract message. In other words, parsers and composers mask the differences between middleware through the concept of abstract messages. The translation logic specifies how to convert the abstract messages of one middleware into abstract messages of the other middleware. This approach decouples the detailed specification of the middleware, which is used to generate the corresponding parsers and composers, from the abstract specification of the translations between middleware solutions.

Summing up, middleware bridges provide a transparent solution to interoperability but are impractical in the long term given the development effort necessary to implement or specify the translation between middleware solutions. Furthermore, in the case of middleware based on different interaction patterns, this translation may become unfeasible in all situations, for example, if one middleware is based on asynchronous communication while the other relies on synchronous communication.

12.4.3 SERVICE BUSES

Like middleware bridges, service buses enable existing components implemented using different middleware to exchange messages transparently, but unlike middleware bridges, the translation between messages is performed through an intermediary representation. This representation can be an abstract proprietary protocol, as is the case with middleware buses, or a message-oriented abstraction layer, as is the case with enterprise service buses (ESBs).

Georgantas et al. [24] define an approach where the developer specifies a set of semantic events common to different middleware. Then, each middleware is associated with a parser that processes the messages of this middleware to produce a semantic event, and a composer that generates a middleware message based on a semantic event. Parsers and composers of different middleware then synchronize based on shared semantic events. For example, to achieve interoperability between SOAP and CORBA, developers define the request and response events. Then, parsers and composers are created per protocol: a SOAP parser triggers a request (respectively response) event upon the reception of a SOAP request (respectively response) and a SOAP composer produces a SOAP request (respectively response) out of a request event (respectively response). The same is true for CORBA parsers and composers. Hence, when a SOAP request is received, the SOAP parser triggers a request event, which the CORBA composer intercepts and transforms into a CORBA request. Once the CORBA response has been returned, the CORBA parser triggers a response event, which the SOAP composer intercepts and transforms into a SOAP response. However, this approach is inapplicable for middleware based on different interaction patterns since it is also necessary to coordinate the message exchange as well as the translation between messages. Furthermore, the approach does not provide any support for the specification or implementation of application-level mediators.

ESBs represent the most mature and widespread solution to enable components using different middleware to interoperate, as is shown by the large number of available industrial implementations, e.g., Oracle Service Bus[4] and IBM WebSphere ESB.[5] An ESB [25] is an open standard, message-based middleware solution that facilitates the interactions of disparate distributed applications and services.

---

[4]http://www.oracle.com/technetwork/middleware/service-bus/.
[5]http://www-01.ibm.com/software/integration/wsesb/.

ESBs generally include built-in conversion across standard middleware technologies (e.g., SOAP, JMS) and provide a set of predefined patterns that can be used to create customized mediators.

However, ESBs takes an enterprise perspective, where interactions between components are planned and long-lived. Hence, the solutions are typically restricted to a set of known middleware standards, and the development effort required to extend them for new protocols or to specify mediators is significant. They are not well suited to situations where interactions must be solved on the fly as in ubiquitous computing environments, which involve short-lived interactions and unforeseen compositions.

12.4.4 ANALYSIS

There exist many middleware solutions to enable components that feature differences at the middleware layer to interact successfully. However, while the implementation of new middleware might be sufficient to deal with the differences at the middleware layer, it is insufficient to deal with differences at the application layer. First, even applications developed using the same middleware are not guaranteed to work together so long as there are differences in their interfaces and behaviors. This is, for example, the case of interoperability in Web Services [26]. Even though both services and clients use SOAP middleware, the differences between their interfaces, which include differences in the operation names, input/output message names and types, the granularity of operations, and the order in which these operations are invoked (or expected to be invoked) hamper independently developed clients and Web Services from working together. Given the countless number of potential cases where a mediator is necessary, any static solution is doomed to fail. We need to generate mediators automatically. Second, while in the case of middleware obeying the same interaction pattern, it suffices to translate the messages sent using one middleware into messages expected by the other middleware, when middleware solutions follow different interaction patterns, e.g., a shared memory and publish/subscribe, the differences can only be solved by considering the characteristics of the applications [27]. Hence, it is necessary to define solutions that are able to reason about the characteristics of applications automatically in order to synthesize the mediator that reconciles the differences between component implementations and enables them to interoperate. In the following section, we present solutions that analyze the behaviors of the components and semi-automatically generate the appropriate mediator that enables their correct interaction.

12.5 THE FORMAL METHODS PERSPECTIVE: MEDIATORS AS CONTROLLERS

Formal methods aim to relieve developers of the burden of designing or specifying mediators, with a special focus on coordinating the behaviors of the components so as to guarantee their correct interaction. Correct interaction may be specified as: (i) the ability of the components to coordinate their behaviors in order to achieve the requirements of the composed system, or (ii) the ability to preserve the meaning of the information exchanged between the components and guarantee that the composed system is free from deadlocks.

12.5.1 CONTROLLER SYNTHESIS USING A SPECIFICATION OF THE COMPOSED SYSTEM

The successful interaction of components results in a composed software system that meets given requirements. By enabling components to interact with each other, mediators can be seen as the missing behavior necessary to realize a specification of the composed system *Goal*.

12.5.1.1 Quotient

Calvert and Lam [28] formulate mediator synthesis as the problem of finding *quotient*. In a similar way to division and product in arithmetics, quotient can be regarded as the adjoint (roughly "inverse") of parallel composition. Given a specification for a system S, together with a component's behavior P, the quotient yields the behavior Q such that $P\|Q$ satisfies S. Applied to mediator synthesis, the mediator is the quotient of the specification of the composed system *Goal* and the parallel composition of the components' behaviors. The authors assume *Goal* to be deterministic and synthesize M by first building the set of all possible coordinations of the actions of the components' interfaces, and then keeping only those that satisfy *Goal*.

Even though the approach can, in theory, always produce a mediator if one exists, it is clear from the algorithm that it is computationally very expensive as it requires exploring all possible traces over the set of actions of both *Goal* and M. Furthermore, it assumes that the same actions are used to define the specification of the composed system as well as the components' behaviors.

12.5.1.2 Planning

Similarly to quotient computation, the planning-based approach defined by Bertoli et al. [29] builds the mediator by identifying among all possible interactions with the components, only those that satisfy *Goal*. Nevertheless, they optimize the search by using a heuristic in order to explore only the interactions that are likely to satisfy *Goal* and use a planning algorithm in order to calculate the traces of the mediator more efficiently.

12.5.1.3 Control theory

Gierds et al. [30] formulate mediator synthesis in terms of controller synthesis. Besides the components' behaviors and the specification of the composed system, they also require the definition of a set of translation patterns between the actions of the components. They create a component whose behavior E is extracted from the specified translation patterns: E represents the behavior of a component able to execute the translation patterns in any order. Then, they use available tools for controller synthesis to generate a controller C for the composition $P_1\|P_2\|E$ to satisfy *Goal*. Finally, they compose the behavior of the controller together with the behavior of the translation component to obtain the mediator, i.e., $M = E\|C$.

Summing up, solutions to mediator synthesis based on quotient computation, planning or controller synthesis are guaranteed to find the mediator if it exists and state its nonexistence otherwise. However, they require the user to have an intuitive understanding of the behavior of the composed system, which can only emerge through the correct interaction of its components. This might be a reasonable assumption when developing a software system by integrating several components, but it is unreasonable to require such understanding from regular users who only seek to interact with the services in their environment, as is the case in ubiquitous computing environments.

12.5.2 CONTROLLER SYNTHESIS USING A PARTIAL SPECIFICATION

The solutions proposed in the following assume that a specification of the correspondence between the actions of the components' interfaces is available and use it to coordinate the components' behaviors in order to guarantee that their interaction is free from deadlocks. This correspondence defines the translations that the mediator must perform in order to reconcile the differences between the components' interfaces. Therefore, we refer to the specification of these correspondences as partial specifications of the mediator.

12.5.2.1 Projection

Lam [31] defines an approach for the synthesis of mediators based on the technique of projections. A projection of a component's behavior P, noted $Proj[P]$ is performed by aggregating some of its states, which induces the definition of an equivalence relation on the actions of the component's interface. Two actions are equivalent if they cause identical state change in $Proj[P]$ while actions that do not cause any state change are not represented in $Proj[P]$. Hence, the projection can be seen as applying relabeling and hiding functions to P.

   If one can define a *useful* common projection of the behaviors of the components, then a stateless mediator M can be synthesized. Useful means that the common projection defines a behavior to achieve some functionality of interest. The common projection can be seen as the lowest common denominator of the behaviors of the components. The definition of the common projection is the responsibility of the developer. The synthesized stateless mediator simply transforms an action required by one component into an action provided by the other component if they cause identical state change in the common projection, and ignores the actions that do not cause any state change. However, this stateless mediator is able to deal with only one-to-one correspondences between actions. Furthermore, no systematic approach for the definition of the common projection is proposed, it depends solely on developers and their understanding of the components' behaviors.

12.5.2.2 Interface mapping

Yellin and Strom [32] define a synthesis algorithm that, besides the behaviors of the components, must be given an interface mapping S, which specifies the correspondence between the actions of the components' interfaces. The interface mapping is required to be complete and nonambiguous. An interface mapping is complete if for every required action of one component, there corresponds a provided action from the other component. It is nonambiguous if for every required action of one component, there corresponds at most one provided action from the other component. Each correspondence in the interface mapping defines an ordering constraint between the required and provided actions. The synthesis algorithm constructs a mediator in two main phases. During the first phase, an initial process A is created which represents all possible coordinations of components' behaviors that verify the ordering constraints imposed by the interface mapping. In the second phase, any execution in A leading to a deadlock is removed. As a result of the second phase, either A is empty, in which case the mediator does not exist, or it is a valid mediator M.

12.5.2.3 Model checking

While interface mapping only specifies one-to-one correspondences between actions, there often exist more elaborate correspondences relating them. In the general case, a sequence of actions of one component may be translated into another sequence of actions of the other component. To specify complex correspondences, Mateescu et al. [33] use an *adaptation contract*, which is an LTS S whose alphabet is a vector composed of the actions of the components' interfaces. The authors then construct the mediator by selecting among all possible executions of the composed system C only those that do not lead to deadlocks. Instead of constructing C then removing the erroneous executions, they use on-the-fly model checking to prune, as early as possible, the executions leading to deadlocks.

12.5.2.4 Semi-automated mapping generation

Nezhad *et al.* [34, 35] define a semi-automated approach to the synthesis of mediators which, rather than considering that the correspondences between the actions of the components are provided, define a series of heuristics to facilitate their computation. First, they focus on the syntax, expressed using XML schema, of the data embedded in the actions. They use existing XML schema matching techniques to evaluate the degree of similarity between sequences of actions in the components' interfaces. Then, they update this similarity based on the first position at which the actions can appear in the behaviors of the components: the similarity score of required and provided actions increases if they are at the same position. The last heuristic consists in selecting the pair of actions with the highest degree of similarity according to the matching of their XML schema and then updating the similarity scores of the other pairs of actions according to their positions relative to the selected pair of actions. The same pair of actions is never selected twice so that the heuristic is guaranteed to terminate. Once the correspondences between actions have been computed, the behaviors of the two components are simultaneously explored in order to identify possible deadlocks. The user is presented with the deadlocks that may occur and has to figure out the appropriate translations that may solve them. The algorithm cannot apply the mapping directly as there is no guarantee that even the actions with the highest similarity score have the same meaning.

12.5.3 ANALYSIS

Formal methods enable a rigorous analysis of components' behaviors in order to synthesize the mediator that coordinates the components' behaviors appropriately. Nevertheless, besides the description of components' behaviors, the synthesis of mediators using formal methods also requires the specification of a single property of the composed systems or the correspondence between actions. The definition of the correspondences between the actions of components' interfaces may be error-prone given the size and the number of parameters of the interfaces involved. For example, the Amazon Web Service[6] includes 23 operations and no less than 72 data type definitions and eBay[7] contains more than 156 operations. Given all possible combinations, methods that automatically compute these correspondences are necessary.

12.6 THE SEMANTIC WEB PERSPECTIVE: MEDIATORS AS TRANSLATORS

When the components are dynamically discovered, and interact spontaneously, as is the case in ubiquitous computing environments, the correspondences between the actions of components' interfaces must also be elicited at runtime. To do so, the meaning of these actions and their relations must be made explicit in order to allow their automated analysis.

---

[6]http://soap.amazon.com/schemas2/AmazonWebServices.wsdl.
[7]http://developer.ebay.com/webservices/latest/ebaysvc.wsdl.

Therefore, the Semantic Web [7] promotes the view that Web resources are augmented with machine-processable metadata expressing their meaning. This vision is supported by ontologies, which provide a machine-processable means to represent and automatically reason about the meaning of data based on the shared understanding of the domain [36]. By relying on ontologies, Semantic Web Services improve the discovery, composition, and mediation of Web Services.

12.6.1 SEMANTIC WEB SERVICES

Web Services are processes that expose their interfaces to the Web so that users can invoke them. Semantic Web Services provide a richer and more precise way to describe the services through the use of knowledge representation languages and ontologies. The aim is to facilitate the service discovery and composition by exploiting knowledge explicitly encoded in the ontology rather than trying to guess the meaning encoded in the schemas, as is the case with XML schemas for example [37]. Major efforts for modeling and using Semantic Web Services include OWL-S [38] and WSMO [39].

OWL-S [38], which was previously named DAML-S [40], is an ontology for formally defining Web Services. An ontology-based description of Web Services has many advantages. First, it promotes the discovery of functionally compatible components through the notion of a capability. In this sense, pioneering work by Paolucci et al. [41] defines an approach to assess functional compatibility between a provided service (advertisement) and a required service (request) by comparing the semantics of the inputs and outputs specified in their respective profiles: an advertisement matches with a request if every input in the request profile subsumes some input in the advertisement profile, and every output in the advertisement profile subsumes some output in the request profile. Second, it eases the construction of composition of services by making explicit the input, output, pre- and postconditions of the services as well as their behaviors. Finally, and most importantly, it facilitates mediation by formalizing both the meaning of the input/output and the behavior of services. Vaculín et al. [42] define an approach for generating mediators between functionally compatible client and service, both of which are modeled using OWL-S. First, they extract a set of representative executions of the client using its process specification. For each execution, they simulate the service process and use a planning algorithm in order to find the corresponding execution such that the client and the service can progress simultaneously. Then, for each pair of client and service executions, they use existing data mediators to perform the translations necessary to compensate for the differences between their input/output.

However, OWL-S only has had a qualified success because it specifies yet another model to define services. In addition, solutions based on process algebra and automata have proven more suitable for modeling and analyzing the behavior of components.

WSMO [39] is another ontology for modeling Semantic Web Services. WSMO considers mediators as first-class concepts and provides a runtime framework, the Web Service Execution Environment (WSMX), to specify, deploy, and execute mediators dynamically.

12.6.2 SEMANTIC MEDIATION BUS

Instead of defining yet another ontology for Web Services, SA-WSDL [43] proposes a cost-effective solution to incorporate ontology reasoning in Web Services by augmenting service descriptions with annotations to: (i) define the semantics of operations and data by referring to concepts in a domain ontology, (ii) map the data syntax to the semantic definition of the associated concept using XSLT,[8] i.e., *lifting*, and (iii) derive the specific data structures from semantic concepts using XSLT also, i.e., *lowering*.

Even though SA-WSDL does not have the expressive power of OWL-S or WSMO as it represents neither the capability of services nor their behaviors, it is easier to integrate in existing systems including ESBs.

The Alion Semantic Mediation Bus [44] brings together SA-WSDL and ESB. While the ESB provides various plugins to support different middleware interaction protocols, services are described using SA-WSDL specifications, which enables the runtime translation of the actions of clients' and services' interfaces using the lifting and lowering functions. Nevertheless, as SA-WSDL does not support the modeling of behavior, the Alion Semantic Mediation Bus focuses on action translations and does not coordinate the behaviors of clients and services. Moreover, as the capabilities are not represented either, the discovery of functionally compatible clients and services cannot be achieved automatically.

12.6.3 ANALYSIS

Semantic Web technologies, and ontologies in particular, enable the precise modeling of and reasoning about the meaning of the information exchanged between components. Semantic Web Services illustrate how ontologies can help to automate the discovery and composition of Web Services and facilitate mediation between them. However, mediation is often based on the definition of new ontologies and their use to infer the translations necessary to ensure the meaningful exchange of information between components. Furthermore, while modeling the behavior of components is recognized as being essential, the logical theory behind ontologies is inappropriate for analyzing components' behaviors. In addition, even though initial attempts to handle differences between components at the middleware layer are beginning to emerge through the concept of semantic mediation buses, they only deal with translations of actions and do not manage behavioral differences between components, at either the application or the middleware layers.

12.7 MEDIATOR SYNTHESIS AS A SERVICE

Over the years, mediation has been the subject of a great deal of work, both theoretical and practical. Table 12.1 summarizes the solutions presented in previous sections. We can notice that although a lot of progress has been made, none of the proposed solutions is able to synthesize and deploy mediators that deal with both application and middleware differences and guarantee that the interaction between heterogeneous components is error-free.

- Software architecture solutions focus on reasoning about the composition of software components and define the requirements for mediation *but* do not specify how to synthesize mediators automatically.
- Middleware solutions facilitate the implementation of mediators *but* do not reconcile the differences between components at the application layer.

---

[8]Extensible Stylesheet Language Transformations—http://www.w3.org/TR/xslt.

Table 12.1 Summary of Mediation Solutions

Pers.	Approach	The Main Idea	Evaluation
Software architecture	Formal reasoning about component interaction [11, 45]	Formal definition of component interaction to detect architectural mismatches	+ Formal basis for understanding mediation − No support for differences at the middleware layer − No automated generation of mediators
	Compositional approaches for connector development [12, 13]	Creating mediators from existing connector instances	
	Self-healing connectors [14, 15]	Recovery from component misuse by deploying connectors on the fly	
Middleware	Universal middleware [20, 21]	Provide an abstraction that masks the differences at the middleware layer	+ Support differences at the middleware layer − Developers need to specify or implement mediators at the application layer
	Middleware bridges [22, 23]	Direct translation between middleware messages	
	Service buses [24, 25]	Dealing with different middleware solutions via an intermediary infrastructure	
Formal methods	Using a specification of the composed system [28–30]	Synthesize the mediator by selecting from all possible coordinations of the behaviors of components only those that satisfy the specification of the composed system	+ Automated analysis and coordination of components' behaviors + Guaranteed correctness of the interaction between components − Require a declarative specification of the correspondences between the actions of components' interfaces − No support for differences at the middleware layer
	Using a partial specification [31–33, 35]	Require the correspondences between actions to be available, and synthesize the mediator that guarantees that interaction between components is deadlock-free	
Semantic web	Semantic Web Services [38–40]	Defining an ontology to support the inference of the necessary translations of the actions required by one component and provided by the other	+ Automated discovery of functionally-compatible components + Automated reasoning about the meaning of information − Partial support for behavioral differences − Partial support for middleware differences
	Semantic mediation bus [44]	Using semantic technologies within an ESB to automate message translation	

- Formal methods provide us with the foundations for coordinating the behaviors of components in order to guarantee the absence of errors in their interactions *but* assume that (i) the components use the same set of actions, (ii) a single specification of the composed system is given, or (iii) the correspondence between their actions is provided.
- Semantic Web solutions allow us to infer the translations necessary to ensure meaningful exchange of information between components *but* do not deal with the differences between components at the middleware layer.

Therefore, we propose to unify these different solutions by considering the various roles of mediators. Mediators act as (i) *translators* by ensuring the meaningful exchange of information between components, (ii) *controllers* by coordinating the behaviors of the components to ensure the absence of errors in their interaction, and (iii) *middleware* by enabling the interaction of components across the network so that each component receives the data it expects at the right moment and in the right format. More specifically, we can use ontology-based reasoning to automate the synthesis of translators, formal methods to synthesize controllers, and middleware solutions to realize and execute mediators. We can combine these solutions in a mix-and-match way to provide mediation as a service (see Fig. 12.3).

The first step consists in using domain knowledge to calculate the correspondences between the actions required by one component and those provided by the other, that is *translator synthesis* (see

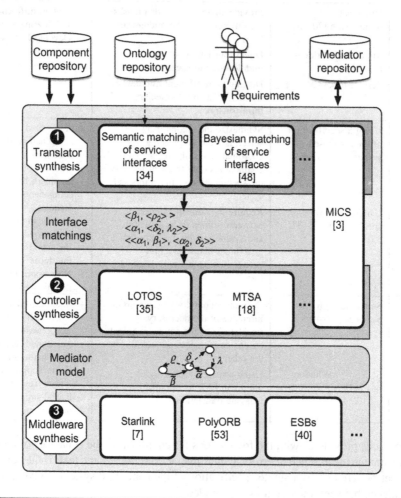

FIG. 12.3

Mediator synthesis as a service.

Fig. 12.3(1)). Indeed, a significant role of the mediator is to translate information available on one side and make it suitable and relevant to the other. This translation can only be carried out if there exists a semantic correspondence between the actions of the components, that is, *interface matching*. The main idea is to use domain-specific knowledge, described within an ontology for example, in order to select from sequences of actions of the components' interfaces only those which retain the meaning of the information exchanged and for which translations can automatically be computed. Interface matchings not only specify one-to-one correspondences between the actions of components but also many-to-many correspondences, which makes their computation very complex.

The second step is to explore the behaviors of the components in order to generate a process that ensures that whenever one of the components chooses a sequence of actions to execute, other components are ready to engage in a sequence of actions while there exist an interface matching relating these sequences of actions, that is *controller synthesis* (see Fig. 12.3(2)). The synthesized controller guarantees the correct interaction between the components by making them progress synchronously and reach a desirable state. Note that solutions such as MICS [46] tackles more than one role of mediators. MICS combines constraint programming and ontology reasoning to compute the correspondences between the actions used by the components, which are then used to synthesize a controller.

The last step entails the instantiation of the data structures expected by each component and their delivery according to the interaction pattern defined by the middleware based on which the component is implemented, that is *middleware synthesis* (see Fig. 12.3(3)). Indeed, to enable the dynamic composition of highly heterogeneous components, i.e., components featuring differences at both the application and middleware layers, a mediator must be synthesized which ensures that each component receives the data it expects at the right moment and in the right format.

12.8 REQUIREMENTS AND MEDIATION

Requirements and mediators may not seem to naturally fit together (see Fig. 12.4). On the one hand, requirements reside primarily in the problem space whereas mediators reside primarily in the solution space. That is, requirements reflect the understanding of the environment, the need of stakeholders and the rationale behind the development of the proposed system. Mediator synthesis, however, focuses on the behavior of individual components and how to enable them to interact with one another. Requirements are often refined by decomposing the problem into smaller ones whereas mediation aim to compose heterogeneous components to make a more complex behavior emerge. On the other hand, the increasing deployment of mobile and ubiquitous computing technology makes the boundary between problem and solution worlds disappear. As a result, realizing requirements through the collaboration of

FIG. 12.4

Requirements vs. mediation.

multiple existing components is more than simply desirable, it is fast becoming a necessity. But the remaining question is: *how to bridge the gap between requirements and mediation?*

Specifying requirements involves making explicit the environment properties under which these requirements must be satisfied [47]. More specifically, Jackson and Zave's framework for requirements engineering [47] makes explicit the relationship between requirements, specifications, and environment properties, which can be formalized as follows.

$$S, E \vdash R$$

where S denotes a system specification, E environment properties, and R requirements. Mediators are synthesized to realize a desirable property/requirement given a set of available components in a specific environment, which can be formalized as follows.

$$E, M \vdash R$$

where M denotes the synthesized mediator and we consider, without loss of generality, that the specifications of the available components are included in that of the environment.

When environment properties change (or the set of available components change) a new mediator must be synthesized to maintain the same requirement satisfied.

$$\text{Synthesize } M' \text{ such that } E', M' \vdash R$$

where E' denotes the updated environment properties and M' the new mediator.

However, it is not always possible to synthesize a mediator that will maintain the requirements satisfied whatever are the environment properties. D'Ippolito et al. [48] propose a multitier framework whereby a stack of mediators are synthesized to satisfy stronger requirements when making stronger assumptions about the environment. For example, a two-level stack would be as follows.

$$\text{Synthesize } M_1 \text{ such that}$$
$$E_1, M_1 \vdash R_1,$$
$$\text{Synthesize } M_2 \text{ such that}$$
$$E_2, M_2 \vdash R_2,$$
$$E_2 \text{ simulates } E_1, \text{ and}$$
$$M_2 \text{ simulates } M_1$$

where in the second tier, some strong assumptions about the environment are made E_2 and strong guarantees provided R_2 while weaker assumptions (E_2 simulates E_1) are made in the lower first tier but also weaker guarantees are provided. Nevertheless, this approach is unable to deal with unrelated environment properties or mediators. Consider for example the case where for the same environment properties, we can synthesize mediators to achieve only one requirement at a time:

$$\exists M_1 \text{ such that}$$
$$E, M_1 \vdash R_1,$$
$$\exists M_2 \text{ such that}$$
$$E, M_2 \vdash R_2, \text{ and}$$
$$\nexists M \text{ such that}$$
$$E, M \vdash R_1 \wedge R_2$$

where R_1 and R_2 are two unrelated requirements. We must then decide which mediator to deploy, which necessitates explicit reasoning about requirements and their relationships.

Goal modeling frameworks such as KAOS [49] or $i*$ [50] are often used represent and reason about the relationships between multiple requirements as well as the associated domain properties. However, while goals, mainly expressed using linear temporal logic (LTL) [51], have been extensively used in controller synthesis, it is not clear how goal modeling can be used for mediator synthesis. Cavallaro et al. [52] propose to extend the KAOS goal models in order to define a specifications of services, which are then instantiated at runtime. In this case, mediators are used to compensate for the differences between the discovered service instance and the service specification. Letier and Heaven [53] propose to use mediator (controller) synthesis to derive a machine specification that satisfies one goal under some domain specifications and then compose them to form a specification that satisfies a set of goals. Hence, combining requirement modeling and mediator synthesis help in dealing with multiple properties of the system composed of the multiple components and mediator.

Yet, rather than the synthesis of a machine specification, we may use requirements analysis to derive the appropriate specification and then implement this specification by using mediation to make multiple components collaborate. One concrete example is that of security. Determining the appropriate mechanisms that need to be deployed in order to protect assets from harm often requires trading off security against other requirements such as performance or usability and considering the value of the assets, and potential threats [54]. Adaptive security (sometimes called self-protection [55]) aims to enable systems to vary their protection in the face of changes in their operational environment. A requirements-driven approach for adaptive security enables the analysis and reasoning about the cost and benefit of the security controls. Salehie et al. [56] propose an approach in which a runtime model that combines goals, threats, and assets models is used to evaluate the cost and benefit of applying each security control (i.e., the mechanism that needs to be deployed in order to protect assets from harm) and choosing the most appropriate one. Collaborative security [57] uses mediation to implement the appropriate security controls by composing components' capabilities at runtime.

12.9 SUMMARY

Ask a software architect about mediation, and she will say that it is about the development of the software connector that enables components to interact successfully. Ask a middleware developer and she will tell you that it is about defining a connectivity infrastructure. Ask a formal methods expert and she will say that it is about computing a controller that enables the components to interact without errors. Ask a Semantic Web expert and she will tell you that it is about defining an ontology that enables reasoning about the meaning of the information exchange. In this chapter, we reviewed the literature on mediation from these four perspectives. We presented a multifaceted approach to mediation, which brings together the solutions of mediation from different perspectives. We also made a case for using requirements to help identify synergies and trade-offs between the many properties that a mediation solution need to deliver.

ACKNOWLEDGMENTS

We acknowledge SFI grant 10/CE/I1855 and ERC Advanced grant 291652 (ASAP).

REFERENCES

[1] R. Fielding, Architectural styles and the design of network-based software architectures, Ph.D. thesis, University of California, California, 2000.

[2] G. Wiederhold, Mediators in the architecture of future information systems, IEEE Comput. 25 (3) (1992) 38–49.

[3] P.K. McKinley, S.M. Sadjadi, E.P. Kasten, B.H.C. Cheng, Composing adaptive software, IEEE Comput. 37 (7) (2004) 56–64. http://doi.ieeecomputersociety.org/10.1109/MC.2004.48.

[4] M. Shaw, Procedure calls are the assembly language of software interconnection: connectors deserve first-class status, in: ICSE Workshop on Studies of Software Design, 1993, pp. 17–32.

[5] N. Medvidovic, E.M. Dashofy, R.N. Taylor, The role of middleware in architecture-based software development, Int. J. Softw. Eng. Knowl. Eng. 13 (4) (2003) 367–393.

[6] E.M. Clarke, J.M. Wing, Formal methods: state of the art and future directions, ACM Comput. Surv. 28 (4) (1996) 626–643.

[7] T. Berners-Lee, J. Hendler, O. Lassila, The semantic web, Sci. Am. 284 (5) (2001) 28–37.

[8] T.R. Gruber, A translation approach to portable ontology specifications, Knowl. Acquis. 5 (2) (1993) 199–220. http://dx.doi.org/10.1006/knac.1993.1008.

[9] S.A. McIlraith, T.C. Son, H. Zeng, Semantic web services, IEEE Intell. Syst. 16 (2) (2001) 46–53.

[10] R.N. Taylor, N. Medvidovic, E.M. Dashofy, Software Architecture: Foundations, Theory, and Practice, Wiley, Hoboken, NJ, 2009.

[11] D. Garlan, R. Allen, J. Ockerbloom, Architectural mismatch or why it's hard to build systems out of existing parts, in: Proceedings of the 17th International Conference on Software Engineering, ICSE, 1995, pp. 179–185.

[12] B. Spitznagel, D. Garlan, A compositional formalization of connector wrappers, in: Proceedings of the 25th International Conference on Software Engineering, ICSE, 2003, pp. 374–384.

[13] P. Inverardi, M. Tivoli, Automatic synthesis of modular connectors via composition of protocol mediation patterns, in: Proceedings of the 35th International Conference on Software Engineering, ICSE, 2013, pp. 3–12.

[14] H. Chang, L. Mariani, M. Pezzè, In-field healing of integration problems with COTS components, in: Proceedings of the International Conference on Software Engineering, ICSE, 2009, pp. 166–176.

[15] G. Denaro, M. Pezzè, D. Tosi, Ensuring interoperable service-oriented systems through engineered self-healing, in: Proceedings of the 7th joint meeting of the European Software Engineering Conference and the ACM SIGSOFT International Symposium on Foundations of Software Engineering, ESEC/SIGSOFT FSE, 2009, pp. 253–262.

[16] V. Issarny, M. Caporuscio, N. Georgantas, A perspective on the future of middleware-based software engineering, in: Proceedings of the Workshop on the Future of Software Engineering, FOSE, 2007, pp. 244–258.

[17] G.F. Coulouris, J. Dollimore, T. Kindberg, G. Blair, Distributed Systems: Concepts and Design, fifth, Addison-Wesley Longman, Reading, MA, 2012.

[18] N.R. Mehta, N. Medvidovic, S. Phadke, Towards a taxonomy of software connectors, in: Proceedings of International Conference on Software Engineering, ICSE, 2000.

[19] G. Blair, M. Paolucci, P. Grace, N. Georgantas, Interoperability in complex distributed systems, in: M. Bernardo, V. Issarny (Eds.), SFM-11: 11th International School on Formal Methods for the Design of Computer, Communication and Software Systems—Connectors for Eternal Networked Software Systems, Springer Verlag, New York, 2011, pp. 1–26.

[20] T. Vergnaud, J. Hugues, L. Pautet, F. Kordon, PolyORB: a schizophrenic middleware to build versatile reliable distributed applications, in: Proceedings of the Ninth International Conference on Reliable Software Technologies Reliable Software Technologies, Ada-Europe, 2004, pp. 106–119.

[21] P. Grace, G.S. Blair, S. Samuel, ReMMoC: a reflective middleware to support mobile client interoperability, in: Proceedings of the OTM Confederated International Conferences CoopIS/DOA/ODBASE, 2003, pp. 1170–1187.

[22] Y.-D. Bromberg, L. Réveillère, J.L. Lawall, G. Muller, Automatic generation of network protocol gateways, in: Proceedings of Middleware, 2009, pp. 21–41.

[23] Y.-D. Bromberg, P. Grace, L. Réveillère, Starlink: runtime interoperability between heterogeneous middleware protocols, in: International Conference on Distributed Computing Systems, ICDCS, 2011, pp. 446–455.

[24] N. Georgantas, V. Issarny, S. Ben Mokhtar, Y.-D. Bromberg, S. Bianco, G. Thomson, P.-G. Raverdy, A. Urbieta, R.S. Cardoso, Middleware architecture for ambient intelligence in the networked home, in: H. Nakashima, H. Aghajan, J. Augusto (Eds.), Handbook of Ambient Intelligence and Smart Environments, Springer, New York, 2010, pp. 1139–1169.

[25] F. Menge, Enterprise service bus, in: Proceedings of the Free and Open Source Software Conference, 2007.

[26] H.R.M. Nezhad, B. Benatallah, F. Casati, F. Toumani, Web Services Interoperability Specifications, IEEE Comput. 39 (5) (2006) 24–32.

[27] M. Ceriotti, A.L. Murphy, G.P. Picco, Data sharing vs. message passing: synergy or incompatibility? An implementation-driven case study, in: Proceedings of the ACM Symposium on Applied Computing, SAC, 2008, pp. 100–107.

[28] K.L. Calvert, S.S. Lam, Deriving a protocol converter: a top-down method, in: Proceedings of the Symposium on Communications Architectures & Protocols, SIGCOMM, 1989, pp. 247–258.

[29] P. Bertoli, M. Pistore, P. Traverso, Automated composition of Web services via planning in asynchronous domains, Artif. Intell. 174 (3-4) (2010) 316–361.

[30] C. Gierds, A.J. Mooij, K. Wolf, Reducing adapter synthesis to controller synthesis, IEEE Trans. Serv. Comput. 5 (1) (2012) 72–85.

[31] S.S. Lam, Protocol conversion, IEEE Trans. Softw. Eng. 14 (3) (1988) 353–362.

[32] D.M. Yellin, R.E. Strom, Protocol specifications and component adaptors, ACM Trans. Program. Lang. Syst. 19 (2) (1997) 292–333.

[33] R. Mateescu, P. Poizat, G. Salaün, Adaptation of service protocols using process algebra and on-the-fly reduction techniques, IEEE Trans. Softw. Eng. 38 (4) (2012) 755–777.

[34] H.R.M. Nezhad, B. Benatallah, A. Martens, F. Curbera, F. Casati, Semi-automated adaptation of service interactions, in: Proceedings of the 16th International Conference on World Wide Web, WWW, 2007, pp. 993–1002.

[35] H.R.M. Nezhad, G.Y. Xu, B. Benatallah, Protocol-aware matching of web service interfaces for adapter development, in: Proceedings of the 19th International Conference on World Wide Web, WWW, 2010.

[36] T. Gruber, Ontology, in: L. Liu, M.T. Özsu (Eds.), Encyclopedia of Database Systems, Springer, New York, 2009, pp. 1963–1965.

[37] P. Shvaiko, J. Euzenat, A survey of schema-based matching approaches, J. Data Semant. 4 (2005) 146–171.

[38] D.L. Martin, M.H. Burstein, D.V. McDermott, S.A. McIlraith, M. Paolucci, K.P. Sycara, D. L. McGuinness, E. Sirin, N. Srinivasan, Bringing semantics to web services with OWL-S, in: Proceedings of the World Wide Web Conference, WWW '07, 2007, pp. 243–277.

[39] E. Cimpian, A. Mocan, WSMX process mediation based on choreographies, in: Proceedings of Business Process Management Workshop, 2005, pp. 130–143.

[40] M.H. Burstein, J.R. Hobbs, O. Lassila, D.L. Martin, D.V. McDermott, S.A. McIlraith, S. Narayanan, M. Paolucci, T.R. Payne, K.P. Sycara, DAML-S: web service description for the semantic web, in: Proceedings of International Semantic Web Conference, ISWC, 2002, pp. 348–363.

[41] M. Paolucci, T. Kawamura, T.R. Payne, K.P. Sycara, Semantic matching of web services capabilities, in: Proceedings of the First International Semantic Web Conference, ISWC, 2002.

[42] R. Vaculín, R. Neruda, K.P. Sycara, The process mediation framework for semantic web services, IJAOSE: Int. J. Agent-Oriented Softw. Eng. 3 (1) (2009) 27–58.

[43] J. Kopecký, T. Vitvar, C. Bournez, J. Farrell, SAWSDL: semantic annotations for WSDL and XML schema, IEEE Internet Comput. 11 (6) (2007) 60–67.

[44] W. Zhu, Semantic mediation bus: an ontology-based runtime infrastructure for service interoperability, in: Proceedings of the 16th International on Enterprise Distributed Object Computing Conference Workshops, EDOCW, 2012, pp. 140–145.

[45] R. Allen, D. Garlan, A formal basis for architectural connection, ACM Trans. Softw. Eng. Methodol. 6 (3) (1997) 213–249.

[46] A. Bennaceur, V. Issarny, Automated Synthesis of Mediators to Support Component Interoperability, IEEE Trans. Softw. Eng. 41 (3) (2015) 221–240. http://dx.doi.org/10.1109/TSE.2014.2364844.

[47] M. Jackson, P. Zave, Deriving specifications from requirements: an example, in: Proceedings of the 17th International Conference on Software Engineering, ICSE, 1995, pp. 15–24.

[48] N. D'Ippolito, V.A. Braberman, J. Kramer, J. Magee, D. Sykes, S. Uchitel, Hope for the best, prepare for the worst: multi-tier control for adaptive systems, in: Proceedings of the 36th International Conference on Software Engineering, ICSE, 2014, pp. 688–699.

[49] A. van Lamsweerde, Requirements Engineering: From System Goals to UML Models to Software Specifications, Wiley, Hoboken, NJ, 2009.

[50] E.S.K. Yu, Towards modeling and reasoning support for early-phase requirements engineering, in: Proceedings of the Third IEEE International Symposium on Requirements Engineering, RE, 1997, pp. 226–235.

[51] A. Pnueli, The temporal logic of programs, in: Proceedings of the 18th Annual Symposium on Foundations of Computer Science, 1977, pp. 46–57. http://dx.doi.org/10.1109/SFCS.1977.32.

[52] L. Cavallaro, P. Sawyer, D. Sykes, N. Bencomo, V. Issarny, Satisfying requirements for pervasive service compositions, in: Proceedings of the Seventh Workshop on Models@run.time, 2012, pp. 17–22.

[53] E. Letier, W. Heaven, Requirements modelling by synthesis of deontic input-output automata, in: Proceedings of the 35th International Conference on Software Engineering, ICSE '13, San Francisco, CA, USA, May 18–26, 2013, 2013, pp. 592–601. http://dl.acm.org/citation.cfm?id=2486866.

[54] C.B. Haley, R.C. Laney, J.D. Moffett, B. Nuseibeh, Security requirements engineering: a framework for representation and analysis, IEEE Trans. Softw. Eng. 34 (1) (2008) 133–153.

[55] E. Yuan, N. Esfahani, S. Malek, A systematic survey of self-protecting software systems, TAAS: ACM Trans. Auton. Adapt. Syst. 8 (4) (2014).

[56] M. Salehie, L. Pasquale, I. Omoronyia, R. Ali, B. Nuseibeh, Requirements-driven adaptive security: protecting variable assets at runtime, in: Proceedings of the 20th IEEE International Requirements Engineering Conference, RE, 2012, pp. 111–120.

[57] A. Bennaceur, A.K. Bandara, M. Jackson, W. Liu, L. Montrieux, T.T. Tun, Y. Yu, B. Nuseibeh, Requirements-driven mediation for collaborative security, in: Proceedings of the Ninth International Symposium on Software Engineering for Adaptive and Self-Managing Systems, SEAMS, 2014, pp. 37–42.

QUALITY ASSURANCE IN SELF-ADAPTIVE SOFTWARE ARCHITECTURES

AN OVERVIEW ON QUALITY EVALUATION OF SELF-ADAPTIVE SYSTEMS

C. Raibulet*, F. Arcelli Fontana*, R. Capilla[†], C. Carrillo[‡]

University of Milano-Bicocca, Milan, Italy[*] Rey Juan Carlos University, Madrid, Spain[†] Polytechnic University of Madrid, Madrid, Spain[‡]

13.1 INTRODUCTION

As software systems are becoming more complex and configurable, self-properties (i.e., self-adaptive, self-management, self-healing, self-optimization, self-protection) have attracted the attention of software engineers to provide adequate validation and verification mechanisms in order to ensure the quality of adaptation [1,2]. In this light, the software engineering discipline has established in time several mechanisms and standards to evaluate the quality of systems from architecture design to implemented solutions. Qualities and Quality in Use are described by the ISO/IEC 25010/2011 standard[1] to provide a consistent terminology to measure and evaluate software product quality. Software quality can be measured at various levels and stages of the software development process, from architecture to code, and it is particularly suited for software-intensive systems. As the evaluation of the quality properties differ in architecture and code and even when the system is running, various evaluation methods and techniques may be used. For instance, the software architecture field has proposed and used a number of quality attribute evaluation methods [3] to evaluate the quality of the architecture in the early stages of the design process; or, a wide range of metrics have been proposed for a qualitative or quantitative evaluation of software.

Nowadays, many modern systems exploit context and ubiquitous properties to adapt their behavior when context changes. In other cases, systems exhibit self-adaptive capabilities to provide autonomous behavior where a runtime manager executes adaptation policies and algorithms based on the information sensed from the environment. Consequently, stringent quality requirements like performance and optimization are expected to be implemented in the architecture and software of such systems. From the perspective of self-adaptive systems that demand a continuous evolution of the adaptation capabilities and that aim to ensure the quality of the performed runtime reconfiguration tasks, there is a clear need to monitor and evaluate the quality of the adaptations and modified behavior. Consequently, this dynamic

---

[1]Systems and software engineering—Systems and software Quality Requirements and Evaluation (SQuaRE)—System and software quality models.

evolution of self-adaptations must be supported by an evaluation of the quality of the adaptations and the success of the runtime changes.

The evaluation and continuous monitoring driving the evolution of self-adaptive systems is difficult as specific metrics are needed to measure the quality of the adaptations accordingly to the variety of self-adaptive systems and runtime needs. Moreover, often it is necessary to evaluate at design time the degree of adaptivity of the self-adaptive system's architecture and self-adaptive properties. Further, it seems necessary to count and identify which concrete metrics provide good evaluation indicators that software engineers may use to test the adequacy of a particular adaptivity mechanism or solution and also, to avoid mismatch problems between architecture and code. While evaluating adaptivity at design time concerns more the specific architectural solution that supports adaptation and self-adaptation in a software system, the evaluation of self-adaptive properties at runtime is closely related to metrics aimed to provide qualitative and quantitative evaluation of the software.

In this chapter we aim to identify general guidelines for the evaluation of self-adaptive systems independent of their type, application domain, or implementation details. To achieve this objective, we propose a taxonomy for the evaluation of the quality of self-adaptive systems based on five dimensions: scope, time, mechanisms, perspective, and type. Further, we identify and describe briefly the main available evaluation approaches and analyze them based on the proposed taxonomy. We describe the evaluation approaches in a common and uniform way in order to be able to easily compare them based on their commonalities and differences. We also discuss several trade-offs concerning each dimension in the proposed taxonomy, trade-offs which should be addressed during the evaluation.

The remainder of this chapter is organized as follows. Section 13.2 describes different points of view to categorize the evaluation of self-adaptive systems and proposes a taxonomy based on five dimensions. In Section 13.3, we describe three evaluation approaches which are based on quality attributes, while in Section 13.4, three evaluation approaches which are based on software metrics. Sections 13.3 and 13.4 end with the analysis of the presented approaches and the related findings. In Section 13.5, we address various trade-offs in the evaluation of self-adaptive systems based on the five dimensions of the taxonomy introduced in Section 13.2. Finally, in Section 13.6 we draw the conclusions and future work.

13.2 EVALUATION OF SELF-ADAPTIVE SYSTEMS

The evaluation approaches for self-adaptive systems proposed so far in the scientific literature may be analyzed from various points of view. Assuming any self-adaptive system is composed of a managed system (which implements the system's functionality) and a managing system (the controller, which implements the self-adaptive functionality), such as Fig. 13.1 shows, we categorize the evaluation approaches for self-adaptive systems in the following two main groups based on their scope:

FIG. 13.1

The managed and managing systems in self-adaptive systems.

1. *Evaluation of the managing system*: The first group concerns the evaluation of the quality of the self-adaptive mechanisms (i.e., the managing part or the controller). This group focuses on self-adaptive mechanisms and on the performance that must be addressed in the early stages of the development process. In this category, the quality of the design influences significantly the overall quality and performance of the self-adaptive system.
2. *Evaluation of the managed system*: The second group pertains to the evaluation of the qualities of a self-adaptive system (i.e., the managed system), often focused on the performance achieved through self-adaptivity. It concerns those quality issues that are measured at runtime during the execution of a system

Furthermore, the evaluation mechanisms of self-adaptive systems may rely on:

(i) *quality attributes*, used to evaluate the quality of a system or part of it, with special focus on those quality properties meaningful for self-adaptive systems (e.g., performance, optimization); and
(ii) *software metrics*, used to evaluate the quality of the adaptation from a local (e.g., adaptivity of a service or agent) or global perspective (e.g., time for adaptation, decentralization degree).

While quality attributes are used for the evaluation of the self-adaptive architecture and system in the early stages of the development process, software metrics provide valuable measures to estimate how good the system performs the runtime adaptations. Metrics are particularly useful for continuous monitoring and evolution of self-adaptive systems. Therefore, we believe there are two important stages where adaptivity and the adaptation mechanisms used can and should be evaluated, that is:

(i) at *design time* during the development of the system when the adaption mechanism is selected; and
(ii) at *runtime* when the system is in fully operationally mode and the quality of adaptations must be continuously monitored.

Moreover, we state that the evaluation mechanisms may interest the entire system (i.e., *global* scope) or a subset of it (i.e., *local* scope), as the objectives of the adaptations may be different in terms of goal and scope.

Last, the evaluation of self-adaptive systems may have *qualitative* or *quantitative* results. Quality attributes offer usually qualitative information about a system. Software metrics may provide both qualitative and quantitative feedback about a system.

The criteria discussed in this section are summarized in Fig. 13.2 in a form of an essential taxonomy for the evaluation of self-adaptive systems. We consider these criteria as key aspects for the evaluation of any kind of self-adaptive system in any application domain. They help software engineers to identify the objectives of the evaluation and the mechanisms necessary to perform the evaluation, as well as to guide the interpretation of the results.

13.2.1 PRESENTATION OF THE AVAILABLE EVALUATION APPROACHES

In this chapter we provide an overview of several approaches for the evaluation of self-adaptive systems available in the scientific literature. We have grouped them based on the evaluation mechanisms they use: quality attributes and software metrics. We have chosen this criterion because it matches best the description of each approach with the presentation provided by its authors and because it enables us to describe each approach only once. The other four criteria do not allow us to easily divide the

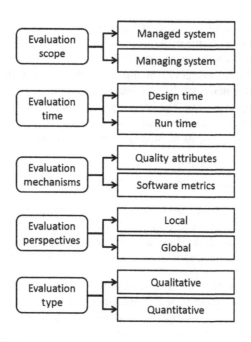

FIG.13.2

A taxonomy for the evaluation of self-adaptive systems.

considered approaches in disjoint groups. Further, we describe the approaches belonging to each group through the main elements of the taxonomy proposed in this section.

13.2.2 SELECTION OF THE AVAILABLE EVALUATION APPROACHES

The selection of the evaluation approaches described in this chapter considers the following premises. Our objective in this chapter is to offer general, but well defined guidelines for the evaluation of self-adaptive systems by inspiring us from the available evaluation approaches. Hence, we tried to identify the available evaluation approaches for self-adaptive systems and to capture their commonalities and differences. This step is hardly achievable through a systematic mapping or review [4] due to the keywords which should be searched (e.g., evaluation, adaptivity, quality, metric) and which are present in many papers and thus provide mostly false positives. As observed also by Brun [5] most of the studies on self-adaptivity are published in specialized venues on self-adaptivity (e.g., ACM Transactions on Autonomous and Adaptive Systems, Software Engineering for Adaptive and Self-Managing Systems) rather than on general software engineering venues (e.g., Transactions on Software Engineering, International Conference on Software Engineering). Therefore, we have investigated all the papers published in the specialized venues to identify those dealing with the evaluation of self-adaptive systems in general independently of the application domain or case study. In this way we have identified four primary studies: three using quality attributes and one using metrics as evaluation mechanisms. Further, we have added two journal papers, which have been published in other venues not focused on adaptivity, but on software engineering in general.

13.3 EVALUATION BASED ON QUALITY ATTRIBUTES

This section presents three evaluation approaches based on quality attributes. McCann and Huebscher [6] focus on the evaluation issues in autonomic computing. Neti and Müller [7] propose the use of quality attributes for the evaluation of self-healing systems. Villegas et al. [8] exploit quality attributes for the evaluation of self-adaptive systems.

Each approach is presented through a brief description which aims to capture the aspects proposed in Fig. 13.2. Further, the description of each approach is summarized in a table which indicates: what is evaluated, i.e., the quality attributes considered in the evaluation, the objectives of the evaluation, i.e., what is expected from the evaluation, the evaluation perspective, the evaluation time, and the evaluation scope (mentioned in Fig. 13.2). The section ends with the findings concerning the described approaches where we summarize the case study considered by the authors of each approach to validate their proposal, the tool support for the evaluation, and the evaluation type (mentioned in Fig. 13.2).

13.3.1 EVALUATION IN AUTONOMIC SYSTEMS

McCann and Huebscher [6] propose nine perspectives (called metrics by the authors) for the evaluation issues in autonomic computing: quality of service, cost, granularity/flexibility, failure avoidance (robustness), degree of autonomy, adaptivity, time to adapt and reaction time, sensitivity, and stabilization (see Table 13.1). The objectives of these perspectives are the evaluation of the autonomicity of software systems by focusing on their performances. This paper provides only hints on how these perspectives may be measured and only some metrics examples which may be used to measure these aspects (see column Metrics in Table 13.1). Further, there are perspectives which cannot be measured immediately, but statistically in time (e.g., people costs in terms of system administration and maintenance). The authors mention that the metrics to be actually applied to a system depend strongly on the application domain, the adaptation goals, and design choices.

These nine perspectives have been identified after the analysis of various self-adaptive solutions, which have been divided in three groups: multi-agent based systems, architecture design-based autonomic systems, and hot swapping components. McCann and Huebscher have tried to identify the commonalities among the analyzed systems and to provide evaluation basis independent of a specific solution or application domain. However, McCann and Huebscher do not describe further the application of the identified perspectives on an actual case study. In Section 13.6, the authors mention that they evaluated Kendra architecture considering some of the quality attributes described in their paper. The evaluation has been a qualitative one with no concrete quantifiable results. No further details are presented; hence we cannot consider this evaluation as a well-described case study. Furthermore, no tool support for the evaluation of self-adaptive systems using these perspectives is mentioned.

From Table 13.1, it results that McCann and Huebscher identify meaningful high-level perspectives for the evaluation of autonomic system. The authors do not mention if these perspectives represent a minimum or complete list. Further, they fail in providing a set of metrics for the evaluation and comparison between autonomic systems. Quality of services, granularity/flexibility, and adaptivity are three perspectives which concern the performances of the managed system. Failure avoidance/robustness, degree of autonomy, and sensitivity concern the self-adaptive mechanisms implemented by a system. The remaining three perspectives involve both the managed system and the self-adaptive mechanisms. Furthermore, all the proposed perspectives are presented by the authors as runtime

Table 13.1 Quality Evaluation in Autonomic Systems

What Is Evaluated	Objective	Metrics	Evaluation Perspective	Evaluation Time	Evaluation Scope
Quality of service	The degree to which the system reaches its goals (e.g., performance improvement, user experience improvement)	Data delivery turn-around time over cost	Global Local	Runtime	Managed system
Cost	The ability to reach a goal / The amount of communication, actions performed, and cost of actions to perform a goal	Cost per performance / Added functionality achievable otherwise not achievable in a nonautonomic system / Cost of extra hardware for the controller / Resource consumption (e.g., battery power in ubiquitous systems)	Global Local	Runtime Design	Managed system Managing system
Granularity/flexibility	The granularity of autonomicity (fine-grained vs. coarse-grained components)	Unbinding, loading, rebinding a component	Global	Runtime Design	Managed system
Failure avoidance/robustness	The ability to cope with failures	Predictability of failures / Mean time before failure	Global	Runtime	Managing system
Degree of autonomy	The ability to be autonomous (e.g., including the ability to learn)	Degree of proactivity	Global	Runtime	Managing system
Adaptivity	The ability to change something (a parameter, a component) in a system	Time needed to change something	Local	Runtime	Managed system
Time to adapt/reaction time	The reconfiguration and adaptation ability of a system / Time to adapt is the time needed to adapt to a change in the environment (between the identification of a change need and the adaptation performed) / Reaction time includes the change occurred in the environment and the time to adapt	Time to adapt/reaction time	Global	Runtime	Managed system Managing system
Sensitivity	The ability to fit with the environment (the ability to notice changes in the environment)	Variations in the environment (e.g., bandwidth)	Global	Runtime	Managing system
Stabilization	The time needed by a system to learn its environment and stabilize its operations	Time taken for the system to learn its environment and stabilize its operations	Global	Runtime	Managed system Managing system

aspects which are measured during the execution of a system. However, several aspects such as cost or granularity/flexibility may be considered also during the design time (e.g., development cost or number of fine-grained or coarse-grained elements).

13.3.2 QUALITY-DRIVEN EVALUATION OF SELF-HEALING SYSTEMS

Neti and Müller [7] propose a subset of traditional quality attributes and a subset of new quality attributes called autonomic-specific quality attributes for self-healing systems focusing on their adaptivity capabilities over long periods of time. Traditional quality attributes based on ISO 9126 exploited in this approach concern maintainability (including modifiability and extensibility) and reliability (including fault-tolerance and robustness). Also availability and survivability are mentioned in the paper, but no further details are presented. Autonomic-specific quality attributes are: support for detecting anomalous system behavior, support for failure diagnosis, support for simulation of expected and predicted behavior, support for differencing between expected and actual behavior, and support for testing of correct behavior (see Table 13.2).

Neti and Müller use a self-managing Java server as a case study for the validation of their proposal. In this case study, the authors consider the following quality attributes: modifiability, support for detecting anomalous system behavior, and support for failure diagnosis. No tool support is mentioned by the authors for the evaluation of these quality attributes.

From Table 13.2 it results that maybe self-adaptive systems need specific quality attributes for their evaluation in addition to the quality attributes defined for traditional software systems. Almost all the quality attributes have a global scope and are exploited to evaluate a system at runtime, during its execution. As stated by [6], the quality attributes are balanced and concern both the managing and the managed systems. Note that no metrics are indicated for the evaluation of self-healing systems by Neti and Müller.

13.3.3 QUALITY-DRIVEN EVALUATION OF SELF-ADAPTIVE SYSTEMS

Villegas et al. [8] propose a quality-driven framework for the evaluation of self-adaptive systems. First, the authors identify a set of analysis dimensions which characterize self-adaptive systems: adaptation goal, reference inputs, measured outputs, computed control actions, system structure, observable adaptation properties, proposed evaluation, and identified metrics. These dimensions have been used to analyze several existing self-adaptive systems. Further, the authors propose four quality attributes which reflect the adaptation goals of self-adaptive systems: performance, dependability, security, and safety. These quality attributes are associated to the adaptation properties of self-adaptive systems. An adaptation property indicates a quality (or characteristic) that is particular to an adaptation approach or mechanism. Adaptation properties for the managing system include: stability, accuracy, settling-time, small-overshot, robustness, termination, consistence, scalability, and security. Adaptation properties for the managed system include behavioral/functional invariants and quality of service (i.e., performance, dependability, security, and safety). Like in the approach provided by McCann and Huebscher, Villegas et al. analyze 16 research solutions for self-adaptive systems in order to identify the quality attributes meaningful for the evaluation of self-adaptive systems. This approach does not describe the application of the identified quality attributes on an actual case study. Neither does it mention tool support for the evaluation of self-adaptive systems through these perspectives.

Table 13.2 Quality Criteria for the Evaluation of Self-Healing Systems

What Is Evaluated	Objective	Metrics	Evaluation Perspective	Evaluation Time	Evaluation Scope
Maintainability	Defined through modifiability and extensibility	N/A	Global	Design	Managed system Managing system
Reliability	Defined through fault-tolerance and robustness	N/A	Global	Runtime	Managed system
Support for detecting anomalous behavior Depends on awareness, observability, and coupling	The ability to monitor, recognize, and address anomalies	N/A	Global	Runtime	Managing system
Support for failure diagnosis Depends on complexity	The ability to locate the source of failure, system degradation or changes	N/A	Global	Runtime	Managing system
Support for simulation of expected or predicted behavior Depends on awareness, correctness, completeness, consistency, and complexity	The ability to accurately model the system and obtain the expected behavior	N/A	Global	Runtime	Managed system Managing system
Support for differencing between expected and actual behavior Depends on the support for simulation of expected or predicted behavior	The ability to detect if the actual behavior differs from its expected behavior	N/A	Global	Runtime	Managed system Managing system
Support for testing of correct behavior Depends on testability	The ability to test and verify that autonomic elements behave correctly	N/A	Local	Runtime	Managing system

Table 13.3 summarizes the information concerning the evaluation framework. From the description of the approach it does not result whether the identified quality attributes form a minimum or complete set of aspects to be considered for the evaluation of self-adaptive systems. Examples of metrics for the evaluation of the quality attributes are also indicated by the authors. However, they fail in providing a complete set of metrics for the evaluation and comparison among autonomic systems. All the quality

Table 13.3 Quality-Driven Evaluation of Self-Adaptive Systems

What Is Evaluated	Objective	Metrics	Evaluation Perspective	Evaluation Time	Evaluation Scope
Performance	Characterizes the timeliness of services delivered by the system	Responsiveness Latency Throughput Capacity	Global	Runtime	Managed system Managing system
Dependability	Defines the level of reliance on the services provided by a system	Availability Reliability Maintainability Safety Confidentiality Integrity	Global	Runtime	Managed system Managing system
Security	Defines the level of security of the system	Confidentiality Integrity Availability	Global	Runtime	Managed system Managing system
Safety	Defines the level of reliance of the system	Interaction complexity Coupling strength	Global	Runtime	Managed system Managing system

attributes are exploited at runtime and concern both the managing and the managed parts of a self-adaptive system.

Geihs [9] exploits the quality-driven framework proposed by Villegas et al. to evaluate three self-adaptive systems from different application domains: ubiquitous computing, autonomous mobile robots, and service-oriented software. He reports that the role of the four proposed quality attributes is not obvious in the evaluation of self-adaptive systems as the adaptation properties should be directly mapped on meaningful metrics, and the use of quality attributes may be avoided. He also states that the framework does not capture the control aspects of the self-adaptive mechanisms (i.e., centralized vs. decentralized adaptation control), which play an important role in the self-adaptive systems [1].

13.3.4 FINDINGS

From our analysis and observations of the quality attributes evaluation approaches for the three types of self-adaptive systems we summarize the following findings. The quality attributes in the "What is evaluated" column of Tables 13.1–13.3 occur just once. Hence, the sets of the quality attributes proposed in the three approaches seem to be totally disjoint. This conclusion may be due to several facts. First, the approaches consider a different granularity of the target systems: autonomic, self-healing, and self-adaptive. While self-healing is considered a property of autonomic computing, self-adaptivity has a more general meaning and may be mapped on one or more properties of autonomic computing.

Second, there is little agreement in the scientific literature on what should be evaluated in self-adaptive systems, and specifically which quality attributes are meaningful for their evaluation. Furthermore, [7] addresses the evaluation of a specific subset of self-adaptive systems (i.e., self-healing systems), while [8] addresses the evaluation of self-adaptive system in general, but they have nothing in common (even if they have one author in common). We expected the quality attributes proposed in [7] (or at least part of them) to be a subset of the quality attributes proposed in [8].

Third, another explanation of this difference among the three approaches may be due to the terminology used for their description. From a deeper analysis it results that quality of service, time to adapt, and reaction time in Table 13.1 have a similar meaning to performance in Table 13.3. In addition, failure avoidance/robustness in Table 13.1 may be mapped on autonomic-specific quality attributes (introduced by Neti and Müller) in Table 13.2 and on dependability in Table 13.3. Alternatively, reliability in Table 13.2 may be mapped on dependability and safety in Table 13.3. Hence, commonalities do exist among the three approaches, even if they have some subtle differences. The works described in [6,8] are the results of the analysis of various self-adaptive solutions available in various application domains. Reference [7] has been inspired by the work presented in [10].

From the point of view of the evaluation scope we notice that all the three approaches consider both the managed and the managing parts of a self-adaptive system. This confirms the hypothesis that in a self-adaptive system both parts are fundamental to ensure its quality. Further, we observe that the evaluation time of most of the quality attribute is runtime, i.e., 19 out of 20 quality attributes in the three tables are evaluated at runtime, 1 out of 20 at design time, and 2 out of 20 at design time and runtime. The evaluation perspective is mostly global, i.e., 18 out of 20 quality attributes have a global perspective, 2 out of 20 a local perspective, and 2 out of 20 may have a local and a global perspective. Table 13.4 summarizes three aspects of these evaluation approaches: case studies on which each approach has been applied by the authors, tool support provided by the authors of the approach, and evaluation computation type on a real example.

We remark that only [8] has been applied on a case study (i.e., a self-managed Java server) by their authors. However, the authors provide minimal details on how quality attributes have been exploited and further analyzed and interpreted. As noticed in Section 13.3.1 McCann and Huebscher [6] mentioned that they applied the identified quality attributes to the Kendra architecture, without providing any detail. Hence, we do not consider it as a case study. We also observed none of the approaches has associated a tool which may hamper the evaluation part.

13.4 EVALUATION BASED ON SOFTWARE METRICS

This section presents three evaluation approaches based on software metrics. Reinecke et al. [11] propose a methodology for the definition of one metric, which can be exploited at runtime to measure the benefits of adaptivity. This metric focuses on the behavioral advantages obtained through

Table 13.4 Summary of the Quality Attribute Based Approaches Considering Their Actual Application

Approach	Case Study	Tool Support	Evaluation Type
McCann and Huebscher [6]	N/A	N/A	N/A
Neti and Müller [7]	A self-managing Java server	N/A	Qualitative
Villegas et al. [8]	N/A	N/A	N/A

self-adaptivity. Kaddoum et al. [12] introduce a set of criteria and software metrics for the evaluation of the self-adaptive systems and their development effort. These metrics focus both on the design and the execution issues in self-adaptive systems. Perez-Palacin et al. [13] introduce software metrics for the evaluation of the adaptability at the architectural level at design time.

Each approach is presented through a brief description which aims to capture the aspects proposed in Fig. 13.2. Further, the description of each approach is summarized in a table which indicates: the name of the metrics, a brief definition for each metric, the computation formula for each metric, the possible range of values, and meaningful observations. The last three columns of each table indicate the evaluation perspective, time, and scope (mentioned in Fig. 13.2).

There are other evaluation approaches based on software metrics in the scientific literature that are not detailed in this section because they have a narrow scope rather than a general purpose. Among these approaches we cite: [14], which evaluates the effectiveness of the Rainbow framework for the development of self-adaptive systems; [15], which identifies the metrics for the performance evaluation in server applications; [16], which focuses on hypermedia systems; [17], which evaluates the complexity of the interaction between users and a self-adaptive system; [18], which introduces three indexes of adaptability at the architectural level. The indexes proposed in [18] are the main inspiration for the software metrics defined in [13] and described in Section 13.4.3.

13.4.1 EVALUATING THE ADAPTIVITY OF COMPUTING SYSTEMS

Reinecke et al. [11] propose a framework and a methodology for the definition of an adaptivity metric (see Table 13.5) through which it is possible to compare systems with respect to their adaptivity. The adaptivity metric is independent of the specifics of the adaptive system, is focused on the behavior of the adaptive system, and provides a quantitative evaluation of the system's adaptivity.

The recipe for defining an adaptive metric consists of the following four steps. First, it is required to identify the system under analysis, its execution environment, and the tasks performed by the adaptive system useful for its clients. Second, it is required to define one or more performance metrics (M) for the tasks implemented by the adaptive system. These performance metrics reflect the usefulness of the adaptive system and they must be measurable by the clients of the adaptive system. Third, it is required to define a payoff metric (P), which captures the usefulness of the adaptive system in a real-valued scalar normalized [0, 1] (i.e., $0 =$ worse case, $1 =$ optimal case). Last, it is required to execute the system and compute the payoff metric and the adaptivity metric.

The authors of the adaptivity metric validate the last through a case study concerning a Web Services Reliable Messaging system, which provides reliable message transports in Web-Services-based service-oriented architectures. The authors have implemented a custom test-bed for this case study. The performance metrics considered in this case study are: the effective transmission time, the unnecessary resource consumption, and savings. No general-purpose tool is provided for the computation of the adaptivity metric, due to the fact that the performance metrics may be different from case study to case study or may be the same for all the case studies which should be compared among them. Note that the proposed metrics are focused on the managed system. Finally, Reinecke et al. mention (without extending the idea) that the quality of the self-adaptive mechanisms (i.e., of the controller) may be evaluated through the Stability, Accuracy, Settling time, and Overshoot (SASO) properties, as sustained also by Villegas et al. Reinecke et al. [11] compare their solution for adaptivity evaluation with architectural or qualitative based approaches. Essentially, the authors sustain that the last approaches do not enable a

Table 13.5 The Adaptivity Metric

Name	Definition	Formula	Values	Observations	Evaluation Perspective	Evaluation Time	Evaluation Scope
Adaptivity metric	Measures how close the benefit accumulated by a system is to that of the optimal system	$$Ad = \frac{\sum_i \Delta i + \sum_i Pi}{\sum_i Pi}$$ where: Δi denotes the benefit of a positive decision of the adaptive system at the ith iteration: $$\Delta i = \frac{Pi + Pi - 1}{2}$$ P is a payoff metric computed as follows during the ith trial: $P : M1 \times M2 \times \ldots \times Mn \to [0, 1]$	$Ad \in Q[0, 1]$	The adaptation process is considered as a sequence of trials It is supposed that the adaptive system has several iterations in time during which it may take positive, neutral, or negative decisions (when the observable performances of the adaptive systems decrease)	Global	Runtime	Managed system

straightforward comparison between self-adaptive systems. In addition, it is difficult to measure architectural aspects, which are not easily observable in a system, being hidden or spread in the entire system.

13.4.2 CRITERIA AND METRICS FOR EVALUATING SELF-ADAPTIVE SYSTEMS

Kaddoum et al. propose 31 metrics (see Table 13.6) based on a set of criteria grouped in four categories (methodological, architectural, intrinsic, runtime) [12]. These metrics and criteria may be used in the description, design, and evaluation of self-adaptive systems. The authors focus on various aspects of the design and execution of self-adaptive systems. They sustain that the proposed evaluation metrics and criteria enable the analysis of the quality of the self-adaptive systems, of the development effort, and of the advantages obtained through self-adaptivity. Attention is given to performance, as well as to homeostasis and robustness issues. These metrics and criteria represent a joint evolution of the work described in [19,20].

The proposed criteria are grouped in four categories: methodological, architectural, intrinsic, and runtime. The methodological category of metrics concerns the development approaches for self-adaptive systems at a high level of abstraction. The first 3 metrics in Table 13.6 belong to this category. The architectural related metrics focus on the connection between the managing and the managed systems, and on the growth of the overall system due to the self-adaptive mechanisms. The next 7 metrics in Table 13.6 belong to this category. The intrinsic category captures the complexity of the self-adaptive process. The next 9 metrics in Table 13.6 belong to this category. The authors propose 12 runtime metrics focused mainly on the performance aspects and resource usage. For each metric in Table 13.6 we indicate in the Definition column its category.

Kaddoum et al. consider that usually self-adaptive systems exploit autonomous entities, called agents, to implement the managing system. The global self-adaptive behavior emerges from the local behaviors of the agents and their interactions. Considering agents, the authors capture also the centralized and/or distributed control aspects of the managing system. Further, the metrics introduced by Kaddoum et al. address both endogenous changes, triggered by the entities inside the system, and exogenous changes, triggered by the entities external to the system.

The authors have identified the evaluation criteria and metrics by analyzing several self-adaptive approaches available in the scientific literature. Further, they have investigated the applicability and usability of the proposed metrics on five systems: a web-based client-server and a videoconferencing system proposed by [21], DAMASCOP [22], an adaptive image server [23], and AHA! [24]. The authors list the metrics which are meaningful for the evaluation of each of these systems, without actually computing them. There is no tool made available by the authors to compute the defined metrics.

Kaddoum et al. propose also several hints on how to exploit the proposed criteria and metrics for the comparison among several self-adaptive solutions. The authors sustain that it is very useful to perform both a comparison among several self-adaptive systems by considering several criteria and metrics, as well as a comparison among several self-adaptive systems by considering a single criterion and/or metric at a time.

For a multi-criteria comparison, Kaddoum et al. advice to choose a subset of the proposed metrics, compute them for the systems under analysis, and compare the results considering all the dimensions/objectives/metrics together. To have a complete view of the measured aspects, Kaddoum et al. propose

Table 13.6 Criteria and Software Metrics for the Evaluation of Self-Adaptive Systems

Name	Definition	Formula	Values	Observations	Evaluation Perspective	Evaluation Time	Evaluation Scope
Adaptivity Agent Identification Index (AAII)	Methodological. Identifies the adaptive functionalities of a system	N/A	N/A	Adaptivity is achieved through autonomous agents, hence the identification of the adaptive functionalities is translated into the identification of the autonomous agents	Global	Design	Managed system
Adaptivity Distribution Index (ADI)	Methodological. Indicates the distribution of the adaptive elements on the physical nodes of an adaptive system	N/A	N/A	Provides information on the additional effort that must be done to deploy an adaptive system	Global	Design	Managed system
Genericity Index (GI)	Methodological. Indicates the genericity of an approach for the development of an adaptive system	N/A	N/A	Indicates the effort to adapt an approach to an actual self-adaptive case study	Global	Design	Managed system
Separation of Concerns Index (SCI)	Architectural. Indicates the degree of dependence between the managing and the managed systems	$SCI = \dfrac{\text{Nr of adaptive elements}}{\text{Nr of functional elem dependent on adaptivity}}$	$SCI \in Q$	Informs about the mean utilization of the potential components for each service	Global	Design	Managed system Managing system

Adaptivity Pattern Index (API)	Architectural. Indicates the separation of concerns between the four steps of the MAPE loop at the architectural level	API = Nr of adaptive conceptual elements	$API \in N$	If API is 0 then the managing system is totally integrated with the managed system If API is 4 then the managing system implements the four steps of MAPE	Global	Design	Managing system
Minimum Adaptivity Growth (MAG)	Architectural. Indicates the minimum number of elements needed to make a system adaptive independently of the number of functionalities it provides	MAG = Min nr of elements for adaptivity	$MAG \in N$	Expresses the fixed growth of the managing system at the architectural level	Global	Design	Managing system
Adaptivity Growth per Functionality (AGF)	Architectural. Indicates the number of elements for the ith adaptive functionality	AGF = Nr of elements for the ith functionality	$AGF \in N$	Indicates the variable growth for introducing adaptivity per functionality at the architectural level	Global	Design	Managing system
Overall Adaptivity Growth (OAG)	Architectural. Indicates the architectural growth in number of elements needed by adaptivity	$OAG = MAG + \sum_{i=1}^{n} AGF_i$	$OAG \in N$		Global	Design	Managing system

Continued

Table 13.6 Criteria and Software Metrics for the Evaluation of Self-Adaptive Systems—cont'd

Name	Definition	Formula	Values	Observations	Evaluation Perspective	Evaluation Time	Evaluation Scope
Average Adaptivity Growth (AvgAG)	Architectural. Indicates the average growth per functionality at the architectural level due to adaptivity	$AvgAGF = \dfrac{OAG}{n}$	$AvgAGF \in Q$		Global	Design	Managing system
Growth of Architectural Elements (GAE)	Architectural. Indicates the percentage growth at the architectural level due to adaptivity	$GAE = \dfrac{OAG}{Nr\,of\,functional\,elements} \times 100$	$GAE \in Q$		Global	Design	Managing system
Domain Factors Influencing Adaptivity (DFIA)	Intrinsic. Indicates the number of domain specific factors taken in input by the managing system	$DFIA = $ Nr of input domain factors in the adaptive logic	$DFIA \in N$	Higher is this value, stronger is the influence of the application domain or contextual aspects on the managing system	Global	Design	Managing system
System Factors Influencing Adaptivity (SFIA)	Intrinsic. Indicates the number of domain specific factors taken in input by the managing	$SFIA = $ Nr of input system factors in the adaptive logic	$SFIA \in N$	Higher is this value, stronger is the dependence between the managed and managing systems	Global	Design	Managing system

Metric	Description	Formula	Range	Notes	Scope		
Factors Influencing Adaptivity (FIA)	Intrinsic. Indicates the total number of factors influencing adaptivity	FIA = DFIA + SFIA	FIA ∈ N		Global	Design	Managing system
Local Computational Complexity (LCC)	Intrinsic. Analyzes the local algorithm of each agent in terms of computational power	N/A	N/A		Local	Design	Managing system
Decentralization Degree (DD)	Intrinsic. Indicates the deciding step of the adaptivity	DD = Control distribution between agents	N/A	Indicates how the decision process is distributed among agents and how many agents are involved in	Global	Design	Managing system
Action Locality Index (ALI)	Intrinsic. Studies the strategies of the agents concerning the information and needs	ALI = Repercussions of local action on the rest of the system	N/A		Global	Design	Managing system
Agent Number Influence (ANI)	Intrinsic. Indicates how efficiency increases or decreases depending on the number of agents	$ANI = \dfrac{\text{Efficiency of the system with } n \text{ agents}}{\text{Efficiency of the system with } p \text{ agents}}$	$ANI \in Q$	p can be higher or less than n	Global	Design	Managing system
Automated Administration Tasks (AAT)	Intrinsic. Indicates the percentage of the automated administration	$AAT = \dfrac{\text{Nr of automated admin tasks}}{\text{Nr of total admin tasks}}$	$AAT \in Q$		Global	Design	Managing system

Continued

Table 13.6 Criteria and Software Metrics for the Evaluation of Self-Adaptive Systems—cont'd

Name	Definition	Formula	Values	Observations	Evaluation Perspective	Evaluation Time	Evaluation Scope
	tasks achieved through adaptivity with respect to the total number of administration tasks required by the system						
Average User Interaction per Functionality (AvgUIF)	Intrinsic. Indicates the average number of interactions users should perform to require a functionality	$\text{AvgUIF} = \dfrac{\sum_{i=0}^{n} \text{Nr of interactions for the } i\text{th functionality}}{n}$	$\text{AvgUIF} \in Q$	n is the total number of functionalities offered by the system	Global	Design	Managed system
Latency (Latency)	Runtime. Indicates the variation of the response time in the presence of self-adaptivity with respect to no adaptivity mechanisms	$\text{Latency} = \dfrac{\text{Response time in a self} - \text{adaptive situation}}{\text{Response time in a nominal situation}}$	$\text{Latency} \in Q$	It may be computed as: number of atomic operations, the computing time, or the number of steps needed by agents to reach a solution	Global	Runtime	Managing system
Working vs. Adaptivity Time (WAT)	Runtime. Indicates the time spent for adaptivity with respect to the time spent for working	$\text{WAT} = \dfrac{\text{Working time}}{\text{Adaptivity time}}$	$\text{WAT} \in Q$	If less than 1, a lot of time is spent for adaptivity	Global	Runtime	Managed system Managing system

Metric	Description	Formula	Measurement	Scope	Time	System
Communication Load (CL)	Runtime. Indicates the communication load among agents for adaptivity needs	$CL = \dfrac{\text{Communication load in self} - \text{adaptive situation}}{\text{Communication load in a nominal situation}}$	$CL \in Q$	It can be measured through the amount of exchanged messages among the agents	Global	Runtime	Managed system Managing system
Quality of Response (QoR)	Runtime. Indicates the variation of the quality of response in the presence of self-adaptivity with respect to the nominal conditions for the same functionality	$QoR = \dfrac{\text{Quality of response in a self} - \text{adaptive situation}}{\text{Quality of response in a nominal situation}}$	$QoR \in Q$	The quality of the response refers to the functional adequacy of the system	Global	Runtime	Managed system Managing system
Non Determinism (ND)	Runtime. Indicates the differences between the obtained solution for the same scenario in distributed asynchronous agent systems	$ND = \text{Distance between different solutions}$	N/A	Provides information about the stability of a system	Global	Runtime	Managed system Managing system
Progress (Progress)	Runtime. Indicates how progressively a complete solution exploiting self-adaptive properties is reached	$Progress = \text{Percentage of a goal reached at each step}$	$Progress \in Q$	Measures the activity in time of a system	Global	Runtime	Managed system Managing system

Continued

Table 13.6 Criteria and Software Metrics for the Evaluation of Self-Adaptive Systems—cont'd

Name	Definition	Formula	Values	Observations	Evaluation Perspective	Evaluation Time	Evaluation Scope
CPU Performance (CPUP)	Runtime. Indicates the variation of the CPU performances for when self-adaptivity is performed with respect to the CPU performances in nominal conditions	$CPUP = \dfrac{CPU\ performance\ in\ a\ self-adaptive\ situation}{CPU\ performance\ in\ a\ nominal\ situation}$	$CPUP \in Q$		Global	Runtime	Managed system Managing system
Storage Dimension Growth (SDG)	Runtime. Indicates the physical growth due to the presence of the self-adaptive mechanisms	N/A	N/A	Self-adaptation mechanisms include agents and their link to the managed system	Global	Design Runtime	Managing system
Storage Dimension of the Agent (SDA)	Runtime. Indicates the physical storage growth to store the agents	N/A	N/A		Global	Design Runtime	Managing system
Storage Dimension of the Connections between Adaptive and Functional Parts (SDCAF)	Runtime. Indicates the physical storage growth due to the link and communication between the managing and managed systems	N/A	N/A		Global	Design Runtime	Managed system Managing system

Robustness Index (RI)	Runtime. Indicates the ability of a system to maintain a stable behavior under perturbations	N/A	To measure RI it may be observed if the system maintains a functional adequacy during perturbations, or reaches a state closed to a previous one, or the changes between the perturbation state and the stable state are minimal	Global	Runtime	Managed system Managing system
Time for Adaptation (TA)	Runtime. Indicates the number of steps needed by the agents to return to a nominal functioning of the system	TA = Time to return to a nominal behavior after a perturbation	$TA \in Q$ It can be measured for each agent or for the system as a whole	Global	Runtime	Managed system Managing system

the use of a radar view, as a meaningful way to analyze the self-adaptive systems. The most suitable self-adaptive system is the one closest of the center of the radar.

For a single-criterion comparison, Kaddoum et al. introduce several typical archetypal behaviors and hints on how to interpret them. The authors sustain that each criterion considered separately may provide valuable information for the comparison of self-adaptive systems.

13.4.3 SOFTWARE ADAPTABILITY AT THE ARCHITECTURAL LEVEL

Perez-Palacin et al. [13] propose a set of five metrics for the evaluation of adaptivity at the architectural level in component-based systems. The metrics are used by software architects during the design phase to evaluate the adaptability of a software system. In particular, four of the metrics are focused on the adaptability characteristics of the services of the architecture and one on the adaptability of the architecture as a whole (see Table 13.7).

The authors of these metrics provide also a tool called SOLAR (SOftware quaLities and Adaptability Relationships) to compute the proposed metrics. Further, they validate the metrics and the tool on a Web application implementing the enrolment of students for an academic year in university.

13.4.4 FINDINGS

As in the case of quality attributes based evaluation approaches, also from the description of these three metric-based approaches it results that the proposed sets of metrics are disjoint. However, there may be established links among the three approaches. For example, for the computation of the adaptivity metric [11], the performance metrics introduced in [12] may be exploited. Further, the architectural metrics defined in [13] may be compared to the metrics belonging to the architectural criteria in [12]. For example, the level of system adaptability (LSA) metric [13] may have as correspondence the overall adaptivity growth (OAG) metric in [13]. The two sets of architectural metrics may be merged together into a single one.

The metrics proposed by the three approaches capture various aspects which may be evaluated in self-adaptive systems:

- Reference [11] focuses on the performances of a self-adaptive system, hence on the behavioral advantages obtained from the self-adaptivity;
- Reference [12] focuses on the design issues in self-adaptive systems (methodological, architectural, and intrinsic criteria), as well as on the execution issues (performance criteria); and
- Reference [13] focuses on architectural aspects addressed at design time of self-adaptive systems.

From these various evaluation aspects, we can remark that there are metrics which are meaningful for the software engineers who are interested both in the design and in the execution of self-adaptive systems, and there are metrics which are meaningful for the users (i.e., final users of a system or software engineers who want to integrate a self-adaptive system into another one that they develop) of self-adaptive systems (i.e., runtime metrics). For example, for a software engineer it is fundamental to know whether the self-adaptive mechanisms are based on a centralized or decentralized control, and on a local or distributed solution. These aspects may be ignored by a final user, who may be interested in the quality of response or in the communication load.

Table 13.7 Metrics at the Architectural Level

Name	Definition	Formula	Values	Observations	Evaluation Perspective	Evaluation Time	Evaluation Scope
Absolute adaptability of a service (AAS)	Measures the number of different alternatives in terms of used components for providing a given service	$AAS = |UC_i|$	$AAS \in N^n$	Quantifies how much adaptable a service is by counting the different alternatives to execute a service, where the service adaptability grows according to the number of components able to provide it	Local	Design	Managed system
Relative adaptability of a service (RAS)	Measures the number of used components that provide a given service with respect to the number of components actually offering such service	$AAS = \dfrac{|UC_i|}{|C_i|}$	$RAS \in Q^n$	Describes how each service stresses its adaptability choices. Informs how much more adaptable the service could be	Local	Design	Managed system
Mean of absolute adaptability of services (MAAS)	Measures the mean number of used components per service	$MAAS = \dfrac{\sum_{i=1}^n AAS_i}{n}$	$MAAS \in Q$	Offers insights into the mean size and effort needed to manage each service	Local	Design	Managed system
Mean of relative adaptability of services (MRAS)	Represents the mean of RAS	$MRAS = \dfrac{\sum_{i=1}^n RAS_i}{n}$	$MRAS \in Q$	Informs about the mean utilization of the potential components for each service	Local	Design	Managed system
Level of system adaptability (LSA)	Measures the number of components in the system with respect to the number of components that the most adaptable architecture would use	$LSA = \dfrac{\sum_{i=1}^n AAS_i}{\sum_{i=1}^n |C_i|}$	$LSA \in Q[0, 1]$	A value of 1 means that the system uses all the components for each service, hence adaptability is to the maximum	Global	Design	Managed system

The metrics proposed in [12] have been defined after having analyzed several approaches for self-adaptive systems and captured what may be meaningful for the evaluation of adaptive systems. Reference [11] started with the idea of having one metric for the evaluation and comparison of self-adaptive systems, while [13] explores adaptability and its influence on other quality attributes.

From the point of view of the evaluation scope, we notice that two (i.e., [13] and [11]) out of the three presented approaches focus on the managed part of a self-adaptive system. Together they define six metrics for the managed part. We suppose there is a greater interest in measuring the benefits obtained through self-adaptive mechanisms than measuring the performance of the self-adaptive mechanisms themselves. The approach presented in [12] proposes 17 metrics for the managing part, 3 metrics for the managed part, and 11 metrics for both parts. Here, the balance goes in favor of the managing part of a self-adaptive system. Further, we observe that [11] focuses entirely on runtime evaluation (i.e., 1 metric), while [25] on design time evaluation (i.e., 5 metrics). Totally, in this section we have presented 24 metrics concerning design time evaluation, 13 metrics concerning runtime evaluation, and 3 for both design and runtime evaluation. The evaluation perspective is mainly global, i.e., 32 out of 37 metrics presented in the three approaches have a global perspective while 5 provide a local perspective.

Table 13.8 summarizes three aspects of these evaluation approaches: case studies on which each approach has been applied by the authors, tool support provided by the authors for the computation of metrics, and evaluation computation performed on a real example.

From Table 13.8, we remark that all the presented approaches have been applied to one or more case studies to outline their applicability and usability. Perez-Palacin et al. propose their tool called SOLAR for the computation of metrics. Further, the authors provide qualitative results for the evaluation of the analyzed case study. Reinecke et al. mention the use of an ad-hoc tool for the computation of the adaptivity metric. They compute a quantitative evaluation of the analyzed case study. Kaddoum et al. do not mention any tool support. They indicate which may be the metrics meaningful for the evaluation of five case studies described in the scientific literature, without actually computing the metrics.

Table 13.8 Summary of the Metrics based Approaches Considering Their Actual Application/ Applicability

Approach	Case Study	Tool Support	Evaluation Type
Reinecke et al. [11]	Web services reliable messaging system	Ad hoc tool, custom test-bed	Quantitative
Kaddoum et al. [12]	Web client-server Videoconference DAMASCOPE Adaptive image server AHA!	N/A	Qualitative
Perez-Palacin et al. [13]	Web application for university enrolment	SOLAR	Qualitative

13.5 **TRADE-OFFS IN EVALUATION OF SELF-ADAPTIVE SYSTEMS**

Maybe the best example to introduce trade-offs is the well-known axiom used in software systems engineering: *Better, cheaper, faster—pick any two!* Essentially, it says that only two of these three issues can be achieved contemporaneously. This axiom is cited also by Taylor et al. in [25] adapted as *Functionality-scalability-performance—pick any two!* when addressing the deployment challenges, mentioning that the software architect's job is to find a solution which minimizes the unhappiness of the users in exploiting the deployed system. We would further personalize this axiom for self-adaptive system as following: *Adaptivity-performance-cost pick any two!* and reading it as achieving adaptivity and performance has a cost.

   From the previous sections of this chapter, it results that various trade-offs should be addressed in the evaluation of self-adaptive systems:

- Evaluation of the managing part or of the managed part? A hint on addressing this trade-off is mainly based on who is interested in the evaluation: software engineers are interested primarily in the managing part or in both of them, while the final users are interested in the managed part. Furthermore, a good result of the evaluation of the managing part leads to the expectation of a good result also for the evaluation of the managed part.
- Evaluation at design time or at runtime? A hint on addressing this trade-off is based on whether we are interested more the in quality of the design or in the quality of the obtained functionality. Usually, it is desired that both qualities are addressed. This trade-off is closely related to the first one on evaluating the self-adaptive mechanisms or the self-adaptive system.
- Quality attributes or software metrics? A hint on addressing this trade-off is similar to the first one being based on who is interested in the evaluation: software engineers are interested in using all the available evaluation mechanisms in order to have an as complete as possible evaluation of a system, while final users are usually focused on part of the system's features. Another possible solution to this trade-off is given by Geihs [9] who prefers metrics (see the last paragraph of Section 13.3.3).
- Local or global evaluation? A hint on addressing this trade-off is based on the objective of the evaluation and on the mechanisms chosen for the evaluation. There are objectives concerning part of a system and there are objectives concerning the entire system. Similarly, there are evaluation mechanisms having a local perspective and there are evaluation mechanisms having a global perspective.
- Qualitative or quantitative evaluation? A hint on addressing this trade-off is based on the following hypothesis: if an evaluation is needed in the early stages of the system's development, a qualitative evaluation (i.e., exploiting quality attributes) is appropriate; if an evaluation is needed after the system has been developed or during its execution (i.e., exploiting software metrics), then a quantitative evaluation should be adopted. Further, when comparing two or more self-adaptive solutions, the objective is to identify the best one; it is of secondary importance to evaluate how much better is one solution with respect to the others.
- Self-adaptivity or other quality attributes? Perez-Palacin et al. [13] discusses the trade-off between the adaptability of a system and its availability quality attribute. The result is that "any architecture that satisfies the availability needs adaptation." There are quality attributes which go hand-in-hand with self-adaptivity (as availability [13], robustness and fault tolerance [6], dependability and safety

[13]) having compatible objectives. Also there are quality attributes which lead to conflicts with self-adaptivity (i.e., cost, performance (i.e., time to adapt and reaction time [6], working vs. adaptivity time, communication load, OAG, quality of response, and computational complexity [12])).

To summarize, self-adaptivity is a complex issue to address. Its evaluation seems even harder. The evaluation can be done from various points of view and through various mechanisms. Hence, to achieve a meaningful result from the evaluation it is important to identify which is the objective of the evaluation and which is the appropriate mechanism through which to achieve this objective.

13.6 CONCLUSIONS AND FURTHER WORK

In this chapter, we have investigated the quality evaluation of self-adaptive systems. We have summarized the available approaches in the evaluation of self-adaptive systems and identified the similarities and the differences among them in order to extract general, common, and well-defined guidelines for the evaluation of self-adaptive systems. Therefore, we have proposed several categorization criteria of the evaluation approaches from various points of view. These criteria should be seen as the main aspects which should be considered both during the development and evaluation of self-adaptive systems. Furthermore, we have described the evaluation approaches in a common and uniform way in order to be able the analyze them. The results of this analysis may be summarized as follows. Each evaluation provides meaningful mechanisms for investigating self-adaptive systems. On the other hand none of them is complete and none manages to capture all the facets and related issues of self-adaptivity. Hence, further refinement of the available solutions is needed and probably novel evaluation mechanisms specific to self-adaptive issues should be defined.

The presentation of case studies on which the evaluation approaches have been applied by their authors plays a fundamental role in understanding both the approach, as well as its usefulness. The same importance is also held by the reports on the application of an approach by other researchers and their feedback (see [9]).

We must note that even if several papers motivate their approach with the need to compare various self-adaptive solutions, just [12] considers more than one case study and proposes a radar view and several archetypical behaviors (and hints on how to interpret them) for the comparison of self-adaptive systems. The other approaches which consider a case study have the objective just to apply their approach.

We stress the importance to have a tool support for the evaluation of self-adaptive systems, as well as the importance to have evaluation mechanisms computable through tool support. A tool support enables the application and the diffusion of the approach by providing an example on how to compute an evaluation mechanism and a way to actually compute it and to obtain a result. Furthermore, it would be easier to compare both the self-adaptive systems and to compare the tools that support the evaluation of self-adaptive systems. Half of the presented approaches do not have any tool support. In addition they do not provide an example of how to calculate the evaluation mechanism and hence who wants to use the proposed evaluation mechanisms may have difficulties to understand them or may not interpret them properly.

The trade-offs mentioned in Section 13.5 are inspired by the taxonomy presented in Section 13.2. The main hint which results from the presented trade-offs is that evaluation should consider the objective of the evaluation, the perspective of whom performs the evaluation, and the available mechanisms which may be used for the evaluation.

The work in this chapter represents a first step in the definition of a taxonomy for the evaluation of self-adaptive systems as well as in the identification of new and enhanced approaches for the evaluation of self-adaptive systems. Another taxonomy for self-protecting systems is available in [26]. This taxonomy considers also the approach quality. The two taxonomies may be merged and may represent a starting point for a more general taxonomy concerning self-adaptive systems. Further work will also concern the application of the identified taxonomy to several case studies in various application domains (e.g., the case studies presented during SEAMS 2015 in the Artifacts session (see website http://www.disim.univaq.it/seams2015/ or the exemplars available at the "Software Engineering for Self-Adaptive Systems" website https://www.hpi.uni-potsdam.de/giese/public/selfadapt/exemplars).

Another future work concerns the metrics for the evaluation of self-adaptive systems. Reinecke et al. [11] reflect that a metric should have at least the following three main characteristics to be considered a good metric: (1) comparability, i.e., the metric allows the comparison between systems (including the comparison of the values computed through the metric); (2) intuitive interpretation, i.e., the metric provides intuitive notions of the system under analysis (including what does it measure and how the result can be interpreted); and (3) simple and efficient computation, i.e., the metric should be computed with little effort, otherwise it will not be used in practice. Based on these assumptions, a future work will analyze the goodness of the metrics proposed for the evaluation of self-adaptivity.

In Ref. [27], the author mentions that besides quality attributes and software metrics, also patterns, antipatterns, and architecture and code smells may provide meaningful information on the quality of self-adaptive systems. Hence, we plan to investigate also the possibility to add other evaluation mechanisms which are used in software engineering for quality evaluation.

REFERENCES

[1] B.H.C. Cheng, R. de Lemos, P. Inverardi, J. Magee, Software Engineering for Self-Adaptive Systems, LNCS, Vol. 5525, Springer, Berlin, 2009.

[2] R. de Lemos, H. Giese, H.A. Muller, M. Shaw, in: Software Engineering for Self-Adaptive Systems II, LNCS, Vol. 7475, Springer, Berlin, 2013.

[3] P. Clements, R. Kazman, M. Klein, Evaluating Software Architectures: Methods and Case Studies, Addison-Wesley, Boston, MA, 2002.

[4] B. Kitchenham, P. Brereton, D. Budgen, M. Turner, J. Bailey, S.G. Linkman, Systematic literature reviews in software engineering—a systematic literature review, Inf. Softw. Technol. 51 (1) (2009) 7–15.

[5] Y. Brun, Improving impact of self-adaptation and self-management research through evaluation methodology, in: Proceedings of the 2010 ICSE Workshop on Software Engineering for Adaptive and Self-Managing Systems, ACM, New York, 2010, pp. 1–9.

[6] J.A. McCann, M. Huebscher, Evaluation issues in autonomic computing, in: Grid and Cooperative Computing—GCC 2004 Workshops, 2004, pp. 597–608.

[7] S. Neti, H. Müller, Quality criteria and analysis framework for self-healing systems, in: ICSE Workshop on Software Engineering for Adaptive and Self-Management Systems, 2007.

[8] N.M. Villegas, H. Müller, G. Tamura, L. Duchien, R. Casallas, A framework for evaluating quality-driven self-adaptive software systems, in: 6th International Symposium on Software Engineering for Adaptive and Self-Management Systems, 2011, pp. 80–89.

[9] K. Geihs, Self-adaptivity from different application perspectives: requirements, realizations, reflections, in: R. de Lemos et al., (Eds.), Self-Adaptive Systems, LNCS, Vol. 7475, Springer, Berlin, 2013, pp. 376–392.

[10] M.J. Hawthorne, D.E. Perry, Architectural styles for adaptable self-healing dependable systems, in: Proceedings of IEEE/ACM International Conference on Software Engineering (ICSE 2005), St. Louis, Missouri, USA, 2005.

[11] P. Reinecke, K. Wolter, A. Van Moorsel, Evaluating the adaptivity of computing systems, Perform. Eval. 67 (2010) 676–693.

[12] E. Kaddoum, C. Raibulet, J.P. Georgé, G. Picard, M.P. Gleizes, Criteria for the evaluation of self-* systems, in: ICSE Workshop on Software Engineering for Adaptive and Self-Managing Systems, 2010, pp. 29–38.

[13] D. Perez-Palacin, R. Mirandola, J. Merseguer, On the relationship between QoS and software adaptability at the architectural level, J. Syst. Softw. 87 (2014) 1–17.

[14] S.W. Cheng, D. Garlan, B. Schmerl, Evaluating the effectiveness of the rainbow self-adaptive system, in: ICSE Workshop on Software Engineering for Adaptive and Self-Managing Systems, 2009, pp. 132–141.

[15] Y. Liu, I. Gorton, Implementing adaptive performance management in server applications, in: ICSE Workshop on Software Engineering for Adaptive and Self-Management Systems, 2007.

[16] H. Sadat, A. Ghorbani, On the evaluation of adaptive web systems, in: Proceedings of the Workshop on Web-Based Support Systems, 2004, pp. 127–136.

[17] S. Weibelzahl, Evaluation of adaptive systems, in: M. Bauer, P.J. Gmytrasiewicz, & J. Vassileva (Eds.), User Modeling 2001, Proceedings of the Eighth International Conference, UM2001, Lecture Notes in Artificial Intelligence LNAI 2109, Springer-Verlag, Berlin, 2001, pp. 292–294.

[18] N. Subramanian, L. Chung, Metrics for adaptability, J. Appl. Technol. Div. (1999) 95–108.

[19] E. Kaddoum, M.P. Gleizes, J.P. George, G. Picard, Characterizing and evaluating problem solving self-* systems, in: Proceedings of the ADAPTIVE 2009 Conference, IEEE Press, 2009.

[20] C. Raibulet, L. Masciadri, Evaluation of dynamic adaptivity through metrics: an achievable target? in: Joint IEEE/IFIP Conference on Software Architecture 2009 & European Conference on Software Architecture, 2009, pp. 341–344.

[21] D. Garlan, S.W. Cheng, A.C. Huang, B. Schmerl, P. Steenkiste, Rainbow: architecture-based self-adaptation with reusable infrastructure, IEEE Comput. 37 (10) (2004) 46–54.

[22] G. Clair, E. Kaddoum, M.P. Gleizes, G. Picard, Self-regulation in self-organizing multi-agent systems for adaptive and intelligent manufacturing control, in: IEEE International Conference on Self-Adaptive and Self-Organizing Systems (SASO), IEEE Computer Society, Venice, Italy, 2008.

[23] I. Gorton, Y. Liu, N. Trivedi, An extensible and lightweight architecture for adaptive server applications, Softw. Pract. Exp. J. 8 (8) (2008) 853–883.

[24] P. De Bra, A. Aerts, B. Berden, B. de Lange, B. Rousseau, T. Santic, D. Smits, N. Stash, Aha! the adaptive hypermedia architecture, in: HYPERTEXT '03: Proceedings of the Fourteenth ACM Conference on Hypertext and Hypermedia, New York, NY, USA, 2003, pp. 81–84.

[25] R.N. Taylor, N. Medvidovic, E.M. Dashofy, Software Architecture: Foundations, Theory, and Practice, John Wiley & Sons, New York, 2010.

[26] E. Yuan, N. Esfahani, S. Malek, A systematic survey of self-protecting software systems, ACM Trans. Auton. Adapt. Syst. 8 (4) (2014).

[27] C. Raibulet, Hints on quality evaluation of self-systems, in: 8th IEEE International Conference on Self-Adaptive and Self-Organizing Systems, London, UK, September 8–12, 2014.

IDENTIFYING AND HANDLING UNCERTAINTIES IN THE FEEDBACK CONTROL LOOP

R.de Lemos[*,†]**, P. Potena**[‡]

University of Kent, United Kingdom [*] *CISUC, University of Coimbra, Portugal* [†]
Fondazione Bruno Kessler, Trento, Italy [‡]

14.1 INTRODUCTION

The key role of the feedback control loop in self-adaptive software systems, like the MAPE-K control loop [1], is to handle changes and uncertainties related to the target system, its goals, and its environment. The MAPE-K control loop, in particular, is characterized by multiple stages, which themselves can equally be a source of different types of uncertainties. Examples of uncertainties that might emerge at a particular stage: (i) users often find it difficult to accurately express quality preferences [2], (ii) distinct techniques can be used at a particular stage [3], or (iii) the analytical models used for assessing the system's quality attributes may simplify, by definition, assumptions that may not hold at runtime [4].

In view of these examples, there is the need for considering uncertainty as a first-class concept for improving the quality, or sometimes, even the correctness of adaptation decisions [4–6].

There have been several contributions in the literature typically focused on identifying and handling uncertainties in self-adaptive software systems. Examples of these contributions are related to: (i) show how uncertainty may impact the system's ability to satisfy its objectives [7], (ii) show how uncertainty may affect the definition and evaluation of software models [8, 9], (iii) specify the behavior of dynamically adaptive systems [10], (iv) express the uncertainty associated with the satisfaction of non-functional requirements given a set of design decisions [11], or (v) support the development and execution of self-adaptive software that handles uncertainty, while satisfying certain non-functional requirements (e.g., response time and the faulty behavior) [12]. Therefore, the identification and handling of uncertainties have been recognized as key factors for enabling systems to make accurate trade-off analysis related to both functional and non-functional requirements.

Although several approaches for identifying and handling uncertainties have been introduced in the last few years, they typically address uncertainties at the Plan stage of the MAPE-K control loop [7] without: (i) considering the different stages of a feedback control loop as a source of uncertainty that could be characterized as non-negligible, or (ii) providing support for collectively handle uncertainties related to the whole feedback control loop, which might be influenced by the dependencies between the stages.

Managing Trade-offs in Adaptable Software Architectures. http://dx.doi.org/10.1016/B978-0-12-802855-1.00014-9

The line taken in this chapter is that there is a need to identify and handle uncertainties locally at the different stages of the feedback control loop. This is essential because at any given stage there are uncertainties related to, for example, goals and inputs to the stage, techniques being used, and assumptions being made. There are several reasons for motivating this approach: (i) if uncertainty is not explicitly captured at a given stage, it might cease to exist or transformed when data is transferred between the stages of the control loop, (ii) if uncertainty is not considered locally at a given stage, the context for that uncertainty might be lost at the loop level, and (iii) if uncertainty is not identified and handled separately at the different stages of the control loop, there is the potential for the curse of dimensionality because of the high number of dimensions that need to be considered (i.e., the goal in decision making is to have fewer dimensions so smaller is the hypothesis space, which allows to obtain faster and more effective decision makers). However, the identification and handling of uncertainty cannot be done in isolation just at the stage level. There are dependencies between the stages of the MAPE-K control loop that need to be taken into account. Hence the motivation for defining an approach in which uncertainty and its propagation are considered in the context of the whole feedback control loop.

As a contribution, this chapter presents an approach that promotes (i) the identification and handling of uncertainty at the different stages of the feedback control loop, and (ii) the analysis of uncertainty propagation between the stages of the loop. The ultimate goal of the proposed approach is to obtain more accurate estimations for the system quality attributes, which are fundamental for the process of decision making. Trade-offs are the core of decision making when evaluating multiple alternatives for selecting one that best fulfils the goals of a stakeholder. In software development, the analysis of trade-offs, between the quality attributes describing different alternatives, has been essentially a development-time activity. However, with the event of self-adaptive software systems there has been a shift towards trade-off analysis at runtime in which decisions are made without any human interference. This cannot be achieved by just using ever more sophisticated techniques since important aspects regarding uncertainty propagation in the feedback control loop may not be captured, hence the contribution of this position chapter.

The rest of the chapter is organized as follows. In Section 14.2, we motivate the need for identifying and handling uncertainty in a coherent way along all the stages of the feedback control loop. Section 14.3 provides a brief overview of the methodology for identifying and handling uncertainty in the MAPE-K control loop. Section 14.4, using a case study of a smartphone application, we identify sources of uncertainty associated with the different stages of the feedback control loop. Related work is described in Section 14.5. Finally, Section 14.6 presents the conclusions, and provides indicative future work in the form of challenges.

14.2 MOTIVATION

This section motivates the need to consider the identification and handling of uncertainties in a staged way, rather than in a single stage, because depending on the feedback loop, its stages might be complex enough that would justify decisions to be made incrementally.

First, we present the stages of the feedback loop in which uncertainty should be identified and handled, next, we introduce some basic concepts regarding uncertainty, and finally, we provide some examples regarding the propagation of uncertainty in a feedback loop.

14.2.1 FEEDBACK LOOP

In this chapter, we adopt as a feedback control loop, the MAPE-K control loop [1], as shown in Fig. 14.1. In this diagram, the main feedback control loop, which embodies the stages of the MAPE-K loop, observes (via probes) and adapts (via effectors) a target system. The *Monitor* stage enables to obtain the state of the target system and its environment. The *Analyze* stage analyzes the state of the target system and its environment in order, first, to decide whether adaptation should be triggered (*Solution Domain*), and second, to identify the appropriate courses of action in case adaptation is required (*Problem Domain*). The *Plan* stage, first, selects amongst alternative courses of action those that are the most appropriate (*Decision Maker*), and second, generates the plans that will realize the selected course of action (*Plan Synthesis*). The *Execute* stage executes the plans that deploy the course of action for adapting the system. Finally, *Knowledge* represents any information related to the perceived state of the target system and environment that enables the provision of self-adaptation. Overall, the MAPE-K loop is appealing due to its simplicity and extendable nature.

In the MAPE-K loop, depending on the diversity of the activities performed at each of the stages, several specific control loops (to be referred as *meta-loops*) can be attached to each of the stages of the MAPE-K loop, as shown in Fig. 14.1. This allows to enforce separation of concerns depending on what

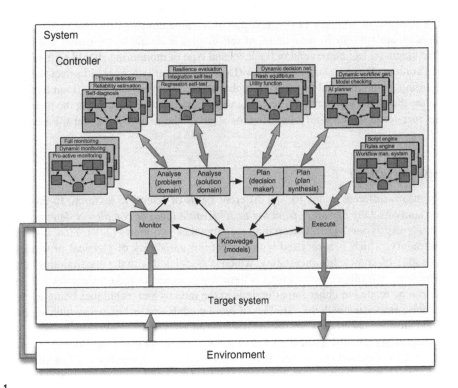

FIG. 14.1

Modified version of the MAPE-K control loop for autonomic computing.

Modified from J.O. Kephart, D.M. Chess, The vision of autonomic computing, Computer 36 (1) (2003) 41–50.

and how should be achieved for a particular stage. For example, for the Monitor stage, different monitoring techniques, like active and proactive, can be used in the different parts of the target system, and each of these might need to be independently self-managed. The same applies to the Analyze (Solution Domain) stage in which specific feedback loops can be associated with the different types of tests, like integration or regression testing, that need to be performed on a particular architectural configuration. In parallel with testing, one could also envisage another feedback loop in which probabilistic model checking is used to analyze whether an architectural configuration is able to satisfy the system properties. The individual outcomes of these meta-loops would be fed into the respective stage of the main MAPE-K loop, and the collective outcome from the meta-loops could be used as evidence for supporting the decisions associated with a given stage.

As an example of a meta-loop, we could associate with the Analyze (Problem Domain) stage a meta-loop responsible for self-diagnosis [13]. Diagnosis is responsible for the localization of faults, which is usually linked to the decision of whether to trigger adaptation. Although diagnosis is usually associated with the Monitor and Analyze stages of the main feedback control loop, its management for the sake of autonomy could be allocated to a meta-loop. In terms of a new meta-loop for self-diagnosis, the Monitor stage would collect data related to architectural configuration, and the operational state of the architectural elements. The Analyze (Problem Domain) stage would localize the faulty components, forward this information to the main feedback control loop, and evaluate whether the confidence levels, or accuracy [14], are within acceptable threshold. In case the confidence level is below an acceptable threshold, adaptation of self-diagnosis should be triggered. The identification of alternative diagnosis techniques and/or the level and type of monitoring should be the responsibility of Analyze (Solution Domain) stage. The Plan (Decision Maker) stage would select the best configuration regarding techniques and monitoring probes to be deployed, and Plan (Plan Synthesis) stage would generate the plan for deploying a new diagnosis. Finally, when processing the plan, the Execute stage of the meta-loop would notify the Monitor stage of the main loop about the new monitoring settings.

14.2.2 UNCERTAINTY

Uncertainty means different things for the different fields of scientific research. In this chapter, we define uncertainty as *"any deviation from the unachievable ideal of completely deterministic knowledge of the relevant system"* [15]. Uncertainty usually takes two views [7, 9]. First, *aleatory*, or stochastic uncertainty, which is associated with the natural variability of physical processes. Second, *epistemic*, or state-of-knowledge uncertainty, which is associated with the uncertainties in knowledge of these processes. A feedback control loop is basically designed to reduce the effects of uncertainty [16]. These can be related to either imperfections in the models and techniques being used, or disturbances and noise associated with the variables of those models and techniques, which are examples of epistemic and aleatory uncertainty, respectively.

The sources of uncertainty, associated with a stage of the MAPE-K loop can either be internal or external to the stage. *Internal sources* are associated with the lack or insufficiency of information, and they are related to internal factors that the stage might exert partial control. Internal sources are associated with epistemic type of uncertainties. *External sources* arise from the environment of a particular stage, and they are related to external factors that the stage has no control. External sources are associated with both epistemic and aleatory type of uncertainties.

Sources of uncertainty might impact the stages of a feedback control loop either explicitly or implicitly. *Explicit* impact of uncertainty occurs when the uncertainty source is clearly expressed or observable. *Implicit* impact of uncertainty occurs when the uncertainty source is implied though not directly expressed, it might be inherent in the nature of the interactions amongst the stages of the control loop.

The flow of the impact that uncertainty sources might have on a stage of a feedback control loop can either be downstream or upstream. The *downstream flow* of the impact follows the usual direction in the processing of the MAPE-K loop stages: initial stages of the feedback loop might affect later stages. The *upstream flow* of the impact follows the counter-direction in the processing of the MAPE-K loop stages: later stages of the feedback loop might affect initial stages.

14.2.3 UNCERTAINTY PROPAGATION IN THE MAPE-K LOOP

In order to demonstrate the impact of the uncertainty propagation in the MAPE-K loop, we present in the following, based on the diagram of Fig. 14.2, some illustrative cases.

Internal uncertainties, associated with a particular stage of the MAPE-K feedback control loop, can be propagated to the other stages of the loop. These uncertainties are usually of epistemic nature, and are related to types of techniques used and the parameters of those techniques. In the context of this chapter, the focus is the Analyze (Problem Domain) stage whose outcome is related to the decision of whether to adapt or not.

Regarding the propagation of external uncertainties, there are several variants amongst the stages of the MAPE-K loop, for example: explicit and implicit upstream propagation, and explicit downstream propagation. The downstream propagation of uncertainties follows the normal flow of the MAPE-K loop stages. As an example, depending how uncertainties are handled at the Monitor stage, these may propagate to the Analyze (Problem Domain) and affect decisions to be made at this stage. The key distinction between explicit and implicit upstream propagation is the fact that in implicit propagation, techniques associated with a particular stage might not be aware of changes elsewhere that may affect their

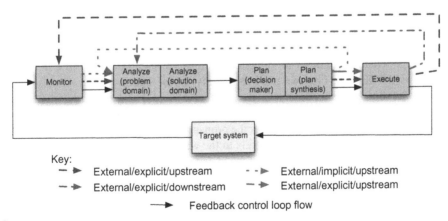

Key:
— ▶ External/explicit/upstream   - -▶ External/implicit/upstream
— ▸ External/explicit/downstream   — ▸ External/explicit/upstream
                    ——▶ Feedback control loop flow

FIG. 14.2

Examples of uncertainty propagation in the MAPE-K loop.

processing. An example for this case is shown in Fig. 14.2 in which the Plan might change the configuration of the target system in such a way that indirectly affects Analyze (Problem Domain). For instance, the new configuration may contain a software component from which less monitoring data is available. Concerning the explicit propagation, there is a direct relation between the changes that occur elsewhere in the MAPE-K loop and the uncertainties associated with a particular stage. For example, in the diagram of Fig. 14.2, the deployment of a plan might imply changes in the monitoring settings for a particular configuration, which then might affect the uncertainties related to Analyze (Problem Domain). Similarly, the Plan stage may not be able to identify a configuration that can be deployed considering the goals of the system, and what it does is to change those goals. For instance, the threshold associated with the trigger of adaptation might need to be lowered if a deployment cannot be found.

Uncertainties associated with the different stages of a feedback control loop need to be handled in order to optimize the quality of the services delivered by the system. In terms of the MAPE-K loop, uncertainties that are associated with its different stages are predominately handled at the Plan stage by the decision maker. However, regarding the MAPE-K loops with more complex configurations [17], such as the one presented above, the uncertainty associated with a given stage needs to be identified and handled at that stage of the feedback loop. The current perspective on software engineering for self-adaptive systems lacks this notion of staged decisions as a manner in which the feedback control loop handles uncertainty. Hence, the challenge being put forward in this chapter is the identification and handling of uncertainty as a function of the stages of the feedback control loop.

In summary, the motivation for dealing with uncertainty in a staged way in the MAPE-K loop is its similarity compared with error propagation in software architectures. Although individual components may work correctly, when these are placed in an architectural configuration, components may fail due to dependencies and relationships with the other components of the configuration [18]. The claim being made regarding uncertainties in a feedback control loop is that, although uncertainty needs to be identified and handled at each stage of the control loop, there is also the need to deal with uncertainty in a collective way because of the explicit and implicit dependencies between the different stages of the control loop.

14.3 METHODOLOGY

Uncertainty is embedded in every facet of adaptation, and the goal of this work is to show how to identify and handle uncertainties in order to mitigate the impact of its propagation in a feedback control loop, like the MAPE-K loop. First we need to identify, in the context of a particular stage of the MAPE-K loop, the sources of uncertainty that may affect the stage. Then, according to the uncertainties and the needs of the stage, techniques need to be identified for handling uncertainty. Even if uncertainty is handled in a staged way, we need to consider the propagation of uncertainty. In the context of a feedback control loop, uncertainty propagation refers to the way in which the uncertainty associated with other stages of the feedback loop might impact the uncertainty of a given stage. The proposition being made in this chapter is to use error propagation techniques as an inspiration for analyzing uncertainty propagation in the MAPE-K loop.[1]

---

[1]Although uncertainty propagation and error propagation are used interchangeably in the scientific literature, the interpretation taken in this chapter for error propagation is that from fault tolerance [19].

14.3.1 IDENTIFYING SOURCES OF UNCERTAINTY

In order to identify the potential sources of uncertainty in the MAPE-K loop, we have used Structured Analysis for Requirements Definition (SADT) [20] for describing the stages of the MAPE-K loop in terms of their *properties*: input and output data, control data, and mechanisms. Based on these properties, the *identification of uncertainties* aims to localize the sources of uncertainty affecting a given stage, which can either be internal or external. Internal sources of uncertainty are associated with those properties that the stage has some control, like mechanisms. Examples of mechanisms are the techniques being used by a stage. On the other hand, external sources are associated with those properties that the stage has no control, such as, input and control data. The control data, for example, may refer to goals (refinement/transformation of the goals associated with the system), constraints and assumptions associated with the stage. Finally, the *handling of uncertainties* aims to manipulate those properties that can be controlled by the stage. Decision making is one of the tools to handle uncertainty in which the sources of uncertainty are transformed by the decisions (i.e., the consequence of decisions may either be propagated or uncertainty mitigated).

For exemplifying how uncertainties can be identified and handled at a given stage of the MAPE-K loop, in the following, we refer once again to the self-diagnosis meta-loop previously described, and in particular, to the Analyze (Problem Domain) stage of that meta-loop. As input data, we identify the monitoring data related to the architectural configuration of the target system, such as, the operational state of its architectural elements, and the environment of the target system. For control data, there is the expected quality (confidence levels/accuracy) of the diagnosis, and constraints related to time and resources. As mechanisms, we identify the technique(s) that can be used to perform diagnosis. Finally, for output data, we expect to obtain a list of potential faulty components with confidence levels.

Regarding the identification of uncertainties, for instances, external sources are associated with the quality of the monitoring data, which might be associated with missing data, or not enough data, or erroneous data, etc. On the other hand, internal sources are associated with the parameters of the diagnosis algorithm being used, or the algorithm being employed.

14.3.2 HANDLING UNCERTAINTY

Concerning the handling of uncertainties, and taking as an example self-diagnosis, uncertainties could be mitigated by: changing the algorithm being used in case assumptions cease to hold, changing the parameters of the algorithm, or employing Monte Carlo simulations to the external sources of uncertainty. In the context of the self-diagnosis meta-loop example, another measure for handling uncertainty would be for the self-diagnosis to request the Monitor stage of the main loop to change its monitoring settings, in order for the self-diagnosis to receive more detailed information about the state of the target system. Another technique for handling uncertainties is that of decision making in which uncertainties are transformed. As already mentioned, the basis of decision making regarding software systems at the architectural level is the trade-off analysis of alternative architectural configurations in terms of their quality attributes—the decision takes place usually at the Plan stage of the MAPE-K control loop. In this case, the inputs to the decision making are the quality attributes, and their confidence levels, associated with the alternative architectural configurations, including the operational status of their components and connectors. Uncertainties associated with the quality attributes might lead to the decisions that might undermine the proper operation of the system. For example, if self-diagnosis identifies the wrong faulty component with a false degree of confidence, this might not trigger adaptation that would reconfigure the system in order to fix the fault localized by the self-diagnosis.

14.3.3 ANALYZING PROPAGATION OF UNCERTAINTY

Associated with each of the stages of MAPE-K loop, there are propagated uncertainties that need to be handled in order to optimize the quality of the services delivered by the system. *Uncertainty propagation* refers to the effects that property uncertainties of other stages might have upon the properties of a given stage. A method for analyzing uncertainty propagation between the stages of a feedback control loop that can be exploited is that of analysis of error propagation [2] between software components [21], which has been proven to be influential for the estimation of system reliability. The same rationale can be applied to uncertainty propagation through the stages of the MAPE-K loop: external sources of uncertainty can affect the processing of a given stage to the point that the outcome of the stage might reflect how uncertainty is handled at that stage. More specifically, error propagation probability [21] from component $Comp_A$ to component $Comp_B$, that are tied through the connector $Conn_X$, is defined by the function $Prob([Comp_B](x) \neq [Comp_B](x') | x \neq x')$, where $[Comp_B]$ denotes the function of component $Comp_B$, and x is an element of the connector $Conn_X$ from $Comp_A$ to $Comp_B$. This property expresses the probability that a component may propagate an erroneous message (uncertainty) when it receives as input an erroneous message (uncertainty).

Similarly, if we consider the stages of a feedback control loop to be like software components (and, thus, their associated decision making process like the function of a component), the uncertainty propagation probability from stage $Stage_A$ to stage $Stage_B$ may also be rooted on the function $Prob([Stage_B](x) \neq [Stage_B](x') | x \neq x')$, where x is an uncertainty source of input data received from stage $Stage_A$ to stage $Stage_B$. In other words, this function may be used for expressing the ability of the stage $Stage_B$ to mitigate uncertainty received form $Stage_A$; therefore, it may give an assessment of the robustness of the decisions made by $Stage_B$ with regard to the uncertainty propagated from the stage $Stage_A$. In fact, the propagation of uncertainty in a feedback control loop refers to the way in which the uncertainty associated with other stages of the feedback loop might impact the uncertainty of a given stage.

In this chapter, the propagation of uncertainty is described in the context of the stages of the MAPE-K control loop, however uncertainties associated with properties of the target system and its environment should also be taken into account depending on what the Monitor is able to observe. These sources of uncertainty should also have an impact on the runtime trade-offs analysis of the decision making not only in terms of the values of the quality attributes, but also on how the trade-off analysis is performed. For example, depending on the level of uncertainty associated with an environmental property, a different technique for trade-off analysis might need to be deployed.

14.4 CASE STUDY: IDENTIFICATION OF UNCERTAINTIES

In this section, we demonstrate the process of identifying sources of uncertainty in the MAPE-K loop in the context of a case study.

---

[2] Error propagation in fault tolerance refers to the successive process of transforming an error into other errors in a given component or between components, until they are either mitigated or possibly affecting the system output [19].

14.4.1 SMARTPHONE APPLICATION

In the following, we describe an example (inspired by [22]) that we devised for illustrating how accurate analysis of uncertainty propagation may influence the estimation of system reliability. In this example, a smartphone user requires the latest news from a service provider (here called Multimedia Service). The news includes text and topical videos available in MPEG2 format. Fig. 14.3A illustrates the software architecture of the system, essentially describing dependencies between components of the system.

It is a client/server system, where the Client is connected via wireless network to the Multimedia Service. The Transcoding component adapts the video content for the smartphone format. The Compression component adapts the news content to the wireless link. The Merging component integrates the text with the video stream for the limited smartphone display. The Locations Database and the Translation components, are used, respectively, for (i) collecting information about the localization of the cells used for user location, and (ii) adapting the text of the smartphone format for showing a user location map.

We consider three services that the system is able to provide. The first service, S_1, provides news in textual format, the second one, S_2, provides news with both textual and video content, and the third service, S_3, provides a user location map. Fig. 14.3B schematically depicts the hardware architecture of the deployment platform.

14.4.2 IDENTIFYING SOURCES OF UNCERTAINTY

For the purpose of the exercise, the goal of the feedback control loop is to control the architectural configuration of the software, and its deployment, in order to maintain the system reliability above a certain threshold (e.g., $R \geq 0.99$). In the following, for each of the stages of the MAPE-K loop, we identify the properties associated with each of the stages, and from these properties, we identify potential sources of uncertainty that may affect the stage.

Monitor stage
This stage monitors the system software architecture, and its deployment on hardware nodes.

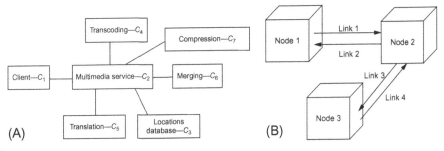

FIG. 14.3

Smartphone application example. (A) Software architecture. (B) Hardware architecture.

Properties

As input data, probes will monitor the operational state of the software components, the hardware nodes and their links, and collect information regarding component invocations. For control data, there is the expected quality (confidence levels/accuracy) of the monitoring data, and constraints related to time and resources. As mechanisms, we identify the technique(s) that can be used to monitoring (e.g., dynamic or static). Finally, as output data, monitoring data (e.g., software component invocations) is obtained from probes or gauges to be used by the other stages of the MAPE-K loop.

Sources of uncertainty

One possible external source of uncertainty is associated with the data coming from the probes, whose quality depends on the quality of the probes. Another possible source is associated with the monitoring settings, these can be changed during runtime, which might affect the selection of probes to be used. Internal sources of uncertainty are related to the techniques employed for managing the monitoring (e.g., static, dynamic, or proactive).

Analyze (Problem Domain) stage

This stage estimates the reliability of the deployed software architecture to decide whether adaptation should be triggered.

Properties

As input data, we identify the monitoring data related to the architectural configuration of the target system (e.g., the operational state of its architectural elements), and the environment of the system (e.g., operational state of the hardware nodes). The control data is related to the reliability estimation threshold (e.g., $R \geq 0.99$) that if violated should trigger adaptation. The mechanisms are related to the technique(s) that can be used to estimate reliability. The output data is the trigger that starts adaptation, and to which a confidence level is associated.

Sources of uncertainty

External sources of uncertainty are associated with the quality of the monitoring data (e.g., missing data, not enough data, erroneous data, etc.). On the other hand, internal sources of uncertainty are associated with the differences in the technique being used to estimate reliability, and the inaccuracies (e.g., due to simplifying assumptions) that may affect the parameters of those techniques.

Analyze (Solution Domain) stage

This stage identifies a set of alternative system configurations that are able to satisfied the specified reliability constraint. These system configurations consist of alternative software architecture configurations and their deployment into hardware nodes.

Properties

The input data comprises a set of available architectural elements and hardware nodes, monitoring data related to the architectural configuration of the target system, and monitoring data related to the environment of the system. The control data specifies the expected quality (confidence levels/accuracy) of the reliability estimation. The mechanisms are related to the technique(s) that can be used to estimate reliability. Finally, the output data will consist of a list of alternative system configurations, with their respective reliability estimations and confidence levels.

Sources of uncertainty

External sources of uncertainty are associated with the quality of the monitoring data (e.g., missing data, not enough data, erroneous data, etc.), and model drift (i.e., accuracy of the models representing the system configuration). Internal sources of uncertainty, similar to the previous case, are associated with the different techniques being used to estimate reliability, and the inaccuracies (e.g., due to simplifying assumptions) that may affect the parameters of those techniques.

Synthesis (Decision Maker) stage

This stage selects the best system configuration depending on the reliability estimation and confidence levels associated with each of the configurations, plus any other criteria (e.g., cost or other non-functional requirement) that might influence the selection.

Properties

The input data consists of a list of alternative system configurations with their respective attributes for the decision making, including their estimated reliability with confidence levels, and any other data related to the target system or the environment that might affect the decision making. The control data are the criteria for selecting the best system configuration, which are related to the system non-functional requirements. The mechanisms are related to the technique(s) that can be used for decision making. Finally, the output data will consist of a single system configuration that will be deployed.

Sources of uncertainty

External sources of uncertainty are associated with the quality of the monitoring data related to the attributes that would be used in the decision making. Internal sources of uncertainty are associated with the differences in the technique being used for decision making, and the inaccuracies that may affect the parameters of those techniques.

Synthesis (Plan Synthesis) stage

This stage generates the plan that will manage the deployment of the selected system configuration.

Properties

The input data comprises the selected system configuration that will be deployed, the operational data regarding availability of software components and hardware nodes, and the actual availability of resources. The control data is related to the system and component constraints that need to be enforced while deploying the system, which might involve its reconfiguration. The mechanisms are techniques to be used in the generation of the plans, and different techniques might generate different plans. The output data is a plan responsible for deploying the selected system configuration.

Sources of uncertainty

The operational data regarding availability of software components and hardware nodes are the main external sources of uncertainty. Internal sources of uncertainty are associated with the different techniques employed for generating the plans, and how those techniques are parameterized.

Execute

This stage is essentially responsible for executing the plan in order to deploy the new system configuration.

Properties

As input data, this stage receives the plan that would manage the deployment of the system configuration, i.e., reconfigure the software architecture and deployment of architectural elements into the hardware nodes. The control data is related to system constraints regarding time for deployment. The mechanisms are associated with the engines responsible for the execution of the plans, such as, workflow management systems. The output data are the commands sent to the effectors for modifying the configuration of the target system.

Sources of uncertainty

The external sources of uncertainty are associated, for example, with the ability of the effectors in carrying out the modifications, and whether software components and hardware nodes remain available during reconfiguration.

14.5 RELATED WORK

It has been claimed that the identification of uncertainty sources is fundamental for obtaining correct adaptation decisions, and trustworthy assessment of the quality of the deployed software [4]. It has been recognized the importance of control theory principles to reason effectively about uncertainty of self-adaptive systems [6]. It has also been recognized that uncertainty can only be controlled by making it explicit [5], and by considering it as a first-class concept. However, in practice, the staged handling of uncertainty is usually implicit, such as, in the self-optimization to reduce energy consumption (e.g., [23]), and in performance-tuning and resource-provisioning scenarios (e.g., [24]).

A quite extensive list of uncertainty sources has been identified for self-adaptive systems (see, e.g., [7–9]). Since not all sources of uncertainty have similar characteristics, this requires the usage of the different techniques for identifying and handling uncertainties [7]. There are several approaches that cater for both types of uncertainty (i.e., classical distinction between epistemic and aleatory uncertainty) [9, 25, 26], as there are approaches that are able to handle specific sources of uncertainty (i.e., problem-state identification, the strategy selection, and strategy success or failure [4]).

Handling uncertainty in the feedback control loop also requires coordination since the loop itself might be also a source of uncertainty [7]. Moreover, this coordination might not be restricted to the typical four stages of the MAPE-K loop since simple MAPE-K loops may not be appropriate to deal with more complex adaptations [27], where MAPE-K loops can incorporate different kinds of coordination [28]. Other approaches for handling uncertainty, instead of focusing on the stages of the MAPE-K loop, have proposed runtime modeling techniques for updating the knowledge data of a control loop, together with an error handling loop on the top of the main loop [8].

There are several contributions in the context of self-adaptive software systems on decision making under uncertainty. Bayesian decision theory has been proposed for capturing the uncertainty associated with the satisfaction of non-functional requirements (NFRs) given a set of design alternatives [11]. Moreover, the exploration of early architectural decisions is also supported by using fuzzy mathematical methods [29], Monte Carlo simulation [30], and game theoretic approaches [31]. Regarding the latter contribution, the outcome of handling uncertainties in a staged way could be fed into a decision maker that would be responsible for performing runtime trade-off analysis for satisfying the system requirements and optimize the quality of services under some cost constraints, for example. These, and other contributions, have mainly focused on analyzing the impact of uncertainties related to input parameters when evaluating architectural alternatives, without considering the joint analysis of sources of uncertainty and their propagation.

Several methods have been introduced to estimate the propagation of the uncertainty on the quality of a system (e.g., [32, 33]). These methods typically address propagation of uncertainties associated with input parameters of architecture-based software quality models, without explicitly considering the propagation of the uncertainty through the architectural elements (e.g., components or services). Examples of such methods include, the analysis of the propagation of parameter uncertainties (e.g., components reliabilities) regarding reliability estimation [32], and the analysis of model-based performance of software architectures under uncertainty of input parameters (e.g., workload, operational profile, and resource demand of services) [33].

14.6 **CONCLUSIONS**

The claim being made in this chapter is that, in self-adaptive software systems, depending on the feedback control loop, uncertainty should be handled according to the complexity of the control loop (whether it is connected with other control loops) and its stages (the number of features associated with a given stage). In simple control loops, just like the traditional four stages of the MAPE-K control loop, uncertainty can be handled in a single place, like the Plan stage. However, in more complex feedback control loops, which might embody complex stages, which on their own might consist of several feedback control loops (i.e., meta-loops), there is a need to identify and handled uncertainty at the different stages of the feedback control loop.

The ideas presented in this chapter, to the best of our knowledge, are a first attempt to investigate the propagation of uncertainty in feedback control loops. For that, we have proposed a method for identifying uncertainties at the stage level, and put forward error propagation analysis as a method for analyzing the propagation of uncertainties in a MAPE-K control loop. The goal of such approach is to maximize the utility of the services to be delivered by the system, which can be achieved, during runtime, by architectural trade-off analysis of the system quality attributes at any stage of the MAPE-K control loop.

In terms of future work, there are several open challenges, and in the following, we identify three of these challenges. First, considering that self-adaptive systems can change themselves, one should expect that sources of uncertainty to change during runtime, and this requires dynamic mechanisms that continuously monitors uncertainty sources, and finds solutions to better handle them. Moreover, the identification of sources of uncertainty, either explicit or implicit, is still an analytical human-based activity, and finding automated tools for this activity is a major challenge. Second, uncertainties associated with each quality attribute should be handled in a specific way, which requires a wide of techniques that need to be made available at runtime. The challenge here is to provide the appropriate support for controller to select autonomously the appropriate technique depending on the identified uncertainty. Finally, the third challenge is related to the ability of the controller to self-manage the orchestration of the activities related to the identification and handling of uncertainties. This should be a runtime activity supported by a wide range of techniques and oracles that should be able to identify where in the feedback control loop trade-off analysis take place, analyze their role and impact, and find ways of improving decision making by providing more accurate quality attributes.

REFERENCES

[1] J.O. Kephart, D.M. Chess, The vision of autonomic computing, Computer 36 (1) (2003) 41–50.
[2] B. Chen, X. Peng, Y. Yu, W. Zhao, Uncertainty handling in goal-driven self-optimization—limiting the negative effect on adaptation, J. Syst. Softw. 90 (2014) 114–127.
[3] I. Gonzalez-Herrera, J. Bourcier, E. Daubert, W. Rudametkin, O. Barais, F. Fouquet, J.-M. Jezequel, Scapegoat: an adaptive monitoring framework for component-based systems, in: Proceedings of the 2014 IEEE/IFIP Conference on Software Architecture (WICSA), 2014, pp. 67–76.
[4] S. Cheng, D. Garlan, Handling uncertainty in autonomic systems, in: Proceedings of the ASE 2007 International Workshop on Living With Uncertainty, Atlanta, GA, 2007.
[5] M. Autili, V. Cortellessa, D. Di Ruscio, P. Inverardi, P. Pelliccione, M. Tivoli, Eagle: engineering software in the ubiquitous globe by leveraging uncertainty, in: Proceedings of the 19th ACM SIGSOFT Symposium and the 13th European Conference on Foundations of Software Engineering, ESEC/FSE '11, ACM, New York, NY, 2011, pp. 488–491.
[6] Y. Brun, G. Marzo Serugendo, C. Gacek, H. Giese, H. Kienle, M. Litoiu, H. Müller, M. Pezzè, M. Shaw, Engineering self-adaptive systems through feedback loops, in: Software Engineering for Self-Adaptive Systems, Springer-Verlag, Berlin, Heidelberg, 2009, pp. 48–70.
[7] N. Esfahani, S. Malek, Uncertainty in self-adaptive software systems, in: Software Engineering for Self-Adaptive Systems II, vol. 7475 of Lecture Notes in Computer Science, Springer, Berlin, Heidelberg, 2013, pp. 214–238.
[8] H. Giese, N. Bencomo, L. Pasquale, A. Ramirez, P. Inverardi, S. Wätzoldt, S. Clarke, Living with uncertainty in the age of runtime models, in: B. Cheng, U. Amann, N. Bencomo, R. France (Eds.), Models@run.time, vol. 8378 of Lecture Notes in Computer Science, Springer, Berlin, Heidelberg, 2014, pp. 47–100.
[9] D. Perez-Palacin, R. Mirandola, Uncertainties in the modeling of self-adaptive systems: a taxonomy and an example of availability evaluation, in: Proceedings of the Fifth ACM/SPEC International Conference on Performance Engineering, ICPE 14, ACM, New York, NY, 2014, pp. 3–14.
[10] J. Whittle, P. Sawyer, N. Bencomo, B.H.C. Cheng, J. Bruel, RELAX: a language to address uncertainty in self-adaptive systems requirement, Requir. Eng. 15 (2) (2010) 177–196.
[11] N. Bencomo, A. Belaggoun, V. Issarny, Dynamic decision networks for decision-making in self-adaptive systems: a case study, in: Proceedings of the Eighth International Symposium on Software Engineering for Adaptive and Self-Managing Systems, SEAMS '13, IEEE Press, 2013, pp. 113–122.
[12] C. Ghezzi, L.S. Pinto, P. Spoletini, G. Tamburrelli, Managing non-functional uncertainty via model-driven adaptivity, in: Proceedings of the 2013 International Conference on Software Engineering, ICSE '13, IEEE Press, Piscataway, NJ, 2013, pp. 33–42.
[13] P. Casanova, D. Garlan, B. Schmerl, R. Abreu, Diagnosing architectural run-time failures, in: Proceedings of the Eighth International Symposium on Software Engineering for Adaptive and Self-Managing Systems, SEAMS 2013, IEEE Press, Piscataway, NJ, 2013, pp. 103–112.
[14] P. Casanova, D. Garlan, B. Schmerl, R. Abreu, Diagnosing unobserved components in self-adaptive systems, in: Proceedings of the Ninth International Symposium on Software Engineering for Adaptive and Self-Managing Systems, SEAMS 2014, ACM, New York, NY, 2014, pp. 75–84.
[15] W. Walker, P. Harremoes, J. Rotmans, J. van der Sluijs, M. van Asselt, P. Janssen, M.K. von Krauss, Defining uncertainty: a conceptual basis for uncertainty management in model-based decision support, Integr. Assess. 4 (1) (2003) 5–17.

[16] K.J. Aström, B. Wittenmark, Adaptive Control, Addison-Wesley, Reading, MA, 1995.

[17] C.E. da Silva, R. de Lemos, Dynamic management of integration testing for self-adaptive systems, in: LADC Workshop on Dependable in Adaptive and Self-Managing Systems (WDAS), Rio de Janeiro, RJ, Brazil, 2013, pp. 3–10.

[18] K. Wallnau, J.A. Stafford, Dispelling the myth of component evaluation, in: Building Reliable Component-Based Software Systems, vol. 8, Artech House, Inc., Norwood, MA, 2002.

[19] A. Avizienis, J.-C. Laprie, B. Randell, C. Landwehr, Basic concepts and taxonomy of dependable and secure computing, IEEE Trans. Dependable Secure Comput. 1 (1) (2004) 11–33.

[20] D.T. Ross, K.E. Schoman, Structured analysis for requirements definition, IEEE Trans. Softw. Eng. 3 (1) (1977) 6–15.

[21] W. Abdelmoez, D. Nassar, M. Shereshevsky, N. Gradetsky, R. Gunnalan, H. Ammar, B. Yu, A. Mili, Error propagation in software architectures, in: Proceedings of the International Symposium on Software Metrics, 2004, pp. 384–393.

[22] M. Alrifai, T. Risse, Combining global optimization with local selection for efficient QoS-aware service composition, in: Proceedings of the of the 18th International Conference on World Wide Web, WWW '09, ACM, New York, NY, 2009, pp. 881–890.

[23] R. Druilhe, M. Anne, J. Pulou, L. Duchien, L. Seinturier, Components mobility for energy efficiency of digital home, in: Proceedings of the 16th International ACM Sigsoft Symposium on Component-Based Software Engineering, CBSE '13, ACM, New York, NY, 2013, pp. 153–158.

[24] M. Litoiu, M. Mihaescu, D. Ionescu, B. Solomon, Scalable adaptive web services, in: Proceedings of the International Workshop on Systems Development in SOA Environments, SDSOA '08, ACM, New York, NY, 2008, pp. 47–52.

[25] X. Chen, E.-J. Park, D. Xiu, A flexible numerical approach for quantification of epistemic uncertainty, J. Comput. Phys. 240 (2013) 211–224.

[26] J.C. Helton, J.D. Johnson, W.L. Oberkampf, C. Sallaberry, Representation of analysis results involving aleatory and epistemic uncertainty, Int. J. Gen. Syst. 39 (2010) 605–646.

[27] P. Vromant, D. Weyns, S. Malek, J. Andersson, On interacting control loops in self-adaptive systems, in: Proceedings of the Sixth International Symposium on Software Engineering for Adaptive and Self-Managing Systems, SEAMS '11, ACM, New York, NY, 2011, pp. 202–207.

[28] D. Weyns, B. Schmerl, V. Grassi, S. Malek, R. Mirandola, C. Prehofer, J. Wuttke, J. Andersson, H. Giese, K. Gschka, On patterns for decentralized control in self-adaptive systems, in: Software Engineering for Self-Adaptive Systems II, vol. 7475 of Lecture Notes in Computer Science, Springer, Berlin, Heidelberg, 2013, pp. 76–107.

[29] N. Esfahani, S. Malek, K. Razavi, Guidearch: guiding the exploration of architectural solution space under uncertainty, in: Proceedings of the 2013 International Conference on Software Engineering, ICSE'13, IEEE Press, Piscataway, NJ, 2013, pp. 43–52.

[30] E. Letier, D. Stefan, E.T. Barr, Uncertainty, risk, and information value in software requirements and architecture, in: Proceedings of the 36th International Conference on Software Engineering, ICSE 2014, ACM, New York, NY, 2014, pp. 883–894.

[31] S. Merad, R. de Lemos, T. Anderson, A game theoretic solution for the optimal selection of services, in: V. Cardellini, E. Casalicchio, K.R.L.J.C. Branco, J.C. Estrella, F.J. Monaco (Eds.), Performance and Dependability in Service Computing: Concepts, Techniques and Research Directions, IGI Global, Hershey, PA, 2012, pp. 172–188.

[32] K. Goseva-Popstojanova, S. Kamavaram, Assessing uncertainty in reliability of component-based software systems, in: Proceedings of the 14th International Symposium on Software Reliability Engineering, ISSRE, 2003, pp. 307–320.

[33] C. Trubiani, I. Meedeniya, V. Cortellessa, A. Aleti, L. Grunske, Model-based performance analysis of software architectures under uncertainty, in: Proceedings of the Ninth International ACM Sigsoft Conference on Quality of Software Architectures, ACM, New York, NY, 2013, pp. 69–78.

GLOSSARY

Adaptation consistency A property of adaptive software that characterizes whether dynamic changes to the software can cause it to fail.

Adaptation disruption Transient unavailability of the managed software due to its adaptation.

Adaptive autonomy Adaptable level of automation that typically depends on changes in environmental conditions.

Adaptive security An adaptation technique that enables systems to vary their protection in the face of changes in their operational environment.

Adaptive software A software system that is easy to modify through human intervention.

Architecting for self-adaptation Designing the software architecture of a system to provide it with the capabilities to detect changes in its relevant context, and in response, decide to perform an adaptation on itself to maintain requirements satisfaction, at runtime and without interrupting its execution.

Architectural framework A coherent set of architecture viewpoints for supporting architecture modeling.

Architectural views Models of a software system architecture, each of which documents a system from the perspective of a particular concern.

Architecture perspective Approach including a collection of activities, tactics, and guidelines that require consideration across a number of the architectural views to address quality concerns.

Architecture view A representation of one or more structural aspects of an architecture that illustrates how the architecture addresses one or more concerns held by one or more of its stakeholders.

Architecture viewpoint A collection of templates and guidelines that represent the conventions for constructing and using a view.

Architecture-based self-adaptation A reflective approach that uses architectural models to reason about the behavior of the system and adapts it at runtime to achieve particular goals.

Automated security adaptation Automatic adaption of the system security configuration and/or capabilities to mitigate reported vulnerabilities or changes of system usage patterns, which most probably indicate that the system is under attack.

Component-based adaptation A method of adapting a software system in terms of changes applied to its components at runtime.

Component-level dependent transaction A transaction whose completion depends on the completion of consequent transactions.

Component-level transaction Exchange of information between two components by which the state of a component is affected.

Compositional adaptation An adaptation technique that aims to change the behavior and the structure of a system in order to make it better fit its environment.

Controller An intermediary software entity that coordinates the behaviors of components to ensure their correct interaction.

Decision making The process of evaluating multiple alternatives for selecting one that best fulfils the goals of a stakeholder.

Dynamic configuration Modification of a software system, while it is running (often used interchangeably with the term "runtime configuration").

Dynamic reconfiguration The capability of a software system to modify its architecture at runtime, without interrupting its execution and without or little human intervention.

Ecosystem A community of managerially and operationally independent organizations interacting with each other and with their environment.

Managing Trade-offs in Adaptable Software Architectures. http://dx.doi.org/10.1016/B978-0-12-802855-1.09985-8

Error propagation In dependability refers to the successive process of transforming an error into other errors in a given component or between components.

Evaluation of self-adaptivity Concerns the evaluation of both the managing part and the managed part of the system. The evaluation of self-adaptivity considers the quality of the self-adaptive mechanisms and the quality of the system's functionalities exploiting self-adaptivity. Evaluation is performed at design time and at runtime.

Feature-oriented adaptation A method of adapting a software system in terms of changes applied to its features at runtime.

Feedback control loop A tool that enables a system to regulate its behavior in order to meet a desired output.

Human-in-the-loop Model that requires human interaction.

Inference-based self-adaptation An approach for engineering self-adaptive software, where the management logic is learned from observations collected from the managed software.

Interoperability Interoperability characterizes the extent to which two software components from different manufacturers, which are functionally compatible, can be made to work together correctly by reconciling the differences in their interfaces and behaviors.

Long-living software Cost-efficiently maintained and evolved software that is capable to endure and preserve its function over an extended period of time.

Mediator An intermediary software entity that enables heterogeneous components to interact despite disparities in their data and/or behavioral models by performing the necessary coordination and translations while keeping them loosely-coupled.

Metropolis model A set of principles for creating and sustaining peer-produced ULS systems.

Multi-objective optimization "The task of finding one or more optimum solutions when an optimization problem involves more than one objective function."

Multi-sidedness A modeling approach that represents the ways that multiple stakeholders within a socio-technical ecosystem interact with each other.

Quality attributes Evaluating the quality of a system or part of it by focusing on the properties meaningful for self-adaptive systems.

Quality requirements The requirements which a system should fulfill in order to satisfy the quality of the software system.

Runtime adaptability A quality attribute related to the capability of a software system to be adapted at runtime according to the changing usage context and constraints.

Runtime configuration Configuration of a software system, possibly by itself, while the system is actually being executed at the operational phase (often used interchangeably with the term "dynamic configuration").

Scalability The ability of a system, network, or process to handle a growing amount of work in a capable manner or its ability to be enlarged to accommodate that growth.

Scalability perspective Architecture perspective for supporting the design and analysis of scalable systems.

Search-based software engineering A research field that approaches software engineering activities (such as design, testing, refactoring, evolution, and others) as optimization problems.

Security analysis The process of analyzing a given system and identify potential security flaws and/or bugs. Security analysis usually has three key tasks threat analysis, attack analysis, and vulnerability analysis.

Security engineering The process of capturing system security requirements, designing system security model, implementing necessary security controls and capabilities, and verifying that the system meets specified security requirements.

Self-adaptation The ability of a system to monitor and modify its runtime behavior in order to achieve particular goals.

Self-adaptive architecture Architecture which automatically configures its components in a way that is compatible with an overall architectural specification while interacting in response to the system goals.

Self-adaptive software A software system that adjusts its behavior at runtime, as automatic as possible, in response to internal and external stimuli.

Self-adaptive software systems Systems that are able to modify their behavior and/or structure in response changes that occur to the system itself, its environment, or even its goals.

Self-adaptive system A system able to perform changes on itself by itself during its execution as a consequence of changes occurred inside the system or in its execution environment.

Self-adaptivity The property of systems to react to varying context conditions and to modify their behavior autonomously.

Self-awareness A capability aiming for more efficient self-adaption, by making the computation node aware of their internal and external states over dimensions related to goals, time, goals, and interactions.

Socio-technical ecosystem An ecosystem combining complementary technological and social systems.

Software adaptability The extent to which a software system can be adapted.

Software architecture "The fundamental organization of a system, embodied in its components, their relationships to each other and the environment, and the principles governing its design and evolution."

Software architecture modeling The process of documenting a software system architecture with a set of models that are specified by conforming to a possibly formal language and notation.

Software modeling The act of creating models for representing all sort of software related aspects such as requirements, structure, behavior, deployment, and evolution.

Software-intensive ecosystem An ecosystem in which the behaviors of the participating organizations are dependent on software.

Systematic mapping study A methodological mean to analyze systematically a research topic, in order to provide an overview of the research area, analyze the quality and type of research conducted, and identify the gaps and research opportunities in this area.

Trade-offs Balance achieved among multiple desirable, but potentially incompatible system qualities.

Ultra-large-scale (ULS) system A system of unprecedented scale used by a wide variety of stakeholders with conflicting needs, evolving continuously, and constructed from heterogeneous parts.

Uncertainties "Any deviation from the unachievable ideal of completely deterministic knowledge of the relevant system".

Uncertainty (1) Dynamic and unpredictable circumstances that can be handled by self-adaptation; (2) the potential consequences of incorporating self-adaptation in a software system.

Uncertainty dimensions Aspects to identify and characterize uncertainty for a self-adaptive system.

Uncertainty propagation In a feedback control loop, this can be defined as the effects on a stage by the uncertainty of one of its properties.

User-driven security adaptation Security engineers can reconfigure or modify the implemented security model to mitigate or prevent a new security risk or realize a new security objective.

Vulnerability analysis The process of analyzing a given system code or binaries to identify existing security bugs such as SQL Injection, Cross-Site Scripting, Improper Authorization, etc. Vulnerability analysis can be conducted using static analysis techniques and/or dynamic analysis techniques.

Vulnerability mitigation The process of patching the system to block or fix a reported security bug. The mitigation could be done manual or automatic.

Author Index

Note: Page numbers followed by "*f*" indicate figures, and "*t*" indicate tables.

Subject Index

Note: Page numbers followed by "*f*" indicate figures, "*t*" indicate tables, "*b*" indicate boxes, and "*ge*" indicate glossary terms.

A

ABAS. *See* Attribute-based architectural style (ABAS)
Acegi, 104
ACM Transactions on Autonomous and Adaptive
    Systems, 256
ACM Transactions on Software Engineering and
    Methodology, 256
Adaptability
    architectural patterns, 8
    MAPE loop, 8
    in modern systems
        cloud computing, 9–10
        cyber-physical systems, 10–11
        service-based adaptations, 10
    queuing theory, 8–9
Adaptable system, architect for, 8–9
Adaptation, 21
    consistency, 369*ge*
    definition, 20–21
    disruption, 369*ge*
    feedback control, 24
    maintainability and policy-driven behavior, 24
    separation of concerns, for dynamic reconfiguration, 24
    time and responsibility, 24
    weather service invocation, 21
Adaptation feedback loop (A-FL), 37–38
Adaptation function uncertainty sources, 65–68, 65*t*
Adaptive autonomy, 369*ge*
Adaptive security, 369*ge*. *See also* Automated security
    adaptation; Runtime security adaptation
Adaptive software, 369*ge*
Adaptive web server, 182
Alion Semantic Mediation Bus, 314
AOSD. *See* Aspect-oriented software development (AOSD)
Application personalities, 306–307
Application specific design space, 309
Architecture-based self-adaptive systems, 369*ge*
    data extraction approach, 53–54
    data items, 54
    description, 47
    limitations and risks, 70
    with multiple quality requirements, 47, 56–57
    quality assessment mechanism
        credibility, 55
        quality of reporting, 55
        rigor, 55

reflective software architecture models, 45
research questions, 49–50
search strategy
    automatic search method, 51
    exclusion criteria, 53
    four-phased search process, 52–53
    inclusion criteria, 53
    publication period, 50–51
    "quasi-gold" standard, 51, 53
    search scope, 50–52
    search strings, 51
    venues, 50–51
uncertainty, 47–48
    classes, 59, 62*t*
    level of uncertainty, 63, 63*t*, 68–69, 69*t*
    nature, 59, 62*t*
    treatment, 63, 63*t*
    variability issues, 69–70
Architecture tradeoff analysis method (ATAM), 1, 207, 249
Aspect-oriented programming (AOP)-static weaving, 105–106,
    118–119
Aspect-oriented software development (AOSD), 93, 242
Attribute-based architectural style (ABAS), 93,
    241–242
Automated inference techniques
    learning-based approach for goal management
        adaptation cycle, 139–140
        emerging pattern caused by database index failure, 140,
          141*f*
        experimental results, 140–141
        learning cycle, 138–139
        objective, 137
        research challenges and risks, 142–143
        similar context, 140, 141*f*
    mining-based approach for change management
        experimental results, 146–148
        research challenges and risks, 148
        runtime dependencies, 144–145, 145*f*
        using mined dependencies, 145–146
Automated security adaptation, 369*ge*
    description, 106
    vulnerability analysis and mitigation, 109
        abstract program representation, 112
        authentication bypass, 111
        improper authorization, 111
        Object Constraint Language, 109–111, 110*f*

Printed in the United States
By Bookmasters